Abbreviation	What You Should Do	Consult
ab	Check, correct, or delete the form.	20C
adj/adv	Check form or position of adjective or adverb.	11A–E
agr	Revise form of verb or number of noun.	13A–D
	Make pronoun and antecedent agree.	15D–G
apos	Check uses of apostrophe.	20B
awk	Untangle sentence; clarify phrasing.	7C, 9A–D
cap	Capitalize it.	20A
case	Identify proper pronoun case; revise.	15H–L
coh	Improve paragraph organization.	5A
cs	Revise to eliminate comma splice.	16A, 17A
d [or dict]	Reconsider the word used.	6A–D
div	Check dictionary for proper syllabication.	18B
dm [or dang]	Attach modifier to a word it can modify.	11F
frag	Expand fragment into a complete sentence.	10A–B
fo	Separate the sentences with punctuation.	10D
ital	Review uses of italics.	18G
lc	Review capitalization; revise.	20A
log	Review fallacies of argumentation.	Ref. Guide
mm	Relocate modifier to avoid a misreading.	11F, A, C
ms	Review specifications for the paper.	22E, Sp. Assign
num	Review use of numbers; revise.	20D
pass	Change the passive verb to an active one.	8E, 13G
pl	Review the item and emend the plural.	14A
pron	Review pronouns or ask for clarification.	15
ref	Clarify the relationship between pronoun and antecedent.	15A–C
rep	Find alternatives, or cut what is repetitious.	8C
sexist	Revise to eliminate sexist overtones.	6D, 15Q
shift	Review consistency in verbs or pronouns.	13E, 15P
sp	Find the correct spelling in a dictionary.	21A
sub	Subordinate one idea to another or review sentence to improve subordination.	9A
trans	Strengthen the transition or create one.	12A–B
var	Vary sentence length and type.	9A
vb	Review verb tense, agreement, form.	13A–I
wdy	Trim the fat.	8A–E
ww	Review your tone; look for another term.	6A–D

THE
SCOTT,
FORESMAN
HANDBOOK
FOR
WRITERS

Maxine Hairston
University of Texas at Austin

John J. Ruszkiewicz
University of Texas at Austin

Scott, Foresman and Company
Glenview, Illinois
Boston
London

monica
Alton

Acknowledgments for literary selections appear on the page on which the copyrighted material appears or in the Credits section at the back of the book, which is to be considered an extension of the copyright page.

Library of Congress Cataloging-in-Publication Data

Hairston, Maxine.
  The Scott, Foresman handbook for writers.

  Includes index.
  1. English language—Rhetoric—Handbooks, manuals,
etc.   2. English language—Grammar 1950–   —
Handbooks, manuals, etc.   I. Ruszkiewicz, John J.,
1950–   . II. Title.
PE1408.H2968   1988   808'.042   87-14681
ISBN 0-673-18542-7

  23456—RRC—91908988

PREFACE

Why is correct grammar important?

Success-conscious Americans are grammar-conscious Americans and for good reasons. They know that if they want to get ahead in almost any business or profession, they are going to have to speak and write reasonably correct English because in the United States, as in other countries, people make judgments (fair or not) about other people by the way they speak and write. For this reason, an important part of education in the United States is and long has been learning the conventions of what is usually called standard English.

Such instruction became particularly important in the United States in the nineteenth century. Correct grammar became almost a moral issue among native-born Americans eager to assert or maintain their positions in society. Similarly, many non-English-speaking immigrants recognized that surviving and perhaps even prospering meant learning to speak and write English. Textbooks of grammar and manuals of style and usage proliferated, offering various versions of "correctness." Predictably, the grammar books usually tried to impose order upon a not-always-cooperative English language, while the style manuals, with titles such as *Handbook of Blunders* and *Everyday Errors of Speech*, railed against mistakes.

Handbooks today tend to teach grammar less formally and to be less preachy about style and usage than their predecessors. To be sure, they remain important tools for writers who want to master standard English, but now they have added sections that emphasize rhetorical concerns—that is, strategies that will help writers write effectively to different audiences for different purposes. Still, the tone, style, and organization of many handbooks convey an intimidating attitude about usage and correctness that can make it difficult for students to use such books easily and comfortably. Our goal in writing *The Scott, Foresman Handbook for Writers* has been to inaugurate a new kind of handbook, one that will give writers the help they need to revise and edit their work effectively, but one that will not overwhelm them with so many rules and injunctions that they become afraid to write. We have tried to create a handbook that is authoritative but informal and as practical and user-friendly as a well-designed computer program.

A major feature of *The Scott, Foresman Handbook for Writers* is a research-based system of marginal icons that marks items of punctuation and usage on a scale of priorities. We surveyed hundreds of English instructors and professional writers and editors to find out which features of standard English they most valued in writing. From their responses we developed a method of rankings that we use to alert writers to those features of usage and style that may cause special problems and also to fine points that could add polish to their work. We believe these icons will help student writers avoid errors and lapses that could be damaging.

What this handbook covers

We have opened the handbook with an overview of **The Writing Process** that makes suggestions about how writers can get started and how they can write and revise their work. We offer tips and checklists arranged to present strategies for approaching different kinds of writing. We don't attempt to cover everything in our discussion of writing strategies. Instead, we emphasize those techniques and methods we believe will improve writing most noticeably.

We follow with a section on **Style** that once again offers selected strategies for choosing language suited to the kind of writing one is doing. Here we discuss paragraphs, sentences, word choice, and sexist language.

The third part of the book deals with **Grammar and Usage**. We have arranged these chapters to help writers identify problems and then solve them. Although writers can benefit from reading this material carefully, we have designed these chapters primarily for quick and easy reference. We consider this portion of the handbook a kind of fix-it manual.

We have taken the same approach with the **Research Guide**. Here writers will find everything they want to know about writing a library paper—and more. The material is arranged to help them locate precisely those points, major and minor, that are causing problems. Users can read the entire section to learn what it means to do research, or they can probe selectively to figure out how to introduce a quotation or how to document a television program.

The fifth section is **Special Assignments**. It is intended to guide users through seven basic writing assignments: *abstracts, essay exams, literary analyses, résumés, reviews, memos,* and *business letters.* We do not intend the material here to be exhaustive. Rather, writers should regard the **Special Assignment** section as a ready reference, sufficient in most cases to point a writer in the direction of a successful paper.

The handbook ends with a **Reference Guide** that includes a glossary of usage and fallacies, an alphabetical list of items dealing with usage and with the most common logical fallacies.

Finally, to add a little zest and fun to our handbook, we have created a cast of characters drawn from a fictional institution called Clear Lake College and the town of Ruralia that surrounds it. They appear in the exercises and examples throughout the book—we hope they will enliven the learning process a little for both instructors and students.

Acknowledgments

We wish to thank all those English professors and other professionals whose work involves writing who responded to our survey about the comparative seriousness of a broad assortment of errors of usage. Their pragmatic responses, which reflected a lively concern about the conventions of language, have helped us establish a research base for our book and make informed judgments about the placement of icons.

Terrie Aamodt
Rose A. Adkins
Dorothea Alexander
Susan Anderson
Rebecca Argall

Rosemary Ascherl
Faren Bachelis
Ralph V. Backman
Leslie G. Bailey
Margaret P. Baker

Arthur D. Barnes
John Bauer
Johnny Bennett
Richard Beckham
Stephen C. Behrendt
Robert Bennett
John Blades
J. Bohlmeyer
Karen L. Bosley
Peter S. Bracher
Patricia Broughton
Brian B. Brown
Alexander J. Butrym
Felicia F. Campbell
Marie Coles Caldwell
Peter Cane
W. L. Cash, Jr.
Diljit Kaur Chatha
William Cole
Oscar Collier
Ann Jennalie Cook
S. Cooney
Paul Connell
Zoe Coulson
C. Michael Curtis
J. R. Dalsant
Vivien Davenport
Ada R. Davis
John T. Day
Susie Day
Layne Dearden
Steven S. Duke
Barbara J. Durkish
Raymond Dumont
D. Dean Dunham, Jr.
Linda Eicken
Ken Emerson
Lynn Fauth
Francis Fike
Bill Fisher
Mary Fleming

B. Floyd Flickinger
Scott Foll
Jerome S. Garger
G. Dale Gleason
Karen Nelson Gleeman
Beverly Graham
Caroline Grannan
Roy Neil Graves
Bob R. Green
Stanley T. Gutman
Stephen Hahn
Lee Hammer
Robert L. Hart
Mary Hatfield
James M. Haule
Werner G. Heim
Jerry Heller
Stephen Herald
Michael B. Herzog
Donald F. Hetzler
Allan Hirsh
Maureen Hoag
Robert Hoover
Richard C. Hovey
Janet B. Hubbs
Barbara Hudson
Geraldine Jacobs
B. Jacobskind
Lee A. Jacobus
A. P. Johnson
Jerry Mack Johnson
Ellen Jones
Jenkin Lloyd Jones
Edwina K. Jordan
Marean Jordan
Lester Kaplan
Dr. Carolyn Keefe
Alice C. Kessler
Sara Lee Kessler
Kate Kiefer
Leonard Bear King

Nina King
Lawrence J. Knapp
George W. Knight
Carole Krysan
Wendell Kurr
Trudy Kutz
Lee S. Laney
Kenneth Larson
Marguerite Larson
Katharine Kyes Leab
Arthur Leible
Robert C. Leitz, III
Bruce H. Leland
Brian D. Lewis
Henry J. Lindborg
Carole M. Lundeberg
Denise E. Lynch
Thomnas A. Maik
Michael Marinetti
Loretta Matulich
Alexander F. McDonald
H. Ray McKnight
Robert E. Mchaffy
Allan A. Metcalf
Helen J. Metcalfe
Sister Virginia Minton, O.S.B.
James A. Moore
Linda Moore-Lanning
Jonathan Morse
Bink Noll
Donald R. Nontelle
Marvin A. Nutt
Charles Owen
Ronald Palosaari
Douglas A. Pearson, Jr.
Charles F. Pelzer
Sr. Ingrid Peterson
Patricia M. Phipps
Susan L. Pratt
Ralph S. Protsik
Jerry E. Quinn

Bennett A. Rafoth
C. Earl Ramsey
Richard K. Rapp
William Reynolds
Dennison G. Rice
Morton D. Rich
Jeremy Richard
Richard H. Roffman Associates
Linda R. Ross
Richard Rouillard
Martha M. Rowlan
Edward Samaha
Marcille M. Sandahl
Arthrell D. Sanders
Ruth Schauer
Nancy Schmitt
Martin D. Schroeder
John Philip Schuyler
Donald N. Schweda
Mary Etta Scott
Sheric L. Sherrill
Michael Skau
John E. Skillen
Edward J. Sims
Audrey N. Slate
Norval D. Smith
Donald J. Sterling, Jr.
Charles Stubblefield
Deborah J. Sulc
Charles Sullivan
Bruce Taylor
Ruthann R. Thomas
Mary E. Thompson
Wayne Tosh
Peter C. Townsend
Walter M. Ulim
Virginia M. Vaughan
Victoria P. Venable
Faye Vowell
David Walker
Denzil Walters

Larry Watson
Mary S. Weinkauf
Monica R. Weis
Myrna Z. Weiss
Regis L. Welch
Alan Whitney
Rita Jacobs Willens
Becky Hall Williams

Thomas J. Wood
Joseph J. Wydeven
Ruth Wyler-Plaut
David J. Yarington
Nancy Yee
Lyle York
John Zoppi

We also wish to thank the many skillful reviewers who read the manuscript at all stages and who, through their advice and wisdom, helped us to shape this book.

Tracey Baker
David Bartholomae
Richard Batteiger
Pam Besser
Jim Berlin
Barbara Carr
Edward P. J. Corbett
Helen Covington
Carol Cyganowski
Carol David
John Dick
Robert DiYanni
George Dillon
Janet Eber
Lisa Ede
Suzanne Edwards
Tahita Fulkerson
Dennis Gartner
Diana George
Joseph Glaser
Joanne Glasgow
Rosanna Grassi
Janice Hall
L. F. Hanley
George Hanson
Sally Harrold
Rosalie Hewitt
Sheryl Horton

Ben Howard
Wayne Hubert
Rose-Ann Jaekel
Ted Johnston
David Kann
Philip Keith
Edward Kline
Joseph LaBriola
Barry Maid
David Mair
Richard Marius
Mike Matthews
Eileen Meagher
Linda Hanson Meeker
Elizabeth Metzger
George Miller
Martha Minter
Robert Moore
Kim Moreland
Robert Noreen
Donald Pattow
Anne Pidgeon
Mary Ellen Pitts
Robert Plec
Michale Raymond
Jerri Scott
Jean Turner Schreier
Charles Schuster

David Schwalm
Jack Selzer
Maxine Singleton
Ronald Sommer
Norman Stafford
William Stull
Donetta Suchon

Mitchell Summerlin
Sally Taylor
Dene Kay Thomas
Marilyn Valentino
William VandeKopple
John White
Joyce Wszalek

We are grateful to the management of the College Division of Scott, Foresman and Company for publishing a handbook that attempts to chart new directions. Their support for our ideas was unwavering and unconditional. We especially want to thank Anne Smith, who initiated this project and sustained it with enthusiasm, energy and wit; and Constance Rajala, our creative, rigorous, and sympathetic editor, who deserves a BMW, but will have to settle for a hearty *brava!* We appreciate the painstaking copyediting of Marisa L. L'Heureux, the brilliant artwork of Bobbye Cochran, the design talents of Barbara Schneider, and the cooperation of the entire team at Scott, Foresman.

Finally, we wish to thank Matthew Atha and James Balur bar, students at the University of Texas at Austin, for allowing us to reprint their drafts and essays as models of the writing process. Indeed, we owe a debt to all our students, past and present, for providing us with the insight and motivation to write this book. Their shadows fall on every page.

Maxine Hairston
John J. Ruszkiewicz

CONTENTS

3

WRITING   47

REVISING AND EDITING 75

PART II   STYLE   103

WHAT MAKES PARAGRAPHS WORK?   105

WHAT KIND OF LANGUAGE CAN YOU USE? 151

CAN YOU MAKE YOUR WRITING CLEARER? 173

CAN YOU BE LESS WORDY? 199

9

PROBLEMS WITH MANAGING SENTENCES? 215

10

PROBLEMS WITH SENTENCE FRAGMENTS, COMMA SPLICES AND RUN-ONS? 231

11

PROBLEMS WITH MODIFIERS? **249**

12

HOW DO YOU MANAGE TRANSITIONS? 273

PART III   GRAMMAR AND USAGE 285

PROBLEMS WITH VERBS AND VERBALS? 287

16

WHERE DO YOU NEED COMMAS?   411

**WHEN DO YOU USE SEMICOLONS AND
COLONS?** 437

HOW DO YOU USE MARKERS? 453

HOW DO YOU PUNCTUATE SENTENCE ENDINGS?   489

PROBLEMS WITH CAPITALIZATION, APOSTROPHES, ABBREVIATIONS, AND NUMBERS? 497

SPELLING, THE DICTIONARY, AND THE COMPUTER 529

A RESEARCH PAPER FROM START TO FINISH   685

PART V   SPECIAL ASSIGNMENTS   731

PART VI   REFERENCE GUIDE   791

FOREWORD

What is a handbook for?
A handbook is a reference book for writers to use when they
want advice about composing or guidance about a point of
grammar or usage. It is one of a writer's basic tools, just as a
word processor or a dictionary is a tool. In three important
ways, we have tried to make this handbook a practical manual,
easy to understand and easy to use.

> First, we have tried to use as little specialized termi-
> nology as possible; when we do use specialized words,
> as we must in many sections, we define them for you.

> Second, we have applied a problem solving approach
> to most parts of the book. **Troubleshooting** sections
> identify the difficulties or questions writers are most
> likely to have. Then we enumerate and discuss solu-
> tions to these problems, beginning with the basic solu-
> tions and narrowing down to matters of **Fine Tuning**.

> Third, we have devised a system of **icons** for marking
> rhetorical and grammatical problems in the handbook
> according to their difficulty so you can tell quickly
> how damaging a certain error may be or how trou-
> blesome some element of the writing process is likely
> to prove. More on this system of icons shortly.

What is damage control?
Most handbooks contain hundreds of conventions, injunctions, and rules; only professional grammarians and rhetori-
cians are likely to appreciate all of them. The problem for the

average person who needs to consult a handbook is how to decide which issues are minor, even trivial, and which are really serious.

What writers need, then, are guidelines for damage control that will tell them which errors are the grammatical or rhetorical equivalent of a **serious blunder**, such as poking a fork in the toaster or turning left from the right-turn lane. And they need to know which issues are significant enough to **warrant special attention** because they play an important role in making writing clear, consistent, and effective. Ignoring such items could cause embarrassment. Writers also need to know which issues of grammar, rhetoric, or usage are just plain **tricky**—those irritating (usually minor) problems that consistently trouble many writers. And finally, it helps to know which conventions of language deal with distinctions so subtle that they might be called **refinements**—the linguistic equivalent of social customs like knowing how to address an ambassador or use a fruit knife. While appreciating such fine points could help you to add a touch of class to your writing, most writers need to think about getting their forks out of their toasters first.

In short, we are suggesting priorities. If you have the time and skill to get everything right every time, fine. But if you don't, we want you to know which problems to concentrate on first.

To do that, *The Scott, Foresman Handbook for Writers* features a system of icons in its margins to help you appreciate the seriousness of certain problems and practices. These icons should help you set priorities in writing and revising. We have not attempted to assign icons to every item in the book; rather, we have put them by only those items we think warrant your particular attention. We had the advice of a panel of experts in deciding which problems deserved what icons, although of course we made the final judgments. Here is what the icons mean.

 Stop!—serious blunder; could be very damaging

Pay attention!—significant item or issue

 Tricky—confusing to many writers

Fine point—nice to know

We hope these icons and the problem-solving arrangement of the text will encourage you to use *The Scott, Foresman Handbook for Writers* as a fix-it manual. In that respect, it is primarily a reference tool. But remember, too, that writing involves much more than just avoiding problems and correcting mistakes. For that reason, the first sections of the book focus on the writing process—getting started, producing a draft, finding your audience and purpose, and revising and editing.

When should you use a handbook?

We advise you not to use the grammar and usage sections of your handbook in the early stages of the writing process. People who write a lot find they work best if they don't worry about grammar, spelling, or rules of usage while composing a first draft. If they do, their best ideas often float away while they are tinkering with details. This "write first and fix it later" attitude makes sense for all writers—novices and professionals. Writing should be fun, not an ordeal, but we know from research that student writers who begin to worry too early about whether they are getting everything correct will bog down quickly. Then writing that could have been exciting and satisfying too often becomes a tedious and discouraging chore.

For this reason, in Part I of the handbook we strongly suggest that you make it your first priority to produce a rough draft of any paper you are writing. If you are preparing one of the assignments discussed in the **Research Guide** or **Special Assignments**, you may want to consult these sections before writing. But, using whatever means work best for you, write down your ideas in some form early—even if they are not fully expressed or well organized. The important thing is to produce a first draft you can then develop into a finished product by revising and editing.

We also suggest you wait to look up specific problems of grammar or usage until after you have finished large-scale revising and are working at small-scale or stylistic revising. (More on these terms in Chapter 4, Revising and Editing.) We think *The Scott, Foresman Handbook for Writers* will help you most if you use it at this stage, after you have made your major decisions about the content of your paper. Then use it again when editing the final version of your paper so that the finished product is as polished as you can make it. Used in this way, the handbook can serve you as a coach, not a dictator.

Finally, a word about the cast of characters in our examples and exercises. You'll find that the lives and activities of people from a mythical school called Clear Lake College and the people from the town of Ruralia that surrounds it have been woven into narratives that develop throughout the handbook. We have created these characters and stories partly to enliven what is often the dullest part of a handbook and partly to remind you that writing usually involves people doing things with or for other people. Writing is a social activity; it doesn't take place in a vacuum. We hope meeting the cast of characters and reading about their triumphs and dilemmas will help to make *The Scott, Foresman Handbook for Writers* interesting and engaging.

PART I   THE WRITING PROCESS

We *write* in order to produce *writing*. That makes writing both a process and a product. In this first section of the handbook, we examine the processes that produce various kinds of writing, and we suggest ways to make composing more productive and, we hope, more enjoyable.

CHAPTER

What Is Writing?

- **A** What is writing?
- **B** What kinds of writing do you do?

WHAT IS WRITING?

Term you need to know

> **Recursive.** Cycling back and forth, not moving in a straight line. The process of writing is more recursive than linear—like a rope curled up upon itself.

Troubleshooting

Writing is not a mysterious activity at which only a few people can succeed; rather it is a craft, like weaving or playing an instrument, that can be learned by almost anyone willing to invest the necessary time and energy. Contrary to popular myth, the main qualities you need to succeed as a writer are not inspiration and talent, but confidence and determination—confidence that you are an intelligent person with something to say and determination to stick with a job until you say it. Consider this. In our information-hungry world, millions of people do a competent job writing every day—so, writing must be manageable. If others can do it, you can too.

▶ **Reject popular myths about composing.** Here are seven common ones.

1A

> **Myth 1.   Good writers are born, not made.**
> Fact: People become good writers through instruction and practice.
>
> **Myth 2.   Good writers work alone.**
> Fact: Good writers frequently rely on other people for advice, suggestions, evaluations, and encouragement.
>
> **Myth 3.   Good writers know what they are going to say before they start writing.**
> Fact: Good writers often begin with only a general idea of what they are going to say. They discover what they want to say as they write because writing is their way of knowing the world.
>
> **Myth 4.   Good writers make complete plans and outlines before they write.**
> Fact: Good writers often make only preliminary plans and outlines. They continue to plan as they write, shifting strategies as their ideas develop, encounter resistance, and change.
>
> **Myth 5.   Good writers get it right the first time.**
> Fact: Good writers almost never say what they want to on the first try. They nearly always plan on revising.
>
> **Myth 6.   Good writing comes from knowing all the rules of grammar.**
> Fact: Learning the rules of grammar won't make anyone a good writer, although it may make someone more relaxed and confident when writing.
>
> **Myth 7.   Writing is writing is writing.**
> Fact: People do many different kinds of writing, ranging from simple notes and notices to complex philosophical essays. Since all writing is *not* the same, writing can't be reduced to simple rules.

In a paragraph or two, explain your reaction to one of the myths listed on page 4. In what ways could that myth shape your attitudes toward writing? Would you be a better writer if you hadn't run into the belief? Can you recall where you first encountered the myth? Do you think someone influenced by a particular myth can shake it? If it helps, discuss how a myth affected a particular piece of your writing.

1A

In the course of this book, you'll be meeting a number of students, faculty, and townspeople associated with Clear Lake College in Ruralia, Illinois—where the grass is always green except in winter and some students turn their papers in on time. Two of those students, Connie Lim and Travis Beckwith, regularly argue about the merits of the writing they do. Connie is a journalist—"a deadline-grubbing sensationalist" in Travis' opinion. Travis is an occasional poet—"very occasional and very minor" replies Connie. (If you want to read specimens of their work, see Sections 18B and 18F.)

Travis considers Connie a hack for turning out lots of writing regularly for the campus paper, *The Daily Toxin*. "She just grinds it out, hands it over to other editors who change it around, and then maybe it says something and maybe it doesn't. All she cares about are readers—so she organizes everything from the top down, practically underlines what she is trying to say so the dullest reader can't miss it."

"That's right," Connie says, "I don't want Travis to miss a thing. I can't rely on inspiration. And I don't have time to think too much about my personal feelings. I've got deadlines to meet and stories to report. The words are just there to get my ideas across. Poetry is fine for people who have nothing better to do. I've got a world to change."

And so the debate goes on. What do you think is the root of their conflict? What myths might each of them be buying into? What kind of writing do you typically do and how would you defend its merit if challenged by someone like Connie or Travis?

▶ **View writing as a process.** Those who have studied how writers work generally agree that most of them move through these stages as they write.

PROCESS MENU

PREPARING
PLANNING
INCUBATING
WRITING
REVISING
EDITING

PREPARATION
In this stage, writers think about what they want to write and look for material.

PLANNING
In this stage, writers consider ways of arranging their materials or developing their subject.

INCUBATION
In this stage, writers give themselves time to let their ideas "simmer" or gestate.

WRITING
In this stage, writers start writing and develop a first draft.

REVISING
In this stage, writers review and re-write.

EDITING
In this stage, writers proofread, polish, and edit their writing.

Though broadly accurate, this summary is sketchy and oversimplified—the process of writing is never as neat and uncomplicated as such a description makes it seem. For one thing, people do many kinds of writing, and they don't do all of them by the same process. For another, writers go about their work differently. Some writers spend much time on preparation and planning, doing extensive research and making elaborate notes and outlines; others may think about their writing for a long time before they do any actual composing, but then they produce copy very quickly. Still others may seem to spend almost no time in preparation. They simply begin to write what comes to them, and that first draft becomes their preparation. In fact, there are no simple formulas that work for everyone. Writers have to figure how to manage the process so that it works best for them.

Writers may also vary the process according to the kind of writing being done. One kind of writing may require a great deal of planning; another may take very little. Or a writer may scarcely revise a particular piece of work, but do several revisions for another more important or more difficult paper. So writers have to learn to adapt to circumstances, following their temperaments. Some writers love to plan; others hate it. Some writers enjoy revising and tinkering with their work; others would rather spend a lot of time on preparation in order to do less revising.

EXERCISE 1.3

Can you recall the most successful piece you have ever written—a letter that may have appeared in the local newspaper, a speech you delivered to a club, a paper for a history class, a note to Grandma that persuaded her to buy you a Suzuki? Try to reconstruct the process of writing that piece. Do you recall how much time you put into it and what strategies you used to make it successful?

▶ **Think of writing as "cycling through stages."** In many cases, successful writers find that they cycle through the stages of writing several times in the course of composing a document. Choosing from the different options on the process menu, they move back and forth, sometimes planning, sometimes writing, sometimes stopping to revise. Most writers begin with some preparation, but they don't try to map out their whole paper ahead of time. Instead, they may plan just enough to get started, do some writing, and then stop to plan again.

They may allow time for incubation before they begin to write, but they also take time out for breaks to reflect on what they have done. Many writers revise their work in chunks, but then also do major revisions after they finish a draft.

1B

So writing is not a straight one-two-three process; it's a dynamic, **recursive** activity in which writers begin by planning and end with editing, but loop in and out of various stages as they work, repeating different operations several times before they produce a finished paper.

EXERCISE 1.4

Stephanie (Big Stevie) Mendelson, the weight-lifting champion at Clear Lake College, writes her papers in her apartment and then revises them in the weight room at Butcher's gym, keeping her legal pad on top of the huge fan blowing across the clutter of Universals and free weights. Maggie Lindstrøm, taking an evening course in philosophy, keeps a pad next to the cash register in the ice cream parlor she owns. That way she is able to sketch out ideas during the day while she works and to write after hours from the ideas she has generated. Darwin Washington, engineering major and captain of the soccer team, can write only in the quiet of the library with his books arrayed in front of him and his numbered notecards flanking the books in parallel rows. He writes papers in one sitting—or so he says.

How do you write a paper? Do you cycle back and forth among the various processes that make up writing—planning, writing, revising, editing?

1B   WHAT KINDS OF WRITING DO YOU DO?

Terms you need to know

> **Type I writing**. Self-limiting writing for which the writer already knows most of the content; the writing task is to present content clearly and effectively. Type I writing tends to be fact-centered.

Type II writing. Reflective, emergent writing for which the writer discovers much of the content while writing; the writing task is to organize and express that content. Type II writing tends to be idea-centered and speculative.

Troubleshooting

People do many kinds of writing—everything from simple notes telling United Parcel where to leave a package to complex analyses of technical data. It would be difficult and tedious to characterize each kind of writing and to analyze how it was produced. But we think most of the writing that students do in college—aside from note taking and lab reports—falls into two general categories: Type I writing and Type II writing.

It may help if you visualize these categories as two towers that bear the weight of a suspension bridge. Though the towers stand apart, they support a span of uninterrupted roadway. Similarly, though Type I and Type II represent distinct kinds of writing, the distance between those categories is spanned by varieties of writing that share features of both types.

► Recognize Type I Writing

Type I writing can be described as **self-limiting** writing; that is, for the most part, its content is fixed. The writer knows what to say before starting to write or at least knows where to look for the information to be conveyed. A good example of Type I writing would be a paper for a public health course in which a student is asked to summarize current medical theory about the relationship between diet and cancer. That student may not know the proper content for her paper ahead of time, but she cannot invent it or discover it within herself. The material already exists, and her job as a writer is to find it and put it in readable form.

Another example of Type I, or self-limiting, writing may be an essay exam in astronomy in which a student is asked to explain and diagram the Doppler effect. The student's job is to gather information about the principle and the supporting facts, organize the material, and present it clearly. Other examples of Type I writing might be a paper describing the functions of the Federal Reserve Board, an essay on what is required to be a good bartender, or an account of how rhetoric developed in ancient Greece. In each case the information exists and the writer presenting it cannot legitimately alter it. The only choices are how to present the information, which points to emphasize or omit, and what attitude or tone to take toward it. Even though an author may learn something while doing Type I writing and find imaginative ways to express his or her points, this kind of writing does not actually involve "discovery."

Type I writing is an important kind of writing both in and out of college. Probably most of the papers students write in college fit into this class, and much of the writing done in businesses and professions—the writing that keeps information flowing and gets jobs done—is Type I writing.

When working on Type I writing, most writers spend some time planning and preparing, making notes about the information they want to present, and writing an outline or a list that will help them organize it. They can use the typical invention strategies such as reviewing common thought patterns or asking the Who?/What?/Why?/When?/Where?/and How? questions to help generate material. (More about such strategies in Section 2B.) They can also count on common organizational patterns such as classification or assertion-and-support to provide a structure for their writing. In general, a systematic, problem-solving approach is likely to work well when you are doing Type I writing.

Type I writing is likely to be fairly audience-directed right from the start. Writers generally know whom they are writing for and consider—at least a little—what their audience expects from them.

EXERCISE 1.5

Try to list at least five examples of Type I writing you have done in the last several months.

▶ Recognize Type II Writing

Type II writing may best be described as **reflective** or **emergent** writing; that is, the writer begins with an idea or a point to make but really doesn't know how that paper is going to develop it or what the specific content of the paper will be. The content will emerge as the writer discovers new ideas and reflects on knowledge or experiences that pertain to the topic. The writer discovers or creates the content by putting old information together in new ways, by having fresh insights, and by tapping into his unconscious. Some typical examples of Type II writing are papers in which people philosophize about their own experiences or feelings; for example, a student from Mexico might write about being both attracted to and repelled by the affluent, materialistic American society. Another example is speculative writing in which the author hypothesizes about the consequences or implications of some event or trend; for example, a man giving up his job to go back to law school might write about his fear of depending on his wife to support him for the three years his education will take.

Other writings that can be classified as Type II are analytical essays in which writers comment on issues or theorize about cause and effect, or original essays in which writers explain an idea or trend. For example, a science writer might present an article speculating about the implications of implanting human embryos in surrogate mothers, or a columnist for a weekly newsmagazine might explain the problems created because business executives were slow to recognize changes in family patterns in the 1980s. Most of the articles you are likely to find in an anthology for a college composition course are apt to be examples of Type II writing.

Writers beginning to work on a Type II piece probably do less planning than when they start a Type I assignment. They may brainstorm, freewrite, or draw diagrams to help them narrow their topic (more about these strategies in Section 2D), but they frequently rely on writing itself to generate ideas and to make connections. They may sketch a rough outline or draw up a list to focus their thinking, but they cannot make a detailed outline before they start writing because they really don't have their content yet. They are going to discover much of it as they work. Writers handling Type II jobs are also less likely to rely on conventional strategies of development, such as cause and effect, definition, or classification, to generate ideas. They might use such tools, however, on subsequent drafts.

The first draft of a Type II paper is often a "discovery draft." That is, the writer writes it to discover what she wants to say, depending on the act of writing to trigger ideas and insights. When she has generated a body of material to work with, she usually prunes and focuses to find a central point she wants to make. Then she writes another two or three drafts to develop her piece. The process is much messier and less predictable than writing Type I papers.

In many cases, writers doing Type II work do not start out with a strong sense of their audience; their first draft is "writer-centered" because they are reflecting and exploring, trying to find their content. When they begin to shape the paper through subsequent drafts, they can begin to think about their readers and how to adapt the writing to their needs.

EXERCISE 1.6

Try to think of some examples of Type II writing you have done recently. What kind of writing do you do more often, Type I or Type II? Why? Do you have a preference for one type over the other? Can you describe kinds of writing that combine features of both these categories?

CHAPTER

Preparing to Write

2A **HOW DO YOU PREPARE TO WRITE?**

▶ Before you start: Be confident!

Almost everything in your life contributes to your preparation for writing: things that have happened in your family or on your job, your hobbies, your experiences in sports or with your car, your social life and your relationships with friends or lovers, your experiences in college—in other words, you have been stocking your memory with a wealth of material that you can draw on for the content of your papers. You also have ideas or opinions you can develop and values you can explain. All this adds up to such a rich stock of resources that you shouldn't run yourself down by saying, "I have nothing to write about." Of course you do!

So approach your writing with confidence. Even if you haven't written much before, you certainly have something to say that other people will be interested in.

Oscar Cupperman, the formidable, graying chair of the English department at Clear Lake, turns away from his computer with an expletive ("Fudge!") as Rusty Smuth, a slim, red-haired freshman English student, pokes his head into the office.

"I'm sorry I'm late sir."

"Well, come in. Have a seat—and put that thing down, won't you?"

"It's a skateboard, sir."

"Well, so it is. You know you may injure yourself on that some day. A young man riding one of those boards in our neighborhood impaled himself on the hood ornament of a Mercedes-Benz. It made a deep impression on him."

"I'm pretty good on the board, sir. I was state champion last year in the high school division."

"Well . . . yes. I must say, I don't appreciate your tardiness."

"Yes sir, but I was down at the drug center. . . ."

"A problem, Smuth?" Cupperman raised an eyebrow.

"No sir, I do counseling. I had a close friend overdose last year and since then I've been helping out at drug centers, usually just manning the phones or talking with kids."

"*Personning*, we say *personning* these days. *Manning* is a sexist term."

"I know, sir. My girlfriend and I fight about that stuff all the time. She's a feminist. Always wants to be treated equal, but never picks up a lunch tab."

Cupperman's computer wheezed, beeped, and ejected a disk.

"Fudge!" he fumed. "The gosh-darn thing keeps asking for the disk I have just shoved in!"

"No, sir. It wants the master disk. Your program is copy-protected and it needs to read a code off the master before it'll open the program, that is, unless you have a program to beat the copy protection . . . sir."

"Oh, I see. You seem to know a lot about these plastic boxes."

"Yes, sir. I've had a computer since I was thirteen. I do some programming and have a part-time job servicing the hardware."

"Well, with one of these machines you should be able to get your papers in more regularly. You are aware that your research paper was late?"

"Yes sir, but my roommate had our place occupied the night before it was due. . . ."

Cupperman smiled knowingly. "Girlfriend?"

"Boyfriend, sir."

"Ahem, well." Cupperman coughed. "What is it that you are here to discuss?"

"I can't think of anything to write about."

What would you suggest Rusty Smuth write about?

▶ **Before you start: Map out a strategy**

Once you have your specific assignment, invest some time on preliminaries that will identify what you need to do and help you map out strategies for getting started.

First, define your writing task and ask yourself these questions:

—Am I going to do mainly Type I or Type II writing?

—Do I have the information I need or do I need to find it?

—What kind of approach will work best for my topic—an organized problem-solving approach or an open, discovery approach?

—How much time can I invest in this paper? How does that limit affect my plans?

Second, define your purpose and ask yourself these questions:

—What do I want to accomplish with the paper?

—What reaction do I want my readers to have?

Try to state your purpose specifically in one sentence. For instance, for a clearly Type I assignment, you might write, "I want to convince my readers that racquetball is an inexpensive, easy-to-learn game that provides a good physical workout and beneficial mental relaxation." For an assignment that seems to call mainly for Type II writing, you might write, "I want my audience to understand what it feels like to have to spend most of one's life in a wheelchair."

Third, define your audience and ask these questions:

—Who would be interested in what I am going to write?

—Why would they read my paper?

2A

—What knowledge of the topic would they already have?

—What questions would they want me to answer?

Knowing and understanding your audience is critically important in any writing situation, and for that reason you need to get in the habit of thinking about readers whenever you write. You may want to postpone thinking about your readers while you are doing the first draft of Type II writing in order to concentrate on generating material about your topic, but by the second draft you should know who your readers are and how you might appeal to them.

EXERCISE 2.2—TYPE I ASSIGNMENT

John Maynard Ringling, retired Army colonel, student at Clear Lake College, and prominent member of the town council, has been commissioned to write a history of Clear Lake College in anticipation of its hundredth birthday in 1989. His report will grace the official Centennial Report—an expensive leather-bound volume to be sent to all alumni and contributors to commemorate the event. What Colonel Ringling has discovered—so far—is this:

> The college was founded by two brothers, Horace and Tobias Elcott, who settled in the vicinity of Clear Lake late in 1888. One cold December evening in Martinich's Saloon and Tonsorial Palace, they announced—over the din of a honky-tonk piano and brawling farmers—that, on January 2, they would be opening a new enterprise, Clear Lake *Haulage*. Everyone's business was welcomed.

The Elcotts bought a barn, three sturdy horses, and two stout wagons, but when the doors of Clear Lake *Haulage* officially opened that snowy day in January, Horace and Tobias met the stares of six young men and two women, carrying satchels, books, and pens, eager to start class. Horace began to explain the mistake, but Tobias quickly interrupted, welcoming the eight students to the opening session of Clear Lake *College*. Teaching students, he figured, must be easier and more profitable than hauling wood and hay. Tobias, with a smattering of the classics, announced that Latin I would meet in the first wagon and the rest, as they say, was History—meeting in the second wagon.

Your Type I assignment will resemble Colonel Ringling's. Over the course of the next several chapters, you will develop, write, and revise a short history of some institution you are either a part of or know something about. It can be a school, city, club, sports team, musical group, business, family, and so on. Your history can draw on your own knowledge, but should also look to other relevant sources: books, newspapers, yearbooks, interviews, videotapes, records. (For library resources, see Section 22B.)

Your history should be based on facts. You can decide what to include and how to organize your information, but you cannot make it up. Unless your instructor specifies otherwise, write your paper for a general college audience. You may want to discuss what writing to such an audience means.

Specific instructions for writing this paper will follow in the course of the next several chapters of this handbook. All you must do now is consider a subject for your history.

EXERCISE 2.3—TYPE II ASSIGNMENT

Wolfgang Rack, Dean of Students at Clear Lake College, has been on a tear about plagiarism. He wants to stamp it out once and for all. His plan is to require that all papers required for courses be written in class—even if that means extending hours of class attendance significantly: "What difference does it make if a student spends two hours writing in the library or an additional two hours in class? The time is the same. But if the paper is written in class under a teacher's supervision, we will know it is original, not bought, stolen, or copied."

2B

"Outrageous," everyone at Clear Lake seems to think, from students who are embittered by a blanket charge of dishonesty to faculty who don't believe all assignments can or should be written in class. Statements, editorials, petitions, letters, and posters blanket the campus in response to the policy Dean Rack intends to impose. Working students point out that they cannot afford to spend more hours in class. Librarians insist that good reports must draw from the resources of the library. Faculty wonder how the greatly extended class periods will affect their time for research.

But Tiffany Shade, President of Clear Lake College, has not been heard from yet, and Rack's opponents have time to sway her opinion. And so the battle rages with words the weapons of choice.

Your Type II assignment is to identify a similar controversy in your school, business, or town and explore the problem in an essay. Aim your essay at a general college audience. Specific instructions for writing this paper will follow at the end of subsequent sections of this handbook. All you must do now is find a subject of controversy for your analysis.

2B   HOW DO YOU GET STARTED?

PROCESS MENU

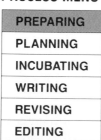

PREPARING
PLANNING
INCUBATING
WRITING
REVISING
EDITING

Troubleshooting

Most writers agree that getting started can be the hardest part of writing. Even professional authors have described the horrible paralysis they sometimes feel sitting before a typewriter staring at a blank sheet of paper. Columnist Russell Baker even tells of pulling one blank sheet out of the typewriter and rolling in another one that may be "friendlier." Today, of course, many of us gaze at a flickering computer screen and a blinking cursor instead of at blank paper, but the problem remains the same: how do you get started?

If you're like most people, you probably dread trying to pry loose those first few sentences. No matter how well prepared you are, you will dawdle and look for excuses to avoid putting words on paper. We have a number of suggestions for getting through that first difficult stage.

To get started . . .

▶ **Clear the decks.** If there are things that you absolutely must do before you start writing, do them. But be honest about those little excuses you find for putting a paper aside. Can't the dog wait another two or three hours for a bath? Do you really have to check out the new cassettes at the video store now? Will the neighbors care if the weeds in your lawn aren't pulled until tomorrow?

▶ **Talk your topic through with a friend** or in a small group to get their ideas and generate material. Or talk about your topic into a tape recorder. Discuss it with yourself just as you would if you were explaining it to a friend.

▶ **Cluster.** In the middle of a blank sheet of paper, write down a word or phrase that summarizes your topic. Circle that word and then, for about ten minutes, do what has been described as "free association." Just write down any words or images that pop into your head as you think about your initial word. Don't edit these ideas; simply circle them, and join them with straight lines either to that first word or to any other word on the page from which they seem to have sprung. When you are done, examine the clusters of words and ideas you have created on the page. See if you can locate a pattern in them that suggests a direction your paper might take.

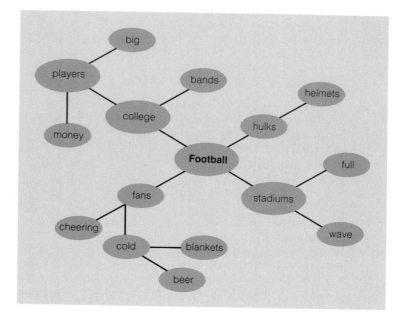

▶ **Brainstorm your topic either in a group or by yourself.** Just write out your topic at the top of the paper or on the board and start free-associating to see what words, phrases, and ideas come into your mind. List those ideas. In brainstorming, one idea piggybacks on another and there are no wrong answers.

▶ **Freewrite by just putting down anything that comes to mind about your topic.** Keep writing sentences for at least fifteen minutes, stop to reread what you've written, and start again if necessary. Don't cross out or censor what you have written—just keep going until you have built up some momentum.

▶ **Don't take beginnings too seriously.** Think of your first paragraph as a device to get you moving—a runway, a starting block, a launching pad. If, later, you don't like your opening paragraph, discard it and write a new one. The important thing is to get going. Write down two or three first sentences, no matter how bad they are.

▶ **Don't criticize yourself as you write.** When you are working on a first draft, give yourself a break. Don't tell yourself, "Oh, this is awful" or "I hate my writing." You wouldn't say that to a friend who was struggling to get a first draft written because you know how discouraging such criticism would be. So don't say it to yourself. Writing anything complex is a slow and difficult business, and you should congratulate yourself when you're getting it done at all. Good writing *evolves*; it doesn't just appear on a first try.

▶ **Don't start editing your writing prematurely.** When you're working on a first draft, try not to worry about punctuation, spelling, or problems like parallelism or sentence fragments—you can go back and fix those later after you have captured your ideas in writing. If you think of a word you want to use or a sentence that sounds good, put it down without stopping to worry whether it's *right*. If you bog down in fussing over details this early in the writing process, two unfortunate things can happen. First, you may lose your momentum; second, you may limit yourself to using only words you can spell and only sentences you know how to punctuate and thus produce a much less interesting paper than you are capable of writing.

▶ **Anticipate rewards.** Promise yourself a trip to the racquetball courts after you have written for two hours. Broil a steak (or make a salad) when you have completed a satisfactory draft.

EXERCISE 2.4

Have you heard or tried excuses like these for not starting a paper?

> —I have only an hour—it's not worth getting started; I'll go watch *Star Trek*.

> —I should call home; I haven't talked to my sister in two weeks. Besides I need to ask someone for a little cash.

> —I'll go the library with Rita and look up another source.

> —Darwin is playing his stereo so loud I can't concentrate. And I can't complain. He's too big. Besides, I like the album he's playing. Maybe I'll wander up there . . .

> —I don't have the right kind of paper. It has to be light green or it hurts my eyes. Better drive out to the mall . . .

> —If I wait until tomorrow to write, I'll be fresher.

> —It's not a long paper—I can write it during Professor Cupperman's class tomorrow. He won't notice.

Can you add at least two more excuses you have used?

2C   HOW DO YOU EXPLORE A SUBJECT?

PROCESS MENU

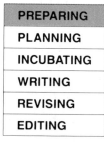

PREPARING
PLANNING
INCUBATING
WRITING
REVISING
EDITING

Invention. In writing, the process of discovering what can or must be said about a topic.

Troubleshooting

You're finally comfortable and ready to write. You even have a subject. What do you do now? It may help to explore your topic by using one or more of the techniques of invention discussed in this section. Although each technique has its strengths, you wouldn't want to apply all of these methods to every subject. Instead, look for those best suited to your subject and your temperament.

To explore a subject . . .

▶ **Use the journalist's questions.** Beginning reporters for newspapers are taught to keep six questions in mind when they write a news story. They are

Who?

What?

Where?

When?

Why?

How?

Not every question is useful in developing every topic, but they can help you generate information for your paper. For example, you could use the journalist's questions this way in developing the "Economics of Football" paper we are going to use as a running example.

Who profits from college football? (Students? Athletic departments? Coaches? Players? Alumni? Faculty? Local businesses?)

What are some of the consequences of college football being a for-profit enterprise? (What effects on athletes? On academic programs? On fund raising? On recruiting?)

Where is it most profitable? (In what parts of the country? In what kinds of institutions?)

When did it start becoming profitable? (Rise of TV? Prominence of the NFL?)

Why has it become so profitable? (Has television had a role? Does football fund other sports? What commercial spin-offs does a successful football program have for a university? Why does football increase alumni contributions?)

How does its being profitable cause problems? (What happens to student athletes? Do they get adequate academic training? Does football distort the basic role of a college or university? Are unpaid student athletes exploited?)

Also look for connections between any of these questions: how **why** relates to **where**, or **who** to **how**.

Why is college football so popular in certain regions (**where**) and less so in others? **How** do the attitudes in different regions of the country affect students who play football?

Who are the people most responsible for deciding **how** college football operates?

EXERCISE 2.5—TYPE I ASSIGNMENT

The journalist's questions work particularly well with factual assignments. Apply these questions, one by one, to the institution whose history you are writing. What kind of approach do the questions encourage you to take? That is, how would a history focusing on the **who** of your subject differ from one that explained **where** or **why**?

Type II papers tend to answer **how** or **why** questions, so these may be the lines to explore as you develop your "exploring a controversy" paper. You can also use the questions to test basic facts and information, making sure you understand the who's and what's of any problem you study.

▶ **Try cubing.**   Cubing is another way of looking at a topic from six different points of view corresponding to the six sides of a cube.

The sides are describe, compare, associate, analyze, apply, and argue for or against.

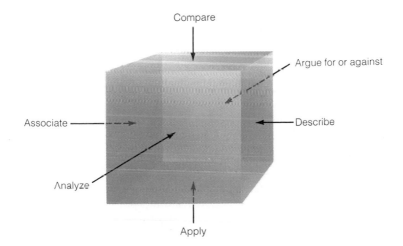

When you "cube" a topic, you work through these processes very quickly, taking no more than a few minutes to respond to each point of view. For example, you might:

> **Describe** the effects of for-profit play on the players: their college drop-out rate, their "working conditions," their time available for study, their attraction to drugs, their success rate in moving into professional sports.

Compare college football when it was strictly amateur to its present state: what were college games like in the *old days*? Who could play? Were high school athletes recruited any differently then?

Associate the change in football with increased television coverage of games or with other aspects of society changed by an influx of big bucks: have athletics become just another form of prime-time entertainment? Is the football hero the same today as the Hollywood idol?

Analyze the various economic aspects of college football: show where the money comes from and where it goes; explore the relationship between a winning team and college revenues; compare the salaries of coaches to faculty salaries.

Apply the logic of professionalized college football to the classroom: what happens to the student athletes there? Does schoolwork mean anything to the sports program?

Argue for or against measures to control some of the effects of for-profit football: suggest or oppose limitations on the relationship between athletes and alumni boosters; advocate or oppose salaries for student athletes; demand or oppose increased entrance or academic standards for all students.

After you run your topic over the sides of the cube, examine your new ideas to locate promising material for your paper. You may have discovered some intriguing issues.

EXERCISE 2.7—TYPE I ASSIGNMENT

In gathering ideas for your history, you may find that the sides of the cube most helpful in generating material are **describing** and **comparing**.

Cubing can be very helpful in exploring a controversy. Explore your subject from the perspectives of **associating** and **arguing**.

▶ **Look at common thought patterns.** People seem to think by processes that fall into distinct patterns. Writers sometimes use these patterns as ways of thinking about their subjects. They produce material by seeing what happens when they weave subject and pattern together. The most familiar are

> Description
>
> Narration
>
> Process
>
> Classification
>
> Definition
>
> Cause and Effect
>
> Comparison and Contrast
>
> Circumstance
>
> Testimony

Here are ways a writer might use these patterns to find material for a paper on college football economics.

Description: Describe a situation you know of in which money played a role in college football—for example, a coach making more money than the governor of the state; the profits from football subsidizing less popular sports in college; the glitz of TV network coverage of a game between traditional rivals.

Narration: Tell the story of a highly successful player whose career was ruined because he accepted $50 from an alumnus of his college. (This kind of anecdote can make an excellent, attention-getting opening for a paper.)

Process: Describe how football has become a for-profit enterprise at many colleges. Show, step-by-step, how television has changed the way we think about college football as a game.

Classification: Set up a system for classifying colleges according to the role money plays in their football programs—for example, private colleges versus public ones; those that generate great income versus those that don't; those that win media coverage versus lesser known institutions that rarely appear on the tube.

Definition: Explain some of the terms and phrases that you hear all the time when people talk about college football. What are sanctions, kickbacks, recruiting violations, under-the-table deals, academic standards, redshirted players? Explaining any one of these terms might furnish material for a full paper.

Cause and Effect: Speculate about the reasons some football programs seem more inclined than others to get involved in illegal deals and sanctions; about the effect on players of knowing that they are making money for their schools while risking personal injury that might prevent them from pursuing professional careers in athletics.

Comparison/Contrast: Compare the football program at a college that emphasizes academic achievement to one where athletics reigns. Contrast the daily schedule of an athlete to that of a student not involved in intercollegiate athletics.

Circumstances: Describe the circumstances that have led to the present situation. How are they different from previous circumstances? You may have to do research to find such material.

Testimony: Use case studies of colleges you are familiar with to illustrate your points. For example, you may be able to find out what the budget is for your school, how it is spent, who decides on how it is divided. Talk to players and ex-players. Get the word of people who are happy with the present system and the testimony of those who aren't.

Some of these patterns discussed above are custom-tailored for examining the history of an institution. For about five minutes, write nonstop on your topic using each of the following patterns as a guide: **description, narration, cause and effect**. In narrating the history of Clear Lake College (Exercise 2.2), for example, Colonel Ringling found an extraordinary **cause and effect** sequence responsible for the institution's founding.

2C

EXERCISE 2.10—TYPE II ASSIGNMENT

Examine your controversy from the perspectives offered by the **classification, cause and effect, circumstances,** and **definition** patterns. For example, the controversy at Clear Lake (see Exercise 2.3) might turn on the definition of *plagiarism*, so a paper might begin by studying the meanings that term can have for different parties in the conflict. Or a study of **consequences** might suggest that the Dean's reaction to campus plagiarism is an extreme reaction to a relatively minor stimulus.

▶ **Discover computer programs for generating material.** In many campus writing centers or writing labs, you may find programs that will help you generate material for your paper. They work by asking you a series of interrelated questions designed to stimulate your thinking on a topic. They help you probe and explore ideas. If you are having a hard time starting a writing project, spend an hour or two in front of a terminal with one of these **invention** programs. They may make you realize how much you already know. Some programs even help you organize and outline material.

2D

PROCESS MENU

PREPARING
PLANNING
INCUBATING
WRITING
REVISING
EDITING

Terms you need to know

Narrowing. Reducing a broad and general topic to a smaller and more specific one.

Focusing. Concentrating your attention on one limited idea or area or one facet of a more complex idea.

Troubleshooting

When you have used some of the strategies outlined in Section 2C for generating material, you should have a great deal of material to work with. Your mind will be buzzing with more ideas than you can possibly use in a short paper. But that's an advantage—better to work from a generous stock of material and have an abundance of examples to choose from than try to eke out a paper from skimpy resources.

Now the job is to find a way to narrow your topic to one you can handle within the limits of your assignment, using specific examples and details that will engage your readers and, you hope, explain something to them. To accomplish that, you will have to avoid bald generalities and also resist the temptation to tell everything you know. If you do not, you can be sure that you will first, write a superficial paper, and second, bore your readers. Two maxims will help you avoid the pitfalls:

—Pick a topic that is small enough to let you use examples and specific details: they are what will interest your readers.

—Write more about less.

Compare narrowing your topic to focusing a flashlight. You can shine the beam over a broad expanse of territory and get a general idea of everything that appears in the range of your light. But if you want to see some part of that territory in detail and find out more about it, you have to narrow the beam so that you concentrate its power on one small and specific area. Similarly, you may have to narrow a topic to a single idea so you can make out the interesting details.

A comparison of the design and operating efficiency of nuclear powerplants in the Soviet Union, Western Europe and North America

Wide angle

A comparison of the design and operating efficiency of nuclear powerplants in the Soviet Union, Western Europe and North America

Narrow angle

2D

▶ **Tree down your topic.** One good way of narrowing your topic to manageable size is to draw diagrams that "tree it down"; that is, make a chart on which you divide and sub-divide the topic into smaller and smaller parts. The tree helps you see how many ideas you can generate under each division and which branch seems to offer the most fruitful material. For example:

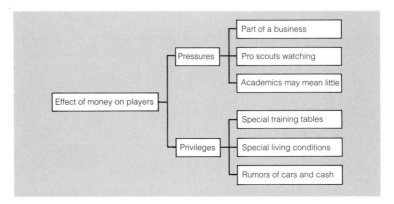

Sometimes you can pick the most promising part of your first diagram and tree it a second time. For example:

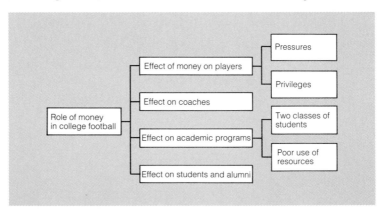

Notice that "treeing" generates as well as focuses material on a subtopic—material you might not have thought of if you hadn't written your ideas down.

Make a tree for your assignment. Remember that your intention is to focus your paper.

If you had been preparing to write a history of rock and roll, you may find now that it makes better sense just to chronicle the rise and fall of a local rock club. If you are writing about a controversy, now is the time to see what perspectives on that controversy you can deal with conscientiously and intelligently within the limits of your paper.

► **Carve out one part of a topic.** Think of your general subject as a large mass from which you intend to carve a topic the same way an artist selects one piece of a stone out of which to fashion a sculpture. The portion selected depends on what the sculptor hopes to accomplish: one part of the stone might work well for one kind of statue, a different part for another. Similarly, you might carve out a single paper from a large mass of material by asking which part of the entire subject best suits your purposes. You don't have to use the whole stone.

If you need to write an argumentative paper, you might focus on some aspect of your subject that provokes people to take sides; if you have been asked to write an informative paper, you might select a historical aspect that enables you to gather data and evidence. Or if you are free to handle your topic in any way you please, you might want to focus on the portion of the topic you find most interesting, perhaps some aspect that would allow you to use your personal experience in a narrative.

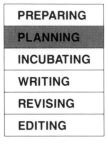

PROCESS MENU

PREPARING
PLANNING
INCUBATING
WRITING
REVISING
EDITING

Troubleshooting

When you write, you need some kind of plan to keep you on track. Maybe you think you have one in your head, but don't trust that. Your map can disappear while you're looking the other way. Fortunately, you can choose from among a number of simple but effective planning strategies. Here are some possibilities:

Sentence outline

Scratch outline

Working list

Thesis sentence.

Once you have a plan, you have to stay flexible. Don't lock out ideas that threaten your original strategy. Plans are supposed to serve ideas, not vice versa.

You'll probably need a specific plan when you are doing Type I writing and have lots of material that needs clear and concise explanation. In such a case, you should sketch out a preliminary pattern for your writing to get the material under control and put it in order for the reader. But you also need at least a tentative plan when you start doing Type II writing and don't yet know just what your content is going to be. Even with reflective or personal pieces, you need a sense of direction for your writing when you start out and some notion of what you want to accomplish.

Compare the difference between planning for Type I and Type II writing to the approaches two different people might use driving from Chicago to Albuquerque. Driver I's objective might be to make the trip as quickly and cheaply as possible with no delays, avoiding cities when possible, and spending only three nights on the road. To do that, he would have to plan ahead carefully, laying out his route on a map, checking a travel guide to find moderately priced motels, and estimating how far he could reasonably expect to drive in a day.

Driver II's objective might be to explore the country along the way, getting off the interstate highways as much as possible, and staying wherever she found an interesting or unusual hotel or resort. She would have to do little specific planning, but at least she has to know in which direction she was heading and what her basic goals are for the trip. She would also have to expect to do some planning as she went along. That's also about the minimum amount of planning a writer can get by with.

To plan a paper . . .

▶ **Make an outline.** For some writers and for some situations, outlining works well. For example, B. F. Skinner, a famous psychologist, swears by outlines. He claims that because he puts so much time into his outlines, he can write much more easily and quickly. But Jacques Barzun, also a famous writer and philosopher, thinks outlines are ridiculous. He favors lists. One author of this book almost always outlines; the other rarely does. Neither is necessarily "right."

Writers sometimes outline when they have to work with complicated Type I writing that contains a lot of information—more than they could possibly store in their heads as they work. Then they may need the support that a detailed, carefully structured outline can provide.

People writing a reflective Type II paper, on the other hand, could scarcely use an outline *before* writing since they would not yet know most of what they were going to say. They might, however, decide to make an outline for their topic *after* they have written a first draft, realizing it is poorly organized and too broad. At that stage, an outline could help focus and shape the revision.

If you have the temperament for it and particularly if you are doing Type I writing, you may find outlining a useful tool. A sentence outline often helps you articulate your main ideas and put them in order. And don't let worries about putting an outline in proper form keep you from making one if you think it will help. Probably no one is going to see it except you, so it's not essential, for example, that if you have an **A** under a main heading, you must also have a **B**. Maybe you have only one subpoint to develop in that division or maybe you'll discover your **B** heading later. Such details are comparatively minor.

Powerful outlining programs are available on personal computers. They allow you quickly and easily to write, revise, expand, contract, and rearrange your ideas in outline form. Some programs even work directly within word processing programs, enabling you to plan, write, and revise all on the same screen. Outlining programs combine the organizational power of the traditional outline with the flexibility and fluidity of less rigid planning strategies. Investigate such programs if your writing center or library has them.

> **Tip: Outlines are only tools to aid organization; they are *not* blueprints that must be followed faithfully once they are written.**

SAMPLE SENTENCE OUTLINE FOR A PAPER

Why Profits in College Football Have Hurt Players

I. When a college earns a million dollars from television rights to football games, players find it hard to remember that they are amateurs.
   A. Television publicity makes star players nationally famous, making academic achievement seem less important than their *real* jobs.

B. Student athletes feel like they are playing professional ball and should be paid accordingly.
   1. When players feel underpaid, it's easy for them to rationalize taking money from alumni.
   2. Scalping tickets can seem like just another part of the college football business.

II. Pressures to win become stronger when it looks as if a college team might win a bid to a bowl game and increase the television revenue of the school.
   A. Players begin to feel that they are part of a big football machine and resent being used.
   B. Players lose their sense of themselves.
   C. Pressures make coaches tough on players, adding to the stress felt by student athletes.

2E

III. College administrators should ask themselves whether the revenue from television is worth the damage done to players and the team.
   A. There are many small schools without television contracts where football thrives on sportsmanship and spirit.
   B. Colleges should cancel their contracts with the television networks and return to radio broadcasts.

Notice that although the outline above uses complete sentences, it is informal in the way it arranges its points, as if its author were sketching out the essay he is planning, not yet sure what his main point will be. In fact, this preliminary plan should help him realize that he has two focal points: a recommendation that college athletes be paid and a recommendation that colleges abandon television broadcasts of their football games. He may not want to tackle both subjects in the same paper.

EXERCISE 2.12—TYPE I ASSIGNMENT

Try your hand now at a relatively formal outline of your subject. See whether the information you have been gathering fits the focus you have decided on. See how the parts fit together. Note places where they don't.

Show your outline to a teacher or fellow student for suggestions.

▶ **Make informal or scratch outlines.** Many writers enjoy working from outlines but dislike the formality and restrictions of formal sentence outlines. For them, informal outlines that give main points in categories and subcategories work just as well as sentence outlines. Not only are they less trouble to make, but they seem more flexible to work with. You don't have as much time invested in an informal outline, so adapting and changing it as you write is easier.

SAMPLE INFORMAL OUTLINE FOR A PAPER

Topic: What Happens to Student Athletes When Profit Takes Over College Football?

Sportsmanship loses out
> Winning becomes more important than playing by rules
> Some players want to grab the spotlight on TV—teamwork goes out the window
> Players lose the sense of playing for their school and play more to catch the eyes of professional scouts
> Idea of football for the students disappears

Players feel like pros
> They think they should be earning money
> Easier for them to rationalize taking gifts and money from alumni and boosters
> Lose sight of why they are supposed to be in school
> Easy to become cynical and think they are part of a business enterprise

With this kind of outline, you have a good working plan that you could start developing with additional information and concrete details. It's also possible that in penning the outline, you might be struck by some part of it—for example, its being easy for college football players to rationalize taking gifts and

2E

money from boosters—and decide to build your paper around that rather than around your original idea. At this stage of your writing, that possibility is still open.

You should know enough about the controversy you are exploring to do a scratch outline. In fact, try to come up with two or three to explore different ways you might approach your subject.

▶ **Make a "working list."** The working list is the most open-ended and flexible of all outlines. It resembles a list you might make at home when planning some activity, perhaps a party or a trip. For instance, if you were preparing a festive Thanksgiving dinner for your immediate family and several friends, you would probably start a list days ahead of time and have several parts to it: one part might be a shopping list; one might be a list of chores to be done, such as cleaning the silver; one might be errands to run, and so on. You could start with only broad categories and add new items as you think of them, keeping the list current as you work by crossing off things as they get done or you decide you don't need them.

You can make plans for your papers in the same way. Start by putting down the key points you want to make, leaving plenty of room under each one. Then working from your brainstorming or freewriting notes, choose subpoints that fit under the various points and write them down. You might want to jot down some "cue notes" in the margin to remind you of anecdotes or examples you could use to illustrate certain points. When you think you have enough material, stop and look it over to decide which point you want to put first and how you can arrange the others. Then start writing and, as you work, refer to your list occasionally to see that you are staying on track and not forgetting important items. But you may also want to cross off some items you decide not to use once you begin to shape your paper through actual writing.

2E

Television has made college football big business

networks can sell millions of $s in air time
colleges profit from TV exposure
  generates interest in games
  sells more tickets
college games become more like pro games

Effect on players

begin to think like pros
more interested in future salaries than in games
worried about being popular
become cynical—take gifts
often poor self-discipline

Effect on coaches

feel more pressure to win
salaries go up as colleges profit
lose track of sportsmanship

Consequences

loss of proportion
athletes don't graduate; jeopardize college careers
depression and personal problems

Possible solutions

pay athletes
reduce the hoopla of television

EXERCISE 2.14—TYPE I AND II ASSIGNMENTS

You guessed it. If you haven't been satisfied with your outline, whether formal or scratch, see if writing and organizing a list helps you focus on your subject better.

▶ **Devise a thesis sentence.** Some writers like to work out a **thesis sentence** that sums up the main idea they want to make in a piece of writing and use that sentence as a working guideline to help them organize their points and keep them moving in the right direction as they work. Such a sentence should be comprehensive but succinct. Here is an example of a thesis sentence with both these qualities:

> In the last fifteen years, television broadcasts of college football have seriously affected the players, the coaches, the students, and the alumni, commercializing the sport and threatening to change college football for the worse.

The sentence still needs a little polish, but a writer who organized a paper according to this sentence and developed its points through expansion and examples should have a tight, easy-to-follow paper.

If you choose a thesis sentence as your main method of organization, remember these two points:

—Invest enough time in your sentence to make it fairly comprehensive. It will be almost worthless to you unless it enumerates the points you intend to develop or sets a direction your readers can follow.

—Don't assume that your thesis sentence must be the first sentence of your paper. Think of your thesis as an aid in planning your paper, a kind of compass, rather than an introduction. You can usually find a more interesting or dramatic sentence with which to open your paper.

To write an effective thesis statement,

—Begin by making a statement about your subject. That means, write a complete sentence (not a phrase, not a fragment) that explains what you expect to write about.

{not} My first week on campus

{but} I learned a lot during my first week on campus. [not a good thesis, but at least it is a complete sentence]

—Examine your statement to determine whether it makes a point. Does your statement provoke reactions? Can someone legitimately disagree with it? If not, modify it to say something that sparks interest or raises expectations. Take a stand.

41

{**not**} John Kennedy defeated Richard Nixon in the presidential election of 1960. [true, but who can disagree?]

{**but**} Suspicious election returns from Cook County, Illinois, may have cost Richard Nixon victory in the presidential election of 1960.

2E

—Examine your statement to determine whether it gives direction to your paper. Does it tell readers what they can expect or what you intend to cover in the paper? If not, check where in your thesis you can break a generality down into more specific parts.

{**not**} Advertising presents to us a world of unreality.

{**but**} Television advertisements for cologne and perfume portray a false world, where everyone is beautiful, rich, happy, and in love.

—Examine your statement to determine whether it is worth making. Read your thesis aloud, and then ask yourself whether an intelligent member of your audience would respond to your point with "So what?" or "Big deal!" If they can, look for a more significant idea, or present a more interesting facet of your original thought.

{**not**} I learned a lot during my first week on campus. [So what?]

{**but**} During my first week on campus, I learned that there's not a dime's worth of difference between looking stupid and being stupid.

—Examine your statement to determine whether it suits your audience. Even a carefully stated and specific thesis may have its limits.

{**Thesis**} Over the next three years, high-tech stocks offer extraordinary opportunities for investors with money they can afford to gamble.

Audience 1: Affluent readers of *The Wall Street Journal*

Great topic!

Audience 2: Readers of *Archie* comic books

So what?

Audience 3: Readers of a newsletter for senior citizens at a public housing project.

Big deal!

For additional material on developing and refining a thesis, see Section 24A, "From Subject Area to Thesis Statement."

2E

EXERCISE 2.15

Review Exercises 2.2 and 2.3 and then assess the quality of the following thesis statements. Which do you think might help focus a paper by summing up main ideas succinctly, specifically, and in ways that make you eager to read the entire essay? Which survive the "So what?" and "Big deal!" tests?

1. Clear Lake College began as a mistake and then things really got bad.
2. The story of Clear Lake College is interesting.
3. We need to cover many aspects of the Clear Lake College story.
4. Probably no institution of higher learning had a humbler beginning than Clear Lake College.
5. Would anyone believe that a college that held its first class in a horse barn would someday count among its alumni a Nobel laureate, a great corporate magnate, and a winner of the Publisher's Clearinghouse Sweepstakes?
6. Dean Rack is a fascist idiot who has no right accusing every student on the Clear Lake campus of plagiarism when the whole problem is in his mind, really.
7. Allowing a few incidents of plagiarism to alter the fabric of education at Clear Lake College undermines the principle of reasonable conversation on which institutions of higher education are supposedly built.

8. In requiring that all papers be written in class, Dean Rack violates the rights of students and undermines the academic freedom of his faculty.
9. The subject of plagiarism is a complicated one and no one is completely right or wrong.
10. The seriousness of the plagiarism problem is great and we must do something about it.

Whatever plans you make to develop a paper, keep them flexible. Actual writing may spark ideas that incinerate your original blueprints. If you can—that is, if you have the time—consider these new ideas and adjust your outlines or lists to accommodate them. Don't moan over the ashes. Don't close down too quickly if you can avoid it. Just because you have a finished plan for a paper doesn't mean you have found the best way to treat a topic. Take time off to assimilate, sort, and connect the ideas you have been working with. Take time out to let your ideas incubate.

2F WHAT IS INCUBATION?

PROCESS MENU

PREPARING
PLANNING
INCUBATING
WRITING
REVISING
EDITING

For many kinds of writing, you will do better *not* to try to work in a methodical one-two-three fashion, moving nonstop from preparation to revising and editing. Interviews with writers and other creative people suggest that it is more productive to allow time after the preliminary writing stages for ideas to incubate or "simmer."

Such interruptions in the process, whether they are over-night or for just a few hours, seem to prompt the subconscious mind to sort through and evaluate material, make new connections, and sometimes arrive at fresh insights or solutions. It's exactly like "sleeping" on a problem to gain a fresh perspective on it. Such time off can be especially useful when you are working on Type II writing and don't know precisely what it is you want to do. When you draw a blank or your ideas dry up, give your mind a rest. Go swimming, clean the closet, or cut the grass.

To take advantage of the subconscious mind's ability to solve problems, you need to begin an assignment far enough ahead of your deadline to allow yourself the leisure of stepping away from a paper. You will usually return to your desk with renewed energy and maybe a new idea.

When you are actually into writing your drafts, take some mini-incubation breaks. When you are stuck for a word or can't think of the example you need to illustrate a point, getting away from the desk long enough to do an errand or get a snack from the refrigerator can trigger a flash of insight that breaks through those barriers that hinder writing. Having confidence that your subconscious will work for you if you let it makes writing a little less stressful, a little more exciting. You never know what you're going to find in the refrigerator.

One warning. Taking time out to allow ideas to simmer assumes you already have ideas and words in the pot. Don't confuse incubation with procrastination.

EXERCISE 2.16

Try to recall a time when you solved what seemed like an insoluble problem after taking a break from worrying about it. (The problem does not have to be connected with writing a paper.) Describe that experience in a short narrative. Was the solution you arrived at an obvious one? If so, why hadn't you discovered it earlier?

EXERCISE 2.17

You need a break from all the hard work you have been doing on your paper. Take one.

CHAPTER

Writing

- **A** Writing situations
- **B** How do you write?
- **C** When is it a draft?
- **D** An essay in progress I

3A WHAT IS YOUR WRITING SITUATION?

PROCESS MENU

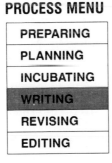

PREPARING
PLANNING
INCUBATING
WRITING
REVISING
EDITING

Troubleshooting

What is your writing situation? Unless you keep a private journal, every time you write you are working with other people. You are trying to:

1. say **something**

2. to **somebody**

3. for **some purpose**.

Unless a piece of writing does those three things, it doesn't really exist *as* writing—it's just an exercise, and you might as well fold it into an airplane and sail it around the classroom.

If you are like most inexperienced writers, however, you may have trouble keeping these requirements in mind when writing for a course. (You probably have less trouble remembering them in more compelling out-of-class situations—for example, writing to appeal a traffic ticket or to correct an error in your transcript.) The first section of this chapter offers tips for conditioning yourself to think of **meaning**, **audience**, and **purpose** every time you compose. Probably no single routine will do more to make you an effective writer. First-class professional writers habitually think in terms of **what** they want to say, **for whom** they are writing, and **why** they are writing. Novice writers usually don't.

To evaluate a writing situation . . .

▶ **Consider the significance of your subject.** Decide whether you have an idea worth your time to write about and worth someone else's time to read. Does it tell your readers what they want or need to know? We don't mean that every time you write you should come up with a fresh idea, or that you always have to write about serious and complex topics. But you should try to tell your readers something interesting or surprising.

Perhaps you can furnish them with useful information, perhaps entertain or amuse them, or just give them fresh insights on a familiar topic. If you were writing an exam for a professor, composing something significant might mean writing a paper that demonstrates you understand a basic concept—for instance, the "red shift" in astronomy. In an essay written for an English class, *significant* could mean a paper that vividly narrates a personal experience.

Don't underestimate your ability to write something other people will enjoy reading. It's rarely true that a person has "nothing to say"—anyone who has held a job, pursued a hobby, traveled, or who simply likes to converse has gathered experiences and information that can be developed into intriguing papers. Chances are good that if you write about something you know well and are curious about—even something as simple as observations about students you see on the bus every day—other people will find your paper worth reading. Chances are also good that if you select a topic that seems easy but bores you, your content will prove trivial, and your readers will yawn. A paper that relies on conventional wisdom and clichés to tell readers what they already know will surely be insignificant writing.

EXERCISE 3.1

Walter's Do-It-Yourself Garage in Ruralia is a favorite Saturday afternoon hangout for the mechanically inclined who like to watch other people work. On any given Saturday afternoon, you're likely to find Big Stevie tinkering with her motorcycle, Jasper Rhodes, Clear Lake College's football coach, dreaming of next season and tightening something or other on his drooping pickup, Colonel Ringling giving orders, and Christy Naomuooon talking about the problem of finding talented jazz musicians to play at her club. Deciding to do a feature story on the garage, Connie Lim made this list of topics discussed at Walter's in the course of a single Saturday afternoon.

What happens when aluminum auto engines overheat?

The age of Mindy Mendelson, owner of The Avant Gardener nursery

The metric system versus good old American measures

Lite Beer commercials

Lite Beer

Passing teams versus running teams in college football

How rock and roll has corrupted American youth

The reasons one might dye one's spiked hair purple

Viet Cong strategy after the Tet offensive

Military pensions

BMW versus Harley versus Honda motorcycles: which has more class?

Who can lift more, Big Stevie or Walter?

Do bulging muscles make either sex more attractive?

Will Clear Lake College win a football game this century?

3A

Which topics do you think might furnish material for intriguing articles? Discuss how you might develop the more promising subjects.

Consider whether the subject of the paper you started developing in the previous chapter is one you can live with. Do you find it interesting and significant enough to spend several days working on? Will it be intriguing to the audience that will read it?

▶ **Consider whom you are writing for.** Commit yourself to writing for somebody. "Somebody" can be an **audience** of one, or it can be a much larger group. (In class, that audience should include people in addition to your writing instructor.) As much as you can, you need to know what your audience expects from you, how much they already know about your topic, what questions they are likely to have about it, and what values and attitudes they have that will affect the way they read your paper.

You also need to consider whether members of your audience have reasons for reading your paper—if they don't, they probably won't bother. In many cases, you have to persuade them shrewdly to read beyond a first sentence or paragraph. To do that, it may help to draw a mental picture of your audience or to make up an individual who represents the important traits of that audience. Keep that portrait—that individual—in mind as you write. The Audience Grid in this section shows how to create such a picture. (Also see the section on Audience Adaptation in Revising, Section 4B.)

Sometimes you may want to postpone an audience analysis until you get to a second draft. This may be the case when you are drafting Type II writing and want to tinker with a subject before aiming your ideas at particular readers. Such a delay may leave you freer to generate ideas.

For instance, if you are furious about a recent proposal to widen a highway through your neighborhood and want to write an editorial about it, you can blow off steam in the first draft, call the mayor who proposed it an idiot, and suggest that everyone picket her office. Such explosions are fun to write and often a good way to start, but they don't do much to impress the people you need to persuade if you want to accomplish something. When you start the second draft, however, you can think about who the readers with power to veto the proposal are and how you can appeal to their concerns. Then you can revise your essay to reach them.

Learning to analyze your audience skillfully takes time, practice, and psychological insights we don't have space to go into here. But we strongly believe that no step in learning to write well is more important than developing a compelling sense of audience. Writing to a professional audience, for example, often means proving that you are ready to become a member of that group. In writing to them, you demonstrate an appreciation for the way they usually write: the level of formality they expect, the organizing patterns they typically employ, the level of knowledge they assume, and the vocabulary they use. In addressing a professional audience successfully, you demonstrate that you are worthy of its attention.

So learn to keep your readers in mind as you work; try to stand in their shoes. Like many professionals, you may have to practice in a mock situation to be prepared for the real thing, so while you are an apprentice writer, learn to think beyond your own viewpoint and to consider the interests and expectations of those you are writing for. The Audience Grid will help you do that.

Would it affect what you wrote if you, like Connie Lim, knew that all the people in Walter's Do-It-Yourself Garage would be reading an article you were writing about them in the local paper (see Exercise 3.1)? In what ways would your writing be influenced by that audience? Describe a time when you had to be especially sensitive or cautious in writing for a particular audience.

3A

▶ **Analyze your readers by using this Audience Grid.**

AUDIENCE GRID

I. Who is going to read this essay?

Is the audience already specified?
Can I specify the audience?
If so, who would be the ideal audience?

II. Are the readers likely to be interested in the topic and willing to read?

Are they likely to be receptive to my ideas? Why?
Do they have the power and ability to act on my suggestions?
Are they going to be willing to learn or be persuaded?

III. What do my readers already know about my topic?

How much experience on this issue can I expect them to have?
Can I use specialized language? Should I?
How much of what I am writing is news to them?
How can I give them new information or ideas?

IV. What attitudes about this issue do my readers have?

What values do we share that I can appeal to?
What biases do they have?

What kind of approach might alienate them?

How will their age, sex, or social, economic, or educational level affect the way they read?

V. What do my readers expect to get from reading this essay?

What specific questions will they have that I should try to answer?

THE AUDIENCE GRID APPLIED TO AN ESSAY

"Paying College Football Players Legally," (Section 3D)

(I–II) In this case, the writer found his topic first and then chose the audience he wanted to address after asking himself, "Who would be interested in this issue and willing to listen to my suggestions?" He decided his best choice would be the university alumni association and the most likely place to publish would be in its monthly magazine. He reasoned that many alumni who join their university's association are likely to be interested in football and issues that affect their football team. They are also influential people in university affairs and could work to change the system if they wanted to. They are probably also willing to be persuaded.

(III) Alumni who keep up with football are likely to be familiar with the problem discussed in the essay—they probably know of specific instances when alumni have given money to players and may even have done it themselves. They also know how severe the penalties can be. So the situation that the writer describes is not exactly news, but they don't mind having their memories refreshed about a serious problem. The proposal to set up a legal fund to give players allowances is probably new, however, and they would definitely be interested in that.

(IV) The readers are sports-minded and share with the writer a concern for the welfare of their alma mater's team. They would certainly hate to have that team barred from conference play or bowl games. They are open to ideas that would help the team and the players. They are particularly sympathetic to the players and may feel that the regulations about what they can receive are too strict. However, the writer could easily alienate his readers by suggesting that they were trying to corrupt players or that they approved of illegal practices. He doesn't accuse anyone directly.

(V) Readers who saw the title of the essay and chose to read it would expect to find out how college football players could be paid legally and why they should be. They would also want to know what situation had prompted the author to raise the issue. At least some of the questions they would probably want answered would be these:

> What are the current problems?
> What has caused them?
> What is happening as a result of those problems?
> What possible solutions are there?

EXERCISE 3.4

Apply the Audience Grid to the readers for whom you intend to write your paper.

EXERCISE 3.5

Here are the titles of several articles. What audience or audiences do you think their authors had in mind?

> Dieting: The Losing Game
>
> Servicing Satellites in Space
>
> Thoroughly Modern Modems: A Ratings List
>
> The Myth, Fable, and Reality of the Working Woman
>
> Making Sense of Agriculture
>
> Gourmet Holidays: The Castles of Scotland

The Art of Rhetoric at the Amphiareion of Oropos

Ruling the World of Money

Why Great Men No Longer Run for President

► **Consider why you are writing—your purpose.** Any time you write you should be doing so for a reason, to accomplish something, achieve some goal. Sometimes, as with an essay exam, the purpose may be set for you. For many writing tasks, however, you will choose your own purpose. In such cases, you'll need to think about what your goals will be—because you are writing to meet your readers' needs as well as your own. Again, before you commit yourself to a specific purpose, you may want to compose a draft from a writer-centered point of view to explore how you feel about your topic and the direction it should take. By the time you get to a second draft, however, you should have a clear idea of where you are going. If you don't, you may waste more time than you can afford writing *around* your topic rather than on it. So try to have a strong sense of what you want to do as you work on your large-scale revision (see Section 4B). The Purpose Grid in this section can help you discover that purpose.

► **Analyze your reason for writing by using this Purpose Grid.**

PURPOSE GRID

I. Why are you writing?

Is your purpose specified for you?
What is it?
Can you specify your own purpose?
What stimulus are you responding to?

II. What do you hope to accomplish with your writing?

To entertain?
To inform?

To share experience?
To influence?
To stimulate?
To provoke emotional response?
To bring about change?
To persuade?
To make readers feel good?
To challenge readers' thinking?
To reinforce existing ideas or attitudes?
To enlighten on some issue?
Several of the above?

III. What action do you want your readers to take as a result of reading?

Join you in a cause?
Reflect on experience?
Consider a new point of view?
Nothing?

IV. What change do you hope to bring about?

Readers will alter their behavior?
Readers will adopt your proposal?
Readers will change or rethink their opinions or attitudes?
None?

THE PURPOSE GRID APPLIED TO AN ESSAY

"Paying College Football Players Legally," (Section 3D)

(I) For this essay, the writer chose his own purpose. He decided he wanted to persuade alumni that giving small amounts of money to individual football players causes serious problems. He also wanted to explain how direct alumni contributions to a school would benefit both the institution and its athletes. The stimulus he is responding to is the way he feels about the problems caused by the present system of supporting college football players. He thinks the system is damaging, and he has a proposal to change it and solve the problem.

(II) The writer is trying to accomplish several goals; he wants to inform, enlighten, persuade, and bring about change. He also wants to make the alumni feel good and reinforce their support of the football program.

(III) The writer wants readers to act by considering a new point of view and joining him in a cause.

(IV) The writer hopes to alter the behavior of some of his readers, those who may have been slipping athletes money under the table. He hopes all of them will change enough to rethink the way the system now operates and work to persuade the NCAA to adopt the proposal he makes.

3A

EXERCISE 3.6

Apply the Purpose Grid to the essay you are developing.

EXERCISE 3.7

Here are the titles of several brochures. What purposes do you think their authors had in mind?

How to Establish Your Credit Rating

Is Exercise for You?

Nutrition and Your Family

Broken French? Repair It at Alliance Française

Your Banking Options

What If the Soviets Get SDI First?

Repent: The End Is Nearer Than You Think!

The Lure and Lore of the Canadian Rockies

You and Alcohol

▶ **Consider how audience and purpose work together.**
Although we have discussed the concepts of audience and
purpose separately in order to define and explain them, experienced writers know that one can never really separate them in
actual writing.

Inevitably, the audience you choose to write for will to
some extent be determined by the purpose you have in writing.
For example, if you want to get your neighborhood rezoned so
that you can open a small jazz club in your house, you will
have to find out who makes rezoning decisions and what
factors they take into consideration, then write to the appropriate people: probably the zoning board, the city council, and
the neighborhood association. You may prefer extolling the
joys of your proposed nightclub in a newsletter to your fellow
jazz fans, but you still have to write to the audience that counts
in this case.

Similarly, if the audience for a letter of protest about doubling the fee for student parking permits has to be the university
vice-president for business affairs, the nature of that audience
is going to affect your purpose in writing a protest letter. For
such a reader, your purpose in writing would be to make a
convincing cause-and-effect argument demonstrating the
harmful results of the increased fee: hardships for commuting
students, reduced enrollment, and so on. If you were writing
the protest as an editorial in the student newspaper, however,
your purpose could be to vent your anger and get other students to join you in trying to get the fee reduced.

EXERCISE 3.8

Review the plagiarism controversy described in Exercise 2.3.
Then, explain the adjustments for audience you might have to
make if you were doing the following kinds of writing.

  a. A letter to the college president urging her to
     reject Dean Rack's proposal.

  b. An editorial in the college paper condemning con-
     niving Dean Wolfgang Rack.

  c. An article in the community paper explaining the
     controversy.

d. A poster urging complacent students to attend a meeting to discuss the proposal.

e. A leaflet blaming students for various kinds of scholastic dishonesty.

f. An argumentative paper in a political science course analyzing the controversy.

g. A report to be issued from Rack's office defending the Dean's position.

3B HOW DO YOU WRITE?

Troubleshooting

There is no one best way to write any paper, nor any ideal paper you are supposed to imitate. Just as people have different ways of learning languages or acquiring other skills, writers take different approaches to writing—any one of which can work well. So you needn't feel guilty if you don't work the same way as some good writer you know—what's best for him or her may not be your style. But you do need to find out what works for you—where do you feel most comfortable writing; what kind of tools or supplies do you require; how long do you need to produce the first draft of a short paper? Must you outline before you can write? Does it help to do several pages of freewriting to get your thoughts moving? Can you write a paper in chunks and organize it later or do you have to work straight through from beginning to end? Do you write quickly or slowly? It's important to discover your own rhythms and style of working and to honor them. It's foolish to make yourself miserable by trying to imitate a method that doesn't suit your temperament.

You may find that your method varies according to the kind of writing you are doing. If you are doing Type I writing and know ahead of time how you are going to organize a paper and what your main points are going to be, you may be able to write your introduction quickly, develop a logical argument with several examples, and have to do only minor tinkering on your second draft. On the other hand, if you are doing Type II, reflective writing, you may need to work very differently, making abundant notes and trying out several different introductions before you find the one that gets you started in what seems like a productive direction. Then your writing may go quickly or slowly, depending on how fast your ideas come to you. So don't assume there is only one effective method for you—there may be several.

To prepare a satisfactory draft . . .

▶ **Set your own pace.** If you are not sure what kind of writing pace suits you best, start by trying to make yourself write quickly. Consult your notes or outline as you go to be sure you're hitting your main points, but concentrate on composing with as few interruptions as possible. To stay on track, you may need to pause occasionally to look over what you've produced, but try not to worry too much about details at this stage.

If you hit a snag and can't think of the precise words you want or the most graphic examples, "island hop" around the troublesome parts and go on, confident that you can return later. Try also not to worry about style or sentence structure—you'll slow yourself down too much. For now, your most important goal is to record your ideas and create a rough first draft. If necessary, you can flesh it out or rearrange it later. Don't lose the momentum writing builds up by pausing to solve minor problems. Tackle the major ones first.

Preparing a first draft quickly will give you a sense of accomplishment. When you are done, you will have ideas on paper—*stuff* to work with.

If, however, you're the kind of writer who just isn't comfortable composing quickly, don't feel bad. Many competent writers work slowly, stopping frequently to reread and reflect on what they've written, changing words and phrases as they go. They pace the floor, look out the window, forage in the refrigerator, and stop to stretch. They may take several hours to turn out a page or two, but their first drafts often are quite polished and so need much less revision than those of faster writers. In the long run, slow writers may not spend any more time composing a paper than writers who seem to be working faster.

Whatever your pace, remember that writing itself is a creative process that stirs up the unconscious mind and generates new material. So even when you know most of your content before you start writing, you should expect fresh ideas or useful examples to turn up as you work. Have a plan to capture them. Such ideas may prove to be the heart of your paper. So stay alert for the flash of insight and be ready to write the thought down immediately—if you don't, it will disappear, perhaps forever.

On some word processors you can jot down and store your brilliant flashes of insight in a scrapbook or on a clipboard. Or you may just want to keep a notepad on your desk for ideas. Either way, don't let good thoughts evaporate because you are afraid to alter your pace or interrupt your writing.

EXERCISE 3.9

Analyze the kind of writer you are by asking yourself the following battery of questions.

—Do you write quickly or slowly? Do you make a lot of changes as you work? How long can you work at one stretch?

—How often do you stop to reread as you are writing? Do such stops seem to be necessary?

—How often do you get up briefly and do other things when you are writing? Do such breaks usually help you think?

—Where do you prefer to write? Do you always write in that place if you can? Is there something about that place that helps you write?

—What time of the day do you prefer to write? Can you work at any time?

—What kind of atmosphere do you like? Must you have quiet? Do you like music while you write? If so, what kind?

—What tools do you use? Pencil and paper? Typewriter? Word processor? Is it very important that you have those tools? Can you switch from one to another without getting disrupted?

—Do you write regularly? How often? Do you keep a journal or diary?

—How do you feel about writing? What words would describe your attitude?

▶ **Organize and shape your thoughts.** We have been saying so much about getting ideas—any ideas—down on paper that we had better remind you that, sooner or later, you have to piece all those thoughts together. As you work, you need to think about ways of keeping your writing unified. You want your writing to give readers an impression of wholeness and direction. You want to be sure that readers can follow your ideas without getting lost or confused. Ideally, readers should not have to stop to reread just to understand your meaning— though they may want to pause to consider your ideas. When they finish, they should feel satisfied, sensing no loose ends. The sentences and paragraphs should fit together so snugly that the reader can't detect joints or seams where you added things or cut words out.

Organizing a paper is challenging—professional writers work hard at it—but here are some suggestions and strategies that may help you.

—*Understand that organization is not optional*. At a minimum, most papers will have a beginning, a middle, and an end. Readers will expect the opening to introduce the subject, the middle to develop it, and the conclusion to round it out and reinforce any major points.

As a writer, you can meet these expectations or reshape them. But you cannot safely ignore them. Meeting these expectations means constructing an opening that lays out a plan for your essay or invites readers to continue reading. It means fleshing out the middle of an essay with ideas, arguments, actions, or illustrations that make your point. And meeting expectations means finding a way out of a subject that doesn't leave readers feeling like they've just run out of tape on their VCR. The basic formula is this simple:

    I. Introduction

   II. Body

  III. Conclusion

Reshaping expectations readers have about organization simply means taking firmer control. You decide precisely how you want your essay to develop and then let the reader in on your game plan. For example, you might decide that the body of your essay cannot simply present arguments that support a thesis. Instead it will have to present two points of view—pro and con—that lead to two tentative conclusions.

    I. Introduction

   II. Pro

  III. Con

  IV. Conclusions

Or perhaps your paper is a narrative that leads to a single conclusion. No introduction is necessary.

    I. First incident

   II. Next incident

  III. Next incident . . .

  IX. Next incident

   X. Conclusion

Fine. You can arrange your essay according to any design, so long as you tell your readers what you are up to. You do that through simple statements that act as roadsigns for your plan *("Both sides of the issue require careful explanation"; "What all these events prove . . .")* and through transitional phrases and paragraphs *("First of all"; "On the other side of the issue"; "Next").*

If you don't make the effort to organize a paper, chances are readers will impose a design on it anyway. They'll fix on a statement that seems to be your main point and then evaluate how well you have supported it. When their expectations aren't fulfilled by what you have written, they'll blame you for the confusion they feel. So don't think that organization is a fine point in an essay; it's a foundation.

3B

—*Find a Controlling Pattern.* The common thought patterns illustrated in Section 2C can provide logical designs for shaping a paper to fit your subject. For example, you might use *definition* and *cause and effect* in writing a paper about the dreadful concerts the Campus Entertainment Committee has scheduled for next semester; that is, start out by defining the problem at your college—the music is saccharine, deadly, and out-of-date—and then analyze its causes and the effects on students.

    I.   Introduction

    II.   The problem defined

   III.   Its causes

   IV.   Its effects

    V.   Recommendations

You might also use a *problem and solution* pattern or a *question and answer* pattern. For the first, you could start out by describing the problem—the horrible concerts scheduled—and then you propose a solution—have student members appointed to the committee; in the second, you could start out by asking the question, "What happened to make the spring concert series such a disaster?" and develop the paper by answering the question.

Two of the most useful of patterns are *comparison* and *contrast*. In fact, they are often treated as a single pattern, especially in examination questions: *Compare and contrast Romanesque and Gothic architecture.* In writing such a comparison or contrast, you'll usually find yourself employing one of two very basic plans, examining the subjects one at a time or feature by feature.

ONE AT A TIME

  I.   Introduction
 II.   Subject 1 (Romanesque Architecture)
       —Feature a (Arches)
       —Feature b (Windows)
       —Feature c (Structure)
III.   Subject 2 (Gothic Architecture)
       —Feature a (Arches)
       —Feature b (Windows)
       —Feature c (Structure)
 IV.   Conclusions

FEATURE BY FEATURE

  I.   Introduction. Romanesque and Gothic
       Architecture
 II.   Feature a (Arches)
       —Subject 1 (Romanesque)
       —Subject 2 (Gothic)
III.   Feature b (Windows)
       —Subject 1 (Romanesque)
       —Subject 2 (Gothic)
 IV.   Feature c (Structure)
       —Subject 1 (Romanesque)
       —Subject 2 (Gothic)
  V.   Conclusions

By employing any of these common thought patterns you tap into the natural thought processes your readers are used to and give them a sense of direction that helps them follow your points. You give them a design that helps them anticipate what to expect from your writing.

—Use Commitment and Response. Another important unifying strategy, one that is useful for almost any paper, is *commitment and response.* Writers using this strategy consciously make a *commitment* or promise to their readers early in a paper and use that commitment as a kind of base or foundation upon which to develop the rest of the essay. The commitment can be direct or indirect. In a direct commitment, the writer might begin the paper with a statement of the problem or issue to be addressed in the paper. For example,

> Yesterday's announcement in *The Daily Toxin* of the concerts the Campus Cultural Entertainment Committee has chosen to inflict on us this year should make every student who was thinking about laying out $25 for a season ticket think again. And again. And again.

Such an opening statement is a commitment because it presents an issue and commits the writer to explaining and developing it in a way that will satisfy expectations raised in a reader's mind.

Another kind of direct commitment can take the form of a provocative question that introduces an issue a writer wants to address. For example,

> Are you planning to put out $25 for the spring concert series announced yesterday by the Campus Entertainment Committee?

A reader who encounters this first sentence knows not to expect a short and specific answer; rather, he or she expects to read more about a controversy.

Indirect commitments can take the form of an anecdote or illustrative narrative. For example,

> Last night I unexpectedly came into a pair of free tickets and found myself sitting in the first balcony of the Ma-

jestic Theatre in Cincinnati waiting for the curtain to go
up for a performance by Bella Boffo and her Blues Band.
Rhythm and blues, I thought. Great! Can't go too far
wrong with that, especially when it's free. That shows
how naive I was. Nothing proved to be a high price to
have paid for a show so bad.

This kind of personal and specific opening raises the
reader's expectations and draws her into the paper to find out
more about the incident it dramatizes. As Johnny Carson's
audiences ask on cue, "How bad was it?"

Two other phrases that describe this kind of opening are to
promise and fulfill and *entice and reward*. All three phrases
suggest that an important function of the opening for a paper is
to **forecast** or **predict** content for the readers. Readers want to
know what to anticipate when they begin to read because it
helps them focus and concentrate on the main idea. They also
don't want to be disappointed when they read a paper—the
writer has either implicitly or explicitly made them a promise,
established a contract, and has an obligation to carry it out.
That's why it is so important for a writer to keep in mind the
second part of these phrases—*respond, fulfill, reward*—as he
or she is writing.

—*Organize in chunks.* Even after you have established a pattern or direction for a paper, you must keep organizing and
shaping. Because readers continuously group and cluster information as they read, every part of an essay needs design. If
you don't supply directions for your readers, they will follow
their own paths (often wrong) or assume that your work is
incoherent.

You can't, for example, simply present ideas at random. If
you supply several examples, you are automatically involved
in a **sequence** that has readers asking which of these ideas is the
most important, which the least. If you don't tell them, they
are apt to assume that your last example is the most important,
whether it is or not. So, within a given chunk of a paper—it
can be a paragraph in a short paper or a whole section in a
longer one—you need to impose a design: one that may be as

simple as a sequence (*first, second, third*) or as complex as a complete thought pattern (*cause and effect*). You need not be terribly self-conscious about outlining such strategies; just be aware that readers benefit as much from the attention you give to individual parts of an essay as to the design of the whole.

Such small-scale strategies of organization offer you opportunities to express ideas powerfully or memorably. In shorter papers, for example, you can emphasize important points, facts, or arguments by placing them where they will get the most attention: at the beginnings or endings of paragraphs or at the beginning or ending of the essay itself. Don't hesitate to announce key ideas with phrases that underscore their significance: *"the chief issue, however, is"; "the most significant development."* In a longer paper, you can highlight new ideas simply by placing them at the beginning of sections or marking them with headings. Consider, too, that what most people remember from a paper is what they have read last, so end a paper—especially an argument—with whatever you want to leave in readers' minds.

Finally, consider the importance of proportions. If you spend two pages discussing a minor point and half a page on a major one, readers are apt to consider the minor point the major one. If your introductory section takes up two-thirds of the paper, it is not an introduction anymore. If you conclude a detailed and complicated essay with one bland sentence, you may trivialize serious work. In short, be aware that readers respond not only to what you say, but how you say it. Be sure that the content and "body language" of an essay send the same message.

—Include Transition Words and Phrases. Successful essays can sometimes seem like those ancient Chinese temples in which all the pieces fit together without nails. But look closely and you'll discover writers using many devices to connect ideas; among the most useful are those words or phrases described as **transitions**. These hooks and directional signals keep writing coherent. They create an impression of ideas flowing smoothly.

But like the welds and bolts that hold a bridge together, transitional words should contribute to structural integrity. They ought not to be treated as afterthoughts. You can't salvage a disorganized argument by tacking a *therefore* to its conclusion. However, you can strengthen a legitimate point by underscoring it with a *consequently* or direct attention to a contrast by beginning *on the other hand.* There are many transitional hooks. Here are just a very few.

also	nevertheless
meanwhile	however
in spite of	on the other hand
consequently	moreover
first of all	although
finally	therefore

Remember that different transition words have different purposes, so use them carefully. More on that later in the transitions section of the handbook.

EXERCISE 3.10

What kind of commitments do the writers of the following openings make? Would these paragraphs prompt you to read the complete articles? Try making a scratch outline for one of the paragraphs, outlining how you might complete the essay.

"Stereotype" is a dirty word among some intellectuals and others who feel that, when used to describe members of a race, religion, or nationality, it indicates prejudices. Perhaps it is time we changed our thinking.
—William B. Helmreich

I knew a man who went into therapy about three years ago because, as he put it, he couldn't live with himself any longer. I didn't blame him. The guy was a bigot, a tyrant, and a creep.
—Ellen Goodman

The buzz is about the men, but put your money on the woman.

The men are Martin Scorsese, who directed *The Color of Money*; Paul Newman, who returns as Fast Eddie Felson in this follow-up to the 1961 movie *The Hustler*; and Tom Cruise, who plays Vincent Lauria, a cocky poolroom wizard by turns befriended, tutored, and challenged by Felson. These are the guys on whom the high hopes are based, about whom the tales of instant camaraderie are told, around whom the Oscar talk revolves. The woman is Mary Elizabeth Mastrantonio, and she has turned what could have been a typical guys' movie—the pool-hall setting, the mentor-student relationship, all that—into something richer and more unexpected.

—Steve Pond

EXERCISE 3.11

If you haven't done so already, write a complete draft of the paper you have been working on, either the Type I history of an institution or the Type II exploration of a local controversy.

3C WHEN IS IT A DRAFT?

Troubleshooting

Your teacher may ask to see a rough version of some paper you are working on by a specified date. How do you know when you have a first draft worth showing a teacher?

As the deadline approaches to turn in that first draft, try to relax and assure yourself that although a paper you are laboring over may not be as good as you'd like, it *is* a draft which you will have the chance to work on again. You can also take comfort in knowing that most other people's first drafts probably aren't in great shape either. If you are in a class where writers exchange papers and comment on drafts, you'll see evidence of that quickly. But how do you know when you have a rough draft you don't have to be ashamed of? How rough may this *rough* draft be?

When you can say "Yes" to the three questions presented below, you probably have a draft that should satisfy you, your instructor, and your classmates reasonably well.

▶ Does the Draft Represent a Good-faith Effort?

Have you made an honest effort to write something worth reading and discussing? If you are tempted to take the easy out of concocting a draft from bald generalizations and obvious comments because you're not going to be graded on this first effort, you're not writing in good faith, and you can't expect anyone else to spend time responding to what you've written. You're also passing up an opportunity you may not get again— the chance to get substantial and useful criticism on your paper before you receive a grade on it.

▶ Is the Draft Reasonably Complete?

Have you stated a thesis or main idea, developed it with some supporting arguments or examples, and finished with some kind of conclusion? If so, you can legitimately claim that you have a working draft that is a starting point. Fragments or an outline and a few paragraphs don't qualify as working drafts. If you want useful feedback from others, you can't give them only part of a paper.

▶ Is the Draft Legible?

Can someone else read the draft without having to struggle to decipher it? If you can, give your readers a break by typing or printing out your paper, double-spaced. If that's not possible, write in ink on every other line. Legibility is especially important if your paper is going to be copied. You can't expect either your instructor or your classmates to give you a sympathetic reading and challenging suggestions if they can't make out what you've written. If that happens, again you are missing your chance to get helpful feedback before you submit the paper for a grade.

EXERCISE 3.12

Evaluate your draft against the three criteria discussed above. Does your paper meet the standards? Or is it back to the drafting table?

WHAT A DRAFT LOOKS LIKE—AN ESSAY IN PROGRESS (PT. 1)

Introduction

Here is the first draft of a student paper for which the author could say "yes" to all the questions in Section 3C. It is also a good draft in other ways. The author makes his main idea clear from the beginning, and he develops it with adequate supporting evidence. He knows quite a bit about his topic and seems genuinely interested in it. He gives reasons for his opinions, uses specific figures to illustrate his points, and proposes a solution to the problem he describes. The paper is certainly readable, with no pretentious language or tangled sentences.

The draft does have weaknesses. It's not clear who the intended audience is, and the organization is rather jumbled. At times the writer repeats himself so that by ¶4 the reader begins to think, "You've already told me this." And the writer has jammed together too much information in the next-to-last paragraph, making it hard to follow. The paper needs fleshing out with more interesting examples. But it's a good start.

Matthew Atha
March 3, 1986

Draft I (no title)

(¶1) Cheating in college football continues to grow at an alarming rate. Alumni often times offer to provide players with cash, cars, homes, and summer jobs to come to State U. and play football. As the problem of cheating becomes almost uncontrollable, a solution must be sought.

(¶2) Currently, the NCAA does not allow players to hold any kind of a job during fall or spring long semesters while attending school. If a student is on full scholarship, he gets his board, books, room, and tuition free. However, after that point, the school's support stops. Many school athletes come from poor families. Their parents cannot afford to give their college age kid extra spending money so he can go out and get a pizza if he gets tired of the dining hall food, or if he needs laundry money. Athletes also enjoy having extra food in their dorm room refrigerator for a late night snack. If athletes can't get money from their parents, where do they turn?

(¶3) Many have questioned even if athletes can't get money from their parents, why can't they save up money earned during the summer. Because college football takes so much time during the school year, football players don't usually take a full load of classes. Because they take fewer hours, many attend summer school. Summer school gives them an opportunity to concentrate fully on their studies and catch up on their hours.

(¶4) Herein lies the dilemma. If they can't work during the summer, and their parents can't support them, where do they get their spending money? For the past couple of decades, alumni have been the illegal providers, but this can change.

(¶5) Coaches have purposed to give each football player a monthly stipend of $100 to $200 for spending money. They reason this would help alleviate the strong temptation to take money under the table. Some believe this would add to the cheating. They reason the players would become greedier. However, if the NCAA imposed harsher penalties for the athletes caught cheating, the monthly stipend might work.

3D

(¶6)   The stipend would allow players with little family support not to worry about money. They would be able to go out on the weekend, do their laundry, and buy some clothes they might need. The cost of putting 90 scholarship athletes on $150 stipend for nine months would be $121,500 annually. This would put a bigger burden on smaller schools with smaller athletic budgets but in the long run the proposal would pay for itself. Instead of alumni pumping money directly to the student illegally, they would begin giving to the school. This would help subsidize the preposal and also give the alumnus a tax break. One BMW would cost an alumnus $25,000, but if he gave the cash to the school instead of the car to the athlete, he would be acting legally and also be rewarded by the government. The proposal might save the school money also. If a school is caught cheating, the NCAA usually sanctions that school and prevents them from having their games televised. One year of television sanctions would cost the University of Texas more than $1,000,000, enough to pay for eight or nine years of stipends for athletes. If the proposal worked ideally, the chance of a school caught cheating would not occur and the likelihood of losing television revenue would decrease.

(¶7)   As cheating at the college level continues to increase, schools must take the initiative to help stop it. Helping athletes meet monthly expenses would be one way schools could help both the athlete and their alumni.

CHAPTER

Revising and Editing

- **A** Revising vs. editing
- **B** Large scale revision
- **C** An essay in progress II
- **D** Small scale revision
- **E** Editing and proofreading
- **F** An essay in progress III

Terms you need to know

Revising. Rethinking and rewriting the draft of a paper, making substantial changes to improve it.

Editing. Correcting and polishing a late draft of a paper; cleaning it up to submit for evaluation.

Proofreading. Checking a finished paper closely to detect any errors in mechanics and usage.

4A **REVISING AND EDITING: WHAT'S THE DIFFERENCE?**

Troubleshooting

Many writers use the terms **revising**, **editing**, and **proofreading** interchangeably. But the words really describe various parts of the larger job of getting a paper into final shape. Understanding the differences can make improving a paper less confusing and intimidating.

▶ Revising and Editing a Paper are Different Processes

When you begin to **revise** your draft, try not to think in terms of *fixing* or *correcting* it—that's really not what you are doing. Rather you are working on a paper in progress, reviewing and rethinking what you have written and looking for ways to improve it. You may well get new ideas and shift the focus of your paper, and you may decide to cut some sections, expand others, and reorganize key parts. You're thinking about several things at once: large concerns such as accuracy, support, and focus as well as lesser ones such as tone, style, and word choice. If you write slowly and stop to reread frequently as you work, you may do substantial revising on paragraphs or sections as you go along; if you write quickly without many pauses, you may finish an entire first draft before you do substantial revising.

When you **edit** a paper, you correct any mistakes, tidy up loose ends or lapses, fix inconsistencies, and try to make the paper look as presentable as possible for its public appearance. You're making cosmetic changes to improve the appearance of the paper, not surgical changes that alter the real nature of the essay. Such editing changes can include correcting spelling and punctuation, fixing sentence fragments or dangling modifiers, straightening out pronoun reference or faulty subject/verb agreement, and **proofreading** to take care of typographical errors and other pesky mistakes that can crop up in a paper. Editing is a kind of quality control check to see that the surface details of a paper are right.

Obviously, editing is an important step for all writers because the appearance of a paper matters. A sloppy paper full of careless mistakes makes a bad impression on readers and biases their opinion of the writer just as a banged-up car with a dirty, interior makes people doubt the competence of a driver. Nevertheless, for most writers it's a good idea to postpone editing and proofreading until the last stages of the writing process. If you start worrying about getting everything correct while you are writing, you are liable to be distracted by little details when you would do better to think about the big picture.

While we urge you to consider writing as a process that normally includes revising, can you list kinds of writing that do not provide opportunities for drafts and serious revision? How might you compensate for not having the chance to rethink what you have done? What role does editing assume in these kinds of assignments or jobs?

4B

4B WHAT DOES LARGE SCALE REVISION INVOLVE?

PROCESS MENU

PREPARING
PLANNING
INCUBATING
WRITING
REVISING
EDITING

Troubleshooting

After completing a draft, you may feel overwhelmed by the prospect of rethinking and correcting what you have done. You are happy with some things you have written, but you also feel that much work remains. At this stage, don't try to revise everything at once or work through the draft paragraph by paragraph. If the paper has serious problems, they are likely to be problems of focus, content, and organization that you need to work on before you start fixing individual sentences. You're wasting your time if you stop now to revise sentences or paragraphs that you may discard entirely in the second draft. At this point, THINK BIG. Don't tinker.

4B

▶ Make Large Scale Changes That Affect Content

You can turn your attention later to **small scale**, mainly stylistic changes. Large scale changes generally include revising for *focus and proportion, commitment and response, purpose, audience adaptation, organization, and sufficient information.*

Terms you need to know

Focus. Concentration on a specific point or area in a paper. A reader feels he or she understands the major point a writer is making either in the paper as a whole or in individual sentences and paragraphs.

Proportion. The distribution and balance of ideas in a paper. The development of ideas should roughly parallel the importance a writer wants them to have in a paper: a major idea gets substantial coverage, a less important point gets less thorough treatment.

Clear purpose. A thesis or main point in a paper that shapes its design. A reader understands the point of a paper or can follow its general direction.

Commitment and response. A statement or suggestion of a writer's purposes in a paper followed by a fulfillment of that promise. The commitment raises expectations in a reader that the writer should fulfill.

Audience adaptation. Adjusting a paper to the needs and interests of its readers.

Effective organization. A design that gets readers from the beginning to the end of a paper without losing them, that treats ideas in proper proportion, that sets ideas in important relationships, and that signals their relative importance.

Sufficient information. Enough evidence, details, and examples to satisfy or convince readers that any assertions a writer has made stand up to the questions or objections they are likely to have.

Working with a paper copy if possible, start by reading over your first draft from start to finish, thinking about these elements of the paper:

> **Focus and proportion**: Ask yourself if you have tried to do too much in the paper. Have you generated more material than you can possibly deal with? Do you need to discard some of it and narrow your topic down to one you can develop adequately? Are the parts of the paper out of proportion? That is, have you gone into too much detail at the beginning and then skimped on the rest of the paper in the later parts?

One of the most common problems with first drafts is that writers try to do too much. They end up with superficial papers full of generalities readers already know. If you find that you have done that, now is the time to focus in on one aspect of your topic and develop it. Sometimes this first reading will make you realize that you have chosen a topic so large that it would be impossible for anyone to deal with it in one paper — the problems of public education, for example. Then you will have to "tree it down" (see Section 2D) and pick out a part of it to work on.

> **Clear purpose**: Ask yourself if early in the paper you have given your readers a clear signal about what to expect from the paper. Do they get a sense of what the paper is about soon after they start reading? Does the paper deal with one central idea that the reader can grasp with little trouble?

You may not have had a strong sense of where you were going when you started your first draft and counted on your purpose emerging as you wrote. That's fine, but now you need to decide what you want to accomplish with your paper and be sure that your intentions are clear to readers. Consider whether they might get to the second or even third page and still be wondering what your thesis is. You also need to ask yourself if the paper has a satisfying conclusion. You don't want readers saying "And so?" or "So what?" when they finish reading.

Commitment and response: Do you make an early commitment—or promise—to your readers that establishes what you are going to write about, that triggers expectations? Then do you finish what you started, follow through on that commitment, keep that promise, and meet those expectations?

Readers like to know what to anticipate when they start reading, so experienced writers usually start off with a commitment: a sentence or a paragraph or a question that makes a promise or holds out bait of some kind that will induce the reader to continue reading. Then it is crucial that the author follow through on the commitment and not disappoint the reader.

Adaptation to audience: Ask yourself who your readers are for this paper. Who would be interested in what you have to say, what do they already know about the topic, and what questions would they have that you need to answer? What changes do you need to make in order to adapt to your audience?

Sometimes a first draft is what we call "writer-centered"; that is, the writer has concentrated mostly on getting his or her ideas down, perhaps doing a discovery draft to get into the topic without really thinking much about the audience. Such an approach can be productive, but a major goal of revising should be to change writer-centered writing to "reader-centered" writing. You do that by trying to shift from your own point of view and to that of your readers. We say "try" because adopting the point of view of your readers is difficult; it's also essential. (See the section on audience, 3A.) Working with the Audience Grid on p. 52 can help you.

Effective organization: Check to see if your writing has a clear plan or pattern that will make it easy for readers to follow your train of thought. Do you move from an opening statement to development of that statement? Is there an obvious natural pattern such as cause and effect, claim/support, or comparison/contrast? Can you make that pattern clear to your readers? What about the order of your ideas? Would the paper work better if you moved some paragraphs around and changed your emphasis?

You really need a typed or printed copy of a draft to appreciate and improve its organization. It's difficult to gain a feeling for organization from a sprawling handwritten paper or, worse yet, from a computer screen. A typed or printed paper also can be cut and pasted, so you can move parts around to test various schemes of organization. Then you can show the cut-and-pasted version to a friend for an opinion.

Sufficient information: At the last stage of this revision, you may find that you need to add information to give your paper more weight and depth, especially if you have decided to narrow your topic and focus on only one of your points. Ask yourself these questions: Do I need more details here to satisfy my readers' curiosity? Can I add specific examples and information that will make my case stronger? Do I need better arguments to challenge my readers' assumptions?

Remember the advice to "write more about less" if you want to hold your readers' interest. That means that, at this point, you may need to stop and think of examples or do more research in order to give your paper authority.

> **When doing large scale revision, you should**
>
> —focus your thesis more sharply,
>
> —test your thesis,
>
> —check the distribution and balance of your ideas,
>
> —analyze the effectiveness of your organization,
>
> —judge whether you have fulfilled your readers' expectations,
>
> —decide how well your essay suits its intended readers, and
>
> —fill in any gaps in information.

Apply the criteria for large scale revision summarized in the box above to the essay you are developing. Don't be intimidated by all the criteria listed. Most people don't revise point by point. Instead, one revision suggests a second, then a third. Use the list to stimulate those initial changes.

4C

4C   LARGE SCALE REVISION—AN ESSAY IN PROGRESS (PT. 2)

Introduction

Here is the second draft of Matthew Atha's paper on paying college football players. He has made a number of large scale changes and improvements. In his first draft (see Section 3D), Matthew spends five paragraphs "discovering" his main point: not until ¶5 does he mention his key proposal to pay college athletes. In this second draft, the focus is much sharper. The proposal to pay athletes is stated in ¶1 and, in effect, controls the paper—Matthew commits himself and the audience to understanding this radical idea.

After stating this proposal, Matthew now writes an entirely new paragraph (¶2) to explain why action needs to be taken promptly. He names six schools already under investigation for violations of NCAA rules, thus involving his audience in his subject by showing how serious the problem is becoming. Throughout the paper, he realizes that alumni make up a critical part of his audience, so he frames arguments to demonstrate how paying athletes openly will benefit boosters and contributors. One key addition in this second draft occurs in the last paragraph where Matthew reminds powerful alumni of "the drastic penalties imposed on athletes" who are caught taking money or cars.

Several paragraphs have been rearranged in the second draft to put ideas in better proportion and to break them up for clearer focus. In the first draft, a single paragraph (¶6) hogged more than one-third of the essay. In the second draft, that huge block has been reshaped into a number of sharper, better focused paragraphs.

Some statistics and numbers have been cut from the second draft, but, in general, Matthew has increased the information he gives his readers. For example, the original version warned rather vaguely that "one year of television sanctions would cost the University of Texas more than $1,000,000." That single line has now been expanded into an entire paragraph (¶8) in the revised version, with the penalties now based on a real NCAA suspension rather than on speculation. He has been attending to the need to provide sufficient information.

4C

Finally, to appreciate how Matthew gives his paper more authority and realism, observe how he sharpens the detail in a sentence that explains why some coaches favor paying athletes:

{1st draft} They reason this would help alleviate the strong temptation to take money under the table.

{2nd draft} They reason this would help alleviate the strong temptation to take a $20 bill from a jubilant alumnus in a crowded locker room after a big win.

Read carefully and watch Matthew's paper evolve.

Matthew Atha
English 325M

Draft II (still no title)

(¶1) Alumni illegally paying college football players continue to grow at an alarming rate. Players receive not only cash, but cards, homes, and summer jobs to play football at State U. As the problem of alumni giving players money becomes almost uncontrollable, a solution must be sought. Some coahces have suggested giving players a monthly allowance would be a start towards helping players say no to the alumni inducements.

(¶2) In the past year, six of the nine Southwest Conference football programs—TCU, SMU, University of Houston, Texas A&M, Texas Tech, and the University of Texas—have been investigated by the NCAA or have been found guilty of illegal recruiting practices. These illegal practices have ranged from giving players money to supplying them with cars.

(¶3) Currently the NCAA does not allow players to hold any kind of job during fall or spring long semesters while attending school. If a student is on full scholarship, gets his board, books, room, and tuition free. However at that point, the school's support stops. Many athletes come from lower income families. Their parents cannot afford to give their college kid extra spending money so he can go out for a pizza if he gets tired of the dining hall food, or if he needs laundry money, or if he wants to go out on a date. Athletes, like any other student, also enjoy having extra food in their dorm refrigerator for a late night snack. However, if athletes can't get money from their parents, where do they turn?

(¶4) Some ask why they can't save up money earned during the summer. Because football takes so much time during the school year, football players don't usually take a full load of classes; thus they have to go to summer school. This gives them an opportunity to concentrate on their studies and catch up on their hours.

(¶5) Herein lies the dilemma. If athletes can't work during the summer, and their parents can't support them, where do they get their spending money from? For the past couple of decades, alumni have been the illegal providers, but this can change.

(¶6) Coaches have proposed to give each football player a monthly stipend of $100 to $200 for spending money. They reason this would alleviate the strong temptation to take a $20 bill from a jubilant alumnus in a crowded locker room after a big win. The stipend would allow players with little family support to go home without worrying about gas money and buy some things they need. The program would put a bigger burden on smaller schools with small athletic budgets, but in the long run the proposal would pay for itself.

(¶7) Instead of alumni pumping money directly to the students, they could give to the school which would set up a fund to finance the athlete's allowance. If school launched a fund raising drive in August every year, schools could draw interest on the funds raised for the nine months they would be used. One hundred and fifty alumni donating $1000 each could fund the program. One BMW for an athlete would cost the alumnus $25,000 but if he gave the cash to school instead, he would be acting legally, help all the athletes instead of one, and be rewarded by the government for giving to a nonprofit organization. The proposal would also save schools money. Now if they are caught cheating, the NCAA can prevent them from having their games televised or from going to revenue producing bowl games.

(¶8) Southern Methodist University recently went on probation for breaking NCAA rules. The two-year penalty stops all television appearances, all bowl appearances, resulted in the firing of one coach and cost the school 30 scholarships. These penalties cost the SMU athletic department over one million in lost revenues, and the football program suffered a tremendous setback because they will not be able to give out scholarships next year.

(¶9) As the amount of money illegally exchanged between alumni and athletes continues to grow, alumni should keep in mind the drastic penalties imposed on athletes caught with their hands under the table. If schools would help alumni resist the temptation by setting up a fund to benefit all athletes, and alumni would cooperate, the schools, the athletes, and the alumni would all benefit.

4D

EXERCISE 4.3

Write an evaluation for Matthew Atha, telling him what you think of his essay. Mention both its strengths and its weaknesses. Be specific in discussing such aspects as organization and sufficient information.

 WHAT DOES SMALL SCALE REVISION INVOLVE?

PROCESS MENU

PREPARING
PLANNING
INCUBATING
WRITING
REVISING
EDITING

▶ Make Needed Small Scale Changes

The large scale changes you have made should provide you with a better-focused draft. You are ready now to revise for features such as the following: *concrete and specific language, word choice, transitions, wordiness, introductions, and conclusions.*

Terms you need to know

Concrete language. Language that describes things so that they can be perceived through the senses: colors, textures, sizes, sounds, smells, actions.

Specific language. Language that names particular people, places, or things.

Abstract language. Language that presents things in general terms, as ideas rather than as objects.

Word choice. Sometimes called "diction"; the kind of words in a paper. They can be formal or informal, standard or colloquial, abstract or concrete, and so on.

Transitions. Hooking or linking terms that show connections between sentences or within and between paragraphs and sections.

Wordiness. Inflated, long-winded quality in writing.

Sentence structure. The way a sentence is put together. Sentence structures can be described in a variety of ways: by the complexity of clauses, by kinds of modification, by length, by rhythms, and so on.

Concepts mentioned in this section are discussed elsewhere in more detail. Here, we present them chiefly as aides to revising.

> **Tip: Now is the time to refer to the handbook if you need to check on details of style, mechanics, or usage.**

Concrete and specific language. Early drafts of a paper often turn out to be too abstract or general because a writer developing ideas may not be thinking about the anecdotes, interesting examples, or vivid language that would enliven a paper. When you start revising your second draft, however, look for ways to add people, objects, and incidents to your essay. Reinforce generalizations with specific details. Give your readers more facts and images. For more suggestions, see Chapter 6, What Kinds of Language Do You Use?

Word choice. Now is the time to tinker with your words to see if they can be improved. For instance, you might consider whether to change "difficult" to "hard" to make your writing simpler or if you want to write "poor" instead of "economically deprived" to make your language more direct. Also check to see if your style is "noun-heavy." (See Section 7D on Style.) If it is, look for ways to substitute verbs or adjectives. And this is the time to be sure you are using words accurately. It's easy to employ trendy words like "interface," "networking," and "scenario" without thinking about what they mean. Check now, and if you're not sure, look them up. Other people who have read your drafts may also have questions about words that you need to resolve now.

Transitions. A notable trait of good writing is smooth transitions from one sentence to another and one paragraph to another. Its "joints" and "seams" don't show. To determine if a paper is choppy and hard to follow, read it aloud. If you pause and stumble, confused by your own words, you've got a problem. Let others read what you've written to see if they lose the thread anywhere. If they do, you may need to add some transitional hooks or to create a pattern that links the parts of your essay. See Section 3B and Chapter 12 for more suggestions.

Wordiness. Many writers produce wordy first drafts, especially when they are generating ideas. Even second drafts—concerned with organization and evidence—may still be overblown. By a third draft, however, you need to start dumping surplus words and extravagant phrases. Perhaps you are trying to explain too much or sound too important? For specific suggestions about how to trim the fat, see Section 8C on wordiness.

Introduction and conclusion. Most of us know instinctively that the introduction of a paper or an article is so important it merits special attention. Nevertheless, it is usually a good idea to postpone revising that first paragraph until after you have dealt with other major problems in your paper. You may make so many changes in the second draft that you will need an entirely new opening. Conclusions also warrant special care, but they may be even harder to write than introductions. So don't fuss too much with them until you have the main part of the paper under control. For more specific suggestions, see Sections 5C and 5D on Introductory and Concluding Paragraphs.

EXERCISE 4.4

Revise the following short draft by Sue Ellen Rizzo, making its language more specific, improving its transitions, cutting unnecessary words, and improving its opening and closing.

(¶1)   There are likely to be many traditions at any school or university, but perhaps the most unique at Clear Lake and one of the most ignored of those traditions is its volunteer fire department. Ruralia is now a town actually large enough to have a competent firefighting force of its own; for many decades the school had to rely on its very own students and faculty personnel for emergency services, yet that tradition continues even to this very day today. Many other traditions continue as well, but they have received considerable publicity in the media while the story of the Clear Lake volunteer fire squad deserves the attention I intend to give it in this essay.

(¶2)   Who serves on this volunteer force that gets so little publicity and works so hard? It's mostly guys and a few gutsy women with intestinal fortitude, mainly the sort who weren't big or quick enough to undertake athletic endeavors or brassy enough to make the cheerleading squad or debating team. They are mostly quiet sorts of individuals, a little more prone to be inclined toward seriousness than most students and likely to be self-motivated. You have to attend meetings and training sessions held weekly on Saturday mornings at 6:00 am before the sun is up. Some students are just dragging themselves in after a wild Friday night then, and this dedicated bunch is practicing CPR, doing hose drills, or polishing Clear Lake College's aging but rugged Niagara fire engine.

(¶3)   How important this dedicated squad is to the college was made emminently evident only last month when a fire in the chemistry lab flared out of control quickly and dangerously, emitting clouds of dark and choking fumes into the corridors of the entire science complex everywhere. There was the danger of real panic and chaos, but suddenly in the midst of this panic, several students took charge—a few members of the volunteer fire department fortunate enough to be in the building at the time when the fire was beginning to occur. There was this mild-mannered Francie Knipstein ordering people twice her size to be still and find their way to the exits. There was Horward Torval, all one hundred ten pounds of him, unlocking cabinets of fire-fighting stuff and moving in the general direction of the smoke, putting on a gas mask. There was Kyle Talbot, locating an injured faculty teaching assistant, and moving her to safety. When the Ruralia Department arrived, the fire was out and a potential catastrophe of major proportions was turned off.

(¶4) Perhaps most indicative of the nature and character of this fighting force was its nixing of a proposal to allow the school to stage a ceremony honoring the heroics of this crew after the disaster had been averted successfully. As a group, the team agreed that they preferred the relative obscurity their group had long enjoyed. If they had wanted glory, one of them explained, they could have joined the football team. Then again, that point is really debatable since the team has not won a game in almost ten years. But that would almost certainly be another story, wouldn't it?

> **When doing small scale revision, you should**
> —sharpen your language,
> —check your word choice,
> —test your transitions,
> —lop out wordiness, and
> —polish your opening and closing.

EXERCISE 4.5

Apply the criteria for small scale revision in the box above to the essay you are developing. Give your essay all the attention to detail it deserves. And don't back away from more complicated revisions when they are necessary.

4E

WHAT DOES EDITING AND PROOFREADING INVOLVE?

PROCESS MENU

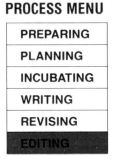

PREPARING
PLANNING
INCUBATING
WRITING
REVISING
EDITING

▶ Edit and Proofread for Quality Control

When you are reasonably satisfied with the content, organization, and style of your paper, you're ready to put it in final form to make a public appearance. Just as people form their first opinion of you from your appearance, your readers are going to be strongly influenced by the surface appearance of your paper. So it's worth your while to invest time in editing and proofreading. Like checking your clothes and grooming in the mirror before an important date or appointment, editing and proofreading provide the final measure of **quality control**. The more you care about the impression a paper makes, the more important it is *not* to neglect this last step.

Here are the minimum editing checks you need to make.

—Check on what you know is your weakest area. If you are a poor speller, look for words that you suspect might be misspelled and look them up or get help in some way. If you can, get a good speller to read your paper. If you are using a word processing program that includes a spelling checker, run your text through it. (See Section 21A on spelling.) If you know you're likely to write sentence fragments, review all your sentences to be sure they have both subjects and verbs. If you are likely to put commas where they're not needed, check all the commas to be sure they're not interrupting the flow of ideas where they shouldn't.

—Check for inconsistencies. If you promised you were going to discuss three points, did you do it? Did you mention issues in the first part of the paper that you never followed through on? (You might remember a director's suggestion to playwrights: never hang a gun on the wall of the set unless someone is going to fire it before the end of the play.) Is the tone of the paper consistent throughout, not light and informal in some places and stiff and formal in others?

—Check punctuation. See that proper names (English, American, and so on) and "I" are capitalized; that you have periods after abbreviations and titles; that you include the second set of quotation marks when you use a first and the second parenthesis at the end of a phrase you're marking off; and that you avoid comma splices—that is, joining a balanced pair of independent clauses with a comma instead of a semicolon. If you have had trouble with punctuation in the

past, get another person to read your paper too. See the various chapters on punctuation in Part III of this handbook.

—*Proofread for typographical errors.* They count even if they aren't your fault (writers tend to blame typists, typewriters, and printers). Look especially for transposed letters, dropped endings, faulty word division, and misplaced or forgotten apostrophes.

4E

—*Check paragraphs to see if they seem too long.* If they are, try to find a place to split them. See Section 5B on bad paragraph appearance.

—*Check on sentence structure* to see if some sentences could be joined together or rearranged to get a smoother, tighter style. See Chapters 7–8.

—*Check the format* of your paper. Be sure to number your pages, keep accurate and consistent margins, underline titles that need to be underlined, put other titles between quotation marks (see Section 18G), and clip your pages together.

EXERCISE 4.6

Edit this excerpt from a draft of Colonel Ringling's history of Clear Lake College. Make changes, as needed, in spelling, punctuation, paragraphing, sentence structure, and so on.

(¶1) An annual event at Clear Lake College has been the annual snowball fight. Following the first major storm of the winter season.

(¶2) This melee regularly pits an outnumbered freshman class against the remainder of the student body. The event seems to have originated around the turn of the century. When a new dormitory was built for upperclasmen to move them out of the Elcott's horsebarn.

(¶3)   Freshman, of course, would share thier studies with cattle until 1910 when thier dormitory, Bovine Hall, was opened.

(¶4)   Year after year for more than a generation, timid freshman were trounced in the snow battle usually centered in the college quadrangle between the living quarters; and sent fleeing into full retreat by barrages of snowballs hurled by triumphant sophmores, juniors, and seniors who then raced into Bovine Hall, pillaging like Vandles and Huns. Freshmen and their possessions' would reign from the lower floor windows. Until the school administrators, finally stirred from an unexplainable lethargy, declared the war over.

(¶5)   The tide turned, however, in 1940 when jolted upperclassmen awoke one night early in december to discover freshman in full dress, armed with snowballs, iceballs, and a few mud-balls, racing through their corridors. Snow had started falling just after midnight, and the freshmen, led by a bold commander, had taken the initiative. While ice missles volleyed and thundered, upperclassmen struggled to some semblence of deceny, feeling, no doubt, a little like the Trojans must have felt the night thier long-triumphant city was assaulted by the greeks.

(¶6)   Sheer numbers enabled the upperclassmen to drive the freshmen into the quadrangle at last and then the tide shifted, or so it seemed—the frosh raced back to Bovine Hall, chased by a furious bands of upperclassmens. But as these elders reached the doors of the building where they had plundered unchallenged for almost forty years, they were blasted by two fire hoses careful positioned at the portals, assaulted on thier flanks by a fresh band of frosh gorillas, and charging from behind a band of frosh women with water ballons! (Women had n'er before taken arms in these struggles.) As the Angle-Saxons are wont to say in their poetry, the frosh soon possessed the slaughterfeild. For the first time in the history of Clear Lake College, the upperclassmen surrendered at the gates of Bovine Hall and were compelled to run a jeering gaunlet across the icy quadrangle, barefeeted.

(¶7) The commander of the freshmen assault in 1940 soon left school to serve his country in World War II and Korea. He made a career in the army, retiring only recently. He has since returned to Clear Lake College to complete his interupted education and; at age sixty five, once again has plans for leading the freshman to gloious victroy.

> **When editing and proofreading, you should**
> —doublecheck spelling,
> —eliminate inconsistencies,
> —get the punctuation right,
> —check grammar and usage,
> —eliminate typographical errors,
> —evaluate the readability of your paragraphs,
> —make last-minute improvements in sentence structure, and
> —check the format of your paper.

Edit and proofread your essay carefully, using the criteria summarized in the box above. As you edit, you are heading for
home plate. But remember the old saw: "The ball game's not
over 'til the last comma's right." Or something like that. If you
need to cycle back to small or even large scale revision—do it.

4F FINISHED—AN ESSAY IN PROGRESS (PT. 3)

Introduction

Get ready for a surprise. With the second draft of his paper on
paying salaries to college athletes (see Section 4C), Matthew
Atha seemed to be working steadily toward a finished essay.
That second draft was better focused, fuller, and more specific
than his initial version. Various additions and changes made it
a little disconnected in places, but Matthew could afford to be
pleased with the direction he had charted. A little judicious
editing and proofreading and his paper would be complete.
Here, for example, is how he *might* have edited ¶1, by refining
the basic issue, improving sentence structures, and eliminating
several obvious errors.

¶1—second draft

Alumni illegally paying college football players continue to grow at an alarming rate. Players receive not
only cash, but cards, homes, and summer jobs to play
football at State U. As the problem of alumni giving
players money becomes almost uncontrollable, a solution must be sought. Some coahces have suggested giving players a monthly allowance would be a start
towards helping players say no to the alumni inducements.

¶1—edited and proofread version of second draft

The practice of alumni illegally paying football players continue**s** to grow at an alarming rate **at colleges and universities around the country**. **If the rumors are true**, players **are regularly** receiv**ing** not only cash, but cards, homes, and **summer** jobs to play football at State U. **Although** the problem of alumni **contributions seems** almost uncontrollable, a solution must be **found quickly to preserve the integrity of college sports**. Some **coaches** have suggested **that** giving players a monthly allowance **might be a way of** helping **athletes** say no to the alumni inducements.

But this competently edited paragraph isn't what Matthew actually wrote. Instead, the version he turned in to his instructor (reprinted below) departs boldly from his first two drafts. Its opening is far longer and more dramatic, its argument shorter but more emotional. Matthew moves his proposal to pay football players to the middle of the essay again, where it was in his first version. He sharpens his language and tone to make his essay harder hitting, more powerful.

This significant revision was prompted by suggestions from students in Matthew's writing course. After reading his second draft, several classmates felt that the paper needed a more dramatic opening and more information about specific schools and players involved in the pay-for-play controversy. Matthew agreed and supplied both. It also seems likely that doing those first two drafts made him believe even more strongly in his subject.

We can't tell you exactly why the process of revision worked so well in Matthew's case, but it did. And that success is exactly the point of revising. Matthew was willing to write and rewrite in response to suggestions and criticism from his instructor and peers. In revising, he found his subject and then his subject took hold of him. It might have been neater to show you a third draft where only editing took place—a misspelling corrected, an apostrophe added, a weak word choice deleted. But that's not the way things happened for Matthew Atha. And the predictable way is not how things will always happen for you when you write. Be prepared for surprises.

You decide if what he has done in his final version isn't significantly better than his first two drafts.

Matthew Atha
English 325M
March 1986

Paying College Players Legally

(¶1)   Texas Christian University's star running back Kenneth Davis entered the 1985 football season riding the crest of a wave. In hopes of capturing the Heisman Trophy, the TCU athletic department printed posters touting him as the "Temple Tornado." In 1984, Davis had helped TCU gain a bowl bid for the first time in more than 15 years as he shattered his school's single season rushing record.

(¶2)   The wave of success abruptly stopped two games into the 1985 season after Davis admitted taking an illegal cash payment from alumni. Because NCAA rules bar players who take money for collegiate competition, his confession ended his college career and severely damaged hopes of a lucrative professional contract. The fate of the TCU football program remains in question following an NCAA investigation.

(¶3) Across the metroplex in Dallas, Southern Methodist University recently went on probation for breaking NCAA rules. The two-year penalty stopped all television appearances, all bowl appearances, resulted in one coach being fired, and cost the school almost 60 scholarships. These penalties resulted in more than one million dollars in lost television, bowl, and ticket revenue. The football program suffered a tremendous setback because it will be unable to give scholarships for the next two years. The school's prestige also undoubtedly suffered.

(¶4) Alumni giving players $50 in the locker room after the game can cause severe penalties such as these. Often an alumnus, caught up in the emotion following a big victory, wants to reward a player for his outstanding performance. Such action can give an alumnus a feeling of self-satisfaction, but it hardly seems worth jeopardizing a player's athletic career and a school's integrity.

(¶5) Although the penalties are severe, alumni illegally paying college football players is a practice that continues to grow at an alarming rate. In the past year, six of the nine Southwest Conference football programs—TCU, SMU, the University of Houston, Texas A&M, Texas Tech, and the University of Texas—have been accused of recruiting violations, have been investigated by the NCAA, or have been found guilty of illegal recruiting practices. Those illegal practices have ranged from giving money to players to supplying them with cars.

(¶6) Currently the NCAA does not allow players to hold any kind of job during fall or spring semester while attending school. If a student is on full scholarship, he gets his room, board, books, and tuition free. At that point, however, the school's support stops. Many athletes come from low income families, and their parents cannot afford to give their youngster extra spending money so he can go out to get a pizza if he gets tired of the dining hall food, or if he needs laundry money or wants to go out on a date. However, if athletes can't get money from their families, where do they turn? For the past couple of decades, alumni have been the illegal providers, but this could be changed.

(¶7) Coaches have proposed giving each football player a monthly stipend of $100 to $200 spending money. They reason this would help alleviate the strong temptation to take $20 from a jubilant alumnus in a crowded locker room after a win. Instead of alumni giving money directly to the student, they could begin giving to the school instead, and the school would set up a fund to finance the athletes' allowance. Such a proposal would benefit the college, help all players instead of a select few, and give the alumni a tax break. One hundred fifty alumni donating $1000 each could fund the program completely. It would also improve a school's credibility and, in the long run, could save it money since, if a school is caught cheating, penalties can cost that institution over a million dollars.

(¶8) If athletic departments and alumni don't work together to come up with some alternative to the present unrealistic system, the amount of money that passes illegally from alumni to players will just continue to grow, and schools will continue to incur the kinds of penalties imposed on Texas Christian University and Southern Methodist University. At this point, shouldn't everyone ask "Is it worth it?" and find a better way?

4F

EXERCISE 4.8

In the second draft of his paper, Matthew moved his proposal from the middle of the paper to the first paragraph—giving the essay a sharp initial focus. In this final version, the proposal is buried again in the middle of the essay. In fact, it doesn't come until ¶7, one paragraph from the end. What do you think of this strategy? Does it work in this particular essay? Or did you prefer version #2?

EXERCISE 4.9

Give the final version of your paper one last reading. Are you satisfied? What do you like most about it?

PART II STYLE

Jonathan Swift defined style as "proper words in proper places." But you'll discover that the meaning of *proper* changes almost every time you write because style is a constant negotiation between you, your subject, and your readers. Style is the shape you give to paragraphs, sentences, and words to lend them your voice.

Style is also *choice*, the selections you make among all those features of language not guided by strict rules and conventions. You decide how long an opening paragraph will be and how its information will unfold. You decide whether sentences should be long or short, plain or fancy, factual or allusive. You decide which words fit your subject—and which do not.

This section is a guide to some of the stylistic choices you can make. Because the subject is large and the options for crafting language so numerous, we concentrate on what we regard as *major opportunities* for enhancing style—those places where investments of time and attention will pay healthy dividends.

CHAPTER

What Makes Paragraphs Work?

- ■ **A** Paragraph sprawl
- ■ **B** Bad appearance
- ■ **C** Opening paragraphs
- ■ **D** Concluding paragraphs

Terms you need to know

Paragraph. A paragraph is a small group of sentences working together to do a job in a paper: to develop a single idea, to show relationships between separate ideas, to move readers from one point to another, to introduce a subject, to conclude a discussion, and so on. Paragraphs are marked by separations (indentions or open spaces) that encourage readers to pause slightly and consider what point a cluster of sentences has made.

¶. A symbol meaning "paragraph." Editors and instructors insert the symbol where a new paragraph is needed in a paper. "No ¶" indicates that an existing paragraph should be combined with another.

Introduction
Paragraphs are a convenience for both readers and writers. For a reader, paragraphs break up information into manageable chunks. For a writer, paragraphs provide vehicles for arranging information strategically and, again, for dividing a large job into smaller, less intimidating, parts.

To manage paragraphs well, you need to know how to handle two common problems that we have termed **paragraph sprawl** and **bad paragraph appearance**. As you'll see, these two concepts cover a lot of ground.

Paragraph sprawl is a problem with the way a paragraph *works*; that is, its sentences do not fit together tightly and focus on a central point. If your paragraphs go off in different directions, if you have put two or three unconnected ideas in one paragraph, or if several sentences in your paragraph could fit just as well in one place as another, you have a problem with paragraph sprawl.

Bad paragraph appearance is a problem with the way paragraphs *look*; that is, paragraphs are either so lengthy that they discourage readers or so short they make writing seem fragmented and disjointed. If you have paragraphs that cover almost a page or more, or if you have several one- or two-sentence paragraphs close together, you may have a problem with paragraph appearance.

Of course, paragraphs do more than just cause problems. They perform special jobs, two of the most critical being *introducing* papers and *closing* them. For that reason, we give special consideration to effective strategies for **introductory** and **concluding paragraphs**.

5A HOW DO YOU ELIMINATE PARAGRAPH SPRAWL?

Troubleshooting

Unlike sentences, paragraphs are not natural units of thought. We don't *speak* in paragraphs the way that we speak in sentences. By traditional definition, paragraphs are units of writing that writers employ to develop their ideas. Again, by tradition, a single paragraph is supposed to house but a single idea. But it's not always easy to decide what constitutes a paragraph, what a paragraph should look like, or where to position paragraph breaks. Yet shaping paragraphs is a key element in fashioning a reader's response to what you have to say.

Readers will feel that your work is out of control if your paragraphs seem to have no design, no point. We call this *paragraph sprawl*. Paragraph sprawl usually results from a writer jotting down several ideas as they occur rather than thinking in terms of developing one idea at a time. The result is a paragraph like the following, filled with intriguing ideas but shapeless:

> {**Sprawling**} There are thousands of school districts across this country, reflecting widely different social, ethnic, and intellectual attitudes. Yet students from all of these districts are admitted to college according to the dictates of a few nationwide placement examinations, chiefly the SAT and the ACT. Examinations of this kind, which tend to reflect the biases of the people who write them, are economically efficient because they are easy to grade. But many students may not be interested in the kind of intellectual and cultural material covered on these examinations. Various services around the country claim to be able to raise SAT scores by a significant number of points, but they are available only at a price. Smaller school districts may not be able to prepare students as adequately as larger districts. Test scores have leveled off in recent years, following a long period of decline. But how can scores from these tests really represent the achievements of four years of high school and the differences between what a student in Vermont, Florida, or Mississippi learns? These are problems.

5A

The reader has trouble following the point of the paragraph because its sentences go off in several different directions instead of focusing on and developing one point. The following revised version eliminates much of the sprawl and makes the paragraph more readable and effective.

> {**Focused**} There are thousands of school districts across this country, reflecting widely different social, ethnic, and intellectual attitudes. Yet students from all

of these districts are admitted to college according to the dictates of a few nationwide placement examinations, chiefly the SAT and the ACT. Standardized examinations of this kind tend to reflect the biases of the people who write them, not the training of the students who take them. How, then, can scores from these tests reflect fairly the differences between what a white student learns in a private Vermont prep school, a Cuban-American student achieves in Miami public school, or a black student accomplishes in rural Mississippi?

5A

Writers also produce sprawling paragraphs when they write several sentences that are all on a high level of generality. (See section on general and specific language, Section 7A.) Instead of making one general statement and then developing it with specific details or examples, they string together a series of generalizations. Even if all of them discuss the same main idea, they don't really develop that idea. For example:

> Everyone is interested in preserving the quality of our environment and natural habitats. The beauty of nature is something almost everyone responds to. Respect for nature comes from a feeling we all share that the environment is something important to our own well-being today and to that of our children and grandchildren tomorrow. Without a healthy environment, we will all find ourselves ravaged by disease and deprived of the beauties of nature. Unless we do something about the environmental crisis in our society today, we soon won't have a society to worry about.

A paragraph like this leaves readers feeling frustrated and bored because they learn little from it. The paragraph lacks design and direction. Any one of its sentences might provide the topic statement for a totally different paragraph, but the paragraph as a whole probably isn't worth salvaging.

To remedy paragraph sprawl, you need to give your paragraphs a feeling of control or design. There are many ways to do that, but three techniques are particularly useful: **commitment and response**, **downshifting**, and **topic sentences**.

To eliminate paragraph sprawl . . .

▶ **Reshape paragraphs according to a "commitment and response" pattern.** We have already described this important strategy in the section on unifying your writing (Section 3B) and will be discussing it again in Section 5C on introductory paragraphs. All commitment and response involves is making a promise to your reader and then keeping it:

commitment

There would seem to be four stages in the composition

response

of a story. First comes the germ of the story, then a period of more or less conscious meditation, then the first draft, and finally the revision, which may simply be "pencil work" as John O'Hara calls it—that is, minor changes in wording—or may lead to writing several drafts and what amounts to a new work.

—Malcolm Cowley, Introduction to *How Writers Work* (Paris Review series)

Cowley begins the paragraph by promising to describe four stages in composing a story. By that simple assertion he raises his readers' expectations and suggests his control over the subject.

Here is a second example:

commitment

A young man might go into military flight training believing that he was entering some sort of technical school in which he was simply going to acquire a certain set of skills.

response

Instead he found himself all at once enclosed in a fraternity. And in this fraternity, even though it was military, men were not rated by their outward rank as ensigns, lieutenant commanders, or whatever. No, herein the world was divided into those who had it and those who did not. This quality, this *it* was never named, however, nor was it talked about in any way.

—Tom Wolfe, *The Right Stuff*

Wolfe makes an opening commitment in this paragraph when he says "a young man might go into military training believing. . . ." His readers immediately expect him to explain why the young man's belief might be wrong, and Wolfe does, thus fulfilling his commitment. Again, the paragraph asserts its style through a simple, but effective device.

Another way a writer can open a paragraph with a commitment is to ask a question. For example:

commitment   response
What is chance? Dictionaries define it as something fortuitous that happens unpredictably without discernible human intentions. Chance is unintentional and capricious, but we needn't conclude that chance is immune from human intervention. Indeed, chance plays several distinct roles when humans react creatively with one another and their environment.
                    —James H. Austin, "Four Kinds of Chance"

Austin obliges himself to answer the question he opens with. He begins with the traditional dictionary definition of *chance*, but then expands it by suggesting that, contrary to what readers might think, chance is not always just random luck. And since this paragraph is also the opening paragraph of an essay, it also serves as a commitment that forecasts what Austin is going to discuss in the complete essay.

As you are no doubt aware, questions can be asked in different ways, hostilely, persistently, humorously, rhetorically. Questions also add a touch of familiarity to a paragraph, especially when they anticipate exactly what a writer might be thinking. Not only, then, do questions give focus to a paragraph, they also set its tone and style.

Example 1. Paragraph from a biting editorial by Connie Lim.

Why, then, were concerned students and citizens not forewarned about the proposed zoning changes? Why were their interests so pointedly ignored? The answers, no doubt, involve large sums of money—some to be invested by the company requesting the zoning change, some to be taxed by a spendthrift city council,

5A

and some to be earned (the new-fashioned way) by a powerful clique of investors and business interests. That's why no one bothered to warn students and citizens of Ruralia that their pristine lakeshore was about to be scarred by a shopping center and condominiums.

Example 2. Paragraph from a comic essay by Sean M. O'Brian.

Did you ever ask yourself who your neighbors might be if you bought into one of those time-sharing or land contracts offered almost daily in the mail? You know the scam I'm talking about—the offers promising you a Cutlass Supreme, sailboat, diamond pendant, or personal aircraft if you'll just drive fifty miles to view some desolate property and listen to a three-hour sales lecture? Your neighbors would be people stupid enough to believe such come-ons, proud owners of 1/24-scale plastic Oldsmobiles, rubber dingies, microscopic carbon chips, and balsa wood 747s. They would probably have subscriptions to *The National Degrader*, send tithes to TV wrestlers, and collect portraits of Elvis done on velvet.

Because an opening commitment sentence for a paragraph does serve that forecasting function, it controls what you write after it and thus helps to prevent paragraph sprawl. You are less likely to let a paragraph wander off the topic if you keep your commitment in your mind as you write. When you complete a paragraph, revise it to eliminate any sentences that don't develop your main idea.

Here is a shapeless, but promising paragraph. Its commitment is boldfaced and sentences not contributing directly to that commitment have been underlined.

{Original paragraph} **Although some recent TV sitcoms may be brasher or more witty, *I Love Lucy* remains among the most creative of all television series.** Many people know whole episodes of this sitcom by heart. Among their favorites are Lucy's adventures in an Italian winery, a chocolate factory, and Hollywood. In one episode, Lucy even steals John Wayne's cement footprints. The appeal of the program lies in its almost perfect combination of likable characters in ludicrous, yet oddly familiar situations. Lucy, the daffy, rubber-faced dreamer, spins her wild schemes with the aid of level-headed but gullible Ethel. Excitable, ambitious Ricky—a band leader from Cuba—struggles about equally with his crazy wife and the English language. We occasionally meet members of his family from Cuba, including his mother and wealthy uncle. His major ally is bald, penny-pinching Fred who earns his income managing the dour apartment building where Lucy and Ricky live in surprising simplicity until almost the end of the series. The Ricardos and Mertzes seem like the neighbors you wish you had, arguing over the washing machine, scheming to manage household accounts, fussing with the baby, yet they toe-tap always on the fringes of show business. Even Fred and Ethel claim a background in show business. Yet it is talentless Lucy who more than anyone wants fame. But only her saxophone playing is worse than her singing.

5A

Refocused, the paragraph might read like this, with a revised concluding sentence.

> {Revised paragraph} **Although some recent TV sitcoms may be brasher or more witty, *I Love Lucy* remains among the most creative of all television series.** The appeal of the program lies in its almost perfect combination of likable characters in ludicrous, yet oddly familiar situations. Lucy, the daffy, rubber-faced dreamer, spins her wild schemes with the aid of level-headed but gullible Ethel. Excitable, ambitious Ricky—a band leader from Cuba—struggles about equally with his crazy wife and the English language. His major ally is bald, penny-pinching Fred who earns his income managing the dour apartment building where Lucy and Ricky live in surprising simplicity until almost the end of the series. The Ricardos and the Mertzes seem like the neighbors you wish you had,

arguing over a washing machine, scheming to manage household accounts, fussing with the baby. Yet, toe-tapping improbably on the fringes of show business, they encourage their middle-class viewers to share their dreams of a more exciting, less predictable world beyond the apartment walls.

EXERCISE 5.1

Rewrite the following paragraphs to eliminate sprawl. Don't hesitate to cut material that leads away from the main idea, or to make major revisions.

1. Several recent surveys suggest that the average American high school and college student is woefully ignorant of geography. When asked to locate Nicaragua, Lebanon, Grenada, Iran, or even France on a map, distressing numbers of students could not. Many were unable to name more than three continents. A few weren't even sure that Washington, D.C., was the capital of the United States. Americans travel all over the world, so you might expect them to be interested in geography. Their ignorance may be traced to a tendency to substitute other more "contemporary" subjects for geography courses in elementary school. Students who formerly took classes in American and world geography now take "Introduction to the Computer," "Life Skills," and "Sex Education." Of course, with the increase in sexually-transmitted diseases and teen pregnancies, classes in sex-education seem quite necessary. But high schools often don't even have a geography teacher and a few universities have closed their geography departments to save money. Surely, basic geography is as important to Americans as knowing how to apply for credit and balance a checkbook—skills now taught in secondary schools. Geography is not a subject Americans dislike, however. The *National Geographic* remains one of the most popular of all magazines and travelogues continue to draw crowds when they are shown on college campuses. The whole issue is serious and complicated.

2. Many people like the idea of volunteering to help others, but dislike actually doing it. Volunteering means giving of yourself for an hour or a day. It means surrendering time you might have spent watching a movie or playing a sport. People can volunteer for many kinds of activities, from helping the aged in retirement centers to serving as candy-stripers at a local hospital. Volunteers reduce the demands on local governments lacking funds to perform necessary services. To volunteer is to perform a service for the community, but also for yourself because volunteering will make you a better person.

5A

3. Characters are important in most films since what most audiences care about are people. Yet they don't always demand unusual personalities. In fact, stereotypes are often quite successful—the athlete who overcomes impossible odds, the grandparent who acts surprisingly youthful, the Vietnam veteran who suffers flashbacks, the faithful but plain girlfriend who wins the hero. Plot is similarly important. People tend to favor plots simple enough to explain in a few words—boy gets girl; girl gets boy; Americans clobber Commies; masked murderer kills everyone. But audiences do expect good plots, and they don't care if matters grow somewhat sentimental. Plots are emphasized through music. The Hollywood musical has almost disappeared, but almost every film now includes one or two musical numbers. The music is usually performed by a popular rock band that uses clips from the film as material for a television video. These musical videos then promote both the movie and the band. Making a successful movie these days requires both shrewdness and simplicity.

EXERCISE 5.2

Explain what you might do with paragraphs that began with these commitments. Write a paragraph based on one of these openings.

1. Who doesn't recall the first time he or she tried to drive a car?
2. Government at the local level should have three priorities.

3. History teaches many lessons, but one of them is almost always ignored.
4. Students entering college expect their lives to change. But they are rarely prepared, emotionally or intellectually, for learning in the fast lane.

▶ **Downshift.** *Downshifting* means developing a paragraph by writing sentences that move from a high level of generality down to lower levels. The writer makes a rather broad statement or assertion in the first sentence and, in the following sentences, enriches and expands that statement by giving more specific and concrete details. Such paragraphs can move through several levels. The process is like subdividing a topic into smaller and smaller details. For example, if we designate a sentence at the highest level of generality as 10, here is how a writer might develop that sentence by moving to lower levels of generality.*

5A

> 10. There are signs that girls are finding their way into the world of computing, despite its male bias.
>
> > 9. A large proportion of the current enrollment in college computing classes is female.
> >
> > > 8. For example, at Mount Holyoke, a women's college, 50 percent of this year's graduates have used computers in their courses—up from 15 percent seven years ago.
> > >
> > > > 7. According to John Durso, professor of computer studies, the number of terminals available to Mount Holyoke students has increased from one to 40 over the same period.
> > > >
> > > > 7. "The basic course in computing, taught twice a year, has quadrupled in enrollment from 30 students seven years ago to 120 today."

—Sara Kiesler, Lee Spoull, and Jacquelynne S. Eccles, "Second Class Citizens?" in *Psychology Today,* March, 1983, p. 47

* The two sentences marked "7" are at the same level of generality.

Here is another example.

10. Preschool children are the single largest television audience in America,

9. spending a greater number of total hours and a greater proportion of their waking day watching television than any other age group.

8. According to one survey made in 1970, children in the 2–5 age groups spend an average of 30.4 hours each week watching television, while children in the 6–11 group spend 25.5 hours watching.

8. The weekly average for adult viewers in 1971 was 23.3 hours.

8. Another survey made in 1971 documented a weekly viewing time of 34.56 hours for preschool boys and 32.44 hours for preschool girls.

8. Still other surveys suggest figures up to 54 hours a week for preschool viewers.

—Marie Winn, *The Plug-in Drug: Television, Children, and Family*

Downshifting is a good cure for those paragraphs made up of several sentences all on the same level of generality. Here is an example of that kind of problem.

The 80s may be remembered as the era when millions of people became obsessed with fitness. For most people, this is the decade in which they think continually about how their bodies function. A preoccupation with one's body is a sign of the times. It is very fashionable to talk about how important it is to be fit.

This is a paragraph that doesn't go anywhere; it merely repeats the same generality four different ways, and that's not paragraph development. If, however, the writer starts with the main idea and develops it by downshifting to lower levels of generality and adding specific details, it can become interesting.

5A

10. The 1980s may be remembered as the era when millions of people became obsessed with fitness.

9. Ambitious young people took up aerobics and weight lifting as a flat belly and sloping shoulders became assets on the career ladder.

9. Others took up running, as comparing marathon times became the approved cocktail party talk.

8. Even the cocktail parties themselves were affected.

7. The boss began drinking Perrier water instead of white wine, and the really strong stuff like martinis brought raised eyebrows from everyone.

6. Smoking at any party made the offending culprit feel like a pariah.

EXERCISE 5.3

Try plotting the levels of generality in the following paragraphs. Mark the first level as "10" and work your way down until all sentences are accounted for. Remember that you may have more than one sentence at any level of generality. After you have diagrammed the paragraphs, decide whether they should be revised to eliminate sprawl.

1. Where, formerly, the average American family showed little interest in the finer points of financial management, a typical family today is likely to be relying on any number of complex investment opportunities. Up until the late sixties, most households managed their money simply. Their single-income portfolios usually consisted of passbook savings accounts, checking accounts, and a variety of insurance policies. Today, a family's finances are apt to be as complicated as those of a small business only twenty years ago. Family savings generated by dual incomes are now regularly invested in mutual funds, tax-sheltered annuities, government securities, and real

estate funds. Retirement monies are channeled to IRA accounts, Keogh plans, and other long-term investment ventures.
Many families invest regularly in the stock market, the futures
market, precious metals, such as gold and silver, and even
collectibles, such as rare coins and classic automobiles. While
precious metals and collectibles lack the security of most of the
financial instruments, they are often more entertaining to family
investors willing to take risks.

5A

2. Computerized writing labs offer students opportunities to
enhance their abilities as writers. These labs are often partially
supported by computer firms eager to introduce students to
their hardware. Many students fear computers because they do
not understand the jargon associated with the machines. Before the invention of word processing, revision was a tedious
and time-consuming process. Many students have problems
with computers because they are not comfortable with a keyboard. But learning how to type is not difficult. Once you have
mastered the keyboard and word processing software, writing
and revising become much more pleasant. The computer will
increase your ability as a writer.

3. Students living in Bovine Hall guessed wildly about what the
time capsule discovered in the garden next to their building
might contain. Some thought it might hold copies of the student
newspaper from an earlier era. Others were sure it would
include coins and photographs of students who had buried the
little iron casket, now deeply rusted, but substantially intact.
The capsule had been unearthed by a crew digging a trench to
lay a cable TV line. Still others speculated that the box might
reveal evidence of a horrible crime. There had long been
rumors that a counterfeiting operation had once operated out of
the freshman dormitory in the 1920s. Might the heavy box
contain the metal plates the freshman class used then to print
fake report cards and transcripts?

EXERCISE 5.4

Develop these opening lines by downshifting through at least
three levels of generality.

1. In America, you cannot escape the influence of advertising.
2. People are rarely neutral about opera.
3. Our attitudes toward the poor are usually shaped by what we, individually, believe are the causes of poverty.

EXERCISE 5.5

Write a paragraph based on one of the commitments made in the sentences below. Use downshifting as a way of keeping the paragraph on track.

5A

1. Celebrities are of two sorts—those who earn fame by what they have done, and those who gain fame by what has been done to them.
2. If I controlled the local school board, I would make three major changes in the high school curriculum.
3. A realistic approach to the drug problem in the United States would acknowledge certain facts largely ignored by the popular media.
4. Why do so few people vote in local and national elections?

▶ **Use topic sentences.** A third useful way to control sprawl is to begin a paragraph with a topic sentence, and then to extend or expand that idea in the following sentences. Here is an example of a paragraph using that pattern.

topic sentence

Shrimping in the Gulf has never been a calling men pursued for the fun of it—or for the easy money. Oh, there was plenty of money to be made once: the lowliest deckhand could return from a fifteen day trip with $3000 in his pocket. But the work was brutal and, most of all, lonely: two or four or six weeks on a pitching boat in the middle of the hostile ocean. Shrimp are elusive creatures, apt to change their feeding grounds from year to year, and some years shrimpers never quite figured out where they were. Those were the years of frustrating summers and lean winters. And then in the good years the crew could work themselves near to death, hauling up the writhing beasts by the ton, working around the clock to get them decapitated and iced down before the sun had a chance to make them spoil.

—Victoria Loe, "Shrimpers," *Texas Monthly,*
April, 1981, p. 128

The topic sentence announces the main idea—shrimping is not fun nor does it bring easy money—and every following sentence develops and supports that idea.

5A

Another name for this kind of sentence is "generative sentence" because it is a sentence that naturally *generates* additional material on the original idea. A writer cannot start out with either a good topic sentence or a generative sentence and then not follow through by adding more information. If she does, she leaves readers saying, "Hey, what happened? You let me down." Here are two more examples of paragraphs with topic or generative sentences.

{**Example 1**} *Until recently, refrigerated whole blood couldn't be stored longer than 35 days.* But two preservatives developed in the past year have extended storage life to 49 days, says James Brassel, blood bank director at New York City's Presbyterian Hospital. This means that a patient can accumulate up to six units before surgery by donating one unit a week for six weeks. Blood constituents can also be frozen; red cells and plasma, frozen separately, can last three years. A mother expecting a Caesarean section, for example, can donate her blood in the second trimester—the safest time—and have it frozen for use months later.

—Royna Prince, "Donating Blood to Yourself,"
Science 85, April, p. 78

The statement made in the first sentence *generates* more sentences—the writer cannot just drop the idea after she has stated it. She must explain.

{**Example 2**} *Women in politics have to pay attention to what they wear; men don't.* If a man politician wears anything approximating the standard male uniform, the people around him focus on what he has to say, not how he looks. Women must keep glancing in the mirror. To get ahead they need a second awareness of themselves in addition to the one that is built into this most demanding of vocations.

—Nicholas von Hoffman, "The Political Woman's Long, Hard Climb," *Esquire*, June, 1984, p. 219

In the first sentence Hoffman *generates* the points he is going to make in the rest of the paragraph—he can't just leave the sentence there and quit.

By now you may have noticed that the three strategies of commitment and response, downshifting, and topic or generative sentences have much in common, and that sometimes writers might have trouble deciding which technique they were using. Well, it really doesn't make much difference. Knowing the exact term for what you are doing is not as important as understanding the principle you're working from. The principle underlying all three of these techniques is this: as a writer, you have an obligation to inform and satisfy your readers. You accomplish that by filling in details, supporting a claim, giving pertinent examples, or doing whatever it takes to follow through on the contract you and your readers enter into when you write and they read. And that's what you are doing in all three of these operations—following through.

EXERCISE 5.6

In the draft of a paper you are writing (or in a finished essay), underline sentences that make commitments to readers. Then consider how you might revise the piece, either to make the commitments you have made more definite or to reorganize paragraphs to support a main idea more consistently.

▶ **Use other paragraph patterns to control sprawl.** Evidence suggests that most writers are conscious of a contract with their readers and, at times at least, think about downshifting or responding to a commitment when they write. But they also use many other kinds of paragraph patterns, some of which may be useful for you to think about when you're writing. We can't say for sure, however, that many writers consciously use these other patterns—perhaps they just emerge as we write because they so closely resemble natural thought patterns.

Those patterns are similar to the organizational patterns discussed in Sections 2B and 3B and to the patterns you may find identified in a college essay anthology. They are

5A

Cause and effect,

Comparison and contrast,

Definition,

Process,

Narration,

Classification, and

Analogy.

Paragraphs using these patterns share some of the features of full essays. For example, a paper analyzing a **cause and effect** relationship might follow this scratch outline.

I.   Introduction

II. The problem defined

III. Its causes

IV. Its effects

V.   Recommendations

A paragraph also exploring a cause and effect problem would use a similar design on a smaller scale, with the introduction (**I.**) perhaps becoming a transitional sentence and the recommendations (**V.**) delayed until later in the paper.

(**I**) Yet another example of the world market working to the advantage of consumers occurred in the automobile industry. (**II**) By the mid-1980s, the prices of economy cars had risen substantially, with the smallest Japanese and American sedans bearing sticker prices that approached or exceeded five figures. (III) American car companies claimed that the profit margins on cheap cars were too small to justify producing vehicles under $6000. The Japanese, who had earned their reputation building well-equipped, high-quality economy cars, pulled away from the market under the pressure of American import quotas. Since they could import only a limited number of vehicles, the Japanese understandably preferred to ship their more profitable luxury and sporty lines to America. (IV) As a consequence, a gap opened at the lower end of the automobile market, leaving room for manufacturers from third world countries, with their reduced labor and production costs, to compete. They introduced to America some of the lowest-priced cars consumers had seen in years.

Similarly, a paragraph can be built quite naturally upon a **comparison and contrast** pattern:

    I.   Introduction

  II   Subject 1

      —Feature a

      —Feature b

  III. Subject 2

      —Feature a

      —Feature b

  IV. Conclusions

Again, the pattern would be modified to fit the needs of the subject developed in the paragraph and the position of the paragraph within a complete essay. But the pattern still works well as a way of organizing information.

(I) Two of the earliest and most publicized of these low-priced third-world automotive imports were the Yugo and the Hyundai. (II) The Yugo looked dated the day it arrived on American shores, not surprising since it was based on a twenty-year-old Fiat design. But the Yugoslavian sedan could claim one feature no other new car available in America offered: a sticker price under $4000. **(III)** The Hyundai introduced to Americans was a brand new car, with a body styled in Europe and an engine based on Japanese technology. Not quite as cheap as the bare-bones Yugo, the Hyundai still managed to offer modern technology at old-fashioned prices. **(IV)** Both manufacturers established a beachhead in the American market within a year, the Hyundai's much larger than the Yugo's.

You can do the same with any of the other patterns of organization. Here are scratch outlines for some of the other patterns.

5A

Definition

   I. Introduction: the term
  II. Its general class
III. Its characteristic features
     —Feature 1
     —Feature 2
     —Feature 3
IV. Conclusion

Process

   I. Introduction: the process
  II. Step 1
III. Step 2 . . .
IV. Conclusion (when necessary)

Narration

   I. Event 1
  II. Event 2 . . .
III. Conclusion (when appropriate)

Classification

  I. Introduction: the material being classified
II. The principle of classification being used

III. The categories
    —Category 1
    —Category 2
    —Category 3 . . .
IV. Conclusion

Analogy

  I. Introduction: the analogy
 II. Comparison 1
III. Comparison 2 . . .
IV. Conclusions

5A

EXERCISE 5.7

Use the patterns above to write one or more of the following paragraphs.

1. A paragraph defining in detail a term you have learned in the last three months.
2. A paragraph explaining how to operate a machine you use regularly.
3. A paragraph narrating something funny that happened to you that you would rather not mention.
4. A paragraph classifying your relatives or the students in one of your courses.
5. A paragraph that employs an analogy to explain the success or failure of a sports team you follow.

▶ **Reduce paragraph sprawl with transitions.** The process of *responding* or *downshifting* or *generating* will usually produce a group of sentences so tightly connected that you don't have to worry about sprawl. Or if you have set up any strong pattern in your paragraphs, the sentences will often fit together naturally, and you won't have to think about putting in hooks and links to control paragraph sprawl. But if the sentences of your paragraphs don't fit together well, and your instructor or another reader says your writing seems choppy, you may need to shape your paragraphs by using the following stylistic techniques.

Use **pointer words**. Set up a pattern for your readers to follow by putting in words like *first, second, next, last*, and so on.

> Kyle, a nonsmoker, argued eloquently before the University Senate that there were many reasons to oppose a campuswide ban on smoking. **First**, such a policy unduly penalized an activity that, though obnoxious, was not, in fact, illegal. **Second**, enforcement of the policy might encourage insidious intrusions upon the privacy of students in their dormitory rooms and faculty in their offices. **Last**, a ban on smoking might set an unfortunate precedent, leading to the elimination of other habits and activities certain groups regarded as similarly offensive or harmful: drinking alcohol or coffee, eating fatty foods, dancing, listening to rock music, or even driving a car.

Use **relationship words**. Connect sentences by using words like *consequently, therefore, nevertheless, yet*, and so on.

> Opinion in the Clear Lake University Senate had generally favored the proposal to abolish smoking on campus. **However**, Kyle's arguments made some proponents waver as they considered the wider implications of their actions. What would happen, **for example**, if one group on campus, citing statistics on heart attacks, demanded a campuswide ban on fast foods? The ban on smoking would provide grounds for such a restriction.

Use **repetition**. Using one or two key words several times throughout a paragraph can tie it together effectively.

> What makes smoking a social problem, not an individual one, Professor Upton argued, is the phenomenon of "**passive smoking**." **Passive smoking** describes the

inhalation of combustion by-products by **nonsmokers** living or working in the vicinity of smokers. Scientific studies suggest a **correlation** between certain health problems in **nonsmokers** and **passive smoking**. Because of this **correlation**, institutions must act prudently to protect their employees and residents from a possible health hazard.

Use **parallel structure**. Establishing a strong pattern of parallel sentence structure in a paragraph is an excellent unifier, contributing to the craft and readability of a paper.

Should smoking be banned because it imposes a health hazard upon individuals who do not smoke? Then **shouldn't drinking** be similarly outlawed, **since alcoholism** victimizes millions of families and drunk driving kills thousands of innocent people every year? **Shouldn't automobiles** be banned **because** they maim hundreds of pedestrians every day? **Shouldn't the printing of controversial books** be halted **because** they plant dangerous ideas in the minds of millions of readers every hour?

5A

More on transitions and achieving links *between* paragraphs in Section 12A.

EXERCISE 5.8

Examine several paragraphs in a published essay, identifying any hooks and transitions the writer has used. If you can, underline those devices, and then try to read the paragraph without them. How is the paragraph hurt by removing the transitional words and phrases?

Now look at an essay you have written recently or a draft you are working on. Underline the transitional devices you have used in several paragraphs. Would the paragraphs benefit from more transitions or have you done an adequate job giving your paragraph coherence?

5B HOW DO YOU IMPROVE PARAGRAPH APPEARANCE?

Troubleshooting

You may not want to worry about paragraph divisions when you are writing your first draft or even the second one. But when you begin to get your paper in shape you need to check on paragraph appearance. Printed material has a kind of body language that affects the way readers respond to it. In fact, the way an essay or article or book *looks* affects the attitude a potential reader has even before he or she reads a word. If the print is small, close together, and goes on for long stretches unbroken by headings, spaces, or segments of dialogue, most readers are going to be a little reluctant to start reading. They assume the subject matter is going to be difficult and the style stiff and not reader-friendly. See if you can find an uninterrupted page of print in a book. Hold it away from you and just look at it, making no attempt to read the words.

One message comes through quickly, doesn't it? That message is *I am hard to read.*

Why do we get that message? From our experience, for one thing. It's just generally true that closely printed, unbroken prose with long sentences and long paragraphs usually deals with fairly difficult topics, and it takes us longer to read and comprehend the material. But we also respond negatively for another reason that we may not be as aware of. That is, our brains process information in chunks, so we like to have it presented to us in manageable units. If the unit is too long or looks too jammed with information, we react negatively and don't want to read it because we suspect we'll have trouble. Of course, a persistent reader can eventually work through long stretches of unbroken print and understand what is being said, but it's tough going and most of us don't want to endure it.

That's why readers are put off by paragraphs that are too long. It is also the reason writers need to think about breaking up their paragraphs frequently in order to help their readers. Your readers are much more likely to take a receptive attitude toward what you write if your paragraphs are fairly short. How short is that? Probably no more than ten sentences—fewer if possible. And it usually is.

We also have a few words to say about when to use one- or two-sentence paragraphs. Many writers have a tendency—perhaps picked up from reading newspapers—to begin a new paragraph every few sentences, without much regard for content. If too many long paragraphs intimidate readers, a lot of short ones in a row tend to distract them or make them feel that the content of a paper is trivial. Yet short paragraphs have their place, too, in shaping and emphasizing ideas. We discuss these matters below.

To improve paragraph appearance . . .

▶ **Break up paragraph blocks that look hard to read.** Of course, you shouldn't just chop up paragraphs arbitrarily to make your paper look friendly. By definition, paragraphs are supposed to develop an idea and it usually takes several sentences to do that. But often, minor divisions within a paragraph will emerge after it is written, and the writer can break it at those junctures. The spots at which such divisions can be made come at these places:

—**Shifts in time**: look for spots where you have written words such as *first, then,* or *afterwards,* or have given other time signals.

—**Shifts in place**: look for spots where you have written *over there,* or *on the other side,* or have used words that point to places.

—**Shifts in direction**: look for spots where you have written *on the other hand, nevertheless, however,* or have indicated contrast.

—**Shifts in emphasis or focus**: look for new emphases or new aspects of your topic sentence.

Here is an example of a long paragraph at the beginning of a paper that has been broken into three shorter ones, each of which still develops a point effectively.

{Original version}

Fire Down Below

While I was in high school I had an unusual summer job working as a chimney sweep's assistant. Even though chimney sweeps have been around for hundreds of years, my partner and I were an odd sight. Clad in black tails and top hat, we would search out jobs in Chicago neighborhoods with lots of chimneys. We always generated an audience as we pulled up in front of someone's house in our old station wagon. In a cloud of soot, we would unload our chimney sweeping equipment and begin preparing for our ascent to the chimney top. At each job we organized our tools to avoid unnecessary climbing, the most dangerous part of our job. I often wondered what I was doing climbing on hot rooftops and risking my neck for a summer job. My partner tried to persuade me that chimney sweeps had a special significance in the world and that I was lucky to be welcomed into people's homes for their yearly sweep. In the past, chimney sweeping was an important industry because people burned considerably more wood and coal for heating and cooking than they do now. Ben Franklin wanted chimney sweeps to be public servants like policemen and firemen. My partner told me of youngsters in England who, like Oliver Twist, were kidnapped in the early 1800s and forced to be "climbing boys." Their job was to squeeze through large chimneys and scrape the walls clean. As the story goes, if a boy got stuck in a chimney, a fire would be lit under his feet to encourage him along.

{Revised paragraphing}

While I was in high school I had an unusual summer job working as a chimney sweep's assistant. Even though chimney sweeps have been around for hundreds of years, my partner and I were an odd sight. Clad in black tails and top hat, we would search out jobs in Chicago neighborhoods with lots of chimneys.

We always generated an audience as we pulled up in front of someone's house in our old station wagon. In a cloud of soot, we would unload our chimney sweeping equipment and begin preparing for our ascent to the chimney top. At each job we organized our tools to avoid unnecessary climbing, the most dangerous part of our job. I often wondered what I was doing climbing on hot rooftops and risking my neck for a summer job. My partner tried to persuade me that chimney sweeps had a special significance in the world and that I was lucky to be welcomed into people's homes for their yearly sweep.

In the past, chimney sweeping was an important industry because people burned considerably more wood and coal for heating and cooking than they do now. Ben Franklin wanted chimney sweeps to be public servants like policemen and firemen. My partner told me of youngsters in England who, like Oliver Twist, were kidnapped in the early 1800s and forced to be "climbing boys." Their job was to squeeze through large chimneys and scrape the walls clean. As the story goes, if a boy got stuck in a chimney, a fire would be lit under his feet to encourage him along.

EXERCISE 5.9

The essay on chimney sweeps continues below, printed as a single paragraph. Use the symbol for new paragraph—¶—to indicate where you might start additional paragraphs in the essay.

Because people today rarely consider having their home's chimney swept, we had to hustle to make any money, carefully explaining to each potential customer why sweeping was necessary to remove creosote, a flammable, tarlike substance, from their chimney walls. Cleaning the creosote encourages proper drafts, removes foul odors from a house, and helps to avoid costly relining in the future if a chimney is heavily used. In our salespitch, we also played on the fears of homeowners by warning them that a build-up of creosote could cause a chimney fire. Since average chimney fires caused $30,000–$40,000 in damage, most people proved eager to eliminate the fire hazard. After convincing the customer that they needed a sweep, we would begin the job. Standing on the chimney top, we pulled our brushes up from the ground with ropes. (Watching a misplaced brush fall off the roof reminded me of the long trip down I would enjoy if I took a careless step over the edge.) We then selected a wiry brush of the right shape or diameter and forced it down the chimney with a snap-together fiberglass extension. The chimney would resist by expelling clouds of thick black smoke in our faces. Reaming the flues several times left us covered in filthy residue. While on the rooftop, we repaired any external damage to the chimney and tried to shake a few pounds of unwanted soot from our formal attire. Before we entered a customer's home for the second half of the job, the lady of the house almost invariably lined our pathway with newspapers and insisted we give our jackets a few more shakes. Inside the house, we covered the area around the fireplace with drop cloths the way a surgeon might surround an incision. I usually had the dirty job of donning a gas mask and climbing as far as possible into the fireplace. With a loud, high-powered vacuum in hand, I cleaned the fireplace, smokebox, and lower flue. As I worked, more clouds of black soot poured out of the chimney into the house. Cleaning up the house when we were done often proved as difficult as cleaning the chimney. Charging forty-five dollars for a two-story house and fifty-five for three, we relied on additional revenue from reconstructing chimneys and selling chimney caps. A chimney cap is supposed to keep debris out of the chimney without blocking rising smoke. To encourage sales of caps, we kept a few dead squirrels in the wagon. Inside the house, we would convincingly pull one of the stiff critters from the fireplace at an appropriate moment. This trick of the trade worked especially well if we evoked a good shriek from one of the family members. Homeowners seemed to enjoy our visit far more than they would the plumber's or electrician's. People often shook our hands for luck, believing that chimney sweeps are bearers of good fortune. Romanticism aside, chimney sweeping is an interesting

5B

job. Few authentic sweepers are around anymore because most people don't consider having their chimney swept. This fact didn't worry my partner and me, however; we could always find jobs in a neighborhood where a chimney fire the past winter had destroyed a house.

—Robert Irmen

▶ **Reconsider short paragraphs.** Paragraphs can be too short as well as too long. A paragraph is, after all, supposed to develop an idea—that is, be a group of sentences that focus on and explain or illustrate a point. That's hard to do in one sentence. So if you are writing a series of one- or two-sentence paragraphs in your paper, you are either not developing your ideas sufficiently or you're chopping what should be a coherent unit into segments that are going to confuse your readers and make it hard for them to follow your ideas. Notice, for instance, how choppy and disorganized this group of short paragraphs seems.

As election time rolls around again, so does all the political hub-bub. Press conferences, debates, degrading commercials, and headlines in newspapers are only a few of the things evident during election time.

All voters are offered a chance to elect their candidate to run their country or state. Everyone seems to know how important it is to participate in the election by voting.

Everyone except young voters.

All through school, young people are taught how their country is run. We learn about Congress and the system of checks and balances. We learn about Presidential elections and responsibilities.

But after high school, just when we reach the voting age, we decide not to take advantage of the opportunity to be heard.

With this kind of organization, it's hard for readers to sense the relationship between the parts. Instead of links, there are gaps. Here are the paragraphs restored to their original shape.

As election time rolls around again, so does all the political hub-bub. Press conferences, debates, degrading commercials, and headlines in newspapers are only a few of the things evident during election time. All voters are offered a chance to elect their candidate to run their country or state. Everyone seems to know how important it is to participate in the election by voting. Everyone except young voters.

All through school, young people are taught how their country is run. We learn about Congress and the system of checks and balances. We learn about Presidential elections and responsibilities. But after high school, just when we reach the voting age, we decide not to take advantage of the opportunity to be heard.

—Brian Mims

Sometimes, of course, short paragraphs work well, particularly when the writer wants to manage a transition, to emphasize or summarize a point, or to introduce a series. Here are examples of single-sentence paragraphs from professional writing.

Tennis has become more than the national sport; it is a rigorous discipline, a form of collective physiotherapy. Jogging is done by swarms of people, out onto the streets each day in underpants, moving in a stolid sort of rapid trudge, hoping by this to stay alive. Bicycles are cures. Meditation may be good for the soul but it is even better for the blood pressure.

As a people, we have become obsessed with Health.

There is something fundamentally, radically unhealthy about all this. We do not seem to be seeking more exuberance in living as much as staving off failure, putting off dying. We have lost all confidence in the human body.

—Lewis Thomas, "The Health Care System"

One sociologist said that you don't have to have a reason for going to college because it's an institution. His definition of an institution is something everyone subscribed to without question. The burden of proof is not on why you should go to college, but why anyone thinks there might be a reason for not going. The implication—and some educators express it quite frankly—is that an eighteen-year-old high school graduate is still too young and confused to know what he wants to do, let alone what is good for him.

Mother knows best, in other words.
—Caroline Bird, "Where College Fails Us"

So you shouldn't be afraid to use one- or two-sentence paragraphs occasionally, but when you do, think about how they are going to affect the body language of your writing and use them sparingly.

EXERCISE 5.10

The remainder of Brian Mims' brief piece on the apathy of student voters has been broken down into short paragraphs and reprinted below. Revise the paragraphing to improve the style and readability of the selection.

Many young voters feel that there are so many other voters in this country, that their one vote won't matter one way or the other.

With this in mind, they decide quite early in a political campaign that they are not going to vote.

Consequently, they don't keep up with the issues, which start forming very early in an election year.

By the time the young voter is finally convinced by all the "Please Vote" commercials, he thinks he is too far behind in the issues to appreciate them and decides not to vote.

Some young people simply decide to let other people run the country for them. They just hope that the better candidate wins, rather than following the issues themselves and casting their votes accordingly.

"I'm too busy to bother myself with all that election junk," they complain. "In the long run, it makes no difference."

You can be sure that these are the first people to complain when student loans are cut or the drinking age is changed.

5C WHAT MAKES AN OPENING PARAGRAPH EFFECTIVE?

Troubleshooting

Opening paragraphs warrant special attention because they introduce you and your paper to the reader and such first impressions are always important. Remember that opening paragraphs serve these functions:

—They make a commitment, either announcing or suggesting the thesis of an essay—or letter, report, brochure, whatever the case may be.

—They set the tone of the essay and indicate the direction in which it will go.

—They draw the reader into the essay and try to get him or her to read it.

These are big responsibilities and that's why first paragraphs are so hard to write. It is also why they are worth spending time on.

We couldn't possibly describe all the kinds of effective first paragraphs a writer could create. We will mention only a few of the most helpful patterns.

To write an effective opening paragraph . . .

▶ **Make a commitment to your reader.** We have already mentioned commitment and response (Section 5A). But nowhere can the technique serve you better than in an opening paragraph, where it may take a variety of forms—an anecdote, a description of a situation, a statement of a problem, even a question. Whatever shape it assumes, a commitment introduces a topic by promising to supply more information. It wins the reader's attention by offering the prospect of material that is valuable, interesting, new, or maybe even amusing.

Here are some examples of opening paragraphs Connie Lim wrote for the *Daily Toxin* to make commitments to her readers and give them strong signals about what to expect from her articles.

Example 1.

Until last week, the closest most Clear Lake College students had ever been to a real country western dance was walking by a juke box that was blaring out Hank Williams' "Honky Tonk Angel." They had never seen anyone dance the Cotton Eyed Joe or Put Your Little Foot, and they wouldn't have known Kicker dancing from a Viennese waltz. As of last Saturday, though, all that has changed with the opening of a new establishment, The Broken Spoke.

In this paragraph, Connie *commits* herself to describing The Broken Spoke and explaining why it can be called a real country western dance hall.

Example 2.

Clear Lake College has always had its share of major league ice cream addicts. Security Officer Klinkhamer, who admits to a six-cone-a-day habit and keeps a computer log on his favorite flavors (the current one is peanut butter/mango), is generally considered one of the top performers. Coach Jasper Rhodes' ice cream consumption is not as steady as Klinkhamer's but on occasions has been more spectacular. Witnesses testify that he devoured three Hot Czech Chocolate Frenzies (ice cream sandwiches made with kolaches and three scoops of double chocolate devil's food ice cream topped with hot fudge sauce) at Maggie's Ice Cream Heaven every time his team lost last fall. But yesterday all records fell as a new ice cream champion—and a woman at that—was crowned at Maggie's.

Here Connie catches the attention of ice cream lovers among her readers and *commits* herself to tell them about what happened at Maggie's to make the woman the new champion.

Example 3.

Shouts of "traitor," "heretic," and "Philistine" and cries of "Standards, by God, standards" filled the air Friday afternoon at the monthly meeting of the English department as the Chair, Oscar Cupperman, tried to contain the controversy that has exploded at every departmental meeting for the past five years. For the benefit of newcomers we should explain the issue that continues to split the department. It is whether the ampersand—the "&" mark that stands for "and"—should be added to the dreaded English Department List of Fatal Errors in Freshman English. After an hour of rather unhumanistic dialogue between the factions that have come to be known as the Tory Grammarians and the Populist Pragmatists, Professor Cupperman was ready to call the question, sure that the Pragmatists finally had the votes to defeat the drive to make the ampersand the thirteenth item on the official Sin List. He had not, however, reckoned with the passion and eloquence of Professor Letitia Warriner.

5C

Here Connie gives her readers enough background information to get them interested in the controversy, then *commits* herself to telling them about what happened when Professor Warriner spoke.

Example 4.

On a recent warm Friday afternoon, Katy Martinich was sitting on the back of a tiger-striped plastic couch in Stan's Blue Note Fern Bar, Laundromat, and Chili Parlor watching her clothes splash around and taking an occasional taste from a bowl of Stan's famous Industrial Strength Cincinnati-style Chili. As she ate, she hummed the theme from Mozart's "A Little Night Music" and energetically conducted her imaginary orchestra, scarcely noticing the tall bearded man in the white leather jacket and designer jeans with a turquoise studded belt who stood across the aisle watching her. He, however, watched Katy intently as she waved an old swizzle stick at the hanging ferns, gesticulated to the potted geraniums, and beckoned to the ficus tree to play louder. And as she turned toward the now-empty chili bowl to motion it to come in *pianissimo*, he stepped forward and spoke to her. "How would you like to make a movie?"

Here Connie creates a narrative, a minidrama, to introduce her topic to her readers; by doing so, she *commits* herself to tell them the rest of the drama and satisfy their curiosity.

EXERCISE 5.11

Choose one of these opening commitment paragraphs and in ten minutes write out a brief summary of what you think Connie Lim said in the rest of the article. Then meet in a small group with other students who have chosen the same paragraph, read each person's summary aloud, and discuss how well it lives up to the commitment of the first paragraph.

FXFRCISE 5.12

Draft an opening commitment paragraph that might begin an essay under one of these titles.

> The College Health Service—Latest Scandal
>
> Rock and Roll Doesn't Live Here Any More
>
> Nuclear Weapons—Do They Assure Peace?
>
> Immigration Today in a Nation of Immigrants
>
> Morality and the First Amendment: Who Censors What?

▶ **Consider making a direct announcement of your intentions.** Sometimes you will do best to open your essay by simply telling your readers exactly what you are going to write about. Such openings work well for many of the papers you write in college courses, for reports that you might have to write on the job, for grant proposals, and for many other kinds of factual, informative writing. Here are some examples.

Example 1. Paper for an American history course written by John Maynard Ringling, retired army officer and history buff.

A New American Hero?

For over 200 years, Americans have honored George Washington for his eloquence, leadership, and courage under fire. He has been called "First in war, first in peace, first in the hearts of his countrymen." A fitting tribute, but one that would not have been possible without the efforts of another great man who was first in his own way: Josiah Stoneridge Ringling, the first man in Virginia to carve wooden dentures. He made it possible for Washington to give the stirring speeches that rallied colonists to join the Continental Army. Perhaps more important, Ringling also enabled Washington to suit actions to words when he admonished his troops to "bite the bullet and press on!" Thus, the story of Ringling's life and how he perfected his wooden dentures is an important one to American history.

Here Ringling has set the context for his paper, shown why his topic is important, and announced to his readers that he is going to tell them about Josiah Ringling's development of wooden dentures.

Example 2. Report submitted by Sue Ellen Rizzo, market researcher for the Clear Lake Potato Chip Factory, to her supervisor.

After spending two weeks interviewing 267 consistent potato chip eaters on the Clear Lake Campus, I have established three reasons for the recent decline in sales for our product. They are, first, the color of our new Blue Chipster potato chips; second, our advertising campaign featuring the word "chippies"; third, our change in recipe to reduce salt. Each reason requires some explanation.

Sue Ellen has told her supervisor immediately what she is going to write about and given her a condensed outline of the points she will cover in the report.

Example 3. Brian McVicker's movie review in the *Daily Toxin*.

The Great Halloween Chainsaw Massacre Part IV: The Final Beginning is the worst movie of the year and possibly the decade. Nevertheless, last night it opened to overflow crowds on two screens at the Regent Theater thanks to a publicity blitz that promised door prizes of plastic chain saws that really can cut your finger and miniature buckets of fake blood for the children to use in their games at home. The concession stand was also offering special Bloody Sunday ice cream treats—vanilla ice cream drowned in crushed maraschino cherries. But however tasteless the preliminaries, they were a treat compared to the gory antics on the screen.

Brian makes a direct statement of his thesis in the very first sentence and lets his readers know what to expect—concrete evidence that the movie is indeed the worst and most tasteless of the year.

EXERCISE 5.13

In fifteen minutes, write a short summary of the material you think would come after these opening paragraphs. When you have finished, get into a group with others who have written summaries for the same topic, compare notes, and discuss your content.

EXERCISE 5.14

Write a "direct statement" opening sentence or paragraph for an article that might support one of these titles

Evolution and the Evidence

Why *Star Trek* endures

Rock and Roll Began in *Cleveland*?

Apartheid and American Political Attitudes

Why America Is Better Off Without Royalty

Psychology and the "Average" Student

5C

▶ **Ask a question.** A third strategy for an opening paragraph is to pose a question that highlights a problem or piques readers' curiosity. Sometimes writers may elaborate on a single question, and sometimes they may raise several questions in an opening paragraph. Not only do questions provide a tantalizing lead-in, but they also make commitments (review Section 5A). Here are some examples.

Example 1. Opening paragraph from an article written by Greta Ericson, co-owner of Wildflowers Good Health Cafe and Market, for the magazine *Hearty Health*.

What distinguishes the sensible, nutrition-minded shopper from the health food nut? Well, I have known some world class health food nuts in my time and I can spot them immediately when they come in the store. The young woman who came in last week wearing a red head band, high-topped black Reeboks, and a purple T-shirt reading "Macrobiotic Mama" had all the earmarks.

Here, Greta leads off with the central question she will answer in her article, assures the reader she has the experience to answer it, and commits herself to doing so in detail.

Example 2. Opening paragraph of an editorial written by Rita Ruiz, student body presidential candidate, for the *Daily Toxin*.

What is it that students at Clear Lake College really care about? What will they spend money for, wait in line for, stay up past midnight for? What means more to them than their waistlines, their cholesterol count, or their complexions? The answer is pizza. Wonderful, fattening, greasy, delicious pizza! They love it and are willing to pay the price to have it. Why then has

President Tiffany Shade threatened to ban pizza deliveries to the dormitories on the Clear Lake College campus? Because, I fear, she has little appreciation for personal liberty. Pizza may be trivial, but freedom is not.

In this opener Rita has caught her readers' interest with a series of provocative questions, given a rousing answer, and then committed herself to arguing against the president's pizza ban.

5C.

EXERCISE 5.15

In no more than ten minutes, sketch an outline of the rest of the paper that might follow either of the two opening paragraphs above. Meet in a small group with two or three others who have done follow-ups on the same paragraph to compare and discuss the content of your outlines.

EXERCISE 5.16

Write opening questions that might make a good lead-in for the following topics.

1. The board of regents of your school proposes to abolish all college sports that are not self-supporting.
2. Only two of the twelve copying machines on campus work.
3. A famous rock star will give a million dollars to the college if it agrees to name the library after her.

Compare and discuss your questions with other students.

▶ **Focus on key facts.** Another good anchor for an opening paragraph is the statement of an important fact that clues the readers into what your topic is going to be and gives them the base of information that they need to continue with their reading. Such a statement of fact (or facts) becomes the take-off point for the essay. Here are some examples of how different students focus on important facts in their opening paragraphs.

> **Example 1.** Abel Gonzalez writing a paper for an advertising course.

> Today 47% of the customers in any grocery store are men. A recent survey published in *Advertising Age* shows that although they don't buy as much per trip as women do, they tend to buy more expensive products and they are more impulsive buyers than women. A person walking through Ericson's health food store last Saturday morning would have seen strong corroborating evidence if she had looked in the baskets of Oscar Cupperman and Hector Stavros as they stood chatting in front of the pasta counter.

Here Abel has started by highlighting the key fact around which his paper will turn, developed the point with an example, and finished his paragraph with a transition sentence into the rest of the paper.

> **Example 2.** Sue Ellen Rizzo, single parent, writing an argument paper.

> Every major industrial country in the western world except the United States has an extensive system of subsidized child care that assures working women their children will be adequately taken care of by qualified people. Every city and town has government-sponsored day care centers and in many countries, factories and corporations provide on-site care that allows women to visit their children during the day. In those companies, absenteeism for both men and women is notably lower than it is in our system. Some of the older business owners of Ruralia, however, still have a dinosaur mentality when it comes to establishing child care facilities.

Here Sue Ellen has focused her opening paragraph on important information about child care policies in other countries and indicated that she is going to use that information to discuss problems with child care in Ruralia.

144

Think of of three important facts you could use as the hook for an opening paragraph. (Check an almanac if you can't locate or recall any pertinent statistics. See Section 21D.) They might be statistics about divorce, the amount of money that the nation spends on cat food, the number of homeless people in Santa Barbara, or the amount spent on athletic scholarships in your college. Or they could be statements such as "In 1986, at the age of thirty-one, Earl Campbell hung up his uniform and quit professional football." Be sure the facts you use are verifiable—not just biases or opinions.

Write an opening paragraph from the most interesting of your facts.

5C

▶ **Avoid "circling the field" or "wheel spinning."** In the struggle to get started, a writer sometimes can't think of anything to say, so he or she strings together generalizations that comment on the topic rather than getting down to business. It's like a pilot circling the field, getting ready to land or someone giving his or her car too much throttle pulling away from a stoplight. There's a lot of noise, tire smoke, and wheel-spinning, but little forward movement. For example, here is a paragraph returning student John Maynard Ringling wrote trying to begin a paper about how buying a computer had changed his study habits.

> In this modern complex world of today, computers play an important role in everyone's lives. There are more computers today than there have ever been before. Whether we like it or not, we are involved with computers. Computers today affect just about every area of our lives. So it is silly to say, "Oh, I'm too old to learn about computers."

All the sentences before the last one would bore the reader. They are filler, a wind-up to get to the point made in the last sentence. They're fine for getting started on a preliminary draft, but you shouldn't waste the reader's time with them in a final version. How much better the opening would be if John

Maynard provided some specific examples of computers becoming a part of his life or told an anecdote about an encounter he had with a computer.

> I was an old-timer in a technical writing class full of nineteen and twenty year olds when I discovered what I had been missing. Most of my classmates were turning in second and third versions of reports they were composing on computers while I was still grinding out an erasure-scarred first draft on my old manual typewriter. Some of those kids' papers looked as if they came out of a printshop, with boldface headings and professional-looking illustrations. The only illustrations on my draft were doodles I had drawn in frustration. For a while, I thought that my typewriter and I suited each other. We both worked kind of slow. Then I recognized that my thinking wasn't old-fashioned— just my technology. I learned quickly that it is silly to say "Oh, I'm too old to learn about computers."

▶ **Tell your readers only what they need to know.** Sometimes a writer gives readers more preliminary information than they need, making them impatient for the main point. Kyle Talbot wrote such a long-winded paragraph for an English paper on white-water canoeing.

> Only a few years ago, you seldom heard of the average person going white-water canoeing, but today it is a hobby that millions of people enjoy. The change began to come about twenty years ago when canoe manufacturers started making fiberglass canoes, replacing the older ones made out of aluminum or wood. Fiberglass was a new material applied over molds in layers that would harden quickly into a very tough surface. It had been used before in industrial applications and for insulation, but no one had thought of putting it on boats. It was also fairly inexpensive as compared to aluminum, although it did raise problems because it posed a health hazard to workers using it. Once the manufacturers learned how to handle fiberglass, it revolutionized the sport of canoeing.

At the beginning of a paper, Kyle's readers probably want to know *how* fiberglass canoes changed canoeing, not details about the material itself. Chances are that they will start skimming to get to the point, and if they don't find it quickly, they'll quit reading. A revised version might be considerably shorter:

> Only a few years ago, you seldom heard of the average person going white-water canoeing, but today it is a hobby that millions of people enjoy. The change occurred about twenty years ago when canoe manufacturers started making fiberglass canoes, replacing the older ones made out of aluminum or wood. Once the manufacturers learned how to handle the difficult material, fiberglass canoes revolutionized the sport of canoeing in three ways.

5D

EXERCISE 5.18

Check the introductory paragraphs in essays you have written recently for wheel-spinning. If your openings seem to move too slowly, try reading the papers beginning with their *second* paragraphs. Quite often, a paper really begins there. Don't be afraid to cut your original introduction if it doesn't move quickly enough.

5D WHAT MAKES A CONCLUDING PARAGRAPH EFFECTIVE?

Troubleshooting

Concluding paragraphs are notoriously hard to write, harder, we think, than opening paragraphs, and more resistant to standard solutions. About all we can say is that the concluding paragraph for a paper should give your readers the sense that you have brought the paper to a satisfactory conclusion, that you have left no loose ends or unanswered questions. You don't want your readers asking "And so?" when they finish or looking on the back of the page to see if they have missed something. There are no simple prescriptions for achieving that important goal; however, we can suggest some patterns that make for stylish endings.

To write an effective concluding paragraph . . .

▶ **Make a recommendation when one is appropriate.** Such a recommendation should grow out of the issue you have been discussing. This approach usually gives a paper a positive ending and closes off the topic. For example:

> **Example 1.** Conclusion from a paper on nutrition by Abel Gonzalez.
>
> But even if you are an athlete who wants quick results, you should not go to extremes in trying to improve your overall nutrition. When you want to start eating better, your motto should be "Eat better," not "Eat perfectly." By increasing carbohydrates and reducing fat in the diet, that is, by eating more fruits, vegetables and whole grains and less whole milk and fat meat, you can improve your energy level rather quickly. You will also feel better, play better, and look better than you ever imagined.
>
> **Example 2.** Conclusion from a paper on starting to lift weights by Stephanie Mendelson (Big Stevie).
>
> Not everyone wants to be a champion weightlifter, but almost everyone can lose weight and inches and gain strength and body tone by lifting weights. The main thing is to get started. Whether you want to be another Scott Madsen or just feel better, you need to start out by finding a partner, choosing a gym for workouts, and getting a routine designed for you. Don't be afraid to try. Every accomplished weightlifter was once a spectator waiting around to get started.

▶ **Summarize the main points you have made.** Sometimes you can bring your paper to a stylish close by re-emphasizing your main points (though not in precisely the same words you have used before) and closing with a wind-up sentence. You want to be careful, however, not to sound as if you're being totally mechanical, tying the paper up in red ribbon and sticking a bow on it. Here are two examples that work fairly well.

Example 1. Conclusion for Richard Wesley's English class paper in which he argues that restaurant customers should tip their waiters.

Anyone who has ever worked in a restaurant knows that sometimes customers don't get very good service, and it's easy to shortchange a waiter by saying "The food wasn't good," or "I had to wait too long." But the bottom line is that tips are part of a waiter's pay, and if you don't tip, you've stolen part of his or her labor.

Example 2. Conclusion for Francie Knipstein's article in the Career Corner of the *Daily Toxin*.

To be a successful television producer takes a combination of talent, training, a lot of hard work, knowing someone, and being in the right place at the right time. This sounds clichéd, but it's true. There are no "accidental" television producers.

▶ **Link the end to the beginning.** Another effective way to end your paper is to tie your conclusion back to your beginning in a way that makes a kind of frame for the paper and unifies it. Notice how the words boldfaced in the examples below forge a connection between opening and closing paragraphs:

Example 1. From a paper on animal myths written by Sue Ellen Rizzo for an English class.

Beginning paragraph:

Ever held a slimy snake in the palm of your hand? Or gotten a wart from a toad? Or been stung by a dragonfly? **If you think you have**, then you believe in **some common myths about animals**.

5D

Closing paragraph:

Although humans have been able to explain most natural phenomena, some animals have habits or appearances that humans do not understand. In an effort to explain those mysteries, **people create myths and superstitions about animals**. When repeated often enough, these myths are taken as fact and become conventional wisdom. But **myths are not facts**, and people who are curious enough to want to know the real facts won't accept superstition as knowledge.

Example 2. A paper by Jenny So for her History of Astronomy course.

Opening paragraph:

In 1931, an event occurred in Holmdel, New Jersey, that was to turn the world of astronomy on its ear. **An electrical engineer named Karl Jansky** was trying to find out what was causing **the static** that was interfering with radio-telephone reception between the United States and Europe. What he found instead was that the heavens were broadcasting! The "static" was caused by radio waves reaching the earth from the center of our Milky Way Galaxy.

Closing paragraph:

If Karl Jansky had not stumbled onto the "static" in the Milky Way and thus led to the development of the radio telescope, we would probably still know nothing about quasars, one of the most astonishing discoveries of our day. And it is doubtful that Jansky himself ever fully realized what a powerful tool he had hit upon for investigating the secrets of our universe.

EXERCISE 5.19

For an editorial for your college newspaper, draft a closing paragraph in which you make a recommendation about changing some absurd college regulation that you ridicule in the editorial.

CHAPTER

What Kinds of Language Can You Use?

- **A** Levels of language
- **B** Denotation and connotation
- **C** Dialects
- **D** Sexist language

Introduction

Few people would choose to use the same kind of language every time they write any more than they would wear the same kind of clothes on every occasion. We instinctively, often unconsciously, adapt our language to our audience situation because we have developed a sense of what is appropriate; we have learned that what works on one occasion may not work as well on another. And, as the person with good clothes sense knows how to choose the right outfit to make the desired impression, skillful writers know how to select language to fit their needs. But to do that, they have to know what choices are available to them. The purpose of this section is to explain what some of those choices of language are.

6A HOW DO YOU CHOOSE A LEVEL OF LANGUAGE?

Terms you need to know

Formal language. Language that is polite, impersonal, and conventional. Most academic, professional, and business writing is formal.

Informal language. Language that is casual and personal. Informal language is still usually quite conventional in grammar and usage, though it uses contractions more regularly and makes use of vocabulary items that might seem more appropriate in everyday speech.

Troubleshooting

The answer to the question "How formal or informal should I be when I write my papers?" is "That depends."

6A

To make appropriate choices about the level of formality for a piece of writing, you have to think about

1. who your readers are,

2. what they expect in that particular writing situation, and

3. what you want to accomplish with that audience.

Only then can you make an intelligent choice about what kind of language is going to work well for that specific paper.

Unfortunately, many writers assume that in order to impress professors, colleagues, or other demanding readers, they must use an excessively formal style. They think writing an "academic style" means writing hard-to-read prose stuffed with big words and ponderous sentences—something so impersonal and dry that it reads as if it came from an insurance policy or a badly written textbook. So they turn out writing like this from the first draft of a paper for a psychology course:

> Neonate infants are realized to have the ability to relate visual sensory perception with motor function. The neonatal visual system is probably the most prefunctional of the senses at birth. Manifestly, this competence is not correlated with time outside the womb for in early months infants have the problem solving ability that comes from linking sensory systems and motor activity. The observation that these subjects manifest visual preference for facial forms upholds the assumption that a connection exists between visual and motor activity.

Writers are often proud of crafting such impressive and impenetrable paragraphs, and so they are crushed when readers complain that the material is overwritten and dull. Readers and instructors are much more apt to be impressed by this fairly formal, but not deadly, revision.

> Observers now realize that newborn infants can coordinate sight and movement. In fact, vision seems to be the sense that is best developed when babies are born for it is evident very early that they can solve problems that require linking vision and motor ability. The fact that they can recognize different facial expressions and respond to them supports this theory.

When you write, you'll often find yourself shifting among various levels of formality, looking for just the right word, phrase, or expression. That is because we cannot make a simple, black/white classification of formal and informal language. You should think of levels of formality in language as a horizontal scale or a continuum.

Levels of Language

Very formal

Legal documents

Technical reports

Scientific magazine articles

Major political speeches

Sermons

Newspaper editorials and columns

Popular magazine articles

Personal experience papers

Notes to friends

Very informal — colloquial or casual

Neither of the extremes on this scale concerns us here since virtually no writing that students do requires them to be either very formal or extremely colloquial. It is, however, useful for you to know something about the general characteristics and uses of at least three of the intermediate levels.

To handle language levels appropriately . . .

▶ **Recognize formal writing.** Formal writing tends to have *long sentences* and usually, though not always, *long paragraphs*. The language is *abstract* (see definition in Section 7A) and *impersonal*, with few references to people or specific instances and very few contractions. Usually there is *little action* in formal writing. The topic tends to be *serious*, not the stuff of everyday letters or casual conversations. The readers feel a considerable *distance* between them and the writer.

Writers who choose a formal style may do so for several reasons. First, they may be writing on a serious and complex topic, one for which a casual, personal style would not be appropriate. Second, they may be writing for a serious formal occasion such as a public speech and don't want their writing to sound too much like everyday speech. Or they may want to sound impersonal and not emotionally involved with their topic, so they adopt a style that puts them at a distance from their reader. Here is an example.

Opening paragraph from Darwin Washington's term paper for an environmental studies course.

An inescapable fact of the world energy situation to-day is that fossil fuel resources are finite, and continued reliance on coal, gas, and oil for generating electricity is not viable. However, meeting future electricity needs requires raising public awareness about finding alternate options. The most important characteristics of these options will be flexibility, cost, and low risk. Three programs currently under investigation are a broader energy information program, cogeneration and small power production, and small renewable power production.

This is an informative paragraph that gets the reader off to a good start, but it's stuffy and not much fun to read because of the formal language. Nevertheless, much of the writing done in Darwin's field of engineering sounds like this, and Darwin's professor wants his students to write this kind of formal prose. So being a bright young man, Darwin does.

▶ **Recognize moderately informal writing.** Although there are many kinds of moderately informal writing, and it occupies a considerable spread across the continuum, we can generalize that it has these characteristics. It has a *variety of sentence lengths* and *short to medium length paragraphs.* Usually we find a *mixture of concrete and abstract language* with *frequent use of personal pronouns and references to people.* *Contractions* and *action verbs* appear fairly often. Topics may range from *serious to casual.* The readers feel *little distance* between them and the writer. The writing in this book is an example of moderately informal prose; so is the work of newspaper columnists like Ellen Goodman and William Raspberry and most of the writing you may read in magazines like *Time, Reader's Digest,* or *People.*

Writers who choose an informal style usually do so because although their topics may be serious, they don't want to sound solemn. They want their readers to feel as if they are talking to them at a close and comfortable distance. An informal style seems more friendly. Here are two examples.

> **Opening paragraph from a paper on educational technology written for an education course by Stephanie Mendelson.**
>
> In the last year, interest in preparing America for its high-tech future has fairly exploded. The current scenario predicts that we will be a huge Information Society, and the current generation of youngsters will need to be familiar with using computers. School districts are now scrambling to meet this need by adding computer courses to their curriculum. They're trying to make as many students as possible "computer literate." A California school system broadly defines that state as "having the ability to function in a computer-oriented society."

Opening paragraph from descriptive paper written by Travis Beckwith III for the campus magazine. (A little more informal)

When you think of tourism in Africa do you think of East Africa, especially big game safaris in Kenya and Tanzania? Most people do. What you and other potential visitors probably don't realize is that West Africa has treasures and wonders to equal, if not surpass, anything on the African continent. Not only treasures and wonders, but mystery and adventure can be found in one country in particular—Mali, the land that is reached by the road to Timbuktu.

6A

▶ **Recognize casual writing.** Casual writing tends to have *short to medium length sentences* and *short paragraphs*. It is likely to have a *high proportion of concrete and specific words* with *many personal pronouns* and *references to people*. It uses *frequent contractions*, *some slang terms*, and many *lively, action verbs*. Usually, though not necessarily, it is written about *light topics*. The reader feels *very little distance* from the writer.

Writers who choose a casual style usually do so when their subject is popular or light, and they want their writing to give a fast-moving, breezy impression. They want to make their readers feel relaxed and comfortable. Here are two examples.

Opening paragraph from a column written by Kyle Talbot for the sports page of the *Daily Toxin*.

Do you wish you could find a fun way to relax and sharpen your body and mind without making your checkbook wince? Ever think about tennis? Probably so, but decided it cost too much and you wouldn't be that good anyway. Well, think again. With a little savvy about shopping at Good Will and a little luck in the bargain corner of Barney Meyers' Jock and Jogger Store, you can get started in tennis for less than $75.

Opening paragraph from a feature article on drinking and driving for the *Daily Toxin* by Rita Ruiz. (Even more informal although the topic is not light.)

You've been hittin' the books all weekend. A new guy from your chem class calls and wants to cruise out to the lake for a swim. He's kind of cute, so you go, picking up a couple of six packs along the way. The afternoon passes, and it's been fun. But now it's time to go home, and your date's had one too many. You're feelin' kind of buzzed yourself. What d'ya do?

Each of these students chose the level of formality for his or her paper by thinking about the purpose of the paper and the audience who would read it. Darwin knew his professor wanted the impersonal and abstract tone of an engineering report—no personal pronouns, no contractions. Stephanie knew that her professor wanted a factual but not stuffy article on computers in the schools, one that might be printed later in a departmental newsletter. Travis wanted to be a little less formal in his article on Mali because he was writing for his fellow students and thought if the article sounded too much like a paper for a course, they wouldn't read it. Kyle wanted an informative but breezy and easy-to-read style for his tennis-playing readers so he chose to sound conversational and casual. Finally, Rita deliberately chose to write her article about drinking and driving in such an informal and colloquial style because she wanted to avoid sounding preachy on a topic that students often feel they have read too much about already. She knows, however, that such a style is much too informal for most papers she would write in college.

EXERCISE 6.1

Using less formal language, rewrite this paragraph from Abel Gonzalez's announcement for student body president in the *Daily Toxin*. Compare your version with that of another student and discuss what changes you made and why.

If elected to the presidency of the student body, I will give high priority to insuring that all Clear Lake College students are guaranteed the right to one pizza a week (large size). Although President Shade's total Pizza Ban has been the object of numerous protests and demonstrations, her unwillingness to negotiate in the face of these manifestations of student displeasure has become more noticeable every day. Therefore it is imperative that we elect someone who will assume firm leadership in this crisis and negotiate a compromise with the administration.

EXERCISE 6.2

6B

Using more formal language, rewrite this memo by Clear Lake College President Tiffany Shade using language it might have if sent as an announcement to the student body in response to a petition that she lift her campuswide ban on pizza sales and consumption. Compare your new version with that of another student and discuss what changes you made and why.

No way am I going to lift my Pizza Ban. The average freshman at Clear Lake College last year ate 3.6 large pizzas a week and gained an average of 12.5 pounds in the first semester. I feel like a mom to those kids, and I'm not going to let them become pizza-eating couch potatoes their first year here. Clear Lake College has an image to maintain.

6B DENOTATION AND CONNOTATION: WHAT'S APPROPRIATE?

Terms You Need to Know

Denotation. A relatively neutral or objective meaning of a term. Sometimes called the "dictionary meaning," the denotation of a word attempts to explain what the word is or does stripped of any individual emotional, political, or ethical associations.

Connotation. The meanings and associations a word has acquired, over and above its dictionary meaning;

its overtones. While any number of words may have roughly the same meaning as the word *beautiful*, for example, and so share the same **denotation**, such words may differ significantly in what they imply—in their **connotations:** *pretty, handsome, lovely, comely, sightly, gorgeous,* and *stunning.*

Troubleshooting

All writers need to learn how to balance denotative and connotative language. Because there seems to be a built-in bias toward logic and facts in the academic world, students sometimes get the idea that denotative language is good and connotative language is bad. Not at all. We need both. Denotative language is necessary for maintaining objectivity when you are writing up experiments, giving data, reporting case studies, writing lab reports, or writing a serious talk.

Connotative language is just as necessary when you are making judgments, giving opinions, writing critical papers in literature or fine arts, or writing arguments. Often it is the connotation and figurative language that gives writing vigor and color. Carefully used, connotative language will help you to express ideas and emotions forcefully and with a strong personal voice.

To understand how words affect readers . . .

▶ **Understand the impression denotative language creates.** Denotative language is limited and specific language that seems to describe an object or a concept as objectively and accurately as possible. You find *denotative* definitions in dictionaries and encyclopedias since those works try to seem factual and give readers straightforward definitions and explanations not colored by associations or emotions. Those books are reference works, and denotative language is *referential.* Often in encyclopedias and larger dictionaries you will find a picture or sketch accompanying a denotative definition in order to make the meaning as clear and specific as possible.

Examples of denotative definitions:

1. **socialism**: a theory or system of social organization that advocates the vesting of ownership and control of the means of production, capital, land, etc., in the community as a whole.

2. **democracy**: a form of government in which supreme power is vested in the people and exercised by them or by their elected agents under a free electoral system.

These are unemotional, limited definitions that seem to give "just the facts."

6B

▶ **Appreciate the power of connotative language.** Connotative language is language that carries additional meanings, a kind of emotional baggage that makes it appeal to readers' senses, feelings, prejudices, or attitudes. Connotation has the power to evoke strong responses from readers because it taps into their whole beings, not just their intellects, and reminds them of experiences, beliefs, or traditions that are meaningful to them. Connotation can be broad and cultural or specific and personal.

Notice, for instance, that though *socialism* has a strict denotative meaning given above, it also has powerful connotative meanings, and they are different for different cultures. In socialist countries such as Holland or Sweden, the term has strong positive connotations; those countries are proud of their socialist governments and traditions. In the United States, however, the term has negative connotations because most Americans believe in the capitalistic system of private ownership and react against anything that is called socialist. *Democracy*, on the other hand, has a strong positive connotation in almost all cultures, so strong that almost all governments claim to be democracies.

Words can also have limited and distinctive personal connotations, specific to an individual or a group. *Safe* and *cautious* could be positive words to a mother, negative ones to a restless young person; *entrepreneur* and *competitive* are good words to people of a certain temperament, bad words to others. This ambiguity of connotative language can make it tricky to use because meaning can shift from one reader to another, and writers have to learn to think ahead about how their audience may respond when they use slanted language. Here are two paragraphs that are heavily connotative.

Front page comment in the *Daily Toxin* written by Coach Jasper Rhodes.

As we head into the new football season with our **valiant** and **beleaguered** team, the Clear Lake College Chiggers, I hope that Clear Lake students will **repent** their **disgraceful** behavior of last year and **vow** that this year they will support their team **wholeheartedly** and **enthusiastically**. Last year's **shocking spectacle** of the only people in the student section being fraternity members dressed in black and wearing Halloween skull masks so **devastated** Hector the quarterback that it is small wonder that he **slunk** under the bench to **sulk** and refused to play any more. Even more **destructive** were the **scurrilous insults** against me emblazoned on the streamers pulled by the **accursed** black plane that **mysteriously** appeared over the half empty stadium during each game. Any **idiot** can see why we ended the season 0–11.

Editorial by Connie Lim for the *Daily Toxin* in response to Coach Rhodes' article.

Coach Jasper Rhodes acts like **a dinosaur standing around waiting for the weather to change.** He seems to think that Clear Lake College students are still **cheerleaders wearing saddle shoes and carrying pompoms** and that their **big thrill of the year is to wave a "Yea Rhodes" pennant at the football game.** The fact is that most students **couldn't care less** about Rhodes' **silly team.** They are **hardworking, harassed students worried about their GPAs and the lousy child care** on this campus, not about the **pitiful morale** of Rhodes' **Neanderthal** players. If he's **nursing a bunch of crybabies, that's his problem.**

Both writers here are using heavily loaded words and metaphors to vent their feelings, and considering that they are writing for the personal opinion column of the paper, they can get by with it. However, the writing is also rather childish and irresponsible, hardly appropriate for most circumstances.

People writing advertising copy are also fond of connotation, particularly words that appeal to the senses. They describe cars as *sleek* and *powerful*, perfumes as *intoxicating* and *sexy*, and clothes as *elegant* and *colorful*. Politicians too are partial to connotative language, telling their audiences they are for *freedom, excellence, responsibility,* and *thrift.* Anyone who has a cause to plead is apt to rely on connotative language as one of his or her major tools and rightly so because it is a powerful one.

6B

● **Fine Tuning**

There is a special group of connotative words that one can call "whoopee" words—terms of exaggeration that are so overused they're virtually meaningless. Here are some of the more popular ones.

fantastic	unbelievable
sensational	fabulous
incredible	marvelous
terrific	tremendous
wonderful	devastating

Words like these are little more than hackneyed buzz words that have little place in college writing except, perhaps, in dialogue.

EXERCISE 6.3

Copy two advertisements from magazines or newspapers and underline the connotative words. Compare the ads you choose with those chosen by some of your classmates and discuss what you think the ad writers are trying to achieve with connotative language.

EXERCISE 6.4

Find and clip a syndicated newspaper column such as those written by Ellen Goodman, George Will, Marianne Means, or William Raspberry. Underline the connotative language. Then clip a news story from the same paper and compare the amount of connotative language with that of the column.

EXERCISE 6.5

Analyze the following paragraphs to decide in which ones connotation and denotation are used appropriately. If you think the language is not appropriate in some of the paragraphs, rewrite them.

1. **Paragraph from a *Daily Toxin* ad for Big Larry's Work-Out Gym**

Today's savvy student knows there's more to being sexy than reading *Playboy* Adviser and wearing Calvin Klein underwear and a Swatch. You also gotta be trim, slim, and have those long, lean muscles that come only from working out under an expert. Just pumping iron with that wornout equipment at the college weight room isn't going to cut it. If you want the real thing, come to Big Larry's where you'll get individualized instruction and work out on the best and newest equipment in town.

2. **Opening paragraph from Natalie Barnard's paper on acid rain for an environmental studies course.**

One of the most terrible scourges of modern times has been visited upon the helpless inhabitants of the Gatlinburg area of Tennessee in the form of acid rain that is devastating their forests and crippling their lumber industry. Because of thoughtless and selfish policies of callous factory owners in the Ohio Valley who care only for their pocketbooks and are willing to recklessly endanger the future of one of the most beautiful areas in the United States, the magnificent national forest at Gatlinburg may be lost to posterity. The burning question that faces all concerned citizens of this heartland is what can we do today to stem this tide of destruction.

3. **Editorial in the *Daily Toxin* calling for a new doctor at the student health service**.

We believe it is time to consider whether changes should be made at the Clear Lake College Health Service. The County Medical Board recently inspected the facilities at the Student Health Service and reported that the X-ray machines had been bought in 1928 and the laboratory equipment was condemned as unsatisfactory two years ago but has not been replaced. The current head of the Health Service, Dr. Janet Salinger, received her license from Paducah Medical School in 1942 and has not taken any additional training since that time. Today Dr. Salinger sees approximately fifty student patients a day and is running the Ruralia Doc-in-a-Box Emergency Medical Service as an additional business.

6C WHEN IS DIALECT APPROPRIATE?

Term You Need to Know

   Dialect. A spoken or written variation of a language.

Troubleshooting

A **dialect** is a *spoken variation* of a language. The written version of a language is generally standardized and uniform, but the dialects of different groups of people within the area in which that language is used are often quite different, sometimes radically so. In some places, such as India or parts of Africa, dialects of various groups and tribes vary so much that they cannot communicate with each other at all.

In the British Isles, someone from Oxford in the south of England might have difficulty understanding the English of a Scottish train conductor, and speakers whose native speech was the Cockney dialect of the East End of London might have trouble making themselves understood in Ireland or in the north of England. In England there are also significant differences in dialects among the various social classes in that still strongly stratified society. The British royal family and the upper classes speak a distinctive dialect that sounds very different from that of the London taxi driver or a clerk in an exclusive shop on Bond Street, yet they can all read the same newspaper with no trouble.

In the United States, our dialects cause fewer communication problems. New Yorkers can understand people from California and someone who has lived all his or her life in Detroit usually has no real trouble understanding natives of Florida, although their accents may sound strange. Moreover, Americans travel and move so frequently that young people often partially lose their early speech patterns and adapt to those of their new regions. But we do have many different dialects in this country—southern dialect, northeastern dialect, midwest dialect, Black dialect, Creole dialect, to mention a few—and their marks are quite distinctive, enough so that foreigners whose command of English is good enough to understand the announcers on television can have serious problems understanding southern or Texan dialect.

You may be an American who has a dialect markedly different from one of the varieties considered "standard." Occasionally you may have problems when some of its features appear in your writing. You may want to use this handbook and other resources to edit out those features so that your readers focus on the content of your writing instead of on features of your dialect. But just because you choose to get rid of those features doesn't mean you should abandon your dialect. Even though it may cause problems at times, it plays an important part in your life. Being bidialectal is often as much of an accomplishment as being bilingual. But all educated people also need to be able to use the standard written dialect of the United States, edited American English, so they can communicate easily with other people.

To give dialects their due . . .

▶ **Recognize their uses and importance.** Dialects are important and useful to the groups that speak them. A dialect helps to hold a group together and gives it a sense of community and identity, a sense of being insiders. Those who belong to a dialect group feel comfortable with each other because it's reassuring to be around other people who "talk your language." Thus, dialects act as a major source of strength within a group and, as such, should be appreciated and protected *for private communication* between individuals within a particular dialect community. Usually such communication is spoken. Here for example is how Bret Easton Ellis represents the dialect of California youth in his novel *Less than Zero*:

> Julian looks really tired and kind of weak, but I tell him he looks great and he says that I do too, even though I need to get a tan.
>
> "Hey, listen," he starts. "I'm sorry about not meeting you and Trent at Carney's that night and freaking out at the party. It's just like, I've been strung out for like the past four days, and I just, like, forgot . . . I haven't been home. . . ." He slaps his forehead. "Oh man, my mother must be freaking out." He pauses, doesn't smile. "I'm just so sick of dealing with people." He looks past me. "Oh, shit, I don't know."

▶ **Acknowledge their limitations.** The problem with some dialects is that, when they show up in *public writing*—and that is what most of the writing you do in college and your profession will be—they can be misunderstood and misinterpreted. Items of vocabulary within a dialect may not be understood by those outside of it. Certain grammatical forms completely natural and logical within a community may be regarded as nonstandard by other users of the language.

For example, in this passage from her novel *The Bluest Eye*, Toni Morrison represents the dialect known as Black English.

> The onliest time I be happy seem like was when I was in the picture show. Everytime I got, I went. I'd go

early, before the show started. They'd cut off the lights, and everything be black. Then the screen would light up, and I'd move right in on them pictures. . . . Them pictures give me a lot of pleasure, but it made coming home hard, and looking at Cholly hard.

The passage shows the character Pauline's most private kind of communication, inner speech to herself.

Here is another example of private dialect in this personal letter between two characters in Larry McMurtry's *Lonesome Dove*, a novel about a cattle drive from Texas to Montana.

> Dear Ellie—
>
> We have come a good peace and have been lucky with the weather, it has been clear.
> No sign of Jake Spoon yet but we did cross the Red River and are in Texas, Joe likes it. His horse has been behaving all right and neither of us has been sick.
> I hope that you are well and have not been bothered too much by the skeeters.
>
> Your loving husband,
> July

In the letter, we read the disarming words of a man not comfortable expressing his feelings in words. The salutation and formal closing show that July knows the form a letter should take, but, since this is a private communication, the vocabulary and rhythms of his day-to-day speech dominate. We don't expect Ellie will criticize the comma splices July uses to link his ideas or his spelling of *piece* and *mosquitoes*. But we can easily imagine situations where such writing would seem out of place and colloquial.

Letting your private dialect intrude into your public writing, then, is not so much wrong as it is inappropriate. When your readers find the marks of your personal language in writing that is directed toward a group of readers who don't share that dialect, they're going to feel that it doesn't belong there. You can, of course, use your dialect in anything you write—but that decision can have serious consequences.

▶ **Use dialect when appropriate.** When can you use your dialect without its interfering with communication in standard English? First, in your private life among friends or others who share the dialect, either in conversation or letters. Second, you might also use it in a first, discovery draft when you are trying to get down ideas and reflections and don't want to make your task more difficult by worrying about the conventions of standard written English. In subsequent drafts, you can edit out dialect features. Finally, you might also use dialect in an anecdote you are adding to your paper to illustrate some point, or you could use it as dialogue that plays a necessary part in a paper. Except for these instances, though, spoken dialect generally doesn't fit into the kind of public writing you'll be doing in college or business.

6D

6D HOW DO YOU AVOID SEXIST LANGUAGE?

Term you need to know

> **Sexist language.** Language that reflects prejudiced attitudes and stereotypical thinking about the sex roles and traits of both sexes, but most frequently about women.

Troubleshooting

Every writer today needs to learn how to identify sexist language in order to avoid it in his or her writing. The idea of sexist language may be new to you, and you may not understand why we are focusing on it and why you should take pains to avoid it. There are at least four good reasons.

1. *Sexist language is often inaccurate and deceptive.* A little more than half the people in the United States are women, not men, and if you consistently write *he* and *him*, you're going to be wrong a large part of the time. If you talk about a doctor or a physicist as *he*, you are ignoring the statistic that a third of today's medical students are women and women now get about one-fourth of the degrees in science.

2. *Sexist language frequently annoys and alienates readers.* Most of the women in the United States today are working women; half of all college students are now women. Such women make up an alert, intelligent, and powerful group of readers, and they're going to be impatient and often angry with writers who they feel are stereotyping and patronizing them—or who are just so unaware that they don't think about what they are doing.

3. *Sexist language can cause legal problems.* Because federal laws now prohibit any discrimination on the basis of sex, anyone who is writing grant proposals, policy statements, credit ratings, or any of the other dozens of working documents we all use from time to time must be sure not to use any language that could be considered discriminatory. To suggest that a scholarship or an award might be open only to *hims* or *hers* is to invite a lawsuit.

4. *Sexist language perpetuates sexist attitudes and behavior.* Social scientists and linguists, as well as politicians, salespeople, and therapists, know that *language shapes thought.* What we say and write can limit how we think and behave. As long as we refer to all scientists and engineers and astronauts as *he*, we will tend to think that women cannot (or should not) aspire to those professions; as long as we write *chairman* and *statesman* and *policeman*, we reinforce the tendency to think of people in power as men. And these thought patterns make it difficult to achieve an equitable society.

To identify sexist language, look for these typical characteristics.

—Watch for the consistent use of the pronouns *he* and *him* as all-purpose pronouns to refer to people in general. For example, "Everyone should remember *he* is a student," or "Any executive enjoys *his* bonus."

6D

—Check for the term *man* used as a catch-all term to refer to all people or all members of a group. For example, "all *men* should vote regularly," or "the recession threw thousands of *men* out of work."

—Learn to spot gender-specific pronouns and terms to refer to individuals in professions or roles that have been traditionally thought of as male or female. For example, "a pilot must be licensed before *he* can fly," but "a secretary should think of *herself* as an administrator."

—Watch for between-the-lines implications that men and women behave in stereotypical ways. For example, *talkative women* and *giggling girls*, *rugged men* and *rowdy boys*.

To avoid sexist language . . .

▶ **Rewrite your sentences to substitute *someone, anyone, person,* or *people* for the terms *man* and *woman* used in a general sense.** For instance, instead of writing "the man who wants to be an astronaut . . . ," write "anyone who wants to be an astronaut." Instead of writing "the girl who hopes to be a ballet dancer . . . ," write "someone who wants to be a dancer." Instead of "men who become professors . . . ," write "people who become professors."

▶ **Identify people by occupation or role, not by sex,** for instance: parent, student, naval officer, voter, consumer, and so on. So instead of writing "mothers who are concerned about their children's health . . . ," write "parents who are concerned about their children's health." Instead of writing "men who want to do their own auto repairs . . . ," write "owners who want to do their own auto repairs." Notice that the second versions are also more accurate; most fathers are concerned about their children's health, and some women repair their own cars.

▶ **When you can, replace job-related terms that use the suffix *man* or *woman* with another, more accurate term.** For instance, write "police officer" instead of "policeman," "mail carrier" instead of "mailman," "custodian" or "janitor" instead of "cleaning woman," and "business executives" instead of "businessmen." Avoid terms like "poetess" and "waitress" when you can; "poet" and "waiter" can be used to refer to either sex.

▶ **Be careful not to stereotype men and women by assuming that they belong in what have traditionally been thought of as men's and women's occupations or roles.** For example, instead of writing "men who hope to become scholarship athletes . . . ," write "men and women (or "young people") who hope to become scholarship athletes." Instead of writing "housewives who want to become better cooks . . . ," write "people who want to become better cooks" or "anyone who wants to become a better cook."

6D

▶ **Find strategies to avoid having to use the pronouns *he* or *him* alone unless the antecedent is clearly a male.** You can use plural nouns, reword your sentence to eliminate pronouns, use *he* and *she* alternately, or occasionally write *he or she*. (For a full discussion of ways to solve the problems of sexist pronouns, see section 15Q.)

> **Tip.** You probably shouldn't worry prematurely about sexist language when you are writing your first or second drafts—it's a problem that you can wait to deal with until you get to the editing stage and are tinkering rather than making large-scale changes. After you have worked to avoid sexist language for a while, you will gradually become more conscious of the problem and, in time, probably find little of it even in your first drafts.

EXERCISE 6.6

Rewrite the following sentences to eliminate sexist language. If necessary, refer to Section 15Q on sexist pronouns.

1. The professor who expects his students to respect him should not come to class in jeans with the knees knocked out.
2. Clear Lake College's athletes are guys used to suffering the slings and arrows of outrageous fortune.
3. Any man who goes into campus politics at Clear Lake College should be ready to take on President Tiffany Shade.
4. A woman who wants to avoid premature wrinkles should stay out of the sun.
5. Most of the policemen at Clear Lake College lead a calm existence.
6. Fortunately many graduate students at Clear Lake College have working wives.
7. The high school music teacher who was trained at Clear Lake College may find some embarrassing gaps in her education.
8. Some of Illinois' most prominent businessmen graduated from Clear Lake College.
9. Any lawyer who thinks he can intimidate Darwin Washington will be in for a surprise.
10. Medical students are often young men who are either very money-conscious or very nurturing types; in either case, they are nearly always bright.

CHAPTER 7

Can You Make Your Writing Clearer?

■ **A**   Being specific
■ **B**   Making your writing visual
■ **C**   Using actor/action sentences
■ **D**   Avoiding bureaucratic prose
■ **E**   Chunking

Introduction

A few lucky people in the world may have bodies that are naturally fit without their having to work at it, but there aren't many. And neither are there many writers whose prose is always clear and easy to read without their investing time and effort in it. If you want to develop a fit body or learn to write clearly you have to care about results and be willing to work to get them. There are no quick fixes. But you can attain both goals by developing habits that, over a period of time, will almost guarantee those impressive results. This chapter and the next give you guidelines for developing routines to enhance the clarity of your writing.

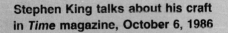

> **Stephen King talks about his craft in *Time* magazine, October 6, 1986**
>
> **On writing.** A matter of exercise. If you work out with weights for 15 minutes a day over a course of ten years, you're gonna get muscles. If you write for an hour and a half a day for ten years, you're gonna turn into a good writer.

CAN YOU BE MORE SPECIFIC?

Terms you need to know

Abstract words. Words that refer to qualities, ideas, attitudes, or beliefs that we cannot see or hear or touch—words like *convenience, treason, generosity, value*, and *mysticism* are abstract. We can *conceive* of abstract qualities only with our minds, and often we need an example to understand just what an abstract term means.

Concrete words. Words that refer to qualities or things that we can touch or smell or see or hear—words like *purple, hot, computer, horse*, and *automobile* are concrete. We *perceive* the things that concrete terms refer to with our senses, and often we use these concrete terms to help illustrate and explain abstract terms.

Troubleshooting

When your instructor or another reader says your writing would be clearer and more interesting if you made it more specific, you may need to learn more about the classifications of *abstract* or *concrete* language, defined above. But language is so complex that it isn't always easy to say, "This is an abstract word," and "This is a concrete word." Words are more or less abstract according to how broad the concept is to which they refer; thus, we have to talk about the different *levels of abstraction*. To appreciate those levels, consider this **ladder of abstraction** that shows how related terms can range from a low level of abstraction to a very high one.

High Abstraction

7. intellectual theories
6. science
5. physical science
4. physics
3. theoretical physics
2. particle physics
1. Heisenberg uncertainty principle

Low Abstraction

Yet even the lowest (and most concrete) item on the scale—
the Heisenberg principle—is still abstract since no one can
actually *perceive* it. Yet the Heisenberg principle is a narrower
and more limited concept than any of the items above it on the
ladder, and only a tiny subdivision of the most abstract category—intellectual theories.

We can also talk about **levels of concreteness** that go from the
very particular to the very general. Again, words are more or
less concrete according to the size of the class of things to
which they refer. For instance:

General

8. vehicles
7. internal combustion vehicles
6. automobiles
5. two-door cars
4. sports cars
3. foreign sports cars
2. Porsches
1. Coach Jasper Rhodes' red Porsche 944S

Concrete

All of these examples are concrete and can be perceived
through the senses, but it's hard to get a clear mental picture of
"vehicles" or automobiles in general. It's much easier to visualize Porsches and especially Coach Rhodes' red 944S.

How clearly you write is also affected by the **levels of
generality** you use. For example, you can write about a topic
on a very high level of generality or you can use extremely
specific examples. A *specific* to *general* scale might look like
this:

General

7. food distributors
6. grocery stores
5. health food stores
4. health food stores owned by nutritionists
3. Ericson's Good Health Food Store
2. fresh produce department in Ericson's store
1. salad counter in produce department

Specific

To make your writing more concrete . . .

▶ **Illustrate your ideas with examples that help readers understand what you are writing about.** Of course, all writers have to use abstract language at times—we could never talk about ideas or concepts or theories if we didn't. But notice how much trouble you have when you encounter uninterrupted stretches of highly abstract language, as in this passage.

> Entropy is one of those seminal ideas that assume mythic proportions in the history of consciousness because it purports to offer an irrefutable argument about ultimate concerns: time, life, and death. An explanation with a pretense to such cogency naturally excites intense interest and controversy. But the entropic perspective does much more than that. It poses a fundamental challenge to the materialistic assumptions that define and justify civilization as an illimitable program of technological expansionism. In that sense, entropy casts a pall over the progressivist values on which civilization relies to vindicate what it extols as the worthiest of contemporary projects, the pervasive extension of modernization.

Unreadable, isn't it? After a few seconds, your mind begins to "hydroplane" across the surface and none of the words make any sense. And it's not because you're stupid. Almost any reader would have trouble because all the words are highly abstract and, consequently, it's difficult to grasp what the writer is talking about. The writer could have made it much more understandable with concrete examples to explain abstractions.

▶ **Move up and down a ladder of abstraction and generality.** As you write, buttress the abstract language you must use to talk about ideas with concrete language that helps your readers visualize and perceive your points. Mix specific and general language and support general statements with specific and concrete examples. Don't shy away from general ideas and abstractions, but be sure your readers know the particular items upon which your generalizations are based.

Writing that relies on generalities is not only hard to read, it can be boring as well. Here is an excerpt from a paper for a human sexuality course.

> In the contemporary picture of sexuality and kinship, the threatened self-sufficiency of females for reproductive purposes has great significance for possible male redundancy. The sophistication of fertility technology is one factor to be taken into account; another necessary consideration is the current tendency for postponement or nonperformance of nuptials.

You might think the paragraph sounds "academic," but most instructors will complain that it makes little sense. It needs to be rewritten, perhaps even "translated."

7A

> In today's sexual picture, men could become surplus commodities. For one thing, *in vitro* fertilization (test tube babies) and artificial insemination could replace traditional sex for reproduction; it almost has in the cattle industry. For another thing, because more and more couples are postponing marriage or not getting married at all, fewer of them are going to want babies.

Notice that the passage immediately begins to make more sense when the author writes specifically and adds concrete examples. Notice also that in order to make it clearer, the writer has to think about what the topic really means. She can't hide behind fuzzy language. Here's another example, an excerpt from a paper for a nutrition course on the problems of overweight people.

> The propensity of overweight people to gain extra adipose tissue at holiday time is due to two factors: greater susceptibility and responsiveness to food stimuli and poor compensatory regulation of food intake. Such individuals seek justification for their behavior by citing the pressures of hospitality and the culinary excellence of the food.

There's no excuse for such inflated, hard-to-read writing. The passage can be easily improved.

> Overweight people gain weight at holidays for two reasons: they like to eat more than normal people do,

177

and they have less self-control. They excuse their overeating by saying their hosts force them to eat and, besides, the food is too good to refuse.

Considerably different, isn't it?

▶ **Start writing with a fairly general statement, but then downshift.** With each shift, you become more specific, explaining and illustrating the preceding level. Here is an example of a passage where downshifting occurs, arranged in a pattern that shows the varying levels of generality.

Example

(**Level 5**) One of the things that continues to astonish Jean-Pierre Capelier, master French baker, about America is our love for the substance called "white bread."

(**Level 4**) Wrapped in plastic packages emblazoned with names like Daisy Wheel, Mother's Joy, or Sandwich Wiz, hundreds of loaves of so-called "enriched" white bread are delivered to American stores every morning.

(**Level 3**) "Enriched, indeed!" Jean-Pierre scowls.

(**Level 2**) To say white bread is enriched when it emerges from the ovens of the Blunder-Bunder Bakery is like saying you have enriched a man when you have taken away all his clothes and then returned his undershorts and tennis shoes.

(**Level 2**) Because that is what has happened to white flour.

(**Level 1**) The mill took away all the vitamins when it bleached the flour, and then the bakery restored two or three so it could print "added vitamins and iron" on the label.

(**Level 1**) When the bakery gets through adding air and preservatives, what's left is fit only to squeeze into small balls and use for sling shot ammunition.

EXERCISE 7.1

Arrange this set of abstract words on a ladder of abstraction, going from the least abstract at the bottom to the most abstract at the top.

panic   negative feelings
phobia about heights   emotions
fear   human reactions

EXERCISE 7.2

Arrange this set of concrete words on a ladder of concreteness ranging from the most concrete at the bottom to the least concrete at the top.

horses   four-legged animals
thoroughbreds   mammals
racehorses   Sun Dancer

EXERCISE 7.3

Arrange the words in this group in order of their generality, putting the most specific word at the bottom of the ladder and the most general at the top.

periodicals   editorial page
printed matter   city newspaper
The New York Times   Jack Anderson's daily
                               column

EXERCISE 7.4

Find an example of writing that makes your mind start to "hydroplane" before you complete the first page. Analyze and discuss what it is about the writing that provokes such a reaction. Be specific.

EXERCISE 7.5

Write three or four sentences to support one or two of these lead sentences, downshifting to a lower level of generality with each sentence.

1. American television entertainment may seem to be free until you consider what viewers endure in order to watch a program.
2. Education means something more than sitting in a classroom five days a week.
3. The influence of religion in public life and politics is increasing in many parts of the world.
4. In most cities, people who ride buses every day quickly learn a number of survival strategies.

7B CAN YOU MAKE READERS SEE YOUR POINT?

Terms you need to know

> **Metaphor.** A comparison between two things that does not use the words *like* or *as*.
>
> All the world's a stage.
>
> Minerva is the Rolls-Royce of chocolates.

Analogy. An extended comparison between something familiar and something less well known. The analogy helps a reader visualize what might be difficult to understand. For example:

A transition in a paper serves *as a roadsign, giving readers directions to the next major point.*

Troubleshooting

You will make your writing clearer and easier to read if you can make your readers *see* something. Most of us are very visually oriented—that's one reason television is so popular and why film strips and educational movies are such popular tools of instruction. All of us also know how much it helps to have sketches or pictures to illustrate the points in a complex article. We like pictures and can learn from them. So it is important sometimes for writers to consider how they can use words to create memorable images.

What you do by adding a visual element to your writing is to give certain parts of it *presence*, that is, you draw your readers' attention to them. The best way to illustrate that quality of *presence* is with an ancient Chinese tale:

A king sees an ox on its way to sacrifice. He is moved to pity by it and orders that a sheep be used in its place. He confesses that he did so because he could see the ox, but not the sheep.

(Cited in C. Perelman's *The Realm of Rhetoric.* University of Notre Dame Press, 1982, p. 35)

In this section, we offer several suggestions for adding *presence* to your writing.

To make your writing more visual . . .

▶ **Describe someone doing something.** You can create a scene or drama; you can show action; you can describe a colorful picture or object—there are dozens of ways of showing ideas in action. This doesn't mean you need to go into extended descriptions. Just a visual touch here and there will help. For example, look at the contrast between the two versions in the following example.

{**First draft**} Professor Alan Gates of the Philosophy Department has long been known for his effort to salvage aluminum cans on campus. He takes the largest collection of cans in Ruralia into the recycling depot every Saturday. When asked about his fine record, the professor modestly said he was just lucky. We think he is too modest. We happen to know that he is as much of an authority on where to find aluminum cans as he is on Kant and Hegel, and that he works very hard at collecting cans at many different locations all over campus.

{**Second, more visual draft**} Anyone who has been on campus for a week has probably seen a white-haired gentleman poking his cane into the trash barrels around campus and fishing out aluminum cans, carefully separating them from bottles. That ecology-minded citizen is known for his one-man salvage campaign, and almost any morning and afternoon you can see him checking out each trash barrel along the campus diagonal, then dropping cans on the sidewalk, stomping on them, and putting them in his briefcase or lunchbox. This campus character is professor of philosophy Alan Gates, authority on Kant and Hegel, but also the hero of the local recycling depot where you may see him drive in every Saturday morning with his yellow pick-up and matching trailer piled high with aluminum cans.

The passage is both clearer and livelier now that you can "see" the professor. Adding a visual element also strengthens the rewritten version of this example.

{**First draft**} Stretching and cardiovascular exercises must be an essential part of the daily routine for any health-minded student whose study habits require him or her to spend many hours sitting in the Clear Lake College library. Because more than half of the study tables and chairs in the library were bought on sale from the local middle school, their height is not suitable for normal sized adults and curvature of the spine may develop in especially conscientious students. Some numbness of the buttocks and cramping in the legs from small chairs also occasionally results, making arising difficult for those affected. Those concerned about their bodies may want to attend the prelibrary warm-up sessions held at 6:45 p.m.

{Second, more visual draft} As a new student on campus, you may wonder why you see so many students emerging from the library bent over and holding their backs. From time to time, one will be rubbing his or her behind and staggering a little. Now and then an older, gray-haired student will emerge looking for a few minutes like the Hunchback of Notre Dame. If you take a look inside the west-side reading and reference room, you will see the reason: rows of students hunched over at tables and chairs that look as if they were made for sixth graders. They were acquired on sale by the Clear Lake College purchasing department several years ago. But you don't have to join the ranks of the cripples—come jump and stretch in the prelibrary warm-up sessions nightly at 6:45.

The second version catches the readers' attention. As soon as readers can *see* something, they get a clearer idea of the writer's point.

▶ **Add people.** One way to add a visual element to your writing is to put people in it. Most of the issues and ideas we write about do involve human beings, after all, and your readers are more likely to understand what you are writing about if you bring those human beings into your writing. Here is an example of a totally impersonal, abstract discussion of an economic issue.

{First draft} During the past decade, consumer activity has been significantly influenced by the inflationary environment. An increased reluctance to use savings or incur new debt has been a trend shown in all surveys of recent years although large discretionary purchases have continued to be responsive to interest rates. Experts feel that consumer motivations have moved toward saving and away from debt, due to lowered price expectations and higher interest rates.

Notice how this rather murky and difficult paragraph becomes easier to read and understand when people are added.

During the past decade, fear of inflation has caused many people to hang on to their savings and avoid debt, even though they still make large discretionary purchases of items such as cars and new homes when interest rates are low. But the experts feel that buyers would rather save than go into debt because they expect interest rates to go up and prices to go down.

The reader understands the point more easily when the writer describes people taking actions like buying and saving and abandons phrases like "consumer motivations" and "lowered price expectations." Such phrases, however, may be appropriate when used in a technical sense for an audience familiar with them.

▶ **Use metaphors and analogies.** You can also give your writing presence by using metaphors and analogies that help readers make connections with something they already know. Notice how the italicized metaphors and analogies work in these examples.

Example 1.

Administrative Memo
From: Dean Rack
To: Clear Lake College Faculty
Subject: Faculty evaluation

Beginning January 1, all Clear Lake College faculty will have the opportunity each semester to be evaluated by students in their classes. I want to stress that participation in the evaluation program is entirely voluntary; we have no desire to coerce faculty into compliance. *You are as free not to have such evaluations as you are free not to take a breathalyzer test if stopped on suspicion of driving while intoxicated.*

184

Example 2.

If you want to be a writer, you had better not just sit around and wait for inspiration. You could wait a long time for that *Muse to come down and whisper in your ear* or for a great idea to spring full blown from your head *like Athena from the forehead of Zeus*. The best thing to do is to just start to write, even putting down something you don't like very much. *The act of writing itself can set off sonar vibrations into your sub-conscious that will sweep through your memory and intuition, picking up signals from things that you never dreamed were there.*

EXERCISE 7.6

Think of a way you could add a visual touch to a discussion of these topics: an editorial about the high cost of housing at your college; an article comparing various kinds of motorcycles; a guide to cheap entertainment in your town.

EXERCISE 7.7

Find metaphors or analogies that would add a visual element to any two of these sentences.

1. Coach Marie Vorhees returned in triumph from the Women's National Volleyball Playoffs yesterday, feeling justifiably exuberant as she got off the plane.
2. When she and the team left Ruralia last Friday, almost no knowledgeable sports enthusiast would have bet any money that there was a chance they would get beyond the first round.
3. In fact, their chances were rated so low that the team had trouble even finding the money for their plane fare since whoever figured out the volleyball budget of $850 obviously didn't anticipate any postseason travel.

4. But a surprisingly large and noisy contingent of fans turned out at the airport to help make up for the neglect Coach Vorhees' women have suffered this season.

5. What they learned to their surprise was that the coach had not only brought home a large silver loving cup and a national small college championship, she had also brought home an offer for a new and much more profitable contract for herself.

7C CAN YOU MAKE YOUR SENTENCES MORE VIGOROUS?

Troubleshooting

Remember that when your readers start reading, they want to find the answer to two questions: What's happening? Who's doing it? They will find out more quickly if you arrange your sentences so that an **actor/action relationship** is at the heart of your sentence, not lost somewhere in a tangle of words. Consider crumpled sentences like these:

> My ultimate goal is the obtainment of a judgeship.

> When the concepts of balance, calorie control, and variety are remembered, a successful diet can be established.

How much clearer they are when revised so you can tell who is doing what to whom:

> Ultimately, I want to be a judge.

> You can establish a successful diet if you remember balance, calorie control, and variety.

To make your sentences more vigorous . . .

▶ **Ask yourself who or what is taking action and make that person or thing the subject of your sentence.** Then find a verb that describes the action. These examples show how much clearer your writing can be once you get the actor/action habit.

(First draft) More than one successful business enterprise has begun as a small operation on a college campus as a response to a student's need to earn his or her way through school. Many of those enterprises could serve as examples that illustrate the classic economic pattern of identifying a hitherto neglected need of some group that has money to spend and devising a way to meet that need. An example to be found close to home is that of Joella and Jason Goodnight's local business, JJ's Good Graces Wake-up and Reminder Service, a computerized system that makes wake-up calls and keeps subscribers from forgetting anniversaries, birthdays, and any other dates that, if forgotten, have the potential for provoking domestic disaster. In ten years, that enterprise has grown from a one-person, part-time operation run by a Clear Lake College undergraduate to a prosperous personal service business that employs five people.

{**Revised to include more actor/action sentences**} Many a successful business began on a college campus when some student found a new way to work his or her way through school. Such students often demonstrate the classic economic strategy of figuring out what some group of people need and are willing to pay for and then devising a way to meet that need. Joella and Jason Goodnight are striking examples. Ten years ago, Joella started her own wake-up and reminder service to help pay her way through Clear Lake College. Today, she and her husband Jason have built that business into JJ's Good Graces Wake-up and Reminder Service, a computerized system that makes wake-up calls and keeps subscribers from forgetting anniversaries, birthdays, and any other dates that, if forgotten, have the potential for provoking domestic disaster. When Joella started the service, she got up early and worked only three hours in the mornings; now the Goodnights employ five people full time in their prosperous personal service business.

The revision is clearer and crisper because the actor/action patterns are easier to read. Consider the reaction (or lack of it) the following announcement might receive if posted in a bar.

{**First draft**} Dependence on false identification for purposes of obtaining alcohol will be considered fraudulent and uncooperative behavior by the manager of this establishment. If determination is made that such behavior has occurred, it will be the privilege of the management to remove the offender and prohibit reentrance.

The notice might attract more attention if rewritten to emphasize who will do what to whom:

{**Revised**} If you use a false I.D. to buy drinks here, I will throw you out and you can't come back.

—The Manager

Naturally you wouldn't want to write all your sentences in actor/action patterns since often you need to write about concepts, theories, or processes that require abstract language. But you can probably use actor/action sentences more often than you realize—after all, even when you're writing about history, philosophy, or economics, people are usually involved. And there is no question that using such sentences frequently will make your writing clearer. You may want to wait until a second draft to fit some of your sentences to an actor/action pattern, but if you work at it, eventually you'll develop the habit of using this kind of sentence even in a first draft.

EXERCISE 7.8

Recast these sentences in actor/action patterns that show more clearly *who* is doing *what* to *whom*.

1. *Take Five*, a local coffee store and campus meeting place, is the brainchild of Christy Rasmussen, to whom the quality of Ruralia's coffee was offensive when she arrived from Norway five years ago.
2. Christy's coffee consumption and her tolerance for caffeine had been a source of amazement for years even among her Norwegian friends.

3. But during the visit of one of those friends after Christy moved to Ruralia, it became apparent that her drinking ten cups a day of the locally-available coffees was ruining her palate and producing more than a slight twitch, yet withdrawal symptoms set in when the coffee drinking was discontinued.

4. In desperation and depression, the decision by Christy was made to open her own Coffee Emporium in order to acquire more bearable brands of coffee.

5. In addition, the shop's fine Scandinavian decor and the fragrant odors that assault passers-by are two reasons for the almost instant success achieved by *Take Five*.

7D

6. Another major reason is the founding of a coffee-tasting club by Hector Stavros, whose fine taste in foods is the envy of Ruralia.

7. Belonging to the *Five O'Clock Club*, as the coffee-drinkers have chosen to call themselves, is almost as prestigious as driving a Yugo.

8. And becoming closer to Christy Rasmussen these days is Hector Stavros, whose caffeine level has begun to equal hers.

9. Their association, however, has brought about Christy's announcement that a water-processed decaffeinated coffee will soon be added to her stock.

10. Their friends' speculation is that when that happens, Hector's bouncing off the walls will decline significantly.

7D ## CAN YOU LIGHTEN BUREAUCRATIC PROSE?

Terms you need to know

Prepositional phrase. The combination of a preposition and a noun or pronoun. The following are prepositional phrases: *on our house; above it; to him; in love; through them; by the garden gate.*

189

Nominalizations. Nouns coined made by adding endings to verbs and adjectives: *acceptability, demystification, prioritization,* and so on. In this handbook, such words are called **heavy-duty** nouns because most have the charm of a Sears Diehard battery.

Troubleshooting

Writers in college and occasionally even in business sometimes protest to us that their readers expect them to write a stodgy, impersonal, and noun-heavy prose—in fact, they expect to be penalized if they don't. This could be true. Certainly, some of the material you read in textbooks or scholarly articles is written in a noun-heavy, preposition-stuffed style, as are many insurance policies and bureaucratic memos. Here is an example of such bureaucratic style. (This kind of writing is sometimes called *jargon*.)

7D

> It is of utmost importance to maintain the vitality of those institutions that serve society as instruments of continuity. Thus, the stability of the country's institutions of higher education should be a high priority with the current administration. The most valuable contributions that authority could make would be (1) predictability and reliability of financing; (2) removal of existing disincentives and the application of new incentives; (3) reduction of regulations about time accountability on federal grants. Actions of this kind would facilitate a welcome disentanglement of higher education and federal bureaucracy.

If you're absolutely convinced your reader expects this style—perhaps you have a professor or boss who writes that way—all right. Go ahead and write like that, but recognize that you are doing it to impress someone, not to communicate. We believe, however, that most of your readers, including most professors, much prefer writing that is clear, lively, and pleasant to read. That is what they claim and what our own experience tells us. In most cases, you will score more points with your readers if you clean out as many of those heavy-duty nouns and prepositional phrases as you can and substitute clear sentences.

To make your writing less stodgy . . .

▶ **Reduce your use of heavy-duty nouns.** Also known as **nominalizations**, these are all those nouns made by adding endings to verbs and adjectives. There are thousands of them in English, too many to list, but this sample will show you what we mean.

authority	reliability
utilization	interference
maximization	impreciseness
specificity	implementation
validity	simplification
reliance	retrogression

7D

Heavy-duty nouns are words created by adding suffixes— -tion, -ity, -ance, -ence, -sion, and others—to a verb or adjective. *Militant* becomes *militancy*, *accountable* becomes *accountability*, *accept* becomes *acceptance*, *specific* becomes *specificity*, and so on.

These heavy-duty words and others like them are perfectly good expressions, useful and often even necessary for conveying your ideas, but in writing they act as a thickening agent, like cornstarch or concrete. A few are fine, but when you begin to use too many of them, they clog up your writing and make it hard to get through.

▶ **Reduce the number of prepositional phrases in your writing.** Prepositional phrases are those little units of writing that join prepositions with nouns to make phrases that show a connection. Again, there are thousands of them, far more than we could list here, but a few samples will refresh your memory about them.

to the limit	*for* the duration
with the exception	*of* the opinion
by the side	*against* the advice
across the board	*until* the next case
above the average	*with* the proviso that

Prepositional phrases are also useful and absolutely necessary, but if you overuse them, your writing will take on a monotonous rhythm—ta-tum, ta-tum, ta-tum—that sounds like tires slapping over expansion joints on a highway. When something you've composed seems especially dull, try underlining all the prepositional phrases. If they begin lining up, one after another, you have detected one cause of your weak prose.

Heavy-duty nouns and prepositional phrases tend to attract each other, and when a writer gets in the habit of using both, the result can be dreary, thick, lifeless writing. Here are two examples of passages made almost unreadable by heavy-duty nouns and prepositional phrases. In both, the heavy-duty nouns are italicized, the prepositional phrases underlined, and a revised version offered.

7D

Example 1.

{**Original**} Most people of today do not have as much *awareness* of sin as the *majority* of people in the past. Their *preoccupation* with conspicuous *consumption* and fleshly *gratifications* may be a sign of their *realization* that there is a growing *possibility* that *obtainment* of the American dream is for many less likely than in the past. The *certitude* of there being a *finitude* of resources available causes a *manifestation* of *self-preoccupation*.

{**Revised**} Today, people don't worry about sin as much as they used to. They seem preoccupied with buying things and enjoying food, drink, and sex, perhaps because, more and more, they realize that their chances of fulfilling the American dream are diminishing. They are frantically indulging themselves because they fear there is going to be less to go around in the future.

Example 2.

{**Original**} The *installation* of Mindy Mendelson, owner of the local nursery, The Avant Gardener, as Grand Marshal and Major General of the Ruralia chapter of Mulchers and Marchers brings to *culmination* a career of *professionalism* and *dedication*. The *magna-*

192

nimity with which Ms. Mendelson has shared her compost pile (25 years in the ripening) with less fortunate gardeners and the *compulsion* and *tenacity* with which she has patrolled the town bridle path for the *obtainment* of the freshest fertilizer for her greenhouse is an *inspiration* to many. Her single-handed *resurrection* of that ancient medieval ritual of the Shovels, Hoes, and Rakes Procession on St. Swithin's Day—now a holiday of great *importance* in Ruralia—her *availability* for directing it, and her *congeniality* in the *imbibance* of mead afterward will be remembered by local citizens.

{Revised} When Mindy Mendelson is installed as Grand Marshal of the Ruralia Mulchers and Marchers Association, the honor will culminate the career of a dedicated professional. Ms. Mendelson has inspired many by the generous way in which she has shared her famed compost pile (25 years in the ripening) with less fortunate gardeners and by the way she has relentlessly patrolled the local bridle path to obtain the freshest fertilizer for her greenhouse. And local citizens remember that she singlehandedly resurrected the medieval ritual of the Shovels, Hoes, and Rakes Procession on St. Swithin's Day—now such an important holiday in Ruralia—and was always available to direct it and congenially imbibe the mead afterwards.

EXERCISE 7.9

Rewrite any two of these sentences to get rid of heavy-duty nouns and excess prepositional phrases.

1. The inaccessibility of registration materials at convenient locations has long been a problem for students in our college.
2. It is beyond the comprehension of this reporter that the implementation of better procedures is beyond the capability of our administration.

3. Improvement is possible if the administration would move toward simplification of their system of distribution.
4. The reliability of the method employed by the IRS should act as a model for Clear Lake College's innovation.
5. In our opinion, Darwin Washington's proposition to institute utilization of the U.S. mails for distribution of registration materials, although radical in its approach, merits the most consideration.

7E   CAN YOU MAKE YOUR WRITING EASIER TO READ?

Troubleshooting

A piece of writing has its own "body language" that gives readers messages affecting how they react to it. (See Section 5B on paragraph appearance.) If you try to jam too much information together into one sentence or one paragraph, you risk alarming readers. Their instinctive reaction may be, "Oh, that's too hard to read. I'm not going try." Even if they are willing to try, you risk overloading the mental circuits by which they process that information. Those circuits may jam so badly that the readers will have to go back and reread what you have written—not because your ideas are subtle but because your language is skewed. If their circuits blow out, your readers will probably quit reading altogether.

To make your writing more readable . . .

▶ **"Chunk" your writing; that is, break it into manageable parts to make it easier to read.**   If you chunk your writing, it becomes much easier to read and the information it conveys becomes easier to process and remember. Chunking is the principle behind dividing telephone numbers; instead of ten numbers jammed together in a long sequence that would overload a reader's memory, they are broken up into three units that the brain can process. If they weren't, you'd have to deal with:

2143280090   *instead of*   Area Code 214 328-0090

And could you ever remember your social security number if it were not divided? Imagine trying to remember:

465189776   *rather than*   465-18-9776

The same principle applies to jamming too many words into one sentence or too many sentences into one paragraph. Consider the body language in the following paragraph.

> {**Original**} Larry Butcher, owner of Butcher's Gym and Muscle Parlor and winner of the 1985 Golden Triceps award for the man in Ruralia whose push-ups and chin-lifts come closest to the standards set by the Swiss gymnast Henreid Madchnik in 1946 when he did 1000 push-ups and 102 chin-lifts without stopping and collapsed into the gym mat not to rise again for three days, believes that the way to championship muscles comes only through exercising six times a week alternating between the Nautilus machines and free weights, immersing one's self in Yoga meditation each morning, and following a diet rich in pasta, yogurt, and quantities of fish. Sporting his white gold Rolex watch on his left wrist, a watch which he informed us cost $6400 and of which the band was stretched to the limit in order to accommodate the 12-inch girth of the wrist, and wearing a gold trimmed T-shirt on which was written "Body by God, Improvements by Butcher's Gym and Muscle Parlor," the proprietor casually demonstrated his right to the award by absent-mindedly chinning himself thirteen times with one hand and then hoisting himself up to the ceiling on one of the climbing ropes and swinging there while ten of the young women working on weights watched him with awe.

Only two sentences, but 93 words in one and 108 in the other. While sentences that long aren't taboo, they need to be divided into manageable parts, or they push readers to limits. A more readable version might cut some of that information and chunk the rest into shorter sentences.

{**Revision**} Larry Butcher, owner of Butcher's Gym and Muscle Parlor, believes that anyone who wants championship muscles must exercise six days a week, alternating between Nautilus machines and free weights. That person should also practice Yoga and eat lots of pasta, yogurt, and fish. Larry should know since in 1985 he won the Ruralia Golden Triceps award for doing the most push-ups and chin-lifts. Wearing a gold Rolex watch and a gold-trimmed T-shirt saying "Body by God, Improvements by Butcher's Gym," Larry demonstrated his own fitness by doing thirteen one-handed chin-lifts. After that, he absent-mindedly climbed to the ceiling on a rope and hung there swaying. As he did, ten young women who were lifting weights watched him with awe.

▶ **Create lists.** Instead of writing overpacked sentences, present your information by chunking it into a list. For instance:

Paragraph from Professor Castor Pollux's statement of rules for papers to be turned in for his class in Astronomy of the Ancients.

{**Original**} Students writing papers for this class must abide by the following rules. All papers must be written on a word processor using 10 point type in Gothic font, double-spaced with side margins of 1.2 inches and top and bottom margins of 1.5 inches, quotations indented to 1.8 inches, all titles of books italicized, dates of books in parentheses after the title, all nouns in the titles capitalized; also required are ivory paper, 20 lb. weight, black ink only, top sheet with name of professor and course, second sheet with name of student, third sheet with title of paper, fourth sheet an acknowledgments sheet; notes must conform to the revised APA style sheet.

It wouldn't be surprising if many students ignored these complicated and barely readable instructions. They might be taken more seriously if put into a list.

Directions for papers in Professor Pollux's course in Astronomy of the Ancients

1. All papers must be written on a word processor.
2. Papers must be typed in 10 point Gothic, double-spaced.
3. Side margins must be 1.2 inches; top and bottom margins must be 1.5 inches.
4. Quotations must be indented 1.8 inches.
5. Titles of books must be italicized.
6. Dates of books should appear after title in parentheses.
7. All nouns in titles must be capitalized.
8. Papers should be typed on ivory paper, 20 lb. weight.
9. All papers must be typed in black ink.
10. Name of the professor and title of course will appear on page 1.
11. Name of student will appear on page 2.
12. Title of paper will appear on page 3.
14. Acknowledgments will appear on page 4.
15. All notes must conform to the APA style sheet.

Breaking down a paragraph that is overloaded with information and rearranging it into a list always helps your reader.

EXERCISE 7.10

Chunk one of the following paragraphs so that it will be more readable. You will have to rearrange several of the sentences considerably.

1. Hundreds of college students swarmed onto the track in front of the Clear Lake College stadium, each of them hoping to be cast in the film spectacle "Grendel Comes to Dinner," a low-budget costume epic written by Grant Geiske, graduate student in Old English and directed by Sean O'Brien, a prize-winning, 21-year-old student filmmaker. Dr. Angus Motherwell, scholar in Old English, who

has recently published a timely mongraph on "Medieval Monsters, Fast Food, and Other Entertainments at the Court of Æthelred the Unready," was on hand as the technical adviser and costume consultant, his responsibilities including checking the actors' helmets for authenticity and their accents for proper vowel pronunciation. Playing the role of Grendel's mother in this piece is to be Melanie Downsouth, senior in the drama department and the veteran of many Clear Lake College productions, whose accent will offer a significant challenge to Dr. Motherwell's determination to put on an authentic production.

7E

2. Residents of Helvetian's Women's Dormitory must observe the following restrictions in order to avoid demerits. All stereos must be fitted with earphones. Refrigerators must be no more than one and one half cubic foot capacity. Posters and pictures may not be attached to walls or to cupboards. Telephones must be shut off at 10:00 p.m.; there will be no exceptions. No food must be carried out of the dining room or brought into the room. Men may visit the dormitory only between 2:00 and 4:30 on Sunday afternoons. Anyone found violating any of these rules will have her privileges taken away.

CHAPTER

Can You Be Less Wordy?

■ **A** Strung-out phrases
■ **B** *Who*, *which*, *that* phrases
■ **C** Redundant phrases
■ **D** Combining sentences
■ **E** Passive verbs

8

Introduction

Wordy sentences use many words to say little. They often sound formal or official—even intimidating. You may find yourself resorting to wordy sentences when you want to impress someone or aren't sure what you are writing about.

> It seems to me that many first-time college students have great difficulty in making the adjustment from high school behavior to college behavior. The classroom maturity level of the average freshman is far below what I have been led to expect.

> The question of whether or not school lunches should or should not be paid for by an agency of the government is a long-standing debate. It is my firm intention to express an opinion on this issue at hand in the paragraphs that follow.

Because most readers don't want to wade through repetitious, wordy stuff that wastes their time, you should try to streamline your writing by getting rid of unneeded verbiage. You can work toward a concise, reader-friendly style by habitually asking yourself, "Do I really need that word or phrase?" Here are some suggestions for making your writing leaner and more economical.

Troubleshooting

In their early drafts, writers sometimes spin rambling, long-winded phrases that use half a dozen or more words to put a point across when one or two words would do. Many of these are "canned" expressions or clichés that slip into a passage barely noticed: *in our society today; at this point in time; come hell or high water; in the process of.* Such overstuffed phrases come in several varieties, but most of them are easy to fix.

To reduce wordiness . . .

▶ **Condense inflated lead-in phrases.** Sometimes writers add useless words as if they are warming up for their main point. But if you're trying to produce a clean, economical style, you will want to be suspicious of such wheel-spinning expressions. For instance,

Why say . . .	When you could just write . . . ?
in the event that	if
if it should happen that	if
in light of the fact that	since
on the grounds that	because
there is a need for	we need
has the ability to	can
regardless of the fact that	although
on the occasion of	when
at this point in time	now
in our society today	today

We are so accustomed to hearing these and similar phrases that we wrongly assume we need the extra words to express our meaning. If, however, you habitually cut such strings of words or condense them, you will improve your writing.

▶ **Condense inflated verb phrases.** Instead of choosing direct and simple verbs, writers sometimes cluster nouns and prepositions to create verb phrases that manage to say less with more. Such phrases make writing cumbersome and rather formal. So,

Why say . . .	When you could just write . . . ?
put the emphasis on	emphasize
have an understanding of	understand
make a comparison of	compare
is reflective of	reflects
give permission to	allow

▶ **Reduce the number of expletive constructions.** **Expletives** are short expressions such as *it was* and *there are* that function like starting blocks for pushing off into a sentence:

> *It was* a dark and stormy night. *There were* five of us huddled in the room.

Habitually using *there is's* and *there are's* at the beginning of sentences or clauses can give your writing a tedious, sing-song rhythm and make it sound amateurish and flat. Sometimes you cannot avoid using expletives (*Gosh, it's cold!*), but, more often, such expressions just divert a reader's attention from your subject. Cutting out expletives usually makes who is doing what to whom clearer. You can usually revise sentences with *there is's* and *there are's* to eliminate these "stretchers" and pep up your prose.

> The night was dark and stormy. Five of us huddled in the room.

So,

Why say . . .	When you could just write . . . ?
there is a desire for	we want
there are several reasons	for several reasons
it is Kevin's job	Kevin's job is
it is obvious that	obviously

201

Rewrite the following sentences and substitute single words for the strung-out phrases. You can rearrange some of them if you like.

1. In the event that Walter Toth's Garage is open after the football game, you should not miss the opportunity to see his latest acquisitions.
2. Walter always has the ability to find bargains and is quick to take cognizance of any chance to add to his stock of memorabilia.
3. It is always possible that in the area in the rear of the shop near the piles of old car magazines and ancient goggles and helmets, you may have an encounter with an aging but venerable car—a rusty-appearing DeSoto, a sagging Packard, a bizarre-looking Nash.
4. And there is a high degree of certainty that Walter will extend you an invitation to come around back to take a look at his special pride.
5. There in the vicinity of the rear fence you will see a monument to one of Walter's heroes in the profession of racing: a signed photograph of Andy Granatelli sitting in a souped-up Studebaker.

8B

8B CAN YOU CUT *WHO'S, WHICH'S,* OR *THAT'S?*

Troubleshooting

Occasionally, writers may have trouble deciding whether they should choose *who* or *whom* (see Section 15L). They also puzzle over when they should use *which* and when they should use *that.*

Toth is a man (who or whom?) everyone likes.

Antique car collecting is a hobby (which or that?) I can understand.

The classic Studebaker coupe is a car (which or that?) antique car buffs cherish.

A passion for old cars is a weakness (which or that?) many former race drivers share.

Certainly it's useful to know those distinctions, but often you can avoid having to make the decision and also get the bonus of cutting out words by simply eliminating unnecessary *who*'s, *that*'s, and *which*'s. Notice these easy changes.

Toth is a man everyone likes.

Antique car collecting is a hobby I can understand.

The classic Studebaker coupe is a car antique car buffs cherish.

A passion for old cars is a weakness many former race drivers share.

To reduce wordiness . . .

► **Eliminate who, which, or that when you can do so without changing the meaning of your sentence.** Your sentences will be tighter and flow more smoothly. For example:

{**Wordy version.**} Brian McVicker felt like the typical freshman who was faced with the awesome task of writing a research paper—overwhelmed. The anxiety that he felt was brought on partly by wondering if he had the skills which he needed to cope with the Clear Lake College Library and partly from worrying over choosing a topic that he wouldn't hate by the time he got through with it. This double dilemma was one which brought on writer's paralysis.

{**Tighter version.**} Brian McVicker felt like the typical freshman faced with the awesome task of writing a research paper—overwhelmed. The anxiety he felt came partly from wondering if he had the skills necessary to cope with the Clear Lake College Library and partly from worrying over choosing a topic he wouldn't learn to hate. This double dilemma brought on writer's paralysis.

8B

Rewrite these sentences to get rid of *who, whom, that, which,* or other phrases when you can do so without altering meaning. Not all of those words should be deleted.

1. Brian's writer's paralysis took a form that many are familiar with: compulsive behavior—in his case, overhauling his bike, which was running beautifully.
2. As he tightened and aligned brakes that he had checked the day before, he wondered if there was anyone who really liked to write research papers.
3. He also wondered who could help students find topics that they liked.
4. He didn't know anyone who was interested in the topics that were on the guideline sheets that were in the library reference room: for instance, consumers' rights, tax reform, funeral rites in ancient Egypt, and other topics equally snooze-producing to an eighteen-year-old.
5. But time was running so short that he couldn't afford to wait much longer.

8C

8C   CAN YOU CUT REDUNDANT WORDS AND PHRASES?

Term you need to know

> **Redundant**. A word or expression that is repetitious or unnecessary.

Troubleshooting

Check your writing to see if you are letting unnecessary filler creep in, words that take up space but add almost nothing to your meaning. The writer and editor William Zinsser calls them "clutter." To identify clutter in your writing, look for places where you have:

—**Used two words where one will do.** For example, *ready and able, fit and trim, hopes and desires, various and sundry, kind and considerate, hope and trust.*

—**Added useless modifiers.** Some adjectives and adverbs only repeat what is already implied in the word being modified; for instance, *completely finished, totally exhausted, awful tragedy, end result, very unique, final outcome, desired goal, consensus of opinion,* and other similar combinations.

—**Added surplus intensifiers.** Avoid padding a word or phrase by attaching a modifying word to it that adds nothing to its meaning; here are some examples with the surplus words underlined: *point in time, purple in color, weather activity, rough texture,* and *area of specialization.* Words such as *practically, absolutely, really, kind of, very,* and *actually* also fall into this category when used routinely and thoughtlessly. Such excess words add unnecessary baggage to your writing.

To reduce clutter . . .

▶ **Seek out and destroy redundant, useless, and empty expressions.**

{**Wordy**} Brian was an absolutely typical kind of Clear Lake College freshman. Although his mind was actually full of the kind of information he could use as the basis for a research paper, he was sure and certain that he had nothing to write about. And by this point in time, he thought his situation was totally hopeless. He could only hope and trust that some wonderful miracle would come along to rescue him from terrible disaster.

{**Leaner version**} Brian was a typical Clear Lake College freshman. Although his mind was full of information he could use as the basis for a research paper, he was sure he had nothing to write about. And by this time, he thought his situation was hopeless. He could only hope that some miracle would come along to rescue him from disaster.

8C

EXERCISE 8.3

Rewrite the following sentences to eliminate unnecessary words and phrases.

1. As Brian tinkered away with the gears on the rear wheel of his bicycle, he thought and pondered about the end result of his present situation.
2. One possible option that occurred to him was joining the Marines. He was absolutely sure they didn't write research papers.
3. The final outcome of that move, however, could be some kind of activity he wouldn't much like in some distant foreign country he really didn't want to visit.
4. Coming back to actual reality, in desperation he began to start looking around hoping against hope for a flash of inspiration.
5. To his great surprise, he found his cleaning activities had triggered one.

8D CAN YOU COMBINE SENTENCES?

Troubleshooting

If the people who are reading your draft suggest that you're writing wordy sentences that tend to ramble and repeat points, one good way to fix the problem is to try combining sentences. Sometimes you can collapse two or three closely related sentences into one. At other times you may be able to make one sentence a dependent (subordinate) clause and join it with another sentence, not only tightening your writing but showing the relationship between ideas more effectively. Here are some examples.

> {**Separate**} Brian McVicker is a good bicycle mechanic. He has been maintaining his own bike since he was nine.

{**Joined**} Since he has maintained his own bike since he was nine, Brian is a good bicycle mechanic.

{**Separate**} He has only recently started getting paid for his tinkering. In his home town, no one took his skills seriously.

{**Joined**} Since in his home town no one took his skills seriously, he has only recently started getting paid for his tinkering.

{**Separate**} He is becoming well known. He could almost open up a bicycle repair shop.

{**Joined**} He is becoming so well known that he could almost open up a bicycle shop.

To combine sentences effectively . . .

▶ **Look for places where simple sentences overlap.** Sometimes you can combine two sentences that have overlapping information to make a single, more effective sentence. When you do, you not only save words, but often you create tighter, more interesting sentences. For instance:

{**Separate**} American cyclists bicycle mainly for sport and exercise. The Chinese are different. The idea of biking for sport wouldn't occur to them. Most ride bikes only because they have to.

{**Combined**} Unlike Americans, most Chinese ride bikes only because they have to and would never consider bicycling for sport or exercise.

{**Separate**} In many third world countries, ordinary one-speed bicycles are prized possessions. They are the major mode of transportation. Private cars are extremely scarce.

{**Combined**} In many third world countries, ordinary one-speed bicycles are the major mode of transportation because private cars are extremely scarce.

{**Separate**} Brian was thinking about all this as he worked on the steering cables. He wondered what it would be like trying to get around China on a rickety old one-speed.

{**Combined**} Thinking about all this as he worked on the steering cables, Brian wondered what it would be like trying to get around China on a rickety old one-speed.

▶ **Look for sentences that can be effectively subordinated.** Sometimes you can not only save words by combining sentences, but by changing one sentence in a pair into a dependent clause and joining the pair, you can improve transitions and clarify your ideas. For example:

8D

{**Separate**} Thinking about those Chinese bikers had made Brian worry less about his problems. They seemed unimportant by comparison.

{**Combined and subordinated**} When Brian compared his problems to those of the Chinese bikers he had been thinking about, his difficulties seemed unimportant.

{**Separate**} He finished squirting grease into the last fitting. Then a wonderful idea struck him. Maybe Chinese bicycle riders and research papers just might go together.

{**Combined and subordinated**} As he squirted grease into the last fitting, a wonderful idea struck him; maybe Chinese bicycle riders and research papers just might go together.

EXERCISE 8.4

Combine sentences in the following passage to eliminate wordiness and improve clarity.

1. The way Brian found a topic for his research paper demonstrates the power of the subconscious mind. It takes in data and makes associations without our being aware of the process.

2. Brian's subconscious was stuffed and overflowing with information he had forgotten he had. He got much of that information from hearing Walter Toth's rambling conversations about the tour he had made to China two years ago.
3. Walter would be a great resource for the research paper. Brian knew he wouldn't find Walter's name in the encyclopedia.
4. Brian's teacher had said they could use interviews for part of their material. He would start by trying to get Walter alone. That wouldn't be easy.
5. Now Brian was excited about his research paper. His major problem was going to be the Clear Lake College Library. He didn't know how much material he could depend on getting from that antiquated place.

8E CAN YOU CHANGE VERBS FROM PASSIVE TO ACTIVE?

Terms you need to know

Passive verbs. Verb forms that show the subject receiving the action instead of doing it. For example:

.   Bicycles *are ridden* by millions of people in China.

Research papers *are written* by millions of college freshmen.

Active verbs. Verb forms that show the subject doing an action. For example:

Millions of people in China *ride* bicycles.

Millions of college freshmen *write* research papers.

Troubleshooting

If you make a habit of using passive verbs, you not only pad your prose with unneeded words, but you slow down your writing and make it less vigorous than it could be. What passive verbs do in many cases is divert attention from the person or agent responsible for the action. For example:

> The bibliography *was left out* of the research paper. (Who left it out? The author? The typist? The copy center?)

> The bicycle *was left unlocked*. (Who left it unlocked?)

> The Chinese *are said* to be unusually industrious people. (Who says so? People who have lived in China? Historians? Sociologists?)

8E

In many situations, your sentences will be stronger if you change passive verbs to active ones. (See Section 13G for an explanation of how to identify passive verbs.) They will also be clearer and give your readers more information because they will know who is doing what to whom.

However, in some kinds of writing, you may want to use passive verbs precisely because you want to emphasize *what* is being done rather than who is doing it. For instance, in scientific and technical reports, writers often know that the results of a process are more significant than the identity of those who carried it out; therefore, they will use mostly passive verbs when writing about that process. Many writers also like to use passive verbs when they want their writing to sound impersonal and rather distant.

To write more active sentences . . .

▶ **Use people as the subject of your sentences when you can.** (See Section 7B on adding people to your writing and Section 7C on actor/action sentences.) You are much less likely to choose a passive verb if you start your sentence off with a person rather than an abstract term. For example:

> {**Passive**} Strong pressures *were felt* by Brian about his first research paper.

{**Active**} Brian felt strong pressures over his first research paper.

{**Passive**} The excitement of doing original research *has not been experienced* by most students.

{**Active**} Most students have not experienced the excitement of doing original research.

{**Passive**} Inattention to detail *is claimed* by most critics to be the primary cause of shoddy research.

{**Active**} Most critics claim that inattention to detail causes most shoddy research.

▶ **Develop the habit of checking your writing for two- or three-word verb forms using *is, are, was, or were,* and** check to see how many of them are passives. (One good way to do this is to put brackets around all the passive verbs in your second draft.) You may find that your writing is thick with them. If so, it's likely not only to be wordy, but also to be heavy and hard to read. For example:

{**Passive style**} Brian's interest and imagination [was instantly captured] by the topic of how bicycles [are used] by the Chinese. Not only [are bicycles used] for commuting long distances to jobs, but they [are rigged up] to pull taxis, serve as delivery vans, and power for machines [is furnished] by them. Protection from the weather [is provided] by the cabs [made] by some riders to fit over their bikes. Side cars for an extra passenger [are added] by others. In many areas, whole families [can be seen] out on their bicycles for a long holiday trip. The potential for a thriving bicycle accessory business with China [is seen] by Brian as one possibility for his future.

{**Active style**} When Brian began to look into how the Chinese used bicycles, the topic instantly captured his interest. Not only do the Chinese ride them for commuting long distances to their jobs, but they rig them up to pull taxis, serve as delivery vans, and even to

211

furnish power for machines. Some riders make little cabs that fit over the bike to protect them from the weather. Others add side cars for an extra passenger. In many areas, one can see whole families out on their bicycles for a long holiday trip. Brian sees the possibility of a thriving bicycle accessory business with China as one future possibility.

(For eliminating unnecessary passive verb constructions, see Exercise 13.8.)

● Fine Tuning

8E

Your writing will be more economical and easier to understand if, whenever you can, you phrase ideas affirmatively instead of negatively. Try to get rid of words like *not* and *never* and prefixes like *un-* and *non*. Use "do" forms instead of "don't" forms. For example,

> {**Negative**} It is not unlikely that Rita Ruiz will be elected president.

> {**Affirmative**} It is likely that Rita Ruiz will be elected president.

> {**Negative**} She is not inexperienced in campus politics and not unattractive.

> {**Affirmative**} She is experienced in campus politics and attractive.

> {**Negative**} Her being a woman will not be a disadvantage either.

> {**Affirmative**} Her being a woman will be an advantage.

EXERCISE 8.5

Untangle and simplify the sentences in this letter of complaint written by the angry residents of Bridge-Over-Troubled-Waters Condominiums to their manager. You can combine sentences (rearrange them if you like), change passive verbs to active verbs, make affirmative statements from negative ones, or eliminate any words you think are unnecessary.

Mr. Shodyworken:

1. There are a number of reasons why this letter is being written to you by the residents of Bridge-Over-Troubled-Waters Condominiums.

2. First of all, it has been noted by one and by all that the lawns and shrubbery in the nearby vicinity of our properties have been nearly neglected completely to the detriment of all concerned.

3. Several of the more elderly members of the condominium association have expressed a certain concern that because of the proximity of overgrown shrubs adjacent to their entrances and walkways, it is conceivable that perpetrators of crimes might be tempted to hide in the shrubberies and, hence, use the foliage as a cover for their intent to mug, rob, and otherwise molest innocent residents.

4. Second of all, we are of the nearly unanimous opinion that due to the fact that you have neglected the maintaining of the swimming pool and surrounding areas, the conditions that exist in the areas are an important factor in the lowerization of our property values.

5. The purchasing of several units in the development has been delayed by buyers who are skeptical about the maintenance aspects of our condominiums.

6. We are able to enumerate numerous other examples of the neglect of routine items of housekeeping and upkeep for which the responsibility lies entirely and completely with you.

7. It seems that until actual monetary and legal pressure is put upon you by the residents of Bridge-Over-Troubled Waters Condominiums that you are unwilling to do what is necessary to restore our properties to the necessary conditions of attractiveness.

8. All six of our previous epistles to you have been in an arrogant manner ignored by you.

8E

213

9. Consequently, we have deemed it incumbent upon ourselves to take prompt and swift action in hiring legal counsel to advise us in this matter and in withholding that portion of our homeowners' fees which go toward recompensing you for your labor.

10. We hope you will act promptly to improve the conditions at Bridge-Over-Troubled-Waters Condominiums.

Sincerely,

8E

The Disgruntled Residents

CHAPTER

Problems with Managing Sentences?

9

- **A** Varying your sentences
- **B** Untangling sentences
- **C** Revitalizing dead sentences
- **D** Making sentences parallel

Introduction

Linguists who study language and try to understand how it works tell a story that several years ago an expert tried to write a clear definition of a sentence. After writing six hundred pages, he gave up and decided it couldn't be done. A whimsical tale, but it suggests how puzzling and wonderful are sentences—those basic units into which we organize thoughts to write them down.

We don't claim to explain everything about sentences in this chapter, but we hope to help you solve some of the typical problems people have with them by describing different kinds of sentence patterns and suggesting how you might use those patterns when you want to improve your writing. We believe, however, that writers don't actually think about sentence patterns when they write a first draft. Rather writers just put down sentences as they think of them. If the sentences don't look right when writers are revising, they look for ways to fix them. Then they may think about what kind of a sentence would work best in that position and use some of the guidelines we offer here. We hope you will also use these sections that way rather than slow down your first draft by worrying about what kind of sentences you should be writing.

9A ARE YOUR SENTENCES MONOTONOUS?

Terms you need to know

Sentence. A group of words that expresses an idea and is punctuated as an independent unit.

Simple sentence. A sentence that has only one clause.

> The Clear Lake College Career Carnival opens March 22.

Compound sentence. A sentence that combines two or more independent clauses.

> Recruiters from industry have set up booths, and several corporations are sending recruiters to interview students.

Complex sentence. A sentence that combines an independent clause and one or more dependent clauses.

> When Rita Ruiz first saw the announcements for the carnival, she began to get nervous.

Phrase. A group of related words that does not include a subject or verb.

Clause. A group of related words that has a subject and verb but is not a sentence.

> The problem she anticipated

Independent clause. A clause that *could* be a sentence.

Dependent clause. A clause that could *not* be a sentence.

Coordinate structure. A sentence arrangement that joins two or more clauses that could be sentences.

Subordinate structure. A sentence arrangement that joins two or more clauses, at least one of which could not be a sentence.

Coordinating conjunctions. Words like *or, and, yet, neither, but,* one of whose functions is to join parts of sentences.

Conjunctive adverbs. Words like *although, nevertheless, however,* one of whose uses is to join the clauses in compound sentences.

Balanced sentence. A compound sentence that has two or more clauses having the same pattern.

> Representatives from corporations like the Career Carnival because it gives them a chance to see students; students like the Carnival because it gives them a chance to meet someone working in a profession.

Troubleshooting

Writers sometimes fall into the habit of writing most of their sentences in nearly the same patterns and of nearly the same length. When they do, not only can their writing seem thin and monotonous, but readers may have a hard time figuring out which ideas are most important and how the ideas in a sentence relate to each other. If you want to fix such sentences, you need to know about different kinds of sentences, understand when to use them, and practice writing a variety of sentences.

To vary your sentences . . .

▶ **Use simple sentences.** When you want to make a straightforward statement, don't hesitate to write one—clear and simple without qualifying clauses.

Here are two examples of simple sentences with no extras. The simple subjects and verbs are in boldface.

subj.   verb

The *Daily Toxin* **has given** the carnival excellent publicity.

subj.   verb

Rita Ruiz will be looking for a job.

But simple sentences aren't necessarily plain. You can add interesting information to them without complicating them with additional clauses. Here are two more simple sentences with the added information underlined.

Rita, <u>who is graduating with high honors</u>, is hoping for a particular interview.

<u>But to her fellow students' surprise</u>, she seems nervous.

9A

EXERCISE 9.1

Write two simple sentences about a job you have had. Write one bare bones, plain sentence and write one with added information.

▶ **Use compound sentences.** When you need to relate two important ideas, you will probably compose a compound sentence. In a compound sentence, two independent but closely related clauses are connected with a conjunction, a conjunctive adverb, or a semicolon. Compound sentences work especially well if the ideas connected in the sentence have approximately the same importance. For example:

Rita knows her nervousness puzzles her friends, but she can't do anything about it.

For the last three and half years, she has been a conspicuously sloppy dresser; Professor Chase, her adviser in the business department, has been telling her to change her image.

When you want to draw special attention to the relationship between ideas in a sentence, you can use a particular kind of compound sentence called the **balanced sentence**—a sentence constructed like an equation with matching parts on each side of the connecting word or the semicolon. Here are two balanced sentences:

> Professor Chase always looks elegant; Rita usually seems unkempt.

> Professor Chase lectures to Rita earnestly; Rita listens to Professor Chase indifferently.

EXERCISE 9.2

Write three compound sentences about friends or people in your family. Make one of them a balanced sentence.

▶ **Use complex sentences.** When you need to show the relationship between two ideas, one of which is more important than the other, you'll probably write a complex sentence. You will indicate the difference between the ideas by *subordinating* one to the other. The main idea will be stated in an **independent clause** and the subordinate idea in a **dependent clause**. Words like *although*, *if*, *before*, *because*, or phrases like *even so*, *in spite of*, and so on typically mark the beginning of the subordinated dependent clause. For example:

> dependent clause
> Although Professor Chase despaired of Rita's ward-
> independent clause
> robe, she admired her quick mind.

> independent clause
> She was afraid that a corporate recruiter would not
> dependent clause
> take Rita seriously, even though she was a superb student of corporate finance.

> dependent clause
> Because she cared about Rita's future, Professor
> independent clause
> Chase explained her own experience as a student.

EXERCISE 9.3

Write two complex sentences about a recent college experience.

By using a combination of simple, compound, and complex sentences and varying their length, you can make your writing easier to follow and more interesting to read. For example, notice the difference in these two versions of a paragraph Connie Lim wrote for the *Daily Toxin*.

{**First draft**} Rita Ruiz has always been a good math student. In grade school, she surprised her teachers. In the second grade, she understood fractions. In the fourth grade, she was experimenting with a slide rule. In the sixth grade, her teacher gave her a geometry book. She sat in the back of the room working problems on her own. Her talents were even more evident in her high school economics class. She understood economic theory better than many college students.

{**Second draft**} Rita Ruiz has always been a good math student. When she was in grade school, she surprised her teachers. In the second grade, she understood fractions, and in the fourth grade, she was experimenting with a slide rule. When she got to the sixth grade, her teacher gave her a geometry book, and she sat in the back of the room working problems on her own. Her talents became even more obvious by high school because she understood economic theory better than many college students.

EXERCISE 9.4

Revise these sentences into a paragraph using a variety of simple, compound, and complex sentences. Be sure to vary their lengths.

1. As a child, Rita was a tomboy.
2. She hated having to dress up for parties or church.
3. She wanted to wear blue jeans all the time.
4. In grade school, blue jeans were especially necessary.
5. At stake was her position on the baseball team.
6. Adults told her she was too pretty to wear boys' clothes.
7. It made no impression on Rita.
8. She knew what was important to her.

9B HOW DO YOU UNTANGLE SENTENCES?

Terms you need to know

> **Complement.** A word or phrase that follows an "is" verb (or some other linking verb) and completes the sentence.

> **Object.** A word or phrase that receives the action of a verb.

Troubleshooting

Sometimes writers try to compose such ambitious sentences that they bog down in hopeless tangles or inflate into unreadable vagueness. Then readers give up on trying to understand them. Sometimes this confusion occurs when a writer tries to include too much information in a single sentence.

> Anyone who has known Professor Chase of the business school, a handsome woman as well as an intelligent one, for the last ten years could tell you that over that period of time she has changed her own image rather remarkably from the one of aggressive dowdiness that she had cultivated when she was a graduate student at a Scottish university and writing her thesis on Adam Smith to that of a sleekly coifed, impeccably dressed, and subtly made-up woman pro-

fessional who has written a famous book and is quite as much at home in the corporate boardrooms of Chicago as she is in the remote stacks of the library.

The reader gets lost before getting halfway through.

Or the writer tries to match up verbs with subjects or objects and complements that cannot fit together.

Professor Chase's *desire* to change her image secretly *longed* to get rid of those shapeless, wooly skirts and sweaters and clunky shoes left over from her days in Scotland.

9B

Notice that it just doesn't work to say "her desire . . . longed to get rid. . . ." This is called a predication error because the subject doesn't fit with the verb (predicate).

When such tangles occur, it's often better *not* to try to fix them. Instead, discard the troublesome sentence and start over. Here are two approaches you can use to manage difficult sentences.

To untangle difficult sentences . . .

▶ **Split them up.** Look for the central ideas in a tangled sentence and incorporate them in two or three shorter sentences. For example, watch what happens when we divide these long, unwieldy sentences into shorter ones.

Example 1.

{**Tangled version**} Even when she was a graduate student wearing a black cap, a droopy skirt, and gray leg warmers with boots because that was the approved outfit for serious students at Scottish universities and also because it was so dreadfully cold in Edinburgh, Marya Chase had a tiny suspicion that she didn't really like looking like an extra from the cast of *Les Miserables*, and she knew that underneath her dowdy, ill-fitting costume which was supposed to be so fashionable burned the soul of a natural clothes horse longing to be free.

The sentence has such a long introductory clause that the reader gets lost before getting to the subject, Marya Chase. It also contains too much information, more than a reader can absorb at one time.

> {**New version**} Even when Marya Chase was a graduate student in Scotland and wearing the approved dowdy costume, she suspected she didn't really like looking like an extra from the cast of *Les Miserables*. She knew that underneath those awful clothes burned the soul of a clothes horse.

Example 2

> {**Tangled version**} Sitting in Professor Chase's class day after day listening to her talk brilliantly about Adam Smith, Karl Marx, and John Maynard Keynes and demonstrate her command of the intricacies of international finance as she paced in front of the class wearing designer shoes and silk blouses was a treat for Rita's acquisitive mind but at the same time an assault on her conviction that women with first class intelligences were not stupid enough to yield to the consumerist passions that her clothes obviously demonstrated.

Not only does the sentence have a 48-word subject that overwhelms the verb *was*, but it is packed with so much information that the reader can easily get the subject and modifying phrases mixed up.

> {**Clearer version**} Although Rita enjoys hearing Professor Chase talk brilliantly about Adam Smith and Karl Marx, seeing her lecture in designer clothes and silk blouses confuses Rita. She thought women with good minds didn't care about fancy clothes.

EXERCISE 9.5

Write another simple version of each of the tangled sentences in the two examples above.

▶ **Be sure your verbs work logically with other parts of the sentence.** Sometimes writers match verbs with subjects, objects, or complements that don't suit them. The resulting sentences don't exactly make sense. This kind of error is called *faulty predication*. Here are some examples.

{**Problem**} Professor Chase's passion to be well dressed yearned for the means to express itself.

[Faulty predication because a *passion* is an abstract idea that can't *yearn*; only a person can yearn.]

{**Improved**} Professor Chase's passion to be well dressed made her yearn for the means to express it.

{**Problem**} Her imagination loved the prospect of shopping at fancy boutiques.

[Faulty predication because *imagination* is an abstract quality that can't *love*; only a person can love.]

{**Improved**} Professor Chase loved to imagine herself shopping at fancy boutiques.

{**Problem**} Her ambitions had to think of some way to make money.

[Faulty predication because *ambition* is an abstract quality that can't *think*.]

{**Improved**} Her ambitions drove her to think of some way to make money.

{**Problem**} The situation called for creative.

[Faulty predication because *creative* is an adjective and cannot act as the object of *called for*.]

{**Improved**} The situation called for creativity.

{**Problem**} Professor Chase's solution wrote a book called *The Joy of Money*.

[Faulty predication because *solution* is an abstract quality and cannot *write* something.]

{**Improved**} Professor Chase's solution was to write a book called *The Joy of Money*.

EXERCISE 9.6

Rewrite each of the following sentences and untangle the predication errors.

1. Professor Chase's example keeps telling Rita about the well-dressed young women executives she meets on her trips to Chicago.
2. Rita's clothes classify themselves as not appropriate for the executive boardroom.
3. Her clothes have no suitability.
4. She thought about the aspects that accompanied her dilemma.
5. Fancy clothes are a difficult decision for her.

9C   ARE YOUR SENTENCES DULL?

Troubleshooting

Sometimes in an attempt to impress a reader or to generate a required number of words, writers produce sentences so abstract and overwritten that they're hard to read and understand. They're also deadly boring. They string together several abstract and vague words and phrases and the sentence spins out of control.

Successfully negotiating a compromise between dowdiness and slavish acquiescence to pressures of the fashion world is a difficult decision for Rita.

Availability of an establishment where she could learn more about the problem she faced was not immediately apparent to her.

You can usually fix such sentences by applying the following guideline.

To enliven dead sentences . . .

9C

▶ **Change the sentence pattern and add people.** If an impersonal or abstract subject of a sentence is combined with a weak verb—and usually it is—you might rethink the sentence to fit an *actor/action* pattern (see p. 186). To create such a pattern, you usually have to add people. Generally, the sentence will improve immediately. In the following examples, the *actor* subjects and *action* verbs are italicized.

{**Dead**} Total indifference to appearance is not characteristic of most people.

{**Revitalized**} Most *people are* not totally indifferent to appearance.

{**Dead**} A scarcity of money is the reason for some students' limited wardrobes.

{**Revitalized**} Some *students have* limited wardrobes because they don't have much money.

{**Dead**} That difficulty may be part of the explanation for Rita's tattered jeans.

{**Revitalized**} *Rita may wear* tattered jeans partly because she has no money.

{**Dead**} The greater likelihood, however, is that shopping for clothes fills her with hatred.

{**Revitalized**} More likely *she* simply *hates* shopping.

Try your hand at rewriting the following passage, untangling and dividing sentences that are too long and confusing, correcting faulty predication, and making changes to revitalize dead sentences.

1. Preparation for their encounter with future employers becomes a preoccupation for many students at Clear Lake College.
2. Some students' anxiety feels very nervous as the time approaches.
3. The excitement of getting to experience face-to-face meetings with employment whose salaries are dazzling is heady stuff.
4. The capability of making such salaries is a great fantasy.
5. Their imaginations do not see the probability for success.

9D HOW DO YOU MAKE SENTENCES PARALLEL?

Term you need to know

> **Parallel structure.** A sentence arrangement that organizes all related phrases or clauses so they have the same pattern.

Troubleshooting

A sentence can confuse your readers if its parts don't fit the predictable pattern that you have led them to expect at the beginning. For that reason, you should construct sentences—and lists, too—so that parts that *do* the same thing also have the same form; that is, they are the same kind of words or phrases—nouns, adjectives, prepositional phrases, and the like. The parts of a balanced sentence should also be parallel.

▶ **Rewrite elements that don't match so that they are alike and form a consistent pattern.** In the following examples, the faulty versions contain elements not consistent with the overall patterns of the sentence. These faulty items are made parallel in the corrected version. The faulty and corrected elements are italicized.

9D

{**Faulty**} However impervious Rita might be to the charms of high fashion, she is not naive, stupid, or *has bad taste*.

{**Parallel**} However impervious Rita might be to the charms of high fashion, she is not naive, stupid, or *without taste*.

{**Faulty**} Rita reluctantly realized it was time for her to grow up and *facing the facts of real life economics*.

{**Parallel**} Rita reluctantly realized it was time for her to grow up and *face the facts of real life economics*.

{**Faulty**} New Horizon Venture Capital, the company she wanted to work for, might expect young women both to look intelligent and *being fashionable*.

{**Parallel**} New Horizon Venture Capital, the company she wanted to work for, might expect young women both to look intelligent and *be fashionable*.

{**Faulty**} Rita was willing to change, but as a shopper she was inexperienced and *no confidence*.

{**Parallel**} Rita was willing to change, but as a shopper she was inexperienced and *had no confidence*.

{**Faulty**} But Rita had four things in her favor:
good research skills,
willingness to learn,
zest for problem solving, and
determined to work for New Horizons.

{**Parallel**} But Rita had four things in her favor:
good research skills,
willingness to learn,
zest for problem solving, and
determination to work for New Horizons.

EXERCISE 9.8

Rewrite these sentences to make all elements parallel.

9D

1. Rita started with a trip to the college library for the book *Women's Dress for Success Book*, then taking out a loan from the college credit union.
2. After that she headed for the Clear Lake College Thrift Shop, Becky's Antique Clothing Boutique, and the last stop at Good Will.
3. At the Thrift Shop she found the perfect Dress for Success outfit: a gray skirt, a blue blazer, and economical.
4. Hanging in the rear of the shop was one of Professor Chase's almost new designer blouses—elegant, cheap, and white silk—and she bought it.
5. On Friday morning Rita dressed for her appointment with Marty McAdoo, the young president of New Horizons Venture Capital, but fortunately realizing in time she couldn't wear her cowboy boots with her new outfit.
6. Borrowing some tan shoes, she hurried to the Career Carnival, found the New Horizons booth, and sees Professor Chase talking to a well-dressed young man she presumed to be Marty McAdoo.
7. "Mr. McAdoo?" she said, putting out her hand and was ready to sit down.
8. "No, I'm McAdoo," said a very young-looking bearded man wearing a faded sweater, jeans ragged at the edge, and the heels on his cowboy boots were run down.

9. "So you're Rita Ruiz," he said. "According to your résumé, you're smart, ambitious, and a good honors thesis on currency manipulation. But all I really want to know is this: Can you write?"
10. Stepping in, Professor Chase immediately said, "This young woman is more than just a fashion plate—I will recommend her as a writer, a leader, and very enterprising."

9D

CHAPTER

Problems with Sentence Fragments, Comma Splices, and Run-ons?

- **A** Sentence fragments
- **B** Minor sentences
- **C** Comma splices
- **D** Run-on sentences

10

Terms you need to know

Sentence fragment. A group of words that does not fully express an idea even though it is punctuated as a sentence. May also be called a *broken sentence*.

Fragment: Since David had never driven a really good car.

Minor sentence. A group of words that does not have all the usual parts of a sentence but can act as a sentence because it expresses an idea fully.

Minor sentence: Not in this world, anyway.

Introduction

Three of the most troublesome and common of sentence problems are the fragment, the comma splice, and the run-on. These faults in sentence structure occur so frequently in writing that we believe they merit a chapter of their own. As you'll see, all three difficulties arise from a problem understanding what the dimensions or boundaries of a sentence are. Once you gain a feel for what a sentence does, you are less likely to write one that doesn't do its job adequately.

Terms you need to know

Verbals. Words or phrases derived from verbs that act as nouns, adjectives, and adverbs. The three kinds of verbals are *infinitives*, *participles*, and *gerunds*.

Gerund. A noun made by adding *-ing* to a verb: *walking*, *disagreeing*, *writing*.

Infinitive. The "to _____" form that is the base of a verb; for instance, *to eat*; *to swim*; *to demonstrate*.

Appositive. A group of words that gives more information about a word that it follows.

> Groupies, *those insatiable fans who surround many rock stars*, are flattering but troublesome.

Troubleshooting

You may be getting your drafts or final papers returned to you with *fragment* written in the margins and don't understand what the problem is or how you can fix it. If so, that's serious because sentence fragments badly distress English teachers, editors, and professional people who deal with language.

This section will show you how to identify sentence fragments or broken sentences and how you can fix them or avoid writing them in the first place.

To eliminate fragments . . .

▶ **Check to see that you have not tried to make a dependent or subordinate clause stand alone as a sentence.** Clauses that start with words like *although*, *because*, *if*, *for*, and *thus* won't work as sentences by themselves even though they have a subject and a verb.

Fragments:

If a rock group has a hit record.

Although one can seldom predict what is going to be popular.

Because a tricky name seems to help a new group.

These are *broken sentences*; that is, pieces of sentences that need something else to go with them. By themselves, they leave the reader up in the air waiting to find out what they should be attached to. It's like waiting for the other shoe to fall. Fragments of this kind can usually be repaired by attaching them to a complete sentence.

Full sentences:

If a rock group has a hit record, it may break into the big time.

Although one can seldom predict what record is going to be popular, wild lyrics seem to help.

Because a tricky name seems to help a new group, David tried to pick something novel to call his band.

Here are some additional examples showing the dependent clause fragments or broken sentences in italics.

{**Fragment**} David Barrett, manager and leader of Microwave Katz, has accepted the latest gift from his fan club. *Although members prefer to think of themselves as supporters of the arts.*

[The clause starting with *although* has been broken off from *fan club* and doesn't make sense by itself.]

{**Fragment eliminated**} David Barrett, manager and leader of Microwave Katz, has accepted the latest gift from his fan club, although members prefer to think of themselves as supporters of the arts.

{**Fragment**} *Even though they have spiked hair, wear leather, and roar through town on noisy motorcycles whenever they get bored.* The group has bank accounts that make it respectable in Ruralia.

[The clause beginning with *Even though* goes on so long that it seems like a sentence, but it's not because you don't know what *even though* refers to until you come to the main sentence.]

{**Fragment eliminated**} Even though they have spiked hair, wear leather, and roar through town on noisy motorcycles whenever they get bored, the group has bank accounts that make it respectable in Ruralia.

10A

EXERCISE 10.1

Write full sentences that incorporate these sentence fragments from dependent clauses.

1. Even if a rock band isn't very talented.
2. Because there is so much money to be made in the music business.
3. Although the major rock stars are usually guitarists.
4. When *Rolling Stone* reviews a new record.
5. Since an amateur group often has minimal musical equipment.

▶ **Check to see that you have not tried to make a relative clause or appositive stand alone as a sentence.** Words like *who*, *which*, *that*, and *where* are frequently used to signal the beginning of a relative clause that must be connected to the main part of the sentence in order for it to make sense.

He was just plain David Barrett. *Who never expected to own a coveted sports car.*

Another kind of clause that frequently turns into a sentence fragment is the appositive clause, one that is really acting as a modifier.

The car itself was super. *The last word in 1960s American sports machinery.*

When either relative clauses or appositives are separated and made to look like sentences, you get sentence fragments. Here are some examples with the fragments in italics.

{**Fragment**} Barrett's fan club bought him a handsome 1963 Corvette Sting Ray. *Which replaced the embarrassing 1958 Borgward he had been driving.*

(The clause starting with *which* is punctuated as a sentence, but it modifies the Corvette and doesn't express a full idea by itself.)

{**Fragment eliminated**} Barrett's fan club bought him a handsome 1963 Corvette Sting Ray to replace the embarrassing 1958 Borgward he had been driving.

{**Fragment**} He never had imagined that he could own such a classic. *The most respected road car in America and the most timeless of all Corvette designs.*

(The long clause beginning with *the most respected* is an appositive that gives more information about *classic* and won't work by itself as a sentence.)

{**Fragment eliminated**} He had never imagined that he could own such a classic, the most respected road car in America and the most timeless of all Corvette designs.

EXERCISE 10.2

Write full sentences that incorporate these sentence fragments derived from relative clauses or appositives.

1. A car that any connoisseur would appreciate.
2. Which was a gift that would impress anyone.
3. A hobby that certainly isn't for the poor.
4. Who is the favorite among local fans.
5. Never having happened to him before.

▶ **Check to see that you have not mistaken a verbal for a verb.** Verbals (see Section 13I) are tricky constructions that can easily confuse a writer into mistaking a phrase for a sentence. Verbals *look* like verbs but they really act as nouns, adjectives, or adverbs. For instance, in the phrase *to look at* *something, to look* is the infinitive of the verb, but it doesn't act as a verb. In the phrase *running for office, running* is the kind of noun made by adding *-ing* to a verb and is called a gerund; it is not a verb. In the phrase *recognizing his weakness, recognizing* can be a noun or an adjective, depending on the context; it is not a verb. To eliminate fragments caused by verbals, it may help to remember that

> An *-ing* word by itself can never act as the verb of a sentence. It must have an auxiliary word such as *have, is, were*.
>
> An infinitive, such as *to run, to go*, and so on, can never act as the verb of a sentence.

10A

Here are examples of how verbals cause sentence fragments. The fragments are italicized.

> {**Fragment**} When Barrett's fan club drove the Corvette up and parked it in front of his house, the usually talkative songwriter suddenly fell silent. *Feeling unworthy of that handsome split-window coupe.*
>
> [The italicized portion is an adverb phrase modifying *songwriter* and cannot act as a sentence.]

> {**Fragment eliminated**} When Barrett's fan club drove the Corvette up and parked it in front of his house, the usually talkative songwriter suddenly fell silent, feeling unworthy of that handsome split-window coupe.

> {**Fragment**} *To hear the rumble of the 327 V-8.* That was magic.
>
> [The entire italicized portion is an infinitive phrase acting as a noun and shouldn't be punctuated as a sentence.]

> {**Fragment eliminated**} To hear the rumble of the 327 V-8 powering the machine was magic.

> {**Fragment**} *Approaching the car cautiously.* David reverently laid his hand on the gleaming fiberglass hood.
>
> [The italicized phrase is a participle phrase acting as an adjective because it modifies *David* and should not be punctuated as a sentence.]

{**Fragment eliminated**} Approaching the car cautiously, David reverently laid his hand on the gleaming fiberglass hood.

{**Fragment**} *Leaving a fingerprint on the finish.*

[This cannot be a sentence by itself.]

{**Fragment eliminated**} He left a fingerprint on the finish.

EXERCISE 10.3

Write full sentences incorporating these sentence fragments derived from verbals or verbal phrases.

1. Given all the trouble he had caused the neighbors.
2. Never realizing those crazy fans had so much money.
3. Considered an outrageous luxury by most people.
4. Believing that it would make his career even better.
5. To see if there had been some mistake.

▶ **Check to see that you have not treated a disconnected phrase as a sentence.** Sometimes—particularly in advertising copy—a disconnected phrase that has no subject or verb is punctuated as a sentence.

The classic Corvette Sting Ray. Muscular and powerful. Timeless design. Above all, performance.

Such constructions are not always puzzling, but they can offend careful readers—especially teachers—so it's a good idea to keep them out of the writing you do for classes. Turning a disconnected phrase into a full sentence is usually a matter of adding a subject or a verb (sometimes both), depending upon what has been omitted from the phrase. Here are some examples of disconnected phrases. The fragments are italicized.

{**Fragment**} *Immediately upset and panicky.* That's what Barrett was when he saw the fingerprint on his Corvette.

[By itself, the phrase isn't clear.]

{**Fragment eliminated**} Barrett was immediately upset and panicky when he saw the fingerprint on his Corvette.

{**Fragment**} David buffed the fingerprint away. *With his new cashmere sweater. Absent-mindedly.*

[The prepositional phrase—*With his new cashmere sweater*—can be joined easily to the end of the sentence. *Absent-mindedly* needs to be attached to what it modifies: David.]

{**Fragment eliminated**} Absent-mindedly, David buffed the fingerprint away with his new cashmere sweater.

EXERCISE 10.4

Write full sentences that incorporate these fragments derived from disconnected phrases.

1. One of the fastest cars in town.
2. Never again.
3. Without looking back.
4. Not in his lifetime.
5. Awesome. Eye-catching.

EXERCISE 10.5

Rewrite these sentences and correct any sentence fragments.

1. Although Barrett's neighbors thought they were used to almost anything. The next day they were startled to see a long covered object in his carport with only a glimpse of white sidewall tires showing at the bottom.
2. The first things that caught their eye were signs saying "Keep Off," "Don't touch," and "Posted." Plastered all over the canvas cover.

3. As they watched, Barrett came out of the house in white overalls and wearing a surgical mask on his face. With two large plastic buckets of warm water and a basket full of car care products.

4. Putting down the buckets and basket, he reached into his pocket. Drawing out a chamois.

5. The very picture of a meticulous specialist at work. That's the impression he conveyed to the neighbors.

6. Carefully he pulled a glove onto each hand. One finger at a time and flexing his wrists as he worked.

7. Then he drew a packet of Q-tips from another pocket and a plastic bag stuffed with tiny cosmetic sponges. From still another pocket, six toothbrushes.

8. The neighbors were consumed with curiosity about his meticulous preparations. Doing things ahead of time being very uncharacteristic of David the musician.

9. At last Barrett approached the Corvette. Standing to one side, being careful not to lean on the car.

10. Before touching the car, David sat down beside it in a cross-legged position. Feeling respectful in the presence of so renowned a vehicle.

10B HOW DOES A MINOR SENTENCE DIFFER FROM A FRAGMENT?

Troubleshooting

You may have noticed sentence fragments appearing frequently in advertising and in some kinds of professional writing and wondered how those writers manage to get away with it.

> Some classic car buffs are fanatics. No moderation. No control. When they restore a car, they'll go to any extreme to see that it's perfect. Total authenticity. That's their goal.

Are sentence fragments considered wrong at some times but not at others? The answer is *yes*.

Certain kinds of fragments can be classified as **minor sentences**; that is, phrases or groups of words that don't have all the traditional ingredients of a sentence but nevertheless work as sentences because they effectively convey a full idea. Such sentences appear frequently in many informal essays, magazine pieces, and advertisements.

> Does such perfectionism mean that they're doomed to failure? Not necessarily. Persistence and luck. If they have those, they can achieve their goal.

Writers can sometimes use fragments effectively when they are writing for certain purposes. For instance, they may want to achieve a quick pace or a staccato effect in their writing, or they may want to create a series of images. One way to accomplish either of those goals is to use a series of sentence fragments.

> The classic car connoisseur with a good eye can always recognize a master's work. The gleaming, immaculate finish. The authentic hood ornament. The perfectly restored hub caps and manufacturer's insignia.

The problem is that both minor sentences and deliberate fragments may look just like the fragments many readers consider to be major errors.

To avoid problems with minor sentences . . .

▶ **Use them sparingly.** Minor sentences and deliberate fragments should not appear regularly in any formal or academic writing you do. You probably wouldn't want to use deliberate fragments in a research paper, report, job application letter, or literary analysis. You might use them in narratives, journal pieces, humorous essays, or personality sketches.

▶ **Be sure readers understand that they are deliberate.** Careful readers who think that fragments or minor sentences are accidental rather than written for some specific effect may object to them strenuously, thinking that they show a mishandling of sentence structure. If you do want to use fragments occasionally, think first what your purpose is in using them and who your readers are. For readers who you know are conservative about grammar, don't use fragments. For other readers, be sure you have some special purpose in mind for using them. You don't want them to look like careless accidents.

In the following passage, for example, Kyle Talbot, writing a sketch of David, uses a series of minor sentences and effective fragments to achieve the upbeat, rapid pace he wants to convey in his portrait.

> One would think that anyone as rad as David Barrett wouldn't be overwhelmed by a car. *Any car. Not so.* But then a Corvette Sting Ray is not just any car. It's a cult item. *An icon. A grunting, pulsing emblem of America. Something every car nut worthy of his tachometer would kill for.* So no wonder David was overwhelmed. *No wonder, indeed.*

EXERCISE 10.6

Find an advertisement that uses minor sentences and deliberate fragments. Rewrite it, eliminating the fragments. Then assess the difference between the original ad and your corrected version. Why did the copywriter of the ad use fragments?

10C HAVING PROBLEMS WITH COMMA SPLICES?

Term you need to know

> **Comma splice.** The punctuation error of using a comma to join two groups of words, each of which could be a sentence by itself. May also be called a *comma fault.*

> Being a member of a fan club is a gratifying experience, it is comparable to being in a football booster club.

Troubleshooting

If the mark CS or *comma fault* is decorating the margins of your papers all too often, and you can't figure out what you're doing wrong or how to fix the problem, it will be worth your time to find out what comma splices are and how you can fix them when they appear in your writing. Basically, the comma splice signals confusion about how to join independent clauses in a sentence. If you can straighten that out, you're on your way to eliminating the problem and perhaps forestalling a serious rage from your teacher.

10C

A comma splice occurs when the writer joins two independent clauses with a comma instead of using a conjunction or a semicolon or separating them into individual sentences.

> David's fans showed great insight about his tastes, they couldn't have chosen a better gift for him.

The comma is a weak mark of punctuation that should be used only to indicate a brief pause or a very slight separation. When it is used to separate two independent clauses (see Section 9A), each of which could be a sentence by itself, it's just not strong enough to do an effective job. Consequently, the reader may become confused about how the sentence works or about the relationship between the two clauses. If the words on both sides of a comma could stand alone as sentences, chances are good you have a comma splice.

> {Comma splice} He carefully put the buckets of warm water on the ground, he began to lay the cleaning tools on a table to the right of the car.

> [The comma joins two sentences. Either one could stand alone.]

> {Comma splice eliminated} He carefully put the buckets of warm water on the ground. He began to lay the cleaning tools on a table to the right of the car.

Only very short sentences, often in threes, are regularly joined by commas.

> I came, I saw, I conquered.

> She ate, I paid, we left.

Identify which of the following sentences have comma splices and indicate how the problem could be corrected.

1. Not many fan clubs could afford fancy cars, the members are generally too young.
2. Usually fans content themselves with just being enthusiastic and loyal, they love shouting and applauding as loudly as possible.
3. They had taste, they had class, they had money.
4. David's fans were devoted, they thought he hung the moon.
5. Not all Ruralia residents appreciate rock music, however, nearly all the college students are ardent supporters of Barrett's group.

10C

To fix a comma splice . . .

▶ **Substitute a semicolon for the comma.**

{Comma splice} As David cleaned his car, every sponge, Q-tip, toothbrush, toothpick, and pipe cleaner was laid out in one neat row, every linen towel, chamois square, cotton ball, and silk handkerchief was laid out in another row.

[The separation between these two closely related independent ideas gets lost among the commas that are separating items in the series.]

{Comma splice eliminated} As David cleaned his car, every sponge, Q-tip, toothbrush, and pipe cleaner was laid out in one neat row; every linen towel, chamois square, cotton ball, and silk hankerchief was laid out in another row.

▶ **Substitute a period for the comma.**

{Comma splice} Like a surgeon going to work, David began to wash one square inch of the car at a time, by the end of the morning he had finished the hood and one fender.

> [These two independent clauses should have a stronger separation to emphasize their difference.]

{Comma splice eliminated} Like a surgeon going to work, David began to wash one square inch of the car at a time. By the end of the morning, he had finished the hood and one door.

10C

▶ **Keep the comma, but insert a conjunction such as *but*, *and*, or *or* after it.**

{Comma splice} His progress was so slow because he probed each door crevice with a Q-tip or a toothpick, after he finished a section, he polished it to a high shine first with a linen towel and then with a silk handkerchief.

> [These two independent clauses need a strong separation to stress that they are in a sequence, and the comma doesn't provide that separation.]

{Comma splice eliminated} His progress was so slow because he probed each door crevice with a Q-tip or a toothpick, *and* after he finished a section he polished it to a high shine with a linen towel and then a silk handkerchief.

▶ **Rewrite the sentence and make one of the clauses a dependent, subordinate clause.**

{Comma splice} David came untangled from the lotus position, he balanced his buckets and basket in his hands.

> [The two clauses of the sentence are not equally important so the first one should be changed to a subordinate clause, and the comma retained.]

{Comma splice eliminated} As David came untangled from the lotus position, he balanced his buckets and basket in his hands.

Rewrite these sentences to eliminate the comma splices.

1. The parents of the young people in David's fan club were perpetually astonished at their children's behavior, nevertheless, they tried to understand their fanaticism.
2. Wearing ear plugs, two of the more adventuresome parents actually attended a concert, afterwards they were more astonished than before.
3. Both of them admitted that Microwave Katz gave a dynamic, energetic performance, they knew in their hearts that groups today just didn't measure up to the bands of their days, Jefferson Airplane, the Supremes, the Strawberry Alarm Clock.
4. They wanted to stay on good terms with their children, however, they were careful not to make any comparisons.
5. Then Lucinda's parents realized that the last thing she wanted was for them to like rock music, that would take all the fun out of it for Lucinda.

10D

10D HAVING PROBLEMS WITH RUN-ON SENTENCES?

Term you need to know

Run-on sentence. The punctuation error of failing to insert a conjunction or a semicolon to separate two groups of words, each of which could be a sentence by itself. May also be called a *fused sentence*.

Troubleshooting

You may be seeing *run-on* or *FS* (for fused sentence—another term for a run-on) in the margins of your papers and not understand what the symbol means. Basically, you just have a punctuation problem, one that is more easily fixed than many.

In run-on sentences, the problem is just the opposite of a comma splice; that is, there is no punctuation at all between two independent clauses, and the reader can't tell how they should be separated. If your instructor has told you several times that you need to be more careful about run-on sentences, you should probably get in the habit of checking any long sentence to see if you have run together two or more sentences that should be punctuated to show a clear separation of ideas.

10D

{**Run-on**} Barrett's fans thought locating the 1963 Corvette Sting Ray would be a major research job they never dreamed Walter Toth would be able to find one for them.

{**Rewritten**} Barrett's fans thought locating the 1963 Corvette Sting Ray would be a major job. They never dreamed Walter Toth would be able to find one for them.

{**Run-on**} The price they paid for the car is a well-kept secret speculation is that it was about the same as Coach Rhodes' recruiting budget.

{**Rewritten**} Although the price they paid for the car is a well-kept secret, speculation is that it was about the same as Coach Rhodes' recruiting budget.

To eliminate run-on sentences or phrases . . .

▶ Insert a period between fused sentences.

{**Run-on**} After four days of cleaning, waxing, and polishing, Barrett was finally satisfied with his Corvette he agreed with his neighbors that it could not have looked any better if it had belonged to Bruce Springsteen.

[The sentence needs to be broken after *Corvette* in order not to confuse the readers. Adding a period makes a natural separation.]

{**Run-on eliminated**)} After four days of cleaning, waxing, and polishing, Barrett was finally satisfied with his Corvette. He agreed with his neighbors that it could not have looked any better if it had belonged to Bruce Springsteen.

▶ **Insert a semicolon between two independent clauses that have been run together.** A semicolon suggests that the ideas in the two sentences remain closely related.

{**Run-on**} David's whole life now revolved around his Sting Ray he could think of nothing else.

[The two clauses are closely related but need to be separated to show they are separate ideas. A semicolon separates the sentences, but preserves a relationship between them.]

{**Run-on eliminated**} David's whole life now revolved around his Sting Ray; he could think of nothing else.

▶ **Make one of the clauses run together dependent on the other clause.**

{**Run-on**} The only problem was that while David "detailed" his 'Vette, his business manager, Maxwell Maverick, had to cancel three concerts for Microwave Katz Barrett had completely lost interest in the group.

[The sentence needs to be rewritten to show the relationship between the two independent clauses.]

{**Run-on eliminated**} The only problem was that while David "detailed" his 'Vette, his business manager, Maxwell Maverick, had to cancel three concerts for Microwave Katz because Barrett had completely lost interest in the group.

Rewrite the following sentences to eliminate any run-on sentences.

1. Desperate, Maxwell Maverick racked his brain to find a way to get David to forget his car he knew they would all go broke unless he did something drastic.

2. Two more days elapsed with Barrett refusing to leave the Corvette except to sleep a revelation finally came to Maverick in a dream.

3. Early on the morning of the seventh day of Barrett's addiction to the Corvette, Maverick called Lucinda Leverage, President of Barrett's fan club he spoke with her urgently for fifteen minutes.

4. At ten o'clock that same morning Lucinda walked into the Ruralia First National Bank she asked to talk to the head cashier.

5. At ten fifteen the head cashier issued a stop-payment order on a check from Lucinda Leverage to Walter Toth's Used Sport Cars at first Toth was outraged but after Lucinda talked to him, he approved her strategy.

6. At eleven o'clock a wrecker from Walter Toth's garage appeared before Barrett's house the red Corvette disappeared down the driveway David was so shocked he was speechless.

7. At nine o'clock that night Barrett gyrated once again with Microwave Katz on the stage of the Clear Lake Coliseum in the first row stood Lucinda Leverage, waving a set of keys.

10D

CHAPTER

Problems with Modifiers?

11

Terms you need to know

Adverb. A word that gives information about verbs, adjectives, other adverbs, and sometimes an entire sentence.

Adjective. A word that gives information about nouns and pronouns.

Linking verb. Forms of the verb *to be* and others like it that *link* the subject to the modifier that describes it. Some other common linking verbs are *seem*, *appear*, and *feel*.

Modifier. A word, phrase, or clause that gives information about another word, phrase, or clause. Writers use modifiers, mainly adjectives, adverbs, and modifying phrases, to make important qualifications in their writing, to make it more accurate, and sometimes to give it color and depth.

Dangling modifier. A modifying phrase that seems unattached because the reader has trouble finding the word or phrase that it modifies.

Misplaced modifier. A modifying word or phrase that is ambiguous because it could modify more than one thing.

Absolute. A phrase that modifies a sentence, but is not part of its grammar. Unlike other modifying phrases, an absolute does not have to modify a specific word in the sentence.

11A

> *absolute*
> **The student presidential campaign beginning**, Abel Gonzalez needed to find a popular issue.

11A WHERE DO YOU PLACE ADJECTIVES?

Troubleshooting

Most adjectives precede the noun or pronouns they modify. The noun acts like a magnet, attaching the adjective to it: **red** *Ferrari*; **uncoordinated** *athlete*. Yet it's possible to place adjectives in such a way that their meaning is ambiguous to a reader:

{**Ambiguous**} Abel sought the always *unpredictable* students' votes. (*unpredictable* attaches itself to *students* instead of to *votes*.)

{**Clarified**} Abel sought the students' votes, always unpredictable.

{**Ambiguous**} He tried to think of some *unpopular* administrator's decision. (*unpopular* attaches itself to *administrator* instead of to *decision*.)

{**Clarified**} He tried to think of an unpopular decision by some administrator.

If your readers say, "I can't tell which noun this word goes with," you need to check to see that your adjectives are next to the noun or phrase they modify.

Adjectives may also follow a noun or pronoun. Placing two or more adjectives after a noun can add style to a sentence and help avoid a piling up of adjectives before a word.

To handle adjectives effectively . . .

▶ **Relocate adjectives that are potentially confusing or ambiguous.** You may have to read your sentences carefully to appreciate how they might be *misread*.

> {**Ambiguous**} The old congressman's records were revealing. (Does *old* go with *congressman* or with *records?*)

> {**Clarified**} The congressman's old records were revealing.

> {**Ambiguous**} The dismal student's room caused quite a furor. (Does *dismal* go with *student* or with *room?*)

> {**Clarified**} The student's dismal room caused quite a furor.

▶ **Consider placing adjectives after the word or phrase they modify.** A sentence may be made more graceful or readable with adjectives placed after a noun or pronoun. When you are managing two or more adjectives, see what happens to the sentence when you move them after the word or phrase they modify.

> In order to mount a strong campaign for student body president, Abel Gonzalez needed a major issue, *popular and dramatic*.

> Cafeteria food, *mediocre and unappetizing*, seemed like a natural rallying point.

Rearrange the adjectives in each of these sentences to make the sentences clearer or more effective.

1. Abel practiced his boring politician's speech on his little brother.
2. Simple and pure food was going to be the center of his campaign.
3. He could try to blame the miserable manager's attitudes for some of the problems.
4. But he needed to find a conspicuous cook's disaster to create true drama.
5. Happily he began to lay his elemental but clever plan.

11B

11B HOW DO YOU HANDLE PREDICATE ADJECTIVES?

Term you need to know

> **Predicate adjective.** An adjective that follows a linking verb and gives more information about the subject of the sentence.
>
> Political campaigns can be *expensive*.
>
> A good candidate feels *confident*.
>
> The prospects for Abel look *bad*.

Troubleshooting

Do you wonder what a predicate adjective is? Do you sometimes find yourself confused about which word you should use to complete sentences that use those pesky linking verbs like *seem*, *feel*, *grow*, *become*, *look*, and others? If so, you have plenty of company. In this tricky area, your first tactic should be to determine which word you want to link the modifier to. If that word is the subject, use an adjective to complete the link.

To handle predicate adjectives correctly . . .

▶ **Be sure to use an adjective to modify a noun, not an adverb.** If you are going to complete the linking verb of a sentence with a word that you want to attach to the *subject* of that sentence, you need to use an adjective because you are modifying a noun. In the following examples, the first version of the sentence shows the incorrect adverb modifier italicized; the second version shows the correct adjective form.

{**Problem**} Abel feels a little *guiltily* about jeopardizing some people's jobs.

[The word describes Abel so it should be an adjective.]

{**Solution**} Abel feels a little guilty about jeopardizing some people's jobs.

{**Problem**} He knows he may look *badly* to the administration.

[Again, the word describes Abel, not the verb *look*.]

{**Solution**} He knows he may look bad to the administration.

{**Problem**} Nevertheless, he feels *confidently* about the outcome.

[The term modifies *he*, so it must be an adjective.]

{**Improved**} Nevertheless, he feels confident about the outcome.

> **Tip:** Remember that most of the time you shouldn't use a word with an *-ly* ending after a linking verb.

11B

Bad/Badly

From an episode of NBC-TV's *Cheers*, first aired December 18, 1986.

The patrons of the bar are watching a videotape of Diane attempting (with little success) to dance ballet.

DIANE
(oblivious to taunts)
Ever since I was a child I wanted to dance so badly.

NORMAN
It looks like you got your wish.

● **Fine Tuning**

Among the trickiest modifiers are *good* and *well*. *Good* is always an adjective; *well* is usually an adverb but sometimes it too can be an adjective. No wonder writers sometimes get confused about which one they should use. Here are some quick guidelines.

—Use *good* after a linking verb when you want to link the modifier to the subject. For example,

> Abel Gonzalez looks **good**.
>
> His scholastic record is **good**.
>
> His karma seems **good**.
>
> He feels **good** about his plan for a demonstration.

—But when you are referring to someone's state of health, you should use *well* to finish the linking verb.

Granted, most students are **well** in spite of the substandard food.

—Except in very casual conversation with your close friends, it's not a good idea to use *good* as an adverb. For example, don't write

Abel's car runs **good**.

The cook's job doesn't pay **good**.

Instead, write

Abel's car runs **well**.

The cook's job doesn't pay **well**.

EXERCISE 11.2

In these sentences, replace the italicized modifier with a better one or move it into the right position.

1. Abel began his campaign against the *unsavory* Santini's Campus Catering Company by putting an announcement in the *Daily Toxin*.
2. In it he asked anyone who thought Clear Lake College cafeteria food was not cooked *good* to meet in front of the cafeteria at 7:00 Sunday night.
3. At first, he felt *guiltily* about his plan because two of his good friends sometimes cooked for Santini's.
4. But after he once more tasted the stuff that Santini's passed off for pizza, he didn't feel so *badly*.

11C WHERE DO YOU POSITION ADVERBS?

Troubleshooting

Adverbs are generally easy to work with because they can take several different positions in a sentence, and you can move them around to get different effects. For instance,

Abel made his plans *carefully*, humming *softly* to himself.

or

Carefully Abel made his plans, *softly* humming to himself.

or

Abel *carefully* made his plans, humming to himself *softly*.

Because adverbs are so flexible, it's easy to get them in an inappropriate place, particularly if the sentence has two verbs and the adverb might modify either one of them. The result may be a confusing or ambiguous sentence like this.

11C

Overcooking pork chops effectively incinerates them. (Does *effectively* go with *overcooking* or *incinerates?*)

To position adverbs accurately . . .

▶ **Check to see that you have placed your adverbs so that your reader can't get confused about which words they modify.** Sometimes you may want to ask a friend to help you double-check for misplaced modifiers.

{**Adverb misplaced**} Watching the crowd gather *quickly* Abel realized he had underestimated students' feelings.

[The reader doesn't know whether *quickly* goes with *gather* or *realized*.]

{**Adverb repositioned**} Watching the crowd gather Abel *quickly* realized he had underestimated students' feelings.

[A comma after *gather* in both sentences would also help.]

{**Adverb misplaced**} To get the crowd to support him *immediately* he began to look for an angle.

[The reader doesn't know if *immediately* goes with *to support* or *to look*.]

{**Adverb repositioned**} To get the crowd to support him he immediately began to look for an angle.

[Again, a comma after *him* would help in both sentences.]

▶ **Be sure the adverbs** *almost* **and** *even* **are next to the words they modify.** These common words are adverbs that can cause confusion in a sentence. Notice the ambiguities they create in the following sentences because they are misplaced.

{**Adverb misplaced**} Abel *almost* knew every dish the cafeteria featured.

[Putting *almost* next to *knew* instead of *every* confuses the meaning.]

11C

{**Adverb repositioned**} Abel knew almost every dish the cafeteria featured.

{**Adverb misplaced**} He had *even* tasted the Lo-Cal Calypso Delight, raw cabbage and cauliflower with coconut and catsup dressing.

[*Even* could modify *tasted* here, but it really goes with *the Lo-Cal Calypso Delight.*]

{**Adverb repositioned**} He had tasted even the Lo-Cal Calypso Delight, raw cabbage and cauliflower with coconut and catsup dressing.

▶ **Place the adverb** *only* **directly before the word you want it to modify in a sentence.** The word *only* has one specific meaning: *this one and no other.* Writers tend to let *only* drift around in sentences, slipping into positions where it can be confusing.

{**Confusing** *only*} Abel *only* knew one person who claimed not to mind the cafeteria food.

[Could be misinterpreted to mean that Abel was the only person who knew someone who didn't mind the food.]

{*Only* **repositioned**} Abel knew only one person, Misty Green, who claimed not to mind the cafeteria food.

{**Confusing** *only*} Misty only thought about whether the food had ever been alive, not how it tasted.

> [Could be misinterpreted to mean that Misty never thought about any other topic except whether the food had ever been alive.]

{*Only* **repositioned**} Misty thought only about whether the food had ever been alive.

EXERCISE 11.3

Rewrite the sentences in which the adverbs are misplaced and could be misinterpreted.

1. Misty thought slaughtering animals cruelly exploited them.
2. Coming upon a dead bug in one's rice unexpectedly disrupts one's meal.
3. The cafeteria manager only seems to remember his days cooking in a commune in the sixties.
4. He doesn't believe his cooking badly upsets anyone.
5. He even thinks the students' parents like his food.

11D PROBLEMS WITH DOUBLE NEGATIVES?

Term you need to know

> **Double negative.** A statement in which a second negative word unnecessarily repeats a negative already in the statement.
>
> Misty *doesn't* like *nothing* with meat in it.

Troubleshooting

Chances are you don't use double negatives like *don't never do that* and *didn't do nothing*. You may, however, have problems with the *concealed* negative adverbs *hardly*, *scarcely*, and *barely*, which don't look like real negatives, but are. When you're editing, watch for such words and then check to be sure you haven't used another negative such as *none*, *never*, *not*, or *nothing*.

To avoid double negatives . . .

▶ **Don't mix the negative adverbs *hardly*, *scarcely*, or *barely* with another negative word or phrase.** If you do, you will have a sentence with a double negative in it, not considered standard English. Here are some examples of such faulty usage.

11D

> {**Double negative**} When Abel realized that the cafeteria issue could be a political gold mine, he *couldn't hardly* wait to get organized.

> {**One negative removed**} When Abel realized that the cafeteria issue could be a political gold mine, he could hardly wait to get organized.

> {**Double negative**} He *didn't scarcely* have time to get much help from other students.

> {**One negative removed**} He scarcely had time to get much help from other students.

> {**Double negative**} He *hadn't barely* thought of a plan himself.

> {**One negative removed**} He had barely thought of a plan himself.

EXERCISE 11.4

Rewrite any of the sentences that contain double negatives to eliminate the problem. Not every sentence is faulty.

1. Some studious souls don't hardly notice what they eat.
2. Others can't barely wait to register a complaint.

3. Abel's friend Melinda scarcely ever makes a fuss about food.
4. But even she can't hardly tolerate the cafeteria's pseudo-pizzas.
5. I don't scarcely see how they have avoided poisoning some-one.

11E PROBLEMS WITH ADVERB FORM?

Troubleshooting

Do you get confused about the difference between *slow* and *slowly*, *tight* and *tightly*, and *quick* and *quickly*, wondering why it seems to be all right to say *Tie it tight* or *Drive slow* instead of using *slowly* and *tightly* to modify the verbs in those phrases? That's hardly surprising. These adverbs have two forms, either of which can be correct in certain situations.

To be sure you are using a correct adverb form . . .

▶ **Remember that many adverbs have both short and long forms.** Here are some examples.

slow/slowly	tight/tightly
quick/quickly	rough/roughly
fair/fairly	deep/deeply

Examples:

The Redskins play *rough*.	The Redskins play *roughly*.
Connie drives *slow*.	Connie drives *slowly*.
Darwin writes *quick*.	Darwin writes *quickly*.
Richard plays *fair*.	Richard plays *fairly*.
Pull that knot *tight*.	Pull that knot *tightly*.

In most cases, the short form of the adverb sounds more casual than the long form. Consequently, in most academic and busi-ness situations you will be better off using the *-ly* form. For example, in these sentences you should use the long form.

Abel thought *deeply* (not *deep*) about what he should do.

He wanted to be sure all the parties involved were treated *fairly* (not *fair*).

Misty turned *slowly* (not *slow*) to see what the protesters were doing.

We cannot give you a fixed rule for deciding when to employ the short form of these adverbs. When in doubt, you're probably better off using the long form.

Troubleshooting

Many adverbs are made by adding *-ly* to an adjective; for instance, words like *considerably*, *differently*, *confidentially*, and *seriously* form one such group. Another group contains words like *surely* and *really*. Although the adjective forms—*considerable*, *different*, *serious*, *sure*, and others—are used frequently in colloquial conversation, they are not generally considered acceptable as adverb forms when one is doing public writing or speaking.

▶ **Use the adverb form ending in *-ly* in most writing situations.** Here are some examples that show the colloquial and formal usages.

{**Colloquial**} Abel worried *considerable* about how President Shade was going to react to his parade around the campus.

[*Considerable* should be *considerably* because it modifies *worried*.]

{**Standard**} Abel worried considerably about how President Shade was going to react to his parade around the campus.

{**Colloquial**} Not that President Shade had been *real* loyal to Santini's food service—she hadn't.

[*Real* should be *really* because it modifies the adjective *loyal*.]

{**Standard**} Not that President Shade had been really loyal to Santini's food service—she hadn't.

{**Colloquial**} Perhaps, then, she wouldn't take it all too *serious*.

[*Serious* should be *seriously* because it modifies the verb *take*.]

{**Standard**} Perhaps, then, she wouldn't take it all too seriously.

EXERCISE 11.5

Rewrite the following sentences, correcting the misplaced adverbs and replacing nonstandard adverb forms with appropriate ones when necessary.

1. Abel was real surprised when more than 500 students showed up in response to his announcement in the *Toxin*.
2. Some of them had already made banners that showed they took the protest serious.
3. A number of them were waving energetically printed signs.
4. Others were thumping cafeteria trays and chanting loud.
5. Abel could see that he needed to get working quick to organize this energy.

11F PROBLEMS WITH MISPLACED OR DANGLING MODIFIERS?

Troubleshooting

As we explained in the first part of this chapter, words tend to act as magnets to modifiers that precede them and inexorably pick up their meaning whether that is what the writer intended or not. If you write a sentence with a modifying adverbial or adjectival phrase that is not next to the word it should modify, your sentence is going to "derail." Two forms of this problem are *misplaced modifying phrases* and *dangling modifiers*.

A misplaced modifier is a modifier that isn't placed next to the word it modifies.

> *Being short of money*, the plan Abel devised had to be modest. (It is Abel, not the plan, who is short of money.)

A dangling modifier occurs when a writer pens a sentence with a modifying phrase but doesn't supply anywhere in the sentence a word it could sensibly modify. As a result the modifier just hangs there with nothing to attach to.

> *Before deciding on a strategy*, a place has to be chosen. (The italicized phrase doesn't fit with anything in the main part of the sentence.)

To eliminate misplaced or dangling modifiers . . .

▶ **Be sure that a modifying phrase is close to the word it modifies.** Ask yourself who or what does what the modifying phrase says. (Often the word or phrase modified will be the subject of the sentence.) Then make any necessary revisions. You may have to supply a word that the phrase can modify; in some cases, the whole sentence may have to be rearranged.

> {**Misplaced modifier**} *Having learned to cook in a commune*, the preferences of Darby the chef leaned toward squash casseroles and bean sprout sandwiches.
>
> > [The italicized phrase doesn't describe *preferences*, the word closest to it, but Darby the chef.]
>
> {**Revision**} Having learned to cook in a commune, Darby the chef preferred squash casseroles and bean sprout sandwiches.
>
> {**Misplaced modifier**} On the other hand, many of the students came from small midwestern towns *that liked beef and pork.*
>
> > [The italicized phrase doesn't describe *towns*, the word closest to it, but the students. Different revisions are possible.]

{**Revision #1**} On the other hand, many of the students came from small midwestern towns and liked beef and pork.

{**Revision #2**} On the other hand, many of the students, coming from small midwestern towns, liked beef and pork.

▶ **Supply a word for a dangling modifier to modify.** This often means rewriting the entire sentence since you must usually add a word or phrase that the sentence alludes to but doesn't actually include. For example:

{**Dangling modifier**} *On leaving the commune*, a job was hard to find.

[There is nothing in the sentence for *On leaving the commune* to modify. In this case, the entire sentence can be revised to include Darby the chef.]

{**Revision**} When Darby the chef left the commune, he had a hard time finding a job.

{**Dangling modifier**} *Considering it one of the less desirable places to work*, his first choice would not have been cooking for college students.

[Again, the italicized phrase dangles; there isn't a noun for it to modify. The sentence must be revised.]

{**Revision**} Considering such a job undesirable, Darby would not have chosen to cook for college students.

> Tip: You are less likely to get yourself in a tangle with modifiers if you consistently use people or concrete things as the subject of your sentences. When you follow that guideline, it's easier to keep modifiers under control.

● Fine Tuning

Some introductory modifying phrases may look like misplaced modifiers but are actually *absolute modifiers*; that is, they are complete in themselves, serving only to give additional information about the sentence of which they are a part. Writers find such absolute modifiers useful so it's important to learn to distinguish them from faulty constructions.

> *Given the circumstances*, no single person was to blame for the bad food.
>
> *To be quite honest*, the manager of the cafeteria hadn't eaten there for years

11F

In order to distinguish an absolute modifier that *does* work from a misplaced or dangling modifier that *doesn't* work, often you will just have to trust your judgment. Ask yourself, "Is there any possible confusion here? Does the sentence work?" If you are satisfied with your answers, the modifier is probably all right.

EXERCISE 11.6

Rewrite these sentences, placing modifiers in appropriate positions. Not all of the sentences need to be revised.

1. Trying to look very official and confident, the efforts to organize the parade got under way.
2. Turning toward the main building, signs began to appear.
3. "Beeves, not Leaves," said one sign, marching happily along in front of the building.
4. "Quash the Squash" and "Ban the Beansprouts" proclaimed other waving vigorously students.
5. To be honest, even the watching cooks had to laugh.

11G PROBLEMS WITH COMPARATIVES AND SUPERLATIVES?

Terms you need to know

Comparative and superlative. Adjectives and adverbs can express three different levels or degrees of intensity—the positive, the comparative, and the superlative. The positive level describes a single object, the comparative ranks two objects, the superlative three or more:

Positive	Comparative	Superlative
cold	colder	coldest
angry	more (less) angry	most (least) angry
angrily	more (less) angrily	most (least) angrily

Troubleshooting

Most of the time you can simply trust your instincts when you use the comparative forms for adverbs and adjectives. As a general rule, you add *-er* and *-est* endings to one-syllable adjectives and adverbs but put the comparative terms *more* and *most* before words of two or more syllables. It seems natural to add endings to *smart* to make *smarter* and *smartest* but to use *more* and *most* when you want to compare a word like *active* or *hostile*.

Two problems typically arise with comparatives and superlatives. The first is mistakenly using a superlative form when comparing only two objects.

Abel was the *tallest* of the two leaders. [should be *taller*]

Francie was the *most talented* of the two writers. [should be *more talented*]

A less frequent error involves doubling the comparative and superlative forms, using both the ending (*-er*, *-est*) and *more* and *most*.

That was the *most unkindest* cut of all. [should be *most unkind* or *unkindest*]

The cooks acted the *least friendliest* about the protest. [should be *least friendly* or *unfriendliest*]

To avoid problems with comparisons . . .

▶ **Be sure to use the comparative form when you are comparing two objects.** Ordinarily that means using an adverb or adjective with an *-er* ending or modified by *more* or *less*.

> {**Faulty comparison**} Darby was the *best* of the two cooks.
>
> > [*Best* is the superlative, not the comparative, form.]
>
> {**Revised**} Darby was the *better* of the two cooks.
>
> {**Faulty comparison**} Celeste, the other cook, was the *most imaginative* although that wasn't necessarily good.
>
> > [*Most imaginative* is the superlative, not the comparative, form.]
>
> {**Revised**} Celeste, the other cook, was the *more imaginative* although that wasn't necessarily good.

▶ **Use the superlative form when comparing more than two objects or qualities.** In most cases when you compare three or more things or qualities, you need to use *-est* adjectives or adverbs or preface the modifiers with *most* or *least*.

> Given a choice of several recipes, Celeste would choose the one that was the *most* vegetarian.
>
> Of all the cooks Santini had ever hired, she was probably the *worst*.

▶ **Do not double the comparative or superlative forms.** Don't confuse your reader by using two comparative forms in the same phrase. When you have made one comparison, that's enough.

{**Confusing**} Celeste was *more happier* at her job than Darby was.

{**Clear**} Celeste was *happier* at her job than Darby was.

{**Confusing**} Abel was the *most angriest* about the food of all the students on campus.

{**Clear**} Abel was the *angriest* about the food of all the students on campus.

EXERCISE 11.7

Rewrite these sentences and correct any faulty comparative or superlative modifiers.

1. Abel couldn't decide which was the worst-tasting dish, barbecued tofu or curried eggs.
2. But he granted that the pizza had to be the most awfullest of all.
3. His plan was to draw the least angriest of the student leaders into his protest.
4. After all, of the two possible leaders for the protest, he didn't want the most radical one.
5. When the time came to negotiate, he would have to deal with either Dean Rack or President Shade, and he needed to figure out which would be the most formidable opponent.

11H PROBLEMS WITH ABSOLUTE ADJECTIVES?

Term you need to know

> **Absolute adjective.** A word like *perfect*, *unique*, *dead*, or *equal* that cannot have degrees. One cannot be *less equal* or *more dead*.

Troubleshooting

A few words express qualities that can't logically be compared; for instance, *unique* means the only one of its kind so it doesn't make sense to say *more unique*; *perfect* means without any faults so it doesn't make sense to say *less perfect*. *Equal* means exactly the same amount so logically we can hardly say something is *more equal* any more than we can say it is *more empty*. A container is either empty or it's not.

To handle absolute adjectives correctly . . .

▶ **Be sure not to add qualifiers to words that already express an extreme: something that cannot be compared or compromised.** In conversation, of course, we frequently use such expressions, but in writing, it's a good idea to be careful not to use comparatives with the following words: *unique, perfect, singular, empty, equal, full, definite,* and, of course, *pregnant.*

11H

Thus it's not good usage to write, "Misty thought it was the *most perfect* vegetable soup she had ever eaten," or "The cafeteria is *emptier* at night than in the morning." Soup is either perfect or less than perfect. A cafeteria is either empty, or someone is in it.

EXERCISE 11.8

Revise any faulty modifiers in the following sentences.

1. With the help of Francie Knipstein, Abel arranged to get all the protesting students to gather in front of the cafeteria again at noon on Monday to stage the most unique march in the history of Clear Lake College.
2. Each carried a red cafeteria tray with an extra full dish of some food and a sign describing that creation.
3. Signs said things like "Murderous Mashed Potatoes," "Pathetic Pasta," "Gruesome Granola," and "Egregious Egg-

plant"—that last was Connie showing off that she had a more perfect vocabulary than the others.

4. Even Dean Rack said the parade was the most singular he had seen.

5. President Shade's comment was milder; she just called it a most definite success.

111 TOO MANY MODIFIERS?

Troubleshooting

Mark Twain once said, "About the adjective—when in doubt, don't use it." That's usually good advice for adverbs too. Sometimes when you intend a passage to be colorful and descriptive, it's easy to get carried away and overdo the modifiers, laying on descriptive words like chocolate frosting. But remember how you groan inwardly when you encounter excessive description. You may enjoy it at first, but then your mind starts to "hydroplane" over the "sparkling" passage, thinking "I don't need to know this," or "this is overwritten."

> Francie claimed that the food at the Mayfield cafeteria downtown was wonderful—superb cheesecake, lovely glazed hams, elegant pies and puddings, mouth-watering molded salads, crisp and crusty breads, and fresh, dewy melons and other fruit.

It's really too much description. You get tired of all those adjectives.

Another problem is that when you use too many modifiers, you're *telling* your readers about something rather than *showing* it to them, and that's not good writing. People don't want to be told everything; they'd rather *see* it.

> The students looked like they thought the parade was lots of fun. They were in high spirits and having a marvelous good time. [Dull sentences that tell you what to think but don't give you a picture.]

Parading round the campus the students laughed, twirled trays on their fingers, and now and then dashed out to dance with the spectators. [This sentence uses active verbs instead of adjectives to create a picture.]

To keep modifiers under control . . .

▶ **Believe in the modifiers you select.** Choose them for what they say, not how they sound. If you find yourself embroidering your writing with adjectives like *shimmering* and *magnificent* or adverbs like *savagely* and *egregiously*, be sure those are the words that best suit your subject. See also our reminder about "whoopee words."

> Abel was *terribly* proud of his work and thought the parade was a *smashing* success. [Such overblown modifiers add little to the sentence.]

> He thought it would be a *magnificent* triumph to be able to say he had changed the *revolting, wretched* food at the cafeteria. [Such strong modifiers overstate the point and clutter the sentence.]

▶ **Cut out those pale but overused adverbs *definitely*, *terribly*, *very*, *really*, *actually*, and *so* as much as possible when you edit.** They are fuzzy intensifiers that seldom add significant information to your papers and can irritate your readers.

> Francie *definitely* hoped that their protests would *really* improve lunch at Clear Lake College.

> She wasn't *terribly* optimistic, however, because she had heard *so* many complaints before and *very* little had *actually* come of them.

Notice that cutting all the italicized words would give you stronger, clearer writing.

> Francie hoped their protest would improve lunch at Clear Lake College. She wasn't optimistic, however, because she had heard many complaints before and little had come of them.

Rewrite these sentences to eliminate overblown modifiers and fuzzy intensifiers.

1. The wonderful parade wound sinuously around the cafeteria, up the steps of the impressive administration building, and came to a full halt before President Shade's office.
2. She looked out over the beautiful green mall, lush and shimmering with the sparkling morning dew.
3. She suddenly felt terribly sad that these fine upstanding young college students were so miserably unhappy with the food at her very own college.
4. She was definitely even more upset when she looked at some of the awful samples of wretched food the students were carrying.
5. "I certainly had not realized the food was so egregiously bad," she said.
6. "Starting this very day I'm going to launch a full-scale, sweeping investigation into this dreadful situation," she said.
7. "Abel Gonzalez and Francie Knipstein, I'm asking you to form an official working committee that will thoroughly and systematically look into every single aspect of the menu planning and cooking operation at the cafeteria."
8. "We must get right to the very heart of this pernicious and intolerable situation."
9. Smiling broadly, she looked out at the crowd, expecting to see sunshiny and happy faces at her wonderful announcement.
10. Instead she noticed that Abel was really frowning glumly, unutterably furious with himself that he had been conned into doing something about his own stupid complaints.

111

CHAPTER

How Do You Manage Transitions?

■ **A**   Diagnosing problems with transitions

■ **B**   Improving transitions

12

Terms you need to know

Transitions. Connecting words and phrases that help readers move from one unit to the next in your writing. They help to hold a piece of writing together, bridging gaps and linking sentences and paragraphs.

Expletive construction. The words *there* and *it* used as lead-ins to sentences.

It is going to be a day to remember.

There were hundreds of spectators watching the demonstrators.

Introduction

When you write, you take your readers on a journey, and you certainly don't want them to get lost. Unfortunately, however, if you give them any opportunity to do so, they usually will. They'll miss turns, go off in the wrong direction, or fall through gaps you have left. If that seems to happen to your readers frequently, it may be because they're not reading attentively, but it may also be your doing. When they say, "Hey, I'm lost," or your teacher tells you that you have problems with transitions, you should acknowledge that you do.

Ask yourself if you have started your readers off in the right direction with a strong first paragraph, and if, as you write, you're *showing them the connections* between sentences by inserting signals and the hooks, links, and signs they need to move them the way you want them to go. The connections between your sentences may seem so obvious to *you* that it's hard to realize your readers need help. This chapter will give you some suggestions about how you can provide that help.

12A WHERE DO PROBLEMS WITH TRANSITIONS OCCUR?

Troubleshooting

The best linking devices are *underlying* and *internal*. That is, the best way to keep readers from getting lost in your writing is to craft it around a pattern or design that lets them know what to expect and carries them along naturally; for example, you might use a cause and effect or a comparison/contrast pattern (Section 3B). But even with such a pattern, you sometimes need to use the *external* transitional terms, those visible hooks, links, and directional signals that give the reader specific pointers to keep them on track. That is the principal kind of transitions we discuss in this section.

Skillful transitions, internal or external, keep your writing from seeming choppy and amateurish. Smooth-flowing, tightly unified writing is one of the unfailing marks of a skilled writer. Your readers will enjoy your prose more if you take the time to sand smooth the joints in a paper. To do that, of course, you need to understand where the joints are.

To diagnose problems with transitions . . .

▶ **Pay attention to the types of sentences you are writing.** Do you frequently write paragraphs made up of a series of mostly simple sentences with very few commas? Do you avoid complex and compound sentences (see Section 9A)? If so, you may be producing a choppy, disconnected style. That's because your simple sentences may not be showing relationships between the ideas they are expressing. You may be doing little more than listing concepts, not analyzing them. Writers who avoid the connections implied by more complex sentences are sometimes leaving the work of thinking to their readers.

Here's an example of a paragraph where the sentence structures seem too simple to connect ideas significantly. All the sentences are fairly short with similar patterns and no commas. And sure enough, although you don't get lost in the paragraph, the style is choppy and graceless. As a result, the writing seems thin and amateurish.

12A

{**Weak transitions**} Ombudsman Hector Stavros' mother, Hilary Stavros, is 58 years old. She is a passionate believer in exercise. She lives by what she preaches. She won a blue ribbon in the Golden Oldies 10 kilometer run last week. She swims a mile before breakfast every morning. She works out on the Nautilus machines. She walks three miles on the treadmills every morning. While she walks, she listens to Perry Como on her Sony Walkman.

Here is a revised version with some sentences combined and others connected with transitional terms (italicized).

{**Revised**} Ombudsman Hector Stavros' mother, 58-year-old Hilary Stavros, is a passionate believer in exercise, *who* lives by what she preaches. *Just last week* she won a blue ribbon in the Golden Oldies 10 kilometer run. *Not only* does she swim a mile before breakfast every morning, *but* she works out on the Nautilus machines, and walks three miles on the treadmill every morning, listening to Perry Como as she exercises.

▶ **Evaluate the structure of your sentences.** Do your sentences have few of the typical dependent clause signals such as *although, if, since, because, so,* and *unless?* If so, you may not be clearly showing connections between your ideas.

{**Weak transitions**} Ms. Stavros has been watching Clear Lake College students' exercise habits. She has decided the kids don't have the right stuff anymore. They should be young and healthy. They claim they don't have the energy to exercise. They are exhausted from studying. They would rather sleep late and ride the bus to school. They are too tired to work out after classes. She thinks the habit becomes a vicious cycle.

You get no sense of the subordination of one idea to another in this paragraph. Does "exhausted from study" relate to "they don't have energy" or to "they would rather sleep late"? Here is a revised version with better connections; the transitional terms are italicized.

12A

{**Revised**} *Since* Ms. Stavros has been watching Clear Lake College students' exercise habits, she has decided the kids don't have the right stuff anymore. *Although* they should be young and healthy, they claim they don't have the energy to exercise. *Because* they are exhausted from studying, they would rather sleep late and ride the bus to school. *Then*, since they are too tired to work out after classes, the habit becomes a vicious cycle.

▶ **Be suspicious of expletive constructions.** Do you tend to write a lot of sentences beginning with the strung-out constructions *There is*, *It is*, and *There are*? If so, you may be putting together groups of sentences that are weakly connected, and you may also be creating a monotonous rhythm in your paper.

{**Weak transitions**} It is Hilary Stavros' personal credo that "Exercise is like money. It's good for almost everything." It is the slogan on her car bumper. There is the same slogan stamped on the back of her workout T-shirts. It is also painted across the back of her running shorts. It is a point of pride with her that she consistently shows that back to runners twenty years younger than she is.

Again, you get little sense of the relationship between these sentences, and the repetitious patterns are boring. Here is the paragraph reworked with sentences streamlined and transitional terms italicized.

> {**Revised**} Hilary Stavros' personal slogan is "Exercise is like money. It's good for almost everything." *That* slogan is on her car bumper, stamped across the back of her workout T-shirts, and painted across the back of her running shorts, *and* it is a point of pride with her that she consistently shows that back to runners twenty years younger than she is.

▶ **Pay attention to sequences of time and order.** Do you have few words that indicate time or sequence, words like *once, when, ago, formerly, finally,* and *after* that help readers position themselves in your article? You may be leaving out important guideposts for your readers.

> {**Weak transitions**} Stavros has not always been an athlete. She started ten years ago. She was a flabby woman who didn't know her biceps from her pectorals. She had hamstrings so tight she could hardly bend over. She had little soft pouches bulging over her belt. She had 30 percent body fat. Her breath was short. She could hardly walk up a hill.

The effect is choppy and disconnected. Here is a revision with hooks and transitions italicized.

> {**Revised**} Stavros has not always been an athlete. *When* she started exercising ten years *ago*, she was a flabby woman who didn't know her biceps from her pectorals *and* whose hamstrings were so tight she could hardly bend over. *With* 30 percent body fat, little pouches bulged over her belt. Her breath was *so* short she could hardly walk up a hill.

▶ **Look for connectives of all kinds.** Does your writing have few of the common connective words like *and, but, or, too, moreover, consequently, nevertheless, therefore,* and *also?* If so, the cracks and seams in your work are probably showing, and your writing will seem fragmented.

{**Weak transitions**} Her inspiration came from her son Hector Stavros. He was in poor condition. She got tired of looking at him falling onto the couch every day after work. He had very little energy. She realized he wouldn't be attractive to women. He might live at home the rest of her life. It was a frightening thought. One of them had to get out of the house on nights and weekends. Hector wasn't interested. It was up to her to act.

You get the feeling of a gap at each period and no strong links between the sentences. Here is the revision with connectives and links italicized.

12A

{**Revised**} Her inspiration came from her son, Hector Stavros, who was *also* in poor condition. He *too* had little energy. She realized he wouldn't be attractive to women *and* might live at home the rest of her life. *That* was a frightening thought. One of them had to get out of the house on nights and weekends, *but* Hector wasn't interested. *Thus* it was up to her to act.

▶ **Check for gaps between paragraphs.** Major transitional problems are most likely to occur as you move from paragraph to paragraph. Be sure you have used some device to link your paragraphs. It can be as simple as repeating a key word at the end of one paragraph and the beginning of the next. Or you might end a paragraph with a question that is answered in the material that follows. Or the gap between paragraphs might be bridged by an appropriate transitional word. Whatever you do, be sure to give your readers some signal of what is to come.

Here are some examples of how a paragraph can be tied in with the one that comes before it.

A. Hilary realized she had a hard task because she had tried to inspire Hector in the past. Then she remembered that sage advice, "You can't change anyone else. You can only change yourself." That was a painful realization, but she felt she couldn't stand to look at Hector any longer.

B. New ideas are hard to come by. It took several tries before she even managed to buy a book to get some help. Then it took another week to decide whether she should try yoga, transcendental meditation, rolfing, or just plain exercise. But at the end of that week she had a plan.

> [Notice the gap between A and B. If paragraph A were to come at the bottom of the page, when you started to read the next page, you would be lost for a few seconds because you can't immediately link "New ideas are hard to come by" with the previous sentence.]

One way is to add a sentence or question at the end of paragraph A.

A1. Where was she going to get a new idea?

or

A2. That was when she began to look for new ideas.

Another way is to rewrite the first sentence of paragraph B so that it contains a link.

B1. *But* Hilary knew that new ideas for *change* are hard to come by.

B2. *So* with an image of Hector in mind, she began to look for ways to *change*.

B3. *So* she set out to *change* herself.

B4. The *realization* made her look for new ideas.

These are only some of the possibilities.

> **Tip:** It's better not to worry too much about transitions while you're writing your first draft. Then you should be thinking about getting down your ideas. While eventually you want those ideas to seem coherent and connected, you will probably do better to wait until your second draft before you start to check for any missing links.

**HOW CAN YOU STRENGTHEN
TRANSITIONS?**

Term you need to know

> **Demonstrative pronoun.** A pronoun that points some-
> thing out: *this*, *that*, *these*, *those*.

Troubleshooting

Once you have learned to diagnose your problems with transitions, you can use a variety of strategies to solve them. The
concept that underlies all of them is this: *Each sentence should
leave a little trace or residue out of which the next sentence
can grow.* An overall plan of organization can be the surest
way of shadowing the entire paper, giving your readers a
confident sense of what lurks in the next section, paragraph, or
sentence. In this section, we offer a few smaller-scale ways by
which you can establish connections between ideas.

To improve your transitions . . .

▶ **Accumulate a stockpile of the conventional transition
words.** When you edit, get in the habit of checking to see if
you need to insert one or more in order to firm up connections
in your writing. But be careful. Transition words and terms
give strong but diverse signals to readers. They say "turn
here," "stop for a qualification," "notice the cause and effect," "here's something similar," or "here's something different." You cannot just grab an expression out of the
transition sack at random and insert it; you have to check the
sense of the sentence you're putting it into and be sure it is the
transitional signal you want.

The most common of these transitional words and phrases
are listed below according to their function.

likewise
similarly   }   showing similarity
in the same way

however instead nevertheless although in spite of on the other hand not only	showing contrast
moreover in addition to for example	showing accumulation
hence consequently therefore as a result of thus	showing consequence
because since for	showing causation
next subsequently after finally first, second, etc.	showing sequence

▶ **Repeat a key idea throughout a paragraph to establish a *motif* or central idea running through it.** An idea can be a key word plus variations. For example, if you are writing a paper about rockets, then *rockets* becomes a key idea that can be repeated through a variety of potential synonyms: *missiles*, *boosters*, *launchers*, *launch vehicles*, and so on. Each word helps to establish a connection to the central topic. In the example below, the key theme of *health* is repeated through synonyms that include *well-being*, *physical condition*, and *vigor*.

On a nasty Monday night in December ten years ago, faced with another evening of Hector and pro football, Hilary Stavros turned to *HEALTH* CLUBS in the Yellow Pages to find some way to get out of the house and work off her frustrations. She located Butcher's Gym and braved the icy streets primarily to save her mental *well-being* but also to improve Hector's *physical condition*. She was afraid she was going to kill him. But the results of that first visit ten years ago have been not only mental *health*, but also physical, emotional, and financial *vigor* for Stavros.

▶ **Use the demonstrative words *this*, *that*, *these*, and *those* within sentences to tie ideas together.** Notice how the italicized pointers in the example hook directly into the previous sentences.

12B

> The change in Stavros has come about gradually, and she points *this* out frequently. Exercise won't turn a flabby 40 + woman with 30 percent body fat into a triathalon champion with 18 percent body fat in a matter of months or even years. *That* kind of claim is ridiculous.

For additional discussion of these important pointers, see Section 15C.

▶ **Use parallel structures and downshifting (see Section 5A) within a paragraph.** Ideas contained within parallel sentences automatically seem equivalent because they share similar arrangements of sentence elements. Ideas that branch off from one another also seem tightly connected. The following example employs both techniques. The first sentence states the topic of the paragraph: the difficulty of a fitness regimen. The next three parallel sentences downshift to develop that main idea. Finally, the last sentence downshifts again to embroider the fourth one, providing one memorable illustration of changed eating habits.

> The middle-aged woman who wants to become really fit *must embark* on a strenuous exercise and diet program that she may find distinctly uncomfortable. She *must work out* at Butcher's Gym at least two hours every day. She *must do* a series of exercises that may leave her muscles sore for a while. She *must change*

her eating habits, trading in chicken salad and choco-late cheesecake for pasta and raw vegetables. At one point, Stavros ate so many carrots that the palms of her hands turned orange.

▶ **Use a semicolon to link two closely related state-ments.** Many writers ignore this useful piece of punctuation. For more details about the semicolon, see Section 17A.

Hilary Stavros no longer worries about what the Methodist Ladies Alliance will think of her pound cake; now her concern is what her classmates at Butcher's Gym will think of her curl-up.

12B

> Tip: We suspect that, for some writers, problems with transitions stem from worrying about how to punctuate sentences. They tend to write simple sentences, but fail to connect them because they're not sure where to put commas and how to use semicolons. They're afraid that if they try to compose the more complex sentences they would prefer to use, their writing will become tangled. So they limit themselves to an immature and choppy style that doesn't do justice to their ideas.
>
> If you think this might be your problem, we suggest that you temporarily forget about the punctuation in those complex or involved sentences and just go ahead and write them. You can figure out how to fix them later, getting help if necessary from an instructor or a writing lab. You'll get more points for a smooth, tightly unified style than you will for having all your commas in the right place.

EXERCISE 12.1

Underline the transitional words and phrases in the following paragraph.

On that December night ten years ago when she trudged to Butcher's Gym to improve her health, Hilary Stavros never dreamed that today she would be famous. She would have scoffed at that possibility as ridiculous. Yet she is now probably the best known citizen of Ruralia, at least among the over-fifty group. Her book *Fit and Foxy After Fifty* is on the best-seller list in Walden's Books, and the next selection for the national Golden Age Book Club. And anyone who gets up as early as she does—5:00 a.m.—can see her on the popular morning exercise program, Dawn Control, jumping and hopping and shouting, "Move it, move it, don't you lose it. Endorphins, endorphins, yea, yea, yea!"

12B

EXERCISE 12.2

Rewrite the following paragraph to improve the transitions.

It is unfortunate that Hector Stavros, Hilary's son, is not pleased with his mother. He is still a couch potato. Monday nights find him glued to the TV screen. He is watching football or reruns of *Newhart*. He would prefer that his mother act her age. It's unseemly for her to wear leotards and work out at Butcher's Gym. He fears that she might take up with a younger man. She might marry again. He might have to move out of her house. On hearing this, Hilary Stavros' only comment was, "He's right."

PART III GRAMMAR AND USAGE

Grammar and usage are the rules of the language game. Like the length of a football field or the number of outs in an inning of baseball, some rules and usages of grammar are relatively stable and unchanging. Other grammatical "conventions" are modified more often, like the size and weight of a baseball or the rules for tackling a quarterback.

What follows is not a comprehensive description of English grammar, but a sort of "playbook" describing the problems you are most likely to encounter when writing—and the ways to solve them.

CHAPTER

Problems with Verbs and Verbals?

13

Terms you need to know

> **Subject**. The word or phrase that names what a sentence is about. The subject ordinarily performs the action described by the verb in a sentence. A **simple subject** is either a noun or a **nominal**—that is, a word that acts like a noun.
>
> subj
> The *music* played on.
>
> subj.
> *It* disturbed the neighbors.
>
> subj.
> *Turning* the volume down proved to be difficult.

A **complete subject** consists of the subject and all its modifiers.

> complete subj.
> *The music David's band played* sounded raucous.

> complete subj.
> *Keeping the volume down* proved to be even more difficult.

Verb. The word or phrase that establishes the action of a sentence or expresses a state of being.

> verb
> The music **played** on.

> verb
> Turning the volume down **proved** to be difficult.

A verb and all its auxiliaries, modifiers, and complements is called the **predicate** of a sentence.

> complete subject
> *The music played by David's band* **would have**
> predicate
> **continued on throughout the night.**

> complete subject
> *Turning the volume down on the band* **proved to**
> predicate
> **be much more difficult than the neighbors had anticipated it might be.**

Auxiliary verb. A verb, usually some form of *be*, *do*, or *have*, that combines with other verbs to show various relationships of tense, voice, mood, and so on. All the words in boldface are auxiliary verbs: **has** *seen*; **will be** *talking*; **would have been** *going*; **are** *investigating*; **did** *mention*; **should** *prefer*.

Linking verb. A verb, often a form of **to be**, that connects a subject to a word or phrase that extends or completes its meaning. Common linking verbs are **to seem**, **to appear**, **to feel**, and **to become**.

> Oscar Cupperman **is** a Professor of English.
> *Marie* **seems** *suspicious*.

Person. A way of classifying personal pronouns in sentences:

> **1st person**: the speaker—*I*, *we*.
> **2nd person**: the one spoken to—*you*.
> **3rd person**: the person or thing spoken about—*he*, *she*, *it*, *they* + all nouns.

Number. The form a word has or takes to indicate whether it is singular or plural.

Agreement. Verbs and nouns are said to agree in number. This means that with a singular subject in the third person (for example, *he*, *she*, *it*), a verb in the present tense ordinarily adds an -*s* to its base form. With subjects not in the third person singular, the base form of the verb is used.

Third person, singular, present tense:	Jasper complain*s*. He complain*s*. She complain*s*.
First person, singular, present tense:	I complain.
Second person, singular, present tense:	You complain.
First person, plural, present tense.	We complain.
Second person, plural, present tense:	You all complain.
Third person, plural, present tense:	They complain.

13A

13A AGREEMENT: IS THE SUBJECT SINGULAR OR PLURAL?

Troubleshooting

English verbs don't change much to reflect an agreement in number with their subjects—just enough to complicate a writer's life. A change occurs in the present tense with subjects in the third person. The modification involves adding an -s or -es to the base form of the verb:

	Singular	Plural
1st person	I go	we go
2nd person	you go	you go
3rd person	he/she/it go*es*	they go

	Singular	Plural
	I smile	we smile
	you smile	you smile
	he/she/it smile*s*	they smile

Some changes also occur in tenses formed by using auxiliary verbs because two important auxiliary verbs—**to have** and **to be**—are irregular. That is, they do not simply add -*s* in the third person singular. **To have** is only slightly irregular, forming its third person singular by changing **have** to **has**.

I have	we have
you have	you have
he/she/it *has*	they have

To be changes more often, in both the present and past tense.

I *am*	we are	I *was*	we were
you are	you are	you were	you were
he/she/it *is*	they are	he/she/it *was*	they were

Remember that (except with the verb **to be**) you need to worry about agreement only when the subject of a sentence is in the third person and the verb is in the present tense or in a tense requiring an auxiliary verb. With subjects in first or second person, the verb does not add -*s* or -*es*.

{**1st person**} **I** nod sympathetically whenever Mr. Butcher complains about David's band.

{**2nd person**} **You** listen patiently to David's defense of artistic freedom.

{**1st person**} **We** endure a lot from those two chronic complainers.

To choose a correct verb form in the third person, however, you must know whether the subject of a sentence is singular or plural. Sometimes it isn't easy to tell.

In the following sentence, for example, a singular subject *David Barrett* is linked to another possible subject *members of his band* by the expression *together with*. Does the complete subject remain singular or become plural?

> *David,* **together with** his band *members,* (**write? writes?**) songs about his irritable neighbors.

Most subjects joined by **and** are plural. But what happens in a sentence like the following?

> *Peace and quiet* (**was? were?**) what all the neighbors wanted.

Is a subject like *peace and quiet* (or *rum and Coke* or *law and order*) really one idea and, consequently, singular or two ideas and plural?

Just as puzzling are subjects joined by *or* and constructions such as *either . . . or* and *neither . . . nor.*

> *Neither the neighbors nor David* (**is? are?**) eager for trouble.

Finally, there are those indefinite pronouns such as *each, every, none,* and *any* which can seem either singular or plural. How do you select a verb to agree with such a pronoun?

> *Each* (**has? have?**) strong arguments supporting his case.

The guidelines below will help you deal with situations like these.

To be sure subjects and verbs agree in number . . .

▶ **When a subject is tied to another noun by expressions such as *along with, as well as,* or *together with,* pay attention only to the subject.** The verb agrees with it, not with the second noun, which is usually the object of a prepositional phrase.

sing. subj.   plural noun   verb
David, **together with** his band *members*, **writes** songs about his irritable neighbors.

plural subj.   singular noun   verb
The neighbors, **along with** Mr. *Butcher*, **circulate** petitions about the noise.

▶ **When subjects are joined by *and*, treat them as plural in most cases.**

subj.   +   subj.   verb
Mr. Butcher **and** *his neighbors* occasionally **call** David's apartment manager to complain about Microwave Katz.

subj.   +   subj.   verb
But *the manager* **and** *his wife* **like** rock and roll music.

However, some subjects joined by *and* actually describe a single thing or idea. Treat such expressions as singular.

subject   verb
Rock and roll **is** their passion.

["Rock and roll" is one kind of music.]

subject   verb
Unfortunately, *peace and quiet* **was** what their neighbors wanted.

["Peace and quiet"—like "law and order" and "rum and Coke"—really expresses one idea.]

subject   verb
Ranting and raving **is** all some people are capable of.

When a compound subject linked by *and* is modified by *each* or *every*, the verb takes a singular form. You'll appreciate this guideline when you see the examples:

subj.   subj.
Every resident and shopkeeper **has** an opinion.

Each store owner and *each* member of the band **intends** to speak his or her mind.

13A

292

However, when *each* follows a compound subject, usage varies.

> The angry resident and the irate shopkeeper *each* **have** their opinions.

> The angry resident and the irate shopkeeper *each* **has** his or her opinion.

▶ **When subjects are joined by *or*, *neither* . . . *nor*, or either . . . *or*, the verb (or its auxiliary) should agree with the subject closer to it.** Take a look at these examples to see how this guideline operates. The arrows point to the subjects nearest the verbs.

13A

                  plural   singular ↲
Neither the neighbors nor *David* **is** eager for trouble.

           singular   plural   ↲
But either David or the *neighbors* **are** likely to hire a lawyer.

  → singular   plural
Does *David* or the neighbors **know** a lawyer?

  →   plural   singular
Do the *neighbors* or David **know** a lawyer?

  plural   plural   ↲
Lawyers or *lawsuits* **cost** lots of money.

   singular   singular ↲
Compromise or *cooperation* **costs** much less.

The rule holds when one or both of the subjects joined by *or*, *either* . . . *or*, or *neither* . . . *nor* are pronouns: the verb agrees with the nearer subject.

                       ↲
Neither Kyle nor *I* **have** any news.

                    ↲
Neither I nor *Kyle* **has** any news.

> [Notice that both subjects are singular. In this case, the verb changes to reflect a shift from a first person subject (*I*) to a third person subject (*Kyle*).]

293

Neither <u>she</u> nor <u>we</u> **admit** ⌐ to an opinion about the dispute.

Neither <u>we</u> nor <u>*she*</u> **admits** ⌐ to an opinion about the dispute.

However, when the resulting construction proves awkward, it should be revised—usually by making the verb plural or rewriting the sentence.

{**Awkward**} Neither *you* nor *I* **am** bothered by the noise of the band.

{**Better**} Neither *I* nor *you* **are** bothered by the noise of the band.

{**Better**} *We* **are** not bothered by the noise of the band.

13A

▶ **When your subject is an *indefinite pronoun*, use the chart below (or a dictionary) to determine whether the word is singular, plural, or variable.** Then select the appropriate verb form. The most troublesome indefinite pronouns are probably *each* (which is always singular) and *none* (which varies, but is usually singular in formal writing).

Singular	Variable, S. or Pl.	Plural
anybody	all	few
anyone	any	many
each	more	several
either	most	
everybody	none	
everyone	some	
neither		
nobody		
no one		
somebody		
someone		

Each **holds** strong arguments supporting
his case. [singular]

Nobody **knows** how the grievance
committee will rule. [singular]

None of the arguments **is** easy to
dismiss. [variable]

None but the brave **are** at the meeting. [variable]

Many in the town **plan** to attend the
meeting. [plural]

Few **intend** to miss the confrontation. [plural]

● **Fine Tuning**

1. Whenever you think a subject joined to expressions such as
along with, as well as, or *together with* sounds awkward with a
singular verb, consider linking the subjects with *and* instead.

{Slightly awkward} David, *as well as* his neighbors,
considers a compromise possible.

{Better} David *and* his neighbors **consider** a compromise possible.

2. Titles should be treated as singular subjects.

Franco Zeffirelli's *Romeo and Juliet* **remains** a popular
film.

Streamers **is** a play about the Vietnam War.

EXERCISE 13.1

Decide which verb in boldface would be correct in academic
writing.

1. The meeting of the Clear Lake College district neighborhood association (**promise/promises**) to be exciting.

2. Grievance panel members, sifting through papers, (**sit/sits**) at a table near the front of the room.

3. As soon as the meeting begins, Mr. Butcher and his allies (**present/presents**) their "noise pollution" case against David and his band, Microwave Katz.

4. David, as well as other members of Microwave Katz, (**sit/sits**) patiently in the audience, waiting for a chance to rebut the accusations.

5. "Common decency and the right of a citizen to a quiet place of business (**demand/demands**) an end to this outrageous music in our neighborhood," Mr. Butcher declares, bringing his muscle-bound arm down on the table in front of the grievance committee.

6. "Neither my band nor I (**make/makes**) as much noise as the patrons of Butcher's Gym, slamming weights until 11:30 every night," David counters.

7. "And (**has/have**) either the neighbors or the police measured the decibel count inside Lindstrøm's Ice Cream Shop when its jukebox, as well as its patrons, (**is/are**) blasting full tilt?"

8. "Peace and quiet, it seems, (**is/are**) in the ear of the hearer."

9. David concludes, however, by acknowledging that neither the neighbors nor he (**was/were**) guiltless of disturbing the peace.

10. Everybody on the grievance committee and neighborhood association (**hope/hopes**) for a compromise.

13B AGREEMENT: IS THE SUBJECT A COLLECTIVE NOUN?

Term you need to know

Collective noun. A noun that names a group: *team, band, orchestra, jury, committee.*

Troubleshooting

With collective nouns used as subjects, you often have the option of treating a subject as either singular or plural, depending on how it is used in a given sentence.

> The grievance *committee* (**expect? expects?**) to resolve the disturbing-the-peace charge against David's band, Microwave Katz.

> The *band* (**feel? feels?**) that their music is an expression of artistic freedom.

Sometimes you must decide which of two acceptable versions of a sentence seems better:

> The *band* **feels** that **its** music is an expression of artistic freedom. [subject treated as singular]

> The *band* **feel** that **their** music is an expression of artistic freedom. [subject treated as plural]

Guidelines for making such choices are provided below.

To be sure verbs and collective nouns agree in number . . .

▶ **Decide whether a collective noun you are using as a subject acts as a single body (the *jury*) or as a group (the *twelve* members of the jury).** Then be consistent. If you decide the subject is singular, be sure its verb is singular. If the subject is plural, the verb should also be plural.

> {**Singular**} The grievance *committee* **expects** to resolve the disturbing-the-peace charge against David's band, Microwave Katz.

> {**Plural**} The grievance *committee* **raise** their hands to vote.

You will run into fewer problems if you usually regard collective nouns as single objects. Notice how awkward the following sentences seem because the collective nouns are treated as plural forms.

The *committee* **seem** unable to make up their minds.

The *band* **feel** that their music is an expression of artistic freedom.

Revise sentences like these either by making the collective subjects singular or more obviously plural.

{**Singular**} The *band* **feels** that its music is an expression of artistic freedom.

{**More clearly plural**} The *members of the committee* **seem** unable to make up their minds.

The following chart may help you manage other collective subjects:

Subject	Guideline	Examples
Measurements	Singular as a unit; plural as individual objects.	*Five miles* **is** a long walk. *Five more miles* **are** ahead of us. *Six months* **is** the waiting period. *Six months* **have** passed.
Numbers	Singular in expressions of division and subtraction.	*Four* divided by *two* **is** two. *Four* minus *two* **leaves** two.
	Singular or plural in expressions of multiplication and addition.	*Two* plus *two* **is/are** four. *Two* times *two* **is/are** four.
Words ending in -*ics*	School subjects are usually singular.	*Physics* **is** a tough major. *Economics* **is** a useful minor. *Linguistics* **is** popular today.

	Other *-ics* words vary; check a dictionary.	His *tactics* **are** shrewd. *Athletics* **are** expensive. *Ethics* **is** a noble study. Her *ethics* **are** questionable. *Politics* **is** fun. Francie's *politics* **are** radical.
data	Plural in formal writing; often singular in informal writing.	The *data* **are** reliable. The *data* **is** reliable.
number	Singular if preceded by *the*; plural if preceded by *a*.	*The number* **has** grown. *A number* **have** left.
public	Singular as a unit; plural as individual people.	The *public* **is** satisfied. The *public* **are** here in great numbers.

13B

EXERCISE 13.2

Choose the correct verb.

1. The five-person grievance committee (**adjourn/adjourns**) to a smaller room to make its decision while the general public (**wait/waits**) in the town hall twiddling their thumbs.
2. A majority of the committee (**is/are**) undecided about how to cast their votes, so they discuss the issues at length.
3. A half hour (**pass/passes**).
4. In the larger room, the crowd (**grumble/grumbles**) restlessly, and Microwave Katz (**remove/removes**) their instruments from cases to practice a little.

5. Meanwhile the members of the grievance committee (**agree/agrees**) that the economics of the case (**support/supports**) banning Microwave Katz' practices but that the ethics of the situation (**is/are**) against such a prohibition.
6. The decibel data supplied by the band (**show/shows**) that the group (**make/makes**) no more noise than other groups or businesses in the vicinity.
7. Thirty more minutes (**pass/passes**) in deliberation.
8. Suddenly the committee (**hear/hears**) a noisy din from the main room.
9. The public (**is/are**) getting restless.

13C

13C AGREEMENT: IS THE SUBJECT SEPARATED FROM ITS VERB?

Troubleshooting

Subject/verb agreement errors tend to occur when subjects are separated from their verbs by modifying words or phrases. Nouns near the verb can sound like subjects.

> <u>David</u>, encouraged by his band members and even a few interested *neighbors*, (**tune? tunes?**) his guitar.

> The <u>neighbors</u>, especially the proprietor of the gym, *Mr. Butcher,* (**feel? feels?**) that David's band Microwave Katz should practice away from their businesses.

Subject/verb agreement difficulties also arise when the subject of a sentence is an indefinite pronoun modified by a prepositional phrase. In cases like these, you have to pay attention both to the pronouns and the modifying phrases before choosing a verb.

> <u>Each</u> of the *boys* (**is? are?**) a skilled musician.

> <u>All</u> of the *music* (**is? are?**) rock and roll.

> <u>All</u> of the *songs* (**is? are?**) rock and roll tunes.

The guidelines below explain how to handle such situations.

▶ **Be sure that a verb agrees in number with its real subject, not with other words that may stand between them.** Modifying words or phrases often stand between subjects and verbs.

> subject   modifying phrase
> <u>David</u>, encouraged by his band members and even a
>   verb
> few bored neighbors, **tunes** his guitar.

But such a separation does not change the subject-verb relationship. In the example above, the verb remains singular because its subject is singular—the plural nouns *members* and *neighbors* have no bearing on subject-verb agreement.

Yet it is easy to mistake such nouns or pronouns for subjects because, standing closer to the verb than the subject does, they seem to determine its number.

> The <u>neighbors</u>, especially the proprietor of the gym,
> *Mr. Butcher*, (**feel? feels?**) that David's band Microwave Katz should practice away from their businesses.

But the phrase between the subject and verb only describes the subject; it is not the subject itself.

>   subject   modifying phrase
> The <u>neighbors</u>, especially the proprietor of the gym,
>   verb
> *Mr. Butcher*, **feel** that David's band Microwave Katz should practice away from their businesses.

▶ **Remember that if a pronoun is always singular (see the chart in Section 15G), it remains singular even if it is modified by a phrase with a plural noun in it.** Confusion is especially likely when the subject of a sentence is an indefinite pronoun such as *each*, *everyone*, *all*, and *none* followed by a prepositional phrase:

13C

{**Problem**} <u>Each</u> of the *boys* (**is? are?**) a skilled musician.

subject   verb
{**Solution**} <u>Each</u> of the *boys* **is** a skilled musician.

If the indefinite pronoun can vary in number (see the chart in Section 15G), the noun in the prepositional phrase determines whether the pronoun (and consequently the verb) is singular or plural.

sing.
{**Noun in prep. phrase is singular**} <u>All</u> of the *music* **is** rock and roll.

plural
{**Noun in prep. phrase is plural**} <u>All</u> of the *songs* **are** rock and roll tunes.

13C

If the indefinite pronoun is plural, so is the verb.

<u>Few</u> in the audience at the meeting **hesitate** to applaud the band's first song.

EXERCISE 13.3

Choose the correct verb.

1. The members of the grievance committee, locked in discussion within the conference room, (**ignore/ignores**) the rock and roll sounds coming from the main hall.
2. Each of them (**feel/feels**) the obligation to weigh the facts in the case carefully.
3. But the noises, like the sounds of an approaching storm, (**grow/grows**) louder and louder. The committee members, especially the chairperson, Greta Ericson, (**decide/decides**) it is time for a decision.

4. All of the committee members, eager to serve the public, (**vote/votes**) to ban David's band from practicing in the neighborhood during or after business hours.

5. The committee members, a proud bunch that feels it has done its civic duty, (**march/marches**) into the main hall with the decision.

13D AGREEMENT: HAS THE SUBJECT GOTTEN LOST?

Troubleshooting

Occasionally you may simply lose track of a subject because the structure of a sentence is complicated or unusual. One such situation involves sentences or main clauses beginning with *here* and *there*.

Here (**is? are?**) a surprising turn of events.

In every corner of the room, there (**is? are?**) dancers.

Another involves singular subjects tied to plural nouns by linking verbs. The verb choice can be baffling:

The *key* to the band's success (**is? are?**) catchy *lyrics*.

The guidelines below discuss these situations as well as several other puzzlers.

To be sure subjects and verbs agree in number . . .

▶ **Don't lose track of your subject. When a sentence begins with *here* or *there*, the verb still agrees with the subject, which usually trails after it.**

	verb	subj.
{Singular subject}	Here **is** a surprising *turn* of events.	

{Plural subject} In every corner of the room, there
verb   subj.
are *dancers*.

	verb	subj.

{Singular subject}　There **has been** a *change* of attitude on the part of the neighbors.

	verb	subj.

{Plural subject}　There **have been** surprising *developments*.

▶ **Remember that when a linking verb connects a singular subject to a plural noun, the verb still agrees with the subject—even if the resulting sentence sounds awkward.**

sing. subj.　　　　　　　　　　　　*linking verb*
The best *tribute* to Microwave Katz' music **is** the
　　　plural noun
dancing *neighbors*.

　　sing. subj.　　　　*linking verb*　　*plural noun*
The *key* to the band's success **is** catchy *lyrics*.

The same is true when a linking verb connects a plural subject to a singular noun, but such sentences sound normal and don't ordinarily raise questions of agreement:

　　　　plural subj. *l.v.*　　　　*sing. noun*
The dancing *neighbors* **are** the best *tribute* to Microwave Katz' music.

　　plural subj. *l.v.*　*sing. noun*
Catchy *lyrics* **are** the *key* to Microwave Katz' success.

▶ **When the verb comes before its subject, the verb still agrees in number with that subject.**

　　　　　　　　　verb　　*subject*
Puzzled by the rapid turn of events **are** the *members* of the grievance committee.

verb　*subject*
Is this *party* a joke on the committee?

▶ **When the subject is a singular word such as *series*, *segment*, *portion*, *fragment*, or *part* that describes a por-**

304

tion of a larger object, the subject remains singular even if modified by plural words. You'll recognize the problem when you see examples:

> A *series* of questions **is** raised by the strange behavior of the crowd.

> A substantial *portion* of Ruralia's population of senior citizens **is** dancing like teenagers.

The words *majority* and *amount* do not fall under this guideline; they can be either singular or plural, depending upon their use in a sentence.

> The *majority* **rules**.   [*majority* treated as singular]

> The *majority* of townspeople **like** music.   [*majority* treated as plural]

● **Fine Tuning**

One of the trickiest subject/verb agreement situations occurs within clauses that include the phrase *one of those who*. In formal English, the verb in such a clause is plural—even though it looks as if it should be singular:

> David is one of those musicians who never **seem** [not **seems**] tired.

The verb is plural because its subject is plural. To understand the situation more clearly, rearrange the sentence this way:

> Of those musicians *who* never **seem** tired, David is one.

Now it is clearer that the subject of the verb *seem* is the pronoun *who* and the antecedent of *who* is the plural noun *musicians*. So, tricky as the construction looks, it actually follows the rule: a plural noun takes a plural verb. Now watch what happens if you add the word *only* to the mix:

> David is the *only* one of the musicians who **seems** tired.

Why is the verb now singular? The subject of the verb *seems* is still the pronoun *who*, but its antecedent is now the singular pronoun *one*, not the plural *musicians*. Again, it helps to rearrange the sentence to see who is doing what to whom:

> Of the musicians, David is the only one who **seems** tired.

Note that the sentence makes little sense if arranged this way:

> Of the musicians who **seem** tired, David is the only one.

EXERCISE 13.4

Choose the correct verb.

1. The chair of the grievance committee (**pound/pounds**) a gavel at the podium to restore order.
2. There (**is/are**) grumbles from the crowd, but the band (**stop/stops**) playing.
3. A portion of the audience (**ignore/ignores**) the call for order, but soon most of the revelers (**is/are**) willing to listen to the grievance committee.
4. Irritated by the sudden return to peace and quiet (**is/are**) many of the citizens who had been enjoying Microwave Katz' rock and roll.
5. "(**Do/Does**) the good people of this town want to hear our decision?" the chair of the grievance group (**want/wants**) to know.
6. The reply (**is/are**) loud hoots and Bronx cheers.
7. Mr. Butcher speaks, "I am one of those townspeople who (**object/objects**) loudest to noise in our neighborhood."
8. "But apparently I am not the only one of these citizens who (**recognize/recognizes**) good music when I hear it. I withdraw my complaint."
9. "(**Do/Does**) anyone here want to disagree?" six-foot six, 250-pound Mr. Butcher asks.
10. Nobody (**do/does**) and the band (**play/plays**) into the night.

Terms you need to know

Tense. That quality of a verb that expresses time and existence. Tense is expressed through changes in verb forms and endings (*see, seeing, saw; work, worked*) and the use of auxiliaries (*had seen, will have seen; had worked, had been working*). Tense enables verbs to state complicated relationships between time and action—or relatively simple ones. For example, a verb in present tense can describe action occurring now, a state of being, or an action happening in the future.

Professor Cupperman **scratches** his mustache.   [action now]

Professor Upton **is** shrewd.   [state of being]

Their play **opens** next month.   [future action]

Verbs in the future tenses can describe—among other relationships—what will happen, or what will continue to happen, or what will have happened already.

The show **will flop**.   [future action]

Travis **will be watching** Jenny carefully.   [continuing action]

By the time you read this sentence, Professor Cupperman **will have retired**.   [action that has occurred]

Tense is a subtle and complicated aspect of verbs.

Sequence of tenses. The way the tense of one verb in a sentence limits or determines the tense other verbs can have.

Voice. Verbs can be either in the **active voice** or the **passive voice**. They are in the active voice when the subject in the sentence actually does what the verb describes.

subject   action
Professor Vorhees **invited** David to write music for the play.

They are in the passive voice when the action described by the verb is done *to* the subject.

subject   action
David **was invited** by Professor Vorhees to write music for the play.

See Section 13G for more details about active and passive verbs.

Troubleshooting

Although choosing the right form for some irregular verbs can be tricky (see Section 13F below), most writers have little trouble finding the tense they need. Even complicated tenses usually fall into place easily.

13E

It **might have been** a more successful production if the audience **had been able** to hear what the actors **were saying**.

Professor Cupperman **will have been teaching** Shakespeare for forty years when **he retires** next decade.

Yet some writers tend to avoid the more complex tenses, latching on, instead, to the simplest tense that comes to mind—even when a more complex tense might better express a relationship between two actions.

{**Vague**} Sue Ellen **was** reading the play an hour when she **dozed** off.

{**More precise**} Sue Ellen **had been reading** the play an hour when she **dozed** off.

More often, writers are inconsistent about tenses, confusing their readers by inappropriately switching from tense to tense in midsentence or paragraph.

Occasionally writers are unsure about the **sequence of tenses**, that is, what tenses may follow each other in a sentence. English is very flexible, allowing all sorts of potential combinations between tenses. Still, certain constructions work while others do not.

All of these problems are discussed below.

To manage verb tenses effectively . . .

▶ **Know what tenses are available and what they do.** Below is a chart of English tenses, past, present, and future in the active voice.

What It Is Called	What It Looks Like	What It Does
Past	I **answered** quickly.	Shows what has happened in the past at a particular time.
Past progressive	I **was answering** when the alarm went off.	Shows something happening in the past.
Perfect	I **have answered** the question often.	Shows something that has happened more than once in the past.
Past perfect	I **had answered** the question twice when the alarm went off.	Shows what had already happened before another event, also in a past tense, occurred.
Present	I **answer** when I must.	Shows what happens or can happen now.
Present progressive	I **am answering** now.	Shows what is happening now.
Future	I **will answer** tomorrow.	Shows what may happen in the future.
Future progressive	I **will be answering** the phones all day.	Shows something that will continue to happen in the future.

13E

What It Is Called	What It Looks Like	What It Does
Future perfect	I **will have answered** all the charges before you see me again.	Shows what will have happened by some particular time in the future.
Future perfect progressive	I **will have been answering** the charges for three hours by the time you arrive at noon.	Shows a continuing future action that precedes some other event also in the future.

These, of course, are only the basic verb forms in the active voice. Verbs look more complicated when they are in the **passive voice** (see also Section 13G):

What It Is Called	What It Looks Like
Past	I **was invited** to her party last year.
Past progressive	I **was being invited** by Alicia when the phone went dead.
Perfect	I **have been invited** to many of her parties.
Past perfect	I **had been invited** to this one too, or so I assumed.
Present	I **am invited** to everyone's parties.
Present progressive	I **am being invited** now! That's Alicia calling, I'm sure.
Future	I **will be invited** tomorrow. Wrong number.
Future perfect	I **will have been invited** by this time tomorrow. You'll see.

One tense some writers seem to avoid is the past perfect in all its forms. The result can be sentences less precise than they might be:

> {**Slightly vague**} Maggie could not believe that Greta actually **divorced** George.

{**More precise**} Maggie could not believe that Greta **had** actually **divorced** George.

{**Slightly vague**} Although the divorce **was granted** two months before, George was still living with Greta.

{**More precise**} Although the divorce **had been granted** two months before, George was still living with Greta.

▶ **Keep your tenses consistent.** Consistency here doesn't mean never changing verb tenses. In almost anything you write, you will have to switch back and forth between past, present, and future time. Just be sure that you don't switch tenses in ways that confuse or distract readers—when you are narrating an event, for example, and have to shift between several tenses:

13E

> David **was surprised** when Marie Vorhees, the drama (and volleyball) coach at Clear Lake College, **summons** him to her office. Although he **had taken** a drama course from her when he was a freshman, he **had not done** well and never **expects** to see her again. He **wasn't** much of a volleyball fan either, so he **has** no idea why he **is called** to her office. She **smiled** when he **walked** in and **asks** him to have a seat. David **was feeling** uneasy, as if he **did** something he **shouldn't have**, but **didn't know** what.

The passage sounds somewhat confusing because it shifts between two time frames. The first time frame presents David's story as if it were happening at the present moment: Professor Vorhees *summons* David; David doesn't know why he *is called* to her office; she *asks* him to sit down. But the second time frame in the passage narrates events as if they have already occurred: David *was surprised*; Professor Vorhees *smiled* when he *walked* in. The paragraph needs to be revised to express a more consistent point of view. Here's one revision of the passage, viewing David's meeting with Marie Vorhees as an event that has happened in the past:

David **was surprised** when Marie Vorhees, the drama (and volleyball) coach at Clear Lake College, **summoned** him to her office. Although he **had taken** a drama course from her when he **was** a freshman, he **had not done** well and never **expected** to see her again. He **wasn't** much of a volleyball fan either, so he **had** no idea why he **had been called** to her office. She **smiled** when he **walked in** and **asked** him to have a seat. David **felt** uneasy, as if he **had done** something he **shouldn't have**, but **didn't know** what.

Now here is the same passage narrated as if David's appearance in Professor Vorhees' office is occurring in present time. Notice, however, that this shift does not simply put all verbs in the present tense. Some events in the paragraph still need to be stated through various past tenses.

13E

David **is surprised** when Marie Vorhees, the drama (and volleyball) coach at Clear Lake College, **summons** him to her office. Although he **had taken** a drama course from her when he **was** a freshman, he **had not done** well and never **expected** to see her again. He **isn't** much of a volleyball fan either, so he **has** no idea why he **has been called** to her office. She **smiles** when he **walks** in and **asks** him to have a seat. David **feels** uneasy, as if he **has done** something he **shouldn't have**, but **doesn't know** what.

▶ **Try not to shift the tenses of parallel verbs within a sentence.** When a single subject is followed by one or more verbs, the verbs should be comparable in form whenever possible. This *parallel* form makes a sentence more readable. See Section 9D on **parallelism**.

{**Lack of parallelism**} Dr. Vorhees **explains** to David that she knows he has a band and **is asking** him to provide the music for the spring Shakespeare festival.

> subject
> *Dr. Vorhees*

>> 1st verb
>> **explains** to David that she knows he has a band and

2nd verb [not parallel to first]
is asking him to provide the music for the spring Shakespeare festival.

{**Revised for parallelism**} Dr. Vorhees **explains** to David that she knows he has a band and **asks** him to provide the music for the spring Shakespeare festival.

subject
Dr. Vorhees

1st verb
explains to David that she knows he has a band and

2nd verb
asks him to provide the music for the spring Shakespeare festival.

● Fine Tuning

1. In most cases, when the main verb in a sentence is in the past or past perfect tense, a verb in an attached subordinate clause will also be in the past or past perfect tense.

main verb
Even Professor Cupperman finally **agreed** *that David*
verb in subordinate clause
had the talent to compose a rock score.

main verb
Dr. Vorhees **had gotten** Dr. Cupperman's approval
verb in subordinate clause
before she offered David the project, a rock version of Shakespeare's least known tragedy, *Timon of Athens.*

A notable exception occurs when infinitives (see Section 13I) follow a main verb in the past tense. In such cases, the present form of the infinitive is preferred.

main verb
{**Problem**} Dr. Vorhees **would have expected** David
past infinitive
to have jumped at the opportunity.

313

main verb
{**Revised**} Dr. Vorhees **would have expected** David
pres. infinitive
to jump at the opportunity.

main verb   past infinitive
{**Problem**} David **had tried** hard *to have seemed* interested but uncommitted.

main verb   present infinitive
{**Revised**} David **had tried** hard *to seem* interested but uncommitted.

2. Participles (see Section 13I) have both present and present perfect forms:

Present	admitting	considering
Present Perfect	having admitted	having considered.

13E

The present participle is used to show that something is happening at the same time as the action of the main verb.

pres. participle   main verb
Admitting his interest, David still **seemed** cool at first to the idea of writing a score.

The present perfect is used to show that something has happened before the action of the main verb.

pres. perfect participle
Having considered the proposal for several days, David
main verb
told Dr. Vorhees that he would write the music for the show.

EXERCISE 13.5

Replace the verb forms in parentheses below with more appropriate tenses. You may need to use a variety of verb forms, including passive and progressive forms. Treat all ten sentences as part of a single paragraph.

1. On the Monday after he (**agree**) to write music for the spring Shakespeare festival, David had lunch with Drs. Vorhees and Cupperman to discuss *Timon of Athens*.
2. Professor Cupperman explained that they would be (**perform**) *Timon* only because he (**make**) a commitment long ago to produce all thirty-seven of Shakespeare's plays.
3. "We (**avoid**) *Timon* for as long as we could, but now we have to perform it to complete the cycle," he (**lament**).
4. David admitted that he never (**read**) *Timon*.
5. In fact he never even (**hear**) of it.
6. Professor Vorhees confessed that she (**read**) the tragedy only recently and that it (**be**) her idea to perform *Timon* as a rock musical to add some life to a dismal work.
7. "In four hundred years, it never (**be**) performed as a musical. In fact it hardly (**perform**) at all.
8. People who attend our show (**watch**) something unique."
9. Professor Cupperman seemed much less enthusiastic, but (**agree**) that his department could not afford to lose money again on this year's Shakespeare play, or it (**spell**) an end to the spring festival entirely.
10. "If it takes a little rock and roll to save future productions of *Hamlet*, *Othello*, *Macbeth*—well, that is just the price we (**pay**)."

13E

EXERCISE 13.6

Revise the verb tenses in the following paragraphs as needed to make the passages more readable. Change only those verbs that appear in boldface type; the other verbs in the passage will help you select appropriate tenses. Several versions of the paragraphs are possible.

1. After his lunch with Drs. Vorhees and Cupperman, David trooped to the Clear Lake Library to read Shakespeare's *Timon of Athens*, the play for which he **agrees** to write a rock score.

The work **has been** just as Professor Vorhees **has been describing** it—dismal. In this tragedy, Timon, a wealthy citizen of ancient Athens, wastes expensive gifts and large sums of money on a bunch of no-account friends until he **will go** broke. Then, in a financial pinch himself, Timon turns to his friends for help, only to discover that they **will not have lent** him the money he needs to get out of debt. Angry, Timon **is skipping** the city of Athens and **will spend** the last two acts of the play in a forest, cursing everybody and everything. Then he dies, offstage, out of sheer spite. In the meantime, Alcibiades, a soldier and friend of Timon, **will be gathering** an army to march on Athens to punish the city for executing one of his war buddies—who just **happened** to be a murderer. But instead of ending the play with a nifty battle, Shakespeare has the city and Alcibiades **agreed** to a peace settlement. Timon **was** practically forgotten, but by this point, nobody **will have cared**.

2. "Well," David thinks to himself after closing his heavy Shakespeare volume, "even if my music **has turned** out to be terrible, this play is going to seem worse." Still, he **has found** himself gradually sketching out ideas for songs and instrumentals. Within a few days he has come up with musical themes for several of the minor characters, and **wrote** a noisy dance number for the lavish banquet scene. The character of Timon proves a problem until David **began** thinking of him as an ancient Mick Jagger. Then, suddenly, the music **will be coming** easily. He finds that even Timon's curses **have made** perfect lyrics for rock and roll anthems. His band members soon join him in the writing and scoring and, before you **could be saying** *Timon of Athens: Superstar*, David **will have dropped** his completed work on Dr. Cupperman's desk. "Let me just warn you," he says, "I**'d been making** a few minor changes."

Terms you need to know

Principal parts of a verb. The three basic forms of a verb from which all tenses are built.

Infinitive (present). This is the base form of a verb, what it looks like when preceded by the word *to*: *to walk*; *to go*; *to choose*.

Past. This is the simplest form the verb has to show action that has already occurred: *walked*; *went*; *chose*.

Past participle. This is the form a verb takes when it is accompanied by an **auxiliary verb** to show a more complicated past tense: *had* **walked**; *will have* **gone**; *would have* **chosen**.

Regular verbs. A verb that forms its past and past participle forms (see **Principal parts of a verb**) simply by adding -*d* or -*ed* to the infinitive.

Infinitive	Past	Past Participle
talk	talk**ed**	talk**ed**
coincide	coincide**d**	coincide**d**
advertise	advertise**d**	advertise**d**

Irregular verbs. A verb that does not form its past and past participle forms (see **Principal parts of a verb**) by adding -*d* or -*ed* to the infinitive. Irregular verbs are important because they are so commonly used. They change their forms in various ways; a few even have the same form for all three principal parts.

Infinitive	Past	Past Participle
burst	burst	burst
drink	drank	drunk
arise	arose	arisen
lose	lost	lost

317

Auxiliary verbs. Verbs, usually some form of *be*, *do*, or *have*, that combine with other verbs to show various relationships of tense, voice, mood, and so on. Auxiliaries are sometimes called *helping verbs*.

Troubleshooting

At one time or another almost everyone stumbles over verb forms:

> By the time Rita had (**drove? driven?**) a hundred miles, her patience had (**wore? worn?**) thin.

> Barry (**hanged? hung?**) the racquets in his display window.

Since the English verbs we use most often tend to be irregular, we gain command over most of the forms quickly. But certain verbs are persistently troublesome. With such verbs, you may need help.

> {Correct} By the time Rita had **driven** a hundred miles, her patience had **worn** thin.

> {Correct} Barry **hung** the racquets in his display window.

To be sure the form of an irregular verb is correct . . .

 ▶ **Consult a dictionary or check the following list of irregular verbs.** The list below of troublesome irregular English verbs gives you three forms: (1) the present tense, (2) the simple past tense, and (3) the past participle. (Remember that the past participle is used with auxiliary verbs to form verb phrases: *I have ridden*, *I had ridden*, *I will have ridden*.)

Most problems occur in distinguishing between the past tense and the past participle (*wore, worn*; *lay, lain*). As you will discover from the list, sometimes these forms will be identical (*brought, brought*; *found, found*). And sometimes there may be more than one acceptable form (*dived, dove*). Your safest bet, when in doubt, is to check the list. Errors in verb form irritate readers.

Present	Past	Past Participle
arise	arose	arisen
bear (carry)	bore	borne
bear (give birth)	bore	borne, born
become	became	become
begin	began	begun
bite	bit	bitten, bit
blow	blew	blown
break	broke	broken
bring	brought	brought
burst	burst	burst
buy	bought	bought
catch	caught	caught
choose	chose	chosen
cling	clung	clung
come	came	come
creep	crept	crept
dig	dug	dug
dive	dived, dove	dived, dove
do	did	done
draw	drew	drawn
dream	dreamed, dreamt	dreamed, dreamt
drink	drank	drunk
drive	drove	driven
eat	ate	eaten
fall	fell	fallen
find	found	found
fly	flew	flown
forget	forgot	forgotten
forgive	forgave	forgiven
freeze	froze	frozen
get	got	got, gotten
give	gave	given
go	went	gone
grow	grew	grown

13F

Present	Past	Past Participle
hang (a person)	hanged	hanged
hang (an object)	hung	hung
know	knew	known
lay (to place)	laid	laid
lead	led	led
leave	left	left
lend	lent	lent
lie (to recline)	lay	lain
light	lighted, lit	lighted, lit
lose	lost	lost
pay	paid	paid
prove	proved	proved, proven
ride	rode	ridden
ring	rang, rung	rung
rise	rose	risen
run	ran	run
say	said	said
see	saw	seen
set	set	set
shake	shook	shaken
shine	shone, shined	shone, shined
show	showed	showed, shown
shrink	shrank, shrunk	shrunk, shrunken
sing	sang, sung	sung
sink	sank, sunk	sunk, sunken
sit	sat	sat
slide	slid	slid, slidden
speak	spoke	spoken
spring	sprang, sprung	sprung
stand	stood	stood
steal	stole	stolen
sting	stung	stung
swear	swore	sworn

13F

Present	Past	Past Participle
swim	swam	swum
swing	swung	swung
take	took	taken
tear	tore	torn
throw	threw	thrown
wake	waked, woke	waked, woken
wear	wore	worn
wring	wrung	wrung
write	wrote	written

The reference guide at the back of the handbook treats various troublesome verbs, including some in the list above, in greater detail. Check for entries for *can/may*; *get/got/gotten*; *lay/lie*; *sit/set*; and so on.

13F

▶ **Special Problem**

A surprising number of writers tend to drop the final *-d* or *-ed* in some words because common pronunciation sometimes hides the "d" sound:

> {**Wrong**} Jenny was **suppose** to make the arrangements.
>
> {**Right**} Jenny was **supposed** to make the arrangements.
>
> {**Wrong**} She is **use** to dealing with theater people.
>
> {**Right**} She is **used** to dealing with theater people.
>
> {**Wrong**} Jenny was not **prejudice** against them.
>
> {**Right**} Jenny was not **prejudiced** against them.

Many readers and editors find these errors irritating.

EXERCISE 13.7

Choose verbs from the list above to complete the following sentences.

1. After Travis had _____ an hour, he _____ on the hammock and slept.
2. When Jenny _____ him there, she _____ the hammock back and forth, slowly at first.
3. Then she _____ to rock it faster, until Travis _____ suddenly from his nap, terrified.
4. He _____ that he was in a fighter jet that had just _____ hit by a heat-seeking missile.
5. As he ejected, his plane _____ apart and _____ toward the horizon in a fiery ball.
6. He had _____ almost a mile when his parachute finally opened, his expression _____ in terror.
7. The parachute _____ him gently at first toward the ground, his body swaying gently.
8. Then he was _____ in a crosswind that _____ from nowhere.
9. He was _____ violently, back and forth, until he _____ out of his harness, and he plunged toward some trees on the ground.
10. For a moment he _____ in the branches; then he _____ to the earth. He _____ to Jenny's laughter.

13G

13G ACTIVE VS. PASSIVE VERBS: WHAT IS THE DIFFERENCE?

Terms you need to know

Transitive verb. A verb that takes a direct object. In a sentence with a transitive verb, the subject acts upon someone or something; without this someone or something—the object—to receive the action, the sentence sounds incomplete:

            subject   verb   object

{**Transitive**} Travis **slugged** *Jenny*. [You can **slug** *someone*.]

                  subject   verb

{**Transitive**} Sister Anne Constance **wrecked** the object van. [You can **wreck** *something*.]

Unlike **intransitive verbs**, transitive verbs can usually be changed from the active to passive voice:

{**Active**}	Travis **slugged** *Jenny*.
{**Passive**}	Jenny **was slugged** by Travis.
{**Active**}	Sister Anne Constance **wrecked** the van.
{**Passive**}	The van **was wrecked** by Sister Anne Constance.

Voice. Transitive verbs can be either in the **active voice** or the **passive voice**. They are in the active voice when the subject in the sentence actually does what the verb describes.

           subject   action

Sister Anne Constance **wrecked** the van.

They are in the passive voice when the action described by the verb is done *to* the subject.

        subject   action

The van **was wrecked** by Sister Anne Constance.

Troubleshooting

Many writers employ the passive voice too often. Appreciating the difference between active and passive voice will help you decide when the passive voice is appropriate and when it simply obstructs your prose. By eliminating passive verbs, you can often turn weak, slow-moving sentences into stronger, more vital ones. (See Section 8E.) To revise effectively, you

13G

323

need to know how to recognize the passive voice and, when appropriate, how to make passive verbs active.

To change a passive verb to an active one . . .

▶ **Identify your passive verbs.** In a sentence with a passive verb, the subject doesn't perform the action. Instead the action is *done* to the subject:

> subject   action
> Jenny **was selected** by Professor Vorhees to be stage manager for *Timon of Athens*.

> subject   action
> She **had been nominated** for the job by Travis.

Passive verbs are always formed with some form of *be* + the past participle.

> *be* + past participle
> The van **had been wrecked** by Sister Anne Constance.

> *be* + past participle
> The accident **was caused** by faulty brakes, or so she had claimed.

Of course, not every sentence with a form of the verb *to be* is passive, especially when *be* is used as a linking verb:

> She **was** unhappy that the damage to the van **had been** so great.

Nor is every sentence with a past participle passive:

> Sister Anne Constance **had driven** for ten years without an accident.

To identify a passive verb form, look for **both** the past participle *and* a form of *be*.

> The minivan **had been loaded** with flats and props for *Timon of Athens* when it **was totaled**.

▶ **After you have identified a passive form, identify the word in the sentence that actually performs the action and make it your subject.** When you revise the sentence this way, the original subject usually becomes an object:

subject action
{Original—passive} Jenny **was selected** by *Professor Vorhees* to be stage manager for *Timon of Athens*.
performer of action

subject action object
{Revised—active} Professor Vorhees **selected** *Jenny* as stage manager for *Timon of Athens*.

Notice that the revised version is a few words shorter than the original. Active sentences tend to be more economical than passive ones. Here are three more examples.

{Original—passive} She **had been nominated** for the job by Travis.

{Revised—active} Travis **nominated** her for the job.

{Original—passive} The van **had been wrecked** by Sister Anne Constance.

{Revised—active} Sister Anne Constance **had wrecked** the van.

{Original—passive} The accident **was caused** by faulty brakes, or so she had claimed.

{Revised—active} Faulty brakes **caused** the accident, or so she had claimed.

However—and this is important—not every passive verb can or should be made active. Sometimes you do not or cannot know what the real subject in a sentence is.

Hazardous road conditions **had been forecast** the morning Sister Anne Constance ventured out. To make things worse, oil **had been spilled** at the intersection where her accident occurred.

She **was convinced**, however, that it was safe to drive.

The van **had been loaded** with flats and props for *Timon of Athens* when it **was totaled**.

In this last example, you might revise the second verb, but leave the first alone:

The van **had been loaded** with flats and props for *Timon of Athens* when Sister Anne **totaled** it.

[Who loaded the van is not particularly important; who wrecked it may be.]

In some cases, who or what did the action may be less important than to whom or to what it was done. A passive verb lets you put the *victim* (so to speak) right up front in the sentence where it gets attention.

Her accident **was featured** on the TV nightly news and in the local paper.

13G

Unfortunately, Sister Anne's insurance premium **was increased** because of the incident.

And all the major props for *Timon of Athens* **were smashed** in the collision.

And finally the passive verb form is customary in many expressions; an active form might even sound peculiar.

Flight 107 **has been delayed**.

The letter **was posted** yesterday.

The boys **were fined** for trespassing.

Even with these exceptions in mind, make an effort to cut most passive verbs from your writing. Your sentences will be livelier without them.

EXERCISE 13.8

Underline all the passive verbs in the following paragraphs. Then revise those sentences that would be stronger with passive verbs stated in the active voice.

1. Students working on Professor Cupperman's production of *Timon of Athens* began to fear that the show had been cursed by the ghost of Timon. It was bad enough that the lead in the show had been given by Professor Cupperman to a mysterious nobody named Kelly McKay. But then strange things began occurring. Such a rash of accidents, bad luck, and bad breaks could be explained by nothing other than an evil spirit. Sister Anne Constance was only the first victim of Timon. Alcibiades' toe was broken on stage by a falling pilaster. Francie Knipstein was arrested by Officer Klinkhamer on her way to practice because she looked "suspicious" in her Timandra costume. Some of David Barrett's music was accidentally shredded by Professor Vorhees' secretary. And the entire cast was sickened one evening by a pizza they were told had been ordered by Professor Cupperman.

2. Professor Cupperman was convinced that more than the cast had been cursed by Timon's spirit. His reputation as a producer was certain to be ruined by this terrible play. The decision to add rock tunes to the show was sorely regretted by him. Attention was only drawn to the weaknesses of the story by the loud and energetic music. But the show was plagued by many other problems, including a Timon (who was being played by a mysterious Kelly McKay) whose lines frequently were dropped or forgotten. A crutch had to be carried by Alcibiades because a toe had been broken by him during rehearsal. The last act of the tragedy had been laughed at by a test audience of Shakespeare students previewing the scene. And a brand-new college van had been destroyed by a nun! Surely the production had been cursed.

3. The scheme was working just as it had been planned by Professor Vorhees. Riot police would have to be hired by the school when *Timon of Athens: Superstar* was seen by paying theatergoers. Professor Cupperman had slyly been convinced by Marie Vorhees to turn a weak Shakespearian tragedy into another burning of Atlanta. He had been maneuvered by her into accepting a rock-musical production. He had been convinced by her to cast the mysterious (and totally unreliable) Kelly McKay as Timon. He hadn't even noticed when a pilaster had actually been nudged by her onto the toe of the one

13G

competent actor in the show. Poor naive Cupperman was unaware that a rebellion was being brewed by a cast subtly stirred up by vicious rumors, planted jealousies, spoiled pizza, and rotten choreography. And Professor Vorhees' plot had been smiled upon even by fortune. A rain-slick highway and a few loose wheel bolts were all that were needed to send a nun careening into a brick wall outside of Butcher's Gym while driving the new van that had been loaned to her by Cupperman. Before long Professor Cupperman was sure to be relieved of his control over the spring drama festival by a reluctant but suitably embarrassed Clear Lake College Board of Directors. She would be put in total control of the festival by the Directors instead. Then things would be changed by her!

EXERCISE 13.9

Select a paragraph you have written and underline all the passive verbs. Then rewrite the paragraph, making passive verbs active whenever such a revision makes a sentence livelier and more economical.

13H WHAT IS THE SUBJUNCTIVE AND HOW DO YOU USE IT?

Term you need to know

> **Mood**. A term used to describe how a writer regards a statement: either as a fact (the **indicative** mood), as a command (the **imperative** mood), or a wish, desire, supposition, or improbability (the **subjunctive** mood). Verbs change their form to show mood.
>
> **Indicative**: The director **was** careful.
>
> **Imperative**: **Be** careful!
>
> **Subjunctive**: If the director **were** more careful . . .

Troubleshooting

Even if you don't know what the subjunctive is you are probably using it correctly at least half the time. You are employing the subjunctive mood whenever you say *God bless* [instead of *blesses*] *you* or use the expressions *If I were* [not *was*] *you . . .* or *As it were* [not *was*]. In English, the subjunctive verb forms survive mainly in expressions like these which people use habitually. Where employing the subjunctive requires more thought, it seems to be fading from usage, replaced by the more familiar indicative forms.

Still, using the subjunctive correctly in the few remaining situations where English preserves it is not difficult. The subjunctive is one of those many points of grammar more troublesome to explain than to employ. You use the subjunctive to express ideas that aren't factual or certain or to state wishes or desires. You also use the subjunctive in clauses that follow statements of request, demand, suggestion, or recommendation. In the abstract, you may find these occasions hard to appreciate; in practice, you can learn easily how to identify situations that require subjunctive verb forms.

13H

To use the subjunctive . . .

▶ **Identify situations where the subjunctive might ·be used.** The subjunctive is often used . . .

In statements that express wishes.

> I wish it **were** [not **was**] bedtime.
>
> Jenny's parents wish she **were** [not **was**] **living** at home.
>
> Would he **were** [not **was**] here.

In **if** *clauses that describe situations that are contrary to fact, hypothetical, or improbable.*

> *If* Kyle **were** [not **was**] a rich actor, he'd drive a Maserati Biturbo.
>
> *If* Jenny **were** [not **was**] to call, Travis would pretend not to hear the phone.

If Officer Klinkhamer **were** [not **was**] thinner, he'd be healthier.

If it **were** [not **was**] to rain, Cupperman would move the meeting indoors.

In **that** *clauses following verbs that make demands, requests, recommendations, or motions.* These sentences will often seem formal or legalistic.

Professor Cupperman demanded *that* his cast **be** silent.

"I ask only *that* each actor **give** his best in the performance," he said.

"It is necessary *that* you all **be** at the dress rehearsal tomorrow."

After Cupperman left, Kyle moved *that* the crew **send** their director a basket of figs.

In certain common expressions.

Be that as it may	**Come** what may
As it **were**	Peace **be** with you

▶ **Select the subjunctive form of the verb.** As the examples above suggest, forms of the subjunctive are relatively simple. For all verbs, the present subjunctive is simply the base form of the verb—that is, the present infinitive form without *to*:

Verb	Present Subjunctive
to be	be
to give	give
to send	send
to bless	bless

The base form is used even in the third person singular where you might ordinarily expect a verb to take another form:

It is essential that *she* **have** [not **has**] her lines memorized by tomorrow.

Professor Cupperman demanded that *Kelly* **give** [not **gives**] the scene more attention.

Cupperman also insisted that *Kelly* **be** [not **is**] on time for rehearsal.

For all verbs except *be*, the past subjunctive is the same as the simple past tense.

Verb	Present Subjunctive
to give	gave
to send	sent
to bless	blessed

For *be*, the past subjunctive is always *were*. This is true even in the first and third person singular, where you might expect the form to be *was*:

{**First person**} I wish *I* **were** [not **was**] the director.

{**Second person**} Suppose *you* **were** the director.

{**Third person**} I wish *she* **were** [not **was**] the director.

13H

EXERCISE 13.10

Underline all verbs in the following passage in the subjunctive mood.

1. Barely two weeks before the opening night of Clear Lake College's Shakespeare Festival production, Marie Vorhees received a terse message from Professor Cupperman: "It is essential that you be in my office at 2:00 p.m. today."

2. "If I were a betting woman," the ambitious Professor Vorhees thought to herself, "I'd guess that Cupperman is about to cancel his show." But much to Professor Vorhees' surprise, Professor Cupperman insisted at the meeting that she take over as director of *Timon of Athens: Superstar*.

3. "You see," he explained, "I insisted that Kelly McKay do a more conscientious job in the lead role, but he missed two

important rehearsals in a row, and so, today, I have given him the axe, as it were. If only he were more responsible! I had no choice."

4. "But doesn't that mean you must cancel the show? I can't recommend that the show go on without someone to play the lead role. And only two weeks remain before opening night. Even bringing me in as director won't save the show."

5. "Be that as it may," Professor Cupperman said, "it is necessary that someone replace me as director because—I will play Timon. And my replacement is you. If I were you, I'd be thrilled at the prospect of directing."

131

EXERCISE 13.11

Write five sentences that include verbs in the subjunctive mood.

131 **WHAT ARE VERBALS AND HOW DO YOU USE THEM?**

Terms you need to know

Verbals. Verb forms that act like nouns, adjectives, or adverbs. The three kinds of verbals are **infinitives**, **participles**, and **gerunds**. Like verbs, verbals can take objects to form phrases and express time (present, past). But verbals are described as **nonfinite** (that is, "unfinished") verbs because they cannot alone make complete sentences. A complete sentence requires a **finite** verb, that is a verb that changes form to indicate person, number, and tense.

{**Nonfinite verb—infinitive**} **To have found** security . . .

{**Finite verb**} I **have found** security.

{**Nonfinite verb—participle**} The actor **performing** the scene . . .

{**Finite verb**} The actor **performs** the scene.

{**Nonfinite verb—gerund**} **Directing** a play . . .

{**Finite verb**} She **directed** the play.

Infinitive. A verbal that can be identified by the word *to* preceding the base form of a verb: *to strive*; *to seek*; *to find*; *to endure*. Infinitives also take other forms to indicate aspects of time and voice: *to be seeking*; *to have found*; *to have been found*. Infinitives act as nouns, adjectives, and adverbs:

> {**Infinitive as noun**} **To direct** a play is not easy. [subject of the sentence]

> {**Infinitive as adjective**} Kyle had many lines **to learn**. [modifies the noun **lines**]

> {**Infinitive as adverb**} Travis smiled **to ease** the pain. [modifies the verb **smiles**.]

An infinitive can also serve as an **absolute**, that is, a phrase, standing alone, that modifies an entire sentence.

> *To be* **blunt**, the play stank.

> *To make* **a long story short**, opening night recalled the sinking of the *Titanic*.

The sign of the infinitive—*to*—is deleted in some sentence constructions.

> The cast and crew purchased aspirin to help them [*to*] **deal** with the disastrous reviews.

Participle. A verb form used as a modifier. The present participle ends with *-ing*. For regular verbs, the past participle ends with *-ed*; for irregular verbs, the form of the past participle will vary. (If you aren't sure about a past participle, check the list on pp. 319–21.)

Participles have these forms:

To perform (a regular verb)

Present, active: performing
Present, passive: being performed

Past, active: performed
Past, passive: having been performed

To write (an irregular verb)

Present, active: writing
Present, passive: being written

Past, active: written
Past, passive: having been written

Participles can serve as simple modifiers:

Smiling, Brian McVicker left the auditorium to write his review. [modifies Brian]

But they often take objects, complements, and modifiers of their own to form verbal phrases that play an important role in shaping sentences:

Writing his review of Timon of Athens: Superstar, Brian smiled at his own cleverness.

Having been criticized often in the past by Professors Cupperman and Vorhees, Brian now had an opportunity for revenge.

The actors, ***knowing they had worked hard***, celebrated despite their dismal show.

Like an infinitive, a participle can also serve as an **absolute**, that is, a phrase, standing alone, that modifies an entire sentence.

All things *considered*, the actors didn't regret their efforts.

Gerund: A verb form used as a noun: *smiling, biking, walking*. Most gerunds end in *-ing* and, consequently, look exactly like the present participle:

{**Gerund**} **Smiling** is good for the health.

{**Participle**} A **smiling** critic is dangerous.

The difference, of course, is that gerunds function as nouns while participles act as modifiers. Gerunds usually appear in the present tense, but they can take other forms:

> **Having been treated** unfairly made Brian angry. [Gerund in past tense, passive voice acting as subject of the sentence]

> **Being asked** to write the review was an opportunity Brian wouldn't have missed. [Gerund in present tense, passive voice]

Gerunds have many functions:

> {**Gerund as subject**} *Being* **fair** posed a problem for Brian McVicker.

> {**Gerund as object**} He enjoyed *reviewing* **movies and plays.**

131

> {**Gerund as appositive**} Brian resisted his weakness, *writing* **scathing reviews.**

>   subj.
> {**Gerunds as subject and complement**} **Reviewing**
>   comp.
> was *seeing* **things critically.**

Troubleshooting

Verbals play an important role in shaping sentences. But they cause relatively few difficulties. One problem, though, is quite famous: the issue of the **split infinitive**. According to some writers, it is incorrect to separate the *to* in an infinitive from its verb. Consequently, by this strict interpretation, the following sentences err grammatically:

> "In *Timon: Superstar*," Brian's review began, "the cast decided *to boldly go* where no actors had been before."

> "To appreciate how bad *Timon: Superstar* is, you have *to actually see* it yourself," Brian wrote.

A second problem involves deciding whether a noun that precedes a gerund needs to be possessive. Two forms are possible:

> pos. noun
> {**Possessive noun**} The audience roared at the **scenery's**
>   gerund
> *collapsing* in the banquet scene.

> com. noun
> {**Common noun**} The audience roared at the **scenery**
>   gerund
> *collapsing* in the banquet scene.

Suggestions for handling nouns that precede gerunds are presented in a fine-tuning section below.

131 **To avoid splitting an infinitive . . .**

▶ **Check that no words separate the *to* in an infinitive from its verb.**
If a sentence sounds awkward because a word or phrase splits an infinitive, move the interrupter.

> {**Split infinitive**} Brian's intention in his review was *to, the best he could,* **warn** other students about the play.

> {**Revised**} Brian's intention in his review was *to warn* other students about the play **the best he could.**

Sometimes split infinitives invite misreadings and need to be revised:

> {**Confusing**} Brian intended *to only describe* the worst parts of *Timon: Superstar.*

> {**Clearer**} Brian intended *to describe* **only** the worst parts of *Timon: Superstar.*

In many cases, however, split infinitives do not sound awkward or confusing, and revising them does not necessarily improve sentences.

> {**Split infinitive**} Words fail *to adequately describe* the incompetence of the acting.

{**Revised**} Words fail *to describe* **adequately** the incompetence of the acting.

{**Split infinitive**} "In *Timon: Superstar*," Brian's review continued, "the cast decided *to boldly go* where no actors had been before."

{**Revised**} "In *Timon: Superstar*," Brian's review continued, "the cast decided *to go* **boldly** where no actors had been before."

Whether to revise split infinitives of this sort is a judgment call. Be warned that some people would sooner split a gut than an infinitive. They react strongly to writers who violate the rule. So use common sense. When a split infinitive sounds more natural than one that isn't split, ignore the guideline. But in other cases, try to keep *to* and the verb together.

EXERCISE 13.12

Find the split infinitives in the following sentences and revise them. Decide which revisions are necessary, which optional. Be prepared to defend your decisions.

1. Brian McVicker decided to immediately tear up the first draft of his review after he read it.
2. He had allowed his personal dislike of Professors Vorhees and Cupperman to too much intrude upon his professional judgment.
3. It was a reviewer's responsibility to always strive for objectivity.
4. His problem was how to frankly convey how bad the show was without seeming to only be responding to his personal feelings.
5. To viciously attack the entire show because of a vendetta would be to unfairly criticize many hard-working students.
6. To too enthusiastically endorse the show would be to badly, almost criminally, misrepresent the production to the people who read the student newspaper.
7. Brian decided to carefully rework his entire evaluation.

● Fine Tuning

Nouns (and pronouns) often precede gerunds. These nouns (which technically serve as subjects to the gerund) can be treated either as possessives or as common nouns:

Possessive nouns	Common nouns
the **curtain's** *closing*	the **curtain** *closing*
the **actor's** *bowing*	the **actor** *bowing*
the **audience's** *hissing*	the **audience** *hissing*

In context, the choices look like this:

pos. noun
{**Possessive noun**} The audience roared at the **scenery's**
gerund
collapsing in the banquet scene.

com. noun
{**Common noun**} The audience roared at the **scenery**
gerund
collapsing in the banquet scene.

Here is a general guideline: use the possessive noun for formal or academic writing; use the common noun in informal situations. But you should use the possessive in *both* formal and informal writing when the subject of the gerund is a proper noun or a pronoun:

> Spectators had little respect for **Richard's** *wielding* a sword. [not *Richard*]
>
> They hissed **his** *acting* tough. [not *him*]

And in the following situations, you should use the common noun even in formal writing.

—When the subject of the gerund is modified by other words:

> Brian admitted that he enjoyed **Francie**, his classmate, *portraying* Timandra as a vamp. [not **Francie's**]

—When the subject of the gerund is either plural or collective:

> But he disliked the other **actors** *prancing* on stage like
> rock stars. [not **actors'**]

> The **band** *playing* original rock songs was innovative.
> [not **band's**]

—When the noun is abstract:

> But the production demonstrated **originality** *getting*
> out of hand. [not **originality's**]

Finally, when you want to emphasize the subject of the
gerund, you should use the common form with nouns and the
object form with pronouns:

> Brian couldn't imagine the **cast** *taking* a bow after this
> show. [not **cast's**]

> He anticipated **them** *ducking* fruit and paper airplanes.
> [not **their**]

131

EXERCISE 13.13

Select the appropriate form for the nouns or pronouns used
before gerunds in the passage below. Gerunds are italicized.
Assume that the passage is written for an academic audience.

1. (**Brian/Brian's**) *reviewing* of the show was the hot topic at
   the (**coffeehouse/coffeehouse's**) *gathering* of the *Timon: Superstar* cast after the performance.
2. Francie thought (**Professor Vorhees/Professor Vorhees's**)
   pretending not to remember (**Brian/Brian's**) *flunking* her
   drama class was amusing.
3. "I'm counting on (**his/him**) *being* fair," Vorhees said.
4. She did not, however, appreciate (**Kyle/Kyle's**), one of her
   current students, *reminding* her that the F had been a mistake.

5. **(She/Her)** *refusing* to rectify the error for several months and the college grievance **(committee/committee's)** *blaming* the error on Brian had only made matters worse.
6. Many students thought that **(Professor Cupperman/Professor Cupperman's)** *chairing* the grievance committee had been high-handed.
7. Only the **(Dean/Dean's)** *intervening* in the case made it possible for Brian to demonstrate convincingly that he had been the victim of a simple error in recording grades.
8. **(Justice/Justice's)** *being* done had almost been prevented by Professors Vorhees and Cupperman, but no one imagined **(their/them)** *admitting* their misjudgments. And they hadn't at the time.
9. Their **(victim/victim's)** *taking* revenge now seemed inevitable.

131

EXERCISE 13.14

Decide whether the words or phrases italicized are infinitives, participles, or gerunds.

1. Professor Vorhees sighed, *regretting* all her *misfired* schemes and plots.
2. *Identified* in the program as the director, she was now completely associated with the *failed* show.
3. *To expect* otherwise had been naive.
4. As it turned out, she was no better at *directing* than Professor Cupperman had been at *acting*.
5. *To be* charitable, his performance in the *leading* role had been almost bearable, *evoking* only a few catcalls and hisses.
6. His *singing* of David Barrett's rock lyrics was another matter.
7. But it hadn't been worse than her choreography. One of her dancers, *tripping* over a riser, had fallen into a flat, *bringing* down half of the set in the fourth act.

8. *To make* matters worse, the audience thought the set *collapsing* was part of the show and applauded.
9. "*Seeing Timon of Athens: Superstar* is *believing* it" the *advertising* posters for the show had proclaimed.
10. Professor Vorhees was inclined *to disbelieve* it.

EXERCISE 13.15

Write two sentences using an infinitive, two using a participle, and two using a gerund.

Anatomy of a Verb: *to pay*

Principle Parts

Infinitive:	pay
Past tense:	paid
Past participle:	paid

Tense

Present:	I pay
Present progressive:	I am paying
Present perfect:	I have paid
Past:	I paid
Past progressive:	I was paying
Past perfect:	I had paid
Future:	I will pay
Future progressive:	I will have been paying
Future perfect:	I will have paid

Voice

active:		passive:	
	I pay		I am paid
	you paid		you were paid
	he will pay		he will be paid

Mood

indicative:	I pay.
imperative:	Pay!
subjunctive:	I suggested that he *pay* me.

Person/Number

1st person, singular:	I pay
2nd person, singular:	you pay
3rd person, singular:	he pays
	she pays
	it pays
1st person, plural:	we pay
2nd person, plural:	you pay
3rd person, plural:	they pay

Nonfinite forms

infinitives:
to pay [present tense, active voice]
to be paying [progressive tense, active voice]
to have paid [past tense, active voice]
to have been paying [past progressive tense, active voice]

to be paid [present tense, passive voice]
to have been paid [past tense, passive voice]

participles:
paying [present tense, active voice]
having paid [past tense, active voice]

being paid [present tense, passive voice]
paid, having been paid [past tense, passive voice]

gerunds:
paying [present tense, active voice]
having paid [past tense, active voice]

being paid [present tense, passive voice]
having been paid [past tense, passive voice]

CHAPTER

Problems with Plurals, Possessives, or Articles?

■ **A** Plural nouns
■ **B** Possessive nouns and pronouns
■ **C** Choosing *a* or *an*

14

Terms you need to know

Noun. A word that names a person, place, thing, idea, or quality. In sentences, nouns can serve as subjects, objects, complements, appositives, and even modifiers.

Pronoun. A word that acts like a noun, but doesn't name a specific person, place, or thing—*I*, *you*, *he*, *she*, *it*, *they*, *who*, *this*, and so on.

Case. The form a noun or pronoun takes to indicate its function in a sentence. Nouns have only two cases: the **possessive** form to show ownership and the **common** form to serve all other uses. Pronouns have three forms: **subjective**, **objective**, and **possessive**.

Articles. The words *the*, *a*, and *an* used before a noun. *The* is called a **definite** article because it points to something specific: *the* book; *the* church; *the* criminal. *A* and *an* are **indefinite articles** because they point more generally: *a* book; *a* church; *a* criminal.

343

Troubleshooting

Most plurals in English are simple. You form them by adding -*s* or -*es* to the singular form of the noun:

> demonstration → demonstration*s*
>
> picture → picture*s*
>
> dish → dish*es*

Yet adding -*s* or -*es* causes spelling complications in words ending in -*y*, -*o*, -*um*, -*us*, or -*f*.

Singular		Plural
bus	→	buses? busses?
video	→	videos? videoes?
memo	→	memos? memoes?
turkey	→	turkeys? turkies?
foundry	→	foundrys? foundries?
Gary	→	Garys? Garies?
chief	→	chiefs? chieves?
curriculum	→	curriculums? curricula?
knife	→	knifes? knives?

Some English words use the same form for both singular and plural meanings; others seldom appear as singular terms.

Singular/Plural	Almost Always Plural
athletics	scissors
mathematics	trousers
sheep	caries
spacecraft	headquarters
Sioux	cattle

A substantial number of words—some of them borrowed from foreign languages—are simply irregular. You couldn't reliably predict what their plurals would be if you didn't know them.

Irregular

man → men
ox → oxen
mouse → mice
goose → geese
child → children
beau → beaux (or beaus)
fungus → fungi (funguses)
parenthesis → parentheses

Finally, the plurals of compound words and of figures can be troublesome:

Singular	Plural
father-in-law →	fathers-in-law? father-in-laws?
chief-of-staff →	chiefs-of-staff? chief-of-staffs?
president-elect →	presidents-elect? president-elects?
VIP →	VIPs? VIP's?
2 →	2s? 2's?

14A

In short, plurals merit your careful attention.

When you are unsure about a plural . . .

▶ **Check the dictionary.** This is the safest strategy. Most college dictionaries give the plural forms of all troublesome nouns. If your college dictionary does not provide a plural form for the noun you are looking up, you should assume that it forms its plural regularly, with -s or -es.

You may eliminate some trips to the dictionary by referring to the following guidelines for forming plurals. But the list is complicated and full of exceptions. So keep that dictionary nearby as your backstop.

▶ **Add -s to most nouns.**

demonstration → demonstrations
picture → pictures

▶ **Add -es when the plural adds a syllable to the pronunciation of the noun.** This is usually the case when a word ends in soft *ch*, *sh*, *s*, *ss*, *x*, or *zz*. (If the noun already ends in *-e*, you add only *s*.)

dish → dish-*es*

glass → glass-*es*

bus → bus-*es* or bus-*ses*

buzz → buzz-*es*

choice → choice-*s*

▶ **Add -s when a noun ends in o and a vowel precedes the o; add -es when a noun ends in o and a consonant precedes the o.** But be warned that this guideline has exceptions. A few words ending in *o* even have two acceptable plural forms:

14A

Vowel before -*o* (add -*s*)	Consonant before -*o* (add -*es*)
video → videos	tomato → tomatoes
rodeo → rodeos	veto → vetoes
studio → studios	hero → heroes

Exceptions (add -*s*)	Two acceptable forms
banjo → banjos	cargo → cargos/cargoes
nacho → nachos	no → nos/noes
soprano → sopranos	motto → mottos/mottoes
alto → altos	hobo → hobos/hoboes
piano → pianos	zero → zeros/zeroes
Frito → Fritos	

When in doubt about the plural of a word ending in *o*, check a dictionary.

▶ **Add -s when a noun ends in y and a vowel precedes the y. When a consonant precedes the y, change the y to an *i* and add -es.**

Vowel precedes the -y (add -s)	Consonant precedes the -y (add -es)
attorney → attorneys	foundry → foundries
Monday → Mondays	candy → candies
boy → boys	sentry → sentries

An exception to this rule occurs with proper nouns. They usually retain the *y* and simply add -s.

Proper names ending in -y (add -s)	Exceptions to the exception
Gary → Garys	Rocky Mountains → Rockies
Nestrosky → Nestroskys	
Germany → Germanys	Smoky Mountains → Smokies

▶ **Check words ending in *f* or *fe*. Some form plurals by adding -s, some change *f* to *ves*, and some have two acceptable plural forms.**

Add -s to form plural	Change -f to -ves in plural
chief → chiefs	leaf → leaves
belief → beliefs	wolf → wolves
roof → roofs	knife → knives

Two acceptable forms

elf → elfs/elves	scarf → scarfs/scarves
hoof → hoofs/hooves	wharf → wharfs/wharves

▶ **Check multisyllable words ending in *us* preceded by a consonant.** Some form plurals by changing -*us* to -*i*. But notice that even these may have a second, regular plural.

Change -us to -i

focus → foci/focuses
cactus → cacti/cactuses
syllabus → syllabi/syllabuses

▶ **Check multisyllable words ending in *um* preceded by a consonant.** Some form plurals by changing *-um* to *-a*. But notice, again, that these often have a second, regular plural.

> Change *-um* to *-a*
>
> addendum → addend*a*
>
> curriculum → curricul*a*/curriculum*s*
>
> stratum → strat*a*
>
> medium → medi*a*/medium*s*

▶ **Check compound words.** The last words in most compounds are pluralized.

> dishcloth → dishcloth*s*
>
> bill collector → bill collector*s*
>
> housewife → housewi*ves*
>
> money changer → money changer*s*

However, the first word in a compound is pluralized when it is the important one. This is often the case in hyphenated expressions.

> father-in-law → father*s*-in-law
>
> chief-of-staff → chief*s*-of-staff
>
> president-elect → president*s*-elect
>
> woman-of-the-year → wom*en*-of-the-year
>
> passer-by → passer*s*-by

Naturally, there are exceptions:

> love-in → love-in*s*
>
> sit-in → sit-in*s*
>
> thirty-year-old → thirty-year-old*s*
>
> set-up → set-up*s*

Words that end with *ful* add *s* to the end of the whole word, not to the term before *ful*.

handfuls [not handsful]

tablespoonfuls [not tablespoonsful]

cupfuls [not cupsful]

▶ **Check letters, abbreviations, acronyms, figures, and numbers.** These constructions usually form their plurals by adding either -*s* or '*s*. The '*s* is used where adding an *s* without the apostrophe might cause a misreading.

three *e*'*s* and two *y*'*s*

several of the *I*'*s* in the paper

twenty V.I.P.'*s* [used here because of the periods in the abbreviation]

Quite often, though, the apostrophe is left out, especially when it might mistakenly indicate possession.

3 mins.   the SAT*s*

42 lbs.   five CRT*s*

In many cases, either form of the plural is acceptable.

the 1960*s*/the 1960'*s*

8*s*/8'*s*

two*s*/two'*s*

EXERCISE 14.1

Form the plurals of the following words. Use the guidelines above or a dictionary as necessary.

basis	gas	soliloquy
duo	loaf	zero
tooth	alkali	mongoose
alumnus	datum	heir apparent
moose	Oreo	court-martial
tomato	tattoo	ferry
monkey	thief	man-of-war

Form the plurals of the italicized words in the passage below. Use the guidelines on plurals above or a dictionary as necessary.

1. George Ericson prepared three *espresso* and two *mocha* and then sat with his wife, Greta, and her friends on one of the comfortable *sofa* at the back of the health food store.
2. The kids were Greta's *classmate* in a philosophy course she was taking at the college.
3. Their almost daily after-class *symposium* in the Ericson's store usually began with debates and *cross-examination* of various *theory*, *phenomenon*, and problems introduced in the course, but almost always ended with Greta lamenting the passing of the *1960*.
4. "Where are the *Bob Dylan* and *Joan Baez* of your generation?" she would inevitably ask.
5. "All you kids care for these days is getting *A* and *B*."

14B   PROBLEMS WITH POSSESSIVES?

Term you need to know

> **Possessive case.** The form a noun or pronoun takes to show ownership: *Greta's*, *hers*, *the students'*, *theirs*, *the pride of the town*, *the tail of the dog*. Sometimes the possessive shows a relationship similar to, but not exactly like, ownership: *the night's labor*, *the city's destruction*, *the senator's strategy*, *the governor's approval*.

Troubleshooting

These days, the major problem with the possessive is remembering it: many writers tend to forget the apostrophe before or after an *s* that indicates ownership. Their possessives look just like plurals: *Gretas opinion, the students concern, the nights labor.* And, more and more, the apostrophe is fading from the marketplace—in signs, in advertising, and in corporate logos: *mens room, Americas finest, Macys, Scarboroughs.*

Despite these tendencies, the apostrophe is not optional when an *s* is used to indicate the possessive case. Even where a possessive without an apostrophe won't be mistaken for a plural, your readers and editors expect to see the correct form: *Greta's opinion.* You cannot afford to omit the apostrophe in academic or business writing.

A problem you may have with possessives is positioning the apostrophe. Difficulties arise, for example, when a singular word ends in *-s* or *-z*.

> Ross's handball *or* Ross' handball?
>
> Oz's wizard *or* Oz' wizard?

14B

Questions can also come up when forming the possessives of plurals:

> the hostesses' *or* the hostesses's?

Then there's the problem of joint possession:

> George's and Greta's shop *or* George and Greta's shop?

Sometimes you must choose between the two possessive forms: *'s* and *of.*

> The eyes **of** Texas *or* Texas' eyes?
>
> Kelly's secret *or* the secret **of** Kelly?
>
> the book's spine *or* the spine **of** the book?

Finally, some pronouns cause possession problems. Unlike nouns, personal pronouns never take an apostrophe, yet they look as if they should:

> The problem is (**theirs? their's?**).
>
> Be sure you know (**its? it's?**) measurements.

All of the issues (and more) are addressed in detail below.

▶ **Add an apostrophe + s to most singular nouns and to plural nouns that do not end in s.**

Singular Nouns	Plurals Not Ending in -s
dog's life	*geese's* behavior
that *man's* opinion	*women's* attitude
child's imagination	*children's* imaginations
the *NCAA's* ruling	

Singular nouns that end in *s* or *z* may take either an apostrophe + *s* or the apostrophe alone. Use one form or the other consistently throughout a paper.

> *Ross's* handball or *Ross'* handball

> *Oz's* wizard or *Oz'* wizard

> *Katz's* music or *Katz'* music

The apostrophe alone is used with singular words ending in *s* when the possessive does not add a syllable to the pronunciation of the word.

> *Texas'* Independence Day

> *Jesus'* words

> *Alexis'* new husband

▶ **Add an apostrophe (but not an s) to plural nouns that end in s.**

> *hostesses'* job

> *students'* opinion

> *dogs'* day

> *senators'* chambers

> *Smiths'* home

> *stewardesses'* protest

14B

► **Indicate possession only at the end of compound or hyphenated words.**

chief-of-staff's arrest

president-elect's decision

fathers-in-law's Cadillacs

court martial's opening

► **Indicate possession only once when two nouns share ownership.**

Greta and *George's* health food store

Vorhees and *Goetz'* project

But when ownership is separate, each noun shows possession.

Greta's and *George's* educations

Vorhees' and *Goetz'* homes

14B

► **Use an apostrophe + s to form the possessive of living things and titled works, use of with nonliving things.** This guideline should be followed sensibly. Many common expressions violate the convention, and many writers simply ignore it.

Take apostrophe + *s*	Take *of*
the *dog's* bone	the weight *of the bone*
Professor Shade's taxes	the bite *of taxes*
Kelly's dark mystery	the lure *of mystery*
Macbeth's plot	the weaknesses *of the plot*
Newsweek's cover	the attractiveness *of the cover*

Use *of* whenever an apostrophe + *s* might be awkward or confusing.

{**Confusing**} The **student** sitting next to Greta's opinion was radical.

{**Revised**} The opinion **of the student** sitting next to Greta was radical.

In a few situations, English allows a double possessive, consisting of both the *'s* and *of*.

That suggestion **of** George**'s** didn't win support, although an earlier one did.

An opinion **of** Greta**'s** soon spurred another argument.

▶ **Do not use an apostrophe with personal pronouns.** Personal pronouns don't take an apostrophe to show ownership: *my/mine, your/yours, her/hers, his, our/ours, their/theirs, whose,* and *its.* Constructions such as *her's, his',* or *their's* don't exist. The forms *it's* and *who's* are contractions for *it is* and *who is* and shouldn't be confused with the possessive pronouns *its* and *whose.*

It's an idea that has **its** opponents in arms.

Who's to say **whose** opinion is right?

14B

Indefinite pronouns—such as *anybody, each one, everybody*—do form their possessives regularly: *anybody's, each one's, everybody's.* For more about possessive pronouns, see 15D.

EXERCISE 14.3

Decide whether the forms italicized in the passage below are correct. Revise any you believe are faulty.

1. "That impression *of your's* is all wrong," Abel Gonzalez replied to *Greta's* assertion that the main concern *of most students'* was getting high grades.
2. Abel continued. "We care about the *society's* problems as much as students did in the *1960s'.* We just don't thumb *our nose's* hypocritically at our *parent's* generation while enjoying *it's* benefits. Our protests aren't paid for by *someone elses* labor."

3. *Greta and George's* temper flared.
4. "Hypocrites! This reminds me of *King Lear's plot* where ungrateful children abuse their *elders* generosity," Greta said with excessive drama. "*Its* a shame!"
5. Sue Ellen Rizzo, a student *of Gretas* generation, tried to calm things down. "Mr. *Gonzalez'es* opinion is no more extreme than *your's*, Greta."

14C IS IT A OR AN?

Troubleshooting

English has only one form for its definite article: *the*. So you cannot choose a wrong form: *the* argument, *the* European, *the* house, *the* historic day. But the indefinite article has two forms: *a* and *an*. Some writers think that they should simply use *a* before all words that begin with consonants and *an* before all words that begin with vowels. In fact, usage is just a bit more complicated, as a few examples show: *an* argument, *a* European, *a* house.

To choose between *a* or *an* . . .

▶ **Use *a* when the word following it begins with a consonant *sound*; use *an* when the word following it begins with a vowel *sound*.** In most cases, it works out so that *a* actually comes before words beginning with consonants, *an* before words with vowels.

Initial consonants	Initial vowels
a **b**oat	an **a**ardvark
a **c**lass	an **E**gyptian monument
a **d**uck	an **i**gloo
a **f**inal opinion	an **o**dd event
a **h**ouse	an **u**tter disaster

But *an* is used before words beginning with a consonant when the consonant is silent, as is sometimes the case with *h*. It is also used when a consonant itself is pronounced with an initial vowel sound (F → *ef*; N → *en*; S → *es*) as often happens in acronyms.

Silent consonant	Consonant with a vowel sound
an hour	an *F* in this course
an heir	an SAT score
an hors d'oeuvre	an X-ray

Similarly, *a* is used before words beginning with a vowel when the vowel is pronounced like a consonant. Certain vowels, for example, sound like the consonant *y*, and in a few cases, an initial *o* sounds like the consonant *w*.

Vowel with a consonant sound

a European vacation (*eu* sounds like *y*)
a unique painting (*u* sounds like *y*)
a one-sided argument (*o* sounds like *w*)
a U-joint (*u* sounds like *y*)

14C

EXERCISE 14.4

Decide whether *a* or *an* ought to be used before the following words or phrases.

1. _____ L-shaped room
2. _____ hyperthyroid condition
3. _____ zygote
4. _____ X-rated movie
5. _____ Euclidean principle
6. _____ evasive answer
7. _____ jalapeno pepper
8. _____ unwritten rule
9. _____ unit of measure
10. _____ veneer of oak
11. _____ EPA investigation
12. _____ euphemistic expression
13. _____ aerobic exercise
14. _____ NASA engineer
15. _____ jellyfish
16. _____ OK from the editor
17. _____ Syrian import
18. _____ D− grade
19. _____ idiosyncrasy
20. _____ FBI investigation

CHAPTER

Problems with Pronouns?

■ **A** Unclear reference
■ **B** Ambiguous reference
■ **C** *This, that, which, it*
■ **D** Lost antecedent
■ **E** *Or, either/or; neither/nor*
■ **F** With collective nouns
■ **G** With indefinite pronouns
■ **H** Case: subject/object/possessive
■ **I** After prepositions
■ **J** In comparisons
■ **K** After linking verbs
■ **L** *Who/whom*
■ **M** Possessive pronouns
■ **N** *Its* or *it's*
■ **O** Reflexive/intensive pronouns
■ **P** Using *I, you, one, we;* consistency
■ **Q** Nonsexist usage

15

Terms you need to know

> **Pronoun.** A word that acts like a noun, but doesn't name a specific person, place, or thing—*I, you, he, she, it, they, whom, who, what, myself, oneself, this, these, that, all, both, anybody,* and so on. Pronouns often stand in for nouns in a sentence: David was proud that *he* [that is, *David*] had written the music.

There are many varieties of pronouns: **personal, relative, interrogative, intensive, reflexive, demonstrative, indefinite, reciprocal,** and **numerical.**

Antecedent. The person, place, or thing a pronoun stands in for: *he = David; it = the radio; they = the bodybuilders in Butcher's Gym.* The antecedent is the word you would have to repeat in your sentence if you couldn't use a pronoun.

Reference. The connection between a pronoun and the noun it stands in for. This connection should be clear and unambiguous. When a reader can't figure out who *he* is in a sentence you have written, or what exactly *this* may mean, you have a problem with unclear reference.

Agreement. Pronouns are said to be in agreement when singular pronouns stand in for singular nouns (*his* surfboard = *Richard's* surfboard) and plural pronouns stand in for plural nouns (*their* surfboard = *George and Martha's* surfboard). However, when pronouns and their antecedents aren't the same in number, you have an agreement problem.

Case. Some pronouns change form according to how they are used in a sentence. They have one form when used as a subject (*he, they, who*), another when used as an object (*him, them, whom*), and a third when they show ownership (*his, theirs, whose*). The **case** of a pronoun is its form, either **subjective** (or **nominative**), **objective**, or **possessive.**

15A PRONOUN REFERENCE: UNCLEAR

Troubleshooting

You have a problem with pronoun reference if readers can't find a word in your sentence that could sensibly replace the pronoun you are using.

Brian liked to study rocketry though he had never seen **one** in his life.

> [*Rocketry* seems to be the word the pronoun *one* refers to, but the sentence doesn't read well if you make the substitution: *Brian liked to study rocketry, though he had never seen rocketry in his life.*]

Passengers had been searched for weapons, but **it** did not prevent the skyjacking.

> [No word in the sentence explains what the pronoun *it* is.]

As for women's view of *Rambo*, **they** are either repulsed by the film or excited by the hero.

> [This example is tricky. The pronoun *they* clearly refers to *women*. But notice that the only word actually in the sentence that might replace *they* is *women's*—and it has a possessive form. If you replaced *they* with *women's*, you'd have nonsense: "As for women's view of *Rambo*, *women's* are either repulsed by the film or excited by the hero."]

15A

In all the above cases, the sentences need to be revised for clarity.

To be sure your pronoun references are clear . . .

▶ **Revise a sentence or passage to ensure that there is an antecedent for any potentially vague pronoun.** When you aren't sure that the pronoun has an antecedent, ask yourself whether another word in the sentence could be put in the place of the pronoun:

> Brian liked to study rocketry though he had never seen **one [?]** in his life.

> Brian liked to study rocketry though he had never seen **[rocketry?]** in his life.

If no word from the sentence can replace the pronoun, you may have to add a word:

> {**Revised**} Brian liked to study rocketry though he had never seen **a rocket** in his life.

Here's another example:

> Passengers had been searched for weapons, but **it [?]** did not prevent the skyjacking.

> {**Revised**} Passengers had been searched for weapons, but **this precaution** did not prevent the skyjacking.

When a word that might stand in for the pronoun is possessive, you may have to rewrite the sentence. In some instances, it is best to eliminate the pronoun entirely.

> As for women's view of *Rambo*, **they** are either repulsed by *Rambo* or excited by its hero.

> {**Revised**} **Women** are either repulsed by *Rambo* or excited by its hero.

15B PRONOUN REFERENCE: AMBIGUOUS

Troubleshooting

You also have a problem with pronoun reference when a pronoun you use could refer to more than one antecedent.

> When Doris talked to Tiffany that noon, **she** did not realize that **she** might be resigning before the end of the day.

> [Who is resigning?]

> We pulled out our umbrella, which was under the seat, and opened **it**. **It** dampened our spirits for a while, but we decided to stick **it** out.

> [What is **it**?]

Such sentences ordinarily need to be modified to eliminate the ambiguous pronoun references.

▶ **Revise a sentence to eliminate confusing or ambiguous antecedents.** You can usually make a confusing sentence clearer by replacing the pronouns with more specific words or by rearranging the sentence. Sometimes you may have to do both:

> When Doris talked to Tiffany that noon, **she** did not realize that **she** might be resigning before the end of the day.

> {Revised} When **they** talked to each other at noon, **Tiffany** did not realize that **Doris** might be resigning before the end of the day.

> *or*

> {Revised} When **the women** talked to each other at noon, **Tiffany** did not realize that **Doris** might be resigning before the end of the day.

Here's another example:

> We pulled out our umbrella, which was under the seat, and opened **it**. **It** dampened our spirits for a while, but we decided to stick **it** out.

> {Revised} We pulled out and opened the **umbrella** stowed under the seat. The **rain** dampened our spirits for a while, but we decided to **stay for the entire game**.

15C

15C PRONOUN REFERENCE: PROBLEMS WITH *THIS, THAT, WHICH, IT*

Troubleshooting

Your readers may be confused if you use the pronouns *this, that, which,* or *it* to refer to ideas and situations you haven't named or explained clearly in your sentence or paragraph. You expect readers to understand what *this* is—and they often do, especially in spoken English. But in written English you must be more specific. This problem is one best explained through examples. Many readers find constructions such as the following confusing or imprecise.

> The novel is filled with violence, brutality, and refined language. I especially like **this**.
>
>> [Readers can't tell whether you like violence, brutality, or refined language—or all three. The *this* in the second sentence could refer to any one of those terms or to all of them.]

> The influx of new residents brings growth, new business, talented people, heavier traffic, and large-scale housing developments. Mayor Carter is responsible for **this**.
>
>> [Readers have to guess what *this* is. What exactly is the mayor responsible for—growth? talented people? housing developments? Or is it some as yet unstated idea related to the influx of new residents?]

> The Supreme Court acted decisively on the Gideon case after the accused had spent time in a Florida jail for a crime he had not committed, **which** is typical of American justice.
>
>> [The *which* here is very confusing. What is typical of American justice—the decisive action of the Supreme Court or the imprisonment of an innocent man?]

Sentences of this kind must be revised to eliminate the vague pronoun references.

To avoid vague references . . .

▶ **Revise a sentence or passage to make it clear what this, that, which, or it means.**   When a reader might mistake what a *this* or *that* means, you can usually remedy the problem by inserting an imaginary blank space after the pronoun (*this* _____ ? or *that* _____?) and filling it in with a word or phrase that explains what *this* or *that* is.

The novel is filled with violence, brutality, and refined language. I especially like **this**.

> [*This* is not clear. Imagine a blank space after the *this*.]

The novel is filled with violence, brutality, and refined language. I especially like **this** _ _____ ?

> [Now fill in the blank.]

{**Revised**} The novel is filled with violence, brutality, and refined language. I especially like **this** *combination of toughness and grace.*

Here's another example:

> The influx of new residents brings growth, new business, talented people, heavier traffic, and large-scale housing developments. Mayor Carter is responsible for **this**.

> > [Insert an imaginary blank space after *this* and fill it in.]

> {**Revised**} The influx of new residents brings growth, new business, talented people, heavier traffic, and large-scale housing developments. Mayor Carter is responsible for **this** *sudden population increase.*

When the unclear pronoun is *which* or *it*, you must either revise the sentence or supply a clear direct antecedent.

> The Supreme Court acted decisively on the Gideon case after the accused had spent time in a Florida jail for a crime he had not committed, **which** (?) is typical of American justice.

> > [When you face a confusing pronoun like the *which* here, you need to understand what sort of problem the vague word is causing your readers. In this sentence, they can't tell *what* is typical of American justice. Revise the sentence to relieve the confusion. Several alternatives are possible, depending upon your meaning.]

15C

{**Revised**} After the accused had spent time in a Florida jail for a crime he had not committed, the Supreme Court acted on the Gideon case **with the decisiveness typical of American justice.**

{**Revised**} The Supreme Court **typified American justice** when it acted decisively on the Gideon case **only** after the accused had **already** spent **long months** in a Florida jail for a crime he had not committed.

Here's another example, with **it** as the vague pronoun:

While atomic waste products are hard to dispose of safely, **it** remains a reasonable alternative to burning fossil fuels to produce electricity.

[What is the alternative to burning fossil fuels? Surely not *atomic waste products*. The *it* needs to be replaced by a more specific term.]

15C

{**Revised**} While atomic waste products are hard to dispose of safely, **nuclear power** remains a reasonable alternative to burning fossil fuels to produce electricity.

● **Fine Tuning**

1. Don't use a pronoun to refer to the title of your paper or a word or phrase in a title.

All the World's a Stage

This is how a character in Shakespeare's *As You Like It* compares reality to the illusion of theater. Both theater and reality are versions of the same dream. . . .

Consider the title as separate from the rest of the paper.

All the World's a Stage

In Shakespeare's *As You Like It*, a character compares reality to the illusion of theater by suggesting that "all the world's a stage." Both theater and reality are versions of the same dream. . . .

2. In academic writing, avoid using *they* or *it* without antecedents to describe people or things in general.

>{**Vague**} You are going to get **it**!

>{**Revised**} You are going to get **in trouble**!

>{**Vague**} In Houston, **they** live more casually than in Dallas.

>{**Revised**} In Houston, **people** live more casually than in Dallas.

3. Don't let a pronoun that is not possessive refer to a word that is possessive.

>{**Inaccurate**} Seeing **Rita's** car, Hector waved at **her**.

>{**Revised**} Seeing **Rita** *in her* car, Hector waved at **her**.

EXERCISE 15.1

Decide whether a reader might find the pronouns in boldface unclear. Revise the sentences as necessary.

1. A little collusion seemed like a good idea at the time, even though Mrs. Ericson was against **it**—complaining that **this** was what was wrong with the younger generation.
2. Nonetheless, Kyle and Richard decided to collaborate on their semester term papers, preparing one paper for both **their** classes, dividing up the labor, and producing a first class research effort, **which** was against school policy.
3. Kyle was especially enthusiastic. He loved doing research and poring through reference books and indexes in the library, although he had not written **one** since high school.
4. After Kyle discussed the topic for the paper with Richard, he agreed to leave **that** to **him**.
5. Richard—neat and efficient as usual—would be responsible for writing the paper itself, organizing **it**, and polishing the final version.

6. **It** suddenly occurred to Richard that **their** paper might also fulfill Francie's history assignment, so he decided to bring **her** in on **it**.

7. After all, no one handled documentation better than Francie, edited more proficiently, or owned a fancier word-processor. **This** would be a major advantage.

8. Francie had some qualms initially, but if Richard were involved, well, she'd do **it**. And she did.

9. Unfortunately, soon after turning in the paper, Francie felt that her teacher was casting accusatory glances her way, although he didn't actually make **one**.

15D AGREEMENT PROBLEMS: LOST ANTECEDENT

15D

Troubleshooting

Pronouns and nouns are either singular or plural. You would ordinarily use a singular pronoun (such as *she, it, this, that, her, him, my, his, her, its*) when referring to someone or something that is singular and a plural pronoun (such as *they, these, them, their*) when referring to plural things. Think of this "principle of agreement" as one way the language helps you keep track of what you are talking about.

You have a problem with **pronoun agreement** when you use a singular pronoun to substitute for a plural noun (or its **antecedent**) or a plural pronoun to substitute for a singular noun (or its antecedent).

In most cases, you will have no difficulties with pronoun agreement when the pronoun and its antecedent stand close together and when the antecedent is clearly either singular or plural.

sing.   sing.

The **carton** was full when I closed **it**.

[No likelihood of a misreading in this sentence. The antecedent of the pronoun *it* is clearly *carton*. Both *it* and *carton* are singular.]

plural   plural
The **football players** gathered **their** equipment while
sing.   sing.
Coach Rhodes looked for **his** car.

But sometimes, words and phrases that come between pronouns and their antecedents cause a kind of "misdirection." A writer loses track of the real antecedent and mistakenly gives the pronoun the wrong number, as in the following examples.

> Even though the typical **student** enjoys a lively social life, parties, and athletic events, our survey found that **they** also work hard on **their** school work.

> > [The plural pronouns *they* and *their* mistakenly refer to a singular noun, *student*. The mistake probably occurs because the writer thinks of a survey as involving more than one student. Consider, too, the possibility that the plural words *parties* and *athletic events* make the writer forget about that singular antecedent, *student*.]

15D

> An **American** always takes it for granted that government agencies will help **them** when trouble strikes.

> > [The plural pronoun *them* mistakenly refers to the singular noun, *American*. This error probably occurs because the pronoun and antecedent are far apart and the plural noun *agencies* causes interference.]

To be sure your pronouns and their antecedents agree . . .

▶ **First, identify the antecedents of any troublesome pronouns. Then be sure that singular pronouns refer to singular antecedents and that plural pronouns refer to plural antecedents.** Here's an example:

> Even though the typical **student** enjoys entertainment, parties, and athletic events, our survey found that **they** also work hard on **their** school work.

367

[*They* and *their* are the pronouns, standing in for the nouns *student* and *student's*. But since *they* is plural and *student* singular, a revision is necessary. Either *student* can be made plural or *they* can be made singular.]

{**Revised—first version**} Even though typical **students** enjoy entertainment, parties, and athletic events, our survey found that **they** also work hard on **their** school work.

{**Revised—second version**} Even though the typical **student** enjoys entertainment, parties, and athletic events, our survey found that *he* also work*s* hard on *his* school work.

Here's another example:

An **American** always takes it for granted that government agencies will help **them** when trouble strikes.

[**American** is singular; **them** is plural. Revision is needed.]

{**Revised—first version**} **Americans** always take it for granted that government agencies will help *them* when trouble strikes.

{**Revised—second version**} An **American** always take*s* it for granted that government agencies will help **him** *or* **her** when trouble strikes.

15E AGREEMENT PROBLEMS: *OR, EITHER/OR, NEITHER/NOR*

Troubleshooting

Quite often, writers have problems with pronoun agreement simply because they aren't sure whether the word or phrase their pronoun refers to is singular or plural. Don't be embarrassed when you find yourself in this situation. The English language supplies many such puzzles.

One puzzler occurs when the antecedents for a pronoun are nouns joined by *or, either . . . or,* or *neither . . . nor.*

> **Sean** or **Darwin** had the coins in (**their? his?**) pocket.
>
> Either the weak **script** or the inept **actors** will take (**its? their?**) toll on the audience.
>
> Neither the **students** nor the **professor** wanted to recalculate (**her? their?**) numbers.

When antecedents are joined by *and,* it is usually apparent that both the pronoun and antecedent are plural.

> When **Richard** and **Francie** finished the paper, **they celebrated.**

To be sure pronouns agree with antecedents joined by *either* and *neither . . .*

► **Examine pairs of nouns joined by** *nor, or, either . . . or,* **neither . . . nor to determine which one of the following guidelines applies in your sentence:**

When both nouns in the pair are singular, a pronoun referring to them should be singular.

> **Maggie** or **Rita** had the script in (**their? her?**) purse.
>
> > [Both **Maggie** and **Rita** are singular, so the **possessive** pronoun describing **purse** should also be singular.]
>
> {**Revised**} **Maggie** or **Rita** had the script in **her** purse.
>
> > [Compare the revised sentence to what happens when *or* is replaced by *and*: *Maggie and Rita had the scripts in their purses.*]

When both nouns are plural, a pronoun referring to them should be plural.

> **Players** or **managers** may file **their** grievances with the commissioner.

When one noun is singular and one is plural, the pronoun should agree in number with the noun nearer to it—except when the resulting sentence sounds unnatural or awkward.

> Either the weak **script** or the inept **actors** will take (**its? their?**) toll on the audience.

>> [**Script** is singular; **actors** plural. The pronoun will be nearer to **actors**, and so it should be plural.]

> {**Revised**} Either the weak **script** or the inept **actors** will take **their** toll on the audience.

> {**Revised**} Either the inept **actors** or the weak **script** will take **its** toll on the audience.

Here's a second example, with a complication:

> Neither the **students** nor the **professor** wanted to recalculate (**her? their?**) numbers.

>> [**Students** is plural; **professor** singular. The pronoun is nearer to **professor**, and so it should be singular.]

> {**Revised**} Neither the **students** nor the **professor** wanted to recalculate **her** numbers.

>> [Notice, however, that it would be easy to assume from this revised sentence that only the numbers of the professor were being talked about—and not those of the students as well. The sentence might need to be revised if a different meaning were intended.]

> {**Revised**} Neither the **professor** nor the **students** wanted to recalculate **their** numbers.

15F AGREEMENT PROBLEMS: COLLECTIVE NOUNS

Troubleshooting

Agreement problems occur frequently with pronouns that refer to nouns describing groups or collections of things: *class,*

370

team, band, government, jury. These so-called **collective** nouns can be either singular or plural, depending on how they are used in a sentence.

The **orchestra** played **its** heart out.

The **orchestra** arrived and took **their** seats.

A pronoun referring to a collective noun should be consistently either singular or plural. That usually means deciding whether to treat the noun as singular or plural.

To handle references to collective nouns . . .

▶ **Identify any collective noun in a sentence to which a pronoun refers.** Decide whether you want to treat that noun as a single body (the *jury*) or as a group made up of more than one person or object (the twelve members of the *jury*). Then be consistent. If you decide it makes sense to treat the word as singular, be sure pronouns referring to it are also singular. If you decide it is plural, all pronoun references should be plural.

15F

The **jury** rendered **its** decision.

The **jury** had **their** photographs taken frequently during the trial.

In most cases, your sentences will sound more natural if you treat collective nouns as single objects. Notice how awkward the following sentences seem because the collective nouns are treated as plural forms.

The **committee** are unable to make up **their** minds.

The **band** are unhappy with **their** latest recordings.

Sentences like these are likely to be improved either by making the collective nouns more clearly plural or by making them singular.

The *members of the* **committee** are unable to make up **their** minds.

The **band** *is* unhappy with *its* latest recordings.

Troubleshooting

A very troublesome agreement problem involves sentences that include pronoun references to words (usually other pronouns) described as *indefinite.* Common indefinite pronouns include *everyone, anybody, anyone, somebody, all, some, none, each, few, most.* It is not always easy to tell whether one of these indefinite words is singular or plural.

> **Everyone** should have (**his? their?**) ticket in (**his? their?**) hand.

> **None** of us intended to leave (**her? our?**) place in line.

Yet a decision usually has to be made before a pronoun can be selected.

15G

To handle problems with indefinite pronouns . . .

▶ **Use the chart below or, better yet, a dictionary to determine whether an indefinite pronoun or noun in your sentence is singular, variable, or plural.** (The list is *not* exhaustive.)

Always singular	Variable, S. or Pl.	Usually plural
anybody	all	few
anyone	any	many
each	more	several
everybody	most	
everyone	none	
nobody	some	
no one		
somebody		
someone		

► **If the indefinite word is always singular, make any pronouns that refer to it singular.**

> Did **anybody** misplace **her** notes?

> **Everyone** should keep **his** temper.

> **No one** has a right to more than **his or her** share.

Using singular pronouns in these cases may seem odd at times because the plural forms occur so often in speech and informal writing.

> {Informal} **Each** of the candidates has **their** own ideas.

> [Informal] We discovered that **everyone** had kept **their** notes.

But in academic and professional writing, you should still respect the principle of consistent agreement between pronouns and antecedents.

> {Revised—formal} **Each** of the candidates has **his or her** own ideas.

> {Revised formal} We discovered that **everyone** had kept **his** notes.

► **If the indefinite word is usually plural, make any pronouns that refer to it plural.**

> **Several** of the aircraft had to have **their** wings stiffened. **Few**, however, had given **their** pilots trouble.

► **If the indefinite word is variable, you'll have to use common sense or your best judgment to determine which pronoun fits your sentence better.** In most cases, the choice will be obvious.

> **All** of the portraits had yellowed in **their** frames. **Some** will be restored to **their** original condition.

> **All** of the wine is still in **its** casks. **Some** of it is certain to have **its** quality evaluated.

None is considered variable because it is often employed as a plural form in informal writing and speech. However, in

15G

formal writing, you should usually treat **none** as singular. Think of **none** as meaning **not one**.

> **None** of the women is reluctant to speak **her** mind.

> **None** of the houses has **its** mortgage approved.

▶ **Rewrite any sentences that simply don't seem to make sense.** You can get into problems when a possessive pronoun referring to two antecedents doesn't explain clearly who owns what.

> Neither Greta nor George is willing to sell (**his? her? their?**) house.

> [What a reader needs to know is whether Greta and George own a single home (in which case *their* **house** would be appropriate) or two separate houses (in which case *his or her* **house** is probably the best choice). Often it makes sense simply to rewrite the sentence entirely to avoid confusion.]

> Neither Greta nor George is willing to sell *the house they jointly own.*

> Greta *won't sell her* house and George *won't sell his.*

Fortunately, sentences with potentially confusing antecedents and pronouns usually make better sense when they are part of a paragraph or full document than when they are examined alone.

● **Fine Tuning**

1. *Everyone* and *everybody* should be treated as singular whenever a possessive pronoun refers to one of these words.

> **Everybody** had received **his or her** allotment of food.

But when a pronoun referring to **everyone** or **everybody** acts as a subject or an object, it will ordinarily be plural because it describes a group.

> **Everybody** had plenty of money and **they** were willing to spend it.

374

Because **everyone** arrived late, Dr. Upton gave **them** a stern lecture on punctuality.

2. *Person* is a singular noun, not a plural one. Don't use *they* to refer to *person*.

If a **person** watches too much television, **they** may become a couch potato.

{Revised} If a **person** watches too much television, **he or she** may become a couch potato.

EXERCISE 15.2

Look for pronouns that do not agree in number with their antecedents. Make whatever corrections are necessary. Sometimes you will need to change only a word; in other cases, you will need to revise the entire sentence. Apply the standards of formal written English even to the passages of dialogue.

15G

1. "I'm sure everyone has done their own work," Mr. Ransom said as he returned the history term papers.
2. "If you have any problems with the essays or my comments on them, feel free to discuss it with me."
3. Francie cringed at his implied accusation—and his grammar. Why had she allowed Richard and Kyle to involve her in their scheme to write one paper for three different classes?
4. She should have known that neither Tricky Dick nor Kyle the Smile would get their knuckles rapped for scholastic dishonesty.
5. No, she was the one with a conscience who felt obligated to tell all. Either the boys or she had to admit their perfidy and face the consequences.
6. Each would have to take their medicine—even if it meant an F.
7. The bell rang and Francie watched as the class left its seats, leaving her alone with Mr. Ransom.

8. Somebody returned for their textbooks left under a seat, but the interruption lasted only a second. She had to speak.

9. "Mr. Ransom?" she began, "Does a teacher remember what it was like when they were in college?"

10. "No one remembers everything they did, but almost all can recall some of his trials and tribulations," Mr. Ransom replied, rubbing his forehead thoughtfully.

11. Francie gulped, then spoke. "Mr. Ransom, I didn't write my paper myself. A group of us put its heads together and produced one paper to turn into its three different classes. I'm sorry. I was just so busy."

12. Francie continued. "All my courses had its term paper due on the same day, so I got a little desperate. You remember how it was. None of us is perfect."

15H PROBLEMS WITH PRONOUN CASE: SUBJECT/OBJECT/POSSESSIVE

Terms you need to know

Case. The form a pronoun takes to show what it is doing in a clause. The three cases are defined below.

Subjective (or **nominative**) **case.** The form a pronoun takes when it is the subject of a sentence or a clause: *I, you, she, he, it, we, they, who.* A pronoun is also in the subjective case when it follows a linking verb as a **predicate nominative**: It is *I*; It was *they* who cast the deciding votes.

Objective case. The form a pronoun takes when something is done to it: Elena broke *them*; Buck loved *her.* This is also the form a pronoun takes after a preposition: [to] *me, her, him, us, them, whom.* For the pronouns *you* and *it*, the subjective and objective forms are identical.

Possessive case. The form a pronoun takes when it shows ownership: *my, mine, your, yours, her, hers, his, its, our, ours, their, theirs, whose.*

Personal pronoun. A pronoun that refers to particular individuals, things, or groups: *I, you, he, she, it, we, they.*

Preposition. A word that links a noun or pronoun to the rest of a sentence. Prepositions point out all kinds of basic relationships: *on, above, to, for, in, out, through, by.* The combination of a preposition and a noun, pronoun, and modifiers is called a **prepositional phrase**. The following are prepositional phrases: *on our house; above it; to him; in love; through them; by the garden gate.*

Troubleshooting

Some personal pronouns (and *who*) change their form according to how they are used in a sentence. They have one form when used as a subject (*he, they, who*), another when used as an object (*him, them, whom*), and a third when they show ownership (*his, theirs, whose*). In most situations, writers are able to select the appropriate case without even thinking about their choices.

Whose book did she give to **him**?

They were more confident of **their** victory than **we** were of **ours**.

But at other times, selecting the right case is no easy matter. The problem is that the correct pronoun choice often sounds or looks wrong.

Pairs of pronouns can be especially puzzling. When you have two pronouns or a noun and pronoun, expect a problem, especially when the choice is between *I* and *me*.

You and **(I? me?)** don't have an effective partnership.

As for **my sister** and **(I? me?)**, we chose not to attend.

The rescuers discovered both **(she? her?)** and **(he? him?)** under the rubble of the gym.

377

▶ **Use the chart below to select subjective forms when pronouns act as subjects, objective forms when pronouns act as objects (especially in prepositional phrases), and possessive forms when pronouns show ownership.**

Subject Forms	Object Forms	Possessive Forms
I	me	my, mine
we	us	our, ours
you	you	your, yours
he	him	his
she	her	her, hers
it	it	its, of it
they	them	their, theirs
who	whom	whose

15H

When you are unsure about what case a pair of pronouns should be in (usually, the second pronoun of the pair is causing the difficulty), imagine how the sentence would read if you dropped one or the other pronoun. With only one pronoun in the sentence, you can usually tell immediately what the correct form should be.

> **You** and **(I? me?)** don't have an effective partnership.
>
> > [The pronouns here are both part of the subject. So you would use the subjective form of the *I*/*me* pair—which is *I*. But even if you didn't recognize the need for a subject form, you could still make the right choice just by examining the two versions of the sentence possible after you dropped *You*.]
>
> **Me** don't have an effective partnership.
>
> **I** don't have an effective partnership.
>
> > [Given this choice, most people will select the correct pronoun—*I*.]
>
> {**Revised**} **You** and **I** don't have an effective partnership.

378

This simple but effective trick works with many confusing pairs of pronouns or even a noun/pronoun combination:

> noun   pro.
> As for **my sister** and (**I? me?**), we chose not to attend.
>
> [Drop the noun phrase *my sister*, and consider the alternatives.]
>
> {**1st version**} As for **I**, we chose not to attend.
>
> {**2nd version**} As for **me**, we chose not to attend.
>
> [Even though the sentence doesn't make perfect sense with *my sister* deleted, version #2 is obviously better than version #1. Notice too that dropping *my sister* makes it clearer that the pronoun you select must be the object of the preposition *for*. Checking the chart above, you see that the object form of *I/me* is *me*.]
>
> {**Revised**} As for **my sister** and **me**, we chose not to attend.

Another example:

> The rescuers discovered both (**she? her?**) and (**he? him?**) under the rubble of the gym.
>
> [You could figure this one out quickly if you recognized that the *rescuers* perform the action in this sentence and, consequently, are the **subject**. The people the rescuers discover become the **object** of the sentence and so must take the objective form—which you can locate in the chart above. Complicated? Not really, but if you find it so, try the deletion procedure explained above, dropping all but one of the pronouns.]
>
> {**1st version**} The rescuers discovered **she** under the rubble of the gym.
>
> {**2nd version**} The rescuers discovered **her** under the rubble of the gym.
>
> [Version #2—with the pronoun in the objective case—is better. You can assume that the same choice would hold for *he/him*.]

{**Revised**} The rescuers discovered both **her** and **him** under the rubble of the gym.

Sentences in the passive voice pose a special problem.

(**He? Him?**) and (**she? her?**) were carried out on stretchers.

[In this sentence, the verb *were carried* is passive, but you might still recognize that the pronouns are the subjects of the sentence and, consequently, in the nominative case: **He/she**. This time, if you try the deletion technique, you will run into a complication.]

{**1st version**} **He** were carried out on stretchers.

{**2nd version**} **Him** were carried out on stretchers.

[Neither version seems correct. That's because of the change from a plural subject or object (he/him + she/her) to a singular one. To figure out the right pronoun, you have to adjust the sentence to a singular form.]

{**1st version**} **He** was carried out on a stretcher.

{**2nd version**} **Him** was carried out on a stretcher.

[Now the correct version is more obvious. Notice that the need to change the verb in itself indicates that the pronoun should be in the subjective form. You can now write the final version.]

{**Revised**} **He** and **she** were carried out on stretchers.

15l PROBLEMS WITH PRONOUN CASE: OBJECTS OF PREPOSITIONS

Troubleshooting

Pronouns that are the objects of **prepositions** are always in the objective case. Difficulties with case are rare when a single pronoun closely follows its preposition.

Come *with* **me** now.

[You would never say: *Come with I now.*]

But add another pronoun or noun after the preposition, and you may suddenly have doubts about the correct form.

Come *with* Travis and (**I? me?**) now.

To be sure you are using the right pronoun form . . .

▶ **Use the objective case when pronouns are the object in a prepositional phrase.** Again, difficulties are most likely to arise when the preposition takes two objects.

Come *with* **Travis** and (**I? me?**) now.

[In this sentence, the preposition *with* takes two objects, *Travis* and a pronoun. A quick glance at the chart shows that the object form of *I/me* is *me*. You can reach the same conclusion by simply deleting *Travis* and considering the alternatives.]

{**1st version**} Come *with* **I** now

{**2nd version**} Come *with* **me** now.

[Once again, the deletion might make it clearer to you that version 2 is correct, and the full sentence can be restored.]

{**Revised**} Come *with* **Travis** and **me** now.

15J

15J **PROBLEMS WITH PRONOUN CASE:
IN COMPARISONS**

Troubleshooting

Be alert to possible problems with pronoun case when you are writing a comparison that includes *than* or *as* followed by a pronoun. You'll recognize this familiar problem immediately:

I am taller **than (him? he?)**.

She is far more active in the organization **than (me? I?)**.

Politics does not interest me as much **as (she? her?)**.

To be sure you are using the right pronoun form after *than* or *as* . . .

▶ **Expand the comparison into a full sentence and then decide what the appropriate pronoun form should be.** Examples furnish the best way of explaining this guideline clearly.

15J

> I am taller **than (him? he?)**.
>
>> [Complete the comparison by assuming that the verb *is* follows the pronoun.]
>
> I am taller **than (him? he?)** *is*.
>
>> [The correct pronoun form is now more obvious. The pronoun functions as the subject of the verb *is*.]
>
> {**Revised**} I am taller **than he**.

Another example.

> She is far more active in the organization than **(me? I?)**.
>
>> [Comparison expanded.]
>
> She is far more active in the organization than **(me? I?)** *am*.
>
> {**Revised**} She is far more active in the organization than **I**.

An example with *as*.

> Politics does not interest me as much **as (she? her?)**.
>
>> [Comparison expanded.]

Politics does not interest me as much **as** it interests **(she? her?)**.

[In this case, the expanded comparison shows that the pronoun could be the object of the verb *interests*. Hence, the objective form is necessary.]

{**Revised**} Politics does not interest me as much as **her**.

But sometimes a sentence can be expanded two ways, with the pronoun you select having an important effect on what the sentence means.

Sean treats Connie better than **(I? me?)**.

{**1st version**} Sean treats Connie better than **I** *do*.

{**2nd version**} Sean treats Connie better than *he treats* **me**.

[Both sentences make sense, so that either pronoun could be used at the end of the original sentence. But the meaning of the resulting sentences would be much different. In a similar situation, you might avoid a misreading simply by filling out the sentence, adding a verb after *than* + the pronoun.]

Politics does not interest me as much **as (she? her?)**.

{**1st version**} Politics does not interest me as much **as it interests her**.

{**2nd version**} Politics does not interest me as much **as she does**.

[Again, both expansions make sense, so that either pronoun could be used at the end of the original sentence. And again, you might want to avoid possible misreadings by using the fuller, more specific version of each sentence.]

PROBLEMS WITH PRONOUN CASE: AFTER LINKING VERBS

Linking verb. A verb, often a form of *to be*, that connects a subject to a word or phrase that extends or completes its meaning. Common linking verbs are *to seem, to appear, to feel,* and *to become.*

Wolfgang Rack **is** Dean of Students.

She **seems** tired.

Subject complement. A word or phrase that follows a linking verb, completing its meaning. Subject complements can be nouns, pronouns, or adjectives.

          subj.   l.v. subj. comp.
Tiffany Shade is **president**.

          subj.   l.v. subj. comp.
The president is **she**.

          subj.   l.v.   subj. comp.
President Shade appears **confident**.

Do you write *It is I* or *It is me*? Many writers have problems deciding what the case of a pronoun ought to be after forms of *to be.*

That is **she? her?**

This is **he? him?**

The director was **he? him?**

It will be **she? her?** who will write the script.

You are **who? whom?**

Spoken English usually tolerates either form. But for written English, readers expect that the pronoun will be treated consistently as a subject complement in the subjective case.

▶ **Use the subjective case when pronouns follow a linking verb.**

> That is **she? her?**
>
>> [**She** is the subject form.]
>
> {**Revised**} That is **she.**

Other examples:

> This is **he? him?**
>
> The director was **he? him?**
>
> It will be **she? her?** who will write the script.
>
> You are **who? whom?**
>
> {**Revised**}
>
> This is **he.**
>
> The director was **he.**
>
> It will be **she** who will write the script.
>
> You are **who?**

● **Fine Tuning**

1. Here's a noteworthy exception to the guideline that pronouns in the subjective case take a subject form: when a pronoun is the subject of an infinitive phrase (*to be, to seek, to employ*), it takes the objective case.

> The corporation expected **him** *to hire more minorities.*
>
> The coach ordered **them** *to look sharp.*
>
>> [*To hire more minorities* and *to look sharp* are infinitive phrases. *Him* and *them* are the subjects of those phrases, even though both are in the objective case.]

2. When a pronoun is followed by a noun that describes or explains it (technically, the noun or noun phrase is called an **appositive**), the pronoun and noun both share the same case.

> **We** *lucky sailors* missed the storm. [Subject]
>
> The storm missed **us** *lucky sailors.* [Object]

15K

385

You may run into a problem when a pronoun in a prepositional phrase is followed by an appositive noun. The proper form for the pronoun is the objective case, even though it may sound odd to the ear.

The New Yorkers decided to join with **us Texans** in supporting the legislation in Congress.

[*We Texans* may sound more correct, but *we* is the subject form and cannot be used after the preposition *with*. Another example follows.]

For **us engineers,** the job market looks promising.

When you are in doubt about the proper form, read the sentence without the appositive.

EXERCISE 15.3

Decide which of the pronoun forms in parentheses is correct in the following sentences.

1. Kyle and Richard sat sullenly in one corner of the Dean's paneled office; Francie sat quietly alone in another. Both **(she? her?)** and **(they? them?)** knew why the Dean had summoned **(they? them?).**
2. For the guys and **(her? she?)** alike, this was a dark day. Yesterday, Francie had admitted to Professor Ransom that two other students had worked with **(she? her?)** on the term paper she turned in for his history class. Ransom had run off immediately to report the case to Wolfgang Rack, the Dean of Students.
3. While Francie was no more responsible than Kyle or Richard for the actual collusion, the guys were doing an expert job of making her feel more guilty than **(them? they?).**
4. Richard finally broke the silence in the tense room. "I thought you and the two of **(us? we?)** could count on each other," he said. "As for Kyle and **(me? I?),** we would

never have gotten you involved even if either **(he? him?)** or **(I? me?)** had gotten fingered for plagiarism.''

5. ''Collusion,'' Francie corrected, and then wished she hadn't. Why couldn't **(her? she?)** be less of a perfectionist? If she had been, neither **(she? her?)** nor the guys would have found themselves in this mess.

6. Kyle, adjusting his glasses, was doing his best to stay calm even while his dream of law school seemed to be drifting away. ''Don't feel guilty, Francie. You don't have any more experience with this kind of situation than **(I? me?)**. **(We? Us?)** overachievers don't expect to end up in Deans' offices.''

7. ''Just between you and **(I? me?)**,'' Kyle continued, smiling a little, ''don't you think that Richard is really the one to blame?''

8. Francie pondered deeply and then spoke. ''If anyone can talk himself and **(us? we?)** out of a mess like this, it's got to be Richard. Let's blame him.''

9. Richard choked at the suggestion that Kyle and **(her? she?)** make **(him? he?)** the scapegoat. He hoped his comrades weren't serious.

10. ''Come on, you guys. You're better at winning sympathy than **(I? me?)**,'' he said. ''Besides, do you want me to face the Rack alone?''

15L SPECIAL PROBLEM: *WHO* OR *WHOM*

Term you need to know

   Clause. A group of words with a subject and predicate.

   In spoken English, the distinction between *who* and *whom* (or *whoever/whomever*) has just about disappeared because keeping track of subjects and objects can be almost impossible as sentences roll along in conversation—though some people try. In written English, however, many readers still expect the distinction to be observed, despite the problems it can cause.

If you can't remember all the fine points of *who/whom* (or can't consult a handbook), you can play it safe by using *who* in most situations—except immediately after a preposition. After a preposition, use **whom**: *to* **whom**; *for* **whom**; *with* **whom**. Using *who* in all other circumstances will mean you are technically incorrect whenever the word is acting as an object. But *who* misused as an object usually sounds less stodgy than *whom* misused as a subject.

{*Who* **misused as an object**} You addressed **who**?

{*Whom* **misused as a subject**} **Whom** wrote this letter?

The actual rule for choosing the form *who/whom* is the same as for selecting the case of other pronouns: *select the subjective form (who) when pronouns act as subjects, the objective form (whom) when pronouns act as objects—especially in prepositional phrases.*

{**Revised**} You addressed **whom**?

{**Revised**} **Who** wrote this letter?

The problem, of course, with *who/whom* is figuring out whether the word is acting as a subject or an object. You often cannot detect much difference; both versions of some troublesome sentences are likely to seem acceptable:

Who did you address?

Whom did you address?

The best you can do is to identify the subject and the object.

{**Correct**} **Whom** did you address?

If you can locate the verb, you can usually figure out who is doing what to whom:

(**Who? Whom?**) is finding this section tricky?

[The verb is *is finding*. *Section* wouldn't make sense as the subject: *Section is finding*. That leaves the subject form of *who/whom: who*.]

{**Revised**} **Who** is finding this section tricky?

15L

Another example.

> (**Who? Whom?**) are you taking with you?
>
> [The verb is *are taking*. The doer of the action is clearly *you: you are taking*. The person receiving the action, then, is the object form of *who/whom: whom*.]
>
> {**Revised**} **Whom** are you taking with you?

But be careful with sentences with passive verbs. In them, the subject does not perform the action, yet it remains in the subjective case:

> (**Who? Whom?**) was accused of collusion by Professor Ransom?
>
> [The subject is the pronoun. Consequently, the pronoun takes its subjective form: *who*.]
>
> {**Revised**} **Who** was accused of collusion by Professor Ransom?

So far, so good. But what happens when *who/whom* (or *whoever/whomever*) is part of a **clause** within a sentence—that is, when *who/whom* is the subject or object of a sentence which is, itself, the object of another sentence? Now, this may sound picky, but constructions of this kind are quite common. The phrases italicized below are clauses within the full sentences.

> The system rewards (*whoever? whomever?*) *works hard.*
>
> The deficit will increase no matter (*who? whom?*) *we elect President.*
>
> (*Who? Whom?*) are you finding *is having difficulty?*
>
> Do you really know (*who? whom?*) *you are?*

In such situations, *who/whom* takes the form it would have in the clause, not in the sentence as a whole. In the first example, the correct version would be the following if you omitted *works hard.*

> The system rewards **whomever.**
>
> [*Whomever* is the object of the sentence.]

15L

389

But when the clause is added, the case of the pronoun changes.

The system rewards **whoever** *works hard.*

> [*Whoever* is now the subject of the clause *whoever works hard*—even though the entire clause functions as an object.]

Three more examples.

The deficit will increase no matter (**who? whom?**) *we elect President.*

> [*Who/whom* here is part of a clause: we elect *whom* President.]

{**Revised**} The deficit will increase no matter **whom** *we elect President.*

(**Who? Whom?**) are you finding *is having difficulty?*

> [This one is tricky because the *who/whom* is separated from its clause. In locating clauses within questions it often helps if you rearrange the sentence as if it were a statement: *You are finding who/whom is having difficulty.* Now you can see more clearly that the clause needs a subject form.]

{**Revised**} **Who** are you finding *is having difficulty?*

Do you really know (**who? whom?**) *you are?*

> [*Whom* might seem like the correct choice when you look at the italicized clause. But remember that after the linking verb *to be,* English takes the subject form: *you are who.*]

{**Revised**} Do you really know **who** *you are?*

Now you can probably appreciate why *who/whom* gives writers fits. Sometimes the simplest strategy is to write around the problem.

Decide which of the pronoun forms in parentheses is correct in the following sentences.

1. Dean Rack looked like a man (**whom? who?**) wouldn't trust a nun with a prayer.
2. He glared at the boys and then at Francie. "(**Whom? Who?**) would like to explain this plagiarism accusation to me?"
3. "We're guilty as sin," Francie blurted out with heart-rending contrition. "I've already confessed to Mr. Ransom, my history teacher, (**who? whom?**) you've probably spoken to, that my friends and I collaborated on a paper for our classes."
4. "May I assume," asked the Dean, "that these young men here, with (**who? whom?**) you wrote the allegedly plagiarized essays, are your friends?"
5. "They might be," said Francie wistfully, "though a person can never really be too certain (**who? whom?**) her friends are."

15M

Terms you need to know

> **Possessive case.** The form a pronoun takes when it shows ownership: *my, mine, your, yours, her, hers, his, its, our, ours, their, theirs, whose, anyone's, somebody's.*

> **Personal pronoun.** A pronoun that refers to particular individuals, things, or groups: *I, you, he, she, it, we, they.*

> **Indefinite pronoun.** A pronoun that does not refer to a particular person, thing, or group: *all, any, each, everybody, everyone, one, none, somebody, someone,* and so on.

Contraction. A word shortened by the omission of a letter or letters. In most cases, an apostrophe is used to indicate the deleted letters or sounds: *it is = it's; they are = they're; you are = you're.*

Troubleshooting

The most common way of showing ownership in English is to add an apostrophe + *s* to a noun: Sarah's book; the dog's owner. The familiar *'s* is not, however, used with **personal pronouns** (and *who*)—and this exception confuses some writers who are inclined to add an *'s* to personal pronouns that don't require it.

This inclination is responsible for one of the most common of all mechanical errors in English: mistaking the possessive pronoun *its* for the **contraction** *it's. Its/it's* will be the subject of a **Special Problem** section below.

Finally, the possessive forms of **indefinite pronouns** can be troublesome. Some indefinite pronouns take the apostrophe + *s* to indicate ownership, but others do not.

To be sure you are using the right possessive pronoun . . .

▶ **Remember that personal pronouns do not require an apostrophe to show ownership.** This is true whether the possessive pronoun comes before or after a noun.

Before the Noun	After the Noun
Whose *book* is this?	The *book* is **mine**.
That is **my** *book*.	The *book* is **yours**.
That is **your** *book*.	The *book* is **hers**.
That is **her** *book*.	The *book* is **his**.
That is **his** *book*.	The *book* is **ours**.
That is **our** *book*.	The *book* is **theirs**.
That is **their** *book*.	What is the *price* **of it**?
What is **its** *price*?	

15M

▶ **Remember that while some indefinite pronouns can form the possessive by adding 's, others cannot.** Among the indefinite pronouns that cannot add *'s* to show possession are the following.

Indefinite Pronoun	Form of the Possessive
all	the opinion **of all**
any	the sight **of any**
each	the price **of each**
few	the judgment **of few**
most	the dream **of most**
none	the choice **of none**

Indefinite pronouns ending in *-body* or *-one* can form the possessive with *'s* or with *of.*

Indefinite Pronoun	Forms of the Possessive
anybody	**anybody's** opinion / the opinion of **anybody**
everybody	**everybody's** wish / the wish of **everybody**
each one	**each one's** jacket / the jacket of **each one**
someone	**someone's** hope / the hope of **someone**

▶ **Remember that the possessive of *who* is *whose*.** Don't mistake *whose* for *who's*—the contraction for *who is* or *who has*.

Whose teammate is on first base?   [possessive form]

Who's on first?   [contraction]

● **Fine Tuning**

1. Deciding whether to place a possessive pronoun before or after a noun is often a matter of style. Some combinations of possessive pronouns are simply awkward.

His and **their** projects were selected for the science fair.

The teaching assistant was curious about **her** and **my** ideas.

In cases like this, try other ways of expressing ownership.

{**Revised**} **His** project and **theirs** were selected for the science fair.

Their projects were selected for the science fair.

{**Revised**} The teaching assistant was curious about **her** idea and **mine.**

The teaching assistant was curious about **our** ideas.

2. *Whose* usually refers to living things and *of which* to nonliving objects. Use *whose*, however, in any sentence where *of which* seems awkward.

It is a country the people **of which** are splendid but the landscape **of which** isn't.

{**Revised**} It is a country **whose** people are splendid but **whose** landscape isn't.

SPECIAL PROBLEM: *ITS* OR *IT'S*

Why do writers so often use the contraction *it's* (for *it is*) where they need the possessive form *its*—and vice versa?

Its unlikely that the aircraft will lose **it's** way in the dark. **Its** equipped with radar.

[**Revised**] *It's* unlikely that the aircraft will lose *its* way in the dark. *It's* equipped with radar.

It may be because the apostrophe makes the contracted form look suspiciously like a possessive. And the possessive form sounds like a contraction. But don't be fooled. The possessive forms of personal pronouns never take an apostrophe, while contractions always require one.

The iron left **its** grim outline on the silk shirt. [possessive]

It's a stupid but popular program. [contraction]

But even without a rule, chances are you can tell *its* from *it's* when you have to. If you consistently misuse *its/it's*, you need to circle these words whenever they appear in your paper, and check them. It may help if you always read or think of *it's* as *it is*. Eventually you will eliminate this error.

Don't even for a moment imagine that such a construction as *its'* exists. It doesn't.

EXERCISE 15.5

Identify and correct any pronoun-related errors in the sentences below. Possible trouble spots are italicized, but not all the words and phrases italicized contain errors of possession or pronoun form.

1. Kyle and Richard would have been content to leave Dean Rack's office with *their* college careers intact even at the cost *of Francie's and their* pride.
2. What strategy the Dean would use to explore the matter was *anybody's* guess. Rack seemed absolutely puzzled.
3. "Exactly *whose* responsible for this plagiarism of *your's?*" he finally asked.
4. Before Francie could make *their'* troubles worse with another one *of her* patented explanations, Kyle volunteered to Dean Rack that the three *of them* had decided to form a team—*it's* purpose to compose collaboratively the best essay in the least time.
5. The task of finding and researching a topic would be *his'*; his roommate, Richard, would organize the paper, sort out the facts, and sketch a rough version *of their's* essays.

6. Francie would document the paper and type the final version. It was *all's* responsibility to polish the papers into final form for *his' or hers'* class.
7. "*That's* what we did; *its* that simple," Kyle concluded.
8. Dean Rack arched *his* eyebrows grimly and placed an essay from *his* file before Francie.
9. "Is this essay *yours'*?" he asked. "And *your's* and *you'rse*?" he continued as he returned *everybodys* papers.
10. Rack's eyes, *of which* the centers seemed like deep pools, softened momentarily.
11. "These papers are *each's of yours*?" he asked once again and the three students nodded apologetically, *all's* eyes cast down.
12. "Then, would one of you explain to me why three supposed plagiarists would each turn in a completely different paper?" The students looked up, *theirs* eyes proclaiming "*Its* a miracle!"

150 PROBLEMS WITH REFLEXIVE/INTENSIVE PRONOUNS

Terms you need to know

Reflexive/intensive pronouns. The pronoun forms created when -*self* is added to singular personal pronouns and -*selves* to plural personal pronouns: *myself, yourself, herself, himself, itself, oneself, ourselves, yourselves, themselves.*

These words are **reflexive** in sentences like the following where both the subject and object of an action are the same person or thing:

subj.   obj.
Corey had only *herself* to rely on.

subj.   obj.
They took *themselves* too seriously.

They are **intensive** when they modify a noun or another pronoun to add emphasis.

noun
Warren *himself* admitted he was guilty.

pro.
I never vote *myself*.

noun
The residents did all the plumbing and wiring *themselves*.

Troubleshooting

Many writers use the more formal-sounding reflexive pronouns, especially *myself* in situations where a simple personal pronoun is more appropriate. Others use the nonstandard forms *hisself* or *theirselves*.

150

To handle reflexive/intensive pronouns correctly . . .

▶ **Don't use a reflexive pronoun to make a sentence sound more formal.**

The gift is for Matthew and **yourself**.

[A simple *you* is adequate.]

{**Revised**} The gift is for Matthew and **you**.

Use the pronoun reflexively only when the subject and object in a sentence refer to the same person or thing.

subj.   obj.
Maggie rediscovered **herself** in her painting.

Use an intensive pronoun where emphasis is needed.

The gift is for you **yourself**.

[In this sentence, *yourself* is used appropriately as an intensive pronoun, emphasizing *you*.]

Problems occur most frequently with the form *myself*. *Myself* is used often in place of a more suitable *I* or *me*.

subj.   obj.

*Cate and **myself*** wrote the lab *report.*

> [In the example above, the subject and the object of the sentence are not the same. So the reflexive pronoun form (*myself*) is not needed. The simple subject form—*I*—suffices.]

{**Revised**} Cate and **I** wrote the lab report.

Compare the sentence above to a similar one using *myself* correctly as an intensive pronoun.

> I wrote the lab report **myself**.

Two more examples:

> Tiffany and **myself** attended the banquet.

> [*I* is the better choice.]

{**Revised**} Tiffany and **I** attended the banquet.

Andrew spoke with Jethro and **myself** about the contract.

{**Revised**} Andrew spoke with Jethro and **me** about the contract.

▶ **Never use the forms *hisself* or *theirselves* in academic or business writing.** The correct forms for writing are *himself* and *themselves*.

> Lincoln **hisself** wrote the memo.

{**Revised**} Lincoln **himself** wrote the memo.

> They saw **theirselves** on television.

{**Revised**} They saw **themselves** on television.

EXERCISE 15.6

Correct any problems with reflexive or intensive pronouns in the following sentences.

1. Kyle tried to explain why the supposedly plagiarized paper he had turned in hisself might differ from Francie's and Richard's.
2. "Myself, I made a few changes in the paper Francie gave me," Kyle began.
3. Richard spoke next: "I know that Kyle and myself weren't completely happy with the paper Francie gave us, so I changed mine a little too."
4. "Me, too," Francie explained. "I wrote our collaborative version myself based on the research materials Richard and Kyle had given me, but even they theirselves would admit that their work had some gaps, so in my own paper, I made a few changes without telling the guys."
5. Dean Rack, scratching hisself on the forehead, now looked more amused than angry. "Let me get this straight," he said, "You, Francie, wrote one version of a paper for Kyle and Richard and one version for yourself while you, Kyle, and you, Richard, both wrote versions for yourselves based on the paper Francie wrote for you but not for herself?"

15P WHEN SHOULD YOU USE *I*, *YOU*, *ONE*, *WE*?

Troubleshooting

Many writers are unsure when—if ever—they may use *I*, *we*, or *you* in professional or academic writing. Some teachers and editors practically outlaw *I* or *you* except in personal essays. As a result, students often retreat in their academic writing to the passive voice ("it is believed"), to unusual constructions ("this writer"; "the author of this piece") or to the pronoun *one*—all of which can make their essays sound awkward or unduly formal.

Pronouns do, in fact, change your relationship with your reader. They aren't interchangeable, nor is it easy to formulate strategies to explain what pronouns to use in every situation. However, you may find the following guidelines helpful.

▶ **Use *I* whenever it makes sense for you or your opinions to appear in a paper.** In general, you should avoid *I* in scientific reports and expository essays where your identity or your personal opinions are likely to be unimportant to readers.

> **I learned** that students who drive a car on campus are more likely to have jobs than those who do not.

> {Revised} **The survey showed** that students who drive a car on campus are more likely to have jobs than those who do not.

However, when you find that avoiding *I* makes you resort to an awkward passive verb, use *I* instead:

> **It is felt** that the play is too long.

> > [If you are the one who believes that the play is too long, say so.]

> {Revised} **I believe** the play is too long.

Still, you can often eliminate an awkward passive without using *I*.

> {Revised without *I*} The play is too long.

The same advice—to use *I* sensibly—applies when you find yourself concocting a word or phrase just to avoid *I*:

> **In the opinion of this writer**, federal taxes should be lowered.

> {Revised} **I believe** federal taxes should be lowered.

> {Revised without *I*} Federal taxes should be lowered.

> **The experience of this researcher** suggests that the research design itself is flawed.

> {Revised} **I am convinced** that the research design itself is flawed.

> {Revised without *I*} The research design itself is flawed.

Be aware that some editors and teachers simply will not allow *I* to be used in academic and scientific writing. When writing for them, follow their rules. However, most writers today recognize that using *I* is both natural and sensible even in formal prose.

▶ **Use *we* whenever two or more writers are involved in a project or when you are writing to express the opinion of a group.**

> When **we** compared our surveys, **we** discovered the conflicting evidence.

> **We** believe that City Council has an obligation to reconsider its zoning action.

Or use *we* to indicate a general condition.

> Almost everyone agrees that **we** live in an age of transition.

> **We** need better control of our health care systems in the United States.

Avoid using *we* or *us* as a chummy way of addressing your reader. When introducing a paper or handling a transition, don't make it sound as if you are taking your readers on a grand tour of Europe:

15P

> Now that **we** have completed our survey of mental disorders, let **us** turn to . . .

In most academic writing, *we* used this way sounds pompous. This is not the case, however, in spoken English.

Do not use the royal *we*—unless you are a high government official or a monarch:

> **We** have directed the Attorney General to select a special prosecutor.

> **We** are not amused.

▶ **Use *you* whenever it makes sense to speak to your readers personally or when you are giving orders or directions.** *You* sounds direct, cordial, and individual. Consequently, when you use *you* in academic writing, be sure that you really want your readers to be a part of what you are talking about:

> A recent student government survey suggested that **you** will cheat in two courses during your college career.

[In this case, the sentence may be too personal. It seems to implicate the reader directly in scholastic dishonesty.

{**Revised**} The student government survey suggested that **most students** will cheat in two courses during their college careers.

Also, be sure that when you write *you*, you aren't describing an experience that would be handled better from a first-person *(I)* or third-person *(he, she, they)* point of view:

You are puzzled by the nature of the ghost when **you** first read *Hamlet*.

{**Revised**} **I** was puzzled by the nature of the ghost when **I** first read *Hamlet*.

{**Revised**} Some people are puzzled by the nature of the ghost when **they** first read *Hamlet*.

{**Revised**} When reading *Hamlet* for the first time, some people are puzzled by the nature of the ghost.

▶ **Use *one* when you want to express a thought that might be yours, but which should be understood more generally.** *One* is often useful for conveying moral sentiments or general truths.

Consider the terror of not knowing where **one's** next meal is coming from.

Reading Tolstoy, **one** senses the presence of a great soul.

[Notice that *one* here gives the sentence more authority than it would have if *one* were replaced by *I* or *you*.]

But sentences with too many *ones* sound like the butlers of British comedy—sneering and superior:

One can never be too careful about maintaining **one's** good reputation, can **one**?

In most cases, *you* or an appropriate noun sounds better and less formal than *one*, especially when giving directions:

If **one** is uncertain about the credibility of **one's** sources, **one** should consult a librarian in the reference room.

{**Revised**} If **you** are uncertain about the credibility of **your** sources, **you** should consult a librarian in the reference room.

{**Revised**} If **students** are uncertain about the credibility of **their** sources, **they** should consult a librarian in the reference room.

▶ **Whatever pronoun forms you use, be consistent.** Don't switch pronouns in the middle of a sentence or paragraph. Problems are most likely to occur with the indefinite pronoun *one*:

One cannot know what **their** future holds.

[Here the pronoun shifts from **one** to the plural form **they**. Several revisions are possible.]

{**Revised**} **One** cannot know what **one's** future holds.

{**Revised**} **People** cannot know what **their** futures hold.

{**Revised**} **One** cannot know what **his** future holds.

[You can shift between *one* and *he or she*, as the example above demonstrates. Notice, though, that in this sentence a reader might assume that *he* is not the same person as *one*.]

Here's another example:

When **one** turns on an aerobics program these days, **you** are likely to see both men and women participating in the exercises.

{**Revised**} When **you** turn on an aerobics program these days, **you** are likely to see both men and women participating in the exercises.

{**Revised**} When **one** turns on an aerobics program these days, **one** is likely to see both men and women participating in the exercises.

15P

Are the pronouns or other expressions in boldface appropriate in the sentences below? Change any that you think are either awkward, unduly formal, or inconsistent. In some cases, you may have to rewrite entire sentences.

1. "**One** might say, Dean Rack, that the three of **us** are as confused as **you** are about the originality of our papers," Richard volunteered, trying to explain why there were three totally different versions of the paper supposedly written in collaboration by Kyle, Francie, and him.

2. "Let **us** read from the opening paragraphs of each of your papers," Dean Rack said. "Shall **we** begin with yours, Richard?"

15P

3. '. . . **I** don't know who invented the water clock, but **I** think the ancient Egyptians were the first to use it with any degree of sophistication. The advantage of the water clock over the sundial was that **you** could measure time at night; the disadvantage was that **you** might wake up in the morning with a frozen timepiece. . . .'

4. "And now from yours, Kyle:

> "In some respects, the modern world began with the invention of the mechanical clock. Let **us** look at three inventions that made the mechanical clock possible, the escapement, the pendulum, and the balance spring. It is the opinion of **this writer** that we do not understand adequately the relationship between these important inventions . . . "

5. "And, lastly, would **you** like me to read from your paper, Francie?" The question was rhetorical, for Rack began reading it immediately:

> . . . **One** can never know what will make **them** a success. Did the Jesuit missionary Matteo Ricci ever imagine that clocks, not religious fervor, would help to gain him access to the Chinese emperor in the six-

teenth century? **You** wouldn't expect the sophisticated Chinese to be impressed by what amounted to little more than a European toy—but **they** were. **This paper** will review how Ricci's missionary exploits were connected to Europe's invention of the mechanical clock.''

6. The Dean put the papers down on his desk. ''**One** hardly knows what to think when **one** encounters work of this sort, does **he**? **You** all wrote on the same general subject, but **you** didn't write the same paper. **One** is led to wonder, is this collusion, or isn't it?''

15Q ARE YOUR PRONOUNS SEXIST?

Troubleshooting
What happens when you need to use a pronoun, but don't know whether it should refer to a man or a woman?

Each of the editors walked to (**his?/her?**) Yugo.

Until recently, you would have been expected to use a masculine pronoun *(he, him, his)* in any such situation—on the grounds that when you are talking about *mankind* you are also thinking about *womankind.*

Each of the editors walked to **his** Yugo.

But, in fact, such male-only constructions excluded women from more than just grammar:

The President begins **his** term in January.

A competent lawyer keeps track of **his** case load.

The chairman has not completed **his** correction of the report.

Applied rigorously, the old male-only rule leads to all sorts of distortions, some even humorous—as in this sentence taken from an actual paper:

One common myth teenagers believe is that a **person** cannot get pregnant the first time **he** has intercourse.

English has a second-person singular form that talks to men and women alike: *you*. But, unfortunately, the third-person singular forms are either male *(he, him, his)*, female *(she, her, hers)*, or neuter *(it, its)*. And *it* just doesn't work as a substitute for a person.

To avoid sexist pronouns . . .

▶ **Assume that all professions and groups may include both men and women.** Get into the habit of thinking that members of either sex may belong to any profession or group—students, athletes, coal miners, truckers, secretaries, nurses. Then let your language reflect that diversity. Obviously, there are going to be exceptions which you should, of course, acknowledge:

15Q

> Each of the nuns received an award for **her** valor.
>
> None of the NFL quarterbacks received a payment for **his** appearance at the benefit.

But in situations where you cannot assume that members of a group will all be male or all be female, be sure your language—in one fashion or another—accommodates both sexes. You can do that in several ways, listed below. Be forewarned, though, that these various strategies are not approved by all writers and readers.

▶ **Use the expressions** *he or she, him or her,* **or** *his or her* **instead of the pronoun of either sex alone.**

> Every secretary may invite **her husband**.
>
>> [Unless you know that every secretary is female, the sentence should be recast.]
>
> {**Revised**} Every secretary may invite **his or her spouse**.

Unfortunately, *he or she* expressions can be awkward and tiring, especially when they occur more than once in a sentence.

> Before **he or she** leaves, each member of the band should take **his or her** instrument with **him or her**.

In many cases, you'll want to try another strategy for avoiding sexist usage.

▶ **Change a singular reference to a plural one.** Because plural pronouns do not have a specific gender in English, you can often avoid the choice between *he* or *she* simply by turning singular references into plural ones:

> **Every** secretary may invite **her husband.**

> {**Revised**} **All secretaries** may invite **their spouses.**

Here's a second example:

> Before **he or she** leaves, **each** member of the band should take **his or her** instrument with **him or her.**

> {**Revised**} Before leaving, **all members** of the band should take **their instruments** with **them.**

> [Notice how the first *he or she* is eliminated entirely.]

15Q

▶ **Eliminate the troublesome pronoun.** The preceding example shows that, in some cases, you can simply cut the feminine or masculine pronoun from a sentence. Here's another sentence that can be revised to avoid the troublesome reference:

> None of the realtors was proud of **his** sales record for January.

> {**Revised**} None of the realtors was proud of sales in January.

This option is useful, but not always available. Notice in the example above how the meaning of the sentence shifts subtly when the pronoun is dropped.

▶ **Use *he* or *she* alternatively.** You can strive to balance the total number of references to males and females in a given piece of writing. This does not mean you should arbitrarily shift gender with every pronoun. In most cases, pronouns can be varied sensibly and naturally within chunks of prose—

between paragraphs, for example, or between the examples in a series. Handled skillfully, the shift between masculine and feminine references need not attract a reader's attention.

Dean Rack knew that any student could purchase **his** term papers through mail-order term paper services. If **he** could afford the scam, a student might construct **his** entire college career around bought papers, even designing **his** course schedule to accommodate the kinds of work the so-called "research services" perform.

Yet Rack also knew that the typical plagiarist was not so grossly dishonest and calculating. **She** tended to resort to such highly unethical behavior only when **she** believed an assignment was beyond **her** capabilities or **her** workload was excessive. Then **she** tended to panic.

15Q However, you should avoid varying pronoun gender within individual sentences.

{**Confusing**} If **he** could afford the scam, a student might construct **her** entire college career around bought papers, even designing **his** course schedule to accommodate the kinds of work the so-called "research services" would do for **her**.

{**Revised**} If **he** could afford the scam, a student might construct **his** entire college career around bought papers, even designing **his** course schedule to accommodate the kinds of work the so-called "research services" would do for **him**.

▶ **Use a plural pronoun with a singular antecedent.** Though this pronoun/referent *dis*agreement—very common in speech—is gaining some acceptance in writing, be warned that most writers still consider such forms simply wrong:

Every skier took **their** turn on the slope.

[Technically, *every skier* is a singular expression which should be referred to by a singular pronoun: *his or her.*]

Here's a second example:

Each candidate for the vice-presidency had Secret Service agents assigned to **them.**

[Again, *each candidate* is singular; technically, the pronoun should be *him or her.*]

Given the widespread objection to such forms, you would be wise to avoid them in academic writing. In fact, there's rarely a reason to use a plural pronoun with a singular referent. Grammatical and nonsexist alternatives are almost always available.

{**Revised**} **All** the skiers took **their** turns on the slope.

{**Revised**} **Every** skier took **a** turn on the slope.

{**Revised**} **All** candidates for the vice-presidency had Secret Service agents assigned to **them.**

{**Revised**} **Each** candidate for the vice-presidency **was assigned** a Secret Service agent.

▶ **Use the feminine pronoun form throughout an essay if you are a woman; use the masculine pronoun if you are a man.** This strategy has the virtue of simplicity, but raises other problems. Readers may appreciate the rationale of a woman using only female references, but a man using only masculine pronouns runs the risk of appearing insensitive to the issue of sexist usage.

EXERCISE 15.8

Revise the following sentences to eliminate any pronouns that might be considered sexist. Treat all examples as if they occurred in written English—even when the pronouns in question occur in dialogue.

1. Francie spoke. "Well, Dean Rack, it looks as if each of us wrote his own paper after all. I have to admit that I didn't like the topic Kyle and Richard chose, so I rethought and reworked my paper without telling them."

2. "None of us is as good a writer or researcher as he thinks he is," Richard observed, "yet apparently each of us believed he could do a better job than our collaborators. Like Francie, I thought I could improve on the topic Kyle originally researched and Francie wrote up, but I didn't want to hurt him or her. I guess each of us realized that a good student ultimately has to rely on his own strengths."

3. Kyle spoke last. "I did the same thing. I was going to write on the problems a timekeeper in ancient Egypt would have had keeping his calendar accurate, but ended up writing about water clocks instead."

4. "So, it seems," said the Dean, "that I have a case of collusion in which each writer chose his or her own topic, did his or her own research, and turned in his or her own paper. What do you think a Dean should do when he is faced with such a complication?"

5. Kyle smiled broadly and suggested that the Dean give each of the three students the warning he richly deserved and then dismiss the case. Rack agreed, spoke sternly for almost fifteen minutes about scholastic dishonesty, and sent Kyle, Richard, and Francie on his or her way. Case closed.

CHAPTER

Where Do You Need Commas?

- **A**   Commas that don't belong
- **B**   Commas that separate
- **C**   Commas that enclose
- **D**   Commas that link

16

▶ Function

The central fact about a comma is that it is an interrupter, a signal to pause. Think of a comma as a kind of stop sign at a juncture or minor intersection in a sentence, placed to keep words from running into each other. It isn't as strong a stop sign as a semicolon, which marks a major intersection (one that warrants a traffic light instead of just a sign), and certainly not as strong as a period, which marks the end of the sentence (rather like a hand signal from a police officer). But it does make readers pause momentarily when they come to it. For that reason, it's just as important *not* to put in commas when they aren't needed as it is to put them in when they are needed to mark separations.

Of course, you need to know the guidelines for placing commas, but the truth is that knowing all the rules isn't necessarily going to solve all your comma problems. Ultimately, you have to develop a *feel* for commas, a sense of when you should interrupt the flow of your sentences and when you shouldn't. That requires you to think about the sense and structure of a sentence, not just stick commas in according to a formula. You need to think about how your *readers* are going to approach a sentence and what punctuation they need to make sense of it. It will also help occasionally if you stop to observe how an author is using commas in an article or story. Analyze why the commas were placed where they are.

▶ Major Uses

—To separate parts of a sentence to avoid confusion in the meaning.

—To mark off parts of a sentence that give information but are not crucial to the main point.

—To break up long sentences that might otherwise be hard to read.

—To mark off items in a series.

▶ Other Uses

—To separate items in dates.

> Sue Ellen and Renaldo were married on February 14, 1978.

> Rodney was born on April 1, 1979.

—To mark off units in an address.

> Both Renaldo and Sue Ellen were born in Ruidosa, New Mexico.

> The Rizzos used to live at 17 Coleridge Place, Kubla Khan Estates.

> Now Sue Ellen and Rodney hope to live at 330 College Drive, Apt. 32.

—To separate proper names from titles and degrees that *follow* the names.

>Renaldo Rizzo, M.D.

>Doris Upton, Ph.D.

—To separate units of three within numbers.

>4,110   99,890   5,325,777

—After the salutation in personal letters.

>Dear Dr. Rizzo,

>Dear Rodney,

—To introduce quotations or follow them

>Rodney always says, "I'll do anything for money."

>"Don't tell me he can't be held responsible," bellowed Judge Carver

16A   COMMAS THAT DON'T BELONG

Troubleshooting

You may get nervous about putting commas in your sentences because you're uncertain about the rules for using them. You may then resort to just sprinkling them through your sentences, hoping they will land in the right place. That system doesn't work very well, and inevitably some of these commas are going to confuse your readers. From their point of view, it's disconcerting to be moving along with a flow of ideas and run into a comma that disrupts a train of thought.

Unnecessary comma

1. Although, Sue Ellen Rizzo is thirty-one, she is an undergraduate student at Clear Lake College.

Unnecessary comma

2. What happened, is that at nineteen she dropped out of college to put her husband through medical school.

Unnecessary comma

3. Ten years later she found herself, without a college degree or a husband, but with a nine-year-old son, Rodney.

16A

▶ **Diagnosis**

At each of the marked places in these sentences an unnecessary comma interrupts the flow of thought and makes readers skid to a stop when they should be moving along smoothly. They expect a comma to mark off part of a sentence *for some reason* and get confused when they can't figure out what the reason is.

In the first example, the subordinating conjunction *although* introduces a subordinating clause: *Although Sue Ellen is thirty-one. . . . Although* needs to be part of that clause, not separated from it by a comma.

In the second example, *what happened* is actually the subject of the sentence and subjects shouldn't be separated from predicates by commas unless a modifying phrase intervenes. Compare these sentences.

subject　　　　predicate

Sue Ellen is determined to complete her education.

[No comma comes between subject and predicate.]

subject　　　　modifying phrase　　　　predicate

Sue Ellen, who just turned thirty-one, is determined to complete her education.

[A pair of commas brackets the modifying phrase.]

In the third example above, the comma provides a pause where one is simply not needed. The sentence reads more easily and naturally without the pause.

▶ **Solution**

If you read the sentences above, you will realize that the misplaced commas interrupt units of thought that shouldn't be divided. So cut the commas.

16A

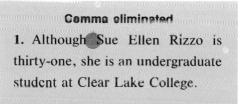

Comma eliminated

1. Although Sue Ellen Rizzo is thirty-one, she is an undergraduate student at Clear Lake College.

Comma eliminated

2. What happened is that at nineteen she dropped out of college to put her husband through medical school.

Comma eliminated

3. Ten years later she found herself without a college degree or a husband, but with a nine-year-old son, Rodney.

Every comma in a sentence should be there for a reason: to mark a pause, to set off a unit, to keep words from running together, or for any of the other purposes discussed in Section 16D. If you tend to use too many commas, check your commas when you edit your writing and ask yourself why you have used them.

▶ **Additional examples**
(In each sentence, the comma underlined is unnecessary and should be eliminated.)

> Sue Ellen says it was quite a shock to find herself with an enormous house and little money, for maintaining it.

> She says that she had never aspired to be a woman, who had a career of her own.

16A

> However, the thought of a full time job, was getting more attractive all the time after nine years at home with Rodney.

Notice that if you read these examples aloud you would not ordinarily pause at the places marked by the underlined commas. The unexpected pauses are like encountering a stop sign positioned without reason in the middle of a block. You slam on the brakes expecting an intersection, but then find there isn't any.

> Tip: When you are drafting and revising, gamble on using too few commas rather than too many and don't just put one in because you think it *might* need to go there. Sentences with commas inserted where they are not needed are often more distressing to a reader than those with a few commas omitted.

Rewrite these sentences to get rid of commas that cause awkward interruptions in the flow of thought.

1. Sue Ellen's principal problems, are coming from having to move out of her neighborhood because of her son, Rodney.
2. Although, he is only nine and not large for his age, he has acquired a formidable reputation.
3. He is reputed to be, very bright, but he has a Mephistophelean imagination.
4. His teachers, have known that for quite a while.
5. Granted, some of his escapades have shown, that, like the kids in *Weird Science*, he has creative genius.
6. However, some of Sue Ellen's neighbors in Kubla Khan Estates, her home right now, have complained, that Rodney is an apprentice terrorist.
7. And according to reports, from independent observers, they may be right.
8. His mother, however, fears that he may end up, in reform school.
9. So Sue Ellen, understandably, would welcome almost any suggestion, that would relieve her anxieties.
10. The only one, who is unconcerned is Rodney.

16A

Comma problem 2: Comma splice

> **Comma splice**
> Two years ago, Sue Ellen returned to college, she knew an education had to be her first goal.

▶ Diagnosis

You may be getting papers back with a comma circled in the middle of a sentence and a big CS written in the margin. If so, you're guilty of the infamous comma splice, a usage lapse that badly upsets many readers. That is, you're joining two independent clauses in a sentence with a comma instead of a conjunction or a semicolon. You're confusing your readers by not signaling a strong enough stop or by not putting in the linking term they need.

▶ Solution

In this case, you could simply replace the comma with a piece of punctuation that provides a complete stop—a semicolon.

16A

> **Comma splice eliminated**
>
> Two years ago, Sue Ellen returned to college; she knew an education had to be her first goal.

In other situations, you might add a conjunction or create separate sentences from the two independent clauses incorrectly linked by the comma. For a fuller discussion of how to avoid and fix comma splices, see Section 10C.

▶ Additional examples

{**Comma splice**} Those two years have been difficult, however, the problems have not been the kind she expected.

{**Comma splice eliminated**} Those two years have been difficult; however, the problems have not been the kind she expected.

{**Comma splice**} She thought courses like philosophy and English would be especially difficult for her, she has done well in them.

418

{**Comma splice eliminated**} She thought courses like philosophy and English would be especially difficult for her, but she has done well in them.

Rewrite these sentences to eliminate comma splices. You may change the punctuation, add conjunctions, or reorganize the sentences.

1. Sometimes it is difficult to tell the difference between imaginative, creative children and rebellious, mischievous brats, the difference can depend on who is describing them.
2. Sue Ellen would like to think Rodney is just mischievous and will outgrow his devilry, she is afraid she can't wait to find out.
3. His father thinks Rodney would be perfect to star in a movie version of O'Henry's "The Ransom of Red Chief," Rodney wouldn't even have to be coached.
4. In that well-known story, two amateur outlaws kidnap a young boy and hold him for ransom, their scheme backfires, however, because the boy is tougher and smarter than they are.
5. The movie *Ruthless People*, starring Bette Midler, was a takeoff on that plot, probably many people didn't know where the story idea came from originally.

16B

16B COMMAS THAT SEPARATE

Troubleshooting

Commas are placed in a sentence not just to satisfy certain conventions, but to help readers understand the relationships between ideas. Commas keep words and phrases in order by separating ideas in various ways.

> **Comma missing**
>
> Although Rodney seems cherubic
> at first glance he excels in creating
> havoc.

▶ **Diagnosis**

A comma is omitted after an introductory subordinate clause. When you forget to put a comma after such an introductory clause, your readers are likely to slide past the place where the main idea of the sentence begins, stop in confusion, and then have to reread from the beginning to understand your sentence. In the example above, the reader runs right through the intersection between *glance* and *he*, wonders whether the phrase *at first glance* goes with the part before or after it, and then has to reconsider the sentence.

▶ **Solution**

Insert a comma after *glance*.

> Although Rodney seems cherubic
> at first glance, he excels in creating
> havoc.

▶ **Additional examples**

If Sue Ellen turns her back, she may soon find Rodney directing a siege from the rooftop and hurling chimney bricks at the house next door.

When she orders him to come down, he threatens to throw himself onto the concrete driveway unless she grants unconditional amnesty.

420

> **Missing comma**
>
> Considering the laws against child abuse the only choice Sue Ellen has is to outwit Rodney.

▶ Diagnosis

The sentence needs a comma at the intersection of *abuse* and *the*. The reader reads right through the intersection between *abuse* and *the* and at first thinks *the only choice* goes with the introductory phrase. One of the important uses of commas is to mark those places in sentences where a speaker would have to pause slightly between words in order to make his or her meaning clear; that is, to keep words from running into each other and causing confusion.

Unfortunately, we can't give you simple rules for identifying all the places where you need commas to keep from confusing the reader—again, try to develop a feel for where commas are needed by keeping in mind how someone else may read your writing.

16B

▶ Solution

Just insert a comma at the intersection after the introductory clause.

> Considering the laws against child abuse, the only choice Sue Ellen has is to outwit Rodney.

(Notice that you are again setting off a nonessential part of the sentence with a comma.)

Rewrite these sentences and insert commas where needed.

1. After some vain fantasizing about the possibility Sue Ellen realized that Rodney's father was not going to try to kidnap him.
2. Instead Dr. Rizzo was going to keep up Sue Ellen's child support payments scrupulously however painful it was to him for fear Sue Ellen might claim she wasn't able to keep Rodney.
3. Unless Sue Ellen gets Rodney under control she will not be able to move into student housing she can afford.
4. She gets nervous when she realizes that other young, defenseless parents who have no inkling of Rodney's destructive capabilities will be her neighbors in the student family complex.
5. Yet if she isn't able to get into student housing she will not be able to continue her education.

Comma problem 5: Commas to mark contrasts

> **Missing comma**
> Sue Ellen's primary concern is for education not glamour.

▶ **Diagnosis**

A comma is needed to set off a contrasting element in the sentence. The reader needs to make a fairly strong pause after *education* to emphasize the shift of ideas; therefore, the intersection requires a comma.

▶ **Solution**
Add a comma to show the contrast.

Sue Ellen's primary concern is for education, not glamour.

▶ **Additional examples**

Getting into student housing is a necessity for Sue Ellen, not a whim.

The Clear Lake College Housing Authority welcomes well-behaved youngsters, but not the likes of Rodney.

COMMAS THAT ENCLOSE

Terms you need to know

Restrictive modifier. A modifying phrase that names some essential characteristic of the word it modifies. Restrictive modifiers can't be removed from a sentence without changing or reducing its meaning significantly.

The boy *who hijacked the police cruiser* was Rodney.

Nonrestrictive modifier. A phrase that enhances our understanding of what it modifies, but does not define the modified expression in any essential way. A nonrestrictive modifier ordinarily can be cut from a sentence without radically altering its meaning.

The police officers, *who seemed more embarrassed than angry*, found their vehicle on a used-car lot.

423

Appositive. A noun or noun equivalent that follows a noun and "renames" or expands on it. Appositives are nonrestrictive modifiers.

> appositive
> Ike Cannon, *neighborhood-watch coordinator*, considers Rodney to be the agent of a foreign power.

Troubleshooting

Within sentences, commas serve the useful function of chunking information so that readers can better appreciate how ideas and phrases are connected. In the cases described below, commas work either in pairs or with other pieces of punctuation to enclose or highlight important words or phrases that operate as modifiers or interrupters.

Comma problem 6: Commas enclosing modifying phrases —nonrestrictive vs. restrictive modifiers

> ### Commas missing
> Rodney particularly excels at kidnapping the neighborhood dogs no matter how large they are and holding them for ransom.

▶ Diagnosis

Here, the nonessential **(nonrestrictive)** modifier is not marked off by commas. The modifying phrase *no matter how large they are* is an interrupting phrase that is not essential to the main idea of the sentence; therefore, it needs to be set off by commas. That's what commas do—they mark separable units.

Mark off with commas that part of the sentence that can be omitted from the sentence without changing its essential meaning.

> Rodney particularly excels at kidnapping the neighborhood dogs, no matter how large they are, and holding them for ransom.

An **appositive**, that is, a noun or noun equivalent that follows a noun and renames or expands on it, is an important kind of nonessential modifier. You should be particularly careful to set appositives off with commas.

16C

> appositive
> Rodney's mother, *the long suffering Sue Ellen*, has gotten so she hates to hear a knock at the door.

> appositive
> And when his father, *now a child pyschiatrist*, learns of Rodney's latest exploit, he grinds his teeth and worries about lawsuits.

However, when a modifying phrase is essential to the meaning of the sentence, it should *not* be set off with commas. Such a modifier is called **restrictive**. You don't want to separate a part of a sentence that will radically alter its meaning. For example:

> It's true, of course, that a boy *who is a showman at such an early age* seems destined for success in America.

The italicized restrictive modifier is essential to the meaning of the sentence; without it, *destined for success in America* makes no sense.

Nonessential modifiers (nonrestrictive)—commas

> Last winter he enticed a Doberman pinscher, one of those dogs that normal people are afraid of, into his garage.

> He then boldly called the owners, who had no idea the dog was even missing from their yard, and demanded a ransom of two Madonna albums and a CD player.

Essential modifiers (restrictive)—no commas

> Some would say that Rodney is just imitating people *who were heroes in the days of Social Darwinism.*

> Others would say, however, that he comes closer to imitating criminals *who deserved to hang from the yardarm.*

16C

Comma problem 7: Commas surrounding interrupting words and phrases

> **Missing commas**
>
> His mother at any rate is not impressed by either observation.

▶ **Diagnosis**

There are no commas around *at any rate* to indicate that it is an interrupting word or phrase in the sentence. Again, the reader tends to run through the intersection because there is no signal. The sentence is easily misread.

▶ **Solution**

Insert commas before and after *at any rate.*

> His mother, at any rate, is not im-
> pressed by either observation.

You need to insert commas around an interrupting phrase or word in a sentence, especially when it is an adverb like *however, moreover, nevertheless, therefore,* and so on (see comma problem 8 below).

▶ **Additional examples**

> Sue Ellen realizes, of course, that Rodney's inappropriate behavior has to be controlled.
>
> She knows, however, that she will have to be wily to deal with him.

16C

EXERCISE 16.4

Rewrite these sentences, inserting commas where you think they are necessary.

1. Child psychiatry a fairly new branch of medicine has only imperfect answers for many juvenile problems.
2. If the truth were known forty percent of parents who are psychiatrists still have problems with their children.
3. Such statistics often cited by people who think psychiatry is a "soft" science are not much consolation to other parents.
4. Although Sue Ellen is a loving parent who wants to do the right thing for her child she sometimes suspects Rodney is smarter than she is.
5. The fact is however that she is in charge and he had better realize it soon.

16C

> **Missing commas**
>
> **1.** The upshot of Rodney's misbehavior is that Sue Ellen may not be able to leave Kubla Khan Estates; *consequently* the Kubla Khan Neighborhood Association has decided to sponsor a contest to help Ms. Rizzo.
>
> **2.** *However* the Association's real intention is to get rid of Rodney.

▶ **Diagnosis**

Commas are missing after the conjunctive adverb *consequently* in the first sentence and after *however* in the second. Commas are needed because conjunctive adverbs (such as *consequently, nevertheless, however, therefore*, and so on) are interrupters that mark a shift or contrast in a sentence.

In the first example, *consequently* is preceded by a semicolon that marks the beginning of the clause. However, a comma is still needed after the conjunctive adverb. (For additional discussion of conjunctive adverbs preceded by semicolons, see semicolon problem 2 in the next chapter.)

In the second example, the adverb *however* marks a contrast and needs to be followed by a comma.

▶ **Solution**

Insert a comma after *consequently*.

> **1.** The upshot of Rodney's mis-
> behavior is that Sue Ellen may not
> be able to leave Kubla Kahn Es-
> tates; *consequently,* the Kubla
> Khan Neighborhood Association
> has decided to sponsor a contest to
> help Ms. Rizzo.

Insert a comma after *however*.

> **2.** *However,* the Association's real
> intention is to get rid of Rodney.

16D COMMAS THAT LINK

Troubleshooting
Though commas usually mark separations, they can also tell readers that certain ideas belong together. When commas stand before conjunctions, they provide a pause between clauses, but also furnish a kind of linkage that lets readers know that the ideas will continue; they aren't as fully stopped as they would be by a semicolon or period. Similarly, commas that mark off and separate items in a series simultaneously help readers appreciate that those items belong together.

Missing comma

The aim of the contest is to figure out how to control Rodney *and* its judges will be Rodney's mother and two magistrates of the juvenile court who live in Kubla Khan Estates.

16D

▶ **Diagnosis**

Commas are ordinarily needed before conjunctions that link independent clauses. Such conjunctions include *and*, *yet*, *but*, *or*, *nor*, and *so*. In the example above, a comma is missing before the coordination conjunction *and*. The comma helps to emphasize the break between the two parts of the sentence and lessons the likelihood of a misreading.

▶ **Solution**

Insert a comma before the first *and*.

The aim of the contest is to figure out how to control Rodney, and its judges will be Rodney's mother and two magistrates of the juvenile court who live in Kubla Khan Estates.

The judges are looking forward to the contest, but at least one of the magistrates is dubious.

That judge, Mary Pearl Carver, is a mother herself, so she knows at first hand what "incorrigible" means.

> **Tip:** Be especially careful not to insert the comma *after* the conjunction that joins independent clauses. In that position, commas can interrupt the flow of your sentences and confuse the reader.

{Incorrect} Rodney's father is enthusiastic about the contest but, he's not pinning his hopes on it.

{Correct} Rodney's father is enthusiastic about the contest, but he's not pinning his hopes on it.

{Incorrect} Dr. Rizzo remembers what a happy hellion he was as a child and so, he knows how intoxicated Rodney must be with his power.

{Correct} Dr. Rizzo remembers what a happy hellion he was as a child, and so he knows how intoxicated Rodney must be with his power.

16D

EXERCISE 16.5

Rewrite the following sentences, adding commas where they are needed and moving those that may be misplaced.

1. In spite of Judge Carver doubts about the success of the contest have not been expressed by any other neighbors.

2. So the Neighborhood Association will go ahead with plans for the contest; however the group does not have the wherewithal to award a prize for suggesting how to neutralize Rodney.
3. At first they thought they might have to abandon their plans but, a thoughtful citizen stepped forward.
4. Rodney's father Dr. Renaldo Rizzo has announced that he will donate a prize but it must provide incentive to elicit entries from embattled parents experienced in dealing with delinquents as formidable as Rodney the terror of Coleridge Place.
5. Of course Dr. Rizzo also hopes that he will get some ideas for dealing with his young patients but, he doesn't want to make his motive obvious.
6. Judge Carver suggested that the incentive might be eight fully-paid weeks at the well-regarded paramilitary summer camp Rambo's Redoubt for not one child but two.
7. When the contest is over and forgotten Rodney's name will be blessed in some quiet household this summer.
8. That is a bonus that several parents are hoping for and, it will undoubtedly help to make the contest a popular one.

Comma problem 10: Commas to mark a series

> **Commas missing**
>
> So the "Let's Get Rid of Rodney" contest kicks off on Monday amidst excitement anticipation and high hopes.

There are no commas to mark off the words in a series, *excitement, anticipation,* and *high hopes.* Again, commas are needed to mark a pause for the reader and to keep the words from colliding.

▶ **Solution**

Add commas after all but the last word in a series of three or more items.

> So the "Let's Get Rid of Rodney"
> contest kicks off on Monday
> amidst excitement, anticipation,
> and high hopes.

16D

In most cases, it is best to use a comma before the conjunction that signals the end of a series (usually *and* or *or*).

> . . . the rack, the wheel, the stocks, and other instruments of correction.

> . . . to pillory, keelhaul, or tar-and-feather.

Some writers, however, omit the comma before the conjunction at the end of a series.

▶ **Additional examples**

> Contestants are asked to write 500 words or less explaining their proposal for getting Rodney's attention, showing him the error of his ways, and giving him motivation to change.

> All proposals submitted must be humane, legal, and relatively inexpensive.

Use commas to mark off *coordinate* adjectives in series; that is, adjectives that all modify the same noun, the one they precede.

> Rodney is an *intelligent, conniving, cantankerous* child.

Notice that these adjectives could be switched around without affecting the sense of the sentence. It could read *cantankerous, intelligent, conniving child* just as well as the other way around. Here's a second example.

> Sue Ellen is a *frazzled, tired,* and slightly *frantic* mother.

These adjectives could also be switched around with no problem.

However, when you have an adjective modifying another adjective, the words are *noncoordinate*, and you couldn't switch them around without changing the meaning. In that case you shouldn't use commas between the adjectives.

> no commas
> At times Sue Ellen thinks longingly of her *good old single* days.

> no commas
> It's a tribute to her *natural good* humor that she doesn't complain.

EXERCISE 16.6

Rewrite these sentences, inserting commas where they are needed. If necessary, consult the section on other uses of commas on pp. 412–13 for guidance.

1. Some of the contest proposals for the reform of Rodney were inexpensive but not humane legal or practical.

2. For instance Otto Klinkhamer suggested that Rodney could be apprenticed out as child labor 8687 miles away in Tanzania.

3. Tong Chai proposed that Rodney be sent to Hampstead England to work with the famous dog trainer Barbara Woodhouse noted for her book *No Bad Dogs*.

4. Other suggestions were so bizarre that the judges concluded their authors were child-haters Mafia hit men Puritans or script writers for horror movies.

5. Finally out of the 1001 proposals emerged one to which both the judges and Sue Ellen were able to say "This sounds as if it might work."

6. It wasn't perfect in every respect but the price was right

7. It also would win the approval of that hard-to-please organization the Kubla Khan Neighborhood Association.

8. When the time came for the judges to announce their decision suspense was high.

9. Everyone agreed that the judges had been courageous confident and perhaps naive to take on the responsibility in the first place.

10. After the contest ended however the neighbors agreed that the judges had done a good job.

16D

Tip: In recent years, many newspaper and book editors have advised their writers not to overpunctuate. That's good advice. If you have several long sentences and you put commas in every single place that the rules specify, you may end up with sentences that make the reader stop every few words. Consequently, your sentences may seem choppy and hard to understand.

Here are sentences from which most commas have been removed. Add commas and then compare your version of the passage with someone else's. Note those places where you disagree about the need for a comma.

1. At the last minute a team Lawrence Butcher and Greta Ericson combined their skills for the ''Let's Get Rid of Rodney'' contest to draft the prize-winning proposal an imaginative yet practical idea.

2. To the judges' satisfaction Butcher and Ericson proposed to combine a sugarless diet with kung-fu martial arts to de-energize Rodney and at the same time give him an outlet for his aggressive competitive but at heart fun-loving nature.

3. Enthusiastically the contest winners predict that unless one of Rodney's kung-fu partners maims him within three years the Rizzo youth will be calm happy and the holder of a black belt.

4. The beauty of the plan as they outline it is that it will keep Rodney away from his terrorist activities for three years at least and also if he works hard make him appreciate the value of self-control and discipline.

5. Rodney however responded to the proposal by spraying the lawns of the winning contestants with herbicide releasing every cat and dog from the Ruralia animal shelter reversing every street sign in his neighborhood and toilet-papering the yards of the judges.

16D

CHAPTER

When Do You Use Semicolons and Colons?

■ **A** Semicolons
■ **B** Colons

17A WHEN DO YOU USE SEMICOLONS?

▶ **Function**

A semicolon is a stronger pause than a comma, but a weaker pause than a period. Think of a semicolon as a connector or an addition sign, joining related ideas. Or picture a semicolon as the center point on a balance because semicolons usually mark off or link items of equal grammatical weight.

▶ **Major Use**

—To join independent clauses (see p. 216) closely related to each other in thought. The semicolon tells us to read the linked clauses as a pair. See Problem 1 below.

> {**Example**} Films are about action and movement; plays emphasize thought and language.

437

► **Other uses**

—To join independent clauses connected by words or phrases such as *however*, *therefore*, *nevertheless*, *nonetheless*, *moreover*, *conversely*, *consequently*, *in fact*, and so on. (Words such as these are called **conjunctive adverbs** when they are used to link sentences.) See Problem 2.

> {**Example**} Films are about action; **consequently**, most memorable films have lively plots.

—To mark off phrases or items in a series that would ordinarily be separated by commas—except that they already contain commas. See Problem 3.

> {**Example**} The characters in Sean's film included Giorgio, a rich Venetian industrialist; Celeste, a society matron in love with Giorgio; Master Laurence, a professor of comparative literature troubled by dark thoughts, an unfaithful wife, and gambling debts; and Maria, a temperamental, dark-haired actress trying to find financial backing for *Acid Grapes*, a film she has written about the wine industry in Germany.

—To separate clauses, phrases, or series that might be confusing if commas alone were used to mark boundaries. These phrases often contain punctuation marks other than commas. See Problem 4.

> {**Example**} Sean's favorite films included *Boom!*; *2001: A Space Odyssey*; *W.U.S.A.*; and *Fire Maidens From Outer Space*.

Semicolon problem 1: Comma used where a semicolon is needed

Comma splice

Sean was a natural director, he liked giving orders.

438

▶ Diagnosis

A comma splice. A comma has been used where a semicolon is needed. A semicolon alone is strong enough to join two independent sentences. But a comma can link them only with the help of coordinating conjunctions—words such as *and*, *but*, *for*, *yet*, *or*, *nor*, and *so*.

▶ Solution

Replace the comma with a semicolon.

> **Use a semicolon**
>
> Sean was a natural director; he liked giving orders.

▶ Additional examples

Though a terrible actress, Rita was a gifted scriptwriter; she had an ear for dialogue.

Rita's script had energy and intelligence; she was sure the actors would love their parts.

Semicolon problem 2: Semicolon needed before conjunctive adverbs

> **Comma splice**
>
> Sean cast Alicia in the title role; however, he preferred Lynda for the part.

▶ Diagnosis

A comma splice. A comma has been mistakenly used before a conjunctive adverb—*however*—where a semicolon is required. This is a common punctuation problem.

► **Solution**

Replace the comma with a semicolon.

> **Use a semicolon**
>
> Sean cast Alicia in the title role; however, he preferred Lynda for the part.

► **Additional examples**

Lynda was the better actress; however, Alicia knew several people who might be willing to finance Sean's production.

Sean had a tight budget; nevertheless, he hoped to produce a professional-looking film.

Casting Alicia in the role of Maria made financial sense; indeed, Sean knew it was probably just the first of many artistic compromises.

● **Fine Tuning**

When a conjunctive adverb begins a clause that could stand on its own as a sentence, check to be sure that a semicolon comes before the conjunctive adverb and a comma follows it.

Frequently Used Conjunctive Adverbs		
therefore	moreover	furthermore
however	consequently	indeed
nevertheless	nonetheless	meanwhile

Sean's film was a parody of foreign movies; *however,* his major target was Fellini's *8-1/2.*

—But when the conjunctive adverb appears *in the middle* of a sentence, it is preceded and followed by commas.

Sean's film was a parody of foreign movies; his major target, *however,* was Fellini's *8-1/2.*

When you are in doubt about the punctuation, see what happens when you capitalize the conjunctive adverb and put a period before it. If the conjunctive adverb *begins* an independent clause, the new version will make sense—and you may use a semicolon before the conjunctive adverb.

{**Original**} Sean's film was a parody of foreign movies; *however,* his major target was Fellini's *8-1/2.*

{**Test version**} Sean's film was a parody of foreign movies. However, his major target was Fellini's *8-1/2.*

If the adverb is in the middle of a sentence, your attempt to create independent clauses usually won't work—and you cannot use a semicolon before the adverb.

{**Original**} The major target of Sean's foreign movie parody, *however,* was Fellini's *8-1/2.*

{**Test version**} The major target of Sean's foreign movie parody. However, was Fellini's *8-1/2.*

▶ **Additional example**   (Compare the versions.)

{**Version one**} Most of Sean's cast hadn't seen *8-1/2*; in fact, they had never heard of Fellini.

{**Version two**} Most of Sean's cast had, in fact, never seen *8-1/2* or heard of Fellini.

Confusing commas

Sean's expenses included the cost of renting lights, costumes, and sound equipment, film and film-processing fees, duplication costs for scripts, contracts, and other paperwork, and money for miscellaneous props.

17A

▶ **Diagnosis**

The commas within a complex list may prove confusing. For clarity, you need to separate the items in the series. But since some of the series items already contain commas, using more commas only makes it harder to tell what goes with what. As a result, the sentence is difficult to read.

▶ **Solution**

Replace the commas between the series items with semicolons. Since semicolons mark stronger pauses than commas do, they are better able to mark off the separate items.

Semicolons replace commas

Sean's expenses included the cost of renting lights, costumes, and sound equipment; film and film-processing fees; duplication costs for scripts, contracts, and other paperwork; and money for miscellaneous props.

Rita wrote a food orgy sequence, planning to film it in the Lindstrøm ice cream parlor; a scene in a health club, intending to use Butcher's Gym as a set; and a midnight swimming episode at Lake Nittani.

Sean decided that Alicia, tall and charismatic, would play Maria, the sophisticated and hot-tempered Italian actress; Sue Ellen Rizzo, a single parent returning to school for a finance degree, would play the rich and ruthless Celeste; Richard Wesley would portray Master Laurence, the troubled professor of comparative literature; and Travis Beckwith would take the role of Giorgio because no one else tried out for the part.

Semicolon problem 4: Clearer boundaries needed

17A

Confusing commas

Sean wanted Rita to include allusions in her screenplay to *Divorce: Italian Style, And the Ship Sails On,* and *400 Blows.*

▶ **Diagnosis**

Confusing commas within a series that contains several kinds of punctuation. Commas have been used where semicolons would provide sharper boundaries between items.

▶ **Solution**

Replace the commas with semicolons to reduce the likelihood of misreading.

Sean wanted Rita to include allusions in her screenplay to *Divorce: Italian Style;* *And the Ship Sails On;* and *400 Blows.*

▶ **Additional example**

The sound track for Sean's parody would include the overture from Wagner's *Tannhaüser*; the Supremes' "Stop in the Name of Love!"; Bob Dylan's "Rainy Day Women #12 & 35"; and Rogers and Hart's "Glad to Be Unhappy."

17A

● **Fine Tuning**

1. In most cases, a comma is strong enough to join a pair of independent clauses linked by a **coordinating conjunction** (*and, but, for, yet*):

The cast and crew for Sean's film were all amateurs, *yet* they worked almost as hard as professionals.

But a semicolon is sometimes used when the independent clauses are lengthy and contain punctuation themselves. The semicolon acts like a traffic signal, letting you know the difference between a brief stop (comma) and a major intersection (semicolon):

The cast and crew for Sean's film were all amateurs, from Rita, the scriptwriter, developing her first screenplay to Abel, the electrician, trying to figure out how to illuminate a lake at night; *but* they worked so hard that Professor Vorhees, the faculty supervisor on the project, decided to investigate whether they might earn course credit for the production.

2. When closely-related independent clauses are very short, they are sometimes linked by commas. Semicolons can seem heavy-handed between short clauses.

> {**With commas**} Travis picked up the costumes, Alicia arranged for transportation, Francie secured the props.

> {**With semicolons**} Travis picked up the costumes; Alicia arranged for transportation; Francie secured the props.

3. Never use a semicolon to introduce a list or dialogue. In most cases a colon or comma is the appropriate punctuation:

> {**Wrong**} The crew were amazed by the props Francie had located; an Art Deco sofa, a stuffed basset hound, a working Victrola, and the bumper from a 1949 Ford.

> {**Right**} The crew were amazed by the props Francie had located: an Art Deco sofa, a stuffed basset hound, a working Victrola, and the bumper from a 1949 Ford.

> {**Wrong**} At rehearsal one afternoon Alicia wondered aloud; "Do European students parody American films?"

> {**Right**} At rehearsal one afternoon Alicia wondered aloud, "Do European students parody American films?"

4. Don't use a semicolon to separate sentences from phrases or dependent clauses (see p. 216):

> {**Wrong**} Never having seen a foreign film; Travis wasn't sure what Sean's movie was poking fun at.

> {**Right**} Never having seen a foreign film, Travis wasn't sure what Sean's movie was poking fun at.

> {**Wrong**} Because he loved having his picture taken; Travis had tried out for the role of Giorgio.

> {**Right**} Because he loved having his picture taken, Travis had tried out for the role of Giorgio.

17A

{**Wrong**} Travis had all the qualities an actor needed; except talent.

{**Right**} Travis had all the qualities an actor needed, except talent.

EXERCISE 17.1

Revise the following sentences, adding or deleting semicolons as needed. Not all semicolons below are incorrect.

1. Maggie Lindstrøm had promised Sean he could use her ice cream parlor as a set if he made a film, however, she hadn't really expected his project to get off the ground when she made the offer.
2. Suddenly they were all there one Saturday morning; crew, actors, and spectators all appeared simultaneously.
3. Indeed, she doubted her shop had ever been so crowded; people were everywhere.
4. She watched; amazed, as Francie Knipstein transformed the ice cream parlor into a decadent European salon.
5. Against the wall, Francie placed a fancy embroidered screen, on the tables she draped elegant lace tablecloths and arranged expensive pieces of crystal and tiny oil lamps, and on the floor she deposited ferns and other plants.
6. In the meantime, Abel Gonzalez was stringing cable, setting up lights, and; occasionally, cursing when the wiring got tangled.
7. Maggie was getting up her courage to ask how long all this would take; when Sean strode up to her and asked; "Would you like to be in the movie?"
8. "Well, I've always thought I'd be a wonderful actress," Maggie admitted, "I played Juliet once in my high school play."
9. "We just need someone to serve drinks behind the counter during the scene, no acting talent is required," Sean said.
10. Maggie; however, didn't care, she was going to be a star!

▶ **Function**

A colon is a strong directional signal. Think of a colon as two small arrows pointing or a pair of eyes staring.

▶ **Major uses**

—To direct a reader's attention to an example or explanation. See Problem 1 below.

> {**Example**} Sean faced a major problem in filming his parody: a cast that didn't take direction well.

—To direct a reader's attention to a list. See Problem 2.

> {**Example**} The screenplay for the scene called for a variety of camera angles: a wide angle shot, an over-the-shoulder shot, a closeup, and a moving shot.

—To direct a reader's attention to a significant remark or conclusion.

> {**Example**} Sean, his cast, and his crew soon discovered the major ingredient in successful film-making: hard work.

—To direct a reader's attention to a quotation or dialogue.

> {**Example**} After a tough morning of shooting and re-shooting, Sean remembered Irving Berlin's line: "There's no business like show business."

▶ **Other uses**

—To join two complete sentences when the second sentence illustrates or explains the first.

> {**Example**} Making a film is like writing a paper: it absorbs all the time you'll give it.

—To separate numbers in various ways.

12:35 p.m.   Matthew 3:1

—To punctuate the salutation in a business letter.

Dear Sir or Madam:

Dear Mr. Iacocca:

—To separate title from subtitle.

Divorce: Italian Style

—To separate place of publication from the name of the publisher in a bibliography entry.

Cleveland: World Publishing, 1961

Colon problem 1: Unnecessary colon

> **Colon misused**
>
> Shoestring budgets have produced many financially successful films, such as: *Flashdance*, *Breaking Away*, *Friday the 13th*, and *Halloween*.

▶ **Diagnosis**

Unnecessary colon. Colons are not ordinarily needed after *such as*, *for example*, and *that is*. In fact, colons are stand-ins for such expressions. Colons are often used, however, with phrases that more specifically announce a list: *such as the following*, *including these*, *as follows*.

▶ **Solution**

Remove the colon. No additional punctuation is needed.

▶ **Additional example.**   (Compare the versions.)

{**Version one—with a colon**} Sean intended to trim his production budget by cutting out the *luxuries:* special effects, fancy titles, salaries for his cast, and lunches for the crew.

{**Version two—without a colon**} Sean intended to trim his production budget by cutting out *luxuries, such as* special effects, fancy titles, salaries for his cast, and lunches for the crew.

{**Version three—with a colon**} Sean intended to trim his production budget by cutting out *luxuries such as these:* special effects, fancy titles, salaries for his cast, and lunches for the crew.

Colon problem 2: Misused colon

17B

449

► **Diagnosis**

Ordinarily, a colon is used to introduce a list chiefly when the list follows a complete sentence. This guideline is somewhat flexible. But in the example above, there is no need to interrupt the sentence with the colon.

► **Solution**

Remove the colon. No additional punctuation is needed.

> **Unneeded colon cut**
>
> Sean's favorite directors were Hitchcock, Carpenter, Antonioni, Fellini, and Pollack.

► **Additional example.**   (Compare the versions.)

{**Version one—with a colon**} The filmmakers Rita admired most were a diverse group: François Truffaut, Mel Brooks, Alain Robbe-Grillet, and David Lean.

{**Version two—without a colon**} The filmmakers Rita admired most were François Truffaut, Mel Brooks, Alain Robbe-Grillet, and David Lean.

● **Fine Tuning**

1. Colons and semicolons are not interchangeable, but you can use both pieces of punctuation in the same sentence. A colon, for example, might introduce a list of items separated by semicolons.

Rita, the scriptwriter on the film, thought that the character of Celeste faced three options: a dramatic suicide from the observation deck of a tall building; remarriage to her fourth husband, the chief executive officer of a nuclear waste disposal company; or a shopping binge at Neiman Marcus.

450

2. Don't allow a colon to separate a preposition from its object(s).

> {**Wrong**} By the end of a week of shooting, the students had filmed in: an ice cream parlor, a funeral home, a police car, a locker room, and a supermarket.

> {**Right**} By the end of a week of shooting, the students had filmed in an ice cream parlor, a funeral home, a police car, a locker room, and a supermarket. [Colon cut.]

3. Short quotations introduced by short phrases don't require colons. Commas or no punctuation at all is usually sufficient. Compare the following sentences.

> Dirty Harry said "Make my day!"

> As Dirty Harry said, "Make my day!"

> Sean recalled Dirty Harry's memorable taunt: "Make my day!"

EXERCISE 17.2

Revise the following sentences, adding or deleting colons as needed. Not all colons below are incorrect.

1. At long last, the crew was ready to film the concluding scene: the midnight swim at Lake Nittani.
2. "We want to film this realistically: so let's meet at the lake about 11:15 pm to set up for the scene," said Sean.
3. At the quiet lake that night, Francie unloaded: towels, a lounge chair, fake pearls, wine glasses, and the old wind-up Victrola.
4. Francie told Sean that she had just one question, what did the scene at the lake have to do with *8-1/2*: the movie they were parodying?
5. Said Sean, "That's precisely my point, my parody has nothing to do with the film I am mocking!"

6. Francie said: "I see." But she didn't.
7. Sean then explained to his cast that in this final scene, the decadent Europeans, recognizing the folly of their lives, threw all their worldly goods into the lake, including: their jewels, their furniture, and their clothes.
8. "Then they plunge into the lake themselves, this midnight swim becomes the symbolic absolution that ends my film."
9. Alicia, Richard, Sue Ellen, and Travis all had the same question, "What are these decadent Europeans wearing while they are absolving themselves symbolically?"
10. "They wear a great deal, their sorrow, their pain, their guilt, their grief, their corruption."

EXERCISE 17.3

Revise the following sentences, adding or deleting colons and semicolons as needed. Not all the punctuation is incorrect.

1. "And their clothes?" asked Sue Ellen; who felt silly enough already: standing on a lake shore at midnight in the role of a tipsy society matron.
2. Sean admitted that he may have failed to mention that his movie ended with a nude scene, however, he promised to film it as discreetly as possible.
3. The film premiered several weeks later in Clear Lake College Auditorium, it was; in fact, a smashing success.
4. At the party after the premier, Professor Vorhees told Sean that she was especially impressed by the symbolic richness of the last scene where the decadent socialites throw everything that had been tormenting them into the lake; their jewels, their music, their alcohol, their director.
5. "Not until that final moment when you are flung into the water; screaming like a scalded cat; stripped of your pretensions and your clothes; did I realize that your film was really a statement about: a film-maker's struggle to create art. Bravo! Have you ever seen Fellini's *8-1/2*?"

CHAPTER

How Do You Use Markers?

- **A** Dashes
- **B** Hyphens
- **C** Parentheses
- **D** Brackets
- **E** Quotation Marks
- **F** Ellipses
- **G** Italics

18A **WHEN DO YOU USE DASHES?**

▶ **Function**

A dash is a bold piece of punctuation. When used alone, a dash attaches one idea to another with more vigor than a comma would. When used in pairs, dashes highlight words or phrases by isolating them from the rest of a sentence. Think of dashes as sparks of energy in a sentence, arcing from idea to idea.

▶ Principal uses

—To join a phrase to the end of a sentence. The phrase might clip on an example, illustration, or summary. Or it might add a surprise, a contradiction, or an exception to the sentence. Like colons, dashes point to ideas. But where colons provide formal introductions, dashes introduce unanticipated guests.

{**Examples**}

Politicians do dumb things—even in small towns like Ruralia.

Late one night, a tired Ruralia town council agreed to a zoning change proposed by a powerful out-of-town developer—a minor variance no one thought much about.

Several weeks later a sign appeared in the glen next to Clear Lake College announcing that the firm of Dumble & Tweed was about to build just what Ruralia needed—another shopping center.

—To insert an idea into the middle of a sentence. The interruption might be an example, explanation, illustration, observation, amplification, or contradiction. In any case, the interrupting phrase, surrounded by dashes, could be lifted out of the sentence without affecting its overall sense.

{**Examples**}

The Daily Toxin—Clear Lake College's noisy and aggressive school paper—trumpeted news of the shopping center in two-inch headlines.

The pristine woodlands next to the college—where students and faculty now relaxed, took walks, studied plants, picnicked, and partied—would soon become a concrete and asphalt eyesore.

The *Toxin* challenged all concerned individuals—and that included almost everyone who lived or worked on campus—to attend an emergency meeting to stop the shopping center.

18A

—To show an interruption, especially in dialogue.

{**Examples**}

"When—perhaps I should say *if*—this shopping center is built, we will lose a natural resource that cannot be replaced," Dean Rack declared at the meeting.

Connie Lim, *Toxin* editor, replied, "For the first time in my three years at Clear Lake College—I can hardly believe it—I agree with Dean Rack."

—To set off items, phrases, or credit lines.

{**Example**}

McDonald's, Burger King, Sears, National Video, H & R Block—the town of Ruralia already hosted all the essential retail outlets.

Participants at the meeting agreed
　　—to oppose the building of the shopping center,
　　—to develop a strategy to publicize their opposition,
　　—to resort to the strongest measures necessary to save the woodlands.

"If we don't have trees, where will the birds sit?"
　　　　　　　　　　　　　　　　　—Wolfgang Rack

—To mark off questions and answers.

{**Example**}

Q.—Did you understand fully the consequences of the zoning change?
A.—To be honest, I did. I don't oppose the new shopping mall. Ruralia needs developments like Sylvan Centre to keep its economy expanding.

18A

> **Hyphen used for a dash**
>
> A committee was established-con-sisting of students, faculty, and administrators-to coordinate campus opposition to Sylvan Centre.

▶ **Diagnosis**

Hyphens { - } have been typed where dashes are intended. Typed dashes are made up of two unspaced hyphens { -- }. No space is left before or after a dash.

18A

▶ **Solution**

Replace the hyphens with dashes.

> **Dash typed correctly**
>
> A committee was established--con-sisting of students, faculty, and administrators--to coordinate campus opposition to Sylvan Centre.

> ### Too many dashes
> Hector Stavros—the college om-budsman—suggested that a variety of tactics—radio talk show ap-pearances, letters-to-the-editor, street-corner petition drives—would persuade the citizens of Ruralia to oppose Sylvan Centre.

▶ Diagnosis
The dashes cause confusion. Dashes are vigorous pieces of punctuation that should be used cautiously—one pair of dashes per sentence.

▶ Solution
Replace some of the dashes with commas.

> ### Some dashes eliminated
> Hector Stavros, the college om-budsman, suggested that a variety of tactics—radio talk show ap-pearances, letters-to-the-editor, street-corner petition drives—would persuade the citizens of Ruralia to oppose Sylvan Centre.

18A

457

▶ **Additional example**

{**Too many dashes**} Connie believed that Stavros' suggestions—which she privately labeled gutless media pandering—would only bore the public, while her more assertive tactics—sit-ins, demonstrations, civil disobedience, boycotts, and guerrilla theater—would galvanize the public into resisting the greed of the developers—and stop Sylvan Centre.

{**Revised**} Connie believed that Stavros' suggestions, which she privately labeled gutless media pandering, would only bore the public. She proposed more assertive tactics—sit-ins, demonstrations, civil disobedience, boycotts, and guerrilla theater—to galvanize the public into resisting the greed of the developers and stopping Sylvan Centre.

18A

EXERCISE 18.1

Add and delete dashes as necessary to improve the passage below. You may rearrange the sentences as necessary.

1. Within a week of the announcement of Sylvan Centre, two campus groups were working hard to oppose the project, one led by Stavros, the other by Connie Lim.
2. The split in tactics led—almost inevitably—toward one result—a confused public.
3. Supporters of the shopping center project a powerful group of developers and politicians were pleased by the divided opposition.
4. Noise, angry words, a few half-filled petitions that's all the campus politicians were able to produce.
5. The public according to a survey published in the town paper seemed to favor Sylvan Centre though support for the project was "soft."

▶ **Function**

The hyphen, a humble but much-used mark, either divides syllables or links words. You might want to visualize these marks as hinges that help things move smoothly.

▶ **Principal uses**

18B

—To divide words at the ends of lines when you run out of space. When typing or writing by hand, try not to divide too many words. If you are using a word processor, "word wrap" will eliminate most divided words. Here are some guidelines for using hyphens to divide words.

1. When you must divide a word at the end of a line, break it only at a syllable. If you are unsure about a syllable break, check a dictionary. Don't guess.

> fu / se / lage   vin / e / gar / y
> lo / qua / cious   cam / ou / flage

2. Never divide a word of one syllable or let a single letter dangle at the end of a line. Divisions like the following would be either wrong or inappropriate:

> mo- uth   cry- pt   cough- ed
> o- boe   e- clipse   i- dea

3. Never strand only a letter or two at the beginning of a new line. Divisions like the following would be inappropriate.

> Ohi- o   clump- y   flatfoot- ed
> log- ic   oversimpli- fy   yo- yo

4. Don't leave a syllable at the end of a line that might be read as a complete word. The following sentences might be misread at first because of faulty division.

> Barry intended to dedicate his life to studying Zoroastrianism.

> Nothing could deter Alicia in her pursuit of a management degree.

5. Don't hyphenate contractions, numbers, abbreviations, or initialisms at the end of lines. The following divisions would be inappropriate.

would- n't	250- 000,000	NA- TO
U.S.- M.C.	Ph.- D.	NB- C

6. Divide compound expressions between words, not syllables. Divide expressions that contain hyphens at the hyphen.

18B

barber- shop	space- ship	hind- quarter
pre- emergent	ex- governor	post- modern

—To link various kinds of compound words and expressions. Hyphens join words together in a variety of situations, but the conventions guiding their use are complicated. Sometimes you'll have to rely on instinct—or a dictionary. Here are some guidelines to sharpen your instincts.

1. Use hyphens when you write out numbers from twenty-one to ninety-nine. Fractions also take hyphens, but only one hyphen per fraction.

twenty-nine	two-thirds	one forty-seventh of a mile
one-quarter inch	ninety-nine	two hundred forty-six

2. Check a dictionary to be sure which compound expressions are typically hyphenated. Usage may vary. Here are some words that do take hyphens.

mother-in-law	son-in-law	great-grand-mother
three-D	walkie-talkie	water-skier
half-and-half	self-government	cross-examine

Note, however, that many compounds do not take hyphens.

hitchhiker	evildoer	yearbook
selfsame	shoofly pie	motorcycle
deer skin	cross current	attorney general

3. Hyphens are often used when modifiers that come before a noun work together.

a sharp-looking suit	a blue-green tint
a stop-motion sequence	a well-known artist
a seventeenth-century vase	a blood-curdling scream

If placing a comma between the modifiers or dropping one of them changes the meaning of the phrase, then the modifiers probably should be linked by a hyphen.

a sharp, looking suit?	a blue tint?
a stop, motion sequence?	a well, known
a seventeenth, century vase?	artist?

However, hyphens are not used with adverbs that end in -ly. Nor are they used with very.

a sharply honed knife	a quickly written note
a bitterly cold morning	a very hot day

4. Hyphens are usually not required when compound modifiers follow a noun.

The artist was **well known**.
The scream was **blood curdling**.
I thought the suit was **sharp looking**.

▶ **Other uses**
—To link prefixes and suffixes to base words.

pre-Columbian
governor-**elect**
post-Reagan era

—To create compound phrases.

Hector Stavros resented Connie Lim's **holier-than-thou** attitude in opposing the Sylvan Centre project.

In Hector's opinion, Connie was of the **make-the-news-if-you-can't-find-any** school of journalism.

Don't use this technique of creating categories or descriptions too often. It can seem gimmicky.

—To prevent words from being misread.

But Connie knew that regaining the confidence of a public **once-burned** by sensational or irresponsible reporting was about as easy as **re-belling** a cat.

Hyphen problem: Faulty division of words at the end of a line

> **Faulty division**
>
> While opponents of Sylvan Centre argued about strategy, archit-ects and engineers on the project were surveying the landsca-pe to prepare for bulldozing.

▶ **Diagnosis**
Words at the end of typed lines are divided wrong.

▶ **Solution**
Divide the words at the end of syllables. Check a dictionary if necessary.

> **Correct division**
>
> While opponents of Sylvan Centre argued about strategy, archi-tects and engineers on the project were surveying the land-scape to prepare for bulldozing.

Sometimes a word or phrase may have more than a single hyphenated modifier. These suspended modifiers look like the following.

> Stavros proposed separate campaigns to reach **low-, medium-,** and **high-income level** citizens in Ruralia.

> Connie, on the other hand, intended to disrupt regular **Democrat-** and **Republican-sponsored** events in town.

EXERCISE 18.2

Most people guess at syllable division when they divide words. Should they consult a dictionary instead? Try your hand at dividing the following twenty words into syllables. Then check your divisions against a dictionary. Tally up the number you got exactly right and enter it in the formula below for figuring your percent correct. Can you afford to rely on your best guesses?

18B

Word	Right	Wrong
1. malfeasance	____	____
2. Aleutian	____	____
3. baboon	____	____
4. cooperate	____	____
5. measles	____	____
6. separate	____	____
7. zoology	____	____
8. flamingo	____	____
9. dyslexia	____	____
10. faucet	____	____
11. writing	____	____
12. mischievous	____	____
13. revelation	____	____
14. parabola	____	____

15. oceanographer   _____   _____
16. license   _____   _____
17. junior   _____   _____
18. hemorrhage   _____   _____
19. grabbed   _____   _____
20. novice   _____   _____

Number right _____ × 5 = _____ % correct

EXERCISE 18.3

18B

Add, delete, or correct hyphens as needed in the following editorial. Consult a dictionary to check your work.

Act Now To Save Forests

by Connie Lim

Citizens of Ruralia have a once in a life-time opportunity to secure today a priceless resource for their children tomorrow. A large wooded tract is about to be stolen from us by out of town developers and pinstripe suited investors—the parcel of land bordering Clear Lake College and Lake Nittani. Today the woods beloved of generations of Clear Lake-College students provide an unspoiled reminder of our debt to nature. The groves, home to wildlife of all varieties, from ruffed grouse to ruby throated hummingbirds, provide a pleasant haven from the pressures of school and work. The lake, cooled and protected by the surrounding forest, is the loveliest place in the county on a humid summer day, free of the hurly-burly of traffic, agriculture, and business. It is where citizens of Ruralia can go when they find the world too much with them. Unless we act promptly and powerfully, this sylvan wilderness will soon become "Sylvan Centre," a concrete-and-asphalt tribute to the I can do what I like with my own attitude. The only green the developer—the firm of Dumble & Tweed—loves can be counted, stacked, and deposited in glass towered banks. Do we really need more video stores, more T shirt shops, more over priced boutiques and junkfood restaurants? Ruralia Mall is only two miles from the site of this most recently-proposed development. Let's work together to stop the abomination upon our natural-resources that Sylvan Centre is sure to be. Call your city-council representatives today and tell them that you're opposed to developing our most beautiful forest-land.

18C WHEN DO YOU USE PARENTHESES?

( )

▶ Function

Both parentheses and brackets act like enclosures. Parentheses are used more often than brackets and more generally— usually to show when something needs to be separated from the rest of a sentence or paragraph. Parentheses lack the snap of dashes; instead, they quietly furnish an extra bit of information, a comment, or an aside. Brackets, on the other hand, are specialty pieces of punctuation used in a few specific situations (see 18D).

▶ Principal use

—To separate material from the main body of a sentence or paragraph. This material may be a word, a phrase, a list, even a complete sentence.

> While lobbying late in the evening at city hall against construction of Sylvan Centre, Hector Stavros learned **(from a sympathetic secretary in the planning office)** that developers planned to bulldoze the construction site early the next morning.

465

To keep a low profile until the job was under way, the developers were bringing in construction people and equipment **(trucks, tractors, bulldozers, flatbeds)** from towns around Ruralia.

Demolition would start early **(5:30 a.m.)** and by noon, a swath would be cut from the heart of the woodland. **(The developers figured students and faculty couldn't mount a protest earlier.)** Once construction was under way, the developers were confident that opposition to Sylvan Centre would fade.

▶ **Other uses**

—To insert examples, directions, or other details into a sentence.

> While still at city hall, Hector left a note for Bernice Kopple, a council member, friend, and former mayor **(1982–86)**.

> Call me at home **(288-0355)** or at my university office **(471-6109)**. Urgent!

—To highlight numbers or letters used in listing items.

> Hector realized that he could **(1)** allow the developers to have their way, **(2)** try to procure a court injunction against the construction (not likely in the time available), or **(3)** encourage Connie and her troops to take direct action against the developers.

18C

Faulty punctuation

Connie was thrilled by the prospect of direct action against the developers. (She had longed for a political confrontation like this.) She swung into immediate action, calling everyone she could think of (including some students she didn't like.)

▶ **Diagnosis**

The periods are misplaced. When a complete sentence standing alone is surrounded by parentheses, its end punctuation belongs inside the parentheses. However, when a sentence concludes with a parentheses, the end punctuation for the complete sentence falls outside the final parenthesis mark.

▶ **Solution**

Move the periods. (See also the Fine Tuning section below.)

Punctuation corrected

Connie was thrilled by the prospect of direct action against the developers. (She had longed for a political confrontation like this.) She swung into immediate action, calling everyone she could think of (including some students she didn't like).

467

1. If parentheses enclose a full sentence within another sentence, the enclosed sentence begins without capitalization and ends without punctuation.

> Connie called the gymnastics squad **(they owed her a favor)**, fraternity and sorority houses **(she wasn't on good terms with most of them)**, and even the college volunteer fire department **(it was, after all, an emergency)**.

2. No punctuation is needed to introduce parentheses within a sentence. However, if necessary, a phrase in parentheses may be followed by a comma.

> {**Wrong**} Amazed as he was by Connie's energy**,** (she worked nonstop throughout the night), Hector was even more impressed by Connie's political savvy.

> {**Right**} Amazed as he was by Connie's energy (she worked nonstop throughout the night), Hector was even more impressed by Connie's political savvy.

3. Parentheses are used around in-text notes when using MLA or APA documentation. See Chapter 23 for details.

18C

EXERCISE 18.4

Add parentheses as needed to the following passage. Pay special attention to punctuation and capitalization.

1. When the construction crews arrived at the construction site in the cool dawn, they were greeted by lights, cameras, television crews, newspaper reporters including one from Chicago, angry local farmers, and even a church choir.
2. Ike Cannon, the crew foreman, grumbled at the protestors under his breath he had seen their kind before in California and ordered his crews to work.

3. His crews about thirty men and women, all told mounted their heavy machines.
4. The forest shook with the rumble of a dozen Diesels clanging to life. The equipment had arrived on schedule from another Dumble & Tweed project site in the north of the state. As soon as the engines started, the choir began singing "We Shall Overcome."
5. Two bulldozers one driven by Ike Cannon moved ruthlessly toward a towering oak, the first of their intended victims.

18D WHEN DO YOU USE BRACKETS?

[ ]

▶ Function

Like parentheses, brackets are enclosures. But they have fewer and more specialized uses. Brackets and parentheses are usually *not* interchangeable.

▶ Principal use

—To insert comments or explanations into direct quotations. You cannot change the words in a direct quotation, but you can add remarks to them by using brackets.

> Waving a sheet of paper, Bernice yelled to Ike Cannon, "This **[a copy of the zoning variance]** doesn't give you authority to start construction."

> "Wanna bet?" he replied still aiming his bulldozer at the oak. "Phil Grymm **[legal counsel for Dumble & Tweed]** says we can, and I take my orders from him."

> "You could face prosecution. He **[Grymm]** is an idiot," Kopple replied.

▶ **Other uses**

—To clarify situations where parentheses fall within parentheses. When possible, avoid parentheses within parentheses. If you cannot, the inner set of parentheses should become brackets.

> Ruralia City Council had granted a zoning variance to the developers (Dumble & Tweed **[parcel no. 34209]**).

—To acknowledge or highlight errors that originate in quoted materials. In such cases the Latin word *sic* ("thus") is enclosed in brackets immediately after the error. The [sic] tells your reader that what may seem to be an error on your part is a faithful copy of the original material. See Chapter 23 for additional details.

> One protestor's sign read "Go home Dumbo **[sic]** and Tweed."

18D

Bracket problem: Parentheses used instead of brackets

Parentheses used instead of brackets

Bernice stood her ground saying, "This piece of paper (the zoning variance) won't move me and neither will your bulldozers."

▶ **Diagnosis**

Your typewriter doesn't have keys for brackets!

▶ **Solution**

Leave a space where the brackets should appear and draw them in after you have typed your paper. But don't forget.

Brackets drawn in

Bernice stood her ground saying, "This piece of paper [the zoning variance] won't move me and neither will your bulldozers."

18E WHEN DO YOU USE QUOTATION MARKS?

Terms you should know

Direct discourse. The actual words of a speaker or writer. You should enclose all direct discourse in quotation marks.

As Ike's bulldozer approached, Bernice yelled "I will not budge!"

Indirect discourse. The substance of what a speaker or writer has said, but not the exact words. Indirect discourse is not surrounded by quotation marks.

As Ike's bulldozer approached, Bernice declared that she would not move.

▶ Function

Quotation marks—which always appear in pairs—highlight whatever appears between them. Conventionally, double marks ("") are used around direct discourse and titles. However single marks appear (' ') with quotations or titles inside quotations.

▶ Principal uses

—To signal that you are quoting word-for-word from printed sources. Notice the capitalization and punctuation before and after the quotations in the following examples.

> "Heroism," says Ralph Waldo Emerson, "feels and never reasons and therefore is always right."

> Emerson reminds us that "Nothing great was ever achieved without enthusiasm."

> "Next to the originator of a good sentence is the first quoter of it," writes Emerson.

For more details about punctuating quotations, see Quotation Problems 1–3. For details about how to introduce direct quotations, how to tailor quotations to the grammar of your sentences, how to handle long quotations, and how to quote from poetry, see Chapter 23.

18E

—To show dialogue. Quotation marks are used around the exact words of various speakers. When you write extended dialogue, you ordinarily start a new paragraph each time the speaker changes.

> As the bulldozer approached her, Bernice quoted from Thoreau: "In the long run men hit only what they aim at."
>
> "Are you aware," Ike replied, stopping his bulldozer momentarily, "that Thoreau also wrote that 'It is characteristic of wisdom not to do desperate things'"?
>
> Bernice said, "Yes, of course."
>
> "Well, then don't you feel foolish planting yourself in front of a six-ton bulldozer?" Ike asked.

However, when dialogue is provided not for its own sake, but to make some other point, the words of several speakers may appear within a single paragraph.

> But Bernice was wondering "Is it really possible that this burly vacuity driving a tractor knows Thoreau well enough to quote him to me?" And Ike was musing on much the same theme: "I bet that *Cosmo*-reading uppity lawyer thinks I haven't got a brain in my head." Love was blooming.

—To cite the titles of short works. These ordinarily include titles of songs, essays, magazine and newspaper articles, TV episodes, unpublished speeches, chapters of books, and short poems. (Longer works appear in *italics*.)

> "Love is Just a Four Letter Word"—song
> "Love is a Fallacy"—title of an essay
> "Love Among the Ruins"—title of a poem

▶ Other uses

—To draw attention to specific words. Italics can also be used in these situations. See 18G.

> Connie whispered to Hector that he was about to see what the "pro" in "protest" meant.

> Hector whispered back that he hoped she could spell "protest" better than one of her sign-carrying colleagues could spell "bourgois swine."

> Ike Cannon liked to think of himself as the "Bill Buckley" of the Caterpillar set.

18E

To signal that you are using a word ironically, sarcastically, or derisively.

> While Ike "studied" Bernice's technique of passive resistance, a coworker maneuvered her bulldozer around Councilor Kopple and headed for the oak.

Quotation problem 1: Periods and commas go inside quotation marks

> **Period and comma misplaced outside quotation marks**
>
> From the top of the oak, eggs suddenly rained down and voices were raised singing "The Battle Hymn of the Republic⬤ Muttering "I don't believe it⬤the driver of the bulldozer stopped her machine.

Both the period and comma are incorrectly placed outside the quotation marks. Commas and periods always go *inside* a closing quotation mark.

▶ **Solution**
Move period and comma inside the quotes.

18E

> **Period and Comma relocated inside quotation marks**
>
> From the top of the oak, eggs suddenly rained down and voices were raised singing "The Battle Hymn of the Republic." Muttering "I don't believe it," the driver of the bulldozer stopped her machine.

▶ **Additional examples**

"Stop all the machines!" Ike yelled. "We don't want anyone hurt."

To the students the protest was a "game," but to Ike the construction delay was serious business.

Quotation problem 2: Colons and semicolons go outside quotation marks

Colon and semicolon misplaced inside quotation marks

It looked like a scene from "Robin Hood:" the trees were filled with students. In a sycamore, members of the gymnastics team unfurled a banner that read "Heck no, we won't go;" in a neighboring pine, three members of the football team tossed a hacky-sack.

▶ **Diagnosis**

Both the colon and semicolon are incorrectly placed inside the quotation marks. Colons and semicolons always go *outside* a closing quotation mark.

▶ **Solution**

Move the colon and semicolon outside the quotation mark.

Colon and semicolon relocated outside quotation marks

It looked like a scene from "Robin Hood": the trees were filled with students. In a sycamore, members of the gymnastics team unfurled a banner that read "Heck no, we won't go"; in a neighboring pine, three members of the football team tossed a hacky-sack.

▶ **Additional examples**

> The fraternities made a rare show of "peaceful coexistence": they commandeered half the threatened grove.

> Even the faculty defended a portion of the "woods in riot"; a stately elm supported two assistant professors.

Quotation problem 3: Placement of question marks, exclamations, and dashes varies

18E

> **Punctuation misplaced outside quotation marks**
>
> When Hector saw the people in the trees, he muttered, "Good grief"?! Then he turned to Connie and said "Can you imagine whose stupid idea this was"? Connie fumed: "Stupid"—but just then two police cruisers lumbered to the site.
>
> **Punctuation misplaced inside quotation marks**
>
> Who was it complained "there's nothing new under the sun?" The police dispatcher should have warned her officers that they were about to journey into the "Twilight Zone!"

476

▶ Diagnosis

The closing punctuation is misplaced. Question marks, exclamation points, and dashes can fall either inside or outside quotation marks, depending on the situation. (1) These punctuation marks fall inside the closing quotation when they are the right punctuation for the phrase inside the quotes, but not to end the sentence as a whole. (2) They fall outside the closing quotation mark when they are the appropriate mark for the complete sentence.

▶ Solution

Move the punctuation inside or outside the closing quotation mark according to the guidelines above.

18E

Punctuation relocated inside quotation marks

When Hector saw the people in the trees, he muttered "Good grief!" Then he turned to Connie and said "Can you imagine whose stupid idea this was?" Connie fumed: "Stupid—" but just then two police cruisers lumbered to the site.

Punctuation relocated outside quotation marks

Who was it complained "there's nothing new under the sun"? The police dispatcher should have warned her officers that they were about to journey into the "Twilight Zone"!

1. Don't use quotation marks to draw attention to clichés. Highlighting a tired phrase just makes it seem more fatigued.

> On the cool morning in Ruralia, "truth seemed stranger than fiction."

> Ike Cannon was angrier than a "cat on a hot tin roof."

2. Use quotation marks very sparingly to indicate irony or sarcasm. The technique loses its punch quickly.

> At the demonstration site, Connie played the part of a "humble" country reporter.

> Ike called his headquarters to report a little "problem."

3. Don't put the title of your paper between quotation marks on the title page or first page.

> {**Wrong**}

> "The Tradition of Civil Disobedience in Illinois"

> {**Right**}

> The Tradition of Civil Disobedience in Illinois

18E

EXERCISE 18.5

Rework the following passage by adding or deleting quotation marks, moving punctuation as necessary, and indenting where you think appropriate.

By noon, the "face-off" between Connie Lim's treed protestors and Ike Cannon's construction crews had attracted national attention. On cue, the demonstrators sang Blowin' in the Wind whenever a TV camera was pointed in their direction. A crew from ABC news interviewed Connie who claimed she had enough supporters to keep teams of students and faculty in the trees for a month. This beautiful forest cannot be replaced she said If the firm of Dumble & Tweed intends to destroy it, we want the whole nation to watch them do it! Do you take seriously the threat by Dumble & Tweed's attorneys to arrest you and anyone on the Sylvan Centre property for trespassing? the reporter asked. She replied that she was perfectly willing to be arrested if that is what it took to save the trees. But at that moment, Phil Grymm, spokesperson for Dumble & Tweed intervened. I think that the public should be aware that this lot is private property—No development that destroys the environment is private! Connie interjected. As I was trying to say, Grymm continued, Dumble & Tweed expects Sylvan Centre to provide the citizens of Ruralia with a wide range of new shopping experiences. In the long run, the people here will be grateful for this development Connie was furious. I want to know one thing. Do you dare name the retailers who intend to build here or are they too ashamed to admit on national television their role in this tragedy? Grymm blushed like a "bride".

EXERCISE 18.6

Write a passage of dialogue in which you complete the argument between Grymm and Connie.

18F WHEN DO YOU USE ELLIPSES?

▶ **Function**

The three spaced periods that form an ellipsis mark indicate a gap in a sentence. Either the writer has left something out or wanted an idea to seem to trail away.

▶ Principal use

—To indicate that material has been left out of a direct quotation. This material may be a word, a phrase, a complete sentence, or more.

> {**Complete passage**} In *Walden* (1854), Henry David Thoreau describes his forest in spring: "Early in May, the oaks, hickories, maples, and other trees, just putting out amidst the pine woods around the pond, imparted a brightness like sunshine to the landscape, especially in cloudy days, as if the sun were breaking through the mists and shining faintly on the hill-sides here and there."

> {**Passage with ellipses**} In *Walden* (1854), Henry David Thoreau describes his forest in spring: "Early in May, the oaks, hickories, maples, and other trees . . . imparted a brightness like sunshine to the landscape . . . as if the sun were breaking through the mists and shining faintly on the hill-sides here and there."

▶ Other uses

—To indicate any gap or pause in a sentence, not necessarily in quoted material.

> We will fight them in the bushes, we will fight them in the poison ivy, we will fight them in the brambles . . . we will not surrender.

—To suggest an action that is incomplete or continuing.

> About to explode in anger, Ike Cannon began counting under his breath, "One, two, three. . . ."

18F

> 1. most   governments . . . are sometimes
> 2. It is excellent, . . . yet this government
> 3. the people can act through it. . . .
> 4. the right to revolution . . ."
> (102).

18F

▶ **Guidelines**

An ellipsis is typed as three spaced periods (. . . not ...).

Be sure to position an ellipsis mark accurately when slipping it into a sentence. Spacing is important, especially when typing. Here are four guidelines for placing an ellipses.

1. When an ellipsis mark appears in the middle of a sentence, leave a space before the first and after the last period. (See # 1 above.)

2. If a punctuation mark occurs immediately before the words you are cutting, you may include it in your edited version if it makes your sentence easier to read. The punctuation mark is followed by a space, then the ellipsis mark. (See # 2 above.)

3. When an ellipsis occurs at the end of a complete sentence, the end punctuation of the sentence is retained in the edited version, followed by a space, followed by the ellipsis. No gap is left between the last word in the sentence and its original end punctuation. (See # 3 above.)

4. When a parenthetical reference follows a sentence that ends with an ellipsis, leave a space between the last word in the sentence and the ellipsis. Then provide the parenthetical reference, followed by the closing punctuation mark. (See # 4 above.)

● **Fine Tuning**

To show that you have left a line or more out of a poem, type a full line of spaced periods.

{**Original**}

Life's a crock, or so they say;
Crocks are mud wrung dry as hay;
Hay's a grass grows fast as weeds;
Weeds are life drawn out of seeds.

—T. Beckwith

{**Line deleted**}

Life's a crock, or so they say;
Crocks are mud wrung dry as hay;
. . . .
Weeds are life drawn out of seeds.

18F

EXERCISE 18.7

Add ellipses to the following passage from Henry David Thoreau's *Resistance to Civil Government* (1849). Try to add at least four ellipsis marks at various points in the passage. Be sure that the passage is still readable after you have made your cuts.

I heartily accept the motto,—"That government is best which governs least"; and I should like to see it acted up to more rapidly and systematically. Carried out, it finally amounts to this, which also I believe,—"That government is best which governs not at all"; and when men are prepared for it, that will be the kind of government which they will have. Government is at best but an expedient; but most governments are usually, and all governments are sometimes, inexpedient. The objections which have been brought against a standing army, and they are many and weighty, and deserve to prevail, may also at last be brought against a standing government. The standing army is only an arm of the standing government. The government itself, which is only the mode which the people have chosen to execute their will, is equally liable to be abused and perverted before the people can act through it. Witness the present Mexican war, the work of comparatively a few individuals using the standing government as their tool; for, in the outset, the people would not have consented to this measure.

EXERCISE 18.8

Add ellipses to the following passage. Try to add at least four ellipsis marks at various points in the passage. Be sure that the passage is still readable after you have made your cuts.

By midafternoon, the protestors in the trees at Clear Lake College had drawn a noisy, festive crowd, one more eager to be on television than to support the survival of the forest. Connie Lim, driven by nervous energy and excitement, completed yet another interview, explaining for the twelfth or thirteenth time how the protestors' action belonged to a long and distinguished tradition of civil disobedience, stretching from Thoreau to Gandhi and Martin Luther King, Jr. Almost every hour, new spokespeople for Dumble & Tweed arrived, each declaring the firm's commitment to the environment and ecology, yet asserting the right to build on the property the company owned. Hector Stavros—carefully staying in the background—spent hours on the phone, talking with members of Clear Lake College's Board of Regents and with Dumble & Tweed executives in Chicago. Hour stretched into hour. Bernice Kopple invited Ike Cannon to dinner. Night fell, and with it, a slow, steady rain. The protestors might have scurried away under cover of darkness, dragging their flimsy rainwear, portable radios, and water-logged signs with them, except for the renewed glare of lights and cameras. A late-night news show from a major network was going to feature the Clear Lake College story.

WHEN DO YOU USE ITALICS?

italics   italics

▶ **Function**

Italics, like quotation marks, draw attention to a title, word, or phrase. But they are even more noticeable because italics change the way words look. In a printed text, italics *are slanted letters*. In typed or handwritten papers, italics are signalled by <u>underlining the appropriate words</u>. In either case, italicized words get noticed.

▶ **Principal use**

—To set off a title. Some titles and names are ordinarily italicized; others appear between quotation marks. The table below explains which is which.

Titles *Italicized*

books	*The Big Sleep*
magazines	*Newsweek*
journals	*Written Communication*
newspapers	*The New York Times* or the New York *Times*
films	*Witness*
TV shows	*Moonlighting*
radio shows	*All Things Considered*
plays	*Measure for Measure*
long poems	*Paradise Lost*

long musical pieces	*Concerto in F*
albums	*Nashville Skyline*
paintings	the *Mona Lisa*
sculptures	Michelangelo's *Pietà*
ships	*Titanic*
	U.S.S. *Saratoga*
trains	the *Orient Express*
aircraft	*Air Force One*
spacecraft	*Apollo 11*
software programs	*MacWrite*

Titles "In Quotations"

chapters of books	"Colons and Semicolons"
articles in magazines	"Life After Thirty"
articles in journals	"Vai Script and Literacy"
articles in newspapers	"Inflation Heats Up"
sections in newspapers	"Living in Style"
TV episodes	"Cold Steele"
radio episodes	"McGee Goes Crackers"
short stories	"Araby"
short poems	"The Red Wheelbarrow"
songs	"God Bless America"

18G

Neither italics nor quotation marks are used for the names of *types* of trains, ships, aircraft, and spacecraft.

DC-10	Boeing 727
space shuttle	Atlas Agena
Trident submarine	

Neither italics nor quotation marks are used with titles of major religious texts, books of the Bible, and major legal documents.

the Bible	the Koran
Genesis	Exodus
1 Romans	The Declaration of Independence
The Constitution	the Magna Charta

485

▶ **Other uses**

—To set off foreign words or phrases. Foreign terms that haven't become an accepted item of English vocabulary and scientific names are given special emphasis.

> Bernice nearly fainted when Ike described the students as *les bêtes humaines*.

> Sitting in a yew, Francie was convinced that a *Passarella iliaca* and a *Cyanocitta cristata* had selected her for target practice.

However, the many foreign words absorbed by English over the centuries should not be italicized.

> crèche   gumbo
> gestalt   arroyo
> bayou   gondola

Common abbreviations from Latin also appear without italics or underscoring.

> etc.   et al.
> i.e.   viz.

—To emphasize or clarify a letter, word, or phrase.

> Does that word begin with an *f* or a *ph*?

> The many foreign words absorbed by English over the centuries should *not* be italicized.

> According to Connie, when PR people talk about *environmental concerns*, they really mean *threats to their profits*.

● **Fine Tuning**

1. You can use italics to highlight words you intend to define in a sentence.

> "A *fascist*," Ike explained, "is apparently anyone who doesn't agree with you, Bernice."

18G

2. You can italicize words to indicate where emphasis should be placed in reading.

"That may be how *you* define fascist," she replied.

Indicate whether the following titles or names in boldface should be italicized, in quotation marks, or unmarked. If you don't recognize a name below, check an encyclopedia or other reference work.

1. Launching a **Titan III** at Cape Canaveral
2. **My Fair Lady** playing at the **Paramount theatre**
3. Watching **I Love Lucy**
4. Sunk on the **Andrea Doria**
5. Returning **A Farewell to Arms** to the public library
6. Playing **Casablanca** again on a **Panasonic** video recorder
7. Discussing the colors of Picasso's **The Old Guitarist**
8. Assigning Jackson's **The Lottery** one more time
9. Picking up a copy of **The Los Angeles Times**
10. Whistling **Here Comes the Sun** from the Beatles' **Abbey Road**
11. Reading **On the Town** in **The Washington Post**
12. Riding on **The City of New Orleans**
13. Working with **Wordstar** on an **IBM-PC**
14. Settling in for an evening with Puccini's **Madame Butterfly**
15. Photocopying **Trouble in Silicon Valley** from a recent issue of **Time**
16. Trying to remember Wyatt's sonnet **Farewell, Love**
17. Writing a paper about the **Edsel**
18. Rereading the **The Grand Inquisitor** from Dostoevsky's **The Brothers Karamazov**
19. Quoting a paragraph from **Gulliver's Travels**
20. Spending an afternoon at the **Hirshhorn Museum** in **Gucci** shoes

18G

487

Add or delete italics and quotation marks from the following passage as needed.

1. Appearing on NightGripes, a network news-talk show, was almost as good, Connie thought, as making the cover of *Life Magazine*.
2. It was the show to be on as far as budding journalists were concerned, the ne plus ultra of TV news.
3. Phil Grymm was less eager about representing the views of *Dumble & Tweed*.
4. He was much relieved to learn that Mr. Dumble himself, speaking from an office in *The World Trade Center* in New York, would be the firm's spokesperson.
5. "Let's skip the *mumbo jumbo* and get right to the heart of the matter," began the slick, cordial host Ian Grumbling.
6. "Mr. Dumble, your bulldozers perched to destroy those trees in tiny Ruralia, Illinois, looked like the helicopters in 'Apocalypse, Now' dropping napalm on defenseless villagers."
7. "You must feel like the biggest villain since Satan in 'Paradise Lost.'"
8. "As for you, Ms. Lim," Grumbling continued without a pause, "I think Antony in Shakespeare's 'Julius Caesar' says something like 'ambition should be made of stern stuff.'"
9. "You must be an ambitious cookie to take the credit for all this trouble while the *real* heroes have been perched in those trees for hours in the rain."
10. "Do you regard them as too *naïve* to see how you intend to parlay all this publicity into articles for the Village Voice or The Nation?"
11. "Makes you feel like J.R. from Dallas, doesn't it, kid?"
12. "Ah, sorry, we don't have time to hear your pathetic replies now. We have to break for a commercial. Pardonez moi."

CHAPTER

How Do You Punctuate Sentence Endings?

■ **A** Periods
■ **B** Question Marks
■ **C** Exclamations

19A WHEN DO YOU USE PERIODS?

▶ **Function**

Periods say "that's all there is." They terminate sentences and abbreviations. Think of a period as a strong stop signal or a stern warning not to cross a boundary.

▶ **Principal uses**

—To end a statement.

> Connie Lim and her demonstrators persuaded Dumble & Tweed not to build Sylvan Centre on the original site.

> A national environmental group decided to give her an award for environmental heroism.

► **Other uses**

—To punctuate abbreviations.

abbr.	anon.	Cong.	natl.
rpt.	sing.	pl.	pp.

Not all abbreviations require periods. When in doubt, check a dictionary.

NASA   HEW   GPO   GOP

—To express decimals.

0.01 $189.00   75.4%

● **Fine Tuning**

1. If a statement ends with an abbreviation, the period at the end of the sentence is not doubled.

> Connie invited Kyle, Richard, and Francie to join her in Washington, D.C.

However, the period at the end of the abbreviation is retained if the sentence is a question or exclamation.

> Had any of the four ever been to Washington, D.C.?

> Their flight departs from Chicago at 6 a.m.!

2. If an abbreviation occurs in the middle of a sentence, it retains its period. The period may even be followed by another punctuation mark.

> Though Connie had not yet earned her B.A., her job prospects looked bright.

▶ **Function**

Question marks not only terminate questions, they form them. Question marks are strong enough to turn statements into inquiries.

> It was a rough flight.

> It was a rough flight?

They can also raise doubts.

> Kyle told the stewardess that he was born in 1960 (?) and was older than he looked.

Drop a question mark into a sentence and you get a reaction.

▶ **Principal use**

—To end direct questions.

> Did they arrive at National Airport or at Dulles?

> Did the plane land on time?

> When?

▶ **Other uses**

—To indicate uncertainty about dates, numbers, or statements.

> Francis Marion 1732?–1795

> The steward said it was absolutely probable (?) that their luggage would be located.

> Hector wondered whether Connie had been to Washington before?
>
> He asked her if she would have time to check some books for him at the Library of Congress?

▶ **Diagnosis**

These sentences have been mistakenly punctuated as questions because there are questions within them. But look more closely and you'll discover that what the sentences really state is that questions have been asked: *Hector wondered; he asked.* Such statements are called **indirect questions**. Compare these versions.

{**Indirect question**} Hector wondered whether Connie had been to Washington before.

{**Direct question**} Hector wondered, "Had Connie been to Washington before?"

{**Indirect question**} He asked her if she would have time to check some books for him at the Library of Congress.

{**Direct question**} He asked, "Could you check some books for me at the Library of Congress?"

▶ **Solution**

Punctuate indirect questions as statements.

> Hector wondered whether Connie
> had been to Washington before. He
> asked her if she would have time to
> check some books for him at the
> Library of Congress.

● **Fine Tuning**

1. Occasionally, you may write a sentence that begins with a statement but ends with a question. In such cases the sentence is punctuated as a question.

> The flight to Washington had been smooth, but would the rest of the trip be as uneventful?

Don't confuse this sort of construction, however, with indirect questions discussed in the preceding *Problem* section.

2. Direct questions that appear in the middle of sentences— usually surrounded by parentheses, quotation marks, or dashes—are immediately followed by question marks.

> The ride from Dulles seemed endless (might the taxi driver be taking the students from Ruralia for another kind of ride?), but eventually they arrived in the federal district.

> "Is that the FBI Building?" Connie asked the driver.

3. Remember that question marks are placed outside quotation marks except when they are part of the quoted material itself.

> Which federal building bears the motto "Equal justice under law"?

> The clerk at the Hilton asked, "Do you have reservations?"

For a more detailed explanation, see quotation mark problem 3, pp. 476–77.

▶ **Function**

Exclamation marks attract attention. They are vigorous marks with the subtlety of a yellow Corvette or a red dinner jacket.

▶ **Principal use**

—To indicate strong reactions or commands.

> They don't have our reservations!
>
> Nuts!
>
> Find us some rooms!

Exclamation mark problem: Too many!

> ### Too many exclamations
>
> This hotel cannot hold rooms past 6:00 p.m. without a guaranteed reservation! Reservations can be guaranteed by credit card only! We strongly recommend guaranteed reservations for all guests planning to visit Washington! Thank you!

▶ **Diagnosis**

Too many exclamation points. Used so often, the mark loses its power. Save exclamations for those occasions—rare in school and business writing—when your words really deserve emphasis.

▶ **Solution**

Revise to eliminate the exclamations. Replace some of them with periods.

Some exclamation marks removed

This hotel cannot hold rooms past 6:00 p.m. without a guaranteed reservation. Reservations can be guaranteed by credit card only! We strongly recommend guaranteed reservations for all guests planning to visit Washington. Thank you.

● **Fine Tuning**

1. Don't use a comma or other punctuation mark after an exclamation in the middle of a sentence.

> {**Wrong**} "Please check your records again!," Connie demanded.

> {**Right**} "Please check your records again!" Connie demanded.

2. Don't use more than one exclamation point.

> {**Wrong**} Don't shout!!!

> {**Right**} Don't shout!

EXERCISE 19.1

Edit the following excerpt from Connie's letter, adding, replacing, and deleting periods, question marks, exclamation points, and any other pieces of punctuation.

1. I made a fool of myself!!!
2. There I was in the lobby of the Washington Hilton, practically screaming at this polite young clerk behind the desk while Kyle, Richard, and Francie—can you guess how assertive they were being—rummaged through the luggage looking for the slip confirming our reservations!
3. I asked the clerk would he please call the manager?
4. He said that he was the reservations manager, but would I like him to call the general manager.
5. "Of course, do it immediately!," I said, trying to look like an experienced traveller who doesn't deal with junior-level flunkies!
6. He asked if I would mind stepping aside until the general manager arrived?
7. Just then, what do you think Kyle found.
8. The reservation slip!!!
9. Without looking at it, I hurled it down on the desk and said "What do you think of that"?
10. The clerk smiled politely and said, "Ma'am, you have two guaranteed rooms reserved".
11. "What did I tell you," I interrupted?
12. "At the Carroll Arms on First St.".

EXERCISE 19.2

Write five more sentences completing the dialogue between Connie and the reservations manager. Try to use exclamation points and question marks as well as periods.

CHAPTER

Problems with Capitalization, Apostrophes, Abbreviations, and Numbers?

■ **A** Capitalization
■ **B** Apostrophes
■ **C** Abbreviations
■ **D** Numbers

20A WHAT DO YOU CAPITALIZE?

Term you need to know

> **Proper noun.** A noun that names some particular person, place, or thing: *Bryan Adams, Asia, Ford*. The first letter in proper nouns is capitalized.

Troubleshooting

Capitalization is required for proper names, for the first words in many expressions, and for titles. The following sections will provide you with the guidelines you need to steer you through the conventions of capitalization. When you aren't sure whether an individual word needs to be capitalized, check a dictionary. Don't guess.

▶ **Capitalize proper nouns according to the guidelines offered below for persons, places, and things.**

Persons

Category 1:   Names of people

Guideline: Capitalize names and initials.

Connie Lim	Travis B. Beckwith III
Kelly McKay	Sue Ellen Rizzo

Category 2:   Titles before names

Guideline: Capitalize titles that precede names.

Dean Rack	President Tiffany Shade
Justice Forall	Uncle Sidney
Grandma Sewell	Sister Anne Constance

Category 3:   Titles after names

Guideline: Don't capitalize titles that follow names unless they refer to a person individually. Don't ever capitalize the titles of relatives that follow names.

Wolfgang Rack, a dean at Clear Lake College
Wolfgang Rack, the Dean of Liberal Arts

Anne Constance, a mother superior from Toledo
Anne Constance, the Mother Superior of her order

Sidney Goertz, Cathy's uncle

Exceptions: Capitalize any academic titles that follow a name.

Doris Upton, **Ph.D.**
Hector Stavros, **Master of Arts**

20A

Category 4:   Titles without names attached

Guideline: Don't capitalize minor titles when they stand alone.

> a commissioner in Cuyahoga County
> a lieutenant in the Air Force
> the first president of the club

Exceptions: Powerful or prestigious titles are regularly capitalized even when they stand alone. Lesser titles may be capitalized when they clearly refer to a particular individual or when they describe a position in some formal way.

> President of the United States
> Chief Justice of the Supreme Court
> the Pope
> the King of Spain
> Secretary of State
>
> the Chair of the Classics Department argued . . .
> the Director of Public Relations at Dumble & Tweed was fired . . .

20A

Category 5:   National, political, or ethnic groups

Guideline: Capitalize them.

Kenyans	Yugoslavs	Chinese
Afro-American	Chicano	Caucasian
Republicans	Democrats	Marxists
Communists	Socialists	

Exceptions: Titles of economic groups or social classes are usually not capitalized.

> the proletariat
> the middle class
> the bourgeoisie

Category 6: Businesses, unions, organizations, and clubs
Guideline: Capitalize them.

Daimler-Benz
Delta Airlines
National Rifle Association
Apple Computer
Amnesty International
American Medical Association

Category 7: Religious figures, religious groups, and sacred books
Guideline: Capitalize them.

God	the Savior	Buddha
Buddhism	Catholics	Judaism
the Bible	the Koran	Talmudic tradition

Exceptions: The terms god and goddess are not capitalized when used generally. Pronouns referring to God are usually capitalized.

The Greeks had a pantheon of gods and goddesses.

The Goddess of Liberty appears on our currency.

The priest praised God and all His works.

Category 8: Academic ranks (freshman, sophomore, junior, senior, graduate, post-grad)
Guideline: Not capitalized in most situations.

The college had many fifth-year seniors.
The freshman dormitory was a dump.
"Hey, frosh, you live in a dump."
The teacher was a graduate student.

Exceptions: Capitalize them when these groups are referred to as organized bodies or institutions.

A representative of the Senior Class
The Freshman Cotillion

Category 9:   Names of places or words based on place names. Names of specific geographic features, lakes, rivers, oceans, and so on.

Guideline: Capitalize them.

Asia	Old Faithful
Asian	the Amazon
the Bronx	the Gulf of Mexico
Lake Erie	Deaf Smith County
Washington	the Atlantic Ocean

Exceptions: Don't capitalize compass directions unless they name a specific place or are part of a place name.

north	North America
south	the South
eastern Ohio	the Middle East
western dress	West Virginia

20A

Category 10:   Names of buildings, structures, or monuments

Guideline: Capitalize them.

Yankee Stadium	Hoover Dam
the Alamo	the Golden Gate
the Sears Tower	Indianapolis Speedway

Category 11:   Abstractions

Guideline: You may capitalize abstractions (love, truth, patriotism, etc.) when you discuss them as concepts or give them special emphasis, perhaps as the subject of a paper.

What is this thing called Love?

The conflict was between Truth and Falsehood.

Several magazines decided to explore the New Patriotism.

Exceptions: No need to capitalize abstractions used without special emphasis.

Travis had fallen in love again.

Act like a man.

Either tell the truth or abandon hope of rescue.

Rita showed her patriotism by buying a flag.

Category 12: Names of particular objects—including ships, planes, automobiles, brand-name products, events, documents, and musical groups

Guideline: Capitalize them.

S.S. *Titanic*	Rolling Stones
Eskimo Pie	Ford Tempo
the Constitution	Super Bowl XX
Boeing 747	Cleveland Symphony
Panasonic	

Caution: In public and business writing, it is important not to violate the right companies have to brand names or trademarks, even familiar ones. Words such as Kleenex, Frigidaire, and Xerox should be capitalized because they refer to specific, trademark-protected products.

Category 13: Periods of time: days, months, holidays; historical epochs and historical events

Guideline: Capitalize them.

Monday	the Reformation
May	World War II
Victorian Age	January
Bastille Day	Fourth of July
Tuesday	the Russian Revolution
Christmas	Pax Romana

Exceptions: Seasons are usually not capitalized.

autumn   winter   spring

Category 14: —Isms

Guideline: Usually not capitalized unless they name specific literary, artistic, religious, or cultural movements.

socialism	Catholicism
Impressionism	classicism
Judaism	Romanticism
capitalism	Buddhism
Vorticism	

Category 15: School subjects and classes

Guideline: Subject areas are not capitalized unless the subject itself is a proper noun.

biology	chemistry	physics
English	Russian history	French

Exceptions: Specific course titles are capitalized.

Biology 101
Chemistry lab
English 346K

Category 16: Acronyms and initialisms (See 20C, p. 513)

Guideline: Capitalize all the letters in acronyms and initialisms.

NATO	OPEC	SALT Treaty
DNA	GM	SAT tests

Exceptions: Don't capitalize the few acronyms that have become so familiar that they seem like ordinary words. (When in doubt, check a dictionary.)

radar	sonar	laser

> **Tip:** Many writers fail to capitalize words that name nationalities or countries—words such as *English*, *French*, or *American*.
>
> > {**Wrong**} Kyle has three english courses.
> > {**Right**} Kyle has three English courses.
> >
> > {**Wrong**} Brian drives only american cars.
> > {**Right**} Brian drives only American cars.
>
> When proofreading, be sure that you capitalize any words derived from the names of countries.

▶ **Capitalize the first word in a sentence.**

Naomi picked up the tourists at their hotel.

Ready? Let's go.

What a great city Washington is!

▶ **Capitalize the first word in a direct quotation that is a full sentence.**

Richard asked, "Where's the Air and Space Museum?"

"Good idea!" Connie agreed. "Let's go there."

Don't use a capital when a quotation merely continues after an interruption.

"It's on the Mall," Naomi explained, "not far from the Hirschhorn Gallery."

 ▶ **Capitalize titles.**   Here are the rules.

The Treasure of Sierra Madre
In Search of Excellence
The Hunt for Red October
"How Cruel Is the Story of Eve"

Articles and prepositions are capitalized when they immediately follow a colon, usually as part of a subtitle.

King Lear: *An Annotated Bibliography*

▶ **Capitalize the first word in a line of quoted poetry.**

Sumer is ycomen in,
Loude sing cuckou!
Groweth seed and bloweth meed,
And springth the wode now.
Sing cuckou!

Don't capitalize the line, however, if the poet has used a lower case letter to open the line.

Ida
ho and, Oh!
io,
places
with spaces
be
tween 'em.
—Travis Beckwith III, "Travels"

1. Always capitalize the pronoun *I* and the exclamation *O*. Don't capitalize *oh* unless it begins a sentence.

2. Don't capitalize a phrase that follows a colon unless it is part of a title:

> They ignored one item while parking the car: **a** no-parking sign.

> *Marilyn: The Untold Story*

Don't capitalize a sentence that follows a colon unless you want to give it unusual emphasis:

> The phrase haunted her: Your car has been towed!

3. Don't capitalize a phrase in parentheses, but do capitalize a full sentence in parentheses when it stands alone. See 18C, p. 468.

20A

> They gazed at the spot (**on** 7th St.) where their car had been parked.

> "We were in the museum only a few minutes," said Kyle. (**They** had actually toured the exhibits for several hours.)

4. Don't capitalize a phrase or sentence enclosed by dashes.

> Naomi's car—**a** brand new Accord—had been parked next to a "no parking" sign.

> Her Accord—she couldn't believe it—was now in the hands of the police.

5. Check out the conventions of letter writing. Salutations and closings need to be capitalized correctly. See Special Assignments, pp. 780–81.

Review the following sentences, capitalizing as necessary.

1. Four students—two of them seniors, two juniors, all pursuing b.a.'s or b.s.'s—and not one had read the stern warning printed on the sign by district of columbia police: cars parked illegally will be towed.
2. Even washington-native Naomi, their ph.d. tour guide, had not seen the sign when they pulled up to the empty space suspiciously near the national air and space museum.
3. "I intend to write the president about this," Kyle muttered. "after all, i voted for the man." (he hadn't.) "or maybe I'll write senator Smith, or my uncle Robert, an under-secretary of something or other."
4. "Please, o please, why not write queen Elizabeth and boy George and be done with it?" Francie snorted.
5. Richard declared, "if you ask me, towing someone's car smacks of marxism. You expect this sort of thing in leningrad or peking, not in the shadow of the Washington monument in the bastion of democracy and free enterprise."
6. While her friends jabbered, Naomi dug through her purse, finding her visa card, her nra membership certificate, and her amnesty international pledge, but no driver's license.
7. "They'll probably throw me in the bastille and I won't be out until thanksgiving," she thought.
8. She sighed, "I've learned my lesson: read signs carefully."
9. "Perhaps we should just follow the instructions—If towed, call 471-2255—printed on the bottom of the sign," Connie suggested, gazing placidly down the mall toward the capitol building.
10. "According to my *Guide to sights and services in Washington*, the nasa building is just down the street. We can find a phone there."

20A

507

Capitalize the following titles.

1. *The history of freedom and other essays*
2. "Thoughts on the present state of american affairs"
3. *Decline and fall of the roman empire*
4. *The spring of civilization: periclean athens*
5. *The theory of the leisure class*
6. *Walden, or life in the woods*
7. "Whoever you are holding me now in hand"
8. *Resistance, rebellion, and death*
9. "Beat! beat! drums!"
10. *The myth of the ruling class*

20B

20B WHEN DO YOU USE APOSTROPHES?

'

Troubleshooting

Apostrophes are troublesome marks because we often forget to put them where they belong. Ironically, one function of apostrophes is to indicate that letters have been left out of a word or phrase. In forming contractions, the letters left out are usually obvious:

can't—can **not**   it's—it **is**   you'll—you **will**

Apostrophes are also used to form possessives. Forgetting to insert an apostrophe where it belongs in a contraction or possessive causes problems. In fact, leaving the apostrophe out of the contraction *it's* turns the word into a possessive form, *its*.

Apostrophes are sometimes used to form the plurals of numbers, symbols, some abbreviations, and individual letters or to signal the omission of the century marker in dates: *1's, 2's, M's, n's,* "Summer of '69."

Finally, apostrophes are also occasionally used by writers who want to write dialogue that mimics speech. The apostrophes again indicate words or syllables typically left out in some dialects.

To use apostrophes correctly . . .

▶ **Place them in contractions where letters have been omitted.**

should not—shouldn't	had not—hadn't
will not—won't	she will—she'll
cannot—can't	have not—haven't

Contractions are employed not because they have fewer letters, but because they are spoken more quickly and sound less formal. They change the tone of what you are writing from black tie to jeans:

Cannot you join us?
Can't you join us?
You **will** enjoy the movie.
You'll enjoy the movie.

You should be aware that many readers object to contractions in academic and professional writing. For this reason, consider your audience carefully before using contractions freely in academic writing.

The apostrophe is not optional in a contraction. Leaving it out can change the meaning of a word or create a misspelling.

it's—its   won't—wont   you're—youre

The *it's—its* problem is a tricky one. See 15N Special Problem for a full discussion of *it's—its.*

▶ **Place apostrophes as needed to form the possessives of nouns and some pronouns.**

Kyle's report	everyone's opinion
Ruralia's mayor	the Rhodes' daughters
Travis' poems	anybody's guess

Personal pronouns do not require an apostrophe to show ownership.

mine	yours	hers
his	ours	theirs

For a thorough explanation of how to form the possessive of nouns and pronouns, see Section 14B Problems with Possessives, and Section 15M Possessive Pronouns.

20B ▶ **Place apostrophes as needed to indicate the plurals of numbers, symbols, individual letters, abbreviations, words used as *words*, and dates.**

2's and 3's	three $5's
five A's	two B.A.'s
two .45's and a .22	two &'s
three *the*'s and four *an*'s	1960's

Quite often the apostrophe is omitted, especially when the *'s* might be mistaken as a possessive.

3600 rpms.

42 lbs.

the ACTs

the CEOs

In many cases, either form of the plural is acceptable.

the 1980s/the 1980's

10s/10's

Try to be consistent in your usage. For more details and an exercise, see Section 14A.

● Fine Tuning

1. Apostrophes are sometimes used to replace the first two numbers in a date:

"Summer of '69"   Spirit of '76   '64 Mustang

However, in most academic and professional writing, you should write out the complete date unless the contraction is part of a familiar expression, such as "Spirit of '76."

2. You may occasionally write or read passages of dialogue in which apostrophes indicate letters characteristically dropped by speakers.

> . . . airline passengers all over America began to hear that awshuckin' driftin' gone-fishin' Mud River voice coming from the cockpit. . . . "Now, folks, uh . . . this is the captain . . . ummmm . . . We've got a little ol' red light up here on the control panel that's tryin' to tell us that the *land*in' gears're not . . . uh . . . *lock*in' into position. . . ."
>
> —Tom Wolfe, *The Right Stuff*

20B

EXERCISE 20.3

Add or delete apostrophes and revise spelling as necessary from the following sentences.

1. The five stranded tourists searched in vain for a Federal Office open after five oclock where they might use a phone.
2. "Its you're fault, Kyle," said Francie, realizing she hadnt yet lay'd blame on anyone for the fiasco.
3. "The fault isnt Kyles or anybody elses," said Naomi.
4. "Lets just find a shop that has a public phone."
5. Wandering a block or so off the Mall, they found a drugstore that looked like a relic from the 50s.
6. As she dropped dime's into the public phone, Naomi asked if anyone recalled the number she was supposed to dial.

7. "All I remember," said Connie, "is that its got two 2s and two 5s."
8. "Thats a big help," groaned Naomi.
9. Richard smiled. "The first three numbers were 471, so lets give 471-2255 a try."
10. To everyones surprise, they reached a pleasant clerk with a southern drawl: "If yalls cars bin towd, youd best git down to the traffic office roght now."

20C   HOW DO YOU HANDLE ABBREVIATIONS?

Terms you need to know

Abbreviation. A shortened version of a word or phrase, usually consisting of part of the original word or phrase and usually punctuated with a period: *Rev.*—Reverend; *Mr.*—Mister.

Acronym. A single word created by joining the first letters in each word used in a full name or description. Acronyms are pronounced as single words: *NATO*—*N*orth *A*tlantic *T*reaty *O*rganization; *NASA*—*N*ational *A*eronautics and *S*pace *A*dministration.

Initialism. A single word created by joining the first letters in each word used in a full name or description. Unlike acronyms, however, initialisms are pronounced letter by letter: *IRS*—*I*nternal *R*evenue *S*ervice; *CIA*—*C*entral *I*ntelligence *A*gency.

Troubleshooting

Abbreviations, acronyms, and initialisms make writing a bit easier and quicker. In themselves, they don't cause many problems. Writers do have to be careful about when they use abbreviations and their kin. Many conventional abbreviations (A.M.; P.M.; Mrs.; Mr.; Dr.; BC; AD) are suited to every occasion. In fact, it would be odd in most cases to write out *anno Domini* or *post meridiem*. Other abbreviations, acronyms, and initialisms are appropriate on forms, recipes, and statistics sheets, but not in more formal writing: *Jan.*—January; *tsps.*—teaspoons; *no.*—number. Some of these issues are discussed below and in the Fine Tuning section.

Deciding when abbreviations need to be punctuated and capitalized can also be difficult, particularly since there is substantial variation in this area. Is it *Tsps.* or *tsps.*; *N.A.S.A.* or *NASA*? The material below offers some guidelines you may find helpful in handling such items.

▶ **Punctuating abbreviations, acronyms, and initialisms**

1. Abbreviations of single words usually take periods: abbrev.; vols.; Jan.; Mr.

2. Initialisms are now commonly written without periods: HBO; AFL-CIO; IRS. You may still use periods with these terms, but be consistent with your usage.

3. Acronyms ordinarily do not require periods: CARE; NATO; MIRV. Acronyms that have become "regular" words never need periods: radar; sonar; laser; scuba.

4. Periods are usually omitted after abbreviations in technical writing unless a measurement or other item might be misread as a word without the period: in.

5. Use three periods consistently or none at all in terms such as the following.

m.p.g.	*or*	mpg
r.p.m.	*or*	rpm
m.p.h.	*or*	mph

▶ Capitalizing abbreviations, acronyms, and initialisms

1. Capitalize abbreviations of words that would themselves be capitalized if written out in full:

   Saint Joan—St. Joan

   Mister Roberts—Mr. Roberts

   98° Fahrenheit—98° F.

   General Motors—GM

   U.S. Navy—USN

   University of Toledo—UT

2. Don't capitalize abbreviations of words not capitalized on their own:

   pound—lb.   minutes—mins.
   miles per hour—mph

20C

3. Capitalize most initialisms: IRS; CRT; UCLA; NBC; EPA.

4. Always capitalize B.C. and A.D.

5. You may capitalize A.M. and P.M. but they now ordinarily appear in small letters: a.m.; p.m. Printers ordinarily set them as small caps: A.M.; P.M.

6. Don't capitalize acronyms that have become ordinary words: sonar; radar; modem.

Use abbreviations, acronyms, or initialisms . . .

▶ **For titles, degrees, and names.** The following titles and degrees are ordinarily abbreviated.

Mr.	Mrs.
Jr. [Junior]	Esq. [Esquire]
Ms.	Ph.D.
St./SS. [Saint(s)]	M.A.
Dr.	M.D.
LL.D.	M.S.
D.D.S.	M.A.

Give credit for degrees either before or after a name—not in both places. Don't, for example, use both Dr. and Ph.D. in the same name.

> {**Wrong**} Dr. Katherine Martinich, Ph.D.

> {**Right**} Dr. Katherine Martinich
> Katherine Martinich, Ph.D.

Abbreviations for academic titles often stand by themselves, without names attached.

> Professor Upton received her **Ph.D.** from Illinois, her **M.S.** from UCLA, and her **B.S.** from Harvard.

Other titles are normally written out in full; they may be abbreviated only when they precede a first name or initial—and then chiefly in informal writing. In most cases, use the full, unabbreviated title.

Reverend	Reverend Falwell	Rev. J. Falwell
General	General Lee	Gen. Robert E. Lee
President	President Reagan	Pres. Ronald Reagan
Governor	Governor Cuomo	Gov. Mario Cuomo
Senator	Senator Gramm	Sen. Phil Gramm
Professor	Professor Upton	Prof. Doris Upton

Never let abbreviated titles of this kind stand alone in a sentence.

> {**Wrong**} The **rev.** agreed to debate the **gov.** at the invitation of the **prof.**

> {**Right**} **Reverend Falwell** agreed to debate **Governor Cuomo** at the invitation of **Professor Doris Upton**.

> [Notice that titles attached to proper names are ordinarily capitalized.]

Initials are suitable abbreviations for given names; don't abbreviate names in other ways unless such abbreviations are nicknames. Periods do not follow nicknames.

Dean Wolfgang Rack   {**Wrong**} Dean Wolf. Rack
                                  {**OK**} W. Rack

George Ericson   {**Wrong**} Geo. Ericson
                                  {**OK**} G. Ericson

▶ **For technical terms.** Abbreviations are often used in professional, governmental, scientific, military, and technical writing. When you are writing to a nontechnical readership, write out in full any unfamiliar term the first time you use it. Then provide the abbreviation you will use in the rest of the paper.

DNA	UHF	EKG	START
SALT	GNP	LEM	kW
P.M.G.	SOP	SDI	SAT

Governor Cuomo and Reverend Falwell debated the effects **SDI** would have on **START**.

{**Version #1**} Governor Cuomo and Reverend Falwell debated the effects **the Strategic Defense Initiative (SDI)** would have on the **Strategic Arms Reduction Talks (START)**.

{**Version #2**} Governor Cuomo and Reverend Falwell debated the effect **the Strategic Defense Initiative, popularly known as SDI or Star Wars**, would have on the **Strategic Arms Reduction Talks (START)**.

▶ **For agencies and organizations.** In some cases, the abbreviation or acronym regularly substitutes for the full name of a company, agency, or organization.

FBI	IBM	MCI	AT&T
CIA	NASA	GPO	GM
AFL-CIO	GOP	PPG	MGM
A&P	BBC	NCAA	MTV

516

▶ **For dates.** Dates are not abbreviated in most writing. Write out in full the days of the week and months of the year.

> {**Not**} They arrived in Washington on a **Wed.** in **Apr.**

> {**But**} They arrived in Washington on a **Wednesday** in **April.**

Abbreviations of months and days are common in notes, lists, forms, and reference works.

▶ **For time and temperatures.** Abbreviations that accompany time and temperatures are acceptable in all kinds of writing:

> 43 B.C.   A.D. 144   1:00 a.m.   4:36 p.m.
>
> 13° C.   98° F.   143 B.C.E.

Notice that the abbreviation *B.C.* appears after a date, but *A.D.* usually before one. Both expressions are always capitalized. Sometimes *C.E.* (Common Era) is substituted for *A.D.* (*anno Domini*), *B.C.E.* (Before Common Era) for *B.C.* (Before Christ).

▶ **For weights, measures, and times.** Technical terms or measurements are commonly abbreviated when used with numbers, but written out in full when they stand alone in sentences. Even when accompanied by numbers, the terms usually look better in sentences when spelled out completely.

> 28 mpg   3 tsps.   40 km.   450 lbs.
>
> 50 min.   30 lbs.   2 hrs.

> Naomi didn't care how many **miles per gallon** her Accord got. She just wished it hadn't been towed so many **kilometers** from where she stood. They had already lost **fifty minutes** locating a phone.

The abbreviation for number—*No.* or *no.*—is appropriate in technical writing, but only when immediately followed by a number:

> {**Not**} The **no.** on the contaminated dish was **073.**

> {**But**} The contaminated dish was **no. 073.**

No. also appears in footnotes, endnotes, and citations.

517

▶ **For places.** In most writing, place names are not abbreviated except in addresses and in reference tools and lists. However, certain abbreviations are accepted in academic and business writing.

USA   USSR

DDR (for East Germany)   Washington, D.C.

All the various terms for *street* are written out in full, except in addresses:

boulevard   road   avenue   parkway

highway   alley   place   circle

But *Mt.* (for *mountain*) and *St.* (for *saint*) are acceptable abbreviations in place names when they precede a proper name.

Mt. Vesuvius   **St**. Charles Street

(but not Rocky Mts.)

In addresses, use the standard postal abbreviations without periods for the states:

Alaska	AK	Illinois	IL
Alabama	AB	Indiana	IN
Arkansas	AR	Kansas	KS
Arizona	AZ	Kentucky	KY
California	CA	Louisiana	LA
Colorado	CO	Massachusetts	MA
Connecticut	CT	Maryland	MD
Delaware	DE	Maine	ME
Florida	FL	Michigan	MI
Georgia	GA	Minnesota	MN
Hawaii	HI	Missouri	MO
Iowa	IA	Mississippi	MS
Idaho	ID	Montana	MT

20C

North Carolina	NC	Rhode Island	RI
North Dakota	ND	South Carolina	SC
Nebraska	NE	South Dakota	SD
New Hampshire	NH	Tennessee	TN
New Jersey	NJ	Texas	TX
New Mexico	NM	Utah	UT
Nevada	NV	Virginia	VA
New York	NY	Vermont	VT
Ohio	OH	Washington	WA
Oklahoma	OK	Wisconsin	WI
Oregon	OR	West Virginia	WV
Pennsylvania	PA	Wyoming	WY

20C

▶ **For certain expressions preserved from Latin.**

i.e. [*id est*—that is]

cf. [*confer*—compare]

e.g. [*exempli gratia*—for example]

etc. [*et cetera*—and so on]

fl. [*floruit*—flourished, did major work during this time]

In most writing, it is better to use the English versions of these and other Latin abbreviations. Avoid using the abbreviation *etc.* in formal or academic writing.

▶ **For divisions of books.** The many abbreviations for books and manuscripts (*p.*, *pp.*, *vols.*, *ch.*, *chpts.*, *bk.*, *sect.*) are fine in footnotes or parenthetical citations, but don't use them alone in sentences.

{**Wrong**} Richard stuck the **bk.** in his pocket after reading **ch.** five.

{**Right**} Richard stuck the **book** in his pocket after reading **chapter** five.

● Fine Tuning

1. The *ampersand* (&) is an abbreviation for *and*. However you should not use it in formal writing except when it appears in a title or name: *Road & Track*.

2. You may use symbols in technical and scientific writing—%
+ = ≠ < >—but in other academic papers, spell out such terms. The only symbol likely to cause a problem is %—*percent*.

> {**Acceptable**} Connie was shocked to learn that **80%** of the cars towed belong to tourists.

> {**Preferred**} Connie was shocked to learn that **80 percent** of the cars towed belong to tourists.

3. You can use a dollar sign—$—in any writing as long as it is followed by an amount. Don't use both the dollar sign and the word *dollar*.

> {**Wrong**} "Just how many **$s** is this fine going to set us back?" Naomi wondered.

> {**Right**} "Just how many **dollars** is this fine going to set us back?" Naomi wondered.

> {**Wrong**} "The fine for parking in a towing zone is **$125 dollars**."

> {**Right**} "The fine for parking in a towing zone is **$125**."

> {**Right**} "The fine for parking in a towing zone is **125 dollars**."

4. The abbreviations *Co.*, *Corp.*, *Bros.*, *LTD*, and *Inc.* in corporate names appear only when the companies themselves use them in their official correspondence, advertising, or other public materials.

> Sony Corporation of America
>
> Kimberly-Clark Corporation
>
> Philip Morris Inc.
>
> BF Goodrich

20C

520

CBS/Fox Company

Lennox Industries, Inc.

U.S. Postal Service

Even then, you can often drop the *Inc.*, *LTD*, *Co.*, and *Corp.*:

> Stephanie got a summer job with **Nautilus**; Kyle expects to work for **Ford**; Abel has applied for an apprenticeship at **Dumble & Tweed**.

EXERCISE 20.4

20C

Read the passage below, abbreviating where appropriate or expanding abbreviations that would be incorrect in academic or professional writing. Check the punctuation for accuracy and consistency. If you insist on periods with acronyms and initialisms, use them throughout the passage.

1. Leaving the Peoples Drugstore, Naomi, Kyle, Connie, Francie, & Rich. hailed a D.C. Cab, no. 108, cruising slowly down the ave.
2. "It's nearly 6:00 Pm," Connie sighed as the five piled into the bl.-green four dr. sedan.
3. "If we don't recover Naomi's car soon, I'll be late for my award banquet at the Vfw Hall in Alexandria, VA."
4. "That's no problem. There's a > 99% chance I'll get you there on time," said Ransom E. Bullet, P.H.D. of College Pk, Maryld., a cabbie who clearly liked to talk.
5. "You see, we just take Constitution Ave. down past the F.b.i. Building, ease onto the 12th Street Expressway, cruise by the Dept. of Agri., and follow I-395 till we get to the Geo. Washington Mem. Pky, which will take us right into Alexandria."
6. While he spoke, Kyle noted a well-worn paperback copy of *The Treasures of Tutankhamen* on the dashboard of the Chevy, open to ch. seven.

7. "You interested in this stuff?" Kyle asked, but Naomi, irritated by the delay and chatter, interrupted. "To hell with King Tut. Take us to this address."

8. The cabbie, a bit miffed, glanced at the address Naomi had thrust at him (i.e., for the traffic office) and paused.

9. "You sure this is where you want to go—ma'am?" "What's the matter, doesn't the good dr. know where it is?" Naomi asked, more sarcastic than Liz Taylor in *Who's Afraid of Vir. Woolf?*

10. "Yes, ma'am, I do," he replied, putting the cab in gear.

11. The six of them in the Chevy made a slow U-turn in the street and stopped at the curb just a few ft from the drugstore, a ride of no more than ten secs.

12. "That'll be $2 dollars," said Ransom Bullet.

13. Richard looked at the address on the building next to the Peoples Drugstore, Inc., then glanced at the st. sign.

14. "We've just hired a cab to take us to the bldg next to the one we were in!" he groaned.

15. Naomi pulled out three $ bills—including one for a tip—stepped out of the cab, and said "I'm volunteering to be a target for S.d.i. research. Anyone care to join me?"

20D HOW DO YOU HANDLE NUMBERS?

Terms you need to know

> **Cardinal numbers**. Numbers that express an amount: *one*, *two*, *three*.

> **Ordinal numbers**. Numbers that express a sequence: *first*, *second*, *third*.

Troubleshooting

Numbers can be expressed either through numerals or through words.

1	one	
100	one hundred	
1/4	one fourth	
.05%	five hundredths of a percent	

Deciding which to use depends on the kind of writing you are doing. Technical, scientific, and business writing tends to employ numerals. Other kinds of writing rely more on words. The guidelines and charts below attempt to help you figure out which form to use.

To be sure your numbers are right . . .

Basic Guideline: Write out numbers you can express in one or two words. Use numerals for more complicated numbers.

20D

one	fifteen	twenty
twenty-one	fifty-nine	one hundred
one thousand	ten million	fifty billion
101	115	220
1021	59,000	101,000
1001	10,000,101	50,306,673,432

This guideline has variations and exceptions discussed below.

▶ **Don't begin a sentence with a numeral.** Either spell out the number or rephrase the sentence so that the numeral is not the first word.

> {**Wrong**} **32** people were standing in line at the parking violation center.

> {**Right**} **Thirty-two** people were standing in line at the parking violation center.

Sentences may, however, begin with dates.

> **1986** was the year Naomi's driver's license expired.

▶ **Combine words and figures when you need to express large round numbers:**

> 100 billion   432 million   103 trillion

20D But avoid shifting between numbers and figures within a sequence of numbers. If you need numerals to express one of several numbers in a sequence, express all the other numbers in numerals as well—even if they might ordinarily be set down in words.

> Kyle considered that there must be **800,000** people in Washington, **50,000** parking spaces, and only **150** tow-away zones.

> [You might ordinarily write *50,000* as *fifty thousand*.]

▶ **Use numerals when comparing numbers or suggesting a range.**

> A blackboard at the traffic office listed a **$50** fine for jaywalking, **$100** for speeding, and **$125** for parking in a towing zone.

> The students' in-pocket cash reserves ranged from a high of **$76** to a low of **$1.43** and some bubblegum.

▶ **Use numerals for dates, street numbers, page numbers, sums of money, and various ID and call numbers.**

July 4, 1776	1860–1864
p. 352	pp. 23–24
Channel 8	103.5 FM
7404 Cannon Mt. Pl.	1900 East Blvd.
$2749.00	43¢
PR 105.5 R8	SS# 111-00-1111

Don't use an ordinal form in dates:

{**Wrong**} May 2**nd**, 1987

{**Right**} May 2, 1987 *or* 2 May 1987

▶ **Use numerals for time with A.M. and P.M.; use words with o'clock.**

2:15 p.m.   6:00 a.m.   six o'clock

▶ **Use numerals for measurements, percentages, statistics, and scores.**

35 mph	13°C.	5' 10"
75 percent	4.2 liters	5.5 pupils per teacher
Browns 42	15%	2 1/2 miles
Bears 0		

● **Fine Tuning**

1. In large figures, commas separate thousands, millions, billions, and so on. Commas are, however, omitted in dates, street numbers, and sometimes in four-digit numbers.

$1,700,000	45673 Sophia Gate
1988	4,453,500,000 protons
4,342 parking spaces	7865 Hershey's Kisses

2. You form the plural of numbers by adding -s or -'s.

> five 6s in a row   five 98's

See Section 14A for more on plurals.

3. In most cases, *ordinal numbers* are spelled out: *first, second, third, fourth*, and so on.

4. Just in case you need one, here's a table of Roman numerals.

Roman Numerals

1	i	29	xxix
2	ii	30	xxx
3	iii	40	xl
4	iv	49	xlix
5	v	50	l
6	vi	60	lx
7	vii	70	lxx
8	viii	80	lxxx
9	ix	90	xc
10	x	99	xcix
11	xi	100	c
12	xii	200	cc
13	xiii	300	ccc
14	xiv	400	cd
15	xv	500	d
20	xx	1000	m
25	xxv		

Decide whether numbers used in the following selection are handled appropriately. Where necessary, change numerals to words, words to numerals. Some expressions may not need revision. Be prepared to explain your choices.

1. 9:00 p.m. had come and gone before Connie crept into the VFW Hall where more than 500 elegantly attired members of the Spirit of Seventeen Seventy Six Society had gathered to honor her and 6 other recipients of its Environmental Heroism award for Nineteen Eighty-Eight.

2. Exhausted, Connie crept to a seat reserved for her at the main table and listened as the President of the three hundred thousand member society proclaimed the virtues of the 1st, 4th, and tenth amendments to the Constitution.

3. All Connie could think of were the fines levied upon her and her friends, including $125 dollars for illegal parking, seventy-five dollars for towing, and another 35 dollars for Naomi's failure to present a valid driver's license

4. Then the 5 of them had been driven in a two-ton government van crowded with fourteen other angry citizens 3/4 of a mile to Georgetown to a depot for towed cars, only to discover that Naomi's Accord was 5 miles away at a 2nd city depot near RFK stadium.

5. Still, she was proud to be at the head table, even though she looked like she hadn't washed in three days and the camera from Channel six was pointing right at her.

6. "1 day we'll laugh about this," Kyle had kept saying as the crowded van bumped noisily toward RFK stadium and it became more obvious that Connie would be late for her 8 o'clock banquet.

7. While Kyle was wrong about things 1/2 the time, on this occasion Connie was sure he was ninety-nine percent right.

8. Connie *was* amused that she and her companions had been able to persuade a $6,000,000,000 investment company not to build a seven hundred and forty thousand square foot

20D

shopping center in their tiny town, but had been helpless in the face of a 2-bit traffic law in the nation's capital.

9. "And that, my friends, is America," the rather long-winded speaker concluded after nearly seventy minutes, pounding a 5-pound gavel to signal the start of the awards presentations.

10. 500 people awoke with a start and Connie Lim soon found herself accepting a fourteen carat gold medal and waving from the podium to 4 weary, penniless, but cheering friends at the back of the hall.

20D

CHAPTER

Spelling, the Dictionary, and the Computer

■ **A** Improving your spelling
■ **B** Choosing a dictionary
■ **C** Using a dictionary
■ **D** A writer's bookshelf
■ **E** Word processing

21

Terms you need to know

Antonyms. Words with directly opposite meanings: *wrong / right; apogee / perigee; clean / dirty.*

Homonyms. Words of different meanings pronounced alike: *altar / alter; to / too / two; hear / here.*

Synonyms. Words of approximately the same meaning: *street / road; angry / mad; home / domicile.*

Connotation and denotation. Connotation is what a word suggests or implies beyond its basic dictionary meaning, or **denotation**. While any number of terms may, for example, describe a *street* and so share the same denotation, such words may differ significantly in what they imply—in their connotations: *avenue, alley, boulevard, lane, court,* and *highway.*

Troubleshooting

The first problem with spelling English right is that English is hard to spell. The second is that misspelled English upsets people far more than you might expect. You'll pay a penalty for every word you misspell. Readers will take you, your facts, and your ideas—whatever their merit—less seriously if your spelling is just slightly askew. If your spelling is atrocious, you may be in serious trouble.

But be clear on this point: good writing and accurate spelling are not the same thing. Too many writers believe incorrectly that accurate spelling automatically translates into good writing. In fact, spelling is only a small, comparatively manageable part of composing. All things considered, spelling should be a minor problem. Words are either spelled right or spelled wrong (most of the time). With the help of a dictionary or spelling checker, you should be able to attack spelling errors with a greater likelihood of success than troubles with organization, development, sentence structure, or style.

Still, spelling poses real problems for many writers because English spelling is highly irregular. As a result, its spelling rules are often too complicated to be useful—and even then they are riddled with exceptions. Hardly anyone gets out of a spelling dilemma by recalling a rule, except perhaps the time-honored "*i* before *e* except after *c*."

To manage a "spelling problem" requires first that you know a word is misspelled and then that you correct it. Classifying spelling problems in order to solve them isn't easy, since potential errors seem as numerous as words in the dictionary. But chances are good that your most persistent misspellings fall into the following categories.

> *Known errors*—You omit, add, or transpose letters in writing or typing, or habitually botch a word you really do know how to spell, or leave out an apostrophe you know belongs in a word, or forget the *s* in a possessive

form. In all these cases, if you looked carefully at the misspelled word, you'd know it was wrong without having to check a dictionary. This category includes all typos and slips of the pen.

Errors due to mispronunciation or mishearing—Because you don't hear the *d* in *supposed to* or *prejudiced* you spell them *suppose to* and *prejudice*. You don't realize there is an *n* in *government* until you find *goverment* circled in a paper you wrote. You add a letter to *athletics* because you pronounce it *atheletics*. *A lot* sounds like one word, so you spell it that way.

Errors due to words sounding or looking alike—Words that sound exactly alike (homonyms) lead to all sorts of errors in English. *Their* appears where you clearly intend *there* or *they're*; a *too* is written as *to*; *principal* is confused with *principle*; *stationary* with *stationery*; *a while* with *awhile*. Even some words that aren't pronounced exactly alike resemble each other enough to tempt writers to choose a wrong version: *access / excess*; *eminent / imminent*; *advice / advise* ; *personal / personnel*. The possibilities for error in this category seem almost endless.

Errors due to faulty judgment—English is full of silent letters, doubled consonants, inconsistent vowel sounds, and words borrowed from foreign languages. Even when you are being relatively careful, you may be unable to decide whether a word takes an *ee* or an *ea*, doubles its consonant or leaves it single, ends with *-ible* or *-able*. When you must rely on your memory or judgment to construct an English spelling, you'll be wrong more times than you'll care to count. Just try some of these demons: *villainy*, *grammar*, *jeopardy*, *irresistible*, *miscellaneous*, *parallel*, *license*, *separate*, *veterinary*—and on and on.

Errors due to sheer hopelessness—English is filled with words that simply evoke despair. Such items may not be as difficult to spell as they sound, but that is small comfort when one of these words demands a place in a sentence you are writing. Consider *adolescent, bourgeoisie, phosphorescence, schizophrenia, naivete, entrepreneur, hemorrhage, occurrence, soliloquy, silhouette.*

Errors due to unfamiliar words—You can't know everything. With its enormous vocabulary, English will often present you with new and unfamiliar terms—some of them technical items—which you haven't encountered often enough to know how to spell. Then there's the whole realm of proper nouns, the names of persons, places, and things, including that single most unspellable category for Americans—the names of Soviet premiers since Stalin.

Strategies for handling each of these problems are offered below.

21A **To be sure your spelling is right . . .**

▶ **Basic guideline: When in doubt, look it up.**
Look up words in the dictionary even when you are mildly suspicious of a misspelling. To keep from interrupting the flow when you are writing a draft, you may want to postpone trips to the dictionary until you have completed a section or need a break. But don't forget to do the checking. While writing, circle words you are unsure of and then return to them.

If you are an especially bad speller, you'll need to verify the spelling of even some words that look right to you. If they are of a type that has given you trouble in the past—words that end in *-ible* for example, or technical terms—go for the security that extra checking will give you.

Keep a dictionary close by while you write, on the same table. A convenient alternative for frequent misspellers might be a word list, which is simply a dictionary stripped of just about everything but its words, accent marks, and syllable divisions. You can locate words much more quickly using this book, which fits in spaces too small for a dictionary. But don't toss out the dictionary. You'll need information other than spellings.

If you can't locate a word you are seeking in a dictionary, don't assume Noah Webster forgot it. You are probably still misspelling it. Here are some strategies when searching in a dictionary for a word you don't know how to spell:

—Look around in the neighborhood. In a dictionary or word list, you can quickly scan several columns near where you expected to find a word. It may turn up.

—Consider alternatives to the way you think a word is spelled. In English, an *f* sound can be spelled *ph*, a *c* can sound like an *s*, a *u* like a *y*, and on and on. Make a list of possible spellings and then check them out.

> fagocite?
> faygosight?
> faigocyght?
> phaygocite?
>
> phagocyte!

Also consider alternatives to the vowel sound after an initial consonant. You are pages away if you expect to find *tyranny* spelled *tiranny*.

—If you know what a word means, look up one of its synonyms in a thesaurus. Chances are the word you are seeking will be listed under the entry. For example, if you can't figure out how to spell *eulogy* (uelegy? yewlegie? huelogy?) but know it suggests a *tribute* or *sermon*, examine those entries in your thesaurus— where you will find *eulogy*. The method is too time-consuming to use regularly, but it can help.

—For technical terms you can't locate, consider the telephone book. You may not be able to locate *Szechuan* in a dictionary, so look under Restaurants (Chinese) in the yellow pages. The Physicians listing may help you with words like *endocrinology*, *gastroenterology*, *geriatrics*, *ophthalmology*, and *urology*. You'll have to be creative, but the alternative may be misspelling a word or avoiding it.

—Check out textbook indexes. These may list technical terms and proper names you need for a particular course and paper.

—Ask someone. But be sure to use a dictionary to verify any spelling offered to you.

Below, three spellings are given for each word. Using memory alone, underline the ones you think are correct. Then check the dictionary. When you are done, compute the percentage you guessed wrong.

21A

1. parrallel	parallel	paralell
2. accommodate	acommodate	accomodate
3. unecessary	unnecessary	unneccesary
4. drunkeness	drunkness	drunkenness
5. miniature	minature	minaiture
6. exstacy	ecstacy	ecstasy
7. rememberance	remembrance	remembrence
8. rhythm	rythmn	rhythmn
9. governement	governmant	government
10. silouette	silhouete	silhouette
11. exxagerate	exaggerate	exagerate
12. ommission	ommision	omission
13. lieutenant	leiutenant	leuitenant
14. ocurrence	occurence	occurrence
15. camoflage	camouflage	camoflaige
16. guarentee	gaurantee	guarantee
17. questionnaire	questionaire	questionnare
18. miscellaneous	miscelaneous	miscelanious
19. pshychology	pyschology	psychology
20. resterant	restaurant	restuarant

Percent wrong: No. wrong × 5 = _____ %

▶ **Proofread carefully to eliminate "known" errors.**
There's no easy way around the need to proofread carefully anything you regard as important. What this means is seeing a text you may have worked on for days as clearly as a reader coming to it for the first time. Reading a draft, you are probably reading by phrases, not letter by letter or word by word.

To proofread, you have to turn off the automatic pilot in your reading, focus on words and syllables, and locate potential trouble spots. These are special operations, separate from other kinds of revising.

> —Read a paper with a pencil in hand, touching on individual words as you read.

> —Read a piece out loud, slowly.

> —Read an article backwards to isolate individual words.

Use one or a combination of these methods to spot the reversed letters, the omitted endings, the accidentally doubled vowels that may appear in something you have written.

Trouble spots to look for include contractions and possessives. Apostrophes can be murder. And check *it's / its*.

EXERCISE 21.2

Edit this newspaper article by Kyle Talbot. Circle misspelled words and mark them with the appropriate proofreading mark {sp} in the margin. One misspelling has been marked for you. Since you are editing the piece, you aren't responsible for providing the correct spellings. Leave that to Kyle.

Grabowskis Kick Tale!

by Kyle Talbot

In the traditoin of it's varsity squad, Clear Lake College's touch football team fell to ignominious defeat in the annual Town and Gown Bowl with residents of the town of Ruralia, loosing 64-7. The townies—who called themselfs the Grabowskis—stymied the offense and steamroled the defense of **sp.** the Clear Lake Baryshnikovs, coached and named by Sister Anne Constance. The Grabowskis scored on every possession. The Barishnikovs' only points came on a last second "Hale Marry" pass from Sister Anne to Darwin Washington.

A tempermental Washington blamed Sister Constance for the defete: "How you expect to win with a name like Brishnikovs?"

The aeriel circus promised by Sister Anne prior to the game fell victim to a tuff pass defense and a driving rainstorm which turned Walter Toth's back lot in to a qagmire. Yet the weather seemed to have no affect on the sanguine Grabowski offense, which pasterized the Berishknihovs' line.

"It would be no exxageration to describe what happened on the feild today as an annihalation," said an embarassed Maggie Lindstrøm, substituting for Francie Knipstein who lost her contacts lences in the viscous mess. Barney Meyer and the indefatigable Mindy Mendelson, cocaptians of the Grabowski's, attributed thier victory to a harangue delivered before the game by quartreback (and master baker) Jean-Pierre Cappelier: "Jean-Pierre dared us to think of the college team as so much doe to punch and need. We made fritters out of them."

▶ **Read more to eliminate errors that result from mispronunciation or mishearing.**

No one spells English right just because he or she pronounces it correctly or consistently. The regional differences in pronunciation that make English vigorous and interesting also make pronunciation an unreliable guide to spelling. (If you think the people in a town you are visiting *talk funny*, rest assured that they are thinking the same about you.) Even if we all spoke the same way, the language itself refuses to be consistent. Just consider what English does with these words spelled roughly the same: en*ough*, c*ough*, thr*ough*, th*ough*. So you shouldn't feel surprised when the English you spell looks different from the English you speak.

The variations of English pronunciation, however, don't liberate you from the responsibility to spell English right. If you consistently drop syllables, add syllables, or leave off endings, you need to identify these tendencies. Examine corrected copies of your papers to discover your typical mistakes. Then, when proofreading, go into an emergency mode whenever you run up against a word you are likely to misspell. Easier said than done.

Let's say you, like many writers, have a tendency to drop the -d or -ed after verbs or verbals or to use *of* instead of *have* as a helping verb.

> {**Original**} Sister Anne Constance thought the lecture sounded confuse. She was convince she could of described the Promise Land better herself.

> {**Revised**} Sister Anne Constance thought the lecture sounded confused. She was convinced she could **have** described the Promised Land better herself.

Your job is to identify such patterns in your misspellings. If the sentence above were edited for you, you would realize that what at first seems like four errors can be reduced to two: the dropped -d (three times) and the mistaken substitution of *of* for *have*. Once you have identified such error patterns or tendencies in your misspellings, you'll know where slip-ups are likely to occur.

Other errors may be harder to categorize and eliminate. You may not recognize some mispronunciation errors until an editor or reader points them out to you:

Wrong	Right
suprise	surprise
knowlege	knowledge
perscription	prescription
hankerchief	handkerchief
temperture	temperature
privlege	privilege
surppress	suppress

Occasionally you may mishear entire phrases, such as writers who complain about a "doggy-dog" world (instead of *dog-eat-dog*) or describe people who are mere "ponds of faith" (instead of *pawns of fate*). Errors of this kind can't be eliminated magically. You have to rely on trial and error—or as one writer preferred it, trial *in* error.

Build up a personal spelling list of words you tend to misspell for reasons of pronunciation.

▶ **Be alert for words that sound or look alike.**

No tricks help here either: too many English words similar in spelling or appearance differ significantly in meaning. The best you can do is gradually accumulate a personal list of troublemakers. When you write *principal*, be sure that you don't mean *principle*; when *affect* seems right, be sure you don't need *effect*. A dictionary or reference guide (see pp. 791–822) are your best tools for checking out these troublesome sets. Here are just a few of the many problem words in English.

Homonyms

all ready	already	
canvas	canvass	
capital	capitol	
cite	sight	site
course	coarse	
complement	compliment	
council	counsel	
desert	dessert	
holy	wholly	holey
principal	principle	
stationary	stationery	
their	there	they're
throne	thrown	
weak	week	
weather	whether	
whose	who's	

Troublesome Pairs

accept	except
access	excess
adverse	averse
advice	advise
affect	effect
allusion	illusion
breath	breathe
elicit	illicit
eminent	imminent
faith	fate
loose	lose
moral	morale
personal	personnel
quiet	quite
than	then

21A

EXERCISE 21.4

Select five pairs of homonyms or troublesome words from the lists immediately above (or other comparable pairs). Then write sentences in which both words in the pair are used correctly in a single sentence. For example:

The air-conditioner was **quite quiet**.

▶ **Check even familiar words whenever you suspect that some part *might* be wrong.**
You may find it tedious to consult a dictionary or word list every time you are unsure about an ending, a vowel sound, a doubled consonant, a possessive or plural form, but until you know how to spell a word, safe is better than sorry.

You can supplement dictionary checks with three other strategies: identifying **trouble spots**, applying **spelling rules**, and, if you have a word processor, using a **spelling checker**.

Identifying trouble spots means being extra careful at those points where English spelling is most apt to go wrong. Review the following list to identify your **trouble spots**.

1. Words that contain *ei* or *ie*: *receive, perceive, relief.*

2. Words with silent letters: p*neumonia,* de*bt,* an*swer.*

3. Words that end in:
   -*able* or - *ible*: *laughable, visible.*
   -*ance* or -*ence*: *guidance, obedience.*
   -*ant* or -*ent*: *attendant, different.*
   -*cede,* -*ceed,* or -*sede*: *precede, proceed, supersede.*

4. Words with double consonants: *occurrence, embarrass, exaggerate, accumulate, accommodate.*

5. Homonyms: *right, write, rite.*

6. Contractions: *who's, it's, you're.* See Section 20B.

7. Possessive forms: *Jones', Boz's.* See Section 14B.

8. Irregular plurals: *geese, media, spaghetti.* See Section 14A.

9. Hyphenated words: *much-loved, mothers-in-law.* See Section 18B.

Spelling rules are complicated, hard to remember, and unreliable. You may want to review a few basic ones listed below. But in most cases, you are better off relying on a dictionary than one of the following cumbersome, exception-ridden guidelines.

1. I *comes before* e *except after* c—except when *ei* has a long *a* sound.

believe	reprieve	piece
receive	perceive	conceive
eight	weigh	sleigh

Significant exceptions weaken this guideline.

counterfeit	either	seize

2. When adding on to a word that ends with *e*, keep the final *e* if the addition begins with a consonant.

ri*de*	ri**der**
absolu*te*	absolute**ly**
reti*re*	retire**ment**

Drop the *e* if the addition begins with a vowel.

ri*de*	rid**ing**
advi*se*	advis**able**
tribu*te*	tribut**ary**

There are significant exceptions to these guidelines, among them:

tru*e*	tru**ly** (instead of *truely*)
argu*e*	arg**ument** (instead of *arguement*)
jud*ge*	jud**gment** (*judgement is a British spelling*)
dy*e*	dy**eing** (instead of *dying*)
cano*e*	cano**eing** (instead of *canoing*)
sin*ge*	sing**eing** (instead of *singing*)

3. When adding a suffix beginning with a vowel or *y* to a word ending with a consonant, double the consonant if the word has only one syllable and the final consonant is single and preceded by a single vowel. This rule makes clearer sense when seen in operation, but it also demonstrates how complicated spelling rules tend to be.

drop	dro**pp**ing
flip	fli**pp**ed
star	star**ry**

You also double the consonant when the word has more than one syllable, if the last syllable is accented, and the final consonant single and preceded by a single vowel.

reset′	rese**tt**ing
uncap′	unca**pp**ed
omit′	omi**tt**ed

In most other situations, a final consonant is not doubled.

lean	leaning
offer	offering
design	designer
combat	combatant

In some cases, either the single or double consonant may be acceptable. American English, however, usually employs the single consonant.

travel	traveled	travelled
imperil	imperiled	imperilled
kidnap	kidnaping	kidnapping

4. When adding to a word that ends in a *y* preceded by a consonant, change the *y* to *i*—except when the addition begins with an *i*.

ci*ty*	cities	
par*ty*	parties	party*i*ng
hap*py*	happiness	
mar*ry*	married	marry*i*ng

Retain the *y* when the *y* is preceded by a vowel.

vall*ey*	valleys
env*oy*	envoys
st*ay*	staying

5. When faced with a decision between *-able* and *-ible* at the end of the word, it may help you to recall that *-able* tends to attach itself to words that could stand alone without it.

comfort**able**	laugh**able**	unread**able**

In contrast, many of the words that take *-ible* would be incomplete without the ending.

hor**rible**	ter**rible**	respons**ible**
eli**gible**	le**gible**	incred**ible**

As always, there are exceptions.

improb**able**   perfect**ible**   forc**ible**

6. When faced with a decision between *-cede, -ceed,* and *-sede,* remember that *-cede* is by far the most common ending. Only three words end with *-ceed.*

proceed   succeed   exceed

Only one word ends with *sede.*

supersede

All others end with *-cede.*

concede   precede   secede

intercede   recede   accede

7. Form plurals and possessives with care. See Chapter 14.

Spelling checkers are great helps if you are writing on a word processor and have access to a checker program. Because these programs compare your writing to the words stored in their internal dictionaries, they will question every word you produce that they don't recognize. All typos and errors in a paper will be found—as long as they don't form legitimate words on their own.

A spelling checker, for example, will let you know if you spelled *supposed* "suposed"; but it won't tell you if you have left off the *d* at the end of the word because *suppose* is a correctly spelled word. It will let you know if you forget an *m* in *imminent,* but it probably will be silent if you mistakenly use *eminent* instead—unless it has a homonym feature that flags potential problems. Some do.

If you use a word not on your spelling checker's dictionary, the word will be highlighted even if it is spelled right. In most cases, you will have the option of adding that new word to your program's dictionary. Some spelling checkers for personal computers have comparatively small dictionaries; this deficiency is becoming rarer as programs grow more sophisticated and computer memories larger. An able spelling checker now surveys as many words as a good college dictionary. Programs vary in their ability to recognize abbreviations, proper names, and suffixes added to common words.

21A

Spelling checkers will catch many errors quickly and accurately. Most will scan a paper after you have completed it or exited your word processing program. A few will actually check your spelling as you write, signaling whenever you type a word the internal dictionary does not register. But even after a spelling checker has read through a draft, you still need to proofread it on your own to detect the kinds of errors computers can't read.

▶ Check all difficult words.

Don't avoid using words that are difficult to spell. But be honest enough to admit that you might need a dictionary to spell words like *entrepreneur*, *espresso*, *quiescent*, *laryngitis*, *separate*, *fluorescent*, or *zucchini*.

21A

Make a list of troublesome words you use often. Then memorize them, using whatever devices help you to visualize the words. For example, it may help to recall that *espresso* has a pair of *es's* (*espresso*), or that there is *a rat* in *sep*arate. Or simply dividing a word into more spellable units may work: *zuc-chini*; *entre-pre-neur*; *fluor-e-scent*.

▶ Get to know the technical terms in a field. Don't guess on proper nouns.

Almost every discipline or profession lays claim to special words and phrases you need to learn to write successfully in that area. The same is true of proper names in any kind of writing. Imagine the impression made by someone who composes a serious paper on Banquo, a character from Shakespeare's *Macbeth*, but spells the name Bango throughout. When it comes to unfamiliar words, technical terms, or proper names, use whatever resources prove necessary—regular dictionaries, dictionaries of technical terms, dictionaries of biography, newspapers, almanacs, indexes, reference librarians—to get the spelling right.

This applies especially to foreign terms and names—Nikita Khrushchëv, Aleksei Kosygin, Leonid Brezhnev, Yuri Andropov, Konstantin Chernenko, Mikhail Gorbachëv.

Make a short list of technical terms, proper nouns, or names of importance either in your major or some personal area of expertise. Which of the words give you a spelling challenge?

● **Fine Tuning**

1. *A lot* is two words, not one. Don't confuse *a lot* with *allot*.

2. Not all words in English have a single correct spelling. Dictionaries will sometimes present you with variant spellings. In most cases, you should avoid spellings labeled *chiefly British* (*colour, judgement, theatre*) or *Archaic* unless you have a special reason for using them. You would use British spellings, for example, in quoting a London newspaper or a speech by the Prime Minister.

3. Avoid spellings made fashionable by the popular media: *nite, lite, thru*.

4. Many writers confuse the following pairs of words that look similar but have different meanings:

altogether	all together
already	all ready
maybe	may be
all right	alright [nonstandard form]

Check their meanings in a dictionary.

21A

The following excerpt from Colonel Ringling's history of Clear Lake College (see Exercises 1.8 and 3.6) contains more than fifty spelling errors. Locate and correct as many as you can.

(¶1) It has long been the source of considerible embarassment to Clear Lake College that one of it's foundors had the missfortune to be hung.

(¶2) In the early years, fiesty entrepreneurial Tobias Elcott mannaged the college almost single-handedly, allowing his slower brother Horace to run only the horsebarns that would become a cherish part of Clear Lake tradition. Yet, while cleaning stables and bailing hay, Horace nontheless slowly develloped notions about how a college should be govermed. When laryngitis exacerbated by pnuemonia promted Tobias to shuffle off his mortal coil in 1901, the mantel of the college presidentcy decended on Horace, dispite the objection's of one Trustee who declared him "plantlife stupid" and another who doubted that the man could "tell rite from left on a windy day."

(¶3) Though a batchelor, Horace was convince that, next to horses and hay, he was most knowlegable about women. And in his inaugural adress to a student body which had included women since Clear Lake Haulage opened in 1889, he declaired that "women ought not be troubled by Latin and Greak when there's bread to be baked and clothes to be washed." Begining the next academic term, Horace decrede pontifically, women would have to absent themselfs from his college.

(¶4) While a few dinosuars on the campus aplauded Horace's adress, the majority of students and faculty were troubled. A formal reception after the speach buzzed with the coughs and stammers of conscientious profesors and bureacrats on Horace's payrole who doubted the wisdome of his action, but considered themselfs powerless to question it. But while the priveleged few at the reception debated the issue, students on campus acted.

(¶5) Leaving the banquet, Horace was siezed by a band of hooded thugs, bundeled into a dirty canvass laundery bag, and dragged down to Lake Nittani where the sack was pounded clean with rocks, Indain-syle—with Horace still in it. He was discovered some hours later flapping in the breaze along with vareous items of laundery on a rope strung across the quadrangle. Patiently whistleing, Horace seemed rather chastened by the experiance.

(¶6) Rescued from the clothesline, Horace decided that he had done enough for the college and would preffer to be put out to pasture with his horses. No one objected, and the college was turned over to a Bored of Directers. Horace's challenge to coeducation was soon forgoten, and women on campuss returned to more feminine activites.

21B   WHAT KIND OF DICTIONARY DO YOU NEED?

Terms you need to know

Unabridged dictionary. A dictionary that attempts to survey the English language comprehensively, providing spellings and meanings for all its standard vocabulary items. No dictionary, however, can be truly complete. At any given time, many technical, regional, slang, colloquial, or newly invented words are absent from even the most authoritative volumes.

Abridged dictionary. A dictionary based on items selected from a more complete dictionary. Many desk or collegiate dictionaries are abridgements of larger dictionaries. For example, *The Random House College Dictionary* is a condensed version of the larger *Random House Dictionary of the English Language.*

Etymology. The history of a word—its origins, developments, and changes in meaning.

Idiom. Any expression in a language that does not seem to make literal sense. Idioms often mean more than the sum of their parts:

The aircraft **bit the big one** over Montana.

Let's **get cracking**. We're late.

Lexicon. A dictionary; or a list of words used in a particular discipline—a political *lexicon*, the *lexicon* of physics.

The name "Webster" is virtually synonymous with dictionaries in the United States. Noah Webster (1758–1843), an influential scholar, author, and language authority, wrote grammars and spellers that served as basic textbooks for Americans throughout the nineteenth century. His most important work was *The American Dictionary of the English Language* (1828). Revised and enlarged many times, Webster's *Dictionary* became a recognized standard. The Webster name, however, has since entered the public domain—which means it cannot be copyrighted. Hence many works today bear Webster's name even though they may have no connection to him or his famous *Dictionary*.

Troubleshooting

21B

Everyone needs at least one dictionary. But which of the many available volumes is right for you? Does the authority and comprehensiveness of an unabridged dictionary make it worth its bulk and expense? Does the portability of a pocket dictionary compensate for its limited lexicon and bare-bones definitions? Is size the only important difference between dictionaries? If not, what should you look for in making a selection?

▶ Own a desk-sized "college" dictionary.

So-called desk or collegiate dictionaries are an almost ideal compromise between large, unabridged volumes and paperback "pocket" dictionaries. They usually contain between 140,000 and 200,000 entries—enough for most writing jobs. Reasonably priced and usually hardbound, collegiate dictionaries offer many helpful features, from brief histories of the English language to style manuals, lists of foreign terms, and addresses of two- and four-year colleges.

Some collegiate dictionaries list meanings *historically*; that is, the first definition given for a word is its earliest known meaning. Subsequent definitions reflect any changes in meaning the word may have undergone over the centuries. A historically based dictionary gives you a perspective on current language by showing you how definitions grow and alter. But you have to be careful. The first meanings listed for an item in a historically organized entry may be archaic or rare—not the way the term is used today.

For that reason, other dictionaries arrange their definitions in order of use, from the most common meaning of a term to the least familiar. In such a dictionary, you lose some of the chronological perspective you gain from a historical arrangement, but you are less likely to use a word in a sense inappropriate or unfamiliar to modern readers.

Dictionaries also differ in their willingness to give you advice about how words ought to be used. A few tend to be *prescriptive*, offering ample advice about how English is properly employed. Most dictionaries, however, offer advice on usage sparingly, preferring to be *descriptive*. They explain how words *are* used, not how they *should* be used.

The most popular desk dictionaries, listed below, vary in their emphases and features. But any one of them will serve you well.

The American Heritage Dictionary of the English Language

 —Approximately 200,000 entries
 —Meanings listed in order of use, most common first
 —Usage notes based on the opinions of a panel of writers, scholars, editors, columnists, and so on
 —Lists the addresses of American and Canadian colleges and universities
 —Ample front matter: history of the language, dialects, computers
 —Numerous illustrations in ample margins

The Random House College Dictionary

 —Based on the unabridged *Random House Dictionary of the English Language*
 —Approximately 170,000 entries
 —Meanings listed in order of use: most common part of speech first and most often encountered meaning
 —Good coverage of scientific, biographical, and geographic items
 —Includes essays on the history of the language, pronunciation, and dialect

—End matter includes directory of colleges and universities, list of names, style manual
—Some illustrations

Webster's Ninth New Collegiate Dictionary

—Based on the unabridged *Webster's Third New International Dictionary*
—Approximately 160,000 entries
—Meanings listed historically, with items dated
—Draws from nearly a century of college dictionary experience
—Biographical, geographical, and foreign terms listed separately at the back of the book
—Lists the addresses of American and Canadian colleges and universities
—Includes a list of abbreviations and a handbook of style
—Some illustrations

21B

Webster's New World Dictionary of the American Language

—Meanings listed "in semantic order from the etymology to the most recent sense."
—Includes an essay on "Language and the Dictionary"
—Provides guides to usage
—Ample coverage of Americanisms
—Geographical and foreign terms included in main listing
—Lists American and Canadian colleges and universities
—Provides sections on punctuation, manuscript form, weights and measures

Webster's II New Riverside University Dictionary

—Definitions arranged by "central meaning clusters"
—Emphasizes American regional terms indicated by boldface daggers
—Definitions illustrated by quotations from American authors
—Provides occasional "word histories"
—Separate listings of abbreviations, biographical terms, geographic terms, and foreign words
—Lightly illustrated

The Concise Oxford Dictionary of Current English

—Based on *The Oxford English Dictionary* and its supplements

—Meanings listed according to "frequency and convenience."

—Appendices on weights and measures, the Greek and Russian alphabets, and monetary units

▶ **Consult an unabridged dictionary when necessary.**

On some occasions you may need more information about a word than your desk dictionary provides. Or the word you are looking for may be a form too rare, obscure, or old to appear in a dictionary designed for daily work. Then you need to consult one of the large unabridged dictionaries—works which attempt to record standard English vocabulary items as fully as practicable. If you have the wherewithal to own one of these imposing collections—some are single books, others are multi-volume sets—you'll enjoy easy access to the wealth of information they contain. Most people, however, examine such books in the reference rooms of their libraries. Here are three you should be aware of.

The Oxford English Dictionary

—Over 500,000 items: 13 volumes and supplements

—One of the greatest dictionaries in any language

—Definitions listed historically, with quotations (about two million of them) providing the earliest recorded use of a word and its subsequent appearances through the centuries

—Entries treated exhaustively; often more useful to scholars than to writers

—Americanisms somewhat scanted in this British project, begun in 1888 and currently being adapted to computer technology

—Complete dictionary available in a convenient micro-printed two-volume set sold with a magnifying glass: *The Compact Edition of the Oxford English Dictionary.* Also available abridged as *The Shorter Oxford English Dictionary.*

Webster's Third New International Dictionary of English

—Approximately 450,000 items in one volume
—Best known American dictionary
—Illustrated
—Definitions listed historically and amply illustrated through quotations
—Descriptive rather than prescriptive; caused great controversy when first published in 1961 because it printed nonstandard and controversial usages without commentary
—Regarded as complete and authoritative

The Random House Dictionary of the English Language

—Approximately 260,000 items in one volume
—Most recent unabridged dictionary; first published in 1966
—Includes many idioms, synonym and antonym lists
—Usage labels steer middle course between fully prescriptive and fully descriptive
—Full-color atlas of the world; gazetteer
—French/Spanish/Italian/German-English dictionaries

▶ **Know that special-purpose dictionaries are available.**
Every field and interest is served by dictionaries. Your library reference room contains dictionaries of art, history, philosophy, physics, social science, photography, film, television, music, sports, opera, theater, ballet, and so on. Rest assured that for any serious subject you can name, someone has compiled an alphabetical collection of significant terms.

Regular English dictionaries survey certain general aspects of language; other dictionaries deal with more specialized interests. The reference room of a large library contains shelves of such special-purpose volumes. A sampler of such books is provided below to demonstrate how they might solve problems you encounter while writing or reading.

What do you do, for example, when you read or hear an unusual word, maybe slang, but can't locate it in your desk dictionary or even in an unabridged volume? For such an item, you might consult a dictionary of slang such as:

Partridge, Eric. *A Dictionary of Slang and Unconventional English.*

Mainstream dictionaries do list many slang and colloquial items, but they don't pretend to cover all the less formal words and expressions English has acquired over the centuries. Instead, you would go to Partridge to discover words and phrases that have not found their way into more respectable lexicons: *beer-slinger, cliffhanger, flip side, give the heat, mosey, pintle-de-pantedly, put the bite on, ratbaggery, undress a sheep, wharf-rat.*

Partridge's huge dictionary contains unconventional items both from the past and present. If you are interested in current idioms and expressions, you'll find a host of dictionaries catering to the subject, including:

Cowie, A. P. *Oxford Dictionary of Current Idiomatic Usage.* 2 Vols.

Wentworth, Harold, and Stuart B. Flexner. *Dictionary of American Slang*

Dictionaries of idioms provide explanations for those expressions in a language that mean something more than the sum of their parts, expressions such as *bite the dust; easy money; full of oneself; a long shot; a slip of the tongue; weak at the knees; stink to high heaven; tee up; waltz off with.* Dictionaries of idioms are not only useful, they can be fun.

If you meet an abbreviation or acronym you don't recognize—perhaps the name of a new government agency or a corporate conglomerate recently merged—where do you go? To a specialized dictionary of abbreviations. One compilation of these terms, updated regularly, is

Towell, Julie E., and Helen E. Sheppard, eds. *Acronyms, Initialisms & Abbreviations Dictionary.* 10th ed. 1986–87, 3 Vols.

The work covers abbreviations from many fields and areas: aerospace, associations, electronics, labor, government, military, religion, sports, and so on.

Perhaps the problem is understanding a proper noun: the name of an unknown person, place, or thing. Regular dictionaries make an effort here, sometimes providing separate geographic and biographical listings. But for the more obscure allusion, literary character, place, or person, you can check a specialized dictionary of proper nouns such as:

> Payton, Geoffrey. *Webster's Dictionary of Proper Names.*

Here you'll find listed terms as varied as *Angkor Wat*, *Birnam Wood*, *Bushido*, *Dear Abby*, *Krazy Kat*, *Mickey Finn*, *Politburo*, *Reynard the Fox*, *Sardi's*, and *Zond*.

Perhaps your problem is less exotic: you need help with your spelling. Your best friend might be a word list, a handy, pocket-sized dictionary without the definitions, pronunciations, etymologies, and other side dishes that fatten collegiate dictionaries. What word lists provide are words, word divisions, and occasional warnings about homonyms. Two you might consider are

> Ellis, Kaethe. *The Word Book.*

> Leslie, Louis A. *20,000 Words.*

If you are a *really* bad speller—so bad that you have trouble locating correct spellings in a dictionary—you might need something like

> *Webster's New World Misspeller's Dictionary.*

This tiny book, which lists 15,000 common errors, lets you locate a correct spelling by beginning with a misspelling. Look up *laggon* and you will find the correct *lagoon*; *auxilary* gives you *auxiliary*; *medecine* or *medisine* gives *medicine*. Of course, the book cannot anticipate every misspelling, especially if you are unusually creative.

Regular dictionaries often make an effort to explain matters of usage, but you may want more guidance than these volumes can provide. If so, consult one of the available dictionaries of usage, such as

> Follett, Wilson. *Modern American Usage: A Guide*

> Fowler, Henry W. *A Dictionary of Modern English Usage*

Morris, William and Mary. *Harper Dictionary of Contemporary Usage*

These volumes and others like them establish their authority on matters of usage and convention in a variety of ways. Fowler's book, for example, relies to a large extent on the authority and good sense of its original author. The *Harper Dictionary*, on the other hand, resolves disputed questions of convention by referring them to 165 writers, editors, and speakers who form a usage panel. Should *author* be used as a verb (as in "Colonel Ringling *authored* the chapter")? The panel votes no. Is *parenting* a useful new word? Again, the panel thinks not. Can *hopefully* be used in the sense of *we hope*? No, not in writing.

If you are interested in the origins of words, several dictionaries will serve:

Onions, C. T. *The Oxford Dictionary of English Etymology*

Morris, William and Mary. *Dictionary of Word and Phrase Origins*

Finally, if you are a poet in search of a rhyme, a dictionary waits for you:

Fergusson, Rosalind. *The Penguin Rhyming Dictionary*

Arranged somewhat like a thesaurus, this computer-compiled volume includes entries for words that have at least one rhyme. Individual words are listed in an index at the back of the volume, keyed to groupings of words with rhyming endings in front.

▶ **What about "pocket dictionaries"?**

Pocket-sized dictionaries are convenient, but they are no substitute for desk-sized volumes. Pocket dictionaries contain many fewer entries than college dictionaries and slimmer definitions. If you carry a pocket dictionary to help with spelling, you might consider using an even more convenient word list. For other information—meanings, pronunciation, etymologies, usage—rely on a full college dictionary.

21C HOW DO YOU USE A DICTIONARY?

Term you need to know

> **Front matter**. Material that precedes the main body of a work. In a dictionary, the front matter may include a guide to the dictionary, a pronunciation key, a history of English, and various essays on language topics.

Troubleshooting

Dictionaries are as dependable as gravity. Once you know alphabetical order, you can usually navigate one with few problems. But a great many writers, put off by all the signs and symbols that seem to clutter entries, ask no more of a dictionary than that it furnish accurate spellings and clear meanings. In fact, a dictionary can tell you a great deal more, if you know how to interpret the information it presents.

▶ Consult the front matter.

Every dictionary includes a kind of owner's manual, usually a several-page description of how to use the information contained in its thousands of entries. You may not want to read all this material every time you consult a new dictionary, but remember that this guide is available whenever you encounter an unfamiliar word, symbol, or feature.

Don't underestimate the number of features a dictionary entry can contain. The guide to *The American Heritage Dictionary* (Second College Edition), for example, lists all these headings (boldfaced items are discussed in the section that follows):

> Guide Words
> **The Entry Word**
> Superscript Numbers
> **Syllabication**
> **Pronunciation**
> Sound-Spelling Correspondences
> **Part-of-Speech Labels**

Inflected Forms
Labels (*Nonstandard, Slang . . .*)
Cross-References
Order of Definitions
Sense-Division
Explanatory Notes in Entries
Illustrative Examples
Variants
Phrasal Verbs
Modifiers
Idioms
Etymologies
Undefined Forms
Usage Notes
Synonyms
Biographical Entries
Geographical Entries
Abbreviations

21C

Each of these headings represents some feature you may encounter when you look up a word.

▶ **Know how to use key features in a dictionary: spelling, syllabication, pronunciation, part-of-speech, usage labels, definitions, etymologies, usage notes, synonyms, and antonyms.**

—*Spelling and Syllabication.* Obviously, the alphabetical listing of words in a dictionary provides you with a guide to accurate spelling. The main entry, printed in boldface type, will be divided into syllables so that you know where to break the word at the end of a line. Spellings will also be given for various forms of the entry: verb endings, unusual or potentially troublesome plurals, suffixes.

com•press   -pressed, -press•ing, - press•es

mouse   pl. mice

lush   -er, -est

trav•el   -eled, el•ing, els *or* - elled, el•ling, els

Many words have alternative spellings. In most cases, you should choose the first spelling listed, which is usually the most common.

mov•a•ble   also move•a•ble

me•di•e•val   also me•di•ae•val

Avoid archaic and British spellings unless you have a special reason for using them.

col•or   also Brit. col•our

lic•o•rice   also Brit. li•quo•rice

—*Pronunciation.* Hearing a word is the best way of learning to pronounce it correctly. However, dictionaries will help you figure out the sound of an entry if you are patient enough to interpret the pronunciation key usually printed at the top or bottom of every page. The front matter will explain how the pronunciation key in any given dictionary works, but all follow the same basic principles.

Each major entry in a dictionary is followed by a pronunciation, which often looks like an odd spelling of the word cluttered with accent marks, strange vowels, and unusual markings: ü, ø, é, û. Every consonant and vowel sound in the pronunciation is keyed to familiar words in the pronunciation guide that also use those sounds.

For example, let's say you aren't sure how to say the word *harlequin.* Checking the American Heritage Dictionary again, you find this pronunciation listed:

(här'lĭ-kwĭn, -kĭn)

It tells you several things even before you check the pronunciation key. The word is accented on its first syllable (här'), and the two unaccented syllables (lĭ-kwĭn), joined by a dash, are pronounced together. You also learn that there are two possible pronunciations, här'lĭ-kwĭn and här'lĭ-kĭn.

The consonants *h, r, l,* and *n* all have their most familiar sounds. But if you were unsure of any of them, you could check the pronunciation key at the bottom of the page and find that they have these values:

h **hat**   l **lid**

r **roar**   n **no** sud**den**

In the first pronunciation, the *qu* in *harlequin* is written as *kw* and pronounced exactly as you would expect.

k **kick**

w **with.**

The key also gives approximate pronunciations for each of the vowels, often the most troublesome sounds in a given word. Because vowels often have different sounds, the marks over them indicate important distinctions. Again, each vowel sound in the pronunciation is explained by a familiar key word:

ä **father**

i **pit.**

Notice especially here that the *e* in *harlequin* appears as an *i* in the pronunciation.

By putting all the sounds together and paying attention to the accent marks and syllable groupings, you can be sure of a reasonably accurate rendering of an unfamiliar word. Seem difficult? Only because this is one feature of a dictionary easier to use than to explain.

Remember that pronunciations vary from region to region. Ohioans fill their crankcases with *oy-al* while Texans pump *awl*. Dictionaries strive to provide "standard" pronunciations, but standard doesn't necessarily mean *only correct* pronunciation.

—*Part-of-speech.* The meaning or pronunciation of a word may change according to the role it plays in a sentence. *Brave*, for example, can be a noun, verb, and adjective.

{**As a noun**} Darwin once dreamed of wearing the uniform of a Milwaukee **Brave.**

{**As a verb**} Instead, he **braved** the difficulties of electrical engineering and chemistry.

{**As an adjective**} It takes a **brave** student to pursue a double major.

21C

559

Dictionaries, of course, must include all these meanings in an entry. Or separate entries may be provided for words with the same spelling but different pronunciations and meanings. Consider, for example, the uses of the word *deserts* in the following sentences.

{**Noun**} The **deserts** were hot and barren, yet full of life.

{**Noun**} Kyle received his just **deserts** for deceiving Alicia.

{**Verb**} If Kyle **deserts** the team, he'll lose some friends.

Most dictionaries provide useful information about verbs, indicating whether they are **transitive** or **intransitive** and furnishing the **principal parts** of irregular verbs.

—*Labels*. The kinds of labels provided for words will vary from dictionary to dictionary.

21C

It is common, for example, to find **field labels** that identify words or meanings with a special significance in a specific discipline or area. For example, the word *floppy* has an ordinary meaning, one that describes the condition of rabbits' ears or soggy pizzas. But it might also be accompanied by a field label in a dictionary: *Computer Sci.* Then *floppy* refers to a magnetic storage disk for computer information.

Other labels describe the status of particular words in the language. The *American Heritage Dictionary*, for example, uses these labels: *nonstandard*, *informal*, *slang*, *vulgar*, *obscene*, *offensive*, *obsolete*, *archaic*, *regional*, and *chiefly British*. Each word is carefully defined in the front matter. You should be aware that such labels are often controversial. People don't agree on how far a dictionary should go in saying what words are acceptable or offensive. Yet such labels can often prevent you from committing blunders in addressing particular groups that might dislike nonstandard, vulgar, or informal language.

Whatever dictionary you use, be sure to check how it defines its labels and when it applies them.

—*Definitions*. Be sure to check the front matter of your dictionary to learn how it arranges the definitions of an entry when more than one meaning is possible. Some dictionaries list the most common meaning first. Others arrange their entries historically, that is, the first meaning records how the word was used when it first appeared in the language. Subsequent meanings record the changes the term underwent over the years. Still other dictionaries use other principles—such as "meaning clusters"—to order their definitions.

You need to know how the entries are arranged so you can be confident about the meaning of a term. The *Oxford English Dictionary*, for example, lists "Strong, powerful, mighty" as its first definition for *crafty*—not a sense we use today, but the first meaning the term had in English. If you didn't know that the *Oxford* arranged its entries historically, you might be confused and misled in this case by what seems like a peculiar definition.

—*Etymologies*. Most dictionaries make an effort to trace the origins of words, explaining what languages they, or their roots, come from. Etymologies may not be supplied for compounds (*homework*, *bloodshot*), words derived from other words (*escapee*), words derived from geographical names (*New Yorker*), and so on. You can usually trace these etymologies by going back to the more basic words (*home*, *work*, *blood*, *shot*, *escape*, *New York*).

Etymologies in desk dictionaries have to be brief, so they rely on various abbreviations and symbols. Some etymologies are easy to interpret, like the following explanation of *kumquat*:

[Cantonese *kam qwat*, golden orange]

Others can seem quite complicated, especially when a word is derived from several earlier forms or several languages. This is how the American Heritage Dictionary traces the history of *rummage*:

[Obs. *rummage*, act of packing cargo<OFr. *arrumage<arumer*, to stow: *a-*, to (<Lat. *ad-*) + *run*, ship's hold, of Germanic orig.]

For help in interpreting such etymologies, check the guide to etymologies usually located in the front matter of your dictionary. It will explain the meaning of the symbols (<, :, +) and the abbreviations (OFr., Lat.).

—Usage notes. Many dictionaries now offer advice about how the more troublesome words and expressions in a language ought to be used. The advice usually follows the main body of an entry. Such short guides can help you decide how or whether to use a word or phrase. For example, *American Heritage* offers this advice about the word *critique.*

> Usage: *Critique* is widely used as a verb, but is still regarded by many as pretentious jargon. The use of phrases like *give a critique* or *offer a critique* will forestall objections.

—Synonyms. You may be accustomed to looking for synonyms in a thesaurus, but in a pinch your dictionary may help. Some desk dictionaries now list synonyms for many important words, and a few even attempt to explain the differences between synonyms—a useful feature.

21C

EXERCISE 21.7

Browse through your dictionary to find examples of the following:

1. A word with a variant spelling.
2. A word you aren't sure how to pronounce. Use the pronunciation key to figure it out; then test your version on someone who is familiar with the word.
3. A word pronounced with a regional slant in your area. Compare your regional pronunciation with the dictionary's version.
4. Several words that can be used as more than one part of speech. Look especially for nouns that can also be used as verbs.
5. A word with a field label. You may want to begin with a technical term you sometimes use (*chip, touchdown*). Check to see whether your dictionary gives it a field label.
6. A word that might be considered slang, vulgar, offensive, archaic, or informal. See how your dictionary treats the entry.

7. A word with a simple etymology.
8. A word with a complicated etymology.
9. A word that includes a usage note (if your dictionary provides such notations).
10. A word for which synonyms are offered (if your dictionary offers synonyms).

EXERCISE 21.8

Pick a full page of your dictionary at random. Read it completely and write a short summary of what you have learned about the words on that page or about your dictionary. What is the most interesting word on that page? Which has the most impressive etymology? The most complicated definition? The most meanings? The oddest or most difficult pronunciation? Do any words on the page require labels or remarks about usage? Are Illustrations on the page (if any) useful?

21D WHAT SHOULD A WRITER'S BOOKSHELF INCLUDE?

Troubleshooting

What books should a writer own and keep within easy reach on a desk top? Any "essential" collection will vary according to your profession and interests. If you are a business major, you might want to keep a reference book like Clark and Gottfried's *University Dictionary of Business and Finance*. If you are a sports nut, you might regard Brander's *Dictionary of Sporting Terms* as essential.

But particular interests aside, we would like to suggest a "core" collection for writers—a personal library of essential information. We think such a desktop library should include works of the following kinds.

▶ A dictionary.

A dictionary is the first and most important item in your collection. Many fine college dictionaries are available. If you can afford an unabridged dictionary (and have the space), consider purchasing one. But for desk use, the dictionaries discussed in Section 21B are more convenient.

▶ A thesaurus.

A thesaurus is a collection of synonyms—a book designed to help you discover a word better than the one you have in mind or simply an alternative to avoid using one word too often.

The first English thesaurus was published by Peter Mark Roget in 1852. In the first part of his book, Roget grouped words by meaning according to a complex arrangement of categories: *Abstract Relations*, *Space*, *Matter*, *Intellect*, *Volition*, *Affections*. Within this scheme, words of similar meaning (and also of opposite meaning) were clustered together. To locate a particular word and its synonyms in the first part of the book, you started by consulting the alphabetical index in the back of the volume.

Roget's arrangement has been retained in some contemporary thesauruses, including:

Roget's International Thesaurus 3rd ed.

The St. Martin's Roget's Thesaurus of English Words and Phrases

The traditional structure has the disadvantage of requiring two steps to find a synonym. In addition, the words listed in the thesaurus are often far from exact synonyms. More than one writer has chosen unwisely from the full plate of synonyms and related words traditional thesauruses offer. Yet the variety of words grouped in meaningful clusters is the strength of these reference books. Many experienced writers find that Roget's groupings stimulate their ideas and consequently they prefer his arrangement to the alternative.

That alternative to Roget's design is a thesaurus arranged alphabetically. Such a book is as convenient to use as a dictionary: to find a synonym for a word, you check a single

21D

alphabetical list. Two alphabetically arranged thesauruses are:

Roget's II The New Thesaurus

Webster's Collegiate Thesaurus

In most cases, you will find fewer but more precise suggestions for synonyms in these works and much more guidance about meaning. *Roget's II* defines words briefly and uses the words in context, lessening the likelihood of choosing an inappropriate synonym. *Webster's* also uses synonyms in context and warns against terms that might be misconstrued. An alphabetical thesaurus is probably the best choice for most writers—at least initially. Eventually, you may want to graduate to Roget's more challenging design.

▶ A handbook of writing, grammar, and usage.

You need a handbook to give you advice and guidance about writing and usage. Consult a handbook when you have questions about composition, punctuation, grammar, usage, format, and documentation. Since you are reading this, you know what a handbook looks like.

▶ A one-volume encyclopedia.

A multivolume encyclopedia is a great reference tool, but too large for a desk top and usually very expensive. Consider, instead, a single-volume work, such as:

The Random House Encyclopedia

The New Columbia Encyclopedia

These handy tools supply you with information about thousands of subjects, from historical personalities to philosophical and scientific concepts. Keeping an encyclopedia within reach can save you dozens of trips to a library.

▶ An almanac.

An almanac provides facts and figures on thousands of subjects. And because paperback almanacs are relatively inexpensive, you can usually afford to buy a new one every few years to keep your information up to date. So when you need to know the population of Lagos, Nigeria, or who won the World Series in 1952, or the per capita income of farmers in Wisconsin last year, you know where to turn. Most almanacs include information about topics as varied as elections, current events, astronomy, aviation, business, disasters, geography, awards (Nobel, Pulitzer, Oscar, Emmy, Grammy), nutrition, science, and weights and measures. They provide statistics on countries and states and often include maps. Two familiar almanacs, updated annually, are:

> *The World Almanac and Book of Facts*
>
> *Information Please Almanac*

▶ An atlas.

21D

When you write about a place, you should know where it is. A good atlas puts the political and geographical world at your fingertips with its full collection of maps. Atlases vary greatly in their focus and coverage. In addition to providing maps, they may also include detailed information about astronomy, geology, history, geography, ecology, and environments. Some atlases worth considering:

> *The Prentice-Hall New World Atlas*
>
> *Rand McNally Illustrated Atlas of the World*
>
> *Rand McNally Cosmopolitan World Atlas*
>
> *The Times Atlas of World History*

▶ A dictionary of quotations.

The most famous advocate for dictionaries of quotations may have been Winston Churchill who wrote:

> It is a good thing for an uneducated man to read books of quotations. *Bartlett's Familiar Quotations* is an admirable work, and I studied it intently. The quotations when engraved upon the memory give you good thoughts. They also make you anxious to read the authors and look for more.

Even if such collections don't inspire "good thoughts," you will still find dictionaries of quotations handy for discovering what others have said about your subject or locating impressive support for your ideas. Such dictionaries are indexed in various ways—usually by some combination of author, date, and subject. As Churchill suggests, *Bartlett's Familiar Quotations* is the best-known work of this kind, but many useful books are available.

▶ A Bible.

No book is as well known or quoted as often as the Bible. Whether a believer or not, a writer should consider including a Bible among his or her reference works. Because of its literary power, the King James Version of 1611 and its subsequent revisions is still the edition of choice for writers of English.

▶ A volume of Shakespeare.

Among speakers of English, only the Bible is better known or quoted more often than the works of Shakespeare. No matter what your discipline or profession, an edition of Shakespeare can be an appropriate and often-used reference tool. There are numerous reliable editions available, among them:

> Bevington, David, ed. *The Complete Works of Shakespeare* (Scott, Foresman)

> Evans, G. Blakemore, ed. *The Riverside Shakespeare* (Houghton Mifflin)

> Barnet, Sylvan, ed. *The Complete Signet Classic Shakespeare* (Harcourt Brace Jovanovich)

21E   HOW DO YOU USE A WORD PROCESSOR?

Terms you need to know

> **Hardware.** The equipment that makes up a computer: a combination of keyboard, screen, central processing unit, and disk drives.

> **Software.** The electronic directions or programs that run the hardware. It is the software that determines

what the hardware will do: process words, crunch numbers, organize files, play games.

Document. A paper, article, or text prepared on a computer.

Word processing. Writing on a computer with a software program specifically designed to produce texts. Word processing programs vary greatly in their features, but all aim to make it easier to write, revise, and print a document.

Disk. A small plastic record that stores information magnetically. You insert a disk into a disk drive. The computer then loads the information it needs from the disk into its memory. Disks carry the software programs that run computers and store the documents you produce while word processing.

21E

Cursor. A line that blinks on a computer screen at the point where you are writing or working on your text. You move the cursor to the place in your document where you want to add or delete words or perform some other operation.

Memory. The capacity of a computer to store information. When you are writing, for example, your computer must keep in its memory portions of the word processing program and portions of the document you are creating. It will select the information it needs from the disks you have inserted. With some computers and programs, you can exhaust the memory the computer has available to do a job. In such cases, you usually have to break up a long paper into shorter parts.

Save. An important command that tells the computer to make a permanent copy of the document you are working on. Until you save a document, it exists only in the computer's memory and can be wiped out if you turn the computer off, experience a power failure or surge, or exit the program you are working in. If you are revising an existing text, the save command copies any changes you have made and makes them permanent.

Troubleshooting

Almost everyone has heard of word processing, but many people are reluctant to entrust their writing to an electronic device. Some writers believe that pounding the keys on their manual typewriter or dragging a pen across a legal pad stimulates their creative juices and adds texture to their ideas and prose. But people who favor word processors suspect that such physical drudgery produces nothing but calluses.

If you have no experience with computers or word processors, you may find the information in this section helpful in deciding whether writing with a computer is for you. Because computers and software develop and change rapidly, you will eventually have to investigate individual systems or products on your own to discover exactly what they offer you. Not all computers or programs have all the features described below. Nor are all the capacities of word processors covered in these few pages.

Understand, though, that computers are nothing to be afraid of. The days when computer users had to be programmers or silicon devotees are long past. You need to know no more about the innards of a computer to process words than you need to understand the mechanics of an automatic transmission to shift gears.

21E

A word processor may help you . . .

▶ **To revise quickly and easily.**   Most people find that writing on a computer takes the busywork out of revising and editing a text. Because a paper you are working on exists on the equivalent of a TV screen, you can make all the changes you want without manually erasing, recopying, or rearranging sentences or paragraphs. The computer takes care of the alterations for you.

When you delete a portion of a paper, the words, sentences, or paragraphs disappear while the rest of the text rearranges itself to fill in the gap. You can just as easily add anything you want at any point in a paper. Left out a word? Just move the cursor to the place where the word ought to be and begin typing. Need to move an entire paragraph? Mark it, then move it wherever you want. Misspell a word? Change it before anyone notices.

When you have made all the changes you want, you can then print out a draft, turning your screen image into *hard copy*, that is, a text on paper. If reading the hard copy suggests more changes, you can go back to your computer, revise the document again, and print out another version. You don't have to retype an entire paper every time you make significant alterations—so revisions aren't nearly as time-consuming or threatening as they were formerly.

Moreover, since to the computer your document is just a series of electronic signals stored magnetically, you can make copies of your documents quickly and easily, saving various versions of a paper on your disks as records, or sending the document via disk or *modem* (an electronic telephone hookup) to anyone who has a compatible computer system.

21E

▶ **To work with several documents or programs at the same time.** Many software programs make it possible for you to work with several documents on the screen at the same time. This would enable you, for example, to compare several versions of the same paper or to move material from one paper to another.

Depending upon the kind of computer you have, you may even be able to copy material from different kinds of programs into your word processing document: a chart from a graphics program, columns of data from a spreadsheet, a design from a drawing program.

▶ **To arrange and rearrange the format of a paper.** Because a word processor allows you to vary such things as margins, tabs, and spacing, you can print out a paper using any format you like: wide margins, narrow margins, single spaced, double spaced, centered, right margin justified, single column, double column, and so on.

You can produce multiple
versions of any paper, one
perhaps double-spaced to
hand in to an instructor,
another single-spaced for
your own records.

If you want the paper to look
especially polished you can use a
"justified" right margin: the
computer will line up the right
margin as flush as the left so that
your words on the page look almost as
neat as those in a printed book.
Almost, because computers sometimes
leave awkward gaps when they justify
a page.

The computer also takes care of moving you

automatically from line to line as you type.

You don't have to return a carriage or watch

your spacing as you near the left margin; what

is termed "word wrap" takes care of spacing for

you, automatically fitting as many words as

possible on a line, dropping down to the next

one while you just keep on typing.

Computers also allow you to place page numbers and running heads where you want them—top, bottom, centered, left-
hand corner of a sheet. More important, word processing
programs keep track of pagination. If you add or cut pages as
you revise a paper, it repaginates itself automatically. No more
fumbling with pages 8a and 8b.

▶ **To arrange and rearrange the appearance of a paper.** Most computers allow you to underline or print words in **boldface**. Others provide even more flexibility, enabling a writer to form on the screen and then print italics, small caps, or any combination of features. Some programs also allow a writer to vary the type style (font) itself as well as its size.

If your computer has this capacity, you may have to resist the temptation to mix fonts and sizes. The appearance of a paper shouldn't attract more attention than its contents. On the other hand, having the ability to produce boldface headings or different type sizes gives you additional control over your contents. You can use bold headings, for example, to signal important sections or select a font or size likely to be pleasing to a given set of readers.

▶ **To check features of a paper.** Most word processors have the ability to **search** for a given word or phrase in a paper. You can use the search feature to locate and replace words you may have used too often or, perhaps, misspelled. Or you can save time with search, typing a short code—sg, for example— in place of a lengthy title that will appear frequently in your essay (*Sir Gawain and the Green Knight*). Then, when you are nearly done, you simply instruct the computer to replace all occurrences of *sg* with the full title, *Sir Gawain and the Green Knight.*

What computers can do to check grammar and style features varies with available hardware and software. But most word processors now are compatible with spelling checkers and thesauruses. Spelling checkers help you to catch spelling and typographical errors (see p. 543 for more details); electronic thesauruses enable you to call up synonyms for words you select in your paper. Some spelling checkers and thesauruses are built right into word processing programs. Others operate separately.

Programs are also available to check selected stylistic features in a paper you have written. Most ''style checkers'' will tell you how many words your paper contains and the average length of your sentences or words. Some will flag clichés and suggest alternative expressions; some highlight *to be* and other weak verbs to encourage you to make livelier choices. Or they will bring to your attention words you have repeated in close proximity. Style checkers vary enormously in their power and features; they can't make you a better writer automatically, but they can provide feedback on aspects of your prose you need to watch.

Other programs widely available to writers with access to personal computers make outlining, note taking, and indexing easier. Again, such programs vary greatly in power and features.

▶ **To print professional-looking texts.** The quality of the hard copy you produce with your computer depends, naturally, on the printer it is hooked up to. Early dot matrix printers earned word processors a bad reputation, producing pages just barely more readable than cash register tapes. Most dot matrix machines today do vastly better jobs, producing copy almost as good as an average typewriter can manage—and without smudges, erasures, and white-outs.

Even more professional-looking copy is possible using a variety of middle-level printers that employ various technologies (daisy wheels, ink jets) to give near "letter quality" output—that is, printing as good as a topline electric typewriter can produce with a carbon ribbon.

Computers can also be hooked up to laser printers that surpass the abilities of even the best typewriters and approximate (but do not equal) letter-press type. Laser printers do a remarkable job producing graphics and some are even used by companies or institutions to print newsletters, brochures, fliers, and other small jobs.

Most computer users find the relatively inexpensive dot matrix printers adequate for a majority of jobs. When a particular assignment (a senior thesis, an annual report, a dissertation) merits special attention, you can usually arrange to print it at a typing service that rents access to letter quality or laser machines. Writing on a word processor thus gives you a variety of printing options even if you are on a limited budget.

▶ **Save you time.** You might get an argument here, but many users of word processors will admit that the machines don't always speed up composing. Instead, writing on a word processor encourages more tinkering with a text and, consequently, more revision. What a writer gains in not having to copy and recopy an essay every time a change is made is lost in the tendency to make more frequent changes and more serious revisions. So, on balance, you aren't likely to save much time by producing a paper on a word processor. But chances are good that you'll end up with a more polished document—one you are likely to be more satisfied with.

Don't dismiss, either, the time it takes to learn how to use a word processor. Some word processing programs are devilishly complex, though most have become more user-friendly in recent years. Even software that is simple to use involves a writer in numerous computer routines that eat up minutes relentlessly: booting the machine, initializing disks, saving copy, backing up disks, transferring files, naming documents, formating paragraphs, positioning running heads, repaginating, and so on. It all adds up. In the long run, a computer will make you more productive, but it won't necessarily save you time.

21E

▶ **Improve the quality of your writing dramatically.** Computers remove many impediments (and excuses) to composing. They make revising simple and painless. They keep track of items (like pagination, spacing, paragraph formats) that writers would just as soon ignore. They can help out with outlining, invention, spelling, and vocabulary. They churn out handsome copy with ease and relative speed.

But word processors don't work miracles. The old rule holds: garbage in, garbage out. You have to furnish the ideas to build a paper. You have to find the statistics that support an assertion or the illustrations that clinch an argument. You have to arrange sentences that suit both your ideas and your audience. The machine doesn't do the writing.

▶ **Find and eliminate your errors.** Computers can help you locate typographical and spelling errors in a paper and suggest

574

alternative vocabulary items. Some programs point out weaknesses in your style and potential grammar difficulties. But computers are a long way from being able to address all the complex issues even a "simple" paper raises. Don't think that a computer can take charge of the writing you do. It can't.

Some Advice About Word Processing.

1. Save the text you are working on at regular intervals, about every fifteen minutes. If you don't, a power surge or blip can erase hours of work.

2. Always make backup copies of important documents, both on disk and in hard copy. A single electronic copy of a paper is vulnerable to many accidents and system errors. Better safe than sorry, especially when copies are so easy to make.

3. Learn how to use your computer and software correctly. You can waste a lot of time—and miss important features in your software—if you hunt and peck your way through it.

4. Whenever you can, print out hard copies of your drafts and edit them for mechanical errors. Typographical and spelling errors tend to be easier to spot in hard copy than on the screen.

5. Take regular breaks when working at the computer. Staring at a monitor is more fatiguing than you might realize. Be sure the screen is at a level comfortable for your eyes and that the keyboard is conveniently located. If you feel cramped or uncomfortable, your writing will show it.

6. Treat your disks with respect. Brush them against a magnetic field (in your printer, a telephone receiver, a stereo speaker) or expose them to undue heat (direct sunlight, radiator) or moisture (shower, spilled coffee) and you may scramble the information on the disk. Goodbye, term paper.

7. Name your documents carefully so you can locate them later. If necessary, keep a list of your file names.

21E

8. Print out important documents on the best quality paper you can find. If you use perforated computer paper, be sure to separate the sheets and to tear off the tractor feed.
9. Change your printer ribbon regularly, especially with a dot matrix printer.
10. Don't bore people who don't use computers with computer stories.

21E

PART IV   RESEARCH GUIDE

This section presents the basic information you need to write a college research paper. To review the research process, see Chapter 22: How Do You Write a Research Paper? If you already know how to prepare a term paper, but have questions about the proper form for notes and documentation, consult Chapter 23: How Do You Document a Research Paper? To see an actual research paper develop from thesis to final version, see Chapter 24: A Research Paper from Start to Finish.

CHAPTER

How Do You Write a Research Paper?

- **A** How do you select a topic?
- **B** Where do you go for information?
- **C** How do you keep track of information?
- **D** How do you write the paper?
- **E** What should the paper look like?

HOW DO YOU SELECT A TOPIC?

Troubleshooting

For many writers, the most difficult part of doing a research paper can be choosing a subject. Yet the importance of a *good* topic can be overestimated: in and of themselves, topics aren't simply *good* or *bad*. What makes the difference is treatment— that is, how well you shape any topic idea to your assignment, your readers, and your abilities. Finding a good subject is not a matter of chance or luck. It involves, instead, deciding what you want to achieve and then carving out a pathway to that goal.

A first step is determining what is manageable. Assigned, for example, to write a 1500 word essay on a subject in contemporary history, you may be so worried about meeting the required length that you gravitate toward subjects as massive as the Holocaust, the U.S. space program, the American auto industry, or modern literary discoveries. But topics like these have hundreds of aspects that can be explored in thousands of ways. Dealing with a huge subject commits you either to writing a book or to narrowing your interests to something more suitable to a 1500–2500 word attempt.

To narrow a subject, you may want to look for an angle or a hook—an idea that grabs and holds an audience. The point seems so simple: a research paper should convey information that surprises readers. Just tossing around a topic idea should arouse curiosity, questions, objections, or enthusiasm: How did the Nazis keep an operation the size of the Final Solution secret? What did the Voyager spacecraft discover about Uranus? Why exactly did Chrysler almost go broke? Have scholars finally identified the "Dark Lady" of Shakespeare's sonnets?

Finding an angle on a subject can transform a research paper from an *assignment* to what it should be—an *investigation* as exciting for the writer as for the reader. Your vague interest in the space program might become a more focused study of the Voyager mission to Uranus, leading to an essay about the bizarre terrain of the Uranian moon, Miranda.

Put simply, when you have the opportunity to choose the subject of your research paper, follow your inclinations and instincts. You will write a better paper if you like what you are researching. If your topic is assigned, well, that's life—sometimes you have to work harder to achieve your goals.

To select a topic for a research paper . . .

▶ **Size up the assignment carefully.** Be sure you understand what you are being asked to do. Read or listen to the assignment carefully, particularly to certain key words. Are you expected to analyze, examine, classify, define, discuss, evaluate, explain, compare, contrast, argue, prove, disprove, persuade? Each of those words means something a little different. Each gives you an idea of how to approach your subject—even how to organize it.

Analyze. Examine. Break your subject into its parts or components. Discuss their relationship or function.

Classify. Define. Fit your subject into some larger categories. Distinguish it from other objects in those categories. What characterizes your subject? What makes it unique? What are its significant features? What makes it recognizable?

Discuss. Talk about the problems or issues your subject raises. Which issues are the most significant? What actions might be taken? Try to be neutral, looking at the subject from several points of view.

Evaluate. Think about the subject critically. What criteria would you use to judge it? How well does it meet those standards? Is it *good, effective, successful, unsuccessful*? How does it compare to other similar subjects?

Explain. Show what your subject does or how it operates. Provide background information on it. Put your subject in its context so that readers will understand it better.

Compare. Show how your subject resembles other things or ideas.

Contrast. Show how your subject differs from other things or ideas.

Argue. Come to a conclusion about your subject and explain why you believe what you do. Try to get others to agree by presenting evidence.

Prove. Provide evidence in support of an idea or assertion.

Disprove. Provide evidence to contradict an idea or assertion.

Persuade. Provide good reasons for someone to think or act in a particular way.

Once you know what your assignment requires, appraise the length of the paper you are expected to produce. Be realistic about how much you can accomplish in five typed pages (roughly 1200 words), eight typed pages (2000 words), ten pages (2500 words), and so on. Your worry shouldn't be finding enough to write, but deciding what you can say within a given length. In general, the shorter the assignment, the sharper the focus of your essay will have to be. But even lengthy essays—say twenty pages—will require a narrowed subject supported by significant research.

▶ **Explore several topic areas.** Topic areas are big subjects that offer many directions for exploration. Here are just a few examples.

anorexia	the Holocaust
the race for the moon	homosexuality
the troubled U.S. auto industry	child abuse
nuclear disarmament	ocean pollution
symphony orchestras	quasars
the aging U.S. population	science fiction
nature photography	consumer fraud
amateurism and the Olympics	tax reform
Scottish poetry	computer theft
artificial intelligence	the family farm

You begin with topic areas when you have no specific subject assigned. Select areas that intrigue you—not topics you vaguely suspect your teacher prefers. Reward yourself with an idea you won't mind exploring for several weeks. (It is a different matter, of course, when your instructor specifies a subject.)

Avoid stale topics: don't be one of a half a dozen students submitting essays on gun control or capital punishment—unless you are sure you can press a new vintage from the old grapes. But be wary, too, of topics drawn from today's newspapers or magazines. They may be fresh and exciting, but the indexes and bibliographies researchers rely on can't keep up with the evening news. You may quickly exhaust your leads and resources in researching what happened last week. Finally, don't try to resuscitate an old essay unless you are so eager to know more about its subject that you will, in effect, produce a new paper.

▶ **Read in that topic area.** Select the topic area you find most promising and do some selective background reading. Background reading does three things: it confirms whether you are, in fact, interested in your topic; it surveys the main points of your subject so you can begin narrowing it; and it suggests whether the resources of your library or community will support the topic you want to explore in the time available.

The most efficient sources for preliminary reading are encyclopedias, beginning with any that deal specifically with your field or subject. The more specialized the encyclopedia, the more comprehensive the audit it can give you of a subject area. If you check the reference room of your library, you will find specialized encyclopedias covering all the major disciplines and majors. Here are just a few.

Doing a paper on?	Begin by checking . . .
Anthropology, economics, sociology	*International Encyclopedia of the Social Sciences*
Law	*The Guide to American Law*
Crime	*Encyclopedia of Crime and Justice*
Ethical issues on life sciences	*Encyclopedia of Bioethics*
Psychology, psychiatry	*International Encyclopedia of Psychiatry, Psychology, Psychoanalysis and Neurology*
Philosophy	*Encyclopedia of Philosophy*
Art	*Encyclopedia of Art*
American history	*Encyclopedia of American History*
Film	*International Encyclopedia of Film*

Science	*McGraw-Hill Encyclopedia of Science and Technology*
Computers	*Encyclopedia of Computer Science and Technology*
Current events	*Editorial Research Reports*
Literature	*Cassell's Encyclopedia of World Literature*

If no such specialized encyclopedia is available or if the specialized volume proves too technical for your level of knowledge, move up to one of the more familiar general encyclopedias.

The Encyclopaedia Britannica

Colliers Encyclopedia

Encyclopedia Americana

Reading about the general topic should provide you with enough perspective to select a narrower subject intelligently. If, after reading about a subject, you find that it does not interest you or is beyond your competence, choose another general subject area and explore it. When you have found an area that you think is workable, you can start narrowing your topic.

▶ **Narrow the topic to a preliminary thesis or hypothesis. Find a question to answer.** You can't stay with a general subject for too long without wasting time. Even a relatively focused general subject—for example, the troubled U.S. auto industry of the 1980s—would be too large to read widely in. You need to find a facet of the subject you can explore in depth. This narrowing will enable you to read more efficiently, using tables of contents and indexes to locate information about your specific topic area. For example, rather than worry about the entire complicated subject of the Holocaust, you might want to consider only how it was concealed from the Allies—if it was.

Any subject you choose at this stage is likely to be preliminary: it will be shaped and reshaped by the reading and re-

search you do later. What you may have now is no more than a
question or issue you'll use to guide your initial efforts:

> Why do women have keener senses of smell than men?

> How were the Nazis able to conceal the Holocaust?

> What did Voyager discover about Uranus' moon, Miranda?

> What makes people abuse children?

> Why did Chrysler almost go broke?

Focusing your topic will save you hours of aimless reading
and supply you with the confidence to write a successful
paper. Don't go on to the next step—**finding sources** until
you have a tentative thesis or a question to answer. Read
Section 24A for more about shaping a research thesis.

22B WHERE DO YOU GO FOR INFORMATION?

Troubleshooting
Efficient research is systematic, strategic, and comprehensive.
It demands at the outset some effort to lay the groundwork for
a project. But it means, in the long run, spending the least
amount of time finding the best, fullest, and most authoritative
sources. More important, good research habits are repeatable:
they produce results every time you call on them.

Many would-be researchers simply ramble to the card catalog in their library, look up their subject, copy down the first
few works listed under an appropriate heading, and then go off
to the stacks, hoping that the books they have listed will get
them started. This method seems easy at first, even natural.
But, in the long run, the haphazard approach wastes time
because it ignores the quickest ways of finding the best information. What it leads to are complaints that the library
"doesn't have any books on my subject" or "all the books I
need are checked out."

Such complaints rarely have substance. For one thing, a writer relying only on books is probably missing half of the best, most current sources—those available in journals and magazines. For another, the resources of a library aren't likely to be exhausted by a quick flip through the card catalog. Finally, books that are checked out can be recalled—if a project is begun early enough. What follows is a "no excuses" approach to research.

To find information on your subject . . .

▶ **Use the card catalog efficiently.** You should probably begin researching your subject by examining the basic holdings your library has in your subject area. Whether your library has a regular card catalog or a computerized file, check to see how subjects are listed. In many libraries, subject catalogs are kept separate from author/title listings.

Most subjects are cataloged according to categories established by the Library of Congress. So you might want to examine the Directory of the Library of Congress (often called the **Subject List**) to determine how your topic is handled in the card catalog and to accumulate a list of related subject headings. These headings will tell you where in the catalog to look directly for your topic or for subjects allied to it.

Inspect the cards in your topic area. If your subject is a large one, you may find the cards broken down into various subcategories. Look for the category most relevant to your working thesis or question. Then scan books on your topic in a preliminary way by title and date. For many subjects, the most recent volumes may be the most trustworthy. Make a bibliography card for any titles that look immediately useful. Be sure to note whether any of the books listed in the card file either is or contains a bibliography. A bibliography on your subject can lead to much pertinent information.

A catalog card itself carries plenty of information. If you examine it closely, it will tell you:

—the call number and library location of a book;

—author, title, publisher, and date of publication of a book;

—its number of pages and physical size;

—whether the source is illustrated;

—whether it contains a bibliography and index;

—what subject headings the book is listed under.

▶ **Author card**

```
HD
9710     Iacocca, Lee A.
U52         Iacocca : an autobiography / Lee
I25      Iacocca with William Novak. — Toronto
UGL      ;  New York : Bantam Books, c1984.
            xv, 352 p., [16] p. of plates  :  ill.
         ;  24 cm.
            Includes index.
            ISBN 0-553-05067-2

            1. Iacocca, Lee A.  2. Automobile
         industry and trade—United States—
         Biography.  3. Businessmen  United
         States—Biography.  1. Novak, William.
         II. Title
```

22B

▶ **Title card**

```
HD         Iacocca
9710
U52      Iacocca, Lee A.
I25         Iacocca : an autobiography / Lee
UGL      Iacocca with William Novak.  Toronto
         ;  New York : Bantam Books, c1984.
            xv, 352 p., [16] p. of plates  :  ill.
         ;  24 cm.
            Includes index.
            ISBN 0-553-05067-2

            1. Iacocca, Lee A.  2. Automobile
         industry and trade—United States—
         Biography.  3. Businessmen—United
         States—Biography.  I. Novak, William.
         II. Title
```

► **Subject card**

```
HD          IACOCCA, LEE A.
9710
U52         Iacocca, Lee A.
I25             Iacocca : an autobiography / Lee
UGL         Iacocca with William Novak.—Toronto
            ;  New York : Bantam Books, c1984.
                xv, 352 p., [16] p. of plates  :  ill.
            ;  24 cm.
                Includes index.
                ISBN 0-553-05067-2

                1. Iacocca, Lee A.  2. Automobile
            industry and trade—United States—
            Biography.  3. Businessmen—United
            States—Biography.  I. Novak, William.
            II. Title
```

► **Subject card**

```
HD          AUTOMOBILE INDUSTRY AND TRADE — UNITED
9710            STATES—BIOGRAPHY.
U52         Iacocca, Lee A.
I25             Iacocca : an autobiography / Lee
UGL         Iacocca with William Novak.—Toronto
            ;  New York : Bantam Books, c1984.
                xv, 352 p., [16] p. of plates  :  ill.
            ;  24 cm.
                Includes index.
                ISBN 0-553-05067-2

                1. Iacocca, Lee A.  2. Automobile
            industry and trade—United States—
            Biography.  3. Businessmen—United
            States—Biography.  I. Novak, William.
            II. Title
```

22B

BUSINESSMEN—UNITED STATES—BIOGRAPHY.

HD
9710
U52   Iacocca, Lee A.
I25   Iacocca : an autobiography / Lee
UGL   Iacocca with William Novak.—Toronto
    ; New York : Bantam Books, c1984.
          xv, 352 p., [16] p. of plates : ill.
    ; 24 cm.
          Includes index.
          ISBN 0-553-05067-2

          1. Iacocca, Lee A.   2. Automobile
    industry and trade—United States—
    Biography.   3. Businessmen—United
    States—Biography.   I. Novak, William.
    II. Title

These factors may help you decide whether a given book is worth examining. So make intelligent judgments about the materials listed in the card catalog. Don't just copy down the titles on the first five or six catalog cards. Look through the stack and compile a working bibliography of the most promising sources. Aim for a dozen or so to get you started.

▶ **Locate suitable bibliographies.** You will save time if you can locate a bibliography—preferably an annotated one—on your subject. Bibliographies are customized lists of books, articles, and other materials dealing with particular subjects or subject areas.

—Complete bibliographies attempt to list all the major works in a given field or subject.

—Selective bibliographies usually list the best known or most respected books and articles in a subject area.

—Annotated bibliographies summarize or evaluate the works they list.

—Annual bibliographies list the works produced within a field or discipline in a given year.

An up-to-date bibliography on your subject will furnish you with a far more thorough list of sources than a run through the card catalog can. To determine whether a bibliography has been compiled on your subject, first check *Bibliography Index* in the reference room of your library. You can also examine Theodore Besterman's older *A World Bibliography of Bibliographies*. Chances are, however, that you may not locate a bibliography precisely on your subject area; instead, you may have to rely on one of the more general bibliographies available in almost every field. The professor of your course or the reference librarian should be able to steer you to an appropriate work. Only a few of the many bibliographies in specific disciplines are listed below.

Doing a paper on?	Check this bibliography . . .
Anthropology	*Ethnographic Bibliography of North America*
Psychology	*Harvard List of Books in Psychology*
Philosophy	*A Bibliography of Philosophical Bibliographies*
Social work	*Social Work Education: A Bibliography*
Art	*Guide to the Literature of Art History*
American history	*Bibliographies in American History*
Engineering	*Science and Engineering Literature*
Music	*Music Reference and Research Materials*
Classics	*Greek and Roman Authors: A Checklist of Criticism*
Literature	*MLA International Bibliography*

▶ **Locate suitable periodical indexes.** You can usually find the books you need for a research paper in the card catalog, but you won't find articles listed there. Yet, for many subjects, magazine stories and journal articles are likely to contain the most up-to-date and concise information. You shouldn't attempt any college-level research paper without examining the periodical literature on your topic.

22B

Fortunately, articles on your subject can be traced through any number of periodical indexes, some quite general and wide-ranging, others more specialized and sophisticated. Indexes—usually located in the reference room of the library—list where you can find articles written about a given subject during a given period of time. For example, if you were writing a paper about the Italian film director Federico Fellini, you might check the *Film Literature Index* for the past three years to discover what he has been doing most recently. As with any reference tool, you should read the front matter of an index to be sure you are using it properly and understand its coverage and limitations. In addition, the front matter will help you decipher the entries in a periodical index—which may seem like code until you learn what the abbreviations mean:

> Venus: global surface radio emissivity [Pioneer radar mapper] P. G. Ford and G. H. Pettengill. bibl. f il *Science* 220:1379–81 Je 24 '83

The index you are most likely to have used is the *Readers' Guide to Periodical Literature* (1949). It directs you to articles on many topics in many popular magazines. Another such general tool is *Magazine Index* (1980). But almost certainly you will want to employ more specialized and powerful indexes for many college papers. As with bibliographies, there are guides to periodical literature in every major academic field. The list below is just a sampling. Check with the reference room librarian for the most helpful index in your subject area. (The dates in parentheses indicate the first year of coverage for the index.)

22B

Doing a paper in this area?	**Check this periodical index . . .**
Biography	*Biography Index* (1938)
Social science/humanities	*Social Science & Humanities Index* (1907–74) *Humanities Index* (1974) *Social Sciences Index* (1974)
Psychology	*Psychological Abstracts* (1980)
Public affairs	*Public Affairs Information Service* (1960)
Art	*Art Index* (1959)

Technology	*Applied Science and Technology Index* (1971)
Science	*General Science Index* (1978)
Music	*Music Index* (1970)
Film	*Film Literature Index* (1973)
Education	*Education Index* (1959)
Business	*Business Periodicals Index* (1973)
Literature	*Essay and General Literature Index* (1900) Contemporary Literary Criticism

▶ **Do a computer search.**   Most libraries are now linked to various data base systems—which are, in most cases, computerized indexes. For a fee, you can have the librarians do a search of available data bases to provide you with a list of articles on your topic. The computer searches, of course, have their limitations. Because the computers have to locate appropriate references through key terms called "descriptors," the list of sources generated can only be as good as the descriptors that guide the search. And many of the data bases are fairly recent. For topics that reach farther back, you may have to revert to printed indexes.

To initiate a computer search, you will usually fill out a form describing your topic, key terms in it, and related subjects. The more specific you are in describing your topic, the more accurate the computer search is likely to be. You may also be asked which years you want to search and whether you want to include foreign language items. You may be permitted to specify a broad or narrow search, depending upon the nature of your subject.

So a computer search may be well worth your consideration and money (they aren't free), particularly if you need to be thorough in examining what has been written on your subject. Remember, too, that data bases now cover most disciplines, not the sciences only.

▶ **Prepare a working bibliography.** As you move through the card catalog, the bibliographies, the indexes, and your computer printout, list your prospective sources on separate index cards (3″ × 5″ cards are ideal) so that you can add, delete, and alphabetize entries quickly. These cards form your preliminary working bibliography—your private data base.

If you have found only a dozen references, you will probably have time to locate and examine all of them. But if you've found several dozen or more, you'll have to make some decisions about which to pursue first. You may think you don't have enough information to make intelligent decisions about your sources when all you have are bald bibliographic entries, but you probably do.

—*Check the title.* How close does it come to approximating your topic or addressing the question you are asking?

—*Check the author.* Is he or she an authority in this area? Did you come across the author's name in your preliminary reading? Does the author have credentials to write in this field?

—*Check the source.* Who is publishing this information? If a book, do you recognize the publisher? Is it an academic press (that is, one affiliated with a college or university)? If a periodical, is the article in a scholarly journal? A popular magazine? Which kind of publication will give you the perspective on the subject you are looking for?

—*Check the depth of coverage.* Is the piece long enough to give you the information you need, or is it simply an overview or a brief news item?

—*Check the date.* Is this source recent enough to reflect the latest research?

Rank the sources in the order of their apparent usefulness, and then begin locating and examining them. If some of your early sources don't pan out, drop down further in your list until you find the materials you need.

22B

▶ **Consider other sources of information.** The resources discussed above are those most often used in researching a college essay. But there are, of course, other techniques and tools for gathering information. A few are discussed below.

—*Experts in the Field.* Sometimes people are better than printed sources. If you can (without being a nuisance) discuss your subject with an expert, you'll add authority, authenticity, and immediacy to a research report. If you are writing a paper about an aspect of medical care, talk to a medical professional. If you are exploring the financial dilemmas of community theaters, try to get an interview with a local producer or theater manager. If you are writing about problems in the building industry, try to find a builder or banker with ten minutes to talk to you.

If you believe that an interview with an expert will add information to your paper you could not get through printed sources, write or telephone for an appointment and make it clear why you want to talk. Be on time for your appointment if you get one, and be prepared. Have a list of questions and possible follow-ups ready. Take careful notes, especially if you intend to quote your source. Double-check direct quotations, and be sure your source is willing to be cited on the record. If you plan to tape the interview, be certain to get your subject's approval before turning the machine on. Promise to send the person you interview a copy of your completed paper.

—*Professional Organizations.* Almost every subject, cause, concept, or idea is represented by a professional organization, society, bureau, or office. If you have time (you'll need lots of it), write to an appropriate organization for information on your topic; ask for pamphlets, brochures, propaganda, tracts, leaflets, reports, and so on. The *Encyclopedia of Associations* published by Gale Research can be your source for addresses. Also remember that the U.S. Government publishes huge amounts of information on just about every subject of public interest. Check the *Index to U.S. Government Periodicals* or the *Monthly Catalog of United States Government Publications* for listings.

—*Abstracts.* Many disciplines now publish collections of abstracts, which are short summaries of the major research articles in a field. These abstracts can help you scan major research areas or sample the content of a long essay you may have to read. Your librarian can direct you to a suitable collection of abstracts in your area of study.

—*Guides to Reference Books.* The reference room in most libraries is filled with helpful materials. But how do you know what the best books are for your needs? Consult one of these guides to reference books:

> Bell, Marion V., and Eleanor A. Swidan. *Reference Books: A Brief Guide*, 8th ed.
> Murphey, Robert W. *How and Where to Look It Up: A Guide to Standard Sources of Information*
> Sheehy, Eugene P. *Guide to Reference Books*, 9th ed.
> Walford, Arthur. *Guide to Reference Material*, 3rd ed.

—*Citation Indexes.* Citation indexes tell you where a given work is mentioned again *after* it is published. By using a citation index, you can trace the influence a particular article or author has had on a field. Indexes are arranged by author, item, and subject. While you may not need to use a citation index for your early college papers, you should know that these interesting tools exist. Three important citation indexes are the *Science Citation Index* (1961), the *Social Sciences Citation Index* (1972), and the *Arts and Humanities Index* (1976).

—*Dictionaries of Biography.* Quite often you will need to find information about famous people, living and dead. There are dozens of sources to help you in the reference room. Good places to start are *Biography Index: A Cumulative Index to Biographic Material in Books and Magazines* (1946/47) and *Current Biography* (1940). There are also a variety of *Who's Who* volumes, covering living British, American, and world notables, and volumes on Blacks, women, politics, and fashion. Deceased figures may appear in *Who Was Who*. Probably the two most famous dictionaries of biography are the *Dictionary of National Biography* (British) and the *Dictionary of American Biography*. More specialized dictionaries cover scientists, authors, architects, scholars, and so on. Again, check with your reference room librarian.

—*Statistics.* Where do you go to find the figures or statistics you need to support or counter an argument? Begin with the *World Almanac* for basic numbers on everything from population to sports. If your focus is on the United States, check out *Statistical Abstract of the United States* or *Historical Statistics of the United States*. For information about the world, examine *The Statesman's Yearbook*, the *National Intelligence Factbook*, *UN Demographic Yearbook*, or the *UNESCO Statistical Yearbook*. For business figures, check the *Handbook of Basic Economic Statistics*, *Survey of Current Business*, or *Dow Jones Irwin Business Almanac*. Also useful for surveys of opinion is the summary of Gallup poll findings called *Gallup Poll: Public Opinion* 1935–1971.

22B

—*News Sources.* Sometimes you'll need to find information in newspapers. If you know the date of a particular event, you can usually locate the information you want. If your subject isn't an event, you may have to trace it through an index. Only a few papers are fully indexed; the one you are most likely to encounter in American libraries is *The New York Times*, usually available on microfilm. *The New York Times Index* (1960) provides chronological summaries of articles on a given subject. Another useful reference tool is *Newsbank*, an index of more than 100 newspapers from across the country keyed to a microfiche collection. You can use *Newsbank* to present a sampling of journalistic coverage and opinion on major issues and notable people. *Facts on File* summarizes national and international news weekly; *Editorial Research Reports* gives background information on major problems and controversies. To report on what editors are thinking, examine *Editorials on File*, a sampling of world and national opinion.

—*Book Reviews.* To locate reviews of books, check out *Book Review Digest* (1905), *Book Review Index* (1965), or *Current Book Review Citations* (1976). *Book Review Digest* does not list as many reviews as the other two collections, but it summarizes those it does include—a useful feature.

22C HOW DO YOU KEEP TRACK OF INFORMATION?

Terms you need to know

Summary. Notes taken on a source that reproduce the gist of the material, but not the structure of an article or its fine points. In a summary, you boil down a source to its key ideas and put them in your own words.

Paraphrase. Notes taken on a source that follow the structure of the original material. When you paraphrase, you work systematically through the source material, listing the main ideas and supporting points as they occur, putting them in your own words.

Troubleshooting

After you have located all your sources, you have to read and evaluate them. And somehow, you have to keep track of *what* you have read and *where*, so that you can locate and use the information when you actually write your paper.

Yet keeping track of what you've read may be more difficult than finding the material in the first place. Initially, at least, it seems easier to rely on luck and memory than system and strategy to get the right information in the right slots. Books borrowed from the library grow thick with markers and slips of paper. The names of articles dutifully recorded from an index get written down somewhere in a notebook. A significant quotation is copied onto a note card someone left on a library table, and then the quote itself gets attached to another book you have to read. In the meantime, you photocopy a dozen pages of your best source, but—when you sit down with it two weeks later to write the paper—you can't recall what the source was and can't cite the material. You couldn't anyway because the page numbers got cut off by the copier. As you try to write, your desk becomes a cluttered mess of slips, borrowed books, photocopies, scattered notes, and lists of important details that don't quite make the same sense they did when you wrote them down. Sound familiar?

Most people drop at least one pass while writing a research paper. But a little forethought and planning can smooth the process and eliminate major problems. As with finding sources systematically, keeping track of information efficiently requires front-end work. The reward comes near the conclusion of the research project—when you are most pressed for time. Then you discover that you have an accurate "Works Cited" list, comprehensive notes, and all the page numbers you need for accurate documentation. Who could ask for anything more?

22C

To keep track of research data efficiently . . .

▶ **Keep an accurate set of bibliography cards.** For every source you examine—whether it ends up in the final paper or not—make a complete bibliography card, one source per card. Don't keep bibliographical information on sheets of paper. You can't shuffle items entered on a list, rearrange them, or enter new ones alphabetically. And paper lists tend to get lost. So when you start a research project, **buy a stack of cards**, preferably 3″ × 5″.

Each bibliography card should contain all the information you will need to record one source in the *Works Cited* list at the end of the paper. Be sure to include a library call number or location (current periodicals may not have call numbers) in case you have to look the source up a second time.

Also consider assigning a simple **code number** to each bibliography card. Then when you begin taking notes from a source, put its unique code number on those notes instead of tediously recopying all the information already on the bibliography card: author, title, publisher, date. The code number will tell you exactly where the notes are from. For example, a note card using information from Brock Yates' *The Decline and Fall of the American Auto Industry* (listed below) would bear code #1.

For a book:

—Call number/location in the library.

—The code number you have assigned this source (#1).

—Name of author(s), last name first, followed by a period.

—Title of work, underlined, followed by a period.

—Place of publication, followed by a colon.

—Publisher, followed by a comma.

—Date of publication, followed by a period.

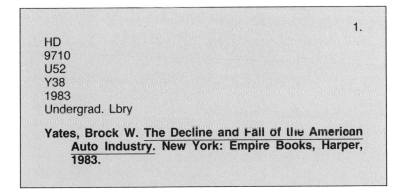

For an article in a scholarly journal:

—Call number/location.

—The code number you have assigned this source.

—Name of author(s), last name first, followed by a period.

—Title of work, followed by a period and between quotations.

—Name of the periodical, underlined.

—Volume number, followed by the date in parentheses, and a colon.

—Page or location, followed by a period.

2.

Undergrad. Lbry
Reading Room

Robinson, Jay L. "Literacy in the Department of English." College English 47 (1985): 482–98.

For an article in a popular magazine or newspaper:

—Call number/location.

—The code number you have assigned this source.

—Name of author(s), last name first, followed by a period.

—Title of work, followed by a period and between quotations.

—Name of the periodical, underlined.

—Date of publication, followed by a colon.

—Page or location, followed by a period.

For the exact *Works Cited* form of any bibliography card
entry, check the MLA or APA Form Directories (p. 647 and
p. 678). If you cannot record the source precisely according to
form (you may not have your handbook with you), at least
copy all the information you will need to transform the card
into a correct *Works Cited* entry when the time comes. If your
bibliography cards *are* accurate, compiling that *Works Cited*
list will require that you do no more than stack the bibliography cards in alphabetical order and type them up.

▶ **Keep a useful set of note cards.** You should put your
research notes on cards for the same reasons you use cards to
keep track of bibliographical information: they are neat,
stackable, and shuffleable. While 3″ × 5″ slips are fine for
bibliography entries, larger cards may be more practical for
notes.

22C

Each note card should have four components:

—a code number to identify what source is being used;

—a heading to identify the kind of information on the
card;

—the actual information itself;

—page numbers accurately locating the information in
the source.

Here is a sample note card from source #3 above:

Vitullo-Martin, Julia. "Chrysler in Chaos: Is the Company Beyond Repair?" <u>Saturday Review</u> 19 Jan. 1980:
22–25.

Many critics—including Ralph Nader—blamed Chrysler's problems on gross mismanagement. Vitullo sums up their arguments this way: "For years Chrysler made reckless decisions at every turn: building big cars when Americans wanted little cars, producing gas guzzlers right before the gas shortage hit and persisting with them long after, and manufacturing inefficient and unattractive cars when consumers were insisting on efficiency and style." (p. 22)

▶ **Summarize or paraphrase your sources.**   Take the kind of notes appropriate to your subject and your research material. A **summary** captures the gist of a source or some portion of it, boiling it down to a few words or sentences. A **paraphrase** will usually run longer than a summary because it is faithful to the structure of a source, listing major and relevant minor points in their original order and with approximately the same emphasis.

22C

An article that supports your thesis but does not provide new information may be a candidate for a summary; another article that goes into more detail about a topic, covering major points your paper will have to deal with, may merit careful paraphrase. In actually taking notes, you will find yourself switching between summary and paraphrase, depending upon what you are reading. Here is an example of a short essay that is first summarized, then paraphrased.

Original Source

Some homeowners in the American Southwest swear by St. Augustine grass for their lawns; others sing the praises of Bermuda. I think both species provide strong arguments for artificial turf, gravel, or green concrete.

To Yankees spoiled by rolling carpets of Kentucky bluegrass, Southern lawns of any variety look like plots of fertilized weeds. At its best, St. Augustine is a coarse lime-green crabgrass that retains its color through the worst heat. Bermuda has a finer texture and appears almost lush in the spring after heavy rains and high-nitrogen feedings. But when the summer sun begins its annual roast, Bermuda sheds its green and fades fast, first to a pale yellow, then to a sandy brown. Come July, the neighbor's St. Augustine frontage sure looks prettier than your patch of well-tended straw. The St. Augustine seems hardier too, spreading like Marxists into disreputable spots of shade where Bermuda (despite its tendency to burn) refuses to grow. Even in open-sun turf battles, stout St. Augustine runners inevitably choke out delicate tendrils of Bermuda.

But wait until August when a week of 100° temperatures compounds the anguish of thirty rainless days. Then, almost over night, huge patches of St. Augustine head towards that great compost heap in the sky—your lawn looks as if Dumbo and his compadres found it after guzzling a trough of Lone Star. Watering won't help. When St. Augustine grass turns brown, it's dead. You might as well roll it up, which you can do easily enough about mid-September when the Chinch Bug larvae have finished severing the roots. Then the rains return, and sprouts of green Bermuda push through the mats of brown to write the moral of this tale: "Better ugly than dead."

I say, so what if concrete cracks?

      —Sam Penguin, "Why I Hate Lawns." *Webworm Review* 4 Sept. 1986: 21.

Summary

Both St. Augustine and Bermuda are less than ideal Southern lawn grasses. Bermuda turns brown in the heat and retreats from the more aggressive St. Augustine, but survives drought. St. Augustine retains its appearance in the sun, but succumbs to drought and insects.

Paraphrase

Neither St. Augustine nor Bermuda are ideal lawn grasses in the South.

St. Augustine, a coarser grass than well-watered and fertilized Bermuda, at least retains its lime-green color well after summer heat has turned Bermuda lawns brown. St. Augustine also thrives in shady spots that won't support the generally less aggressive Bermuda.

Unfortunately, extended heat waves and droughts can kill large patches of St. Augustine lawns. St. Augustine grass also falls prey to Chinch Bug larvae, which feed on its roots in the late summer. In contrast, fall rains revive Bermuda.

Whether writing a summary or a paraphrase, be certain your notes are in your own words (see p. 683 on **improper paraphrase**). Direct quotations, of course, are the exception.

Exactly how you list the information on any given card is up to you, but keep the following points in mind.

22C

—*Be sure to record page numbers for all material.* You will eventually have to cite page numbers for all ideas and quotations you find in your sources. So, to save yourself trips back to the library, get page numbers for ideas and quotations you think valuable enough to record on your note cards.

—*Try to record only one major point per card.* Don't crowd too much information onto a single slip. Later, when you use the cards to help organize your paper, you'll find it much easier if you can move ideas, arguments, statistics, and quotations independently—even if they come from the same source. If you crowd three or four ideas onto a single card, they are locked together—unless you later expend time recopying them.

—*Write on only one side of a note card.* Information on the flipside is easily forgotten. Moreover, at some point you may want to lay out your notes as a sort of outline. You won't be able to do that as easily with two-sided cards.

—*Write your notes legibly in ink.* Always take notes that are legible enough for someone else to read. Be especially careful in recording numbers and dates. It is easy to reverse figures or write one number that looks like another.

—*Photocopy passages you know you will quote from directly and extensively.* Since most libraries are equipped with copying machines, it makes sense to copy your most important information. Be sure, though, that your copy is complete and legible and that you record bibliographical information directly on the material so you don't forget where it came from. You may find it useful to highlight passages you expect to return to later or quote. Keep your copies in reasonable order in a folder.

22D HOW DO YOU WRITE THE RESEARCH PAPER?

Troubleshooting

Because a research paper takes more preparation than most college essays and usually counts more toward a grade than other assignments, students sometimes panic when it comes to composing the paper itself. They freeze at the prospect of turning research into words; they catch "writer's block" just at the moment when they are best prepared to write.

The fact is, however, you don't start writing a research paper when you set down that opening paragraph. The process started long before, when you began auditioning possible subjects for your paper. You were *writing*—in a sense—when you were narrowing your topic, thumbing through indexes, mustering books and articles, and reading them. You were composing when you took notes—putting the words of your sources into your own language. You were composing when you set up a survey or conducted an interview. Mentally, as you did your research, you were examining ideas, discriminating between major and minor points, sorting through evidence.

When you start writing the body of your paper, you'll feel more confident if you remember how much writing you've already done. Your jottings, notes, scratch outlines, and even your "false starts" are all words that contribute to your final product.

That is not to say that writing the paper itself will be easy. You really haven't wrestled with your ideas until you move from what others have told you about your subject to what *you* think about it. And that occurs when your jottings start to take the shape of a first draft. But writing that draft won't require skills significantly different from those outlined at the beginning of this handbook for composing any kind of college essay.

To write a successful research paper . . .

▶ **Make sure you have a point to make.** All the while you are reading and taking notes, you should be testing your preliminary thesis. Is it a significant issue? Can you deal with the whole topic in a short essay? Would you be better off writing about only one aspect of the preliminary subject? Will readers care about the subject you have selected? How can you make them care? These and questions like them are normal in the early stages of composing a research paper. They may prompt you to revise your preliminary hypothesis several times before you are done—or discard it entirely. (See 24A.)

But you can't remain indecisive forever. Sooner or later (sooner is better) you have to fix on the point you want your paper to make. It may not be the best point, or the most profound subject, or the most memorable topic in your class— but it is yours, and you still have lots of time to massage it into shape. Don't hesitate to ask your instructor and classmates what they think of your idea. Get second and third opinions. An outsider may see an exciting side to your subject you have missed.

So you needn't rush into a topic, but neither should you dawdle, expecting a great notion to drop from the sky. As you prepare to write a first draft, you should have a reasonable idea of what you want to say. You may end up arguing something different, but you have to start somewhere.

▶ **Draw the major ideas in your paper from several sources.** Don't rely on a single source for any large portion of your paper. Among the least successful research papers are those that simply clump the opinions of five or six authors together like a five-course meal, one author per paragraph. For a successful essay, you have to do a lot more than reprocess books and articles in the order you have read them. You have to consider how the sources work in relationship to each other. Do they agree? Disagree? Offer different points of view? Support each other? Suggest new issues?

Your job is to create the relationship between the authors you have read, and to add your own ideas. Odds are good that your sources have never been examined in exactly the way you have read them. Your perspective on the subject is unique, but only if you take the time to think seriously about your materials, your topic, your readers, and yourself. (See 24B, "From Notes to Ideas.")

▶ **Make scratch outlines for the whole paper and for smaller parts of it.** Working from a plan, even a rough one, is easier than writing without any direction at all. Begin by flipping through your note cards. Stack them, arrange them, and rearrange them until their facts and ideas start to fall into place. Then, with the cards as a guide, make a scratch outline for the whole paper—nothing elaborate, just your thesis, followed by the four or five major subpoints.

22D

Put your thesis on the page in front of you as a reminder of what you want to write. Then check to see how each of your main points helps to explain or support that thesis. Consider the order of your subpoints. Would a reader understand why your first point comes before your second one, and the second before the third, and so on? If not, do you *have* a good reason for the order you selected? If so, how can you help your readers figure out your thinking? If not, you may want to reconsider your original scratch outline.

It may help if you ask yourself what your readers need to know first about your subject. Where does this background information lead? What ideas do you want your readers to be thinking about at the end of the essay? How can you get them there?

It isn't likely you can resolve all these issues before you begin writing. Ideas have a way of following their own paths once they get moving. So don't hesitate to modify your original scratch outline while drafting a paper. And as you work through that draft, keep making tentative outlines for sections or paragraphs of the essay. These interim outlines needn't be complicated (or neat). Draw up several at a time to test your options; don't feel committed to any of them. Toss them out as soon as you think up something better. But do try scratch outlines as a way of plotting your ideas while you navigate the not-always-placid trails of a first draft. For examples of scratch outlines, see 24C.

▶ **Write a first draft early.** Think of the first draft as the testing ground for your thesis. Many months before new automobiles are introduced to the public, hand-built prototypes are run thousands of miles on test tracks that simulate road conditions. In a similar way, your draft tests your thesis under difficult situations: will it stand up to demands for facts, evidence, and proof? Will it sustain itself against possible counterarguments? Will it be interesting and surprising enough to keep readers on the road?

22D

You really won't know until you try your ideas out. So get them down on paper early—perhaps even before you have completed all your research. Remember that you don't have to write any paper—especially a long one—straight through from beginning to end. While you are doing your research, write any portion of the paper that seems "ready." But as your research draws to a preliminary conclusion, commit yourself to composing a full draft. Plan on finishing this draft about halfway through the time allotted for the paper. If, for example, you have a month for the paper, resolve to have a draft in hand in two weeks.

Why so early? Because you'll want time to fill in gaps and solidify your positions. You may have to return to the library to read more and gather additional facts. You may need to revise your stance entirely or restructure your essay. You will also want to polish your style. Early versions can afford to be ragged and cluttered; a final draft cannot. The more time you allow yourself between a first attempt—even a very rough draft—and the version you turn in, the better your research paper is likely to be.

Remember, too, that the final stages of producing a research paper may involve steps not required in other essays: doing an outline, managing documentation, preparing a *Works Cited* page, and so on. You have to allocate time for these extras as you bring the paper to market. So get the prototype— your first draft—on the test track as early as possible.

▶ **Test your conclusions against your introduction and make any needed modifications.** Sometimes the end of your essay will not agree with your opening. What has happened is that your original idea has matured and developed: you have learned or discovered something.

Yet, a surprising number of writers don't bother to readjust their opening paragraphs to reflect their new conclusions. They aren't lazy; they just don't realize how far they have moved since they wrote that introduction hours or, more likely, days earlier. When you've completed a draft, put it aside for a day or two, and then reread the entire piece. Does it all hang together? If not, revise.

22E WHAT SHOULD A RESEARCH PAPER LOOK LIKE?

Terms you need to know

> **Abstract.** A prose summary of an article or paper, usually no more than a hundred words long.

> **Appendix.** A section or sections at the end of a paper incorporating information important to the essay, but indirectly related to the main subject or too long to incorporate into the essay itself. An appendix might

include statistics, figures, charts, long quotations, and so on. Rare in undergraduate essays, appendixes usually follow the text of an essay and precede the *Works Cited* page.

Front matter. Any material that precedes the body of an essay: dedication, table of contents, foreword, preface, acknowledgments, introduction, abstract, and so on. These features are usually optional in undergraduate essays.

Outline. A formal plan of an entire essay, showing, in skeletal fashion, the thesis, the major divisions of the paper, and the major points of evidence. Outlines, when required, usually precede the body of an essay.

Troubleshooting

You can recognize a research paper almost as much by appearance as by what it says. Because these essays represent a first level of serious academic and professional research, most teachers expect research papers to have features not found in ordinary essays and to look more formal. These requirements vary from discipline to discipline and from teacher to teacher. Some instructors are flexible about their standards, provided that the handling of textual matters (margins, headings, documentation) is reasonably consistent throughout a paper. Other instructors allow little deviation from prescribed standards. To play it safe, be consistent and careful when writing a research paper.

Many writers, however, worry excessively about format requirements and forget that the most important feature of a research paper is its content—what it has to offer. A beautiful text is worthless if it presents no new ideas. Yet neither is it good strategy to do fine research and then make yourself appear incompetent—especially when the format requirements of a research paper are relatively easy to manage.

 ▶ **Type your paper.** If you type only one paper during a term, this should be it. If you aren't a good typist, you may want to take this essay to a typing service. A research paper shouldn't look like an amateur effort, full of strike-overs, white-outs, and wandering margins. Also, be sure the keys in your typewriter are clean and the ribbon has some ink in it—and don't experiment with colors. Use good quality paper, type only on one side, and double-space the body of your essay and the notes. If you can see through the paper, don't type on it.

If you write your research paper by hand, try to approximate a typed text: neat margins, clean surface, legible sentences. Use dark ink (blue or black), double-space (unless your instructor says otherwise), and write on only one side of the paper. Try to put a reasonable number of words on a page. Some students who sprawl their words fit no more than three or four sentences on a sheet. Such handwriting is difficult to read and looks juvenile.

If you use a word-processor, be sure your printer produces acceptable copy. If your machine produces print that is difficult to read, show your instructor a page of copy to be sure he or she will accept your paper. Some computers can vary type faces and produce boldface and italics. Keep the type faces simple and use boldface strategically to highlight important headings. Never type an entire paper in boldface. In bibliographies and notes, you may use italics for titles you would have underlined on a typewriter. Buy good quality computer paper, and be sure to separate the pages and pull off the tractor tabs before handing in an essay.

▶ **Be consistent.** Whatever scheme or format you decide upon for your research essay, stick with it throughout the paper. Keep your margins even, all around the page: a one-inch margin works well top, bottom, left, and right. Don't change typewriters or paper. Don't vary the way you handle titles or headings.

Locate page numbers in the same place throughout an essay (usually in the upper right-hand corner, one inch from the right margin, half an inch from the top of the page). Beginning with page two, include your last name and first initial before the page number just in case the body of your paper gets separated from its title page.

Corporation's near-bankruptcy in 1979–80 was a concept called "the sales bank" which exemplified the lack

▶ **Include all the parts your assignment requires.** Before
you turn a paper in, reread the assignment sheet to review your
instructor's requirements for the essay. In some cases, the
assignment will require you to follow a documentation scheme
or style sheet different from the MLA form used in this text.
Be sure to do so.

Check to see what leeway (if any) you have in handling title
pages or other features. The sample research essay on pp.
701–29 presents you with a model for a research essay based
on MLA style. Three features are discussed below.

——**Title Page**. Title pages are not ordinarily required for
undergraduate essays following MLA style. But if your
teacher requests an outline for your paper, you will probably
also need a title page. A reasonable format for a separate title
page appears in the sample research essay, p. 702.

22E

More typically, you may combine the title page and first
page of your essay, as in the sample page reproduced (in
reduced form) below. Your name should appear one inch from
the top of the page, flush with the left-hand margin (also one
inch). The information beneath your name (instructor, course
title, date) should be double-spaced. The title of the essay
appears, centered, a double space below the date. The essay
begins a quadruple space beneath the title. Note that only the
major words in a title are capitalized and that it is neither
underlined nor placed between quotation marks. A page
number appears one inch from the right margin, half an inch
from the top.

——**Outline/front matter**. Some teachers may ask you to include an outline of your research paper. The outline is inserted
immediately after the title page on a separate sheet. It is not
numbered unless it goes beyond a single page (it probably
shouldn't) or there is additional front matter. Front matter,
which would include the table of contents, an introduction,

James Balarbar

Professor Ruszkiewicz

English 101

10 November 1985

Chrysler's Sales Bank

The old Chrysler Corporation was an
excellent example of how not to run a
business. Its management was shortsighted
and disorganized; its method of conducting
business, completely unorthodox. In fact,
according to Lee Iacocca, chairman of the
reformed company,

> . . . Chrysler didn't really
> function like a company at all.
> Chrysler in 1978 was like Italy in
> the 1860's - the company consisted
> of little duchies, each one run by
> a prima donna. It was a bunch of
> mini-empires, with nobody giving a
> damn about what anyone else was
> doing. (152)

However, if a business is to prosper, it
must have a central authority, "coordination
and a unity of purpose" (Albers 206).

acknowledgments, outline, and so on, is numbered in small Roman numbers—*i.*, *ii.*, *iii.*, *iv.* Arabic numerals begin with the first page of the body of the essay.

The outline you insert in the completed research paper may differ from the scratch outlines you used in writing the paper. Those earlier outlines were flexible skeletons, designed to test organizational strategies for your essay. The paper you wrote probably veered from your original plan.

The outline you hand in with the paper should accurately reflect the structure of the finished essay. Hence, it should be written after the paper is completed and list the thesis of the essay, its major points, and its significant evidence. The outline gives a reader an overview of your essay, not a detailed anatomy.

Whether you use a sentence or phrase outline, be sure it is correctly structured. See the sample research essay, pp. 706–7.

—**Abstract**. Your teacher may ask you to prepare an abstract of the paper you wrote. The abstract ordinarily appears on a separate page after the outline and immediately preceding the body of the essay. It is not paginated. The word "Abstract" is centered on the page, one inch from the top. The abstract itself begins a double or quadruple space below this title.

For advice on how to write an abstract, see Special Assignments, p. 734. An abstract appears in the sample research essay, p. 708.

▶ **Assemble the parts of your essay in the proper order.** Your paper may not have all the parts listed below, but here is the order a typical undergraduate essay follows:

 —Title page (optional with instructor or assignment);

 —Outline (optional; begins on its own page; requires separate title page);

 —Abstract (optional; usually on its own page);

—Body of the essay (Arabic pagination begins with body of the essay);

—Appendixes (if any; not common in undergraduate essays);

—Content or bibliographic notes (begin on their own page);

—Works Cited (begins on its own page).

For a more complex paper such as a Master's thesis or dissertation, follow the order recommended either by an instructor or a volume such as *The MLA Style Manual*.

▶ **Follow the rules for documentation right down to the punctuation and spacing.** Accurate documentation is part of professional research. Instructors and editors notice even minor variances in documentation form. Perhaps the two most common errors in handling the MLA format are placing a comma where none is needed in parenthetical documentation and forgetting to put a period at the end of entries in the *Works Cited* list.

22E

> {**Wrong**} (Clancy, 368–369)
>
> {**Right**} (Clancy 368–369)
>
> {**Wrong**} Clancy, Tom. The Hunt for Red October. Annapolis: Naval Institute, 1984
>
> {**Right**}   Clancy, Tom. The Hunt for Red October. Annapolis: Naval Institute, 1984.

You will survive both errors, but they are easy to avoid. For full coverage of documentation, refer to the next chapter.

▶ **Edit the body of your research essay carefully.** Below is a list of some of the most common slips you are likely to make.

—Check spelling: look for transposed letters, slips of the pen, illegible words, and omitted endings, especially *-ed* and *-s*. See Section 21A.

—Check possessive forms. Don't forget the apostrophe (') before or after the -s: boy's, boys'. Don't confuse *its* (possessive form) with *it's* (contraction for *it is*). See Section 14B.

—Check capitalization. See Section 20A.

—Check punctuation. Eliminate comma splices and fused sentences. See Sections 10C–10D.

—Check to see that titles of books, plays, and other long or major works are underlined: <u>The Hunt for Red October</u>. (If you have a printer that can produce italics, all underlined words can be printed as italics.) See Section 18G.

—Check to see that titles of articles, songs, and short poems are set between quotation marks: "Straight from the Heart." See Section 18G.

—Check for words or phrases that have been omitted from your text or words that have been inadvertently repeated.

—Check for errors that crop up regularly in essays you write.

22E

▶ **Check special research paper requirements.**
As you finish up, run through this roster of questions.

—Name, date, course on first or title page?

—Title centered? Only major words capitalized? (Your title should not be underlined.)

—Did you number the pages? Are they in the right order?

—Have you used quotation marks and parentheses correctly and *in pairs*? The closing quotation mark and parenthesis are often forgotten.

—Have you placed quotation marks (" ") around all direct quotations shorter than four lines? See Section 23B.

—Have you indented all direct quotations over four lines long? (Remember that indented quotations are not placed between quotation marks.) See Section 23B.

—Did you introduce all direct quotations with some identification of their author, source, or significance? See Section 23B.

—Did you use the correct form for parenthetical notes? See Section 23C or 23D.

—Did you include a list of *Works Cited*? Is your list of *Works Cited* alphabetically arranged? Did you indent the entries correctly? See Section 23C or 23D.

▶ **Bind your paper sensibly.** You should be proud of your research paper, but don't treat it like a Gutenberg Bible. Bind it together modestly with a paper clip. Nothing more elaborate is needed—unless your teacher also asks you to hand in all the drafts, bibliography cards, note cards, photocopies, and other materials used in preparing the essay. If that is the case, place the essay (still clipped) and related materials in a sturdy envelope or in a folder with pockets.

Check with your instructor before stapling a research paper; some teachers like to read essays with the outline or *Works Cited* list placed alongside the body of the paper so that they can keep track of your organization and references. If you staple the essay, they can't do this as easily.

Don't even consider handing in an essay that is not clipped together.

▶ **Examine a sample research paper.** It may help you to check your paper against the sample essay provided in Chapter 24: A Research Paper from Start to Finish. The paper demonstrates many of the features discussed in this section.

● **Fine Tuning**

Some computers and printers can set italic letters as easily as they can underline words. If your word processing equipment has this capacity, you may italicize any titles that you would otherwise have underlined.

> {**Underlined**} Kenneth Clark's <u>Civilisation</u> surveys . . .

> {**Italicized**} Kenneth Clark's *Civilisation* surveys . . .

One complication of the *Works Cited* page: when an underlined or italicized title (*Hamlet*) becomes part of another title (<u>The Question of</u>), it is no longer underlined or italicized:

> {**Underlined**} Levin, Harry. <u>The Question of</u> Hamlet.

> {**Italicized**} Levin, Harry, *The Question of* Hamlet.

22E

CHAPTER

How Do You Document a Research Paper?

■ **A** What do you document?
■ **B** How do you handle quotations?
■ **C** MLA form
■ **D** APA form
■ **E** How do you avoid plagiarism and collusion?

Terms you need to know

> **Common knowledge.** Facts, dates, events, information, and concepts generally known to an educated public.
>
> **Documentation.** The evidence you provide a reader to support an idea or fact you present in a research paper. Documentation usually directs readers to printed sources of information: books, articles, tables of statistics, and so on. But it may also cite interviews, software, films, television programs, and other nonprint media. Various systems for handling documentation have been devised. Presented in this handbook are systems used by the Modern Language Association (**MLA**) and the American Psychological Association (**APA**). The sample research paper and most examples in the text follow MLA form.

Parenthetical documentation. A form of documentation that places information about sources between parentheses right in the body of an essay itself, instead of in **footnotes** or **endnotes**. With a few exceptions, parenthetical notes have largely replaced the older footnote and endnote systems.

Footnote/endnote documentation. A form of documentation that places information about sources outside the body of an essay either in notes at the bottom of a page or in a list of notes at the end of a paper. Raised numbers appear in the text, keyed to the individual notes.[3] Parenthetical documentation has generally replaced footnotes and endnotes, except for occasional **content notes** used to explain some point in the essay more fully and **bibliographic notes** employed to give readers facts about the sources used in preparing the essay.

Works cited. An alphabetical list of the works used in preparing a research essay. The list is called *Works Cited* if it consists only of materials actually mentioned in the essay itself and *Works Consulted* if it also includes materials examined in preparing the paper, but not actually noted in the body of the essay. *Works Cited* is now the standard title for research paper bibliographies.

23A WHAT DO YOU DOCUMENT?

Troubleshooting
You give credit to your sources in a research paper so that readers can assess the quality, credibility, and originality of your work. Citations let them know how thorough and up-to-date your investigation of a topic is. Source citations also direct readers to additional information on a subject should they be interested in reading more about what you have written.

But writers sometimes find it hard to decide what exactly has to be substantiated through documentation. Do you credit every fact, figure, and idea that appears in a paper? If a subject is new to you, doesn't that mean that virtually every sentence will have to include a citation? When does documentation become excessive?

Sometimes you need to provide readers with information that is, strictly speaking, not a part of your essay or argument. How do you do that without distracting the reader from the main body of your report? Is it scholarly to have lengthy explanatory footnotes in an undergraduate research paper—or just fussy?

To document a paper adequately . . .

▶ **Provide a source for every direct quotation.** A direct quotation is any material repeated word-for-word from a source. Most direct quotations in a college research paper require some form of parenthetical documentation—that is, a citation of author and page number (MLA) or author, date, and page number (APA).

> {MLA} It is possible to define literature as simply "that text which the community insists on having repeated from time to time intact" (Joos 51–52).

23A

> {APA} One researcher questions the value of attention-getting essay openings that "presuppose passive, uninterested (probably uninteresting) readers" (Hashimoto, 1986, p. 126).

You should also give credit for any diagrams, statistics, charts, or pictures in your paper that you reproduce from a source.

You need not document famous sayings, proverbs, or biblical citations ("A bird in the hand is worth two in the bush"; "The truth shall make you free"), but you should identify the author of any quotable phrases you include in your paper. A simple credit line is often enough for quotations used at the beginning of a paper or at chapter divisions:

> I remember your name perfectly, but I just can't think of your face.
>
> .   —William Archibald Spooner

▶ **Provide a citation for all ideas, opinions, facts, and information in your paper that you acquire from sources and that cannot be considered *common knowledge*.** In preparing a research paper, you need to record both what you have learned and where you learned it. In writing the paper, you'll use parenthetical notes to identify those portions of your essay based on the work of other authors. You'll also use these references to add authority and credibility to your assertions. The forms for parenthetical notes differ from discipline to discipline; two major systems are explained in Sections 23C and 23D below.

Many writers aren't sure what they must document in a research paper and what information they can assume is common knowledge—which does not require a note. The difficulty increases when writing on a totally new, unfamiliar subject. In such a case, everything in a paper is borrowed, in one way or another, from a book, article, encyclopedia, or other source. Is it necessary to document every fact, concept, and idea since they are, indeed, someone else's material?

23A

To answer this question, begin with the definition of **common knowledge**: facts, dates, events, information, and concepts generally known to an educated public. No individual owns the facts about history, physics, social behavior, geography, current events, popular culture, and so on. You may need to check an encyclopedia to find out that the Battle of Waterloo was fought on June 18, 1815, but that fact belongs to common knowledge. You don't have to cite a source to assert that Neil Armstrong was the first man to land on the moon, that Freud was the founder of psychiatry, that Charlie Chaplin was a famous comedian, or that the Protestant Reformation was both a religious and political movement.

But if our culture shares a body of common knowledge, so does each discipline. And in writing a paper on a particular subject, you may also make some assumptions about *common knowledge within a field*. When you find that a given piece of information or an idea is shared among several of the sources you are using, you need not document it. If, for example, you were writing a paper on anorexia nervosa and discovered that most of your authors define the condition in approximately the same way and describe the same five or six symptoms, you could talk about these basic facts without providing a credit for every one. (You might, however, want to quote a particular definition of the condition from one of your sources.) Experts on anorexia nervosa know what the condition is and does. What the experts know collectively constitutes the common knowledge within the field about the subject; what they assert individually—their opinions, studies, theories, research projects, and hypotheses—is the material you *must* document in a paper.

▶ **Provide a citation for all ideas, opinions, facts, and information in your paper that your readers might either want to know more about or might question.** The discussion above suggests that you do *not* have to document laboriously every fact and idea in a research paper just because it is new to you or your readers. Your strict responsibility is to credit material that is not—so far as you can tell—common knowledge in your topic area.

But you should ordinarily go somewhat beyond your strict responsibilities, anticipating where readers might ask the questions: **Is this true?** or **Who says so?** The more controversial your subject, the more you may want to provide documentation, even for material that might be considered common knowledge within a discipline. Suppose, for example, you are writing a paper about witchcraft and make some historical assertions well-known by scholars within the field but liable to be surprising or suspect to nonspecialists. If you are writing to the audience of nonspecialists, you should certainly provide documentation for the historical assertions. If you are writing to experts on witchcraft, however, you would not have to cite sources for what they would consider basic information.

▶ **Provide content notes as needed, but sparingly.** Both major systems of documentation—MLA and APA—have done away with footnotes and endnotes for most routine citations of sources. MLA, however, preserves **content notes** located in a list at the end of a paper (immediately after the body of the essay and before the *Works Cited* page). They are identified in the paper itself by superscript numbers at the end of a sentence:

. . . the matter remains undecided.[3]

Content notes might be used:

—to discuss a point made in the text,

—to furnish a definition,

—to provide an explanation for a statistic or calculation,

—to expand upon what is said in the body of the essay,

—to acknowledge assistance, grants, and support.

In general, if the discussion of an idea is important enough to merit a lengthy note, it probably belongs in the body of the essay itself. Even short content notes can be distracting, especially if they are numerous. Rely on content notes only when you absolutely need them: that is, when the information is essential to understanding your paper, yet would interrupt the flow of the essay if inserted within the text itself.

MLA also permits **bibliographical notes**. Like content notes, bibliographical notes are identified by raised superscript numbers and located in a list at the end of a paper. (An essay that contains both content and bibliographical notes would combine them in a single list and number them, consecutively, from the beginning of the essay.) Bibliographical notes are used:

23A

—to evaluate sources,

—to direct readers to other sources,

—to list multiple sources when necessary,

—to name a work or edition that will appear many times in parenthetical citations.

Sources (books, articles, newspapers) mentioned in a content or bibliographic note are also listed on the *Works Cited* page. Here are notes from the sample research paper reproduced in the next chapter. The first is both a content and bibliographic note, the second a content note only.

[1]Lee Iaccoca joined Chrysler in November, 1978 after Henry Ford II removed him from the presidency of

the Ford Motor Company. See Iacocca 120-53; Moritz and Seaman 196-97.

²According to Stuart Reginald, within his first year as president of Chrysler, Iacocca had abolished the sales bank: "Come hell or high water, we are never going to do it again!" (15).

Content and bibliographic notes are relatively rare in undergraduate essays. Use them whenever your paper requires the extra explanations or sources they can provide. But don't get carried away. Notes distract from the body of your essay.

▶ **Provide dates, identifications, and other information to assist the reader.** When writing a research paper, particularly on a topic from history, philosophy, literature, drama, art, communication, government, or law, you will do readers a service if you date important events, major figures, and works of literature and art. Also be careful to identify any individuals readers might not recognize:

23A

After the great fire of London (1666), the city was . . .

Henry Highland Garnet (1815–82), American abolitionist and radical, . . .

Pearl (c.1400), an alliterative elegy about a daughter, . . .

[The c. before the date stands for *circa*—which means "about"—see p. 669 for a list of other abbreviations common in documentation.]

When quoting from literary works, provide information readers would need to locate any lines you are citing. For novels, you should supply page and chapter numbers; for plays give act/scene/line information; for long poems provide line numbers and, when appropriate, division numbers (book, canto, or other division).

Troubleshooting

Some writers want to treat direct quotations like electronic modules: plug them in at the appropriate spots in the circuit board and the device should operate. Unfortunately, quotations don't work that way. You have to select them purposefully, introduce them intelligently, and tailor them to fit your language. Never think of quotations as an easy substitute for your own words. If you do, you are misusing them. The last thing a research paper should be is a patchwork of quotations. If yours looks that way, you've got a problem.

To handle quotations effectively . . .

▶ **Select them carefully.** Every direct quotation in an essay should be there because it contributes something to the paper that your own words could not. You may want to **use a quotation . . .**

—as a focal point for an essay. Here James Balarbar, author of the sample research paper on pp. 701-29, uses a quotation early in his essay to describe a company plagued with management problems. This is his first paragraph:

> The old Chrysler Corporation is an excellent example of how not to run a business. Its management was shortsighted and disorganized; its method of conducting business, completely unorthodox. In fact according to Lee Iacocca, chairman of the newly reformed company,
>
> > . . . Chrysler didn't really function like a company at all. Chrysler in 1978 was like Italy in the 1860's— the company consisted of little duchies, each one run by a prima donna. It was a bunch of mini-empires, with nobody giving a damn about what anyone else was doing. (152)

626

—as a representative statement of an opinion or idea. In a portrait of Wesley Poriotis, a campaigner against age discrimination, the author of the passage Brian Hickey quotes a few lines of dialogue to explain the basic problem.

> "He told me, 'Anyone over 50 I throw away.' I asked him, 'How old are you?' he said, 'Forty-six.' Then he looked at me again and said, 'Wow. I didn't think of that.'"

> It is one of many stories Poriotis tells of a condition in the American work place diagnosed as chronic age discrimination.

—as an assertion of facts. Here, in his research paper on the safety of nuclear plants, Darwin Washington uses a quotation to report some surprising facts.

> Despite the accident at Chernobyl, many people still believe that nuclear powerplants are inherently less life-threatening than fossil fuel plants. Roger Starr makes a graphic point about the dangers of nuclear radiation:

> > The radioactive discharges at the gates of a nuclear power station are so minor that, in one year, someone living next to a nuclear station would be exposed to no more extra radiation than on a single flight from New York to California and back, at altitudes partly above the atmosphere that filters out cosmic radiation. Similarly, the ambient radiation readings from the granite in St. Peter's Square in Rome are higher than the permitted radiation at the gates of a nuclear power plant (373).

—as a voice that adds authority to an assertion you have made. Barbara Neilson, in an article for *Exxon USA* magazine, quotes an expert to prove that the fishing in Louisiana is superb:

The Pelican State, like its state bird, depends on what it can pull out of the sea. From Louisiana's offshore waters come a rich harvest of oil and gas and about one-third of America's fishery products. So bountiful is the resource that commercial fishers flock from Texas, Mississippi, Alabama, Georgia, and especially Florida to fish Lousiana waters.

"Without a doubt, Louisiana is number one in the nation in fish and shellfish production," says tall, lanky Corky Perret, assistant secretary of the Coastal and Marine Division of the Lousiana Department of Wildlife and Fisheries. **"In 1984, the dockside value for our commercial fisheries was around $263 million and weighed nearly two billion pounds."**

—to show a diversity of opinion. Here, John J. Putnam, writing about Switzerland for the *National Geographic*, builds almost an entire paragraph out of quotations that express Swiss self-criticisms.

One has to admire what the Swiss had done with so few people, so little land. I knew all the criticisms, those of the Swiss themselves. In a nuclear age, the army was **"damned expensive folklore." "This trying to be safe alone, to be preserved no matter what happens to others, is a kind of blindness." "We try to stack our lives as neatly as we stack our firewood." "There is always among us the necessity to go to Paris, to Munich, to Milan, and then the necessity to come back; the desire to be universal, but also particular."**

A paragraph this dependent on quotations would be rare in most research papers, but there are times when you can make an effective point by piling quotation upon quotation. Readers begin to feel the weight of your evidence.

—to clarify a point. Tom Callahan, writing about the Army's remarkably successful recruiting slogan, uses the words of Craig Reiss, an advertising expert, to examine the campaign:

Be All You Can Be started in 1981 when studies showed that young people were most interested in

23B

628

learning technical skills and being personally challenged. Explains Craig Reiss of *Advertising Age* magazine:

> The army's approach to advertising changed with the end of the [Vietnam] war and the decline of the effectiveness of the bachelor's degree to get you job skills and an entry-level position. They began to use technology in their ads to position themselves as a big high-tech training school. That proved to be very effective because what else can you do in a peacetime army? You really can't use the emotional argument that you have to join to defend the country.

—to demonstrate the complexity of a point. Here Daniel Boorstin lets famous scientist William Harvey use his own words to describe the motions of the heart:

> When [William] Harvey began to study the heart, doctors were not yet agreed on whether the heart was at work when it expanded, which seemed to coincide with the expansion of the veins, or when it contracted He starts with a rudimentary description of how the heart works.

> In the first place, then, in the hearts of all animals still surviving after the chest has been opened and the capsule immediately investing the heart has been divided, one can see the heart alternating between movement and rest, moving at one time, devoid of movement at another. . . . Muscles in active movement gain in strength, contract, change from soft to hard, rise up and thicken; and similarly the heart. . . .

▶ **Never use a quotation as a way to avoid writing.** Quotations should not be devices for padding your paper. Nor should you rely on them to say something you could have said competently in your own words. Respect your sources. Don't turn them into the academic equivalent of junk food restaurants—where you dine without paying attention to what you are eating.

▶ **Introduce all direct quotations in some way.** Quotations are special. When reading a direct quotation, readers should realize that they are encountering words that aren't yours. To be sure they do, even well-selected and purposeful quotations need to be introduced or framed. While quotation marks or indentions help identify material as borrowed, these typographical devices don't tell a reader who wrote a passage, why it is significant, or in what relationship it stands to the rest of an essay. A short introduction or a few words of commentary can supply this strategic information.

In most writing, quotations are either **integral** parts of sentences or they are framed by words or phrases **preceding** them, **following** them, or **interrupting** them. The frames need not be in the same sentence as the quotation; they are often part of the **surrounding** paragraph.

{**Quotation integrated with sentence**—selection by Daniel Yankelovich}

The study concludes that a faulty work ethic is not responsible for the decline in our productivity; quite the contrary, the study identifies "a widespread commitment among U.S. workers to improve productivity" and suggests that "there are large reservoirs of potential upon which management can draw to improve performance and increase productivity."

{**Frame precedes quotation**—selection by Douglas Colligan}

In one report to earth, the first [Skylab] crew crossed chili off their eating schedule. **Every time they opened a container of it, there was an explosion of food:** "Great goblets of chili go flying all over; it's bad news."

{**Frame follows quotation**—selection by Barbara Lang Stern}

"One reason you may have more colds if you hold back tears is that, when you're under stress, your body puts out steroids which affect your immune system and reduce your resistance to disease," **Dr. Broomfield comments.**

{**Frame interrupts quotation**—selection by Kevin Strehlo}

"In principle," **says John Kert**, "dolphins can spell a word as fast as we can say it . . . ."

{**Surrounding sentences frame quotation**—selection by Douglas Colligan}

Even taste is affected by zero-g. "Body fluids migrate to your upper body, and you end up with engorged tissue around the nasal passages and ear," **explains Gerald Carr, who was commander of the third and longest (eighty-four days) Skylab mission.** "You carry with you a constant state of nasal and head congestion in weightless environment. It feels pretty much like you have a cold all the time."

What this means for your own writing is that you should habitually frame or introduce every quotation in your paper. Either identify (directly or indirectly) the author, speaker, or the work the passage is from, or explain why the words you are quoting are significant.

A quotation may, however, stand alone at the head of a chapter or essay—as a focal point for subsequent discussion. Here, Arthur Schlesinger, Jr., opens an essay of his own with a line borrowed from George Orwell.

> In our time, political speech and writing are largely the defence of the indefensible.
>
> —George Orwell

It takes a certain fortitude to pretend to amend Orwell on this subject. But "Politics and the English Language"—which I hereby incorporate by reference— was written more than a generation ago. In the years since, the process of semantic collapse has gathered speed, verified all of Orwell's expectations, and added new apprehensions for a new age . . . .

▶ **Tailor quotations to fit the focus of your paper or argument.** Occasionally, you may find that only part of a long quotation suits your essay. Or sometimes a word or phrase

23B

crucial to understanding an idea may not appear in a passage you intend to quote. In such cases, you may:

—use ellipses (three spaced periods . . .) to indicate where you have cut material from direct quotations. Ellipses might be used, for example, to trim the lengthy passage below if a writer quoting from it wanted to focus primarily on the oldest portions of the biblical text. The ellipses would tell a reader where words, phrases, and even whole sentences have been cut.

> {**Original passage**} The text of the Old Testament is in places the stuff of scholarly nightmares. Whereas the entire New Testament was written within fifty to a hundred years, the books of the Old Testament were composed and edited over a period of about a thousand. The youngest book is Daniel, from the second century B.C. The oldest portions of the Old Testament (if we limit ourselves to the present form of the literature and exclude from consideration the streams of oral tradition that fed it) are probably a group of poems that appear, on the basis of linguistic features and historical allusions contained in them, to date from roughly the twelfth and eleventh centuries B.C. . . .

> —Barry Hoberman, "Translating the Bible"

> {**Passage as cut for use in an essay**} Although working with any part of an original scripture text is difficult, Hoberman describes the text of the Old Testament as **"the stuff of scholarly nightmares."** He explains in "Translating the Bible" that while **"the entire New Testament was written within fifty to a hundred years, the books of the Old Testament were composed and edited over a period of about a thousand. . . . The oldest portions of the Old Testament . . . are probably a group of poems that appear . . . to date from roughly the twelfth and eleventh centuries B.C. . . ."**

When ellipses occur in the middle of a sentence, leave a space before the first period and after the third one. (Remember that the periods themselves are spaced.)

> "We the people of the United States . . . do ordain and establish this Constitution for the United States of America."

When they occur at the end of a sentence or passage, place the first period immediately after the last word, and add a fourth period to mark the end of the sentence.

> "These are the times that try men's souls. The summer soldier and the sunshine patriot will, in this crisis, shrink from the service of his country. . . ."
>
> —Thomas Paine

The same form (four periods) is employed when entire sentences or paragraphs are omitted.

Occasionally, ellipses appear at the beginning of quoted sentences to indicate that an opening clause or phrase has been omitted. Three spaced periods precede the sentence, with a space left between the third period and the first letter of the sentence. Any punctuation occurring at the end of the clause or sentence preceding the quotation is retained:

> The text of the Old Testament is in places the stuff of scholarly nightmares. . . . the books of the Old Testament were composed and edited over a period of about a thousand [years].
>
> —Barry Hoberman, "Translating the Bible"

23B

You needn't use an ellipses, however, every time you break into a sentence. The quotation in the following passage, for example, reads more smoothly without the ellipses.

> In fact, according to Lee Iacocca, ". . . Chrysler didn't really function like a company at all" when he arrived in 1978.

> In fact, according to Lee Iacocca, "Chrysler didn't really function like a company at all" when he arrived in 1978.

Whenever you use ellipses, be sure your shortened quotation still accurately reflects the meaning of the uncut passage.

—use square brackets [ ] to add necessary information to a quotation. Sometimes, for example, you may want to explain who or what a pronoun refers to, or you may have to provide a short explanation, furnish a date, and explain or translate a puzzling word.

Some critics clearly prefer Wagner's *Lohengrin* to *Tannhäuser*: "the well-written choruses [of ***Tannhäuser***] are combined with solo singing and orchestral background into long, unified musical scenes" (Grout 629).

As one source explains, "No battle was ever more hard-fought than Hastings [**1066**]; no battle has had more momentous results" (Dupuy 289).

And so Iacocca accepted Chrysler's offer: "We agreed that I would come in as president but would become chairman and CEO [**Chief Executive Officer**] on January 1, 1980" (Iacocca 145).

But don't overdo it. Readers will resent the explanation of obvious details. If, for example, most of your prospective readers would know that the Battle of Hastings was fought in 1066, such an explanation would be unnecessary.

—use [sic] to indicate an obvious error copied faithfully from a quotation. Quotations must be copied accurately, word-by-word from your source—even including obvious errors. To show that you have copied a passage faithfully, place the expression sic (the Latin word for *thus* or *so*) in brackets one space after any mistake.

23B

Mr. Vincent's letter went on: "I would have preferred a younger bride, but I decided to marry the old window [**sic**] anyway."

If sic can be placed outside of the quotation itself, it appears between parentheses, not brackets.

Molly's paper was entitled "Understanding King Leer" (**sic**).

▶ **Tailor your language so that direct quotations fit into the grammar of your sentences.** To do this, you may have to tinker with the introduction to the quotation or modify the quotation itself by a careful selection, an ellipsis, or a bracketed addition.

{**Awkward**} The chemical capsaicin that makes chili hot: "it is so hot it is used to make antidog and anti-mugger sprays" (Bork 184).

{**Revised**} Capsaicin, the chemical that makes chili hot, is so strong "it is used to make antidog and antimugger sprays" (Bork 184).

{**Awkward**} Computers have not succeeded as translators of languages because, says Douglas Hofstadter, "nor is the difficulty caused by a lack of knowledge of idiomatic phrases. The fact is that translation involves having a mental model of the world being discussed, and manipulating symbols in the model."

{**Revised**} "A lack of knowledge of idiomatic phrases" is not the reason computers have failed as translators of languages. "The fact is," says Douglas Hofstadter, "that translation involves having a mental model of the world being discussed, and manipulating symbols in the model" (603).

▶ **Place quotations shorter than four typed lines between quotation marks.**

> In *On Liberty* (1859), John Stuart Mill declares that "If all mankind minus one were of one opinion, mankind would be no more justified in silencing that one person than he, if he had the power, would be justified in silencing mankind."

▶ **Indent ten spaces any prose quotations longer than four typed lines.** Quotation marks are not used around the indented material. If the quotation extends beyond a single paragraph, the first lines of subsequent paragraphs are indented an additional three typed spaces. In typed papers, the indented material—like the rest of the essay—is double spaced.

> Mill elaborates his point by explaining in a careful way exactly what is lost when any opinion—right or wrong—is forced into silence:

> . . . the peculiar evil of silencing the expression
> of an opinion is that it is robbing the human
> race, posterity as well as the existing genera-
> tion—those who dissent from the opinion, still
> more than those who hold it. If the opinion is
> right, they are deprived of the opportunity of
> exchanging error for truth; if wrong, they lose,
> what is almost as great a benefit, the clearer
> perception and livelier impression of truth pro-
> duced by its collision with error.
>
> It is necessary to consider separately these
> two hypotheses, each of which has a distinct
> branch of the argument corresponding to it. We
> can never be sure that the opinion we are en-
> deavoring to stifle is a false opinion; and if we
> were sure, stifling it would be an evil still.
> (62-63)

23B

You may indent passages of fewer than four lines when you want them to have special emphasis. But don't do this with every short quotation or your paper will look choppy.

▶ **Indent more than three lines of poetry.** Up to three lines of poetry may be handled just like a prose passage, with slashes marking the separate lines. Quotation marks are used.

> As death approaches, Cleopatra grows in grandeur and
> dignity: "Husband, I come! / Now to that name my cour-
> age prove my title! / I am fire and air" (V.ii. 287-89).

More than three lines of poetry are indented ten spaces and quotation marks are not used. (If the lines of poetry are un-usually long, you may indent fewer than ten spaces.) Double space the indented passage. Be sure to copy the poetry accurately, right down to the punctuation.

> Among the most famous lines in English literature are those that open William Blake's "The Tyger":
>
> > Tyger tyger, burning bright,
> > In the forests of the night;
> > What immortal hand or eye,
> > Could frame thy fearful symmetry?

When possible, you should attempt to duplicate any special typographical arrangement in the original text.

> George Herbert's poem "Easter Wings" (1633), among the most famous of the seventeenth century's "shaped poems," recognizes the weakness of human nature:
>
> > My tender age in sorrow did begin
> > And still with sickness and shame
> > Thou did so punish sin,
> > That I became
> > Most thin.

23B

▶ **Refer to events in works of fiction, poems, plays, movies, and television shows in the present tense.** When discussing passages from novels, scenes from a movie, or events in a poem, think about the actions as performances that occur over and over again.

> In his last speech, Othello **orders** those around him to "Speak of me as I am. Nothing extenuate, / Nor set down aught in malice" (V.ii.338–39). Then he **stabs** himself, and **dies, falling** on the bed of the innocent wife he has murdered only moments before: "I kissed thee ere I killed thee. No way but this, / Killing myself, to die upon a kiss" (354–55).

Troubleshooting

In most college English courses, you will be expected to follow the conventions of documentation and format recommended by the Modern Language Association (MLA). The basic procedures for MLA documentation are spelled out in the following section. If you encounter documentation problems not discussed below or go on to do advanced work in a discipline that follows MLA rules, you may want to refer to the *MLA Handbook for Writers of Research Papers* or *The MLA Style Manual*, both edited by Walter S. Achtert and Joseph Gibaldi. These books are available in most college libraries.

For typical sources (books, magazines, articles by single authors), systems of documentation are almost always more difficult to explain than to use. Once you get the hang of MLA style, you'll find it easy and efficient. But it is important to follow the rules carefully. Seemingly small matters, such as spacing and punctuation, do count when you are preparing notes and bibliographies. And be prepared to check this handbook frequently when you encounter a less than typical source: a computer program, a movie, a government document, an interview.

So the best advice for efficient documentation is this: know the basic procedure and check the details.

To use MLA documentation . . .

▶ **Overview: Follow these two steps.**

1. Insert an in-text note for every passage you need to document.

   While Beethoven enjoyed prosperity and success through 1815, his deafness continued to grow until he became "morose, irascible, and morbidly suspicious even toward his friends" (Grout 540).

2. Record every source mentioned in a parenthetical note (or used in the preparation of your paper) in an alphabetical list of *Works Cited* at the end of your essay.

23C

Works Cited

Grout, Donald Jay. <u>A History of Western Music</u>. 3rd. ed. New York: Norton, 1980.

▶ **Insert an in-text note for every passage you need to document.** The basic form of the MLA note consists of the author's last name and a page number between parentheses. A single typed space separates name and page number(s). No other punctuation is needed; the page number is not preceded by p. or pp.

(Grout 540)

(Iacocca 254–55)

The note is ordinarily located conveniently after a passage requiring documentation, preferably at the end of a sentence and within the final punctuation mark. However, with an indented quotation, the parenthetical note falls outside the final punctuation mark.

> While Beethoven enjoyed prosperity and success through 1815, his deafness continued to grow until he became "morose, irascible, and morbidly suspicious even toward his friends" (**Grout 540**).

Problems in the Chrysler factories grew steadily worse, as quality took a back seat to meeting production quotas:

> Sometimes the quality deteriorated to such an extent that the [assembly] lines were stopped. One engineer (now retired) made some spot checks. He discoverd a Plymouth sitting at a Detroit railhead with no engine mountings, the engine just resting on the frame. (**Moritz and Seaman 92**)

You can shorten a note by naming and identifying the author of the source in the body of the essay; then the note consists only of a page number.

> **Grout, a musicologist**, explains that while Beethoven enjoyed prosperity and success through 1815, his deaf-

23C

ness continued to grow until he became "morose, irascible, and morbidly suspicious even toward his friends" (**540**).

If two or more sources are used in a single sentence, the notes are inserted as needed conveniently after the statements they support.

While the ecology of the aquifer might be hardier than originally suspected (**Chesney 42–48**), there is no reason to believe that "the best interests of all the people of the county" (**Horus 62**) would be served by the creation of a mall and shopping district in a vicinity described as "one of the last outposts of undisturbed nature in the state" (**Munoz 28**).

Notice that a parenthetical note is placed outside of quotation marks but before the period ending the sentence.

Again, if the name of an author appears in the text of your passage, you don't have to repeat the author's name in a note.

23C

While **Harriett Chesney** argues that the ecology of the aquifer might be hardier than originally suspected (**42–48**), there is no reason to believe that "the best interests of all the people of the county" (**Horus 62**) would be served by the creation of a mall and shopping district in a vicinity described by naturalist **Raoul Munoz** as "one of the last outposts of undisturbed nature in the state" (**28**).

Similarly, you don't have to repeat an author's name in second and subsequent references to the same source provided that no other sources are mentioned between these references. After the first reference, page numbers are sufficient until another citation intervenes:

. . . the creation of a mall and shopping district in a vicinity described by naturalist **Raoul Munoz** as "one of the last outposts of undisturbed nature in the state" (**28**). The aquifer area provides a unique environment for several endangered species of birds and plantlife (**31**). The birds especially require breeding areas free from the encroaching signs of development: roads, lights, and human presence (**Harrison and Cafiero 189**). The plantlife is similarly susceptible to the plague of building and exploitation that has followed growth in other areas of the county (**Munoz 41**).

If a work has more than one author, you can either put the names of all the authors in the note or just the name of the first author followed by the expression **et al.** (Latin abbreviation for **"and others"**). The form you use should match your entry on the *Works Cited* page.

Note with all authors named: (Brooks and Heilman 24)

Works Cited:

Brooks, Cleanth, and R.J. Heilman, eds. Understanding Drama: Twelve Plays. New York: Holt, 1945.

Note with *et al.*: (Eastman et al. xxi–xxii)

Works Cited:

Eastman, Arthur M., et al., eds. The Norton Reader. 5th ed. New York: Norton, 1980.

23C

If you use more than one work by a single author in a paper, a parenthetical note that listed only the author's last name could refer, reasonably, to any entry on your *Works Cited* page by that author. To avoid such confusion in your note, simply place a comma after the author's name and add the title of the work you are using, followed by the page number. You may use a very shortened version of the title.

Works Cited

Altick, Richard D. The Art of Literary Research. New York: Norton, 1963.

—The Shows of London. Cambridge: Belknap-Harvard, 1978.

—Victorian People and Ideas. New York: Norton, 1973.

—Victorian Studies in Scarlet. New York: Norton, 1977.

Possible parenthetical notes:

(Altick, Shows 345)

(Altick, Victorian People 190–202)

(Altick, Victorian Studies 59)

Of course, if you mention the name of an author with multiple titles, you do not have to repeat it in the parenthetical note.

> Richard Altick reports that a record of the trial of Victorian murderer William Corder bound in his own skin is on exhibit at Moyse's Hall Museum in England, making Corder "one of the select company of murderers who were hanged, drawn, and quartoed" (*Victorian Studies* 64n).

> [The *n* following the page number indicates that the quotation is found in a footnote on p. 64.]

If you want to refer to a complete work, not just to certain pages, omit page references from the parenthetical note. Let us say that this is an article you use in preparing a paper on *Hamlet*:

Works Cited form:

Wentersdorf, Karl P. "Hamlet's Encounter with the Pirates." Shakespeare Quarterly 34 (1983): 434–40.

To cite the contents of the entire essay in your paper (not any particular pages), give only the author's name in parentheses.

Whole articles have been written even about Hamlet's encounter with the pirates in Act IV (Wentersdorf).

If you must document a work without an author—an article in a magazine, for example, or a newspaper story—simply list the title, shortened if necessary, and the page number.

("Aid to Education" 11)
("Subtle Art" 62)

Works Cited

"Aid to Education and Health Cut by $38-Million." The Chronicle of Higher Education. 18 Dec. 1985: 11.

"The Subtle Art of Stubble." Newsweek. 9 Dec. 1985: 62.

One basic rule for all parenthetical notes is to make them as inconspicuous and short as possible. Don't make your notes so intrusive that the text becomes hard to read. You may, however, cite more than a single work in a note by separating the citations with a semicolon.

(Polukord 13–16; Ryan and Weber 126)

But if a parenthetical citation grows so long that it interrupts the smooth reading of a sentence, a **bibliographical note** (see p. 624) may be a reasonable alternative. In a bibliographical note, you may string together as many sources as you need and comment on them:

[3]On this matter see Polukord 13–16; Granchi and Guillen 126; Valusek and Syrek 188–94; and Shortell 23–24. Holding the opposite view are Lyon 120–28 and Greely 148–49.

The particular forms for many kinds of parenthetical notes (books, articles, movies, collections, and so on) and their accompanying *Works Cited* entries are provided in the **MLA Form Directory** on pp. 647-48.

▶ **Record every source mentioned in a parenthetical note in an alphabetical list of *Works Cited*.** The *Works Cited* page appears at the end of your paper, after and separate

23C

from the body of the essay itself and a footnote page—if there is one. The format for a *Works Cited* page is given on p. 728. Be sure to double-space all entries in your list. The first line of each entry touches the left-hand margin and subsequent lines are indented five spaces.

Entries on the *Works Cited* page are listed alphabetically, by last names of authors. If a work has no given author, it is listed by title and alphabetized by the first word, excluding *a*, *an*, and *the*. Several works by a single author are listed alphabetically under that author's name.

A typical MLA *Works Cited* entry for a book includes the following basic information:

—Name of author(s), last name first, followed by a period and two spaces.

Altick, Richard D.

—Title of work, underlined, followed by a period and two spaces.

Victorian Studies in Scarlet.

—Place of publication, followed by a colon.

New York:

—Publisher (not necessary for works published prior to 1900), followed by a comma.

Norton,

Publisher's names should be shortened whenever possible. Drop words such as *Company, Inc.*, *LTD, Bro.*, *Books*, and so on. Abbreviate *University* to *U* and *University Press* to *UP*. When possible, shorten a publisher's name to one word. Here are some suggested abbreviations:

George Allen and Unwin Publishers, Inc.	Allen
Barnes and Noble Books	Barnes
Doubleday and Co., Inc.	Doubleday
Harvard University Press	Harvard UP
D. C. Heath and Co.	Heath
Rand McNally and Co.	Rand

Scott, Foresman and Co.   Scott
University of Chicago Press   U of Chicago P

> —Date of publication, followed by a period
>> 1977.

>> Altick, Richard D. Victorian Studies in Scarlet. New York: Norton, 1977.

A typical MLA *Works Cited* entry for an article in a scholarly journal (where the pagination is continuous through a year) includes the following basic information:

> —Name of author(s), last name first, followed by a period and two spaces.
>> Robinson, Jay L.

> —Title of work, followed by a period and between quotations. Leave two spaces after the closing quotation mark.
>> "Literacy in the Department of English."

> Name of the periodical, underlined.
>> College English

23C

> —Volume number, followed by the date in parentheses, and a colon.
>> 47 (1985):

> For the date, you usually need to supply only the year; however, if necessary to avoid confusion, you may add the season or month of the issue:
>> 33 (Fall 1984) or 27 (May 1962):

> —Page or location, followed by a period. Page numbers should be inclusive, from the first page of the article to the last, including notes and bibliography.
>> 482-98.

>> Robinson, Jay L. "Literacy in the Department of English." College English 47 (1985): 482-98.

A typical MLA *Works Cited* entry for an article in a popular magazine or newspaper includes the following basic information:

—Name of author(s), last name first, followed by a period and two spaces.

Hoberman, Barry.

—Title of work, followed by a period and between quotations. Leave two spaces after the closing quotation mark.

"Translating the Bible."

—Name of the periodical, underlined.

The Atlantic

—Date of publication, followed by a colon. Abbreviate all months except May, June, and July.

Feb. 1985:

—Page or location, followed by a period. Pages should be inclusive.

43–58.

Hoberman, Barry. "Translating the Bible." The Atlantic Feb. 1985: 43–58.

There are so many variations to these general entries, however, that you will want to check the **MLA Form Directory** below for the correct format of any unusual entry.

Below, you will find the MLA *Works Cited* and parenthetical note forms for more than sixty kinds of sources:

1. A book, one author
2. A book, two or three authors
3. A book, three or more authors
4. A book revised by a second author
5. A book, edited—focus on the editor's work
6. A book, edited—focus on the editor's work, more than one editor
7. A book, edited—focus on the original author
8. A book authored by a group
9. A book with no author
10. A foreword, introduction, preface, or afterword of a book
11. A work of more than one volume
12. A translation—focus on the original author
13. A translation—focus on the translator
14. A book in a foreign language
15. A book, republished
16. A book, part of a series
17. A collection or anthology
18. A work within a collection or anthology
19. A chapter within a book
20. A book published before 1900
21. A book issued by a division of a publisher—a special imprint
22. A book whose title includes the title of another work normally between quotation marks
23. A book whose title includes the title of another work normally underlined

23C

24. A dissertation—published

25. A dissertation—unpublished

26. The published proceedings of a conference or meeting

27. An article in a journal paginated by the year or volume, not issue by issue.

28. An article in a journal or magazine paginated issue by issue

29. An article in a weekly or biweekly magazine

30. An article in a monthly magazine—signed

31. An article in a monthly magazine—unsigned

32. An article reprinted in a collection citing original place of publication

33. An article in a newspaper—signed

34. An article in a newspaper—unsigned

35. An editorial in a newspaper

36. A letter to the editor

37. A cartoon

38. An entry in a familiar reference work or encyclopedia

39. An entry in a less familiar reference work

40. A bulletin or pamphlet

41. A government document

42. A map

43. Computer software

44. A computer disk

45. Material from an information service or data base

46. Microfilm or microfiche

47. A videotape

48. A biblical citation
49. A movie
50. A television program
51. A radio program
52. An interview, personal
53. A musical composition
54. A recording
55. A public address—no printed text
56. A public address—printed text
57. A lecture
58. A letter—published
59. A letter—unpublished
60. A work of art
61. A book review—titled
62. A book review—untitled

23C

1. A Book, One Author—MLA

   Works Cited form:

   Clancy, Tom. The Hunt for Red October. Annapolis:
   Naval Institute, 1984.

   Parenthetical note: (Clancy 368)

2. A Book, Two or Three Authors or Editors—MLA

   Works Cited form:

   Altick, Richard D., and Andrea A. Lunsford. Preface to
   Critical Reading. 6th ed. New York: Holt, 1984.

   [Notice that only the name of the first author—
   Altick, Richard D.—is reversed for purposes of

alphabetization. Names of additional authors and editors follow their normal order—Andrea A. Lunsford.]

Parenthetical note: (Altick and Lunsford 76-77)

3. A Book, Three or More Authors or Editors—MLA

Works Cited form:

Abrams, M. H., et al., eds. <u>The Norton Anthology of English Literature.</u> 3rd. ed. 2 vols. New York: Norton, 1974.

[Although a Latin abbreviation, **et al.** is not italicized or underlined. Commas are needed around **et al.** only when it is followed by a specification such as **eds.** (editors) or **trans.** (translators).]

Parenthetical note: (Abrams et al. 1: 9)

[Because this is a work in two volumes, the note must specify which volume is referred to. So, the volume number follows et al., which is, in turn, followed by a colon and the page numbers.]

4. A Book Revised by a Second Author—MLA

Works Cited form:

Altick, Richard D. <u>The Art of Literary Research.</u> 3rd. ed. Rev. John J. Fenstermaker. New York: Norton, 1981.

Parenthetical note: (Altick 205)

5. A Book, Edited—MLA [Focus on the editor's work.]

Works Cited form:

Noyes, George R., ed. <u>The Poetical Works of John Dryden.</u> Boston: Houghton, 1950.

Parenthetical note: (Noyes v-vi)

23C

6. A Book, Edited—MLA [Focus on the editor's work; more than one editor.]

    Works Cited form:

    Lamson, Roy, and Hallett Smith, eds. The Golden Hind: An Anthology of Elizabethan Prose and Poetry. Rev. ed. New York: Norton, 1956.

    Parenthetical note: (Lamson and Smith 3)

7. A Book, Edited—MLA [Focus on the original author.]

    Works Cited form:

    Dryden, John. Of Dramatic Poesy and Other Critical Essays. Ed. George Watson. 2 vols. Everyman's Library. London: Dent, 1962.

    [*Everyman's Library* is a series name. If a book is part of a series, the series name appears, as above, just before the publishing information and followed by a period. Series are not underlined.]

    Parenthetical note: (Dryden 1: 93)

    [Here, the citation includes a volume number, followed by a colon and then the page number.]

8. A Book Authored by a Group—MLA [The author may be a committee, commission, board, publisher, and so on.]

    Works Cited form:

    Reader's Digest. Fix-It-Yourself Manual. Pleasantville, NY: Reader's Digest, 1977.

    Parenthetical note: (Reader's Digest 54-55)

    [It may make for a clearer note to cite the name of the author or work in the sentence and put only the page numbers between parentheses:

23C

The Reader's Digest Fix-It-Yourself Manual explains the basic tools you need for furniture repair (54-55).]

9. A Book with No Author—MLA

Works Cited form:

Illustrated Atlas of the World. Chicago: Rand, 1985.

Parenthetical note: (Illustrated Atlas 88-89)

[Be sure if you use a shortened title that it begins with the same word by which the title is alphabetized in *Works Cited*. In this case, for example, if the title had been shortened to Atlas, a reader would expect to find the full citation under the A's in the *Works Cited* list.]

10. A Foreword, Introduction, Preface, Afterword—MLA

Works Cited form:

Percy, Walker. Foreword. A Confederacy of Dunces. By John Kennedy Toole. New York: Grover, 1980.

Parenthetical note: (Percy 11-13)

11. A Work of More Than One Volume—MLA

Works Cited form:

Champion, Larry S. King Lear: An Annotated Bibliography. 2 vols. New York: Garland, 1980, Vol. 1.

[A title that would normally be underlined or italicized (in this case, *King Lear*) is no longer highlighted when it becomes a part of a title that is underlined or italicized. See #23 below and Fine Tuning, p. 617 for additional examples.]

Parenthetical note: (Champion 266-67)

[Notice that it is not necessary to give a volume number here since the item in the *Works Cited* list specifies Volume 1. If both volumes are used in the paper, then individual citations *would* include the volume number: (Champion 1: 266–67); (Champion 2: 185).]

12. A Translation—MLA [Focus on the original author.]

Works Cited form:

Zola, Émile. Germinal. Trans. L. W. Tancock. Harmondsworth, Eng.: Penguin, 1954.

Parenthetical note: (Zola 468–69)

13. A Translation—MLA [Focus on the translator.]

Works Cited form:

Tancock, L. W., trans. Germinal. By Émile Zola. Harmondsworth, Eng.: Penguin, 1954.

Parenthetical note: (Tancock 15)

14. A Book in a Foreign Language—MLA

Works Cited form:

Bablet, Denis, and Jean Jacquot. Les Voies de la création théâtrale. Paris: Editions du Centre National de la Recherche Scientifique, 1977.

[Copy the title of the foreign work exactly as it appears on the title page, paying special attention both to accent marks and capitalization, which may differ from English conventions.]

Parenthetical note: (Bablet and Jacquot 59)

15. A Book, Republished—MLA

Works Cited form:

Herbert, Frank. Dune. 1965. New York: Berkley, 1977.

[The date of the original publication follows the title. Then cite the edition you are using, giving full publication information.]

Parenthetical note: (Herbert 146)

23C

16. A Book, Part of a Series—MLA

Works Cited form:

Whitelock, Dorothy. The Beginnings of English Society. The Pelican History of England 2. Baltimore: Penguin, 1952.

> [*The Pelican History of England* is a series name. If a book is part of a series, the series name appears, as above, just before the publishing information and followed by a period. Series are not underlined.]

Parenthetical note: (Whitelock 204-05)

17. A Collection or Anthology—MLA

Works Cited form:

Howard, Maureen, ed. The Penguin Book of Contemporary American Essays. New York: Penguin, 1985.

Parenthetical note: (Howard xix-xx)

> [The small Roman numerals indicate that the passage is probably in the introduction or preface of the volume.]

18. A Work Within a Collection or Anthology—MLA

Works Cited form:

Thomas, Lewis. "Computers." The Penguin Book of Contemporary American Essays. Ed. Maureen Howard. New York: Penguin, 1985. 153-55.

> [Notice that page numbers are provided for the article ("Computers") within the collection. Compare with #17 above.]

Parenthetical note: (Thomas 153-55)

19. A Chapter Within a Book—MLA

Works Cited form:

Clark, Kenneth. "Heroic Materialism." Civilisation.
New York: Harper, 1969. 321-47.

Parenthetical note: (Clark 321)

20. A Book Published Before 1900—MLA

Works Cited form:

Bowdler, Thomas, ed. The Family Shakespeare. 10
vols. London: 1818.

[The name of the publisher is usually omitted in
citations to works published prior to 1900. In addition, the lengthy titles and subtitles of older books
are often trimmed to manageable length. The full
title of Bowdler's edition of Shakespeare, for example, includes this explanation: ". . . *nothing is
added to the original text but those words and
expressions are omitted which cannot with pro-
priety be read aloud in a family.*"]

Parenthetical note: (Bowdler 2: 47)

21. A Book Issued by a Division of a Publisher—a special
imprint—MLA

Works Cited form:

Fulbright, J. William. The Arrogance of Power. New
York: Vintage-Random, 1966.

[The special imprint, Vintage in this case, is attached to the publisher's name by a hyphen.]

Parenthetical note: (Fulbright 50)

22. A Book Whose Title Includes the Title of Another
Work Normally Between Quotation Marks—MLA

Works Cited form:

Crossley-Holland, Kevin, and Bruce Mitchell, eds. "The
Battle of Maldon" and Other Old English Poems.
London: Macmillan, 1965.

Parenthetical note: (Crossley-Holland and Mitchell 29)

23C

655

23. **A Book Whose Title Includes the Title of Another Work Normally Underlined—MLA**

Works Cited form:

Levin, Harry. The Question of Hamlet. London: Oxford UP, 1959.

[Hamlet, the title of a play, would ordinarily be underlined if it stood alone. But as a part of a title, it is not underscored. If you use a computer capable of setting italics, the title would look like this: *The Question of* Hamlet.]

Parenthetical note: (Levin 10)

24. **A Dissertation—published (including publication by UMI)—MLA**

Works Cited form:

Rifkin, Myra Lee. Burial, Funeral and Mourning Customs in England, 1558-1662. Diss. Bryn Mawr, 1977. Ann Arbor: UMI, 1977. DDJ78-01385.

[Many dissertations are made available through University Microfilms International (UMI). If the dissertation you are citing is published by UMI, be sure to provide the order number, as shown in the example above.]

Parenthetical note: (Rifkin 234)

25. **A Dissertation—unpublished—MLA**

Works Cited form:

Altman, Jack, Jr. "The Politics of Health Planning and Regulation." Diss. Massachusetts Institute of Technology, 1983.

[Titles of unpublished dissertations appear between quotation marks. The abbreviation *diss.* indicates that the source is a dissertation, in this

656

case, one written at the Massachusetts Institute of
Technology.]

Parenthetical note: (Altman 150)

26. The Published Proceedings of a Conference or Meeting—MLA

Works Cited form:

Hairston, Maxine, and Cynthia L. Selfe. Selected Papers
   from the 1981 Texas Writing Research Conference.
   24-25 Mar. 1981. Austin: Dept. of English, U. of
   Texas, 1981.

Parenthetical note: (Hairston and Selfe iii-iv)

27. An Article in a Journal Paginated by the Year or Volume, Not Issue by Issue—MLA

Works Cited form:

Wentersdorf, Karl P. "Hamlet's Encounter with the
   Pirates." Shakespeare Quarterly 34 (1983):
   434-40.

Parenthetical note: (Wentersdorf 434)

28. An Article in a Journal or Magazine Paginated Issue
by Issue—MLA

Works Cited form:

Lemonick, Michael D. "Jupiter's Second Ring." Science
   Digest Dec. 1985: 13.

Parenthetical note: (Lemonick 13)

29. An Article in a Weekly or Biweekly Magazine—MLA

Works Cited form:

Pangle, Thomas L. "Patriotism, American Style." National Review 29 Nov. 1985: 30-34.

Parenthetical note: (Pangle 32)

23C

657

30. An Article in a Monthly Magazine—signed—MLA

Works Cited form:

Graham, Don. "When Myths Collide." Texas Monthly Jan. 1986: 42+.

[The plus sign following the page number (42+) indicates that the article continues beyond p. 42, but not necessarily on consecutive pages. You will also see the plus sign appear in citations to newspaper articles, which also often continue across several pages.]

Parenthetical note: (Graham 98)

31. An Article in a Monthly Magazine—unsigned—MLA

Works Cited form:

"Engineered Plants Resist Herbicide." High Technology Jan. 1986: 9.

Parenthetical note: ("Engineered Plants" 9)

32. An Article Reprinted in a Collection—MLA

Works Cited form:

Liebert, Herman W. "Reflections on Samuel Johnson." Journal of English and German Philology 47 (1948): 84–88. Rpt. in Samuel Johnson: A Collection of Critical Essays. Ed. Donald J. Greene. Twentieth Century Views. Englewood Cliffs, NJ: Prentice, 1965. 15–21.

[Notice that the book in which the article is reprinted is part of a series: Twentieth Century Views. The name of the series is not underlined.]

Parenthetical note: (Liebert 17)

33. An Article in a Newspaper—signed—MLA

Works Cited form:

Branson, Louise. "Soviet TV Changing." The Dallas Morning News 13 Jan. 1986, sec. A: 1+.

23C

[The plus sign following the page number (1+) indicates that the article continues beyond the first page, but not necessarily on consecutive pages.]

Parenthetical note: (Branson 4)

34. An Article in a Newspaper—unsigned—MLA

    Works Cited form:

    "Nervous Robber Accidently Shoots Himself in the Mouth." Houston Chronicle 15 Jan. 1986, state final ed., sec. 1: 17.

    Parenthetical note: ("Nervous Robber" 17)

35. An Editorial in a Newspaper—MLA

    Works Cited form:

    "How to Honor Dr. King and When." Editorial. New York Times 15 Jan. 1986, nat. ed.: 23.

    Parenthetical note: ("How to Honor" 23)

36. A Letter to the Editor—MLA

    Works Cited form:

    Cantu, Tony. Letter. San Antonio Light 14 Jan. 1986, southwest ed., sec. C: 4

    Parenthetical note: (Cantu 4)

37. A Cartoon—MLA

    Works Cited form:

    Mathis, Miles. "Squib." Cartoon. Daily Texan 15 Jan. 1986: 19.

    Parenthetical note: (Mathis 19)

    [It might be better to describe the cartoon in the text of your essay, rather than in a parenthetical note: "In 'Squib' by Miles Mathis . . . ."]

23C

659

38. An Entry in a Familiar Reference Work or Encyclopedia—MLA

Works Cited form:

Benedict, Roger William. "Northwest Passage." <u>Encyclopaedia Britannica: Macropaedia.</u> 1974 ed.

[With familiar reference works, especially those revised regularly, you need only identify the edition you are using by its date. You may omit the names of editors and most publishing information. The authors of entries in the Britannica and other reference works are sometimes identified only by initials. To find the full names of authors you will need to check an index or, in the case of Britannica, the *Guide to the Britannica* included with the set.]

Parenthetical note: (Benedict)

[No page number is given when a work is arranged alphabetically.]

23C

39. An Entry in a Less Familiar Reference Work (see #38 for comparison)—MLA

Works Cited form:

Kovesi, Julius. "Hungarian Philosophy." <u>The Encyclopedia of Philosophy.</u> Ed. Paul Edwards. 8 vols. New York: Macmillan, 1967.

[Notice that with less familiar reference tools, a fuller entry is provided, including the name of editors and publishing information.]

Parenthetical note: (Kovesi)

40. A Bulletin or Pamphlet—MLA

Works Cited form:

<u>Finding Film Reviews.</u> UGL Study Guide. Austin: The General Libraries, 1984.

[Treat pamphlets as if they were books: underline titles and provide publishing information.]

Parenthetical note: (Finding Film 4)

41. A Government Document—MLA

Works Cited form:

United States. Cong. Joint Committee on Printing. 1985-86 Official Congressional Directory. 99th Cong. Washington: GPO, 1985.

[Give the name of the government (national, state, local) and agency issuing the report; title of the document; publishing information. If it is a congressional document (as in the case above), identify the Congress and, when important, the session (99th Cong., 2nd sess.) after the title of the document.]

Parenthetical note: (United States. Cong. Joint Committee on Printing 182-84).

[Because the parenthetical note would be so long, you would probably be better off identifying the work in the body of a sentence and placing only the relevant page numbers between parentheses: "These facts are based on information gathered from the 1985-86 Official Congressional Directory (182-84)."]

42. A Map—MLA

Works Cited form:

Cosmopolitan World on Mercator's Projection. Map. New York: Rand.

[Provide a year of publication if listed on the map.]

Parenthetical note: You would refer to the map directly in the body of your essay, not in a parenthetical note: "Rand McNally's Cosmopolitan World map warns of the distortion in a Mercator projection...."

23C

43. Computer Software—MLA

Works Cited form:

PageMaker. Computer software. Aldus Corporation, 1985. Macintosh, 512K, disk.

[If the author of the software is known, his or her name precedes the name of the product. After the name of the manufacturer, you may specify the computer(s) the software is written for, the amount of memory it requires, and the form of the software.]

Parenthetical note: (Page Maker)

[It might be better to name the software in the body of your essay, rather than in a parenthetical note: "Software, such as Aldus' Page Maker. . . ."]

44. A Computer Disk—MLA

Works Cited form:

"Enrollment and Placement—Math 302" Disk 47. Austin: The University of Texas Department of Mathematics, 1985.

[An actual file name might be given to locate the material on the document directory.]

Parenthetical note: The source of the information might be conveniently given in the text of your essay rather than in a parenthetical note.

45. Material from an Information Service or Data Base—MLA

Works Cited form:

Croll, Valerie J., and Kathleen S. Shank. Teacher Training Resources: Preparing Teachers for Mainstreaming. A Selected Bibliography. Charleston, IL: Eastern Illinois U, 1983. ERIC ED 232 971.

[ERIC is the name of the information service; the numbers following identify the particular article in case readers wish to order it.]

Parenthetical note: (Croll and Shank 10-15)

46. Microfilm or Microfiche—MLA

Works Cited form:

"How Long Will the Chemise Last?" Consumer Reports Aug. 1958: 434-37.

[Material seen on microfilm or microfiche is listed exactly as if it were seen in the original hard-copy publication. You need not mention that you used microfilm or microfiche unless the source you are using was originally printed on microfilm or microfiche.]

Parenthetical note: ("How Long" 434)

47. A Videotape—MLA

Works Cited form:

Othello. The Shakespeare Plays. Videocassette. By William Shakespeare. Dir. Jonathan Miller. With Anthony Hopkins and Penelope Wilton. London: BBC Television, 1981.

[The amount and order of information you give in this entry could vary depending upon who or what you intend to emphasize. If your focus is on the author, the entry could begin:

Shakespeare, William. Othello. The Shakespeare Plays. . . .

If your paper focuses on the director of the production, your entry would begin this way:

Miller, Jonathan, dir. Othello. The Shakespeare Plays. . . .

23C

You could also give more (or less) information about the producer, designer, performers, and so on. Note that the series title—The Shakespeare Plays—is not underlined.]

Parenthetical note: (Othello)

48. A Biblical Citation—MLA

Works Cited form:

The Jerusalem Bible. Ed. Alexander Jones. Garden City: Doubleday, 1966.

[If you make frequent references to the Bible, let your reader know what edition you are using.]

Parenthetical note: (John 18:37–38)

[Your parenthetical note does not have to indicate the edition you are using.]

49. A Movie—MLA

Works Cited form:

Tender Mercies. Dir. Bruce Beresford. With Robert Duvall and Tess Harper. EMI Films, 1983.

[The amount and order of information you give in this entry could vary depending upon who or what you want to emphasize. If your focus is on the screenwriter for example, the entry would begin:

Foote, Horton. Tender Mercies. Dir. Bruce Beresford. . . .

If your paper focuses on the director of the production, your entry would begin this way:

Beresford, Bruce, dir. Tender Mercies. With Robert Duvall. . . .

You could also give more (or less) information about the producer, designer, performers, and so on.]

Parenthetical note: (Tender Mercies)

50. A Television Program—MLA

   Works Cited form:

   "Heroic Materialism." Civilisation. Created by Sir Kenneth Clark. PBS. 26 Dec. 1971.

   Parenthetical note: ("Heroic Materialism")

   [Naming the program in the essay itself would probably be preferable to a parenthetical reference.]

51. A Radio Program—MLA

   Works Cited form:

   Death Valley Days. Created by Ruth Cornwall Woodman. NBC Radio. 30 Sept. 1930.

   Parenthetical note: (Death Valley Days)

   [Naming the program in the essay itself would probably be preferable to a parenthetical reference.]

52. An Interview, Personal—MLA

   Works Cited form:

   Michener, James. Personal interview. 4 Oct. 1984.

   Parenthetical note: [Refer to the interview in the body of your essay rather than in a parenthetical note: "In an interview, James Michener explained. . . ." If the person you are interviewing is not widely known, explain his or her credentials in your essay.]

53. A Musical Composition—MLA

   Works Cited form:

   Joplin, Scott. "The Strenuous Life, A Ragtime Two Step." St. Louis: John Stark & Son Sheet Music Publishers, 1902.

   [If you don't have a score or sheet music to refer to, provide a simpler entry:

   Porter, Cole. "Too Darn Hot." 1949.]

23C

665

Parenthetical note: (Joplin)

[Naming the musical work in the essay itself would probably be preferable to a parenthetical reference.]

54. A Recording—MLA

Works Cited form:

Pavarotti, Luciano. Pavarotti's Greatest Hits. London PAV 2003, 1980.

[Notice that the "publishing" information for a recording includes the record label and recording number: London PAV 2003.]

Parenthetical note: (Pavarotti)

[Naming the recording in the essay itself would probably be preferable to a parenthetical reference.]

55. A Public Address—no printed text—MLA

Works Cited form:

Reagan, Ronald. "The Geneva Summit Meeting: A Measure of Progress." U.S. Congress. Washington, D.C., 21 Nov. 1985.

Parenthetical note: If you do not have a copy of an address, refer to it by name or speaker in your essay itself and avoid the need for a parenthetical note: "When President Reagan delivered his Geneva Summit address to Congress. . . ."

56. A Public Address—printed text—MLA

Works Cited form:

Reagan, Ronald. "The Geneva Summit Meeting: A Measure of Progress." U.S. Congress. Washington, D.C., 21 Nov. 1985. Rpt. Vital Speeches of the Day. 15 Dec. 1985: 130–32.

Parenthetical note: (Reagan 130)

23C

57. A Lecture—MLA

Works Cited form:

Emig, Janet. "Literacy and Freedom." Opening General Sess. CCCC Annual Meeting. San Francisco, 18 Mar. 1982.

Parenthetical note: (Emig)

58. A Letter—published—MLA

Works Cited form:

Eliot, George. "To Thomas Clifford Allbutt." 1 Nov. 1873. In Selections from George Eliot's Letters. Ed. Gordon S. Haight. New Haven: Yale UP, 1985: 427.

Parenthetical note: (Eliot 427)

59. A Letter—unpublished—MLA

Works Cited form:

Newton, Albert. Letter to Agnes Weinstein. 23 May 1917. Albert Newton Papers. Woodhill Library, Cleveland.

Parenthetical note: (Newton)

[It would probably be better to refer to the letter in the body of the essay: "In a letter to Agnes Weinstein, dated 23 May 1917, Albert Newton blames. . . ."]

60. A Work of Art—MLA

Works Cited form:

Fuseli, Henry. Ariel. The Folger Shakespeare Library, Washington, D.C.

Parenthetical note: (Fuseli)

[It would be better to refer to the painting in the body of your essay rather than in a note: "Fuseli's Ariel depicts. . . ."]

23C

61. A Book Review—titled—MLA

Works Cited form:

Keen, Maurice. "The Knight of Knights." Rev. of
William Marshall: The Flower of Chivalry, by
Georges Durby. Trans. Richard Howard. The New
York Review of Books 16 Jan. 1986: 39-40.

Parenthetical note: (Keen 39)

62. A book review—untitled—MLA

Works Cited form:

Baym, Nina. Rev. Uncle Tom's Cabin and American
Culture, by Thomas F. Gossett. The Journal of
American History 72 (1985): 691-92.

Parenthetical note: (Baym 691-92)

23C

A Table of Abbreviations

You may encounter or want to employ the following abbreviations in notes or a *Works Cited* page. Limit these abbreviations to such uses; spell the words out fully whenever they occur in the body of your paper—except in parenthetical notes or explanations. Don't use abbreviations you think might confuse your readers.

adapt.	adaption
anon.	anonymous
app.	appendix
assn.	association
attrib.	attributed to
bibliog.	bibliography
biog.	biography
bull.	bulletin
©	copyright (usually followed by a date)
c.	"about" (usually followed by a date)
ch.	chapter
col.	column
coll.	college
colloq.	colloquial
Cong.	Congress
DAB	*Dictionary of American Biography*
dir.	director, directed by
diss.	dissertation
div.	division
DNB	*Dictionary of National Biography*
ed(s).	editor(s)
e.g.	for example
et al.	and others

etc.	and so forth
ex.	example
fig.	figure
fwd.	forward
govt.	government
GPO	Government Printing Office
i.e.	that is
illus.	illustration, illustrated by
introd.	introduction, introduced by
jour.	journal
l., ll.	line, lines
mag.	magazine
misc.	miscellaneous
mo., mos.	month, months
ms., mss.	manuscript, manuscripts
nar.	narrator, narrated by
n.d.	no date
ns	new series
obs.	obsolete
OED	*Oxford English Dictionary*
orig.	original
p., pp.	page, pages
PhD	Doctor of Philosophy
pl.	plural
pref.	preface
proc.	proceedings
PS	postscript
pseud.	pseudonym

23C

pub.	publisher, published by
publ.	publisher, published by
rev.	review, reviewed by
rpt.	reprint, reprinted by
ser.	series
sess.	session
sic	thus
sing.	singular
soc.	society
supp.	supplement
trans.	translator, translated by
U	University
UP	University Press
var.	variant
vol., vols.	volume, volumes
yr., yrs.	year, years

23D HOW DO YOU USE APA DOCUMENTATION?

Troubleshooting

In many college courses (anthropology, astronomy, business, education, home economics, linguistics, political science, psychology, sociology), you may be expected to follow the conventions of documentation recommended by the American Psychological Association (APA). The basic procedures for APA documentation are spelled out in the following section. For a fuller explanation of APA procedures, you should refer to *The Publication Manual of the American Psychological Association* (1983). It is available in most college libraries.

It is important to realize that while MLA and APA documentation will be generally acceptable for most of the papers you write while in college, almost every field and major follows its own conventions in acknowledging sources. You will be expected to learn and follow these variations—especially when you begin to do more advanced work. Always ask your instructor what form of documentation you are expected to follow in a given paper.

To use APA documentation . . .

▶ **Overview: Follow these two steps.**

1. Insert an in-text note for every passage you need to document.

   While Beethoven enjoyed prosperity and success through 1815, his deafness continued to grow until he became "morose, irascible, and morbidly suspicious even toward his friends" (Grout, 1980, p. 540).

2. Record every source mentioned in a parenthetical note in an alphabetical list of *References* at the end of your essay.

References

   Grout, D. J. (1980). <u>A history of western music.</u> 3rd. ed. New York: Norton.

▶ **Insert an in-text parenthetical note after every passage you need to document.** The basic form of the APA parenthetical note consists of the author's last name and a date. A page number may be given for indirect citations and *must* be given for direct quotations. A comma follows the author's name. A comma also follows the date if page numbers are given. Page numbers are preceded by **p.** or **pp.**

   (Grout, 1980, p. 540)

   (Iacocca, 1984, pp. 254–55)

   The note is ordinarily located conveniently after a passage requiring documentation, often at the end of a sentence.

While Beethoven enjoyed prosperity and success through 1815, his deafness continued to grow until he became "morose, irascible, and morbidly suspicious even toward his friends" (**Grout, 1980, p. 540**).

Despite some initial production problems and slow sales at first, the K-cars provided Chrysler with the cash the company needed to develop additional products (**Iacocca, 1984**).

When possible, the necessary information can be distributed throughout the passage:

Grout (1980) observes that while Beethoven enjoyed prosperity and success through 1815, his deafness continued to grow until he became "morose, irascible, and morbidly suspicious even toward his friends" (**p. 540**).

If two or more sources are used in a single sentence, the notes are inserted as needed conveniently after the statements they support.

While the ecology of the aquifer might be hardier than originally suspected (**Chesney, 1981**), there is no reason to believe that "the best interests of all the people of the county" (**Horus, 1985, p. 62**) would indeed be served by the creation of a mall and shopping district in a vicinity described as "one of the last outposts of undisturbed nature in the state" (**Munoz, 1982, p. 28**).

23D

Notice that a parenthetical note is placed outside of quotation marks but before a period ending a sentence.

If the name of an author appears in the text of your passage, you don't have to repeat the author's name between parentheses.

While **Chesney (1981)** argues that the ecology of the aquifer might be hardier than originally suspected, there is no reason to assume that "the best interests of all the people of the county" (**Horus, 1985, p. 62**) would indeed be served by the creation of a mall and shopping district in a vicinity described by **Munoz** as "one of the last outposts of undisturbed nature in the state" (**1982, p. 28**).

Similarly, you don't have to repeat an author's name in second and subsequent references to the same source provided that no other sources are mentioned between these references. After the first reference, page numbers are sufficient until another citation intervenes:

> . . . the creation of a mall and shopping district in a vicinity described by **Munoz** as "one of the last outposts of undisturbed nature in the state" **(1982, p. 28)**. The aquifer area provides a "unique environment for several endangered species of birds and plantlife" **(p. 31)**. The birds especially require breeding areas free from the encroaching signs of development: roads, lights, and human presence **(Harrison & Cafiero, 1979)**. The plantlife is similarly susceptible to the plague of building and exploitation that has followed growth in other areas of the county **(Munoz, 1982)**.

If a work has two authors, include both names in all references:

> (Harrison & Cafiero, 1979)

Notice that an ampersand (&) is used between the authors' names rather than the *and* used in MLA.

If a work has three or more authors, name all of them in the first parenthetical note:

> (Harrison, Cafiero, & Dixon, 1979).

Then abbreviate subsequent notes with **et al**. (Latin abbreviation for **"and others"**):

> (Harrison et al., 1979)

If you use more than one work written by an author in a single year, a parenthetical note that listed only the author's last name and date could refer, reasonably, to more than one entry on your *References* page.

> (Harrison, 1981)

> (Harrison, 1981)

To avoid such confusion, assign a small letter after the date to distinguish between the author's works from the same year.

(Harrison, 1981a)

(Harrison, 1981b)

The question is raised by Harrison (1981a), quickly answered by Anderson (1981), and then raised again (Harrison, 1981b).

If you must document a work without an author—an article in a magazine, for example, or a newspaper story—simply list the title, shortened if necessary, and the date. For a direct quotation, provide a page number.

("Aid to education," 1985)

("Subtle art," 1985, p. 62)

References

Aid to education and health cut by $38-million. (1985, December 18). *The Chronicle of Higher Education*, p. 11.

The subtle art of stubble. (1985, December 9) *Newsweek*, p. 62.

23D

▶ **Record every source mentioned in your paper in an alphabetical list of *References* at the end of your essay.** The *References* page appears at the end of your paper, after and separate from the body of the essay itself. The list of references is double-spaced. The first line of each entry touches the left-hand margin and subsequent lines are indented three spaces.

Entries on the *References* page are listed alphabetically, by last names of authors. If a work has more than one author, all authors are listed in the entry, last name given first. An ampersand (&) is used where MLA documentation uses *and*.

Clark, M. & Stadtman, N.

If a work has no given author, it is listed by title and alphabetized by the first word in the title, excluding *a*, *an*, and *the*. Several works by the same author are listed alphabetically under that author's name.

A typical APA *References* entry for a book includes the following basic information:

—Name of author(s), last name first, followed by a period and two spaces. Initials are substituted for first names unless two authors mentioned in the paper have identical last names and first initials:

Peterson, R. T.

—Date in parentheses, followed by a period.

(1963).

—Title of work, underlined, followed by a period and two spaces. Only the first word and proper nouns are capitalized.

A field guide to the birds of Texas.

—Place of publication, followed by a colon.

Boston:

—Publisher, followed by a period.

Norton.

Peterson, R. T. (1963). A field guide to the birds of Texas. Boston: Norton.

23D

A typical APA *References* entry for an article in a scholarly journal (where the pagination is continuous through a year) includes the following basic information:

—Name of author(s), last name first, followed by a period and two spaces. Initials are substituted for first names unless two authors mentioned in the paper have identical last names and first initials:

Robinson, J. L.

—Date in parentheses, followed by a period and two spaces.

(1985).

—Title of the article, followed by a period and two spaces. Only the first word and proper nouns are capitalized. The title does not appear between quotation marks.

Literacy in the department of English.

—**Name of the periodical, underlined, followed by a comma**. All major words are capitalized.

College English,

—**Volume number, underlined, followed by a comma, page numbers, and a period.**

47, 482-98.

Robinson, J. L. (1985). Literacy in the department of English. College English, 47, 482-98.

A typical APA *References* entry for an article in a popular magazine or newspaper includes the following basic information:

—**Name of author(s), last name first, followed by a period and two spaces.** Initials are substituted for first names unless two authors mentioned in the paper have identical last names and first initials:

Clark, M., & Stadtman, N.

—**Date in parentheses, followed by a period and two spaces.** Give the year first, followed by the month (do not abbreviate it), followed by the day, if necessary.

(1985, December 9).

—**Title of work, followed by a period and two spaces.** Only the first word and proper nouns are capitalized. The title does not appear between quotation marks.

A bad drug's benefit.

—**Name of the periodical, underlined, followed by a comma.** All major words are capitalized.

Newsweek,

—**Page or location indicated by the abbreviation p. or pp., followed by a period.**

p. 84.

Clark, M. & Stadtman, N. (1985, December 9). A bad drug's benefit. Newsweek, p. 84.

23D

There are so many variations to these general entries, however, that you will probably want to check *The Publication Manual of the American Psychological Association* (1983) if you do a major APA-style paper.

APA Form Directory

Below, you will find the APA **Reference List** and parenthetical note forms for some basic sources:

63.   A book, one author

64.   A book, two or three authors

65.   A book, edited—focus on the editor's work

66.   A book with no author

67.   A work within a collection or anthology

68.   A chapter within a book

69.   An article in a journal paginated by the year or volume, not issue by issue

70.   An article in a journal or magazine paginated issue by issue

71.   An article in a weekly or biweekly magazine

72.   An article in a monthly magazine, signed

73.   An article in a monthly magazine, unsigned

63.   A Book, One Author—APA

Reference list form:

Clancy, T. (1984). The hunt for Red October. Annapolis, Maryland: Naval Institute Press.

Parenthetical note: (Clancy, 1984)

64.   A Book, Two or Three Authors—APA

Reference list form:

Altick, R. D. & Lunsford, A. (1984). Preface to critical reading. New York: Holt.

Parenthetical note: (Altick & Lunsford, 1984)

65. A Book, Edited—APA [Focus on the editor's work.]

Reference list form:

Appelman, P. (Ed.). (1979). <u>Darwin: a Norton critical</u>
    <u>edition.</u> (2nd ed.). New York: Norton.

Parenthetical note: (Appelman, 1979)

66. A Book with No Author—APA

Reference list form:

<u>Illustrated atlas of the world.</u> (1985). Chicago: Rand.

Parenthetical note: (<u>Illustrated atlas,</u> 1985, pp. 88-89)

67. A Work Within a Collection or Anthology—APA

Reference list form:

Thomas, L. (1973). Computers. In M. Howard (Ed.),
    <u>The Penguin book of contemporary American</u>
    <u>essays</u> (pp. 153-55). New York: Penguin.

Parenthetical note: (Thomas, 1973)

68. A Chapter Within a Book—APA

Reference list form:

Clark, K. (1969). Heroic materialism. In <u>Civilisation,</u>
    (pp. 321-47). New York: Harper.

Parenthetical note: (Clark, 1969)

69. An Article in a Journal Paginated by the Year or Volume, Not Issue by Issue—APA

Reference list form:

Kroll, B. (1084) Audience adaptation in children's
    persuasive letters. <u>Written Communication</u> 1,
    407-27.

Parenthetical note: (Kroll, 1984)

70. An Article in a Journal or Magazine Paginated Issue by Issue—APA

Reference list form:

Lemonick, M. D. (1985, December). Jupiter's second ring. Science Digest, p. 13.

Parenthetical note: (Lemonick, 1985)

71. An Article in a Weekly or Biweekly Magazine—APA

Reference list form:

Pangle, T. L. (1985, November 29). Patriotism, American style. National Review, pp. 30-34.

Parenthetical note: (Pangle, 1985)

72. An Article in a Monthly Magazine, Signed—APA

Reference list form:

White, C. P. (1986, January). Freshwater turtles—designed for survival. National Geographic, pp. 40-59.

Parenthetical note: (White, 1986)

73. An Article in a Monthly Magazine, Unsigned—APA

Reference list form:

Engineered plants resist herbicide. (1986, January). High Technology, p. 9.

Parenthetical note: (Engineered plants, 1986)

23D

HOW DO YOU AVOID PLAGIARISM AND COLLUSION?

Terms you need to know

Plagiarism. Presenting someone else's words or ideas as your own.

Collaboration. Working with one or more people to produce a paper clearly designed and presented as a group project

Collusion. Allowing other people to write or revise a paper that is supposed to be your work alone.

Troubleshooting

Most students understand that it is wrong to buy a paper, to let someone heavily edit a paper, or to submit someone else's work as their own. This kind of activity is simply dishonest and most institutions have procedures for handling such scholastic dishonesty when it occurs.

But many students do not realize that acknowledging sources inadequately or taking notes carelessly may also raise doubts about the integrity of a paper. Such concerns are easily avoided if you take good notes and follow the guidelines discussed in this section. In fact, you will find that time spent carefully summarizing and paraphrasing sources in your own words pays off later when you sit down to write a draft. You gain authority and confidence that animates every paragraph you write.

Collusion is a different issue, clouded by the fact that good writing often results from people working together. Much professional writing done in business, government, and academia is produced by teams. But effective team members also demonstrate high personal competence. That's what your instructors expect you to demonstrate when you write a paper. Your signature on a paper certifies not only that you wrote the essay but that you could produce comparable work again, on your own. If you rely on editing services or friends to correct your grammar, polish your sentences, flesh out your ideas, your writing isn't really your own.

To avoid plagiarism . . .

 ▶ **Acknowledge all direct or indirect uses of anyone else's work.** Suppose, for example, that in preparing a research paper on the life of Beethoven, you come across the following passage from *A History of Western Music* by Donald Jay Grout:

> {**1**} The years up to 1815 were, on the whole, peaceful and prosperous for Beethoven. His music was played in Vienna, and he was celebrated both at home and abroad. Thanks to the generosity of patrons and the steady demand from publishers for new works, his financial affairs were in good order, despite a ruinous devaluation of the Austrian currency in 1811; but his deafness became a more and more serious trial. As it caused him to lose contact with others, he retreated into himself, becoming morose, irascible, and morbidly suspicious even toward his friends.

23E

If you decide to quote all or part of the selection above in your essay, you must use quotation marks to indicate that you are borrowing the writer's exact words. You must also identify the author, work, publisher, date, and location of the passage through a parenthetical note keyed to a list of *Works Cited* {2}.

> {**2**} While Beethoven enjoyed prosperity and success through 1815, his deafness continued to grow until he became "morose, irascible, and morbidly suspicious even toward his friends" (Grout 540).

Works Cited

Grout, Donald Jay. *A History of Western Music*. 3rd. ed. New York: Norton, 1980.

You must use *both* quotation marks and the parenthetical note when you quote directly. Quotation marks alone would not tell your readers what your source was. A note alone would acknowledge that you are using a source, but would not explain that the words in a given portion of your paper are not entirely your own.

You may need to use the selection above in **indirect** ways, borrowing the information in Grout's paragraph, but not his words or arrangement of ideas. Here are two acceptable **summaries** (see p. 602) of the passage on Beethoven that report its facts appropriately and originally. Notice that both versions include a parenthetical note acknowledging Grout's *A History of Western Music* as the source of information.

> {3} Donald J. Grout reports that Beethoven's life was prosperous in Vienna but, after 1815, his deafness became a major problem affecting his mental attitude and his relationship with friends (540).

> {4} Beethoven, enjoying a steady demand for his work and a measure of prosperity, was relatively untroubled by the Austrian monetary problems of 1811 (Grout 540).

Without documentation, both versions above might be considered plagiarized even though only Grout's ideas—and not his actual words—are borrowed. You must acknowledge ideas and information you take from your sources unless you are dealing with common knowledge (see p. 622).

23E

▶ **Summarize and paraphrase carefully.** A proper summary or paraphrase of a source should represent your own work and employ your own language (as in examples #3 and #4 above). But some students think that they can avoid a charge of plagiarism by changing a few words in a selection they are borrowing. They cannot. The following passage based on Grout's original would be considered plagiarism—with or without a parenthetical note:

> {5} The years to 1815 were mainly quiet and prosperous for Beethoven. His music was played a lot in Vienna, and he was famous both at home and abroad. Because of the goodness of patrons and the steady demand from music publishers for new works, his financial affairs were sound, despite a terrible devalua-

tion in 1811 of the Austrian currency. Unfortunately, his deafness became a growing problem. As it caused him to lose contact with others, he retreated into himself, becoming depressed, irritable, and morbidly suspicious even toward his friends (Grout 540).

To avoid collusion . . .

▶ **Be sure that your instructor knows about any help you receive on a paper.** Naturally, it is best to talk to your instructor before asking for assistance—whether from a friend, a writing lab, or a tutoring service.

But you should also understand that there is nothing inherently wrong with asking people to read and comment on what you have written. Most professional writers regularly ask others to review their manuscripts. They want the feedback of honest critics so that they will have a clearer idea how to revise their essays. Notice, however, that they are soliciting opinions, not corrections.

If your purpose in asking for assistance is to find someone to correct or edit your work, you are avoiding responsibility for your own writing—and you may be accused of collusion.

23E

▶ **Be sure to pull your weight in any legitimate collaborative writing.** A great deal of professional writing is done by groups of people working together. You may be a part of such a collaborative project while in college. If you are, be sure to contribute your strengths to the effort. Don't rely on other people in the group to do all the work. If you sign your name to a project that you really had no part in, you are being scholastically dishonest.

CHAPTER

A Research Paper from Start to Finish

■ **A** From subject area to thesis statement
■ **B** Sources and notes
■ **C** Outlines and drafts
■ **D** Annotated final version

Troubleshooting

In autumn, 1985, James Balarbar, a freshman at the University of Texas, was assigned to write a 1200-word research paper for his "Rhetoric and Composition" class. Provided with a list of twenty-five topic areas, detailed information about finding books and articles, and an ample library collection, he eventually produced the paper reprinted as a model essay in section D below, "Final Version." To reach that point, he went through 199 notecards, twenty-four sheets of scratch paper, dozens of photocopies, and three drafts. Portions of his research process are outlined below to give you an idea of how you might go about finding and developing an idea into a completed paper.

24A FROM SUBJECT AREA TO THESIS STATEMENT

▶ **Finding and developing a topic.**

The twenty-five topic ideas given to James included broad subjects such as child abuse, animal communication, the fashion industry, rock climbing, and robotics. James quickly moved toward one broad subject: the U.S. auto industry. His research notes show that he explored the outlines of his subject in *Collier's Encyclopedia* and *Encyclopaedia Britannica.* Perhaps prompted by the popularity of Lee Iacocca's much-publicized autobiography, James quickly narrowed his topic to Chrysler Corporation and Lee Iacocca.

His earliest notes show wide reading in numerous periodicals covering the near-bankruptcy and recovery of the Chrysler Corporation in 1978–82 and the rise of Iacocca. His notes don't report what indexes he used, but he lists the titles of over fifty articles from *Time, Newsweek, The Saturday Evening Post, Business Week, Motor Trend,* and *Forbes*—and twelve from *The New York Times* in 1978 alone. He labels many of the articles "not useful," but begins moving toward a topic. At this stage, his reading produces a list of terms that seem important to his subject:

> Iran crisis
>
> gas crunch
>
> leasing to rental agencies
>
> sales bank
>
> Townsend
>
> Riccardo
>
> Simca and UK Chrysler
>
> management
>
> quality
>
> morale and loyalty
>
> gas guzzlers

After some additional reading that includes *Going for Broke: Lee Iacocca's Battle to Save Chrysler* by Michael Moritz and Barrett Seaman, he makes another list and then free-writes to focus his preliminary ideas.

> bankruptcy
>
> banks

Chrysler Loan Guarantee Act

advertising

Fraser

mergers

marketing

Mitsubishi

Reagan

Reconstruction Finance Corporation

sales

launchings

UAW

U.S. Congress

The near bankruptcy of the Chrysler Corporation is attributed to the poor sales, poor management, poor styling of the cars, and increased production costs. The company was saved by a change in the management. Lee Iacocca took over the company and helped put it back on its feet. He and many members of the Ford company composed the staff. Two others came from competition such as Volkswagen.

24A

The changes in the staff brought the company into competition again. Apparently the staff brought new ideas and new techniques that bettered the company. Their ideas included the styling of the cars, financing the company, production projects, and sales. . . . Iacocca refers to the different image of the company as the "New Chrysler Corporation."

What were some of the problems of the styling, financing, sales?

Contrast the two managements?

Only after this much reading and thinking is James ready to formulate a preliminary thesis statement to guide his future explorations.

▶ Shaping a Thesis.

The first thesis statement to appear in James' notes already reflects substantial reading. It offers an ambitious prospect.

> *Thesis 1*: Chrysler nearly fell into bankruptcy because of increased production costs, poor sales, and management difficulties; however, a change in the management placed the company back on its feet.

What James has committed himself to in this carefully shaped first attempt is a short history of an entire company—more than he can manage within the 1200-word limit of his assignment. Notice that his thesis actually has two parts, signaled by the presence of the semicolon. If he wrote a paper based on this idea, it would probably have two major divisions: near-bankruptcy and recovery. But his notes reflect a quick change, and a new thesis soon emerges, with only half the scope of the original.

> *Thesis 2*: Lee Iacocca saved Chrysler with his changes in its management and his strong leadership.

More reading and notes follow, much of it designed to explore exactly how Iacocca saved the company. James seems particularly careful about keeping his ideas focused, because his notes are full of attempts to summarize his findings.

> Lee Iacocca helped Chrysler survive by restructuring the company's management.

> Lee Iacocca saved the Chrysler Corporation and restored the company's credibility simply by changing and restructuring the company's management.

> Five men from Chrysler's rival competitor, Ford, three of them retired, two of them fired from Ford, saved the Chrysler Corporation.

> Six men, all previously from Ford, saved the Chrysler Corporation.

He continues to read, adding to his stack of bibliography and note cards. His sources now include Iacocca's book: *Iacocca: An Autobiography*. He reads portions of it, taking full notes. One page includes this reference to what will soon become a major focus of his paper:

24A

Sales bank—factory inventory.

It was "nothing more than an excuse to keep the plants running when we didn't have dealer orders for the cars."

"At regular intervals the Manufacturing Division would tell the Sales Division how many and what types of vehicles they were going to produce. Then it would be up to the Sales Division to try to sell them."
p. 162

Reading portions of *Iacocca: An Autobiography* seems to have shifted James' interest away from how Chrysler was saved to why it failed. Changes in focus of this kind are common in the course of research papers. However, the effort leading up to them isn't lost; instead, this preliminary reading and research often furnishes background information that confers confidence and authority on a writer. James' next attempt to shape a thesis reflects his changing point of view:

> *Thesis 3*: Chrysler's near-bankruptcy is largely accredited to its poor and disorganized management.

This version is modified almost immediately to add two particular examples of Chrysler's mismanagement. The language, too, is sharpened.

> *Thesis 4*: The weak and disorganized former management of the Chrysler Corporation nearly threw the company into bankruptcy with its automobile sales bank practice and its ventures into the foreign market.

Notice that the original spark for the paper—an interest in Lee Iacocca—is now nearly extinguished. The paper is developing in a direction James Balarbar couldn't have predicted at the outset because, when he began, he knew virtually nothing about Chrysler's previous management, the sales bank, or the foreign auto market. Yet James isn't satisfied yet. Another rendering of his thesis appears in his notes, emphasizing the sales bank just a bit more. He shows this version to his teacher, wondering whether it might now be too narrow for an effective paper.

24A

Thesis 5: The weak and disorganized former management of the Chrysler Corporation nearly threw the company into bankruptcy with its unwise ventures into the foreign market and its foolish practice of the automobile sales bank.

The instructor tells James that the thesis is fine. In fact, it might be made even more specific, focusing on either the foreign auto market or the sales bank. "Do you think I can find enough information to write a whole paper on one of those subjects?" James asks. But he, better than his instructor, is in a position to judge the depth and quality of material available on Chrysler's management problems. Almost without realizing it, James has become the expert.

By the time he composes his first full draft, James has made his choice:

Thesis 6—first draft: The sales bank, which displays the disintegration between the management, manufacturing, and sales, was a major cause in Chrysler's near downfall.

From here on, the thesis remains basically unchanged as James completes his reading and research and assembles the information he needs to prove that the sales bank was, indeed, a major factor in Chrysler's much publicized decline. Here are the final two versions of an idea developed with care, thoroughness, and ingenuity by a conscientious student.

Thesis 7—second draft: A major cause of Chrysler's near-bankruptcy was a concept called "the sales bank," which illustrates the disintegration between the management, manufacturing, and sales. Although this method of conducting business was designed to better the company, it actually drained the company of its finances as well as its credibility.

Thesis 8—final version: A major cause of the Chrysler Corporation's near-bankruptcy in 1979–80 was a concept called "the sales bank" which exemplified the lack of coordination between the company's management, manufacturing, and sales divisions.

24A

▶ Hidden Sources.

On the *Works Cited* page of his research paper, James Balarbar lists eleven books and articles that contributed directly to the essay he turned in to his instructor. His sources show a nice balance between the immediate accounts of newspapers and magazines reporting Chrysler's problem as it unfurled and the more thoughtful perspectives of books written with the advantage of hindsight.

But a quick review of his bibliography cards and notes also reveals that James examined and benefitted from materials other than the eleven works cited in his paper. Some contributed little to the final product; others provided background information not requiring documentation; still others helped him focus and narrow his thesis. The six or seven pages of his complete research paper represent the apex of a pyramid built from dozens of books, journal pieces, magazine articles, and reference work entries.

His research began with entries on the automobile industry and Chrysler from two encyclopedias: *Collier's* and *Britannica*—useful sources for a quick survey of any general subject area. Since Chrysler's problems didn't occur in a vacuum, James examined at least three books reviewing the history of the automobile industry.

> Richard M. Langworth. *Kaiser-Frazer, The Last Onslaught on Detroit: An Intimate Behind the Scenes Study of the Postwar Car Industry.* New York: Dutton, 1975.
>
> John B. Rae. *The American Automobile.* Chicago: U of Chicago P, 1965.
>
> Lawrence White. *The Automobile Industry Since 1945.* Cambridge: Harvard UP, 1971.

Though written prior to Chrysler's near-failure, these books would explain the major forces at work in the American auto industry and the fierceness of the competition—a major factor in the Chrysler story. James also checked *Who's Who in America* for basic information about key players in the bankruptcy struggle: Lee Iacocca, Lynn Townsend, Douglas Fraser, and Gene Cafiero. He even glanced at a book or two on management theory, including

> James R. McGiver and R. Charles Moyer. *Managerial Economics*. New York: West, 1979.

Periodical indexes guided James to dozens of articles on the Chrysler story which he dutifully listed in his working bibliography. More than two-thirds of these entries eventually proved "not useful" for the paper he finally wrote. But just knowing this information existed enabled James to maneuver until he found exactly the thesis he wanted to develop. Had he decided to write about Lee Iacocca or Douglas Fraser or foreign auto markets or loan guarantees instead, he could be confident from his working bibliography that resources were waiting.

None of the articles or books discussed above could be traced directly from the paper itself, nor did James get direct credit for examining them. But they were all part of a process that produced a competent and authoritative essay.

24B

▶ From Notes to Ideas.

As you might expect by now, James Balarbar took careful and extensive notes. His earliest jottings were recorded on regular sheets of paper, and they seem loose and open-ended. Once he settled on his thesis, however, all subsequent notes appear on 3″ x 5″ cards. As recommended on p. 599, he keys his note cards to his bibliography cards through code numbers and keeps careful track of direct quotations. He also made photocopies of several important newspaper and magazine articles, using a highlighting pen to mark key passages.

More important than how James took notes is what he did with them. The sources gave James a confident overview of his subject. He learned about the people involved in the corporate struggle for survival, the mistakes they made, and the strategies they devised to pull out of a nosedive. When he decided to write about the "sales bank," he did it understanding exactly how this faulty management technique fit into the bigger picture.

As he assembled his short essay, he drew from a variety of sources to construct individual paragraphs. For example, the sixth paragraph of his final version combines ideas from five different writers. But the paragraph doesn't seem like a patchwork because all the different sources are marshaled to prove one point— that the sales bank concept was a disaster. Each source simply provides evidence that enables James to draw his conclusions at the end of the paragraph:

> As an indirect result of the sales bank, between September 1966 and July 1978, Chrysler made "2447 recalls involving 71 million cars, some of which were recalled several times" (**Yates** 236). The company at one time was widely respected for the dependability of its cars and for engineering innovations such as the high compression engine, the alternator (**McDowell**, "Behind Chrysler" 12), automatic transmission, power brakes, and power steering (**Vitullo-Martin** 23). However, the corporate reputation was tarnished after the introduction, in 1975, of the Plymouth Volaré and Dodge Aspen, which both earned the Center for Auto Safety's "Lemon of the Year" citation in 1977 (**Sobel** 253-54). According to **Iacocca**, the Volaré and Aspen were introduced while they "were still in the development phase" and "should have been delayed a full six months" before they were released to the marketplace (160). Engines stalled, brakes failed, hoods flew open at "high speeds," and fenders rusted because of improper galvanization (**Sobel** 254). Chrysler lost $200 million "and much of its good will" because of the costly recalls the Volaré and Aspen required. *These recalls and losses, however, could have been prevented had the company concentrated more on quality rather than quantity as prescribed by the sales bank practices. Hence, even Lynn Townsend's objective of smooth-running plants was defeated.*

After learning from his sources, James takes command of them, extracting from these books and articles the material he needs to support his ideas. The result is a paper that belongs primarily to him—even though it is based on information borrowed from sources. He is the one who chooses to write on the sales bank problem; he is the one who, in a sense, gathers together Lee Iacocca, Brock Yates, Robert Sobel, and others to discuss that management technique for the benefit of his readers.

You should strive for the same creative collaboration in writing your research paper. Don't allow just a few sources to dictate the contents, point of view, and organization of your essay.

24C OUTLINES AND DRAFTS

▶ Scratch Outlines.

James is the kind of writer who prefers to prepare thoroughly before penning even a rough draft. As the previous sections show, he brainstormed, read widely, freewrote, and took lots of notes before tackling the paper itself. He also wrote the three scratch outlines reproduced below. As you see from these examples, scratch outlines really can be sketchy—full of abbreviations, vague phrases, and tentative ideas. Compare these experiments at organization with the more formal outline that accompanies the final version of the paper.

Scratch Outline 1: Only one major point from this trial outline will make it into the final paper, Point D—the sales bank. But the value of this tentative plan is that it locates that idea and focuses on it. James probably wrote this outline while he was in the process of shaping his thesis statement.

A. Start on money lost each yr.

B. Examples of disorganization

　　1.　Secretaries

　　2.　President's office was a thoroughfare

3. Who saved the company and basically how?

—restructuring the management

—hiring from Ford

4. Giant used-car business (Hertz and Avis story)

5. Basic shortsightedness—surviving day to day

C. Venture into foreign markets

D. Sales bank

Scratch Outline 2: Several of the main points of the previous plan have been collapsed into the introduction here. The sales bank idea now dominates everything but that introduction.

Intro.—describe disorganization, a few e.g.'s, and how sales bank failed

1. Decision to enter foreign market

2. No communication between the engineering, manufacturing, and sales

3. Sales bank intro.

I. Definition

1. Townsend's financial weapon

2. Discuss how the operation worked

3. Costs

II. Engineering and manufacturing difficulties

1. Cuts made in the engineering department responsible for poor cars

2. Affected credibility and finances of company

III. Effects of sales bank

1. Push-pull principle

2. Fire sales

3. If sales didn't work, cover up

4. $400 rebate offer by Iacocca to alleviate the sales bank mess

24C

695

Scratch Outline 3: This final scratch outline cuts the reference to foreign markets and briefly sketches a final plan for the paper. Yet even this sketch proves to be provisional. The completed paper, for example, says nothing about cars that appeal mainly to the elderly (Point II.2).

Intro.—teamwork to save company

I.   What sales bank is—millstone effect

II. Effects on engineering

    1. Recalls—poor quality, shipping junk

    2. Cutbacks on engineering—appealing to elderly

III. How they got rid of inventory

IV. What the sales bank cost the company, financially and reputation

▶ **Drafts.**

James Balarbar wrote two drafts before handing in a final version of "Chrysler's Sales Bank." (The paper that appears in 24D below is a refined version of the final paper.)

The first draft reflected James' detailed preparation and planning. Based on the third scratch outline above, it already contained most of the major ideas that would appear in the completed version. The style was polished, too. What the draft required, above all, was some reworking to define the "sales bank"—a concept familiar perhaps only to marketing experts—more clearly for the average reader. James took care of this problem in his second draft.

Rather than reprint the drafts in their entirety, we reproduce here that portion of James' paper where he defines the sales bank: Draft 1, Draft 2, and Final Version.

▶ **Draft 1.**

In his first draft, James does a good job getting down the basic facts.

¶3 The idea of a sales bank was conceived by Lynn Townsend, chairman of Chrysler from 1960 to 1975. By this procedure, the manufacturing division would build a specific number of cars regardless of whether the dealers ordered them or not. Manufacturing produced the cars at regular rates, filled their production quota, and passed the responsibility for the cars onto the sales division. The method was supposed "to compensate for the disadvantages of [Chrysler's] relatively small size," "to keep plants running smoothly," and "to keep pressure on the salesman and dealers" (Moritz and Seaman 87). However, the sales bank backfired because manufacturing geared themselves toward filling the inventory quota rather than providing cars with the customer's specifications in mind. In 1969, the sales bank inventory had 408,302 automobiles (96). Ten years later, operations still focused on the sales bank. Over 80,000 cars occupied the central inventory, and 355,000 automobiles where still sitting in the Chrysler dealer showrooms "at the close of fiscal 1979" (Vitullo-Martin 22). Those 80,000 cars alone were worth $700 million in merchandise. Moreover, the cost of storing those cars in the inventory lots was a staggering $2 million per week (22) because of maintenance and repairs due to the weather and rising interest rates (Moritz and Seaman 93).

The paragraph packs lots of interesting information. But James struggles to explain what the sales bank is and how it operates. A second draft will need to work harder to make readers as familiar with the concept as James already is. He'll also need to resolve these problems:

—Confusing pronoun references to "manufacturing": it is singular, not plural.

—Confusing figures comparing the 1969 and 1979 sales banks.

—Confusing last sentence: packs too much information.

—Formidable appearance: should the ¶ be broken up?

▶ **Draft 2.**

James revises his work, turning one paragraph into two and expanding his explanation of the sales bank concept. His additions and other revisions appear in boldface.

¶3 **Before Lee Iacocca arrived at the company, the sales bank was Chrysler's method of manufacturing and selling automobiles**. The idea was conceived by Lynn Townsend, chairman of **the company** from 1960 to 1975. By this **method**, the **management would set a quota on the number of cars to be built**. Manufacturing produced the cars at regular rates, filled their production quota, and **stored the cars on lots. Then, unloading the cars was left to the sales division.** The method was supposed "to compensate for the disadvantages of [Chrysler's] relatively small size," "to keep plants running smoothly," and "to keep pressure on the salesman and dealers" (Moritz and Seaman 87).

¶4 However, the sales bank backfired. **To begin with, the management almost never consulted the sales division or the dealers for forecasts or customer orders of the cars to be built.** Manufacturing, **which primarily** geared **itself** toward filling the inventory quota, **haphazardly added automobile options on each car. Consequently many of the cars were not**

sold. Because of the sales bank routine, over 80,000 cars occupied the central inventory, and 355,000 automobiles where still sitting in the Chrysler dealer showrooms "at the close of fiscal 1979" (Vitullo-Martin 22). Those 80,000 cars alone were worth $700 million in merchandise. Moreover, the cost of storing those cars in the inventory lots was a staggering $2 million per week (22). **These costs were due to rising interest rates on the storage lot rentals and to regular maintenance and repairs on the cars, such as "recharging batteries, pumping and changing tires, [and] replacing broken windshields"** (Moritz and Seaman 93).

This second draft does a better job than the first draft of explaining what the sales bank is. Notice that James' revision entails more than just tinkering with a few words. He adds whole sentences, cuts others, and then breaks the original paragraph into two, the first defining the sales bank, the second showing where it failed. He also eliminates the confusing (and unnecessary) reference to the 1969 sales bank. Yet problems remain:

24C

—Confusing explanation of customers' reluctance to buy sales bank cars.

—Some awkward sentences.

—Pointless quotation: "at the close of fiscal 1979."

▶ **Final Version.**
Here are the paragraphs as they appear in the final version of the paper, printed in its entirety in section 24D below. Once again, additions and changes are boldfaced.

¶3 Before Lee Iacocca arrived at the company, the sales bank was Chrysler's method of manufacturing and selling automobiles. The idea was conceived by Lynn Townsend, chairman of the company from 1960 to 1975, **described as a good manager, "a long ball hitter who occasionally struck out" (McDowell, "Reassessing Townsend" 7)**. By this method, the management would set a quota on the number of cars to be built. Manufacturing produced the cars at regular rates, filled **its** production quota, and stored the cars on **huge** lots—**sales bank lots. Marketing these** cars was left to the sales division. The **sales bank** method was supposed "to compensate for the disadvantages of [Chrysler's] relatively small size," "to keep plants running smoothly," and "to keep pressure on the salesman and dealers" (Moritz and Seaman 87).

¶4 However, the sales bank **strategy** backfired—**disastrously**. To begin with, the management almost never consulted the sales division or the dealers **before deciding what kinds of cars to produce**. Manufacturing, which primarily geared itself toward filling the inventory quota, haphazardly added options to each car. Consequently many of the cars were not **equipped the way buyers wanted them to be and proved difficult to sell. At the close of 1979, the sales bank routine had piled** 80,000 cars **into Chrysler's** central inventory, and 355,000 automobiles **sat** in dealer**'s** showrooms (Vitullo-Martin 22). Those 80,000 cars **in inventory** alone were worth $700 million in merchandise. Moreover, the cost of storing **the vehicles** in the inventory lots was a staggering $2 million per week (22). **The money covered** rising interest rates on the storage lot rentals and regular maintenance and repairs on the **stored** cars, such as "recharging batteries, pumping and changing tires, [and] replacing broken windshields" (Moritz and Seaman 93). **These were all expenses Chrysler didn't need, especially in times of economic slowdown (Reginald 15).**

The final version adds a line of revealing information about the man who conceived the sales bank idea. It adds a new observation at the end of the second paragraph, suggesting that the sales bank technique made Chrysler particularly vulnerable during economic recessions. And it smooths out some confusing passages in version 2, notably the reason why cars produced by the sales bank technique often weren't saleable: they were "not equipped the way buyers wanted them to be."

These paragraphs show how one student revised one portion of an essay; your method of revision may be different. For example, many writers produce less polished first drafts than James did in this case and then revise more intensively. But whatever your mode of revising, you should be willing to recast, rephrase, add, and delete until what you write serves both the ideas you want to convey and the readers you want to reach.

24D

24D ANNOTATED FINAL VERSION

This final version of James Balarbar's essay has been reworked slightly to enhance its usefulness as a model; most of these modifications occur in quotations and notes. As a result of these additions, some transitions have been changed and James' original paragraphing is altered in one place. Phrases have been tightened and mechanical errors edited. Yet the bulk of the essay remains just as James Balarbar wrote it in his freshman year. The numbers circled in the margin are keyed to the annotations on the facing page.

Chrysler's Sales Bank

by

James B. Balarbar

24D

English 101

Prof. John J. Ruszkiewicz

10 November 1985

► **Annotations**

1. Separate title page. A separate title page of this kind is usually optional. Check whether your instructor wants one. If so, follow the pattern shown on the facing page, providing and centering all the information shown. If you include a separate title page, do not repeat your name, instructor's name, date, and course on the first page of your essay.

You will ordinarily need a separate title page if any **front matter**—outline, preface, abstract—precedes the body of your essay. If your paper does not include such items, you may dispense with the title page and open your paper using this format:

ı

```
James Balarbar

Professor Ruszkiewicz

English 101

10 November 1905

            Chrysler's Sales Bank

    The old Chrysler Corporation was an excellent

example of how not to run a business.  Its
```

24D

Opinion is divided on whether such a first page should be numbered. The *MLA Handbook for Writers of Research Papers* does number the first page as shown above, but some instructors prefer that the first Arabic number appear on page two.

Beginning with page two, be sure to type your first initial and last name before page numbers. This will protect you against loss should your pages become separated.

J. Balarbar 2

2. Title of paper. Do not underline the title, place it between quotation marks, spell it out entirely in capital letters, or conclude it with a period. Refer to the following guide for capitalizing words.

Your paper title may, however, include other titles or phrases that require underlining or quotation marks:

Marriage and Mirth in Shakespeare's <u>As You Like It</u>

Dylan's "Like a Rolling Stone" Reconsidered

Eisenhower the General: "Nothing Is Easy in War"

Titles may also end with question marks:

Who Really Wrote <u>Hamlet</u>?

3. Instructor's name. Try to be accurate about listing your instructor's academic title. Check the college catalog to find out what rank your instructor holds. Assistant, associate, and full professors alike are addressed as professor or, if they hold a doctorate, Dr. When you can't determine an instructor's rank, simply use Mr or Ms, or no title at all:

Professor Doris Upton

Dr. Leroy Jones

Dean Wolfgang Rack

Ms Kelly Witherspoon

Mr Carter McCleary

Be sure to spell your instructor's name right.

Outline

<u>Thesis</u>: A major cause of the Chrysler Corporation's near-bankruptcy in 1979-80 was a concept called "the sales bank" which exemplified the lack of coordination between the company's management, manufacturing, and sales divisions.

    I.   Introduction
         A. Chrysler's poor management
         B. The sales bank
   II.   Definition and purpose of Chrysler's sales bank concept
  III.   Problems with sales bank
         A. No input from dealers or consumers in deciding what kinds of cars to manufacture
         B. High cost for storing and maintaining inventories of unsold cars
         C. Poor quality of cars built under quota pressures
   IV.   Consequences of sales bank
         A. Loss of the goodwill of consumers
         B. Loss of leverage over dealers
         C. Loss of control over accounting procedures
    V.   Conclusions
         A. Drain on Chrysler's finances
         B. Erosion of consumer confidence in Chrysler as an auto manufacturer

4

24D

4. Outline. Outlines are optional. If you include one, keep it short, highlighting the major points treated in your essay. Be sure the form of your outline is both consistent and accurate. It helps your reader if you begin with a clear statement of your thesis.

If you use a sentence outline, every entry in the outline is a complete sentence in the same tense. Lines begin with capital letters and end with periods. Questions are inappropriate in outlines of this sort.

For most papers, a phrase outline—as employed by James Balarbar—is probably more appropriate. Here, each entry is a phrase. The phrases begin with capital letters, but are unpunctuated. No complete sentences (with the exception of the thesis) appear in the outline.

Both sentence and phrase outlines should be double-spaced and consistently aligned, following this pattern:

```
I.   -------------------------
   A.   -------------------
   B.   ---------------
        -------------------
        1.   --------------
        2.   --------------
        3.   --------------
             a.   --------
             b.   --------
   C.   -------------------
II.  -------------------------
```

An outline preceding a short paper will probably not need to go beyond the second or third level.

Be sure to keep the levels carefully aligned and punctuated. If a line runs beyond the right margin, it carries over to the left and picks up at a point directly below where it started (see line **B.** above). No number or letter at any level of a formal outline stands alone: If you have a point **A.**, there must be a point **B.**; a point **1.** requires a corresponding point **2.**

An outline that runs only a single page is not numbered. One that requires more pages is numbered—along with other items in the front matter—in small Roman numerals (i, ii, iii, iv).

Abstract

5

One major cause of Chrysler Corporation's near-
bankruptcy in 1979-80 was a management concept called
the sales bank. Originally intended to keep
Chrysler's auto plants running smoothly by building
autos according to quotas, the sales bank revealed a
near-fatal lack of coordination between the
corporation's management, manufacturing, and sales
components. The quotas pressured the company into
building low-quality vehicles consumers didn't want
which then had to be stored at great expense until
sold at fire-sale prices to dealers profiting by
Chrysler's overstock. For a while, Chrysler's losses
were hidden by creative accounting methods, but the
sales bank idea eventually cost Chrysler millions of
dollars and the goodwill of many customers.

24D

5. Abstract. This optional feature (see pp. 614 and 734) is included on a separate page immediately before the body of the paper and is ordinarily not numbered. The word *Abstract* is centered above the summary.

24D

Chrysler's Sales Bank

¶1   The old Chrysler Corporation was an
excellent example of how not to run a business. Its
management was shortsighted and disorganized; its
method of conducting business, completely unorthodox.
In fact, according to Lee Iacocca, chairman of the
reformed company,

24D

> . . . Chrysler didn't really function like a
> company at all. Chrysler in 1978 was like
> Italy in the 1860's — the company consisted
> of little duchies, each one run by a prima
> donna. It was a bunch of mini-empires, with
> nobody giving a damn about what anyone else
> was doing. (152)[1]

¶2   However, if a business is to prosper, it
must have a central authority, "coordination and a
unity of purpose" (Albers 206). Unfortunately, the
company lacked this focused collaboration and was
almost financially destroyed. A major cause of the

6. Pagination. The first page of an essay with a title page is paginated in the upper right-hand corner, one half inch from the top, one inch from the right margin. Don't use a period after any page number.

7. Title again. Even if you have used a title page, repeat the title on this page, exactly as it appears the first time. The title is centered, four spaces above the body of your text.

If your title runs long enough to require two lines, double-space it and center both halves:

> Chrysler's Sales Bank: "Come Hell or High Water, We
> Are Never Going to Do It Again!"

8. The first quotation in the paper is lengthy enough to require indention. Such passages are placed ten spaces from the left margin and *are not* surrounded by quotation marks. They are followed by a parenthetical note —in this case **(152)**. The parenthetical note falls outside the period ending the quotation when a passage is indented (but see also #16 below). For an explanation of the raised footnote number at the end of the passage, see #10.

9. The quotation opens with an **ellipsis mark** to show that the borrowed passage begins in midsentence. The writer wants to let the reader know that Lee Iacocca's remark is incomplete. Partial quotations ordinarily do not require an ellipsis mark when what is quoted is clearly a chunk. But here, the passage continues on for several complete sentences, so it is helpful to let the reader know that the first sentence has been edited.

10. The footnote number at the end of the passage signals that there is a content/bibliographic note (see p. 623).

> a bunch of mini-empires, with nobody giving a damn
> about what anyone else was doing. (152)[1]

This raised number directs the reader to the note page which follows the body of the essay and precedes the *Works*

24D

Chrysler Corporation's near-bankruptcy in 1979-80 was
a concept called "the sales bank" which exemplified
the lack of coordination between the company's
management, manufacturing, and sales divisions.

¶3   Before Lee Iacocca arrived at the company,
the sales bank was Chrysler's method of manufacturing
and selling automobiles. The idea of a sales bank
was conceived by Lynn Townsend, chairman of the
corporation from 1960 to 1975, described as a good
manager, "a long ball hitter who occasionally struck
out" (McDowell, "Reassessing Townsend" 7). By this
method, the management would set a quota on the
number of cars to be built. Manufacturing produced
the cars at regular rates, filled its production
quota, and stored the cars on huge lots—sales bank
lots. Marketing of these cars was left to the sales
division. The sales bank method was supposed "to
compensate for the disadvantages of [Chrysler's]
relatively small size," "to keep plants running
smoothly," and "to keep pressure on the salesman and
dealers" (Moritz and Seaman 87).

¶4   However, the sales bank strategy backfired—
disastrously. To begin with, the management almost
never consulted the sales divison or dealers before
deciding what kinds of cars to produce.

24D

12

13

14

15

16

Cited page (see p. 726). The note provides the following information on Iacocca which the writer decided was important enough to include with the paper, but not in the main body of the essay. It also provides two source citations.

> [1]Lee Iaccoca joined Chrysler in November, 1978, after Henry Ford II removed him from the Presidency of the Ford Motor Company. See Iacocca 120-53; Moritz and Seaman 196-97.

The information on Iacocca could probably have been incorporated unobtrusively into the essay, but the two citations would have cluttered the page. Hence the information is placed in a note.

11. A conventional parenthetical reference, including the last name of an author and the page number on which the direct quotation preceding the note would be found.

12. Thesis statement.

13. The paper uses two newspaper articles by Edwin McDowell. So parenthetical notes need to include a short title to clarify which of the two articles is being cited. In this note, "Reassessing Townsend" is a slightly truncated form of the full title "Reassessing Lynn Townsend."

14. The expression "Chrysler's" is added to the quotation to make it clearer. The brackets tell the reader that the word does not appear in the original passage.

15. The note here refers to a work by two authors, Michael Moritz and Barrett Seaman.

16. Notice that when a quotation falls at the end of a sentence, it is followed by the closing quotation mark, a space, the parenthetical note, and only then, a period. Compare this punctuation to what happens at #8 above when a long quotation is indented.

24D

Manufacturing, which was geared primarily toward
filling the inventory quotas, haphazardly added
options to each car. Consequently many of the cars
were not equipped the way buyers wanted them to be
and proved difficult to sell. At the close of 1979,
the sales bank routine had piled 80,000 cars into
Chrysler's central inventory and 355,000 automobiles
sat in dealer showrooms (Vitullo-Martin 22). Those
80,000 cars in inventory alone were worth $700
million. Moreover, the cost of storing the vehicles
in the inventory lots was a staggering $2 million per
week (22). The money covered rising interest rates
on the storage lot rentals and regular maintenance
and repairs on the stored cars, such as "recharging
batteries, pumping and changing tires, [and]
replacing broken windshields" (Moritz and Seaman 93).
These were all expenses Chrysler didn't need,
especially in times of economic slowdown (Reginald
15).

¶5 Unfortunately, the storage costs were not
the only drain on Chrysler's resources. Because the
manufacuring division was pressed for time in filling
its quotas, it built poor-quality automobiles. In

24D

17

18

19

17. Vitullo-Martin is the hyphenated last name of a single writer, not two authors. Notice, too, that the note here documents the information in this paragraph, not a direct quotation.

18. The page reference here (22) is still to the article by Julia Vitullo-Martin.

19. Brackets indicate that *and* does not appear in the quotation from Moritz.

24D

Going for Broke, Moritz and Seaman explain how bad
the production situation could get:

> Sometimes the quality deteriorated to such
> an extent that the [assembly] lines were
> stopped. One engineer (now retired) made
> some spot checks. He discovered a Plymouth
> sitting at a Detroit railhead with no engine
> mountings, the engine just resting on the
> frame. (92)

¶6 As an indirect result of the sales bank,
between September 1966 and July 1978, Chrysler made
"2447 recalls involving 71 million cars, some of
which were recalled several times" (Yates 236). The
company at one time was widely respected for the
dependability of its cars and for engineering
innovations such as the high compression engine, the
alternator (McDowell, "Behind Chrysler's Decline"
12), automatic transmissions, power brakes, and power
steering (Vitullo-Martin 23). However, the corporate
reputation was tarnished after the introduction, in
1975, of the Plymouth Volare and Dodge Aspen, which
both earned the Center for Auto Safety's "Lemon of
the Year" citation in 1977 (Sobel 253-54). According
to Iacocca, the Volare and Aspen were introduced

20. Brackets indicate that *assembly* does not appear in the quotation from Moritz.

21. Here, both the name and authors of the cited passage are named in the sentence introducing it. So the parenthetical note at the end of the indented quotation gives a page number only: (92).

22. The parenthetical notes come thick and heavy in this section because of the numbers and statistics drawn from a variety of sources.

24D

while they "were still in the development phase" and
"should have been delayed a full six months" before
they were released to the marketplace (160). Engines
stalled, brakes failed, hoods flew open at "high
speeds," and fenders rusted because of improper
galvanization (Sobel 254). Chrysler lost $200
million "and much of its goodwill" because of the
costly recalls the Volare and Aspen required. These
recalls and losses, however, could have been
prevented had the company concentrated more on
quality rather than quantity as prescribed by the
sales bank practices. Hence, even Lynn Townsend's
objective of smooth-running plants was defeated.

¶7 Not only did Chrysler lose goodwill, it lost
respect as an automobile supplier as well. Dealers
learned to take advantage of the company. Since the
manufacturer immediately sold its cars to the
wholesalers who stored them on the inventory lots,
the retailers bargained directly with the
wholesalers. Because the sales bank foolishly
focused on quantity and kept putting cars into the
inventories, monthly "fire sales" were needed to make
room for the new incoming units. The dealers soon
learned that the wholesalers became desperate to move

24D

23

24

23. This is a helpful transitional sentence. It summarizes the previous paragraph ("not only did Chrysler lose good will . . .) and announces the topic of the new one (. . . it lost respect as an automobile supplier as well").

24. Although James chooses to highlight the term "fire sales" and probably found it in one of his sources, he does not have to provide a reference for it since the term is a common expression.

24D

the older cars. So the retail marketers capitalized
on that panic by waiting until the last week of each
month to barter for less than the regular "wholesale
price" (Iacocca 163). The sales bank system, in
effect, removed from sales personnel and dealers the
pressure it was designed to create. The retailers
were in control. The company lost more money.

¶8 When the sales bank inventory became too
large and the sales division could not unload all of
the cars to the dealers, the company covered up its
losses on quarterly sales reports with stealthy
accounting tricks. The manufacturing division
concealed its losses by recording its profits
immediately after passing the inventory to the sales
division even though the cars had not actually been
sold to customers (Moritz and Seaman 91).
Furthermore, the corporation shuffled the excess
inventory between its major divisions, such as the
Chrysler Leasing Company, so that the corporation
could show sales to balance its sales reports. One
leasing official conceded that "We were robbing Peter
to pay Paul" (93). Ronald Horwitz, a business
professor at the University of Michigan, observed at
the time that this type of action makes the company

720

25. This sentence includes a reference to the second of McDowell's articles used in preparing the paper. See #13 above.

24D

"look better on the profit-and-loss statements
but . . . does great harm over the long haul"
(McDowell, "Behind Chrysler's Decline" 12).

¶9   The old Chrysler did eventually have to pay
Peter. The management was only fooling itself with
its cover-ups and inefficient sales bank practices.
Although the sales bank was designed to improve
Chrysler, it actually drained the corporation of both
its financial resources and its credibility. The
unusual business procedure had put the company under
the "millstone effect" (Skinner 533-34). According
to this business theory, the old corporation failed
to "recognize the relationship between manufacturing
decisions and corporate strategy [so it became]
saddled with seriously noncompetitive production
systems which [were] expensive and time-consuming to
change" (533-34). The sales bank's inability to
pressure retail dealers, the production of poorly-
built vehicles, and the chaotic shuffling of
inventories were all results of Chrysler's
"noncompetitive production systems."   The bottom
line is that the sales bank and other management
mistakes eventually cost the old Chrysler Corporation
$3.3 billion (Nicholson and Jones 64). It took Lee

26

27

24D

26. Notice how this transitional sentence refers back to a quotation in the previous paragraph: "We were robbing Peter to pay Paul."

27. Notice that the conclusion does not merely restate what the paper has already said, but draws out and explains the consequences of Chrysler's use of the sales bank.

24D

Iacocca and a new team of managers more
than five grueling years to reform the company,
deliver it from red ink, and restore the goodwill of
its customers.[2]   But that's another story.

28

24D

28. Here is a second content note.

24D

Notes

[1] Lee Iacocca joined Chrysler in November, 1978 after Henry Ford II removed him from the presidency of the Ford Motor Company. See Iacocca 120-53; Moritz and Seaman 196-97.

[2] According to Stuart Reginald, within his first year as president of Chrysler, Iacocca had abolished the sales bank: "Come hell or high water, we are never going to do it again!" (15).

29. Content notes. Most undergraduate essays will not contain content notes. But if yours does, they appear on a separate page immediately following the body of the essay. The page is numbered consecutively with the rest of the essay and headed by the title *Notes* at the center of the page.

The notes themselves appear two lines below the heading, double-spaced. The first line of the note is indented five spaces, followed by the footnote number raised half a space above the line.

24D

30

Works Cited

Albers, Henry H. _Principles of Management_. 3rd ed.
    New York: Wiley, 1969.

Iacocca, Lee. _Iacocca: An Autobiography_. New York:
    Bantam, 1984.

McDowell, Edwin. "Behind Chrysler's Long Decline:
    Its Management and Competition." _New York Times_
    17 Aug. 1979, sec. 1: 1+.

---. "Reassessing Lynn Townsend." _New York Times_ 12
    Aug. 1979, sec. 3: 7.

Moritz, Michael, and Barrett Seaman. _Going for Broke:
    Lee Iacocca's Battle to Save Chrysler_. Garden
    City, New York: Anchor-Doubleday, 1984.

Nicholson, Tom, and James C. Jones. "Iacocca's Little
    Miracle." _Newsweek_ 3 Aug. 1981: 64-65.

Reginald, Stuart. "On the Firing Line at Chrysler."
    New York Times 16 Sept. 1979, sec. 3: 7+.

Skinner, Wickman. "Manufacturing Link in Corporate
    Strategy." _Harvard Business Review on
    Management_. New York: Harper, 1975.

Sobel, Robert. _Car Wars_. New York: Dutton, 1984.

Vitullo-Martin, Julia. "Chrysler in Chaos: Is the
    Chrysler Company Beyond Repair?" _Saturday
    Review_ 19 Jan. 1980: 22-25.

Yates, Brock W. _The Decline and Fall of the American
    Automobile Industry_. New York: Empire, 1983.

31
32

24D

33

30. Works cited. The *Works Cited* page follows the body of the essay and any content notes. It begins on its own page. The title *Works Cited* is centered at the top, with the alphabetical list beginning two spaces below. Everything is double-spaced. Do not quadruple space between items unless requested to do so by your instructor.

Notice that the first line in each entry touches the left margin and subsequent lines are indented fives spaces so that the author's last name is always highlighted—an important design feature of an alphabetical roster. Notice, too, that each entry consists of three parts, each terminated by a period and separated from the next by two spaces:

—the name(s) of the author(s).

—the title of the work.

—publication information.

A *Works Cited* list contains only books, articles, and other materials actually used or mentioned in the body of the paper. If you want to credit works you read but did not use directly in your paper, entitle the reference list *Works Consulted.*

31. The plus sign (+) following the page number for this newspaper article by Edwin McDowell indicates that the article continues on subsequent pages.

32. McDowell's name isn't repeated for his second article. It is replaced by three typed hyphens followed by a period.

33. Vitullo-Martin is a hyphenated last name.

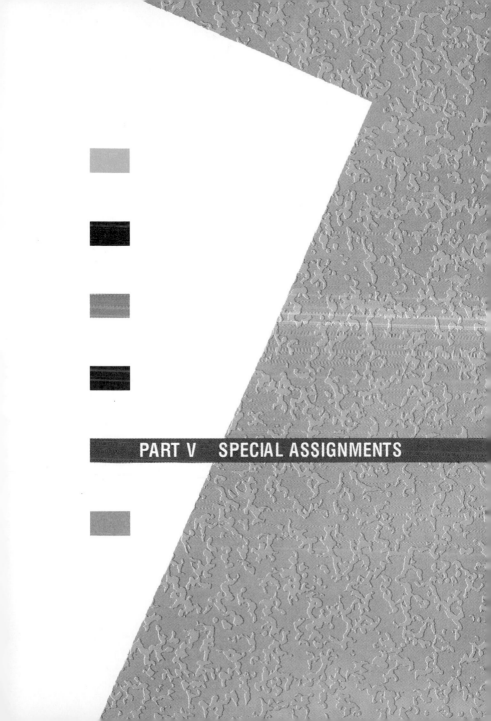

PART V   SPECIAL ASSIGNMENTS

This inventory outlines the distinctive features of seven special writing assignments. For each type of writing, you will find a guide or *template* that includes

> a rationale,
>
> a discussion of criteria for a successful piece,
>
> a list of components or varieties,
>
> a standard form,
>
> some pointers, and
>
> a sample or model.

Consult these sections for the same reasons a pilot reads a preflight checklist: to be sure all major systems are operating smoothly and to be certain nothing important has been forgotten. For more detailed discussions of writing strategies, refer to Parts I, II, and III of this handbook.

The special assignments are discussed in the following order:

- **A** How to write an abstract
- **B** How to write an essay examination
- **C** How to write a literary analysis
- **D** How to write a review
- **E** How to write a résumé
- **F** How to write a memo
- **G** How to write a business letter

Terms you need to know

Abstract. A summary of the argument and evidence in a paper. An abstract should be short—usually less than one hundred words.

Essay examination. A test requiring extended written answers, usually of a paragraph or more in length.

Literary analysis. A paper that examines a literary work—a poem, play, novel, short story. A literary analysis can explore the text of the literary work itself (its plot, characters, style) or related issues such as its historical background, genre, author, influences, or sources.

Review. An essay that evaluates an object, event, person, or work of art according to criteria of quality or performance, exposing strengths and weaknesses. A review often makes its point by comparing and contrasting similar objects.

Résumé. An outline of a person's academic and employment history, also listing personal information (when relevant), achievements, and available references. Prospective employers often ask for résumés.

Memo. A short factual message between individuals or offices in businesses or other institutions.

Business letter. A formal written communication between individuals or institutions dealing with professional or commercial issues.

ABS

733

A   HOW TO WRITE AN ABSTRACT

- **1**   What is the point?
- **2**   What makes an abstract successful?
- **3**   What are its components?
- **4**   What is the standard form of an abstract?
- **5**   Some advice
- **6**   Sample abstracts

1. What is the point of an abstract?

— to summarize accurately the contents of a journal article or paper.

— to help researchers decide whether to examine an article in its entirety.

— to help readers follow the argument of an essay. When articles and their abstracts appear in the same journal, the abstracts function like outlines, highlighting the main ideas and conclusions of the papers.

2. What makes an abstract successful?

ABS

—a clear representation of the abstracted article, outlining its major ideas and how they were arrived at.

—an organization faithful to the structure of the abstracted essay; major points in the abstract should follow the same order as major points in the paper.

—a concise style that nonetheless reflects the wording of the original piece.

—an adherence to any word-limit imposed upon the abstract.

3. What are the components of an abstract?
An abstract usually has only two parts:

a title (optional)

a body.

An abstract preceding an article may carry no title since readers will naturally assume that it is an abstract of the essay to follow. Abstracts separated from their original articles are often identified by the word *Abstract* followed by the title of the original piece:

Abstract: Characteristics of Rejection Letters and
Their Effects on Job Applicants

In an undergraduate essay, the word *Abstract* may be the only title necessary (see model below).

4. What is the standard form for an abstract?

The correct form of an abstract is usually determined by where it will appear. A professional journal, for example, may have specific requirements for abstracts, especially concerning length.

An abstract included in an undergraduate essay is typed on a separate page placed immediately before the body of the essay. The word *Abstract* appears as the title, centered on the page, a double or quadruple space before the body of the abstract. The abstract page ordinarily is unnumbered. The abstract itself should be a single paragraph, double-spaced, of approximately one hundred words.

5. Some advice about preparing an abstract

To prepare an abstract of a paper

—read through the article carefully,

—underline or write down its main points and major supporting evidence,

—extract the gist of each section or cluster of related paragraphs; give special attention to introductory and concluding paragraphs,

—shape your abstract from the points you have underlined or the summaries you have made of each major part of the article,

—link your points with helpful transitions,

—test the abstract against the article, evaluating how well it reflects what the article contains.

Be sure your abstract is easy to read. Keep it short, but don't compress your style so much that the abstract sounds like a want ad. Avoid abbreviations and sentence fragments.

Don't use direct quotations from the article in the abstract.

Try to follow the pattern of organization used in the original article. Don't attempt to restructure an article, even if you discover a more economical way of organizing its material. However, you need not discuss every topic discussed in an essay; you may, for example, explain how one type of analysis is applied to a variety of subjects rather than describe each subject individually (see abstract #2 below).

6. Samples

1. Abstract from an undergraduate research paper (see Chapter 24 for the complete paper):

Abstract

One major cause of Chrysler Corporation's near-bankruptcy in 1979–80 was a management concept called the sales bank. Originally intended to keep Chrysler's auto plants running smoothly by building autos according to quotas, the sales bank revealed a near-fatal lack of coordination among the corporation's management, manufacturing, and sales components. The quotas pressured the company into building low-quality vehicles consumers didn't want. The cars then had to be stored at great expense until sold at fire-sale prices to dealers profiting by Chrysler's overstock. For a while, Chrysler's losses were hidden by creative accounting methods, but the sales bank idea eventually cost Chrysler millions of dollars and the good will of many customers.

2. Abstract from a professional research journal:

Abstract: Expanding Roles for Summarized Information

At least seven types of summaries have emerged in common usage, especially during the past 250 years. They may be classified as either sequential summaries

ABS

that retain the original order in which information was presented or synthesizing summaries that alter this sequence to achieve specific objectives. Each type of summary developed in response to challenges facing professions, government, business, and ordinary citizens—all of whom have sought to absorb increasing quantities of information being generated in a society that is becoming more complex. This taxonomy offers a definition and brief history for each of the seven techniques, describes the growth of corporations or other organizations that can be considered leading practitioners, and comments on the potential continuing role for each type of summary. The article also focuses on several contemporary issues that will affect future research, classroom writing instruction, and information management in modern computerized offices.

—Oswald M. T. Ratteray, *Written Communication* 2 (1985): 457.

B HOW TO WRITE AN ESSAY EXAMINATION

EX

Oswald M. T. Ratteray, from "Expanding Roles for Summarized Information," *Written Communication*, Vol. 2 No. 4, October 1985, pp. 457–472. Copyright © 1985 Sage Publications, Inc. Reprinted by permission of Sage Publications Inc.

1. What is the point of an essay examination?

—to prove that you command the facts in a subject area.

—to show that you can interpret and relate concepts.

—to show that you can use information to support or refute assertions or to discuss and evaluate ideas.

—to show that you have grasped the vocabulary and idiom of a subject.

—to pass.

2. What makes an essay examination successful?

—attention to the questions posed.

—clear, strategically organized answers.

—sufficient evidence to support your assertions.

3. What are the components and form of an essay examination?

There are no set forms for essay exams. But because such exams are both written and read under pressure, it makes sense to follow an organization that makes writing efficient, reading easy, and a worthy grade inevitable.

Use a **commitment and response** design (see Section 5C) to outline your entire essay in your first paragraph. State your major point, repeating key words in the question, and indicate what line of development you will follow. Break the question down into parts you can discuss in separate paragraphs. If you don't complete an essay, the opening paragraph should make it possible for a reader to construct what your finished essay would have looked like had you time to write it.

Treat one major idea per paragraph. State the main point of each paragraph in the first sentence—a topic sentence. Consider the possibility that an instructor may skim your essay and read only these topic sentences.

Use transitions, numbers, and lists. They help organize

EX

information and direct readers to important points: *first, second, third, consequently, as a result, by contrast,* and so on.

Provide specific supporting evidence for your conclusions. Because time is limited, choose your facts carefully. Look for evidence that will suggest you know more than you can write about in the time you have to complete the test.

4. Some advice when taking an essay examination.
Read the questions carefully. Underline key verbs that tell you what to do with the topic: *describe, analyze, classify, compare, contrast, discuss, evaluate.* Each of these words means something a little different (see pp. 580–81). If you don't understand a question, ask your instructor if a clarification is possible under the ground rules of the examination.

Answer the questions your instructor actually asked, not the ones you were hoping for.

Plan ahead. Read over the entire exam, estimate the time you can give to each question, make quick scratch outlines of your essays, work through them with an eye on the clock, and stick to your schedule. Answer every required question—even minimally if you have to. Instructors may give you a few points for a tentative answer, but no points at all for a blank space.

Use the terminology and names you have heard in lectures and come across in your reading—and be sure you know how to spell them.

Don't pad your answers and don't wander from your subject. Instructors recognize a snow job.

EX

Write clearly or print. Illegible handwriting can drop a grade almost as fast as weak content.

Don't be embarrassed to revise, cross out, and rearrange the elements of your paper. Such changes show you are thinking. If necessary, use arrows or balloons to insert or relocate whole sentences or paragraphs. Be as neat as possible.

Allow time to edit and proofread your answer. Instructors will appreciate the concern you show for correct spelling, punctuation, and grammar.

5. Sample essay exam answer

The following response to an essay question in a government course might be written in forty-five minutes to an hour. As a model, it is reproduced in a form and style more polished than might be possible given such a time restriction. But the major features of the answer, explained in the comments, would be manageable within those limits.

Question: *Explain* the system of *checks and balances* operating in the *federal* government.

> {The italicized key words in the question suggest that an effective answer will need to show what the checks and balances do. The question is specifically limited to the federal government only. Examples or illustrations from local or state government would be off the subject.}

To prevent any one group or individual from seizing control of the American federal government, the framers of the Constitution established a system of checks and balances that *imposed specific limitations* upon the *executive, legislative,* and *judicial* branches of government.

> {Again, key words in the reply are italicized. Immediately and briefly, the answer explains what the checks and balances do: they "impose specific limitations upon . . . branches of government." The three branches of government are named in order of their treatment in subsequent paragraphs, one paragraph per branch—executive, legislative, and judicial. This opening paragraph thus addresses the basic examination question and sketches out the organization for the remainder of the reply.}

The executive branch of the federal government is limited in its actions first by the authority of Congress, which controls the federal budget and passes laws, and secondly by the actions of the courts. The President can veto laws passed by Congress, but the Congress can, by two-thirds majorities of both houses, override any veto. Similarly, while the President and executive branch

EX

control foreign policy and the military, treaties must be ratified by the Senate, the military budget is controlled by Congress, and only Congress can declare war. Domestic policies and federal appointments are administered by the executive branch, yet presidential authority is again limited by Congressional review and budgetary power. In much the same way, actions of the executive branch fall under the scrutiny of the federal courts; the Supreme Court can declare presidential actions unconstitutional.

> {The answer first deals with the executive branch, explaining both its powers and its limitations—first those imposed by the Congress, and then those imposed by the judiciary. The writer shows command of the subject by referring to specific powers: foreign policy, treaties, federal appointments. But notice that particular historical examples aren't used. If this were a two-hour examination, such examples might be appropriate and workable. But they are probably too time-consuming to include here.}

The legislative branch of the federal government is limited by the authority of the President and the federal courts. The President can veto all acts of Congress; the Supreme Court can declare them unconstitutional. Moreover the President can command the attention of the American people in ways simply not available to more than five hundred congressional representatives from different and antagonistic parties.

> {Just as the opening paragraph promises, this paragraph is about the checks on the legislative branch.}

The judicial branch of the federal government—particularly the Supreme Court—exercises enormous authority through the power of judicial review of laws passed by the Congress and signed by the President. Theoretically, one vote on the Supreme Court (in a 5-4 split) could override the unanimous opinion of the Congress and the approval of the President. Yet members of

EX

the court are appointed by the executive branch and approved by the Senate. And ultimately, any act of the Supreme Court is subject to the power of the Congress, the President, and the people acting in concert to change the Constitution itself.

{The paragraph explores checks on the judicial branch.}

Thus, the American federal government is an elaborate system of checks and balances that has worked reasonably well for two hundred years to control the ambition of any one branch or person. Each of the branches has enjoyed periods of enhanced power and prestige, but none has been able to dominate or seize the government for any sustained period.

{This effective conclusion suggests to a reader that the writer knows even more about checks and balances—and American history—than the essay contains.}

C   HOW TO WRITE A LITERARY ANALYSIS

1. What is the point of a literary analysis?

—to heighten your appreciation for works of literature.

—to demonstrate your ability to support a thesis about a literary work.

—to enhance your skill at close reading and interpretation.

2. What makes a literary analysis successful?

—a clearly stated purpose in analyzing the literary work—that is, having an assertion worth demonstrating or a point worth making.

—convincing evidence to support the assertion. Evidence may come both from within the literary work itself and from outside readings and secondary sources.

—an appropriate and correct style.

3. What are the kinds of literary analysis?

There are many kinds of literary analysis; a few of the basic types are outlined below. When you write a literary paper, you will ordinarily limit yourself to one or two of these types of analysis.

Close reading of a text. When doing a close reading, you carefully explain the meaning and possible interpretations of a literary passage, sometimes line by line. You look carefully at how the language of the work makes a reader experience or think about certain images. You might do a close reading of a short poem, a speech from a play, or a passage from a longer work.

Analysis of theme. You examine the ideas or messages a literary work conveys to readers. A literary work may explore any number of themes (some general ones might be *anger, jealousy, ambition, hypocrisy, greed*), but most poems, plays, and novels sound one or two consistent notes.

Analysis of plot or structure. You study the way a work of literature is put together and why a writer chooses a particular arrangement of ideas or plot elements to say what he or she wants.

Analysis of character. You study the behavior of characters in a novel, poem, play, or short story to understand their motivations and the ways characters can relate to each other. Or you explore how a writer creates a character through description, action, reaction, and dialogue.

LIT

Analysis of setting. You study setting to figure out how the environment of a literary work (where things happen in a novel, short story, or play) affects what happens in the plot or to the characters.

Analysis of literary type or genre. You study a particular literary work by evaluating it as what it is intended to be: a tragedy, a comic novel, a sonnet, a detective story, an epic, and so on. You compare the work to other similar literary pieces, looking for likenesses and differences.

Historical analysis. You study a literary work as it reflects the society which produced it or as it was accepted or rejected by that society when it was published. Or you study the way historical information makes a literary work from an earlier time clearer to a reader today.

Biographical study. You study how a writer's life is expressed in or through a literary work.

Study of the creative process. You study how a work was written, examining early sources, notes, influences, manuscripts, and revised texts.

4. What is the standard form for a literary analysis?

A literary analysis may take many forms, but academic essays generally follow the conventions of the research paper, including careful documentation (see especially pp. 636–37). However, a few special conventions should be observed.

Use the present tense to refer to events occurring in a literary work: Hester Prynne *wears* a scarlet letter; Hamlet *kills* Polonius. Think of a literary work as an ongoing performance.

Identify passages of short poems by line numbers: ("Journey of the Magi," lines 21–31). Do not, however, use the abbreviations *l.* or *ll.* for *line* or *lines* because they are sometimes confused with Roman numerals; spell out *line* or *lines* completely.

For long poems with major divisions (books, cantos, parts), give both the division and page numbers in citations, separated by periods. You may abbreviate the titles of familiar works such as Chaucer's *Troilus and Criseyde* or Milton's *Paradise Lost* (*Troilus* 2.540–46); (*PL* IX.163–70). Citations usually are placed immediately after short selections occurring in the text of the paper or immediately below longer selections indented from the body of your essay.

Give act and scene divisions (and line numbers as necessary) for passages from plays. Act and scene numbers are now usually given in Arabic numbers, although Roman numbers are still common and acceptable: *Ham.* 4.5.179–85 or *Ham.* IV.v.179–86. The titles of Shakespeare's works are commonly abbreviated in citations: *Mac.* I.ii; *Oth.* 2.2 Check to see which form your teacher prefers.

Make an effort to introduce all direct quotations. Do not insert a quotation from a literary work or a critic into your paper without identifying it in some way. And be sure quotations fit into the grammar of your sentences. Here are some examples:

> When an audience hears the king call his cowering servant a "cream-fac'd loon" it begins to understand why Macbeth's men hate and distrust him.

> As we watch Lady Macbeth sleepwalking, we share the fears of the doctor who warns the gentlewoman: "you have known what you should not" (V.i.46–47).

> Commenting on the play, Frank Kermode observes that "*Macbeth* has extraordinary energy; it represents a fierce engagement between the mind and its guilt."

Provide a date of publication in parentheses after your first mention of a literary work: Before publishing *Ulysses* (1914), James Joyce had written . . .

Use technical terms accurately. Spell the names of characters correctly. Take special care with matters of grammar and convention.

5. Some advice about preparing a literary analysis

It is not possible to provide a formula for writing a literary analysis since the variety of subjects and analytical approaches is enormous. However, you may find the following thirteen-step strategy helpful.

1. Read the work (or works) through once, writing down your reactions or major questions. Don't interrupt your reading to take detailed notes yet. Instead, savor the literary experience.

2. Now, think about what you have just read. What issues interest you immediately? What questions did the piece raise that you'd like to explore more? Examine your preliminary list of issues and questions.

> The problem of ambition in Shakespeare's *Macbeth*
>
> The relationship between Lady Macbeth and her husband
>
> How old are the Macbeths?
>
> Is the story of the Macbeths true?
>
> Why are some lines in this tragedy funny?
>
> The nature of Shakespearian tragedy.

3. To stimulate questions, consider comparisons and contrasts with other similar works you have read (or seen).

> What makes both *Macbeth* and *Hamlet* tragic plays?
>
> Is Macbeth as ambitious as King Claudius in *Hamlet*?
>
> Is Lady Macbeth a more influential character in *Macbeth* than Queen Gertrude is in *Hamlet*?
>
> Does Macbeth resemble Darth Vader?
>
> Why does Shakespeare use comedy in *Hamlet*, *King Lear*, and *Macbeth*?

This would be a good time to use one of the techniques described in Section 2C for finding and focusing ideas: freewriting, brainstorming, cubing.

4. If reading the work itself hasn't raised questions in your mind, examine some secondary sources where you may discover issues you hadn't been aware of.

> Are some scenes missing from *Macbeth*?
>
> Did Shakespeare write *Macbeth* to please King James I?

> What did the term *equivocation* mean to the audience of Shakespeare's *Macbeth*?

To locate secondary sources on literary topics, begin with the following indexes, bibliographies, and guides available in a library reference room.

Essay and General Literature Index

MLA International Bibliography

New Cambridge Bibliography of English Literature

The Oxford Companion to American Literature

The Oxford Companion to English Literature

The Oxford Companion to Classical Literature

Holman, C. Hugh. *A Handbook to Literature*

5. Formulate a preliminary question about the literary work you are studying. Be sure the question is one you are willing to explore in greater depth.

6. Test the energy of your question. Is its answer so obvious that it isn't likely to interest or surprise anyone?

> Is Shakespeare's *Macbeth* a great play?

If so, discard the question. Try another. Look for a surprising, even startling question whose answer you don't already know. Test your question on a friend or instructor.

> Could Shakespeare's *Macbeth* actually be a comedy?

7. Now turn your question into an assertion—your preliminary thesis statement.

> Shakespeare's *Macbeth* is really a comedy.

Is this an assertion you are interested in proving? Is it a statement other readers might challenge? If so, write it on a notecard and go on. If not, modify it or explore another issue.

8. Test the scope of your statement. Freewrite for ten minutes on your subject. Do you think you can deal with it adequately within the limits of your paper—five pages? ten pages? If necessary, narrow and refocus your statement. When you are satisfied with your thesis, copy it onto a notecard.

LIT

9. With your thesis statement on a card in front of you, reread the literary work again, more slowly and analytically this time. Look for characters, incidents, descriptions, speeches, and dialogue that support or refute your thesis. Take careful notes. If you are using your own textbook, highlight significant passages in the work.

10. Evaluate the evidence you have gathered from a close reading of the piece. Modify your thesis to reflect what you have learned or discovered. In most cases, your thesis will be more specific and limited after you have gathered and assessed evidence.

> The many unexpected comic moments in *Macbeth* emphasize how strange the world has become for the Macbeths.

11. If necessary, return to secondary sources to supplement your close reading. (For some kinds of analysis, most of your reading will be in secondary sources and journals of literary criticism.) Do other writers tend to agree or disagree with your thesis? If you use secondary sources, take careful notes. Be sure to prepare accurate bibliography cards for your "Works Cited" page.

12. Read through all your notes, and prepare scratch outlines for your paper. Choose the one you think might be most effective.

> *Thesis*: Comic moments in *Macbeth* emphasize how strange the world has become for the Macbeths.
>
> I. Comic moments after the murder of King Duncan
>
> II. Comedy at the feast for Banquo
>
> III. Comedy in the sleepwalking scene
>
> IV. Conclusion

13. Now write a draft. Stay open to new ideas and refinements of your original thesis. (To see how the paper on *Macbeth* sketched above might develop, see the sample literary paper on pp. 750–61.)

Be sure that the bulk of your essay consists of material that supports or proves your statement about a literary work. Don't wander off into a biography of the author or a discussion of the historical period unless such material relates directly to what you are trying to prove.

Avoid the kind of paper that simply paraphrases the plot of a literary work or praises its author for a job well done. Avoid impressionistic judgments: "I feel that Hemingway must have been a good American. . . ."

Don't expect to find a moral in every literary work.

Don't think a literary analysis requires you to search for "hidden meanings." Respond honestly to what you are reading—not the way you think your teacher expects you to.

1

Travis Beckwith III

Professor Cupperman

English 321 Shakespeare

10 November 1986

The Comedy of <u>Macbeth</u>

Unlike Greek or French tragedians, Shakespeare was
rarely reluctant to add a lively comic scene to even his
most serious plays. Everyone recognizes the humor of the
gravedigger in <u>Hamlet</u>, the fool in <u>King Lear</u>, the porter in
<u>Macbeth</u>. Yet <u>Macbeth</u> (1606?) also contains other less
overtly comic moments, when its lines or characters <u>seem</u>
funny, but actors and audiences are not exactly sure what
to make of them. Bolder actors might be tempted to play
these troublesome moments comically, but at the risk of
offending critics who expect <u>Macbeth</u> to be serious. The
same lines make some spectators want to chuckle, but they
usually remain silent, fearing to look as foolish as the
person who applauds at the wrong place in a symphony. In
my view, Shakespeare creates these uneasy comic situations
in <u>Macbeth</u> deliberately, to emphasize the absurdity of the
world created by the Macbeths after they decide to murder
King Duncan.

Annotations

1. Introductory paragraph. A problem is raised: some scenes in *Macbeth* seem funny, but not in the way typical of other Shakespearian tragedies. What gives? The paper provides a close reading of *Macbeth* to answer this question. No secondary sources are explored, although some might have been appropriate.

The question mark after the year provided for *Macbeth* (1606?) indicates some uncertainty about the date. It is not always possible to date literary works precisely.

2. This statement is a refined version of the thesis developed on pp. 747–48.

LIT

The first few such comic lines come early in the play and could pass unnoticed if actors play them with straight faces. Yet is is hard not to smile when Lady Macbeth boldly claims victory after drugging the grooms who guard Duncan's bedchamber, discovering that "That which hath made them drunk hath made me bold" (<u>Mac</u>. II.ii.1). Then, just the way a slightly drunk person would, she goes on to apologize gruesomely for not killing Duncan herself, almost surprised by her reluctance to murder: "Had he [King Duncan] not resembled / My father as he slept, I had done't" (12-13).

Macbeth has the next comic line, this one his reaction to Lennox's description of the horrible storm that blows while Macbeth is murdering Duncan. Deadpans Macbeth: "'Twas a rough night" (II.iii.61). The audience laughs sympathetically, knowing much better than Lennox how rough it has been for the new Thane of Cawdor. Then when a horrified Macduff discovers that Duncan has been murdered, Lady Macbeth screams: "Woe, alas! / What, in our house?" (II.iii.87-88). Any audience that hears those lines wants to laugh at Lady Macbeth's self-centeredness. Even Banquo notices her inappropriate concern for her household's reputation when he replies: "Too cruel any where" (88). The remainder of the scene has a comic edge to it, as Duncan's sleepy sons rouse themselves to learn that their

LIT

3

4

5

6

3. The paper follows the scratch outline on p. 748. Here is the first of two paragraphs developing point I: "Comic moments after the murder of King Duncan."

4. All the references in the paper are to lines from *Macbeth*. This is the only note that includes the abbreviation *Mac*. Readers can assume that all subsequent act and scene numbers also refer to *Macbeth*.

5. Because the quotation here is short (fewer than four lines), it is incorporated right into the body of the paper. Notice that the period at the end of the quotation follows the parenthetical reference:

> I had done't" (12–13).

6. The parenthetical reference contains only a line number because it refers to the same act and scene mentioned in the previous citation.

father has been assassinated: "O, by whom?" (100). Then
Macbeth almost gives away the whole plot by trying to
explain why he killed the grooms, the only possible
witnesses to the murder. Lady Macbeth understands the
problem, so she faints to draw attention away from her
babbling husband. The entire ghastly episode teeters on
the brink of explosive laughter.

For several scenes afterward though, the action turns
serious enough to make an audience almost forget the
moments of comedy in the play, as Macbeth consolidates his
power and hires men to kill his friend Banquo. But then at
the feast visited by Banquo's ghost (III.iv), the comedy
revives as desperate Lady Macbeth tries to convince the
assembled thanes that her husband's odd behavior when
seeing Banquo is not unusual: "my lord is often thus, / And
hath been from his youth" (52-53), little comfort for men
now serving a king who talks to chairs. Lady Macbeth
admits as much when she criticizes her husband: "Why do
you make such faces? When all's done, / You look but on a
stool" (66-67). Macbeth's major complaint is that the
murdered Banquo isn't playing fair. Macbeth longs for the
good old days:

> . . . the time has been,
> That when the brains were out, the man would die,

7. Here is the paragraph developing point II in the scratch outline: "Comedy at the feast for Banquo."

8. This quotation is long enough to warrant indention from the body of the paper. The left margin of the quotation is moved ten spaces from the margin of the essay itself.

4

> And there an end; but now they rise again
> With twenty mortal murthers on their crowns,
> And push us from our stools. (77-81)

If Macbeth sounds absurd in these passages, Lady Macbeth suffers the same fate in her famous sleep-walking scene (V.i), most of which is pathetic and serious. But in recalling the sight of murdered Duncan, whose blood she earlier smeared on the grooms, she speaks one comic line: "Yet who would have thought the old man to have had so much blood in him?" (39-40). "Old man" seems to mean about the same thing here as "old geezer." The remark suggests that all the blood on Duncan surprises Lady Macbeth, in much the same way that the ghost of Banquo—also bloody—surprises Macbeth.

Is it possible to tie all these comic examples together? One last example hints at the connection. The line occurs very near the end of the play when Macbeth realizes exactly how the witches have lied to him (V.viii). Thinking he can't be killed by one born of woman, Macbeth fears no man during the battle with the rebels who have come to dethrone him. But then Macbeth's sworn enemy Macduff reveals that he was "untimely ripped" (14) from his mother's womb, making it possible for him to slay the tyrant. Macbeth curses the witches for deceiving his

9. Here is the paragraph developing point III in the scratch outline: "Comedy in the sleep-walking scene."

10. Notice that most of the verbs in this paragraph describing action in *Macbeth* are in the present tense. In this paragraph, those verbs include *sounds*, *suffers*, *speaks*, and *surprises*.

hopes, and then, like an angry little boy quitting a game
and carrying his football home, he tells Macduff "I'll not
fight with thee" (22). The remark sounds as absurd as all
the others cited in this paper because Macbeth here feels
the same emotions he and his wife have been experiencing at
intervals throughout the play: surprise, outrage, and
insult. Time and again, the Macbeths become comically
absurd in the tragedy because they don't realize that their
murderous actions have changed the world. After they seize
the throne of Scotland, they expect everything to stay as
it was before they killed Duncan, but they soon discover
that the old game is being played according to rules they
haven't learned yet. Repeatedly they must respond to
situations they haven't anticipated:

> "Had he not resembled my father. . . ."
>
> "'Twas a rough night"
>
> "What, in our house?"
>
> "Why do you make such faces . . .?"
>
> "Now they rise again . . . and push us. . . ."
>
> "Who would have thought . . .?"

Macbeth's comically pathetic "I'll not fight with thee" is
a logical but futile attempt to escape a game the Macbeths
themselves have invented, one so horrible that, time and
again, it frightens them out of their wits. Spectators
feel the horror, but also detect the humor in the Macbeths'
confusion. That's why they want to laugh, but usually don't.

11

LIT

11. The conclusion links all the separate examples cited in the paper to support the thesis and refine it: "After they seize the throne of Scotland, they [the Macbeths] expect everything to stay as it was before they killed Duncan, but they soon discover that the old game is being played according to rules they haven't learned yet."

6

12

Work Cited

The Riverside Shakespeare.   Ed. G. Blakemore Evans.

   Boston: Houghton, 1974.

LIT

12. The *Works Cited* page mentions only the text of Shakespeare used in preparing the essay. No other works contributed directly to the analysis.

LIT

1. What is the point of a review?

—to judge the quality of a performance, a product, or an idea.

—to evaluate a person's work or achievements.

—to establish criteria for measuring quality or success.

—to compare persons, objects, performances, or ideas in order to make preferential judgments.

2. What makes a review successful?

—demonstrated standards of quality that make sense to readers.

REV

—convincing evidence that the object being reviewed either meets or fails to meet accepted standards.

—a reasonable tone—one that suggests the reviewer is being fair.

3. What are the parts of a review?

A review has three basic parts: the criteria of evaluation, the evaluation itself, and the evidence.

Criteria of evaluation are simply measures of quality—the standards we apply to decide how good something is. Criteria can be very simple or complex: a good photograph is *sharp*; a quality steak is *marbled*; a successful movie *reflects the beliefs and styles of its time.* Criteria of evaluation are not always stated outright in an article, especially when reviewers can safely assume that their readers agree with the standards they are applying.

Criteria are more likely to be discussed directly when readers either don't know what the standards are (as might be the case in judging an unfamiliar sport or technical material) or might disagree with them. In these situations, reviewers might explain the criteria in detail, as is common in consumer magazines that rate various products. Or reviewers might spend time justifying their standards, proving they are the best ones to apply.

The central point of any review is the evaluation itself. Just as criteria vary, so do statements of evaluation. Objects may be described (good/bad; effective/ineffective; sensitive/insensitive), classified (****, ***, **), ranked, graded, or judged in some other way.

The bulk of a review presents the evidence supporting the evaluation. The writer must show how and why particular persons, ideas, or objects do or don't live up to the standards that apply to them.

4. What is the standard form for a review?

REV

The forms reviews take vary. An evaluation written in class assessing a painting, a musical composition, or a lecture may take the form of a simple essay. A restaurant review written for a local newspaper or magazine may follow a given format and conclude with a checklist. A road test of an automobile might include comparison charts, performance statistics, and graphs. When you are assigned to write a review, look for examples of similar reviews in magazines, journals, newspapers, and pamphlets.

When reviewing objects or products, you might need to gather data, make measurements, and do comparisons. Information of this kind is usually conveyed most efficiently to readers through charts, tables and graphs. Don't hesitate to use them.

Some advice about writing a review

Writing a review requires that you do more than merely state an opinion. You have to convince readers that your evaluation is worth believing. It is often said that everyone is entitled to an opinion, but opinions supported by good reasons and facts are more respected and powerful than simple expressions of preference. If you are asked to prepare a review, you might want to begin with this ten-step routine.

1. Decide what you are going to evaluate. When the choice of topic is yours, begin with an object or area you know something about. If you know tennis, evaluate tennis players, rackets, tournaments, or clubs. If you cook expertly, evaluate restaurants, cooking utensils, food markets, or frozen cuisine. If you read voraciously or love films, evaluate a novel, an author, a film, a theater, or a director. Everyone is an expert on some subject. Don't underestimate the value of your expertise.

2. List the general criteria that might be used in evaluating your subject. At this stage, list all the criteria you can think of. If you were evaluating a play, for example, your list might include:

acting	lighting
scenery	costumes
pace of action	interpretation of play
blocking	projection of voices
starting on time	use of music

3. Now decide which of these general criteria apply specifically to your subject. Which might be most useful in guiding you toward a judgment? If you already have a strong opinion about your subject, which of the criteria do you think you'll have to examine to support your opinion?

4. Examine the general criteria applicable to your subject more specifically. For each general criterion, define specific standards you think your readers will accept or you are willing to defend.

acting	good acting seems natural
	good acting is subtle
	good acting makes an audience forget the actor
	good acting interprets a character in a unique way
scenery	effective scenery doesn't intrude on the action
	effective scenery highlights the action
	effective scenery creates an appropriate mood
	effective scenery looks realistic

5. Now study your subject in terms of the specific criteria you have listed. For each criterion, list specific evidence that shows that your subject either meets or fails to reach that standard. Look for as much evidence as you can, and be specific.

Good scenery doesn't intrude upon the action of a play.

The scenery in *Timon: Superstar* kept getting in the way.

—Platforms in the banquet scene were at too many levels.

—Several actors almost collided with fake pillars.

—A table kept the actors too far apart during the trial scene.

—Part of the scenery collapsed during the banquet scene.

6. After assembling the evidence, come to a firm judgment about your subject or decide whether your initial opinion is supported by the facts you have assembled.

Timon: Superstar is a failure.

REV

7. Write a preliminary thesis statement that expresses your opinion.

> *Timon: Superstar* is a failure because of faulty staging, performances, and conception.

8. Now consider possible objections to your opinion. Few evaluations are totally one-sided. What contradictory arguments do you need to anticipate in your review? If necessary, refine your thesis.

> The director of *Timon: Superstar* had to work with a weak play.

9. Write a scratch outline that develops that thesis. The outline should arrange the criteria you'll be presenting to support your thesis. But be sure to find a place in your paper to acknowledge and deal with possible objections and contrary opinions. In most cases, you will be more persuasive if you deal with potential opposition first and then present your own evidence. Put your strongest argument where your readers will remember it best—near the end of the paper.

> I. Describe what Shakespeare's *Timon of Athens* is about.
>
> II. Admit the play itself is weak—dull main character and little action.
>
> III. Evaluate the staging.
>
> IV. Evaluate the acting.
>
> V. Evaluate the basic conception of the production—rock musical.
>
> VI. Conclude.

10. Write a draft. (The sample review below develops the thesis and scratch outline used as examples in this section.)

Be sure to define your evaluative terms as precisely as possible. If necessary, describe what your expectations are in short sentences or a paragraph. Don't, for example, simply say that the movie should have "good action." Explain to your readers how they might recognize good action when they see it—what are its "earmarks"?

Use graphic examples. Whatever you are evaluating—person, place, or thing—help the readers to see or understand it by placing it in front of them.

Be tactful, yet honest.

6. Sample review

Timon: Superstar
Worse Than It Has to Be

by Brian McVicker

[The opening paragraph identifies the play being reviewed and its author. Because this review is published in a newspaper, the paragraphs tend to be short. This opener, for example, runs only a single sentence.]

Timon of Athens, a tragedy Shakespeare wrote late in his career, proves that even the author of such masterworks as *Hamlet*, *King Lear*, and *Romeo and Juliet* could pen a really bad play.

[Next, Brian supplies some much-needed background information. Since he assumes that most readers aren't familiar with the play he is reviewing, Brian supplies basic plot information.]

Performed even more rarely than read, *Timon* tells the story of a rich Athenian who wastes his wealth on greedy friends who promptly abandon him to his creditors when he runs out of gold. Timon spends one half of the play giving his money away, the other half angrily cursing those he gave it to—hardly the stuff of memorable drama. While some of the verse is of a high order, the work contains virtually no action, intrigue, emotion, or character development. It is unrelentingly grim.

[Before criticizing the production of *Timon* he watched, Brian acknowledges the difficulties of producing the play. He also points out why the college decided to perform *Timon* to begin with: its "long-term commitment to staging all of Shakespeare's plays."]

REV

So, predictably, Professor Vorhees' current Clear Lake College staging of *Timon of Athens*, renamed *Timon: Superstar*, suffers from all the weaknesses inherent in the work, but those problems could be forgiven, in light of the college's long-term commitment to staging all of Shakespeare's plays, even the clunkers.

> [The evaluation starts in earnest here. The second sentence in the paragraph below suggests one set of criteria for the evaluation. The last sentence is the thesis statement for the entire review.]

Less easily defended are the innovations, updates and clumsy stage business concocted to make the bitter play more appealing to a contemporary audience. Feeble as *Timon of Athens* may be, it merits at least a faithful, reasonably dignified production. What Professor Vorhees gives us, instead, is a jazzed-up MTV nightmare, faulty in its staging, performances, and basic conception.

> [The criticism of ineffective staging begins below with a statement of criteria: "details of staging . . . establish the credibility of a performance." Brian then presents evidence that the staging of *Timon: Superstar* was flawed.]

At the full dress rehearsal, attended by a large group of invited guests, even the little things, those details of staging and stage-craft that establish the credibility of a performance, went wrong. Two distinguished members of the ancient Athenian senate were wearing digital watches and eyeglasses. Carved pillars that figured prominently in the architecture of the city were still on stage when Timon stormed into the forest—a glade of oak, elm, and Greek columns? During the elaborate banquet sequence, part of the set collapsed, just missing a chorus line that looked like ten sweaty Amazons tripping over a volleyball net. The audience cheered. It was a high point.

> [What follows is the first of two paragraphs evaluating the performances in the show. No specific criteria for good acting are discussed, but none seem necessary. Brian assumes most readers will agree that good actors

REV

768

are enthusiastic and well-spoken. The paragraph balances criticism against an admission that two actors did a respectable job. The tone is sharp.]

Professor Vorhees succeeded only a little better with her actors who, by and large, seemed not to understand what the play was about. All played their roles with enthusiasm, but many might as well have spoken Greek for all the audience could discern from slurred syllables, garbled syntax, and unsteady warbling. Darwin Washington swaggered and bellowed convincingly in the soldierly role of Alcibiades, and Sue Ellen Rizzo brought a welcome touch of pathos to the faithful servant Flavius.

[The assessment of the acting continues, with the tone of the review growing harsher and excessively personal. In this paragraph, Brian might be accused of doing a "hatchet job" on Professor Cupperman.]

But neither performance could compensate for the sheer ineptness of Timon played by Professor Cupperman—the biggest ham since Hormel. Every word he spoke was accompanied by a gesture, every gesture by a twitch, every twitch by a leap, left or right, as if he were stomping roaches on the stage floor. In fact, Cupperman seems to have been counting syllables, delivering Shakespeare's iambic pentameter with a maddening regularity that defied both sound and sense. Instead of a misanthrope, we got a metronome. Yet insensitive as his delivery was to the nuances of the character, nothing compares to Cupperman singing. You have not lived until you have heard a full professor crooning rock and roll.

REV

[The next paragraph is also sharply critical, but less personal than the previous one. The evidence Brian presents seems to justify the questions he raises about staging the play as a rock musical. Notice that the criticism here near the conclusion is the most serious and fully developed in the review.]

Singing? Yes, this Shakespearian tragedy has been transformed into a rock opera—and that is its biggest problem. There is nothing wrong, per se, with setting Shakespeare to music. Verdi did it. So did Leonard Bernstein. Such adaptations are fine when they are written to explore new aspects of Shakespeare's dramas, not compensate for their flaws. Professor Vorhees seems to be using the rock music in her production to disguise a weak story and unappealing main character. She doesn't succeed. The problem isn't even the music—which is, on balance, quite good. Most of David Barrett's songs make you want to get up and dance. But Athenian senators sentencing a soldier to death shouldn't wiggle like Elvis. Neither should an army of mercenaries threatening a city's gates. For some reason, I think Shakespeare is abused by a musical Timon moaning: "What a drag it is being poor!" And it defeats the whole point of tragedy to have an audience standing and clapping to the beat of a rock requiem when Timon's death is announced. At this cathartic moment, the invited audience of reporters and theater majors cheered.

> [The conclusion attempts to moderate the harsh criticism of the play by applauding those involved in the play for their effort. But the final judgment is clear: "innovation doesn't guarantee a successful play."]

Professor Vorhees, her cast, and her crew deserve credit for trying to make Shakespeare lively and interesting. But innovation doesn't itself guarantee a successful show—only a controversial one. That *Timon: Superstar* surely will be.

RES

E   HOW TO WRITE A RÉSUMÉ

1. What is the point of a résumé?

—to outline your academic and employment history in a concise, readable, and favorable way.

—to convince a prospective employer to consider your qualifications for a job.

—to win you a job interview.

2. What makes a résumé successful?

—an intelligent selection of those items in your background most relevant to the job you are seeking and most representative of your personal and educational achievements.

—an accurate and well-organized presentation of your qualifications, background, and experience.

—an attractive format that highlights essential information, presenting it in language that is correct and spelled right.

3. What are the parts of a résumé?

A résumé may be tailored for a specific job or employer; a standard résumé would include the following items:

your name, current address, and phone number. You may also want to list a second, more permanent address if your current address (an apartment, a dormitory) is likely to change during the period of your job application.

Relevant personal data. Use your judgment in this area. You need not mention your age, marital status, physical condition unless such factors are important to the job you are seeking. You should not include a picture with your résumé.

Educational background. In most cases, include the dates and institutions of your college and university

RES

degree(s) and other post-high school training. List this information either in chronological order, most recent first, or in order of importance for the job you are seeking. Elementary and secondary school information should not be mentioned unless directly relevant to the job application.

List your academic major or areas of concentration, language skills, and significant academic honors, especially competitive scholarships, grants, and fellowships.

Job experience. List in chronological order, most recent first, or in order of relevance to the job you are seeking, most important first:

> —your position,
> —your employer,
> —the dates of employment for full-time and part-time jobs relevant to the position you are seeking.

Make sure that all recent years are accounted for; don't leave a gap in your employment history that a prospective employer might worry about. Your job history should give an employer a sense of your experience, qualifications, and dependability.

A résumé prepared right out of college might list significant positions held while in school: on committees, in programs, and in clubs and social organizations.

Recommendations, credentials, or employment services. Let a prospective employer know whom he or she can write or call to get more information about you. Be sure you check that the persons you list as references on your résumé *are* willing to speak in your behalf.

Optional features in a résumé:

A list of personal achievements or community service, especially when such activities are pertinent to your job application.

A statement of your specific career intentions. Give this in as few words as possible. A job title usually suffices: junior accountant; medical examiner; dental hygienist.

4. What is the standard form for a résumé?

Most résumés resemble an outline, but there is no single accepted form. Arrange the items on your résumé so that major points stand out clearly. Use headings to highlight major divisions. Allow for ample margins and plenty of white space. Don't use colored paper.

Don't crowd your résumé. Try to fit everything onto a single page; a longer résumé is acceptable if you have a long employment history and significant experiences to chronicle.

The typical order of items on a résumé is as follows:

1. Personal information

2. Educational background

3. Job experience

4. References

A handsomely typed résumé reproduced on high-quality paper is all an employer expects. You need not have your résumé professionally printed—though such services are widely available and relatively inexpensive.

5. Some advice about preparing a résumé

Proofread your finished résumé several times, then get someone else to review it. Errors on a résumé make you look careless and irresponsible and can cost you a job interview.

RES

Never send your résumé alone as a job application. A résumé should always be accompanied by a typed cover letter explaining your interest in a position, your specific qualifications for the job, your willingness to meet for an interview, and so on. Like the résumé itself, the job application letter should ordinarily not exceed one page.

Use the job application letter to draw attention to the best reasons an employer should consider you for a job or interview. The letter can be more specific about these major points than the résumé. Don't merely repeat information already on the résumé in your application letter.

6. Sample résumé

                        Sean M. O'Brian
                        2853 Sophia Ave.
                        Ruralia, IL 61802
                        (217) 123-4567

OBJECTIVE   Beginning position as cinematographer, film editor,
                script writer

EDUCATION   Seminar Participant: The American Cinema
                American Film Institute, Los Angeles, CA,
                June-July, 1986. Worked with Francis Ford Coppola and
                Sydney Pollack. Won "Outstanding Film Student" citation.

                B. A. in Radio, Television, Film, 1987
                Clear Lake College, Ruralia, IL
                Senior Thesis: "The Art of Paddy Chayefsky"
                Courses in Film Production, Script Writing,
                History of the Film I, II, & III, Editing.

                President: Clear Lake College Film Club, 1985-87
                Founded college film journal: "Frame & Shoot," 1985.
                Coordinated Central Illinois Film Fest, 1986.

                Manager: Clear Lake Photography Lab, 1985-87
                Managed campus photo lab. Held informal classes on
                photography, lab work. Maintained and repaired
                cameras and equipment.

AWARDS   Best Student Film: "Treed" 35mm. 13 min.
                Central Illinois Film Festival (1987)

                Best Animated Film: "Bayou By You" 16mm 7 min.
                Midwestern Film Conference (1985)

EXPERIENCE   1986-87. Production Assistant
                University Films, Inc., Ruralia, IL 61803.
                Gained experience with casting, script writing and revision,
                crew management, film stocks, development, editing.

                Summer, 1984. Intern, KYUU-TV, Cleveland, OH.
                Worked as editor, guest coordinator, newswriter.

                Summer, 1983. Gofer, Heliotrope Studios, Los Angeles, CA

REFERENCES   Professor Hart Anderson   Jacob Levin
                Department of Communications   Universal Films, Inc.
                Clear Lake College   101 Faigley Circle
                Ruralia, IL 61802   Ruralia, IL 61802

                    Academic dossier available from:

                        Student Placement Office
                        Clear Lake College
                        Ruralia, IL 61802

7. Sample job application letter

2853 Sophia Avenue
Ruralia, IL 61802
May 23, 1987

Mrs. Carina Obregon
Director of Personnel
Lamontier Films and Documentaries
5400 E. 133 St.
Garfield Heights, OH 44125

Dear Mrs. Obregon:

I would like to be considered for the assistant production
supervisor position advertised by Lamontier Films in the current
issue of Film Monthly.

As my resume demonstrates, I have a recent degree in cinema and
wide-ranging practical experience in movie production. I have
worked and studied on the West Coast with major film companies and
directors and I have been active in movie productions, companies,
and clubs in the Illinois area.

My job experiences include a summer internship at KYUU-TV in
Cleveland, where I first became familiar with Lamontier Films. At
KYUU, I worked on several projects that involved filmmakers from
Lamontier who helped us develop stories on local area businesses and
institutions, including a feature on the Western Reserve Historical
Museum. Such experiences have made me particularly eager to be
involved with the kind of film production Lamontier specializes in—
locally supported, community-oriented documentaries.

Having worked part-time with a small local film company, I believe I
have the skills required of an assistant production supervisor—
especially the ability to handle on-the-spot assignments. I have
handled more than a few crises in the field, from revising a
shooting script to accommodate the sudden laryngitis of an actor to
repairing a jammed film transport on a camera forty feet off the
ground. I have also managed more routine tasks. I am confident I
can be the "adaptable and ingenious" employee your job notice says
you are seeking.

Since I expect to be in Cleveland early in June, an opportunity for
an interview then would be ideal. But I can be available at any
time convenient to Lamontier Films.

I look forward very much to talking with you.

Sincerely,

Sean M. O'Brian

Sean M. O'Brian

Encl.

RES

HOW TO WRITE A MEMO

1. What is the point of a memo?

—to convey information between individuals or offices in an institution or business.

—to make recommendations.

—to establish or affirm policies.

—to establish a record of actions, recommendations, or policies.

2. What makes a memo successful?

—a clear statement of its purpose or recommendations.

—an arrangement that highlights key information.

MEM

3. What are the parts of a memo?

A memo has two basic parts: a heading and a body.

The heading outlines whom the memo is from, to whom it is directed, what its subject is, and the date of the communication (see form below).

The body contains the message. It often begins with an action-oriented statement that makes a recommendation, states a policy, or summarizes the results of an investigation, report, or analysis. This statement may then be followed by more information, explaining or justifying what is proposed.

Memos vary greatly in length and complexity. Depending upon their audience and purpose, memos can range from short and casual to lengthy and formal.

4. What form does a memo take?

Memos are often sent on forms designed expressly for institutional communication. These printed forms specify what information must be contained in a heading. Headings almost always require the following information:

To:

From:

Subject:

Date:

Other information may be requested.

The body of the memo can be arranged like an outline, with major points flush with the left margin and supporting evidence indented neatly below (see sample). Use headings in longer memos to minimize the time readers spend searching for information. A memo should never look crowded. Information should be chunked and surrounded by plenty of white space.

Whenever possible, arrange information into readable lists. Items in a list should be parallel (see Section 9D).

The foot of a memo ordinarily contains notations (in the lower left) explaining

—who typed the memo,

—whether it is accompanied by other documents (enclosures),

—who will receive copies. Copies are indicated by the abbreviation c. (singular) or cc. (plural).

5. Some advice about writing memos

Remember that a memo may be filed as a record of some report or transaction within a company. Be sure to consider who may read the memo not only now but in the future.

Don't think that mentioning a subject in the heading of the memo replaces the need to identify your subject in the body of the memo itself. The subject heading is designed to make filing the memo easier. Many readers simply ignore these headings and read the body of the memo. If you don't state your purpose there, you may confuse your readers.

6. Sample

```
To:        Barry Meyer, Mgr.              10 Dec. 1987

From:      H. Ross Pinkerton

Subject:   Christmas sales at XXX Sporting Goods stores
```

XXX Sporting Goods has set three priorities for the 1987 holiday sales period:

    1. Successful introduction of XXX-brand nutrition supplements.

    2. Successful introduction of XXX-brand of sporting clothes for men and women.

    3. A 30% increase in sales of upscale exercise machines, including exercise cycles, self-contained gyms, abdominal machines, and slant boards.

The first two items reflect XXX's intention to develop a full line of its own low-priced athletic/health products as an alternative to higher-cost national brands currently offered in our stores. Sales literature and suggestions for displays will follow.

The third item reflects a need to correct an overstock in what has proven to be the relatively low-volume home gym equipment area. Because of the overstock, we can offer you substantial discounts (see attached wholesale list) on home gym devices, which you may pass on to your customers.

Healthy sales during this important season!

```
HRP/dw
Enclosure: 1

cc. B. Twombly
    J. Velz
    K. Frost
```

MEM

1.   What is the point of a business letter?

—to communicate *with* an institution or company.

—to communicate *for* an institution or company.

—to establish a record of some transaction.

2.   What makes a business letter successful?

—a clear message conveyed efficiently.

—accurate information.

—a formal, yet cordial tone.

—an acceptable, usually conventional, format.

3.   What are the components of a business letter?

A business letter has eight major components:

Heading. It includes the address of the person sending the letter followed by the date.

> *The Daily Toxin*
> 102 Rebhorn Hall
> Ruralia, IL 61803
> 31 May 1987

Inside address. It is the name and address of the person or institution to whom the letter is written. When you don't know exactly to whom you are writing, you can address the letter to an office or a position: *Office of Admissions, Director of Personnel, Manager.*

> Dr. Tiffany Shade, President
> Clear Lake College
> Mammoth Hall 201
> Ruralia, IL 61802

Salutation. In business letters, the conventional greeting is followed by a colon, not a comma. The most common titles are abbreviated (Mr., Mrs., Ms., Dr.), but others are spelled out in full (Senator, President, Professor, Reverend).

> Dear President Shade:
>
> Dear Sister Constance:
>
> Dear Professor Upton:
>
> Dear Mr. Kuanahura:
>
> Dear Mrs. Vorhees:
>
> Dear Ms. Lim:

When you don't have a particular person to write to at a company or institution, your greeting can be simply:

> Dear Sir or Madam:

In circumstances when you need to make a general announcement, you can use the formal greeting:

> To Whom This May Concern:

Body. This is where the message of the letter is conveyed. The information here should be arranged to highlight important information. Keep paragraphs short and chunk the important points you want to make—giving each major idea its own paragraph.

Closing. The closing, like the greeting, is a conventional expression. A variety of closings is available to you, some formal, some less so:

More formal	Respectfully yours,
	Yours very truly,
	Yours truly,
	Sincerely yours,
	Sincerely,
	Yours sincerely,
Less formal	Best regards,

Notice that only the first word in the closing is capitalized and the phrase is followed by a comma

Signature. The letter is signed in ink just beneath the closing. Because signatures can be hard to read, the writer's name is typed below the signature. A title or position is often included.

Yours truly,

Connie Lim

Connie Lim

Editor, *The Daily Toxin*

Notations. Beneath the signature but nearer the left margin, it is common to include a pair of initials, the first identifying the person who dictated the letter, the second the secretary who typed it. The letter may also indicate whether any other materials are enclosed and to whom copies of the original have been sent:

CL/dw

Enclosures: 2

cc: Oscar Cupperman

Doris Upton

Marie Vorhees

Envelope. The envelope includes the inside address found on the letter plus the writer's return address in block form:

```
Connie Lim
The Daily Toxin
102 Rebhorn Hall
Ruralia, IL 61803


                        Dr. Tiffany Shade, President
                        Clear Lake College
                        Mammoth Hall 101
                        Ruralia, IL 61802
```

4. What is the form of a business letter?

In the **Samples** section below, you will find models of the three most common formats for business letters:

> the block form (letter 1),

> the modified block form (letter 2),

> the indented form (letters 3 and 4).

Whichever form you select for a letter, follow it consistently.

Business letters should always be typed on a standard 8 ½ × 11 inch paper of good quality. If you are writing for a firm or institution, use its printed letterhead.

Use wide margins (1″ or more) all around the letter to form a kind of frame. A business letter should not appear crowded. If necessary, break up long paragraphs into more readable chunks.

5. Some advice about writing a business letter

Business letters vary as much as people and institutions do. Some letters are extremely formal. Others may be almost as casual as personal notes—though they still arrive in business form. That form is the common element, however, because it provides information necessary to make a communication clear, significant, recordable, and (if necessary) continuing: institutional names and addresses, dates, titles, issues, questions, and problems, signature(s), routing information, and so on. Don't regard business letter *form* as a mere *form*ality.

When writing a business letter, put yourself in your readers' shoes. Ask yourself what readers need to know to respond to your letter appropriately. Consider how you would feel if you received a letter like the one you intend to write.

If you are writing a job application letter, for example, (see p. 775 for a model), you will want to assure the prospective employer that you are qualified for the position and eager to have it. But how do you show that? By taking time to find out what you can about your prospective employers and demonstrating that your strengths fill their needs. You wouldn't write the same job application letter to General Motors that you would to Joe's Auto Supply because the needs and scale of the two operations would be vastly different.

Similarly, if you are writing a letter of complaint, you need to consider the point of view of the person likely to read your letter. Even if you are outraged and upset, what will you accomplish by venting your anger on that employee? You are likely to achieve more satisfactory results by recognizing that your reader is, in most cases, being paid to resolve complaints like yours. A calm but firm explanation of your problem is more likely to be effective than an insulting diatribe.

BUS

Be sure your reader understands *why* you are writing. Anticipate the who, what, where, when, and why questions your readers might have when they pick up your letter. Give all the necessary information as briefly as possible: name names; provide dates; explain circumstances. It may help if you spell out your basic request or problem before you present any background information. Don't make readers plow through paragraphs of narrative before getting to the point.

Not:

Dear Ms. Flowers:

The accident occurred last week when my cat knocked over a soft drink into the keyboard of my computer, causing a short circuit which then ignited some papers on my desk, leading to a fire which destroyed my computer, hard disk, and printer. Fortunately I was able to put out the fire before it spread beyond the desk. But the computer and related equipment are, I am afraid, a total loss.

My roommate called the local fire department, which provided a full report on the incident (enclosed), but by the time they arrived there really wasn't anything for them to do.

Fortunately, I carry full apartment owner's insurance with a separate rider covering my computer. Consequently, I am asking you to explain to me how to make a claim under that policy to replace my computer, printer, and other properties damaged in the fire on September 15. . . .

But:

Dear Ms. Flowers:

On September 15, my computer, printer, hard disk, and other related equipment were destroyed by a small fire in my office. This equipment is covered by a special rider to the apartment owner's insurance policy I carry with your company: Policy No #342-56-88709-3.

Please inform me how to make a claim against that policy.

The fire occurred as a result of an accidental short circuit caused when a household pet spilled liquid onto the computer keyboard. I am enclosing a copy of the fire department's report on the incident which provides full details. . . .

BUS

Spell out the action you anticipate as a result of your letter. Don't leave readers wondering what you want. Tell them.

> Please inform me how to make a claim against that policy.

> Please send me information explaining New Zealand's current immigration policies.

> If you do not make payment by the end of this month, we will be forced to take legal action to recover the property we sold you.

Keep paragraphs short. Present information in chunks. Use lists if you need them.

> I have enclosed the information you have requested:
>
> —a copy of my birth certificate
>
> —copies of my medical and dental records
>
> —my high school and college transcripts
>
> —letters of recommendation from two previous employers

Keep the style natural, personal, and positive. Avoid canned expressions such as

> pursuant to
>
> at your earliest convenience
>
> the aforementioned document
>
> as per your letter of . . .
>
> enclosed please find

Be polite. Many business letters end with a pleasantry that affirms the good will or good intentions of both parties.

> I am confident we can resolve this problem promptly.
>
> I look forward to seeing you in Chicago next month.
>
> Let me know if I can be of any further help.

Anticipate that your letter might be read by several people or become part of a permanent record. Keep these other possi-

BUS

ble readers in mind as you write your letter. And provide enough background information so that your communication would make sense if examined several weeks, months, or years in the future.

Not

Con,

Got the stuff and will have it back to you soon.

JR

But

Dear Ms. Rajala:

I received the proofsheets of Chapter 85 of *Spelling Made Simple* today. I will return them to you with my corrections before March 21.

Sincerely,

Jordan Ross

6. Samples

Letters 1–4 are part of a sequence relating to a problem caused by the sample review on pp. 767–70. As you read, notice that each letter is written with more than one reader in mind: check the notations to learn who receives copies.

You might also notice the degree of formality in these letters. They are written by people who know each other well enough to sit down and talk their problems out. Once the issue is put in writing, however, the stakes are raised and these communications become serious matters. Notice how carefully phrased letter 3 is. President Shade attempts to resolve the dispute firmly and judiciously. She balances praise and blame between both parties, but also takes firm action. Letter 4 implies a personal conversation to follow, so it is far less detailed.

Business letters you write may not be as complicated as those presented here. But every business letter—even a simple request—entails acting strategically and with consideration for the reader.

▶ **#1 Full Block Form**

The Daily Toxin
102 Rebhorn Hall   Ruralia, IL 61802

23 April 1987

Dr. Tiffany Shade, President
Clear Lake College
Mammoth Hall 101
Ruralia, IL 61802

Dear President Shade:

I request that you promptly review recent actions by Professors
Vorhees and Cupperman restricting freedom of the press on this campus.

As you may know, several days ago Brian McVicker, a reporter from The
Daily Toxin, reviewed the current English and drama department
production of the annual Shakespeare play. McVicker's review of the
dress rehearsal of Timon of Athens, an obscure and unpopular work even
in Shakespeare's time, sharply criticized the acting, directing, and
staging of Professors Vorhees and Cupperman's production. A copy of
the review is enclosed.

Because of McVicker's unfavorable review of Timon of Athens, renamed
Timon: Superstar, Professor Vorhees has established a policy banning
Daily Toxin reporters from all future drama department dress
rehearsals. She has also warned students in the drama department not
to talk with reporters and denied backstage permissions freely granted
to Toxin reporters in the past.

Professor Cupperman has taken similar action in the English department,
even warning Brian McVicker, an English major, that his work in an
English course might be reviewed as harshly as Timon of Athens.

I am asking you to investigate these attempts by Professors Vorhees and
Cupperman to limit freedom of expression at Clear Lake College. I hope
specifically that you will rescind the gag orders imposed by the drama
and English departments on The Daily Toxin.

Respectfully yours,

Connie Lim

Connie Lim
Editor, The Daily Toxin

Enclosure

cc. Oscar Cupperman
    Marie Vorhees
    Brian McVicker
    Central Illinois ACLU

BUS

1425 Laudanum Dr.
Ruralia, IL 61802
25 April 1987

Dr. Tiffany Shade, President
Clear Lake College
Mammoth Hall 101
Ruralia, IL 61802

Dear President Shade:

I have just read—with mounting outrage—the letter Connie Lim, editor of
The Daily Toxin, sent you on April 23, demanding that you rescind the
guidelines Professor Vorhees and I have promulgated to define the
relationships our departments and faculty will have with the local press.

I strongly urge you to deny the petition and to consider taking further
action against the Toxin for its unprofessional and damaging attacks upon
my reputation and that of Professor Vorhees. To permit the editor of the
Toxin to dictate how the departments and faculties under our authority
will behave toward reporters would set a dangerous precedent for this
college.

The production of Timon of Athens supervised by me and directed by
Professor Vorhees may have had flaws, not the least of which was a weak
text provided us by Mr. Shakespeare. But we were obligated to perform
the play to complete the commitment I made thirty-six years ago to
perform all the Shakespeare plays during the annual Spring Shakespeare
Festival, which I initiated and developed into the event it is today.

I would point out that Brian McVicker's review of Timon strayed well
beyond the margins of good taste and criticism. May I remind you that he
described Professor Vorhees' choreography of the Masque of Cupid as "ten
sweaty Amazons tripping over a volleyball net"? And, for agreeing to
play the title role, I have been branded as "the biggest ham since
Hormel."

While I will admit that the Daily Toxin's review has not hurt attendance
at the festival production, the students and townspeople jamming our
auditorium are attending for all the wrong reasons. I deeply resent the
cheers that news of my character's death raises from this mob.

I hope you will act with your characteristic speed and determination to
show Ms. Lim and Mr. McVicker the difference between anarchy of the press
and reasonable supervision exercised by those who know better.

Yours truly,

Oscar Cupperman

Oscar Cupperman
Professor of English
Chair, Department of English

c. Marie Vorhees

788

▶ #3 Indented Form

Clear Lake College
Office of the President
Mammoth Hall 101
27 April 1987

Oscar Cupperman
Chair, Department of English
Clear Lake College
12 Praline Hall
Ruralia, IL 61802

Dear Oscar:

Like you, I was startled by the unusual sharpness of Brian McVicker's review of your and Professor Vorhees' production of Timon: Superstar. I regret the personal tone he takes in the piece, but let us attribute that to his youth and a subject ripe for shaking.

It pains me to be this blunt, but the Timon of Athens I watched last week was quite the worst play I have ever seen. McVicker's review, in most respects, accurately describes a troubled and unintentionally humorous production. Let us just say that your decision to transform Timon into a rock-tragedy was not a wise one.

Yet even if the play had been entirely successful and The Daily Toxin review were as irresponsible a piece of journalism as your letter (25 April) suggests it to be, I would feel obligated to rescind the restrictions you and Professor Vorhees have imposed upon the college paper. I understand your personal feelings in this matter and applaud your professional regard for good order within your department. But the authority of a chair—even of a university president—must always take second place to the principles of free speech and a free press.

Consequently, I am directing you and Professor Vorhees to give reporters from The Daily Toxin full access to your departments. I am confident that neither you nor Professor Vorhess will take action of any kind against Ms. Lim and Mr. McVicker. I will, however, talk to both students and urge greater sensitivity in reviewing nonprofessional theatrical productions in the future.

Should you have any questions about my actions, please do not hesitate to discuss them with me.

Sincerely,

Tiffany Shade

Tiffany Shade
President, Clear Lake College

TS/cr

c. Marie Vorhees

BUS

789

▶ **#4 Indented Form**

                                        Clear Lake College
                                        Office of the President
                                        Mammoth Hall 101
                                        29 April 1987

Connie Lim, Editor
The Daily Toxin
Clear Lake College
102 Rebhorn Hall
Ruralia, IL 61803

Dear Ms. Lim:

    Responding to your letter of 23 April, I have reviewed the restrictions placed on Daily Toxin reporters as a result of Brian McVicker's recently published review of Timon: Superstar. I am directing Professors Vorhees and Cupperman to rescind those limitations immediately. Daily Toxin reporters are to have the same access to the drama and English departments they have always enjoyed.

    I would, however, like to discuss this entire issue with you and Brian McVicker sometime soon. Please call my secretary to arrange a time when the three of us can talk this week.

    I appreciate your action and your concern for The Daily Toxin.

                            Sincerely yours,

                            Tiffany Shade
                            Tiffany Shade
                            President, Clear Lake College

BUS

PART VI   REFERENCE GUIDE

This Reference Guide explains matters of usage, providing advice about certain words or phrases that can cause problems for writers. We have also included a short section on fallacies of argument; being aware of these pitfalls can help you craft organized, cogent writing.

a, an. Indefinite articles. *A* is used when the word following it begins with a consonant sound: *a house, a year, a boat, a unique experience. An* is used when the word following it begins with a vowel sound: *an hour, an interest, an annoyance, an illusory image.*

Notice that you choose the article by the *sound* of the word following it. Not all words that begin with vowels actually begin with vowel sounds, and not all words that begin with consonants have initial consonant sounds.

accept/except. Very commonly confused. *Accept* means to take, receive, or approve of something. *Except* means to exclude, or not including.

> I *accepted* all the apologies *except* George's.

accidently/accidentally. *Accidently* is a misspelling. The right spelling is *accidentally.*

ad/advertisement. In most situations, you should write out the full word: *advertisement.*

adverse/averse. Often confused. *Adverse* describes something hostile, unfavorable, or difficult. *Averse* indicates the opposition someone has to something; it is ordinarily followed by *to.*

> Travis was **averse to** playing under **adverse** field conditions.

advice/advise. These words aren't interchangeable. *Advice* is a noun meaning an opinion or counsel. *Advise* is a verb meaning to give counsel or advice.

> I'd **advise** you not to give Maggie **advice** about running her business.

affect/effect. A troublesome pair! Both words can be either nouns or verbs, although *affect* is ordinarily a verb and *effect* a noun. In its usual sense, *affect* is a verb meaning "to influence" or "to give the appearance of."

> How will the stormy weather **affect** the plans for the outdoor concert?

> The meterologist **affected** ignorance when we asked her for a forecast.

REF

Affect is only rarely a noun—a term in psychology meaning "feeling" or "emotion." On the other hand, *effect* is usually a noun, meaning "consequence" or "result."

The **effect** of the weather may be serious.

Effect may, however, also be a verb, meaning "to cause" or "to bring about."

The funnel cloud **effected** a change in our plans.

[Compare with: The funnel cloud **affected** our plans.]

aggravate, irritate. Most people use either of these verbs to mean "to annoy" or "to make angry." But formal English, preserves a fine—and useful—distinction between them. *Irritate* means "to annoy" while *aggravate* means "to make something worse."

It **irritated** Greta when her husband **aggravated** his allergies by smoking.

ain't. It may be in the dictionary, but *ain't* won't get you anywhere in academic or professional writing. Avoid it.

all ready/already. Tricky, but not difficult. *All ready*, an adjective phrase, means "prepared and set to go."

Rita signaled that the camera was **all ready** for shooting.

Already, an adverb, means "before" or previously."

Rita had **already** loaded the film.

all right. The only acceptable form. *Alright* isn't all right.

allude/elude. Commonly confused. *Allude* means to refer to. *Elude* means to escape.

Kyle's joke **alluded** to the fact that it was easy to **elude** the portly Officer Klinkhamer.

allude/refer. A not-so-subtle distinction here. *To allude* is to mention something indirectly; *to refer* is to mention something directly.

The boys were not sure to what dark secret Kelly McKay was **alluding.**

McKay did, however, **refer** to ancient undergraduate traditions and the honor of Clear Lake College.

allusion/illusion. No excuse for confusing these terms. An *allusion* is an indirect reference to something. An *illusion* is a false impression or a misleading appearance.

The entire audience missed Professor Cupperman's **allusion** to the ghost in *Hamlet*.

Professor Cupperman entertained the **illusion** that everyone read Shakespeare as often as he did.

a lot. Often misspelled as one word. It is two.

among/between. Use *between* with two objects, *among* with three or more.

Francie had to choose **between** Richard and Kyle.

Francie had to choose from **among** a dozen actors.

amount of/number of. Use *amount* for quantities that can be measured, but not counted. Use *number* for things that can be counted, not measured: the *amount* of water in the ocean; the *number* of fish in the sea. The distinction between these words is being lost, but it is worth preserving. Remember that *amount of* is followed by a singular noun while *number of* is followed by plural nouns.

amount of money   number of dimes

amount of paint   number of colors

an. See **a/an**.

and/or. A useful form in some situations, but many writers regard it as clumsy. Write around it if you can.

angry/mad. The distinction between these words is rarely observed. But some people use **angry** to describe irritation, **mad** to describe insanity.

anyone/any one. These expressions mean different things. Notice the difference highlighted in these sentences:

I doubt that **anyone** will be able to find a solution to **any one** of the equations.

anyways. A nonstandard form. Use **anyway**.

> {**wrong**} It didn't matter **anyways**.

> {**right**} It didn't matter **anyway**.

awful. In most writing, inappropriate as a synonym for *very*.

> {**inappropriate**} The findings of the two research teams were **awful** close.

> {**better**} The findings of the two research teams were **very** close.

awhile/a while. The expressions are not interchangeable. *Awhile* is an adverb; *a while* is a noun phrase. After prepositions, always use *a while*.

> Rusty stood **awhile** looking at Mr. Hutton.

> Mr. Hutton asked Rusty to keep the secret he was told for **a while**.

bad/badly. These words are troublesome. Remember that *bad* is an adjective describing what something is like; *badly* is an adverb explaining how something is done.

> Stanley's taste in music wasn't **bad**.

> Unfortunately, he treated his musicians **badly**.

Problems usually crop up with verbs that explain how something feels, tastes, smells, or looks. In such cases, use *bad*.

> The students felt **bad** about the disappearance of Rusty Smuth, the Clear Lake football team's yell leader.

> The situation looked **bad**.

REF

being as/being that. Wordy expressions when used in place of *because* or *since*. Stick to *because* and *since*, especially in formal and academic writing.

> {**inappropriate**} **Being that** her major was astronomy, Jenny was looking forward to the eclipse.

> {**better**} **Since** her major was astronomy, Jenny was looking forward to the eclipse.

beside/besides. Beside is a preposition meaning "next to" or "along side of"; *besides* is a preposition meaning "in addition to" or "other than."

> **Besides** the fingerprint evidence, the detectives had a clue in the burlap sack found **beside** the lake.

Besides can also be an adverb meaning "in addition" or "moreover."

> Professor Vorhees didn't mind assisting the athletic department, and, **besides**, she actually liked coaching volleyball.

bunch. A term too informal for academic and formal writing.

> {**too casual**} President Shade reported that the college faced a **bunch** of problems.

> {**better**} President Shade reported that the college faced **many** problems.

but what. In most writing, **that** alone is preferable to the more colorful but colloquial **but that** or **but what**.

> {**colloquial**} There was little doubt **but what** he'd learned a few things.

> {**revised**} There was little doubt **that** he'd learned a few things.

can/may. Respect the difference between the auxiliary verbs *can* and *may*. Use *can* to express the ability to do something:

> Darwin **can** work differential equations.

> According to the Handbook of College Policies, Dean Rack **can** lift the suspension.

Use *may* to express either permission or possibility:

> You **may** compare my solution to the problem to Darwin's.

> Dean Rack **may** lift the suspension, but I wouldn't count on him.

cannot. *Cannot* is ordinarily written as one word, not two.

REF

can't hardly. A common expression in speech that is, technically, a double negative. Use *can hardly* instead when you write.

> {double negative} I **can't hardly** see.

> {revised} I **can hardly** see.

censor/censure. These words have different meanings. As verbs, *censor* means *to cut*, *to repress*, or *to remove*; *censure* means *to disapprove* and *to condemn*.

> The student editorial board voted to **censor** the four-letter words from Connie Lim's editorial and to **censure** her for attempting to publish the controversial piece behind its back.

complement, complementary/compliment, complimentary. The words are not synonyms. *Complement* and *complementary* describe things completed or compatible. *Compliment* and *complimentary* refer to things praised or given away free.

> Travis' sweater *complemented* his green eyes.

> The two parts of Greta's essay were **complementary**, examining the same subject from different perspectives.

> Travis **complimented** Greta on her successful paper.

> Greta found his **compliment** sincere.

> She rewarded him with a **complimentary** sack of rice cakes from her store.

conscience/conscious. Don't confuse these words. *Conscience* is a noun referring to an inner ethical sense; *conscious* is an adjective describing a state of awareness or wakefulness.

> Mr. Hutton felt a twinge of **conscience** after knocking Rusty **unconscious**.

consensus of opinion. This expression is redundant because *consensus* itself implies an opinion. Use *consensus* alone.

> {redundant} The student senate reached a **consensus of opinion** on the issue of censorship.

{revised} The student senate reached a **consensus** on the issue of censorship.

contact. Some people object to using *contact* as a verb meaning "to get in touch with" or "to call." The usage is common, but you might want to avoid it in formal writing.

could of/would of. Nonstandard forms when used instead of *could have* or *would have.*

> {wrong} Coach Rhodes believed his team **could of** been a contender.

> {right} Coach Rhodes believed his team **could have** been a contender.

couple of. A casual expression you should avoid in formal or academic writing.

> {informal} The article accused the admissions office of a **couple of** minor errors.

> {revised} The article accused the admissions office of a **few** minor errors.

credible/credulous. *Credible* means "believable"; *credulous* means "willing to believe on slim evidence." (See also **incredible, incredulous.**)

> Klinkhamer found Mr. Hutton's account of Rusty's disappearance **credible.** However, Klinkhamer was known to be a **credulous** police officer, capable of accepting almost any story.

criteria, criterion. *Criteria* has a singular form—*criterion.*

> John Maynard, age sixty-four, complained that he was often judged according to a single **criterion,** age.

> Other **criteria** ought to matter in hiring.

curriculum, curricula. *Curriculum* is the singular form, *curricula* the plural.

> President Shade believed that the **curriculum** in history had to be strengthened.

> Indeed, she believed that the **curricula** in all the liberal arts departments needed upgrading.

data/datum. *Data* has a singular form—*datum*. In speech and informal writing, *data* is commonly treated as both singular and plural. In academic writing, use *datum* where the singular is needed. If *datum* seems awkward, try to rewrite the sentence to avoid the singular.

> {**singular**} The most intriguing **datum** in the study was the percentage of population decline.

> {**plural**} In all the **data**, no figure was more intriguing than the percentage of population decline.

different from/different than. *Different from* is sometimes preferred in formal writing, but *different than* is usually acceptable.

> Ike's narration of his marriage proposal was **different from** Bernice's.

> Ike's narration of his marriage proposal was **different than** Bernice's.

disinterested/uninterested. These words don't mean the same thing. *Disinterested* means neutral or uninvolved; *uninterested* means not interested or bored.

> Kyle and Richard sought a **disinterested** party to arbitrate their dispute.

> Stanley was **uninterested** in the club's management.

due to the fact that. Wordy. Replace it with *because* whenever you can.

> {**wordy**} Coach Meyer was almost fired **due to the fact that** he won no games.

> {**revised**} Coach Meyer was almost fired **because** he won no games.

effect/affect. See **affect/effect**.

elicit/illicit. These words have vastly different meanings. *Elicit* means to "draw out" or "bring forth"; *illicit* describes something illegal or prohibited.

> The detective tried to **elicit** an admission of **illicit** behavior from the Huttons.

eminent/imminent. These words are sometimes confused. *Eminent* means "distinguished" and "prominent"; *imminent* describes something about to happen.

> The arrival of the **eminent** detective is **imminent**.

enthused. A colloquial expression that should not appear in your writing. Use *enthusiastic* instead.

> {**unloved**} Francie was **enthused** about Bruce's latest album.

> {**better**} Francie was **enthusiastic** about Bruce's latest album.

equally as. The expression is redundant. Use either *equally* or *as* to express a comparison—whichever works in a particular sentence.

> {**redundant**} Sue Ellen is **equally as** concerned as Hector about bilingual education.

> {**revised**} Sue Ellen is **as** concerned as Hector about bilingual education.

> {**revised**} Sue Ellen and Hector are **equally concerned** about bilingual education.

etc. This common abbreviation for *et cetera* should be avoided in most formal writing; use *and so on* or *and so forth*.

everyone/every one. These expressions mean different things. Notice the difference highlighted in these sentences:

> **Every one** of those problems could develop into a crisis **everyone** would regret.

> I doubt that **everyone** will be able to attend **every one** of the sessions.

except/accept. See **accept/except.**

the fact that. Wordy. You can usually replace the entire expression with **that.**

> {**wordy**} Rusty was aware of **the fact that** he was in a strange room.

> {**revised**} Rusty was aware **that** he was in a strange room.

faith/fate. A surprising number of students confuse these words and their combinations: *faithful/fateful, faithless/fateless*. Check a dictionary if you are not aware of the difference between the terms.

farther/further. The distinction between these words is not always observed, but it can be useful. Use **farther** to refer to distances that can be measured.

> It is **farther** from El Paso to Houston than from New York to Detroit.

Use **further**, meaning *more* or *additional*, when physical distance or separation is not involved.

> The great detective decided that the disappearance of Rusty Smuth warranted **further** investigation.

fewer than/less than. Use *fewer than* with things you can count; use *less than* with quantities that must be measured or can be considered as a whole.

> The express lane was reserved for customers buying **fewer than** ten items.

> Mindy had **less than** half a gallon of gasoline.

> She also had **less than** ten dollars.

flaunt/flout. These words are confused surprisingly often. **Flaunt** means to *show off*; **flout** means to *disregard* or *show contempt for*.

> Mr. Butcher **flaunted** his muscles at every opportunity.

> **Flouting** a gag order, the *Daily Toxin* published its exposé of corruption in the city council.

get. The principle parts of this verb are:

Present	Past	Past Participle
get	got	got, gotten

Gotten usually sounds more polished than *got* as the past participle, but both forms are acceptable:

> Rita had **gotten** an A in microbiology.

> Rita had **got** an A in microbiology.

Many expressions, formal and informal, rely on *get*. Use the less formal ones carefully.

get ahead   get straight

get along   get real

get away from   get outa here

get it together

good and.   An informal expression. Avoid it in writing.

> {**informal**} The lake was **good and** cold when the actors threw Sean in.

> {**better**} The lake was **icy** cold when the actors threw Sean in.

good/well.   These words cause many problems (see Section 11B). As a modifier, *good* is an adjective only; *well* can be either an adjective or an adverb. To see the difference between the words used as adjectives, consider the difference between these sentences:

> Katy is **good**. (adj.)

> Katy is **well**. (adj.)

Good is often mistakenly used as an adverb.

> {**wrong**} Katy conducts the orchestra **good**.

> {**right**} Katy conducts the orchestra **well**.

> {**wrong**} The bureaucracy at Clear Lake College runs **good**.

> {**right**} The bureaucracy at Clear Lake College runs **well**.

The complication occurs when writers and speakers—eager to avoid using *good* incorrectly—substitute *well* as an adjective where *good* used as an adjective may actually be more accurate.

> {**wrong**} After a shower, Coach Rhodes smells **well**.

> {**right**} After a shower, Coach Rhodes smells **good**.

> {**ok**} I feel **good**.

> {**also ok**} I feel **well**.

great.   Don't use this vague word to describe every appealing object and circumstance.

> The band did a **great** update of "Positively 4th Street." David was especially **great** on the lead guitar.

hang up.   A slang term when used to mean *problem*. Avoid it in academic writing.

> {**slang**} Kyle has a **hang up** about learning French.

> {**revised**} Kyle has a **problem** about learning French.

hanged, hung.   *Hanged* has been the past participle customarily reserved for executions; *hung* is used on other occasions. The distinction is a nice one, probably worth observing.

> Connie was miffed when her disgruntled staff decided she should be **hanged** in effigy.

> Portraits of the faculty were **hung** in the student union.

hassle.   Used either as a noun or verb, *hassle* is too informal for most academic writing.

hisself.   A nonstandard form. Don't use it.

hopefully.   As a sentence modifier, *hopefully* has been attacked as fiercely as the beaches of Normandy. Unless you want to get caught in the crossfire, avoid using *hopefully* when you really mean "I hope" or "it is hoped."

> {**not**} **Hopefully**, the weather will improve.

> {**but**} **I hope** the weather will improve.

Use *hopefully* when you mean "with hope."

> Margery watched **hopefully** as the safe was pried open.

illicit/elicit. See **elicit/illicit.**

illusion/allusion. See **allusion/illusion.**

imminent/eminent. See **eminent/imminent.**

imply/infer. Think of these words as opposite sides of the same coin. *Imply* means to "suggest" or to "convey an idea without stating it." *Infer* is what you might do to figure out what someone else has implied: you examine evidence and draw conclusions from it.

> By acting calm, Mr. Hutton sought to **imply** that Rusty Smuth was safe.

> But the detective **inferred** that Mr. Hutton was, in fact, covering up what he knew about the disappearance of Mr. Smuth.

incredible/incredulous. *Incredible* means "unbelievable"; *incredulous* means "unwilling to believe" and "doubting." (See also **credible/credulous.**)

> Francie and Kyle regarded Mr. Hutton's story as **incredible.** You could hardly blame them for being **incredulous** when Hutton told them he had left Rusty at an emergency medical center after a Picasso had fallen on his head.

into. Avoid using this word in its faddish sense of being "interested in" or "involved with."

> {**informal**} The college was finally **into** computers.

> {**more formal**} The college was finally involved with computers.

> The college finally showed an interest in computers.

irregardless. Nonstandard. Use *regardless.*

irritate/aggravate. See **aggravate/irritate.**

its/it's. Don't confuse these terms. *It's* is a contraction for *it is. Its* is a possessive pronoun meaning "belonging to it." See Section 15N for a discussion of this problem.

judgment/judgement. The British spell this word with two *e*'s. Americans spell it with one: *judgment.*

kind of. This expression is colloquial when used to mean "rather."

> {**colloquial**} The college trustees were **kind of** upset about the publicity.

> {**more formal**} The college trustees were **rather** upset about the publicity.

less than. See **fewer than/less than.**

lie/lay. These two verbs cause much trouble and confusion. Here are their parts:

Present	Past	Present Participle	Past Participle
lie (to recline)	lay	lying	lain
lay (to place)	laid	laying	laid

Notice that the past tense of *lie* is the same as the present tense of *lay.*

It may help you to remember that *to lie* (meaning to recline) is *intransitive*—that is, it doesn't take an object. You can't lie *something*.

> Travis **lies** under the cottonwood tree.

> He **lay** there all afternoon.

> He was **lying** in the hammock yesterday.

> He had **lain** there for several weeks.

To lay (meaning to place or to put) is *transitive*—it takes an object.

> Jenny **lay** a *spider* on Travis' chest.

> Yesterday, she **laid** a plastic *snake* on his forehead.

> Jenny was **laying** the *arachnid* on Travis' T-shirt when he awoke.

> Travis had **laid** a *punch* on Jenny before he realized who she was.

like/as. Many people object to *like* used to introduce clauses of comparison. *As, as if,* or *as though* are preferred in situations where a comparison involves a subject and verb:

> {**not**} Mr. Butcher is self-disciplined, **like** you would expect a champion weightlifter might be.

> {**but**} Mr. Butcher is self-disciplined, **as** you would expect a champion weightlifter might be.

> {**not**} It looks **like** he will win the local competition again this year.

> {**but**} It looks **as if** he will win the local competition again this year.

Like is acceptable when it introduces a prepositional phrase, not a clause.

> Francie looks **like** her mother.

> The sculpture on the mall looks **like** a rusted Edsel.

literally. When you say something is *literally* true, you mean that it is exactly as you have stated. If you write, for example,

> Bernice **literally** steamed when Ike ordered her to marry him.

you are saying that Bernice emitted heated water vapor, an unlikely event no matter how angry she was. *Literally* does not imply fiction of a literary kind.

lose/loose. Be careful not to confuse these words. *Lose* is a verb, meaning to "misplace; be deprived of; be defeated." *Loose* can be either an adjective or verb. As an adjective, *loose* means "not tight"; as a verb *loose* means to "let go" or "untighten."

> Without its mascot Sempronius, Schneider College might **lose** its game with Clear Lake College for the first time in forty years.

> The latch holding Rusty in the empty dormitory room was **loose**.

> He **loosened** it further and slipped away into the night.

REF

mad/angry. See **angry/mad**.

majority/plurality. There is a useful difference in meaning between these two words. A *majority* is more than half of a group; a *plurality* is the largest part of a group when there is *less than a majority*. In an election, for example, a candidate who wins 50.1% of the vote can claim a majority. One who wins a race with 40% of the electorate may claim a plurality, but not a majority.

many times. Wordy. Use *often* instead.

may/can. See **can/may**.

media/medium. *Medium* is the singular of *media*.

> Connie believed that the press could be as powerful a **medium** as television.

> Sean argued that film was the most important of all visual **media**.

Media is commonly used now to refer to the electronic press:

> President Shade declined to speak to the **media** about the disappearance of Sempronius, the mascot of rival Schneider College.

might of. A nonstandard form. Use *might have* instead.

> {**not**} Mrs. Hutton **might of** never admitted the truth.

> {**but**} Mrs. Hutton **might have** never admitted the truth.

moral/morale. Don't confuse these words. As a noun, *moral* is a lesson. *Morale* is a state of mind.

> The **moral** of the fable was to avoid temptation.

> The **morale** of the actors was destroyed by the terrible review.

must of. Nonstandard. Use **must have** instead.

> {**not**} Mr. Hutton suggested that someone from Schneider College **must of** kidnapped Rusty in retaliation for the seizing of Schneider's mascot, Sempronius.

{**but**} Mr. Hutton suggested that someone from Schneider College **must have** kidnapped Rusty in retaliation for the seizing of Schneider's mascot, Sempronius.

nice. This adjective has almost no impact: It was a *nice* day; Sally is a *nice* person. *Nice* is damning with faint praise. Find a better word or expression.

nohow. Nonstandard version of **not at all**.

> {**colloquial**} Mrs. Hutton wouldn't talk **nohow**.

> {**more formal**} Mrs. Hutton wouldn't talk **at all**.

>> Mrs. Hutton couldn't be persuaded to talk.

nowheres. Nonstandard version of *nowhere* or *anywhere*.

> {**colloquial**} The Schneider College mascot was **nowheres** to be found.

> {**revised**} The Schneider College mascot was **nowhere** to be found.

number/amount. See **amount/number**.

off of. A redundant expression. *Off* is enough.

> Kyle drove his Bronco **off** the road.

O.K., OK, okay. Not the best choice for formal writing. But give the expression respect. It's an internationally recognized nod of approval. OK?

on account of. Wordy. Replace it with *because* whenever you can.

personal/personnel. Notice the difference between these words. *Personal* refers to what is private, belonging to an individual. *Personnel* are the people staffing an office or institution.

> President Shade thought drug testing of all her **personnel** would infringe upon their **personal** freedom.

persecute/prosecute. *Persecute* means to "oppress" or "torment"; *prosecute* is a legal term, meaning to "bring charges or legal proceedings" against someone or something.

> Connie Lim felt **persecuted** by criticisms of her activism.

> She swore to **prosecute** anyone who interfered with her First Amendment rights.

phenomena/phenomenon. You can win friends and influence people by spelling these words correctly and using *phenomenon* as the singular form.

> Buck Avery regarded the appearance of Professor Cupperman at the Broken Spoke as something of a **phenomenon**.

> Then again, Buck lived in a world cluttered by strange **phenomena**.

plus. Don't use *plus* as a conjunction or conjunctive adverb meaning *and* or *moreover, besides, in addition to.*

> {**not**} The Huttons and Kelly McKay admitted to kidnapping Sempronius, the Schneider College mascot. **Plus** they acknowledged that Rusty Smuth was being held at Schneider College until Sempronius was returned.

> {**but**} The Huttons and Kelly McKay admitted to kidnapping Sempronius, the Schneider College mascot. **Moreover**, they acknowledged that Rusty Smuth was being held at Schneider College until Sempronius was returned.

precede/proceed. Spelling, not meaning, is the problem with these terms. Though their second syllables sound alike, they aren't spelled the same. Check these puzzlers in the dictionary when you are stumped.

prejudice/prejudiced. Many writers and speakers use *prejudice* where they need *prejudiced*. *Prejudice* is a noun; *prejudiced* is a verb form.

> {**wrong**} Joe Kamakura is **prejudice** against Liberals.

> {**right**} Joe Kamakura is **prejudice*d*** against Liberals.

{**wrong**} **Prejudice** people are found in every walk of life.

{**right**} **Prejudice***d* people are found in every walk of life.

principal/principle. Two terms commonly confused because of their multiple meanings. *Principal* means "chief" or "most important." It also names the top gun in elementary and secondary school (remember the **princi***pal* is your pal?). Finally, it can be a sum of money lent or borrowed.

Ike intended to be the **principal** breadwinner of the household.

Bernice accused Ike of acting like a power-mad high school **principal.**

She argued that they would need two incomes to pay off their mortgage, interest, and **principal.**

A *principle*, on the other hand, is a guiding rule or fundamental truth.

Ike declared it was against his **principles** to have his wife work.

Bernice said he would just have to be a little less **principled** on that issue.

real. Often used as a colloquial version of *very*: I was *real* scared. This usage is too informal for academic writing.

really. An adverb too vague to make much of an impression in many sentences: It was *really* hot; I am *really* sorry. Replace *really* with a more precise word or expression or cut it.

reason is . . . because. The expression is redundant. Use one half of the expression or the other—not both:

{**redundant**} The **reason** the cat is ferocious is **because** she is protecting her kittens.

{**revised**} The **reason** the cat is ferocious is **that** she is protecting her kittens.

{**revised**} The cat is ferocious **because** she is protecting her kittens.

REF

811

relate to.   A colloquial expression used vaguely and too often.

> {**vague**} Rusty Smuth could **relate to** being a Clear Lake campus hero after his escape from his captors at Schneider College.

> {**better**} Rusty Smuth liked being a Clear Lake campus hero after his escape from his captors at Schneider College.

set/sit.   See **sit/set**.

should of.   Mistaken form of *should have*. Also incorrect are *could of* and *would of*.

sit/set.   These two verbs can cause problems. Here are their parts:

Present	Past	Present Participle	Past Participle
sit (to take a seat)	sat	sitting	sat
set (to put down)	set	setting	set

It may help you to remember that *to sit* (meaning to take a seat) is *intransitive*—that is, it doesn't take an object. You can't sit *something*.

> Travis **sits** under the cottonwood tree.

> He **sat** there all afternoon.

> He was **sitting** in the hammock yesterday.

> He had **sat** there for several weeks.

To set (meaning to place or to put) is *transitive*—it takes an object.

> Jenny **set** a *spider* on Travis' chest.

> Yesterday, she **set** a plastic *snake* on his forehead.

> Jenny was **setting** the *arachnid* on Travis' T-shirt when he awoke.

> The next day, Jenny discovered that Travis **had set** a *subpoena* on her desk.

REF

so. Vague when used as an intensifier, especially when no explanation follows *so*: Sue Ellen was *so* sad. *So* used this way can sound trite (how sad is so sad?) or juvenile: "Professor Cupperman's play was *so* bad." If you use *so*, complete your statement:

> Sue Ellen was *so* sad she cried for an hour.

> Professor Cupperman's play was *so* bad that the audience cheered the scenery.

stationary/stationery. *Stationary*, an adjective, means "immovable, fixed in place." *Stationery* is a noun meaning writing material. The words are not interchangeable.

supposed to. Many writers forget the *d* at the end of *suppose* when the word is used with auxiliary verbs:

> {incorrect} Maggie was **suppose to** check her inventory.

> {correct} Maggie was **supposed to** check her inventory.

than/then. These words are occasionally confused. *Than* is a conjunction, *then* an adverb.

> If the film is playing tomorrow, Shannon would rather go **then than** today.

theirselves. A nonstandard form. Use *themselves* instead.

> {incorrect} All the strikers placed **theirselves** in jeopardy.

> {correct} All the strikers placed **themselves** in jeopardy.

throne/thrown. A surprising number of writers use *thrown* when they mean *throne*.

> Charles I was **thrown** from his **throne** by an angry army of Puritans.

thusly. A fussy, nonstandard form. Don't use it. *Thus* is stuffy enough already.

till/until. *Until* is used more often in school and business writing, though the words are usually interchangeable. No apostrophe is used with *till*. You may occasionally see the poetic form *'til*, but don't use it in your writing.

to/too. Most people know the difference between these words, but the adverb *too* often gets cut down to the size of the preposition *to* because of hasty writing or careless proofreading. If you are prone to make this error, check for it when you edit.

> {**incorrect**} Coach Rhodes was **to** surprised to speak after Clear Lake beat Schneider College for the first time in forty years.

> {**revised**} Coach Rhodes was **too** surprised to speak after Clear Lake beat Schneider College for the first time in forty years.

toward/towards.   Either form is fine, but **towards** gets the nod in some quarters.

try and.   An informal expression. In writing, use *try to* instead.

> {**incorrect**} After the victory, the Clear Lake team decided to **try and** thank the Huttons for kidnapping Sempronius, the Schneider mascot.

> {**revised**} After the victory, the Clear Lake team decided to **try to** thank the Huttons for kidnapping Sempronius, the Schneider mascot.

TV.   This abbreviation for *television* is common, but in most writing it is still preferable to write out the entire word. The abbreviation is usually capitalized. You may, of course, abbreviate the names of television networks and services: CBS, ABC, NBC, CNN, MTV.

type.   You can usually cut this word.

> {**wordy**} Hector was a polite **type** of guy.

> {**revised**} Hector was polite.

uninterested/disinterested.   See **disinterested/uninterested.**

unique.   Something *unique* is one of a kind. It can't be compared with anything else, so expressions such as *most* unique, *more* unique, or *very* unique don't make sense. The word *unique*, when used properly, can stand alone.

{**incorrect**} Joe Rhodes' coaching methods were **very unique**.

{**revised**} Joe Rhodes' coaching methods were **unique**.

Quite often, though, *unique* appears where another adjective is more appropriate.

{**incorrect**} The **most unique** merchant on the block was Tong-chai.

{**improved**} The **most inventive** merchant on the block was Tong-chai.

used to.   Many writers forget the *d* at the end of use:

{**incorrect**} Darwin was **use to** studying after soccer practice.

{**correct**} Darwin was **use*d* to** studying after soccer practice.

utilize.   Many readers prefer the simpler term *use*.

{**inflated**} J. M. Ringling **utilized** his gavel to regain the crowd's attention.

{**better**} J. M. Ringling **used** his gavel to regain the crowd's attention.

very.   Many teachers and editors will cut *very* almost every time it appears. Overuse has deadened its impact. Whenever possible, use a more specific word or expression.

{**weak**} I was **very angry**.

{**stronger**} I was **furious**.

well/good.   See **good/well**.

who/whom.   Use *who* when the pronoun is a subject; use *whom* when it is an object.

Who wrote the ticket?

To whom was the ticket given?

See Section 15L.

-wise.   Don't add *-wise* to the end of a word to mean "with respect to" or "as far as the _____ is concerned." Many people object to word coinages such as *weatherwise, sportswise*, and *healthwise*. However, a number of common and acceptable English expressions do end in -*wise*: clockwise, lengthwise, streetwise, otherwise. When in doubt about an expression, check the dictionary.

with regards to. Drop the *s* in *regards*. The correct expression is *with regard to*.

would of. Mistaken form of *would have*. Also incorrect are **could of** and **should of**.

you all. Southern expression for *you*, singular or plural. Not used in academic writing—to its detriment.

your/you're. Homonyms that sometimes get switched. *You're* is the contraction for *you are*; *your* is a possessive form.

> **You're** certain Richard has been to Paris?

> **Your** certainty on this matter may be important.

Fallacies of Argument

Fallacies of argument are forms of argumentation generally considered to be illogical, inappropriate, or indefensible. Recognizing these fallacies will make you a shrewder analyst of persuasive writing. Avoiding these errors in logic will make your own writing more mature and compelling.

But be warned that, in a given circumstance, what one critic considers a fallacy another may accept as a valid argument. Such disagreements often stem from incompatible assumptions about basic values, especially when arguments deal with politics, law, and social policy. Merely branding a notion a fallacy will not send it tumbling like the walls of Jericho. For some readers, you will have to defend the principle behind your objection and hope readers share your values.

Here are some common types of logical fallacies.

Argument ad hominem. The latin term means "to the man." An *ad hominem* argument is an attack on the character of an individual rather than on what he or she stands for. It is often an attempt to divert attention from an issue. For example, a candidate for the U.S. Senate who is regarded as weak on defense issues might defend himself with an *ad hominem* attack on his opponent, pointing out that she has never served in the armed forces. The accusation may be true, but it would not necessarily affect the positions or records the two candidates have on defense matters.

As you might expect, *ad hominem* arguments can get more than a little brutal as people attempt to tear down the good character of their opponents. Such attacks are powerful because we must first trust and respect people before we'll listen to their arguments. Destroy that respect and you have destroyed an opponent's ability to persuade. One protection against *ad hominem* attacks is the frequency with which they return to plague their inventors: audiences deeply resent accusations they regard as unfair or cheap.

REF

> A glowing hearth warmed the cabin while snow fell silently outside. Ike Cannon and Bernice Kopple sipped buttered rum and glowed. Contented and effusive,

Ike suddenly sighed: "Can you imagine a better president than Ronald Reagan?"

Bernice nearly bit her cup. **"That divorcé? Preaching about family and religious values while estranged from some of his own children? And when was he seen in the vicinity of a church?"**

Non sequitur. A *non sequitur* is an assertion that does not follow logically from previous statements or evidence. A non sequitur can sometimes slip through in an argument because it often has a degree of plausibility, but the assertion falls apart under more careful scrutiny.

If, for example, a writer claimed that the economy must be healthy because inflation is under control, the assertion might sound reasonable. But it does not follow necessarily that an economy with low inflation must be thriving. Low inflation might be the result of slow growth, recession, or other conditions. Other factors would have to be considered and the relationship between the economy and inflation drawn more precisely.

Ike gasped. "How could you strike so low, Bernice? **Well . . . you were born in Massachusetts. I guess you can't help being a knee-jerk liberal."**

"Look who's talking," said Bernice, "Mr. Lincoln Town Car, mountain cabin, and Keogh plan. **If you didn't have a six-figure income, maybe you wouldn't be a Republican."**

Hasty generalization. A conclusion based on too little evidence. While a single experience may suffice to teach that fires burn and cats scratch, most issues require fuller demonstration. You usually cannot construct a broad generalization from just a few examples, incidents, or illustrations: *Flying can't be safe: two jets crashed last month.* Nor should you try to reduce a complicated issue to a single statement: *Everyone knows most politicians are on the take.* Most generalizations need the precision that qualifying words and phrases add: *some; many; a few; in many cases; in some situations; almost.*

"Democrats have more money than Republicans. Look at the Kennedys in Massachusetts, Jay Rockefeller in West Virginia, and Barbra Streisand," said Ike.

"At least they aren't crooked," replied Bernice. "Or have you forgotten Agnew and Nixon?"

"So **all Republicans are crooked?**"

"If the shoe fits . . ." said Bernice, arching her brow.

"Better crooked than **war-mongering!**" Ike bellowed. "**Every American war this century was initiated by a Democratic administration!**"

False analogy. A false analogy is a comparison that does not hold true or proves misleading. Analogies are useful tools for argumentation and explanation. They work by comparing something unfamiliar to something better known and understood. A writer, for example, might explain how the turbocharger in an automobile works by comparing it to a windmill, waterwheel, or compressor.

A false analogy trades on the fact that readers can sometimes be steered into believing a comparison that is only partially true. Because one part of an analogy works, readers tend to buy the entire comparison, even when it misrepresents or simplifies the truth. Thus the familiar analogy predicting that America, like Rome, will decline for tolerating "pagan" ways grossly simplifies the history of two vastly different political entities to make a point that is finally not very worrisome. (The Roman empire, after all, lasted many centuries.) Yet analogies that don't work aren't always easy to spot or refute.

"Yeah, well then why are your people so eager to drag us into **another Vietnam War in Central America?**" Bernice asked Ike.

"That's a false comparison," Ike replied. "The threat, scale, and logistics of the problem in Central America are entirely different from what we faced in Asia. What I'm worried about is how you Democrats **coddle leftwing dictators the way Chamberlain appeased Hitler.**"

Bernice gasped: "Not that stale analogy again! Hitler was a fascist racist militarist, not a revolutionary defending the people."

"**Like Stalin?**"

Begging the question. Assuming that something is a fact when it is precisely the issue in question. A lawyer begs the question, for example, when he defends an embezzler by insisting that the accused is an honest woman: he wants a jury to accept as a fact what is very much in doubt. Sometimes it is difficult to spot this fallacy because assertions can be phrased to hide plausible but unproven assumptions. If you argued, for example, that the lives saved by the fifty-five-mile-per-hour speed limit made it a good traffic law, you are assuming that the law had, indeed, saved lives. That's possible, but hardly proven.

> **"How can you accuse me of defending Stalin? I'm not a communist,"** said Bernice.

> Ike sipped his buttered rum cautiously.

> "If you aren't a left-wing radical, why are you so nervous?"

> "I'm not nervous," said Bernice, twisting her handkerchief into tight knots. **"Besides, how can I be a communist when I am so passionate a defender of individual liberties?"**

> "Are you?"

> **"If you were a gentleman, you wouldn't even ask such a question!"**

Either/or. Reducing a complicated problem to two overly-simple alternatives. This is a favorite ploy of politicians trying to tar the opposition. They suggest that an issue comes down to two choices, only one of which is really acceptable to an audience: war or peace; poverty or prosperity; repression or freedom; death or life. They, of course, side with the favorable alternative while their opponent offers war, poverty, repression, and death. The easiest way of breaking down an "either/or" situation is to show that other alternatives are possible.

> "Let's not be subtle, Bernice. **Either you are a communist or you aren't.**"

> "Grow up, Ike." said Bernice. "Just because I favor government programs to help the needy and am

against nuclear war doesn't make me a communist. Anyone who opposes helping the poor and favors nuclear war **is either a criminal or an idiot.**"

"You're the one who needs to grow up, Bernice. No one is against the poor or for war. The question is how to deal with the poor without impoverishing the whole country and how to eliminate nuclear weapons without destabilizing the balance of power. There are no easy solutions."

"That's better. Now you sound like me."

Red herring. Red herrings are distractions in an argument—facts, statements, accusations that have no bearing on the main point. They serve to throw an opponent off balance or readers off course. Lady Macbeth employs the equivalent of a red herring when she faints at a critical moment in *Macbeth* to draw attention away from suspicions that her husband murdered the king. An accused car thief uses a red herring when she blames her theft on the owner leaving his keys in the vehicle. Politicians may be employing a red herring when they attempt to blame a political problem on the press or other media: terrorism occurs because of news coverage; drugs are rampant because movies glamourize them.

"Heaven forbid I should sound like you, Bernice," said Ike. "Fortunately, I know the difference between political realities and bleary-eyed idealism. **Besides, you don't even vote.**"

"I missed one election. One election. At least I have a social conscience. I want to make the world a better place for everyone, not just for people who spend their autumn weekends **stalking Bambi's mother!**"

"Huh? What's hunting got to do with this?"

"What are we arguing about?"

"I don't remember."

Post hoc, ergo propter hoc. The Latin expression means *after this; therefore because of this.* It describes the faulty assumption that anything that happens after some phenomenon is caused by it. In its most extreme form, this fallacy produces superstitions: breaking a mirror causes seven years' bad luck; finding a penny brings good fortune. More subtly, *post hoc, ergo propter hoc* reasoning can induce belief in plausible but unproven causal relationships. For example, when traffic deaths fell the year after the imposition of a national 55 mph speed limit, safety zealots immediately credited the slower highway speeds with saving the lives. Yet subsequent studies showed that the dip in highway fatalities was more accurately related to Americans driving significantly fewer miles because of high gas prices and an economic recession.

Post hoc, ergo propter hoc is among the most common, tempting, and persuasive fallacies because the facile solutions it finds for serious problems are often more appealing than more realistic answers. Thus it is easier to blame rock and roll for rising teen pregnancies than to try to understand complex social and economic relationships; it is easier to blame foreigners for domestic factory closings than to examine labor and management relationships, productivity, and quality control.

> **"We haven't been happy since you bought the Lincoln."** Bernice observed. "Why don't you sell it?"
>
> "That's not the problem. We have never agreed about anything. **Before I met you, I had hair.** Now look at me. **You've made me go bald.**"
>
> **"You made me gain twenty pounds."**
>
> Ike and Bernice sipped their buttered rum thoughtfully.

CREDITS

The sources of quotations used for illustrative purposes are indicated in the text. Special acknowledgment is due for permission to reprint the following selections:

American Heritage Dictionary—From *The American Heritage Dictionary, Second College Edition*, 1982. Copyright © 1982 by Houghton Mifflin Company. Reprinted by permission from The American Heritage Dictionary, Second College Edition.

Austin—James H. Austin, "The Roots of Serendipity," in *Saturday Review/World*, November 1974. Saturday Review/World, Inc., p. 61.

Balarbar—"Chrysler's Sales Bank" by James B. Balarbar. Copyright © 1985 by James B. Balarbar. Reprinted by permission.

Bird—From "Where College Fails Us" by Caroline Bird. Copyright © 1975 by Caroline Bird. Reprinted by permission of the author.

Boorstin—Daniel J. Boorstin, *The Discoverers*. Vintage Books/Random House, 1983, p. 364.

Bork—Robert H. Bork, "Give Me a Bowl of Texas," in *Forbes*, September, 1985, p. 184.

Callahan—From "Advertising The Army" by Tom Callahan, *American Way*, November 26, 1985, Vol. 18, No. 24. Reprinted by permission of the author.

Colligan—From "The Light Stuff" by Douglas Colligan, *Technology Illustrated*, February/March 1982. Reprinted by permission of the author.

Cowley—Malcolm Cowley, "How Writers Write," in *Writers at Work* Viking Press, 1959, p. 7.

Dupuy—R. Ernest Dupuy and Trevor N. Dupuy, *The Encyclopedia of Military History*. Harper & Row, 1970, p. 289.

Ellis—Brett Easton Ellis, *Less Than Zero*. Simon and Schuster, 1985, p. 47.

Goodman—From "It's Failure, Not Success" from *Close to Home* by Ellen Goodman. Copyright © 1979 by The Boston Globe Newspaper Company/Washington Post Writers Group. Reprinted by permision of Simon & Schuster, Inc. and The Washington Post Company.

Grout—Donald Jay Grout, *The History of Western Music*. W. W. Norton, 1980, pp. 540, 629.

Helmreich—From "Stereotype Truth" by William B. Helmreich, *The New York Times*, October 15, 1981. Copyright © 1981 by The New York Times Company. Reprinted by permission.

Hickey—Quote by Wesley Poriotis in, "In Praise of Older Executives" by Brian Hickey, *American Way*, November 26, 1985. Reprinted by permission of American Way, inflight magazine of American Airlines, copyright © 1985 by American Airlines.

Hoberman—From "Translating The Bible" by Barry Hoberman as originally published in the February 1985 issue of *The Atlantic Monthly*, Vol. 255, No. 2. Reprinted by permission of the author.

Hofstadter—Douglas Hofstadter, *Gödel, Escher, Bach: An Eternal Golden Braid*. Vintage Books/Random House, 1979, p. 603.

Iacocca—Lee Iacocca with William Novak, *Iacocca: An Autobiography*. Bantam Books, 1984, p. 145.

Irmen—"Fire Down Below" by Robert Irmen. Copyright © 1984 by Robert Irmen. Reprinted by permission.

Kiesler—Sara Kiesler, Lee Sproull, and Jacquelynne S. Eccles, "Second-class Citizens," in *Psychology Today*, March 1983. American Psychological Association.

King—From "The Novelist Sounds Off," *Time*, October 6, 1986. Copyright © 1986 by Time, Inc. All Rights Reserved. Reprinted by permission of Time, Inc. and Stephen King.

Loe—From "Shrimpers" by Victoria Loe, *Texas Monthly*, April, 1981. Copyright © 1981 by Texas Monthly, Inc. Reprinted by permission.

McMurtry—Larry McMurtry, *Lonesome Dove*. Simon and Schuster, 1985, pp. 386–387.

Mims—"Politics? Who Cares?" by Brian Mims. Copyright © 1984 by Brian Mims. Reprinted by permission.

Morrison—Toni Morrison, *The Bluest Eye*. Pocket Books, 1970, p. 97.

Oxford English Dictionary—"Crafty" from *The Compact Edition of the Oxford English Dictionary*, Vol. I, A–O, 1971, p. 1129. Copyright © 1979 by Oxford Univeristy Press. Reprinted by permission.

Perelman—Chaim Perelman, *The Realm of Rhetoric*. University of Notre Dame Press, 1982, p. 35.

Pond—From "Newman, Cruise . . . Mastrantonio" by Steve Pond from *Rolling Stone*, November 20, 1986. Copyright © 1986 by Straight Arrow Publishers, Inc. All rights reserved. Reprinted by permission.

INDEX

829

831

834

Memo
definition of, 733
example of, 778
how to write a, 776–78
Memory (of computers), 568
Metaphor, 184–85
definition of, 180
Methods for writing, 59–62
might of, 808
Minor sentences, 239–41
cautions about, 240–41
definition of, 231
Misplaced modifiers, 262–65
definition of, 250
MLA documentation, 638–68
abbreviations for, 669–71
bibliography and content notes in,
623–25
parenthetical notes for, 639–43
Works Cited entries, for, 643–46
MLA documentation directory,
647–49
Modem, 570
Modern Language Association documentation. *See* MLA documentation
Modifiers,
definition of, 249
hyphenated, 460–61
nonrestrictive, 423
problems, with, 249–72
absolutes, 265, 333–34
adverb forms, 260–62
comparatives and superlatives, 266–68
dangling modifiers, 262–65
double negatives, 258–60
excessive, 270–72
good/well, 254–55
placement of adjectives, 250–52
position of adverbs, 255–58
predicate adjectives, 252–55
restrictive, 423
suspended, 463
Months of the year
abbreviations for, 517
capitalization of, 502
Monuments, capitalization of, 501
Mood of verbs, 328
subjunctive, 328–32
Movies, italics for titles of, 484
moral/morale, 808
Musical groups, capitalization of, 502

Musical pieces
how to document, 665–66
long, italics for titles of, 485
See also Songs
must of, 808
myself, misused as reflexive pronoun,
397–98

▶

Names
capitalization of, 498
dictionary of proper, 553
of instructors, 705
Narration, as a pattern of development, 27,
124
organization of, 63
Narrowing a topic, 30–33
Nationalities, capitalization of, 504
Negatives
double, 258–60
reducing the number of, 212
Neither/nor constructions, agreement prob-
lems, with, 368–70
Newspaper articles
how to document, 658–59
quotation marks around titles of, 485
Newspapers, italics for titles of, 484
News sources, for research, 596–97
The New York Times Index, 596–97
nice, 809
nohow, 809
Nominals, 287
Nominalizations (heavy-duty nouns),
190–91
when to revise for, 88
Nominative case. *See* Subjective case
none, agreement with, 373–74
Nonfinite verbs, 332–33
Nonliving things, possessive forms of, 353
Nonrestrictive modifiers, 423–27
Non sequitur, 818
Notations, in business letters, 781
Note cards, for research paper, 601–02,
604–05, 692
Notes, taking effective, 602–05
Nouns
collective, 296–98
common, 343
definition of, 343
possessives, forms of, 350–54
proper, 497

Plays. *See* Dramas
Plot, in literary analysis, 743
Plurals, 343–50
  of abbreviations and numbers, 349
  apostrophes for, 510
  of compound words, 348–49
  of figures, 349
  irregular, 345
  of numbers, 349, 526
  and possessives, 352
  of pronouns to avoid sexism, 407
  of proper names, 347
  regular, 344
  in subject/verb agreement, 289
plus, 810
Plus sign, in documentation, 659, 729
"Pocket" dictionaries, 555
Poems
  capitalizing lines of, 505
  ellipses in, 482
  indenting and typing, 636–37
  italics for titles of long, 484
  line numbers for citing, 744–45
  quotation marks for titles of short, 485
  quoting from, 636–37
"Pointer words," 126
Political groups and parties, capitalization
  of, 499
portion, as singular subject, 304–05
Possessive case, 350–55
  of compound words, 352–53
  definition of, 350
  double ('s + of), 354
  of hyphenated words, 352–53
  of indefinite pronouns, 393–94
  of personal pronouns, 354–55
  of plurals, 352
  preceding gerunds, 338–39
  of pronouns, 391–96
Post hoc, ergo propter hoc, 821
precede/proceed, 810
Predicate, definition of, 288
Predicate adjectives
  definition of, 252
  guidelines for correct use, 253–55
  problems with, 252–55
Predication, faulty, 222, 224–25
prefixes, hyphenated, 461
prejudice/prejudiced, 321, 810
Preparation for writing, 13–45

Prepositional phrases
  in bureaucratic prose, 191–94
  case of objects, 380–81
  no colons in, 451
  definition of, 189
Prepositions
  capitalization of in titles, 505
  definition of, 377
Presence, in writing, 181
Present participle, 314, 333–34
Present perfect participle, 314
Present progressive tense, 309
Present subjunctive, 330
Present tense, 309
  for describing literary action, 637
Principal parts of a verb, 317
principal/principle, 811
Printing and printers, 573
Problem and solution, as a pattern of
  organization, 64
Process, as pattern of organization, 28, 124
Process of writing, stages in, 6–9
  editing, 92–94
  incubating, 44–46
  planning, 34–44, 62–69
  preparing, 13–33
  revising, 75–89
  writing, 47–61, 70–71
  See also Writing process
Professional organizations, as sources, 594–95
Pronouns, 357–410
  agreement with collective nouns, 370–71
  ambiguous reference of, 360–61
  antecedents of, 359–76
  case of, 376–91
    with appositives, 385–86
    in comparisons, 381–83
    after linking verbs, 384–85
    in prepositional phrases, 380–81
  consistent use of, 403
  definition of, 343
  I, we, one, we, when to use, 399–405
  indefinite, 391
    agreement with, 294–95, 372–76
    possessives of, 393–94
    as subjects, 294–95
  intensive, 396–99
  its, 394–95
  after linking verbs, 383–85
  personal, 377, 392

Salutations
  in business letters, 780
  colons after, 448
Sarcasm
  signaled by quotation marks, 473,
  478
scarcely, 259
Scientific names, italics for, 486
Scientific writing. *See* Technical writing
Scratch outlines. *See* Outlines, informal
Screenplay, how to document, 664
Sculptures, italics for titles of, 485
segment, as singular subject, 304–05
Selective bibliographies, 589
Self-limiting writing, 9
Semicolons, 437–46
  comma splices corrected by, 438–40
  in complex lists, 442–43
  with conjunctive adverbs, 439–41
  and coordinating conjunctions, 444
  between lengthy clauses, 444
  with quotation marks, 475
  to relate sentences, 283
  with short clauses, 445
Sentence, definition of, 216
Sentence fragments, 232–41
  appositives as, 234–35
  causes of, 232–38
  definition of, 231
  disconnected phrases as, 237–38
  and minor sentences, 239–41
  relative clauses as, 234–35
  verbals as, 235–37
Sentence outlines. *See* Outlines, sentence
Sentences
  actor/action, 186–89, 226–27
  balanced, 227–28
  broken, 232–33. *See also* Sentence fragments
  capitalizing first word in, 504
  combining, 206–09
  complex, 216, 219–21
  compound, 216, 218–19
  definition of, 216
  generative, 120–21
  length of, 154, 155, 156, 223
  minor, 239–41
  parallel, 227–30
  rhythm of, 192
  simple, 216

  topic, 119–21
  writing vigorous, 186–89
Sentences, management of, 215–29
  changing pattern of, 226
  complex, 219–21
  compound, 218–19
  dividing for clarity, 222–23
  revitalizing dull, 186–88, 225–27
  simple, 217–18
  tangled, 221–25
Sentences, problems of, 231–48
  comma splices, 241–45, 417–19,
  438–40
  fragments, 231–41
  minor sentences, 239–41
  run-ons, 245–48
Sequence
  in organization, 67–68
  of research paper components, 614–15
  for transitions, 277
Sequence of tenses, definition of, 307
series, as singular subject, 304–05
series, commas between items in, 429,
  432–33
set/sit. See sit/set
Setting, in literary analysis, 744
Sexist language, 168–72
  characteristics of, 169–70
  definition of, 168
  and gender of pronouns, 406
  pronouns and, 405–10
  reasons for avoiding, 168–69
  ways to avoid, 170–71
Shakespeare, dramas of
  as writer's reference, 567
  abbreviations of titles, 745
Shared ownership, to indicate possession,
  353
Ships
  capitalization of, 502
  italics for names of, 485
Short stories, quotation marks around titles
  of, 485
should of, 812
sic
  brackets surrounding, 470
  use of, 634
Signatures, in business letters, 781
Simple sentences, 217–18
  definition of, 216
Simple subject, definition of, 287

845

847

FIRST AID FOR COMMON PROBLEMS OF WRITERS

How do you overcome writer's block?	Check 2B
How do you write a thesis sentence?	Check 2E
When do you have a "complete" first draft?	Check 3C
What is sexist language?	Check 6D
How do you eliminate wordiness?	Check 8A–E
What is a comma splice? Fragment? Run-on?	Check 10
What's the difference between *good* and *well*?	Check 11B
When do you use *who* and when do you use *whom*?	Check 15L
What's the difference between *its* and *it's*?	Check 15N
Can you use *I* in academic writing?	Check 15P
Which words do you capitalize in a title?	Check 20A
How useful are spelling rules?	Check 21A
What books belong on a writer's bookshelf?	Check 21D
Do you have to document *everything* in a research paper?	Check 23A
Where are the MLA Forms for documenting books, articles, magazines . . . ?	Check 23C
What are the best strategies for writing an essay examination?	Check Spec. Assign. B